THE
CAMBRIDGE BIBLIOGRAPHY
OF
ENGLISH LITERATURE

IN FOUR VOLUMES
VOLUME IV

THE
CAMBRIDGE BIBLIOGRAPHY
OF
ENGLISH LITERATURE

Edited by

F. W. BATESON

VOLUME IV
INDEX

CAMBRIDGE
AT THE UNIVERSITY PRESS
1966

PUBLISHED BY
THE SYNDICS OF THE CAMBRIDGE UNIVERSITY PRESS
Bentley House, 200 Euston Road, London, N. W. 1
American Branch: 32 East 57th Street, New York, N. Y. 10022
West African Office: P. M. B. 5181 Ibadan, Nigeria

First Printed in Great Britain at the
University Press, Cambridge
Reprinted by Offset Lithography in Hungary

INDEX

Entries in roman type are authors, e.g. Dryden, John (1631–1700). A leaded page-number, e.g. II, **312**, indicates relatively full treatment; other references are not indexed unless they add something material, if it is only a minor work, a fuller title or another reprint, to the main section. English editors, critics, etc. appearing incidentally in sections devoted to other writers have only been included up to 1870, and foreign writers are normally omitted altogether except where they specifically figure as influences on or sources of English writers. Printers, publishers and illustrators have not been indexed as such unless they are the subject of a separate section. The *floruit* dates derive from the dates of publication of the books listed and are only included to make their authors easier to place. Non-English writers can be distinguished by the omission of such dates.

Entries in italics are anonymous works, e.g. *Zepheria* (16 cent.). It has been impracticable to index more than the following types of *anonyma*: (i) plays, poems and novels of unknown or uncertain authorship, (ii) poetical miscellanies, (iii) newspapers, magazines and other periodical publications of multiple authorship. Normally as a rough guide the century when the work was written follows the title, but books with the same title and all periodicals have been distinguished by the addition of the year of their first publication. They are all indexed under the first word (other than either article) of the title, which generally derives from the title-page of the first edition.

Entries in capitals are sections or subjects, e.g. CHILDREN'S BOOKS.

'A.' (1820), III, 647
A., A. (*fl.* 1856), III, 347
A., B. (*fl.* 1750), II, 82
A., D. (*fl.* 1683), II, 120
A., E. (*fl.* 1673), II, 813
A., I. (*fl.* 1566), I, 765
A. L. O. E.', i.e. Charlotte Maria Tucker (1825–1893), III, 568
A., M. (*fl.* 1699), II, 791
A., Ma. (1724), II, 538–9
A., R. (*fl.* 1615), I, 654
A., R. (*fl.* 1634), I, 799
A., R. (*fl.* 1825), III, 246
A., S. (*fl.* 1664), II, 778
A., S. (*fl.* 1673), II, 777
Aa, Pieter van der (*fl.* 1706), I, 764
Abbadie, Jacques, II, 769
Abbey of the Holy Ghost (M.E.), I, **186**, 683
Abbot, Charles, Baron Colchester (1757–1829), III, 149
Abbot, George (1562–1633), I, 766
Abbot, John (*fl.* 1623), I, 473
ABBOTSFORD CLUB, III, 86
Abbott, Charles, Baron Tenterden (1762–1832), II, 24; III, 985
Abbott, Edwin (1808–1882), II, 304
Abbott, Edwin Abbott (1838–1928), I, 17; III, 109, 850
Abbott, Evelyn (1843–1901), III, **1003**
Abbott, Joseph C. (1789–1863), III, 1088
Abbott, W. H. (*fl.* 1867), III, 1068
ABC (15 cent.), I, 264
Abdul Quadir, Ahmadi Sa'di (*fl.* 1895), III, 1078

À Becket, Arthur William (1844–1909), III, 782, 811, 820
À Beckett, Gilbert Abbott (1811–1856), III, **598** f., 820, 828
À Beckett, Gilbert Arthur (1837–1891), III, 610
'Abednego' (1820), III, 759
Abeken, B. R., III, 895
Abercrombie, H. R. (*fl.* 1900), III, 1092
Abercrombie, John (1780–1844), III, **861**
Abercromby, David (d. 1701–2?), II, 15, 130
Abercromby, Patrick (1656–1716?), II, 997
Aberdare, H. A. Bruce, Baron (1815–1895), III, 108, 900
ABERDEEN
  Libraries, II, 104 f.
  Magazines, II, 687 (1761–98)
  Newspapers, II, 732; III, 806 f.
  Printing in, I, 354 (17, 18 cents.)
  University, III, 123, 837 f. (magazines)
Aberdeen Daily Free Press, The (1872), III, 806
Aberdeen Evening Express (1879), III, 806
Aberdeen Free Press, The (1853), III, 806
Aberdeen Intelligencer, The (1752), II, 732
Aberdeen Journal, The (1748), II, 732
Aberdeen Journal, The (1782), II, 732
Aberdeen Journal (1876), III, 792, 806
Aberdeen Journal and North-British Magazine, The (1768), II, 732
Aberdeen Magazine, The (1761), II, 687
Aberdeen Magazine, Literary Chronicle and Review, The (1788), II, 687
Aberdeen Magazine; or, Universal Repository, The (1796), II, 687
Aberdeen Press and Journal, The (1922), III, 806

Aberdeen's Journal (1748), II, 732
ABERDEENSHIRE, II, 89 (bibliography)
Aberigh-Mackay, George Robert (*fl.* 1880), III, 1070
ABINGDON, I, 372 (schools)
Abingdon, Willoughby Bertie, Earl of (1740–1799), II, 634
Abingdon, Chronicon Monasterii de (M.E.), I, 120
Abingdon Cartulary (M.E.), I, 38
Ab Isselt, Michael, I, 528
Abraham, W. H. (*fl.* 1892), III, 977
Abraham and Isaac (*Brome*) (M.E.), I, 278 f.
Abraham and Isaac (*Dublin*) (M.E.), I, 279
Abrahams, Israel (1858–1928), III, 834, 850
Abram, W. A. (*fl.* 1887), III, 806
Abree, James (1691?–1768), II, 694
Absalon (16 cent.), I, 661
Abstract and Brief Chronicle of the Time, The (1782), II, 715
Abstract of a Sermon [etc.], *An* (18 cent.), II, 194
Academiae Cantabrigiensis Luctus in Obitum Frederici Walliae Principis (18 cent.), II, 214
Academiae Cantabrigiensis Luctus in Obitum Georgii II (18 cent.), II, 219
Academica (1858), III, 834
Academical Contributions of Original and Translated Poetry (18 cent.), II, 250
Academy, The (1869), III, 818
Academy of Complements, The (17 cent.), II, 174 (2), 175, 179 (2), 186, 213, 219, 243, 250
Accomplish'd Courtier, The (18 cent.), II, 230
Account of the Chief Occurrences of Ireland, An (1660), II, 733
Account of the Proceedings of the Meeting of the Estates in Scotland, An (1690), II, 705
Account of the Publick Transactions in Christendom, An (1694), II, 706
Accountant, The (1874), III, 822
Achard of Bridlington (d. 1171), I, 287
Achelly, Thomas (*fl.* 1576), I, 810
Achilles Tatius, I, 799
Achillini, Claudio, II, 67
Ackerman, Rudolph (1764–1834), I, 372; III, 97, 825
Acland, Sir A. H. D. (1847–1926), III, 106
Acland, Sir Henry Wentworth (1815–1900), III, 695
Acland, Sir Thomas Dyke (1809–1898), III, 126, 136
Acosta, José de, I, 794
Acta Eruditorum, II, 51
ACTING
    Art of, II, 409 f. (17, 18 cents.)
    Extemporal, I, 506 (16, 17 cents.)
Acting Drama, The (1834), II, 393
Acting National Drama, The (1837), III, 585

Acton (or Ayton), John (d. 1350), I, 312
Acton, John (*fl.* 1789), II, 822
Acton, John Emerich Edward Dalberg, Baron (1834–1902), III, 828, 911
Acton, William (*fl.* 1691), II, 744
Actor, The (1780), II, 665
ACTORS, I, 503 f. (16, 17 cents.); II, 407 f. (17, 18 cents.); III, 580 f. (19 cent.)
    Biographical dictionaries of, II, 922 f.
    Costume, etc., I, 506 (16, 17 cents.); II, 405 f. (17, 18 cents.); III, 580 f. (19 cent.)
Acuña, C. d', II, 782
Acworth, H. A. (1850–1925), III, 1073
Acworth, Sir W. M. (*fl.* 1900), III, 985
Adair, James (*fl.* 1775), II, 756
Adam, Alexander (1741–1809), II, 932
Adam, James (d. 1794), II, 161
Adam, James (1860–1907), III, 1003 f.
Adam, Robert (1728–1792), II, 161, 745
Adam and Eve (Norwich Grocers' Play) (M.E.), I, 279
Adam du Petit Pont (d. *c.* 1181), I, 288
Adam of Dryburgh (d. *c.* 1212), I, 297
Adamnan (d. 704), I, 102
Adams, Arthur Henry (*fl.* 1899), III, 1096
Adams, Francis (1796–1861), III, 993
Adams, Francis William Lauderdale (1862–1893), III, 1096
Adams, George (1698?–1768?), poet and translator, II, 763, 780
Adams, George, the elder (d. 1773), mathematical instrument-maker, II, 622
Adams, George, the younger (1750–1795), mathematical instrument-maker, II, 960
Adams, George (*fl.* 1810), Worcestershire farmer, III, 970
Adams, J. (*fl.* 1700), I, 442
Adams, J. (*fl.* 1897–1922), educationalist, III, 106
Adams, John (1750?–1814), compiler of children's books, II, 741
Adams, John (*fl.* 1799), writer on horsemanship, II, 818
Adams, John Couch (1819–1892), III, 944
Adams, Orion (*fl.* 1769), II, 721
Adams, Roger (d. 1741), II, 694
Adams, S. (*fl.* 1795), II, 915
Adams, Sarah Fuller, née Flower (1805–1848), III, 275
Adams, T. (*fl.* 1823), III, 200
Adams, Thomas (*fl.* 1612–53), I, 680, 724
Adams, W. E. (b. 1832), III, 782
Adams, William (d. 1620), I, 784
Adams, William (1706–1789), II, 951
Adams, William Davenport (1854–1904), III, 707
Adams, William Henry Davenport (1828–1891), III, 574, 577, 1077
Adams, William T. (*fl.* 1881), III, 578
Adams's Weekly Courant (1732), II, 722

Adamson, Henry (d. 1639), I, 899
Adamson, John (d. 1653), I, 899, 906
Adamson, John (1787–1855), III, 242
Adamson, Robert (1852–1902), III, **861**
ADAPTATIONS (dramatic), II, 484 f. (17, 18 cents.)
Adcock, A. St John (.1900–30), III, 831
Addington, Henry, Viscount Sidmouth (1757–1844), III, 149
Addington, John Gellibrand Hubbard, Baron (1805–1889), III, 979
Addington, Stephen (1729–1796), II, 149
Addington, Sir William (*fl.* 1773), II, 473
'Addison, Mr.' (1793), II, 248–9
Addison, A. C. (*fl.* 1906), III, 1092
Addison, Charles Greenstreet (d. 1866), III, 985
Addison, G. A. (*fl.* 1837), III, 1083
Addison, John (*fl.* 1735), II, 759, 767
Addison, Joseph (1672–1719), II, 37, 40, 43, 61, 66, 74, **601** f.
Addison, Lancelot (1632–1703), II, 748
Addison, Thomas (1793–1860), III, 963
Additions to the Works of Alexander Pope (18 cent.), II, 231
Addresses of Soul to Body (O.E.), I, **79**
Adelard of Bath (*fl.* 1120), I, **284**
Adelung, Johann Christoph, II, 30
Adis, Henry (*fl.* 1661), I, 718
Adlard, J. E. (*fl.* 1859), I, 530
Adlington, William (*fl.* 1566), I, 799
Admiralty and Horse Guards' Gazette, The (1884), III, 821
Adolphus, John (1768–1845), II, 408, 922
Adolphus, John Leycester (1795–1862), III, 379
Adrichom, Christian van, I, 778
Adson, John (d. 1640?), I, 486
ADULT EDUCATION, III, 117
Adventurer, The (1752), II, 664
Adventurer or London University Magazine, The (1833), III, 836
Adventures of a Hackney Coach (18 cent.), II, 548
Adventures of a Silver Threepence, The (18 cent.), II, 562
Adventures of an Author (18 cent.), II, 546
Adventures of Catullus, The (18 cent.), II, 187
Adventures of Covent Garden, The (17 cent.), II, 532
Adventures of Master Headstrong and Miss Patient, The (18 cent.), II, 563
Adventures of the Helvetian Hero (17 cent.), II, 531
Adventures of the Little Girl in the Wood, The (19 cent.), III, 575
Advertiser's ABC, The (1898), III, 780
Advertiser's Daily Magazine, The (1805), III, 798
Advertiser's Journal, The (1898), III, 780
Advertiser's Monthly Circular, The (1895), III, 780

Advertiser's Review, The (1899), III, 780
ADVERTISING, II, 716 f. (advertisement papers, 18 cent.); III, 779 f. (19 cent.)
Advertising (1891), III, 780
Advertising Notes (1897), III, 780
Advertising Register, The (1886), III, 780
Advice from Parnassus (1681), II, 703
Advice from the Scandalous Club (1705), II, 661
Adviser, The (1797), II, 666
Advocate, The (1720), II, 662
ADVOCATES' LIBRARY (Edinburgh), II, 104
'A. E.' or 'Æ', i.e. George William Russell (1867–1935), III, **1058** f.
Aedler, M. (*fl.* 1680), II, 50
Aelfric, called Grammaticus (*fl.* 1006), I, 25, 27, 31, 34 f., **89** f.
Aelian, I, 799; II, 758
Aelred (d. 1166), I, **286**
Aelred of Rievaulx (*fl.* 12 cent.), I, 116
Aeneas Silvius (Piccolomini), I, 809; II, 785
Aeschines, II, 758
Aeschylus, II, 758
  Nineteenth century translations, III, 249, 260, 280, 284, 362, 888, 999, 1001, 1004, 1006, 1011
Aesop, I, 262, 799; II, 759
Aesop in Select Fables (17 cent.), II, 184
AESTHETIC THEORY (writings on), II, 14 f. (17, 18 cents.)
Aethelwald (*fl.* 700), I, **103**
Aethelwulf (*fl.* 802), I, **106**
Aflalo, Frederick George (1870–1918), III, 767, 772 (2)
AFRICA
  Descriptions of, I, 785 f. (16, 17 cents.)
  English-South African Literature, III, 1088 f.
  Voyages to, I, 781 f. (16, 17 cents.); II, 748 f. (1665–1800)
Africanus, Johannes Leo, I, 785
Agar-Ellis, George James Welbore, Baron Dover (1797–1833), II, 837
Agas, Ralph (1540?–1621), I, 389
Agatharchides, I, 785
Age, The (1825), III, 811
Age and Argus, The (1843), III, 811
Agg, John T. (*fl.* 1816), III, 205 (2)
Aggas, Edward (*fl.* 1564–1601), I, 807, 815–6
Agitator Anotomiz'd, An (17 cent.), I, 724
Aglionby, William (*fl.* 1669–89), II, 811, 813–4
Agnew, Sir William Fischer (*fl.* 1876), III, 985
Agnostic Journal, The (1889), III, 819
AGNOSTICISM, III, 59 f.
Agreeable Companion: A Collection of Polite Tales and Fables, The (18 cent.), II, 236
Agreeable Companion, An (18 cent.), II, 209
Agreeable Companion, The (18 cent.), II, 211
Agreeable Medley, The (18 cent.), II, 212
Agreeable Miscellany, The (1749), II, 684

Agreeable Variety, The (18 cent.), II, 193, 197, 209
Agricultural Gazette, The (1874), III, 820
Agricultural Magazine, The (1802), II, 683
AGRICULTURE (books on)
    Middle English Period, I, 123 f.
    Renaissance to Restoration, I, 391 f., 845 f.
    Restoration to Romantic Revival, II, 927 (dictionaries of agricultural terms). See also under LITERATURE OF SPORT, II, 814 f.
    Nineteenth Century, III, 819 f. (weekly papers), 969 f. (principal writers)
Agrippa, Heinrich Cornelius von Nettesheim, I, 326, 809; II, 805
Ahasuerus (in German), I, 336
Ahiman Rezon (18 cent.), II, 217, 222, 233, 235, 240, 250
Aickin, Joseph (*fl.* 1693), II, 931
Aiken, C. F. (*fl.* 1900), III, 1082
Aikin, Anna Laetitia, later Barbauld (1743–1825), II, 23, **352**
Aikin, John (1747–1822), II, **23**, 671
    Critical essays by, II, 26, 306, 309, 317, 328, 352, 648
    Edited by, I, 464; II, 257, 682, 841, 922, 925
    Miscellaneous works, II, 140, 768–9
Aikin, Lucy (1781–1864), III, 570, **882**
Aikman, John (*fl.* 1835), II, 686
Aileran the Wise (d. 665), I, 102
Ailesbury, Thomas Bruce, Earl of (1655?–1741), II, 149
Ailly, Abbé d', II, 785
Ainger, Alfred (1837–1904), III, **732**
Ainslie, Hew (1792–1878), II, 984
Ainsworth, Henry (1571–1623?), I, 679, 856
Ainsworth, Robert (1660–1743), II, 107, **935**
Ainsworth, William Francis (1807–1896), III, 825
Ainsworth, William Harrison (1805–1882), III, **471** f., 825
Ainsworth's Magazine (1843), III, 828
Aird, Andrew (*fl.* 1830–90), III, 782
Aird, Thomas (1802–1876), II, 732; III, **276**
Airy, George Biddell (1801–1892), III, 129, **943**
Aitchison, Sir Charles Umpherston (1832–1896), III, 1078
Aitken, E. H. ('Eha') (*fl.* 1881), III, 1084
Aitken, George Atherton (1860–1917), III, **1035**
Aitkin, Thomas Johnstone (*fl.* 1838), III, 963
Aiton, John (1797–1863), I, 908
Aiton, William (1766–1849), III, 379, 959
À Kempis, Thomas, I, 266
Akenside, Mark (1721–1770), II, 22, 45, 57, 67, 221, **350** f.
Akerby, George (*fl.* 1729), II, 407
Akerman, John Yonge (1806–1873), III, 770
Alabaster, William (1567–1640), I, 655
Alamanni, Luigi, I, 339
Alamode Musician, The (17 cent.), II, 184
Alan of Melsa (*fl.* 1212), I, **297**

Aland, John Fortescue, Baron Fortescue (1670–1746), II, 920
Alane, Alexander (Alesius) (1500–1565), I, 900 f.
Alardis, J. (*fl.* 1664), II, 795
Alarum for London (17 cent.), I, 539
Albanis Beaumont, Jean François, II, 769
Albany, G. (*fl.* 1834), III, 374
Albemarle, George Thomas Keppel, Earl of (1799–1891), III, 152, 1079
Alberic of London (*fl.* 1217), I, **298**
Alberti, Leon Battista, I, 809; II, 807
Albery, James (1838–1889), III, **625**
Albion, The (1830), III, 801
Albion and Evening Advertiser, The (1799), II, 711; III, 800
Albion and Star, The (1831), III, 801
Albrecht, Heinrich Christoph (*fl.* 1786), II, 71
Album, The (1822), III, 832
Album of Streatham, The (18 cent.), II, 241–2
Albyon Knight (16 cent.), I, 515
ALCHEMY AND CHEMISTRY, I, 885 f. (16, 17 cents.)
Alciati, Andrea, I, 479
Alciphron, II, 759
Alcock, John (1430–1500), I, 314, 680, 683 f.
Alcuin (d. 804), I, **106** f.
Aldam, W. H. (*fl.* 1876), III, 771
Alday, John (*fl.* 1566), I, 806
Aldenham, H. H. Gibbs, Baron (1819–1907), I, 146; III, 974
Alderson, Amelia, later Opie (1769–1853), II, 666; III, **411** f.
Aldhelm (d. 709), I, **103**
Aldiboronti Phoskyphorniostikos (19 cent.), III, 575
Aldine Magazine of Biography, The (1839), III, 97
Aldrich, Henry (1647–1710), II, 938
ALDSTONE, II, 684 (magazine)
Alemán, Mateo, I, 343, 809
Alembert, Jean le Rond d', II, 28, 769
Aleph, Johan (*fl.* 1530), I, 677
Alesius (Alexander Alane) (1500–1565), I, 900 f.
Alessio, I, 809
Alexander, Caleb (*fl.* 1792), II, 932
Alexander, Cecil Frances, née Humphreys (1818–1895), III, **291**
Alexander, Henry (*fl.* 1870), III, 806
Alexander, P. P. (*fl.* 1866), III, 306, 657
Alexander, Robert (*fl.* 1828), III, 799
Alexander, Samuel (1859–1938), III, **861** f.
Alexander, W. F. (*fl.* 1906), III, 1093
Alexander, Sir William, Earl of Stirling (1567?–1640), I, 432, 679, 794, 866
Alexander, William (1824–1911), III, **276**, 807
Alexander Anglicus (*fl.* 1429), I, **302**
Alexander of Hales (d. 1245), I, **291** f.
Alexander and Dindimus (M.E.), I, 143
Alexander Cassamus Fragment (M.E.), I, **144**
Alexander Fragments, Alliterative (M.E.), I, **143**

ALEXANDER THE GREAT, ROMANCES OF, I, **142f.**
Alexander's Letter to Aristotle (O.E.), I, **94**
Alexis of Piedmont, I, 888
Aleyn, Charles (d. 1640), I, 473, 818
Alfieri, Vittorio, III, 38
Alford, Henry (1810–1871), I, 441; III, 257, **276**, 830
Alfred, H. J. (*fl.* 1859), III, 770
Alfred, King (849–901), I, 27, 35, **85f.**
Alfred of 'Sereshel' (or the Englishman) (*fl.* 1200), I, **296f.**
Alfred and Westminster Gazette, The (1810), III, 800
ALFREDIAN PROSE (O.E.), I, **85f.**
Algarotti, Francesco, II, 65, 807
Alighieri, Dante, I, 340; II, 67, 809f.; III, 39, 229 (2), 298, 310, 724
Alimony Lady, The, or Lady Alimony, I, 652
Alisaunder (M.E.), I, **143**
Alisaunder, Lyfe of, or Kyng Alisaunder (M.E.), I, **143**
Alison, Archibald (1757–1839), metaphysician, II, 20
Alison, Sir Archibald (1792–1867), historian, II, **907f.**
Alison (or Allison), Richard (*fl.* 1606), I, 485
Alison, William Pulteney (1790–1859), III, 975
Alken, Henry (1787–1851), III, 82, 90
ALL SOULS COLLEGE (Oxford), I, 368
All the Favourite Oratorios (18 cent.), II, 243
All the Year Round (1859), III, 818
Allais, Denis Vairasse d', II, 802
All-Alive and Merry (1740), II, 708
Allan, Charles Stuart Hay (*fl.* 1848). See Allen
Allan, G. (*fl.* 1834), III, 374
Allan, John Hay (*fl.* 1848). See John Carter Allen
Allan, Robert (*fl.* 1790), II, 731
Allan, Sir William (1782–1850), III, 379
Allardyce, Alexander (1846–1896), III, 1070
Allde, Edward (*fl.* 1555–92), I, 352
ALLEGORICAL POETRY, II, 44f. (French-English)
Alleine, Joseph (1634–1668), II, **846**
Alleine, Richard (1611–1681), II, 846
Alleine, Theodosia (*fl.* 1672), II, 846
Allen, Adam (*fl.* 1798), II, 971
Allen, Benjamin (1663–1738), II, 154
Allen, Charles Manning (*fl.* 1848), afterwards Charles Stuart Hay Allan, III, 763
Allen, David O. (*fl.* 1856), III, 1076
Allen, Grant, i.e. Charles Grant Blairfindie Allen (1848–1899), III, **534f.**
Allen, Henry Ellis (*fl.* 1836–74), III, **996**
Allen, John (1771–1843), political and historical writer, I, 119; II, 952; III, 879 (2)
Allen, John (*fl.* 1825), equestrian, III, 764
Allen, John Carter (*fl.* 1848), afterwards John Hay Allan, III, 763
Allen, John Hensleigh (*fl.* 1788), II, 666

Allen, M. (*fl.* 1841), III, 219
Allen, Thomas (1803–1833), III, **885f.**
Allen, W. (*fl.* 1824), clergyman, III, 219
Allen, William (1532–1594), I, 366, 737
Allen, William (1770–1843), II, 856; III, 113
Allestree, Richard (1619–1681), II, 119, **846**
Alley, William (1510?–1570), I, 508
'Allgood, Nurse' (1780), II, 562
Allibond, John (1597–1658), I, 369
Allingham, William (1824–1889), III, **276f.**, 826
Allison, A. (*fl.* 1885), III, 799
Allison (or Alison), Richard (*fl.* 1606), I, 485
Allison, Thomas (*fl.* 1699), II, 743
ALLITERATIVE VERSE
    Old English. See under PROSODY, I, **13f.** and OLD ENGLISH POETRY, I, **60f.**
    Middle English, I, **195f.** (and references there to PEARL GROUP, PIERS PLOWMAN SERIES, and ROMANCES)
Allman, George James (1812–1896), III, 957
'Allnight, Bumper' (1763), II, 222, 224
Allon, Henry (1818–1892), III, 833
Allott, Robert (*fl.* 1599), I, 404, 715
Allsop, Thomas (1795–1880), III, 176
Ally Sloper's Half Holiday (1884), III, 820
Alma Mater [Cambridge] (1900), III, 835
Almanack of the Month, The (1846), III, 828
Almar, George (*fl.* 1830–40), III, **599**
Almon, John (1737–1805), II, 671, 923
    Biographies and compilations by, II, 164, 167, 230, 340, 631
    Periodicals edited by, II, 679 (2), 680, 708, 716
Almond, Hely Hutchinson (1832–1903), III, 106, 136
Almond, Robert (*fl.* 1673), II, 816
'Almonides' (1751), II, 303
Alms (O.E.), I, **82**
Alney, John (*fl.* 1744), II, 760
ALNWICK, II, 86 (printing)
Alpe, E. N. (*fl.* 1890), III, 985
Alpers, O. T. J. (*fl.* 1900), III, 1093
Alphabet of Tales, An (15 cent.), I, 266
Alphabetical List of the Freemen of Chester [etc.], *An* (18 cent.), II, 237
Alphonsus, Emperour of Germany, The Tragedy of (17 cent.), I, 651
Alpine Journal, The (1863), III, 830
Alsop, George (*fl.* 1666), II, 751
Alsop, Vincent (d. 1703), II, 941
Alston Miscellany; Or, Gentleman's Magazine, The (1799), II, 684
Altar of Love, The (18 cent.), II, 198, 201
Alter et Idem (1794), II, 685
Alves, Robert (1745–1794), II, 916
Always Happy! (19 cent.), III, 575
Amadace, Sir (M.E.), I, **154f.**
Amadis of Gaul, I, 509
Amaryllis (18 cent.), II, 211 (2), 212–3, 219, 233
Amateur Gardening (1884), III, 821

Amatory Pieces (18 cent.), II, 254
Amatory Poems (19 cent.), II, 255
Amberley, John Russell, Viscount (1842–1876), III, 146
Ambrose, I, 857
Ambross, — (*fl.* 1790), II, 408
Amcotts, V. (*fl.* 1866), III, 920
AMERICA
    Descriptions of, I, 794f. (16, 17 cents.)
    Voyages to, I, 786f. (16, 17 cents.); II, 751f. (1660–1800)
American Magazine, The (1851), III, 828
American Mock Bird, The (18 cent.), II, 219
American Repository; Or, Lottery Magazine of Literature [etc.], *The* (1777), II, 680
American Songster, The (18 cent.), II, 241 (2)
Ames, Henry (*fl.* 1727), II, 765
Ames, Joseph (1689–1759), II, **881**
Ames, Richard (d. 1693?), II, **277**f.
Ames, William (1576–1633), I, 875
Amherst, Jeffery, Baron (1717–1797), II, 755
Amherst, William (*fl.* 1758), II, 755
Amhurst, Nicholas (1697–1742), II, 117, **309**, 662 (3), 663, 713
Amiel, III, 562
Amir Ali, Sayyed (*fl.* 1873), III, 1081
Amis and Amiloun (M.E.), I, **154**
Ammath, The Tragedy of (17 cent.), I, 661
Ammianus Marcellinus, I, 804
Amner, John (d. 1641), I, 486
Amory, Thomas (1691?–1788), II, 545 (2)
Amos, Andrew (1791–1860), III, 106
Amott, J. (*fl.* 1865), III, 882
Amours of Messalina, The (17 cent.), II, 531
Amours of the English Gallantry in Several Historical Poems, The (17 cent.), II, 177
Amours of the Sultana of Barbary, The (17 cent.), II, 531
Amphion Anglicus (17 cent.), II, 184
Amphion or the Chorister's Delight (18 cent.), II, 234
Amphlett, James (d. 1860), II, 694
Amsterdam Slip, The (1697), II, 706
Amundesham, Johannes (*fl.* 1421–40), I, 115
Amusement for the Ladies (1780), II, 234, 245–7
Amusement for the Ladies (1793), II, 247
Amusing Instructor, The (18 cent.), II, 562
Amyot, Jacques, I, 331, 804
Amyot, Thomas (1775–1850), I, 488; III, 148
Anacreon, I, 799; II, 759
Anacreon Done into English (17 cent.), II, 179, 191
Anacreontic Magazine (18 cent.), II, 246, 248–9
Anacreontic Song, as sung by Mr Bannister [etc.], *The* (18 cent.), II, 240
Anacreontic Songs (18 cent.), II, 238
Analytical Review; Or, History of Literature, The (1788), II, 681
ANATOMY AND SURGERY (writings on), I, 890f. (16, 17 cents.)

Anatomy of the Separatists, The (17 cent.), I, **723**
Anburey, Thomas (*fl.* 1789), II, 756
Ancient and Modern Scots Songs, The (18 cent.), II, 225, 231, 245
Ancient Ballads, Songs, and Poems (18 cent.), II, 251, 254
ANCIENT HISTORY, III, 894f., 913f. See also under CLASSICAL and ORIENTAL SCHOLARSHIP
Ancient Scotish Poems (1786), II, 239
Ancient Scottish Poems (1770), II, 226
Ancient Songs (18 cent.), II, 243, 246
ANCIENTS AND MODERNS CONTROVERSY, II, 10
Ancren Riwle (M.E.), I, **179**f.
Anderdon, John (*fl.* 1662), II, 861
Anderdon, John Lavicount (1792–1874), III, 769
Andersen, Hans Christian, III, 576, 612
Anderson, Adam (1692?–1765), II, 997
Anderson, Aeneas (*fl.* 1795), II, 751
Anderson, Alexander (1845–1909), III, 327f.
Anderson, Christopher (1782–1852), I, 672
Anderson, G. (*fl.* 1859), III, 302
Anderson, George (1676?–1756), II, **994**
Anderson, George William (*fl.* 1784), II, 741
Anderson, J. D. (*fl.* 1895), III, 1073
Anderson, J. W. (*fl.* 1797), II, 449
Anderson, James (1662–1728), II, 610, **876**
Anderson, James (1739–1808), II, 671, 686, **999**
Anderson, Michael (*fl.* 1812), II, 732
Anderson, Philip (*fl.* 1854), III, 1076
Anderson, R. Patrick (*fl.* 1861), III, 1071
Anderson, Robert (1750–1830), editor and biographer, II, 260, 523, 525, 625, 686, 924, 929
Anderson, Robert (1770–1833), Cumbrian poet, III, **225**
Anderson, William (*fl.* 1796), II, 310
Anderson, William (1805–1866), III, 187, 233
Andreas (O.E.), I, **77**
Andreini, Giovanni Battista, II, 807
Andrewe, Lawrence (*fl.* 1510–37), I, 819, 892
Andrewes, John (*fl.* 1615), I, 473
Andrewes, Lancelot (1555–1626), I, 680, 684, 845
Andrews, Alexander (*fl.* 1859–66), III, 782, 790
Andrews, James Pettit (1737?–1797), II, 378, 807
Andrews, Miles Peter (d. 1814), II, 457, **459**
Andrews, Robert (d. 1766), II, 23, 768
Andrews, Thomas (1813–1885), III, 125, 947
Andrews, W. (*fl.* 1744), II, 793
Andrews, William (*fl.* 1656), I, 890
Andrews, William Eusebius (1773–1837), III, 819
Andromana, The Merchant's Wife (17 cent.), I, 651
Andronicus (17 cent.), I, 661
Androse, Richard (*fl.* 1569), I, 809, 888
Aneau, Barthélémi, I, 732
Anecdotes of a Little Family (18 cent.), II, 563

Anello, Paulillo, I, 340
Angel, Moses (*fl.* 1841), III, 819
Angell, John (*fl.* 1758), II, 621
Angelo, Domenico (*fl.* 1763), II, 823
Angelo, Henry Charles William (1760–1839), II, 138, 823; III, 778
'Angelo, Master Michael' (1776), II, 562
'Angeloni, Battista' [i.e. J. Shebbeare], II, 141
Angerianus, Hieronymus, I, 328
Angiolini, Luigi, II, 141
Angler's Note-Book, The (1880), III, 768
ANGLING (books on), I, 393f. (16, 17 cents.); II, 818f. (1660–1800); III, 768f. (19 cent.)
Angliviel de la Beaumelle, Laurent, II, 769
ANGLO-INDIAN LITERATURE, III, 1067f.
    Fiction, III, 1069f.
    Geography, Topography and Travel, III, 1079f.
    History, Biography and Politics, III, 1074f.
    Philology, III, 1017f., 1073f.
    Poetry and Drama, III, 1068f.
    Religion and Philosophy, III, 1080f.
    Social and Miscellaneous, III, 1082f.
    Translations, III, 1070f.
    Works of Reference, III, 1067f.
ANGLO-IRISH LITERATURE, III, 1045f.
    Dramatists of the Irish Revival, III, 1063f.
    Gaelic Sources, III, 1047f.
    Poets of the Irish Revival, III, 1051f.
    Yeats and Synge, III, 1059f.
ANGLO-SAXON PERIOD, I, 53f. See for details under OLD ENGLISH
Anglo-Saxon Review, The (1899), III, 834
Angoulême, Madame Royale, Duchess of, III, 665
Angove, J. (*fl.* 1910), III, 1092
Angus, Joseph (1816–1902), I, 17, 680; III, 106
Annales Ricardi II et Henrici IV (15 cent.), I, 115
ANNALS. See under CHRONICLES
Annals and Magazine of Natural History, The (1840), III, 826
Annals of Agriculture (1784), II, 673
Annals of Agriculture and other Useful Arts (1784), II, 680
Annals of Europe, The (1739), II, 684
Annals of King George (1716), II, 683
Annals of Medicine (1796), II, 686
Annals of Philosophy, The (1813), III, 825
Annals of Sporting and Fancy Gazette, The (1822), III, 758, 826
Annals of the Fine Arts (1817), III, 825
Annand, James (1843–1906), III, 782, 802 (2), 806
Annand, William (1633–1689), II, 992
Anne, Queen of England (1665–1714), II, 149
Annesley, George, Viscount Valentia (*fl.* 1809), III, 1079
Annet, Peter (1693–1769), II, 664, 945
Annual Anthology, The (18 cent.), II, 254–5

Annual Hampshire Repository, The (1799), II, 685
Annual Harmony, The (18 cent.), II, 242
Annual Register, The (1758), II, 673, 684
ANNUALS, II, 683 (1702–1800); III, 839f. (19 cent.)
Anonimalle Chronicle, The (14 cent.), I, 115
ANONYMOUS PLAYS, I, 520f., 521f., 537f. (16 cent.), 651f. (17 cent.), 661 (university plays)
Anquetil, Louis Pierre, II, 769
Anselm (d. 1109), I, **282**f., 461
Anson, George, Baron (1697–1762), II, 741
Anson, Sir William Reynell (1843–1914), III, **920**
Anster, John (1793–1867), III, **225**f.
Anstey, Christopher (1724–1805), II, **351**f.
'Anstey, F.', i.e. Thomas Anstey Guthrie (1856–1934), III, **535**, 835
Anstey, John (d. 1819), II, 115, 351
Answers (1888), III, 814
Antes, John (*fl.* 1800), II, 749
Anthologia Hibernica (18 cent.), II, 248–9
Anthologia Hibernica; Or, Monthly Collections of Science [etc.] (1793), II, 688
ANTHOLOGIES, I, 12f.
    Old English, I, 54, 62, 85. See also READERS, I, 36, 46
    Middle English, I, 114, 254f. (Middle Scots), 264 (15 cent.), 267f. (lyrics)
    Renaissance to Restoration, I, 380 (prose), 405f. (verse)
    Restoration to Romantic Revival, II, 133 (prose), 257f. (verse)
    Nineteenth Century, III, 13f. (prose), 162f. (verse)
    See also COLLECTIONS and MISCELLANIES
Anthonie, Francis (*fl.* 1610), I, 886
ANTHROPOLOGY (writings on), III, 966f., 1092f. (native races of South Africa), 1097f. (Australia, New Zealand)
Anti-Aulicus (1644), I, 756
Anti-Cobbett, The (1817), III, 816
Antidote against Melancholy, An (17 cent.), II, 173, 175, 179 (2)
Antidote against Melancholy, An (18 cent.), II, 213
Anti-Gallican Monitor and Anti-Corsican Chronicle, The (1811), III, 811
Antigallican Songster, The (18 cent.), II, 248 (2)
Anti-Jacobin; Or, Weekly Examiner, The (1797), II, 390, 698, 716
Anti-Jacobin Review and Magazine, The (1798), II, 683; III, 824
Anti-Levelling Songster, The (18 cent.), II, 248 (2)
Anti-Pamela; or, Feign'd Innocence Detected (18 cent.), II, 543
Antiquarian Repertory, The (18 cent.), II, 230, 233–4, 237

ANTIQUARIES, I, 823f. (1500–1660); II, 864f. (1660–1800, especially 879–81, 890–2); III, 877f. (19 cent., especially 882–6, 902–6, 927–30)

Antiquities of St. Peter's, The (18 cent.), II, 190–2, 196, 208–9

Anti-Roman Pacquet, The (1680), II, 657, 702

Anti-Theatre, The (1720), II, 662

Anti-Union, The (Dublin, 1798), II, 736

Anton, Robert (*fl.* 1616), I, 481, 731

Antoninus Bassianus Caracalla (17 cent.), I, 661

Antonio of Ragusa (17 cent.), I, 651

Anwykyll, John (*fl.* 1483), I, 125

Apel, J. A., III, 649

Apollo, The (1759), II, 218

Apollo, The (1791), II, 245, 249

Apollo: Or, The Songster's Universal Library (18 cent.), II, 220, 228

Apollo's Banquet (17 cent.), II, 182

Apollo's Cabinet (18 cent.), II, 217 (2), 218

Apollo's Delight (18 cent.), II, 217

Apollo's Feast (18 cent.), II, 186

Apollo's Lyre (18 cent.), II, 248, 252–3

Apollonian Harmony (18 cent.), II, 243, 250, 254

Apollonius of Tyre (O.E.), I, **94**f.

Apollonius Rhodius, II, 759

Apperley, Charles James ('Nimrod') (1779–1843), III, 759f.

Appian, I, 799; II, 759

Applebee, F. (*fl.* 1713), II, 712

Applebee, J. (*fl.* 1713), II, 712

Applebee's Journal (1720), II, 662

Applebee's Original Weekly Journal (1720), II, 712

Applegath, A. (*fl.* 1857), III, 78

Appleton, C. E. C. B. (1841–1879), III, 782, 818

Après de Mannevilette, J. B. N. D. d' (*fl.* 1781), III, 1079

Apthorp, S. F. (*fl.* 1859), I, 6

Apuleius, I, 799; II, 764

Aquila, Serafino Dell', I, 339

Arabian Nights Entertainments, II, 540, 565; III, 353

ARABIC SCHOLARS, III, 1020f.

Arago, Dominique-François, III, 675

Arber, Edward (1836–1912), II, 258; III, **1035**f.

Arbor of Amorous Devises, The (16 cent.), I, 404

Arbroath Magazine, The (1799), II, 687

Arbuckle, James (1700–1734?), II, 16, 593, 662, 734

Arbuthnot, Alexander (1538–1593), I, 896

'Arbuthnot, Archibald' (1746), I, 1002

Arbuthnot, Forster Fitzgerald (1833–1901), III, 1078

Arbuthnot, George (1802–1865), III, 972

Arbuthnot, James (*fl.* 1900), III, 1080

Arbuthnot, John (1667–1735), II, 536 (2), **576**f.

Arbuthnot, John (*fl.* 1773), II, 149

'Arcandam' (1562), I, 883

Arcaeus, I, 891

Archaeologist and Journal of Antiquarian Science, The (1841), III, 1034

ARCHAEOLOGY

Anglo-Saxon Period, I, 56f.

Nineteenth-Century writings on, III, 913f.

Archbold, John Frederick (1785–1870), III, 985

Archdale, John (*fl.* 1664–1707), II, 753

Archenholtz, Johan Wilhelm von, II, 141, 688 (2), 805

Archeological Review, The (1888), III, 834

Archer, E. C. (*fl.* 1833), III, 1080

Archer, Thomas (*fl.* 1622), I, 744

Archer, William (1856–1924), III, **732**f.

Archer's Bath Chronicle (1768), II, 720

Archer-Hind, Richard Dacre (1849–1910), III, **1004**

ARCHERY (books on), I, 394f. (16, 17 cents.); II, 822 (1660–1800); III, 775f. (19 cent.)

Architect, The (1869), III, 822

Architectural Magazine and Journal of Improvement in Architecture [etc.], *The* (1834), III, 827

Architectural Review, The (1896), III, 831

ARCHITECTURE (books on), I, 392f. (16, 17 cents.); II, 30f. (17, 18 cents.), 161 (17, 18 cents.)

Arden of Feversham, The Lamentable and True Tragedie of M. (16 cent.), I, 579

Arderne, James (1636–1691), II, 24

Arderne, John (b. 1307), I, **312**, 891

Aresti, J. (*fl.* 1856), III, 83

Aretino, Pietro (Bruni), I, 339, 677, 679

'Argas, Arabella' (1810), III, 571

Argences, — d', II, 534

Argens, Jean Baptiste de Boyer, Marquis d', II, 35, 543, 552, 772

Argentine, Richard (*alias* Sexten) (d. 1568), I, 817 (2), 820

Argonaut, The (1874), III, 830

Argosy, The (1865), III, 830

Argument of the Pastorall of Florimene, The (17 cent.), I, 652

Argus, A. (*fl.* 1813), III, 135

Argus, The (1789), II, 709

Argus, The (1828), III, 801

Argus, The (1839), III, 814

Argus, The [Brighton] (1880), III, 805

Argus of the Constitution, The (1792), II, 709

Argus, The House-Dog at Eadlip (18 cent.), II, 549

Argyll, Archibald Campbell, Duke of (1682–1761), II, 102

Argyll, George Douglas Campbell, Duke of (1823–1900), III, 283, **862**, 954

Argyll, John Douglas Sutherland, Duke of (1845–1914), III, 155

Arias Montanus, I, 679

Ariosto, Ludovico, I, 339–40; II, 66, 808; III, 243

Aris's Birmingham Gazette (1742), II, 721

Aristophanes, I, 658, 799; II, 362, 759; III, 229, 999, 1005, 1009–10

Aristophanes (18 cent.), II, 233
Aristotle, I, 264, 799f., 889; II, 27, 759; III, 1001, 1002 (3), 1004, 1007
ARITHMETIC TEXTBOOKS OF, I, 377f. (16, 17 cents.); II, 125 (17, 18 cents.)
Arliss's Pocket Magazine (1818), III, 825
Armand, Jacques, II, 769
Armand de Bourbon, Prince of Conti, II, 769
Armies Intelligencer, The (1651), I, 761
Armies Modest Intelligencer, The (1649), I, 759
Armies Painfull-Messenger, The (1649), I, 760
Armies Post, The (1647), I, 757
Armies Scout, The (1653), I, 761
Armies Weekly Intelligencer, The (1649), I, 759
Armiger, Charles (*fl.* 1830), III, 759
Armin, Robert (*fl.* 1588–1610), I, 640, 715
Arminian Magazine, Consisting of Extracts on Universal Redemption, The (1778), II, 680
Armistead, J. J. (*fl.* 1895), III, 772
Armistead, Wilson (*fl.* 1850), II, 856
Armstrong, C. (*fl.* 1519), I, 846
Armstrong, G. E. (*fl.* 1894–1907), III, 800
Armstrong, Sir George C. H. (1836–1907), III, 800
Armstrong, H. E. (*fl.* 1898), III, 106
Armstrong, Hopkins (*fl.* 1898), III, 1085
Armstrong, John (1709–1779), II, **309**, 399, 745
Armstrong, R. A. (*fl.* 1880), III, 834
Armstrong, Sir Walter (1850–1918), III, **733**
Armstrong, William George, Baron (1810–1900), III, 71
ARMY, II, 151f.
Army and Navy Gazette, The (1860), III, 821
Arnall, William (1715?–1741?), II, 663, 694, 708, 713, 879
Arnaud, Pierre Baculard d', II, 552 (2)
Arnauld, Antoine, II, 769, 785, 792
Arne, Thomas Augustine (1710–1778), II, 222, 224, 812
Arno Miscellany, The (18 cent.), II, 237
Arnold, Sir Arthur (1833–1902), III, 801
Arnold, Sir Edwin (1832–1904), III, **328**, 799, 1071
Arnold, F. (*fl.* 1862), III, 685, 818
Arnold, J. M. (*fl.* 1859), III, 1081
Arnold, John (*fl.* 1753), II, 216, 224, 226, 230, 232, 239, 245, 248
Arnold, Mary (*fl.* 1845), III, 888 (2)
Arnold, Mary Augusta, later Mrs Humphry Ward (1851–1920), III, **561**f.
Arnold, Matthew (1822–1888), III, 106f., 121 (2), 161, **265**f.
Arnold, Richard (d. 1521?), I, 823
Arnold, Robert (*fl.* 1710), II, 110
Arnold, Samuel (1740–1802), II, 238
Arnold, Samuel James (1774–1852), II, 378; III, 566, **586**
Arnold, T. W. (*fl.* 1896), III, 1082
Arnold, Thomas (1795–1842), Rugby headmaster, III, 33, 122, 134, 136, **888**f.

Arnold, Thomas (1823–1900), literary historian, III, **1028**f.
Arnold, Thomas James (1804?–1877), barrister, III, 985
Arnold, William Delafield (1828–1859), III, 1069, 1084
Arnold, William Thomas (1852–1904), III, **916**
Arnot, D. (*fl.* 1875), III, 1092
Arnot, Hugo (1749–1786), II, 157–8
Arnould, Sir Joseph (1814–1886), III, 985
Arraignment of Lewd Women, The (18 cent.), II, 186
Arrian, II, 759
Arrowsmith, J. P. (*fl.* 1819), III, 107
Arrowsmith, R. (*fl.* 1898), III, 1073
Art and Letters (1888), III, 834
Art and Poetry (1850), III, 833
Art Journal, The (1849), III, 828
Art of Courtship, The (1662), II, 174
Art of Courtship, The (1686), II, 180 (2)
Art of Dress, The (18 cent.), II, 193
Art of English Poetry, The (18 cent.), II, 185–6, 188–9, 191, 194, 197 (2), 206–7, 220
Art of Poetry Made Easy, The (18 cent.), II, 211, 213, 221, 226–7, 231
Art of Poetry on a New Plan, The (18 cent.), II, 220
Art of Story-Telling, The (18 cent.), II, 243
Art Union Monthly Journal of the Fine Arts etc., The (1844), III, 828
Arthour and Merlin (M.E.), I, **133**
Arthur (M.E.), I, **136**
Arthur, Archibald (1744–1797), II, 105
ARTHUR, KING (Legend of), I, 131
ARTHURIAN ROMANCES (M.E.)
    Early Chronicle Treatments, I, **132**f.
    General, I, **130**f.
    Particular Phases and Heroes, I, **131**f.
    Romances in English, I, **133**f.
Arthus, Gothard, I, 785
Artist's Repository and Drawing Magazine, The (1785), II, 681
ARTS, FINE
    Influence on literature, II, 13, 14f. (17, 18 cents.)
    Treatises on, I, 392f. (1500–1660), II, 30f. (1660–1800)
Arundel (or Arundell), — (*fl.* 1720), II, 196
Arvieux, Laurent d', II, 769
Arwaker, Edmund (*fl.* 1684), II, **278**
Asbjörnsen, Peter Christian, III, 576
Ascham, Roger (1515–1568), I, 45, 365–6, 383, **671**, 864
Aschrott, P. F. (*fl.* 1880), III, 976
Asgill, John (1659–1738), II, 84, 958
Ash, John (1724?–1779), II, 931–2
Ashbee, E. W. (*fl.* 1868), I, 318, 711
Ashburnham, John (1603–1671), I, 842
Ashburton, Alexander Baring, Baron (1774–1848), III, 684, 972

Ashburton, John Dunning, Baron (1731–1783), II, 631
Ashby, George (d. 1475), I, **253**
Ashe, Simeon (d. 1662), I, 748, 756
Ashe, Thomas (*fl.* 1600–13), legal writer, I, 849
Ashe, Thomas (*fl.* 1682), writer on America, II, 752
Ashe, Thomas (1836–1889), poet, III, **328**
ASHENDENE PRESS, III, 86
Ashlet, A. (*fl.* 1849), III, 82
Ashley, Sir Anthony (1551–1627), I, 778, 885
Ashley, Maurice (*fl.* 1770), II, 764
Ashley, Robert (1565–1641), I, 785
Ashmole, Elias (1617–1692), I, 386, **886–7**; II, **871**
ASHMOLEAN MUSEUM, II, 104
Ashmore, Francis (*fl.* 1779–89), II, 790, 804 (2)
Ashmore, John (*fl.* 1621), I, 803
Ashton, John (*fl.* 1639), I, 383
Ashton, Robert (*fl.* 1725), II, 592
Ashwell, Arthur Rawson (1824–1879), III, 833
Ashwell, George (1612–1695), II, 533
Ashwick, Samuel (*fl.* 1750), II, 761
Ashworth, Francis (*fl.* 1782), II, 783
ASIA
  Descriptions of, I, 785 f. (16, 17 cents.)
  Voyages to, I, 781 f. (16, 17 cents.); II, 749 f. (1667–1800)
Asiatic Annual Register for the Year 1799, *The* (1800), II, 684
Asiatic Journal and Monthly Register for British India, The (1816), III, 825
Asiatick Miscellany, The (18 cent.), II, 238–40
Askham (or Ascham), Anthony (*fl.* 1552), I, 882, 892
Askwith, G. R., Baron (*fl.* 1897), III, 764
Aspinwall, S. (*fl.* 1765), II, 776
Aspland, Robert (1782–1845), III, 56, 824, 846
Aspley, John (*fl.* 1624), I, 885
Assarino, Luca, I, 732
Assembly of Ladies, The, (M.E.), I, 254
Asser (d. 910), I, **107**
Assheton, Nicholas, of Downham (1590–1625), I, 385
Association Medical Journal, The (1853), III, 821
Associator, The (1792), II, 666
Assumption of Mary (M.E.), I, **175** f.
ASSYRIOLOGISTS, III, 1015 f.
Astell, Mary (1668–1731), II, 121, 131
Astell, Mary (*fl.* 1763), II, 835
Astley, John (d. 1595), I, 393, 814
Astley, Sir John Dugdale (1828–1894), III, 767
Astley, Philip (1742–1814), II, 817, 827
Astley, Thomas (*fl.* 1745), I, 764
Aston, Anthony (*fl.* 1712–31), II, 407, 409
Aston, E. (*fl.* 1611), I, 765
Aston, John (*fl.* 1639), I, 772
Aston, Joseph P. (1762–1844), III, 471
Aston, R. (*fl.* 1661), II, 962

Aston, Walter Hutchinson, Baron (*fl.* 1789), II, 666
Astrey (or Astry), Sir James (*fl.* 1700), I, 478; II, 261
Astrologer's Magazine and Philosophical Miscellany, The (1793), II, 681
Astrological Observator, The (1701), II, 659
ASTROLOGY, I, 883 f. (16, 17 cents.)
ASTRONOMY, I, 882 f. (16, 17 cents.); III, 943 f. (19 cent.). For 1660–1800 see under LITERATURE OF SCIENCE, II, 959 f.
Asty, John (1672?–1730), I, 699
Asylum for Fugitives, An (18 cent.), II, 231, 233
Asylum for Fugitive Pieces, An (18 cent.), II, 238 (3), 239, 248, 250, 253
Asylum; Or, Weekly Miscellany, The (1793), II, 687
Atalanta (1887), III, 578
Athanasius, St, III, 689
Athelston (M.E.), I, **150** f.
Athenae Redivivae (18 cent.), II, 186
Athenaeum, The (1828), III, 818
Athenian Gazette, The (1690), II, 698
Athenian Gazette; Or, Casuistical Mercury, The (1690), II, 658
Athenian Mercury, The (1690), II, 658
Athenian News; Or, Dunton's Oracle (1710), II, 660
Athenian Oracle, The (1703), II, 186 (2), 187, 189, 199, 658
Athenian Sport (18 cent.), II, 187
Athenianism (18 cent.), II, 189
Atherstone, Edwin (1788–1872), III, **226**
Athletic News, The [Manchester] (1875), III, 820
Athletic Record, The (1875), III, 776
ATHLETICS (books on), III, 776
ATHLONE, II, 736 (newspapers)
Athlone Chronicle, The (1770), II, 736
Athlone Herald, The (1785), II, 736
Athlone Sentinel, The (1798), II, 736
Atkins, John (1685–1797), II, 742
Atkins, Maurice (*fl.* 1672), II, 288
Atkins, Sir Richard (*fl.* 1664–9), II, 84
Atkinson, Frederick, II, 243, 245–6, 253
Atkinson, H. G. (*fl.* 1851), III, 497
Atkinson, H. K. (*fl.* 1858?), III, 822
Atkinson, J. L. (*fl.* 1872), III, 1081
Atkinson, James (1780–1852), III, 1070
Atkinson, John Augustus (b. 1775), II, 160
Atkinson, Joseph (1743–1818), II, 452
Atkinson, Robert (1839–1908), III, 1050
Atkinson, Thomas (1600–1639), I, 655
Atkinson, W. (*fl.* 1833–40), III, 978, 982
Atkyns, Sir Robert (1621–1709), judge, II, 962
Atkyns, Sir Robert (1647–1711), topographer, II, **879**
Atkynson (or Atkinson), William (d. 1509), I, 266
Atlas, The (1826), III, 811
Atlay, James Beresford (1860–1913), III, **920**

Atterbury, Francis (1662–1732), I, 455; II, 15, 21, 503, **851**, 866

Atterbury, Lewis (1656–1731), II, 784

Atterburyana (18 cent.), II, 198

Attey, Joan (d. 1640?), I, 486

Attic Miscellany, The (18 cent.), II, 242, 243 (2), 245 (2)

Attic Miscellany; Or, Characteristic Mirror of Men and Things, The (1789), II, 681

Attick Wit (13 cent.), II, 245

Attwood, Thomas (1783–1856), III, 973

Atwood, Thomas (d. 1793), II, 757

Atwood, William (d. 1705?), II, 876

Auber, P. (*fl.* 1837), III, 1075

Aubert, David, I, 266

Aubert de Vertot d'Aubeuf, René, II, 769

Aubignac, François Hédélin d', II, 39, 782

Aubigné, Françoise d', later Madame de Maintenon, II, 769

Aubigné, Theodore Agrippa d', II, 770

Aubin, Penelope (*fl.* 1721), II, 537, 538 (2)

Auborn, A. d', II, 532

Aubrey, John (1626–1697), I, 872; II, **866** f.

Auckland, William Eden, Baron (1744–1814), II, 138, 963

Auction Register and Law Chronicle, The (1813), III, 821

AUCTIONS, BOOK, II, 97 f. (1660–1800); III, 103 (19 cent.)

Audelay, John (*fl.* 1420), I, 264

Audiguier, Vital d', I, 334, 732

Auditor, The (1733), II, 663

Auditor, The (1762), II, 665

Audland, W. F. (*fl.* 1843–7), III, 856

Audley, Thomas (*fl.* 1643), I, 748, 755, 757

Augier, G. V. Emile, III, 598

Augustine, I, 810; II, 764

Augustine, of Ireland (*fl.* 655), I, 102

Aulne, Anne Robert Jacques Turgot, Baron de l', II, 802

Aulnoy, Marie Catherine de la Mothe, Comtesse d', II, 46, 149, 534, 541, 565, 785

Aulus Gellius, II, 765

Aulus Sabinus, II, 182

Aumer, Jean, III, 592

Aumont, J. B. d', II, 774

Aunt Judy's Magazine (1866), III, 578, 830

Aurelius, Marcus, I, 800; II, 759 f.; III, 1000

Aurora and British Imperial Reporter, The (1807), III, 798

Aurora and Universal Advertiser, The (1781), II, 709

Aurora Borealis (1821), III, 811

Aurora; Or, The Dawn of Genuine Truth (1799), II, 683

Ausonius, I, 800

Aussy, Pierre Jean Baptiste Le Grand d', II, 787

Austen, Henry Thomas (1771–1850), II, 666; III, 381 (2)

Austen, James (1765–1819), II, 666

Austen, Jane (1775–1817), III, 23, **381** f.

Austen-Leigh, J. E. (*fl.* 1870), III, 382

Austin, Alfred (1835–1913), III, 161, **328** f., 831

Austin, Henry (*fl.* 1613), I, 805

Austin, John (1613–1669), I, 473

Austin, John (1790–1859), III, **862**, 985

Austin, R. (*fl.* 1819), III, 74

Austin, Sarah, née Taylor (1793–1867), III, 107, 576, 680

Austin, Stella (*fl.* 1875), III, 573

Austin, William (1587–1634), I, 725, 801

Austin, William (*fl.* 1802), II, 142

AUSTRALIA

Literature of, III, 1093 f.

Voyages to, II, 749 f.

Author, The (1890), III, 831

AUTHORS

Biographical dictionaries of, II, 922 f.

Guides to publication for, III, 96 f.

Authors and Artists (1881), III, 830

AUTOBIOGRAPHIES, I, 381 f. (16, 17 cents.), 826 f. (16 cent.), 840 f. (17 cent.); II, 133 f. (17, 18 cents.), 156 (17, 18 cents., Scottish), 158 f. (17, 18 cents., Irish); III, 14 f. (19 cent., literary), 149 f. (19 cent., general)

Avaux, Jean Antione de Mesmes, Count d', II, 791

Avebury, Sir John Lubbock, Baron (1834–1913), III, **915**, 958

Averell, William (*fl.* 1584), I, 729

Avery, Benjamin (d. 1764), II, 662

Aviary, The (18 cent.), II, 210, 213, 217, 221

Avila, Juan de, II, 69

Ávila y Zúñiga, Luis de, I, 810

Avison, Charles (1710?–1770), II, 895

Avity, Pierre d', I, 766

'Avon' (1882), III, 767

Avowynge of King Arthur (M.E.), I, **138**

Awdeley, John (1559–77), I, 717, 845

Awdry, J. W. (*fl.* 1854), III, 128

Awntyrs off Arthure (M.E.), I, **136**

À Wood, Anthony (1632–1695), II, **867**

Awsiter, John (*fl.* 1768), II, 154

Ayenbite of Inwyt, The (M.E.), I, **184** f.

Aylett, Robert (1583–1655?), I, 473

Ayliffe, John (*fl.* 1714), II, 117, 153

Ayloffe, William (*fl.* 1702), II, 275

Ayre, J. (*fl.* 1843), I, 682, 683 (2), 684

Ayre, R. (*fl.* 1783), II, 716

Ayre (or Eyre), William (*fl.* 1734–45), II, 301, 303, 808, 811, 814

Ayre's Sunday London Gazette and Weekly Monitor (1783), II, 716

Ayres, Daniel (*fl.* 1723), II, 129

Ayres, Philip (1638–1712), II, 120, **278** f., 533

Ayrton, William (*fl.* 1853), III, 770

Ayscough, George Edward (d. 1779), II, 321, 485, 746

Ayscough, Samuel (1745–1804), II, 103, 694, 916

Ayton (or Acton), John (d. 1350), I, **312**

Ayton, Richard (1786–1823), II, 161; III, 220
Ayton (or Aytoun), Sir Robert (1570–1638) I, 474
Aytoun, William Edmondstoune (1813–1865), III, **277**f.
Azarias (O.E.), I, **75**

B., A. (*fl.* 1630), I, 715
B., A. (*fl.* 1672), II, 176
B., A. (*fl.* 1680), II, 178
B., A. (*fl.* 1751), II, 303
B., A. (*fl.* 1856), III, 704
B., B. (*fl.* 1680), II, 534
B., C. (*fl.* 1653), I, 781
B., C. (*fl.* 1661), II, 173
B., F. (*fl.* 1661), I, 719
B., F. (*fl.* 1688), II, 127
B., F. H. (*fl.* 1817), III, 196
B., H. B. (*fl.* 1659), I, 654
B., I. (*fl.* 1583), I, 737
B., I. or J. (*fl.* 1657) [misprinted J. B. Gent, I, 378]
B., J., Gentleman (*fl.* 1572), I, 774
B., J., Merchant (*fl.* 1589), I, 779
B., J. (*fl.* 1642), I, 719
B., J. (*fl.* 1652), I, 718
B., J. (*fl.* 1665), II, 800
B., J. (*fl.* 1673), II, 788
B., J. (*fl.* 1674), II, 811
B., J. (*fl.* 1842), III, 193
B., J. L. (*fl.* 1808), III, 566
B., M. (*fl.* 1714), II, 875
B., M. (*fl.* 1725), II, 788
B., M. A. (*fl.* 1844), III, 577
B., P. (*fl.* 1668), II, 781
B., R. (*fl.* 1575), I, 523
B., R. (*fl.* 1583), I, 738
B., R. (*fl.* 1619), I, 771
B., R. (*fl.* 1639), I, 812
B., R. (*fl.* 1671), II, 816
B., R. (*fl.* 1672), II, 176
B., R. (*fl.* 1684), II, 179, 202
B., R. (*fl.* 1784), II, 774
B., R. G. (*fl.* 1862), I, 416
B., S. (*fl.* 1683), II, 179
B., T. (*fl.* 1641–4), I, 752 (2), 754, 756
B., T. (*fl.* 1649), I, 653
B., T. (*fl.* 1654), I, 819
B., T. (*fl.* 1683), II, 776
B., W. (*fl.* 1578), I, 799
B., W. (*fl.* 1658), I, 717
B., W. (*fl.* 1701), II, 398
B., W. (*fl.* 1807), III, 566
B., W. G. (*fl.* 1796), II, 252
Ba., Ro. (*fl.* 1540?), I, 668
Babbage, Charles (1792–1871), III, 85, 97, 941, 978
Babees Book, The (15 cent.), I, 264
Babington, Benjamin Guy (1794–1866), III, 1070

Babington, Charles Cardale (1808–1895), III, **960** (2)
Babington, Churchill (1821–1889), I, 817; III, **996**
Babington, Gervase (1550–1610), I, 508, 684
Babington, John (*fl.* 1635), I, 886
Babington, John (*fl.* 1883), III, 761
Babington, T. (*fl.* 1814), III, 107
Babler, The (1763), II, 665
Babo, Josef Marius von, II, 59
Bacchanalian, The (18 cent.), II, 217, 219
Bacchanalian Songster, The (18 cent.), II, 236
Bacchus and Venus (1737), II, 206
Bacchus and Venus (1770), II, 227
Bachelor (or Batchelor), Thomas (*fl.* 1809), I, 44
Bacon, Anthony (1558–1601), I, 398
Bacon, Francis, Viscount St Albans (1561–1626), I, **868**f.
    Foreign translations and influence, I, 332, 337; II, 31f., 37,
    Minor writings, I, 679, 693, 849
    Special studies of, I, 30, 546, 865
Bacon, Matthew (*fl.* 1736), II, 962
Bacon, Montague (1688–1749), II, 24
Bacon, Nathaniel (1593–1660), I, 849
Bacon, Sir Nathaniel (*fl.* 1580–1620), I, 381
Bacon, Phanuel (1700–1783), II, **310**
Bacon, Richard Mackenzie (1775–1844), III, 832
Bacon, Robert (d. 1248), I, **295**
Bacon, Roger (d. *c.* 1292), I, **293**f., 886
Baconthorpe, John (d. *c.* 1346), I, **311**f.
Baculard d'Arnaud, François Thomas, II, 770
Badcock, John (*fl.* 1816–30), II, 449
Badcock, Samuel (*fl.* 1780), II, 903
Baddeley, John (*fl.* 1834), III, 769
Baddeley, William (*fl.* 1895), III, 775
Baden-Powell, B. H. (1841–1901), III, 1085
Badham, C. D. (*fl.* 1854), III, 770
Badham, Charles (1813–1884), III, **996**
Badminton Magazine of Sports and Pastimes, The (1895), III, 759
Baers, Jan (*fl.* 1623), I, 791
Baert, A. B. F., i.e. Baron Charles Alexandre Balthazar François de Paule de Baert-Duholant, II, 142
Baffin, William (d. 1622), I, 790
Bage, Robert (1728–1801), II, 548 (2), 549 (2), 550 (2)
Bagehot, Walter (1826–1877), III, 125, 379, **707**f., 820, 833, 974
Bagford, John (1650–1716), II, 101, 103
Bagnall, Gibbon (1719–1800), II, 799
Bagnall, J. N. (*fl.* 1855), I, 886
Bagnall's News (1733), II, 724
Bagot, A. G. (*fl.* 1879), III, 767
Bagshaw, William (1628–1702), I, 369
Bagshawe (or Bagshaw), Edward, the elder (d. 1662), I, 845

Bagshawe (or Bagshaw), Edward, the younger (1629–1671), II, 123, 928

Bagster, Samuel (1772–1851), I, 673; II, 260; III, 97

Bagwell, William (*fl.* 1645), I, 717

'*Bagwell Papers*' (1716), II, 662

Baildon, John (*fl.* 1570), I, 346

Baildon, John (*fl.* 1651), I, 816

Bailey, B. (*fl.* 1818), III, 223

Bailey, Nathan (or Nathaniel) (d. 1742), II, 32, 127, 767, 815, 930

Bailey, Philip James (1816–1902), III, **278**

Bailey, Samuel (1791–1870), III, **862**, 972, 974, 980

Bailey, William (*fl.* 1857), III, 770

Baillie, Lady Grisell (1665–1746), II, 156

Baillie, Joanna (1762–1851), II, **226**

Baillie, John (*fl.* 1747), II, 16

Baillie, Robert (1599–1662), I, 386, 909

Baillie, Sir William (*fl.* 1648), of Lamington, I, 909

Baily, Francis (1774–1844), II, 580, 757; III, **943**, 980

Baily's Magazine of Sports and Pastimes (1860), III, 759

Bain, Alexander (1818–1903), II, 956; III, **862**

Bainbridge, George C. (*fl.* 1816), III, 768

Bainbridge, John (1582–1643), I, 765

Baines, Edward (1774–1848), III, 118, 782, **885**, 981

Baines, Sir Edward (1800–1890), III, 107, 120, 782, 803

Baines, Talbot (*fl.* 19 cent.), III, 803

Baird, George Husband (1761–1840), II, 990

Baker, Ada Bartrick (b. 1854), III, **329**

Baker, Anne Elizabeth (1786–1861), III, 219

Baker, Charles (*fl.* 1837), III, 134

Baker, Charles (*fl.* 1898), III, 780

Baker, Daniel (1654?–1723), II, **279**

Baker, David [Augustin] (1575–1641), I, **695**

Baker, David Erskine (1730–1767), II, 96 (2), 430, 803, 923

Baker, Geoffrey le (*fl.* 1350), I, 115

Baker, George (1540–1600), I, 813, 888, 890

Baker, George (*fl.* 1797), translator, II, 766

Baker, George (1781–1851), topographer, III, 885

Baker, Henry (1698–1774), II, 22, 206, **310**, 663, 794 (2)

Baker, Humphrey (*fl.* 1562–87), I, 880, 884

Baker, J. (*fl.* 1712), publisher, II, 707 (2)

Baker, John (b. 1712), II, 136–7

Baker, M. (*fl.* 1828), III, 572

Baker, Sir Richard (1568–1645), I, 800, 810, **839**

Baker, Robert (*fl.* 1768), II, 225, 932

Baker, Samuel (*fl.* 1749), II, 97

Baker, Sir Samuel (1821–1893), III, 989

Baker, T. H. (*fl.* 1883), II, 972

Baker, Thomas (*fl.* 1642), publisher, I, 753

Baker, Thomas (1656–1740), antiquary, I, 124, 681; II, 108, 132; III, 993

Baker, Thomas (1680?–1710?), dramatist, II, **434**, 661

Baker's News; Or, The Whitehall Journal (1722), II, 713

Bakewell, Mrs J. (*fl.* 1849–64), III, 828

Bakewell, Robert (1725–1795), grazier, III, 969

Bakewell, Robert (1768–1843), geologist, III, 949

Balcanquhall, Walter (1586?–1645), I, 839

Bald, R. (*fl.* 1808), III, 980

Baldwin, A. (*fl.* 1704–12), II, 707, 719

Baldwin, Charles (1774–1869), III, 782

Baldwin, Edward (*fl.* 1843), III, 798

Baldwin, Edward T. (*fl.* 1879), III, 985

Baldwin, Henry (*fl.* 1762), II, 221

Baldwin, J. L. (*fl.* 1864), III, 777

Baldwin, Richard (*fl.* 1695), II, 706

Baldwin, Sir Timothy (1620–1696), I, 772

Baldwin, Walter (*fl.* 19 cent.), III, 782

Baldwin, William (*fl.* 1547), I, 413, 715, 728, 873

Baldwin's London Journal; or, British Chronicle (1762), III, 813

Baldwin's London Weekly Journal (1803), III, 813

Baldwyn, C. (*fl.* 1824), I, 488

Bale, John (1495–1563), I, 359, 363, **514**, 515, 774, 819

Bales, Peter (1547–1610?), I, 377

Balfour, Sir Andrew (1630–1694), II, 998

Balfour, Arthur James, Earl (1848–1930), III, **862**, 974

Balfour, Clara Lucas (*fl.* 1862), III, 573

Balfour, Francis Maitland (1851–1882), III, 958

Balfour, James (1705–1795), II, 951

Balfour, John Hutton (1808–1884), III, **960**

Balfour, Mary, later Brunton (1778–1818), III, 389

Balguy, Charles (1708–1767), II, 808

Balguy, John (1686–1748), II, 945

Ball, Edward, later Fitzball (1792–1873), III, 22, **586**

Ball, J. (*fl.* 1729), II, 781

Ball, John (1818–1889), III, 991

Ball, Richard Francis (*fl.* 1896), III, 761

Ball, Sir Robert Stawell (1840–1913), III, **942**, 944

Ball, Thomas (*fl.* 1697), II, 766

Ball, W. (*fl.* 1651), I, 357

BALL-GAMES, III, 772 f.

BALLADS
Collections, I, 403 f. (16, 17 cents.)
Discussions of, III, 159 (19 cent.)
Metre. See under PROSODY, I, 13 f.
Traditional ballads, I, **272** f.

Ballads and some Other Occasional Poems (18 cent.), II, 192–3, 198

Ballantyne, A. (*fl.* 1838), III, 375

Ballantyne, James (1772–1833), II, 694, 732–3
Ballantyne, James Robert (d. 1864), III, 1071, 1081
Ballantyne, John (*fl.* 1856), II, 984; III, 694
Ballantyne, Robert Michael (1825–1894), III, 568
Ballantyne, Thomas (1806–1871), III, 652, 802 (2), 809, 814
BALLANTYNE, HANSON & CO., III, 86
Ballard, George (1706–1755), II, 925
Ballot, The (1859), III, 817
Bally, George (*fl.* 1747), II, 289, 762
Balm of Gilead (1714), II, 661
Balmanno, M. (*fl.* 1858), III, 634
Baltimore, Frederick Calvert, Baron (1731–1771), II, 745
Balzac, Honoré de, III, 21, 339
Balzac, Jean Louis Guez, Sieur de, I, 810; II, 35, 782
BAMBURGH CASTLE LIBRARY, II, 105
Bamford, A. J. (*fl.* 1888), III, 1084
Bamford, R. W. (*fl.* 1822), III, 107
Bampfylde, John Codrington (1754–1796), II, 352
Banbury's Weekly Journal (1727), II, 734
Banchieri, Adriano (*fl.* 1595), I, 713
Bancks (or Banks), John (1709–1751), II, 16, 208
Bancroft, Edward (1744–1821), II, 755
Bancroft, John (d. 1696), II, 417
Bancroft, Richard (1544–1610), I, 687, 691
Bancroft, Thomas (*fl.* 1633–58), I, 474
Band, Cuffe, and Ruffe: A Merrie Dialogue Betweene (17 cent.), I, 661
Bandello, Matteo, I, 341, 810–1; II, 537; III, 353
Bandinel, Bulkeley (1781–1861), II, 864, 875
Banfield, Edmund James (1852–1923), III, 1098
Banfield, T. (*fl.* 1852), III, 978
Banfield, T. C. (*fl.* 1843), III, 982
Banier, Antoine, II, 770
Banim, John (1798–1842), III, 387
Banim, Michael (1796–1874), III, 387
Banister (or Bannister), James (*fl.* 1791), II, 760, 762
Banister, John (1540–1610), surgeon, I, 891
Banister, John (1630–1679), musician, II, 178
Banker's Circular, The (1854), III, 820
Bankes, G. N. (*fl.* 1882), III, 835
Bankes, H. (*fl.* 1813), III, 83
BANKING (writings on), III, 972f.
Banks, Allen (*fl.* 1680–99), II, 703, 711
Banks, John (*c.* 1650–*c.* 1700), dramatist, II, 417
Banks (or Bancks), John (1709–1751), miscellaneous writer, II, 16, 208
Banks, Sir Joseph (1743–1820), II, 741
Banks, T. (*fl.* 1641), I, 752–3
Banks, Thomas Christopher (1765–1854), II, 864

Banks's Currant Intelligence (1680), II, 703
Bankton, Andrew MacDowall, Lord (1685–1760), III, 157
Bannac (or Bannoc), Adolphus (pseud.?) (1756), II, 545
Bannatyne, Richard (d. 1635), I, 901
BANNATYNE CLUB, III, 86
Bannerjea, K. (*fl.* 1831), III, 1083
Bannister (or Banister), James (*fl.* 1780–91), II, 760, 762
Bannister, William (*fl.* 1668), II, 717
Banquet for Gentlemen and Ladies, A (18 cent.), II, 535
Banquet of Dainty Conceits, A (16 cent.), I, 404
Banquet of Musick, The (17 cent.), II, 180 (2), 181 (2), 182 (2)
Banquet of Thalia, The (18 cent.), II, 241, 243, 245–6, 253
Banquet of the Muses, A (18 cent.), II, 211
Baptist Magazine, The (1809), III, 825
Baptist Times and Freeman, The (1899), III, 819
Baptist Union Magazine, The (1892), III, 824
BAPTIST WRITERS, II, 862f.
Baratariana (18 cent.), II, 229, 232
Barbaro, Francesco, II, 808
Barbaro, Giosafatte, I, 781
Barbauld, Anna Laetitia, née Aikin (1743–1825), II, 26, 352
Barbé, Daniel, III, 348
Barber, Francis (*fl.* 1787), II, 625
Barber, John (*fl.* 1720), II, 100
Barber, John Thomas (*fl.* 1803), II, 140
Barber, Margaret Fairless ('Michael Fairless') (1869–1901), III, 544
Barber, Mary (1690?–1757), II, 310
Barbeyrac, Jean, II, 770
Barbier, Jean (*fl.* 1617), I, 375
Barbier, Jules, III, 608
Barbon Mazarini Mancini, Louis Jules Henri, Duke of Nivernois, II, 770
Barbon, Nicholas (d. 1698), II, 958
Barbour, Sir D. (*fl.* 1885), III, 974
Barbour, John (1316?–1395), I, 29, 39, 166f.
Barckley, Sir Richard (*fl.* 1598), I, 714, 874
Barclay, Alexander (1475?–1552), I, 411, 807, 810, 813, 818
Barclay, James (*fl.* 1743–74), II, 108, 626, 931
Barclay, John (1582–1621), I, 329, 779, 859; II, 31
Barclay, John (*fl.* 1828–41), II, 855, 856 (2)
Barclay, Patrick (*fl.* 1735), II, 740
Barclay, R. (*fl.* 1881), III, 974
Barclay, Rachel (*fl.* 1795), II, 251
Barclay, Robert (1648–1690), II, 856
Barclay, Sir Thomas (b. 1853), III, 782
Barclay, William (1546–1608), Scottish jurist, I, 909
Barclay, William (1570?–1630?), miscellaneous writer, I, 718, 911
Barcroft, R. (*fl.* 1725), I, 701

Bardwood, James (*fl.* 1690), II, 493
Baret (or Barret), John (d. 1580?), I, 375
Baret, Michael (*fl.* 1618), I, 393
Baretti, Giuseppe (1719–1789), II, 29, 65, 129, 621 (2), 745
Bargrave, John (1610–1680), I, 457
Barham, Francis Foster (1808–1871), II, 875
Barham, R. H. D. (*fl.* 1849–60), III, 226–7, 400
Barham, Richard Harris (1788–1845), III, **226** f.
Barham, Thomas Foster (1794–1869), I, 21
Baring, Alexander, Baron Ashburton (1774–1848), III, 684, 972
Baring, Sir Francis (1740–1810), III, 973
Baring-Gould, Sabine (1834–1924), III, **535** f.
Barker, Andrew (*fl.* 1609), I, 769
Barker, Christopher (1529?–1599), I, 357
Barker, Edmund Henry (1788–1839), I, 471; II, 632, 935, 937
Barker, Henry (*fl.* 1700), II, 15
Barker, Jane (*fl.* 1688–1718), II, 279, 536–8, 799
Barker, John (*fl.* 1774–6), II, 151
Barker, Ralph (*fl.* 1695), II, 850
Barker, Thomas (*fl.* 1651), I, 394
Barker, William Burckhardt (1810?–1856), III, 1071
Barker, William (*fl.* 1560), I, 809 (2), 813
Barkley, Henry C. (*fl.* 1891), III, 767
Barksdale, Clement (1609–1687), I, 457; II, 130
Barksted, William (*fl.* 1607–17), I, 474, 627, 803
Barlas, John Evelyn (1860–1914), III, **329** f.
Barlow, Edward (*fl.* 1659–1703), II, 742
Barlow, Francis (1626?–1702), II, 818
Barlow, George (1847–1913), III, **330**
Barlow, J. (*fl.* 1793), II, 950
Barlow, Jane (1857–1917), III, **1056**
Barlow, Peter (1776–1862), III, 941
Barlow, Roger (*fl.* 1541), I, 765
Barlow, Thomas (1607–1691), II, 101
Barlow, William (d. 1625), I, 885
Barnard, Lady Anne (1750–1825), II, 990; III, 1091
Barnard, Caroline (*fl.* 1813), III, 571
Barnard, Sir John (1685–1764), II, 120
Barnavelt, The Tragedy of Sir John van Olden (17 cent.), I, 651
Barnes, — (*fl.* 1548), I, 714
Barnes, Ambrose (1627–1710), II, 134
Barnes, Barnabe (1570?–1609), I, 640, 432 f.
Barnes, Edward (*fl.* 1852), III, 790
Barnes, George (*fl.* 1760), II, 765
Barnes, Joshua (1654–1712), II, 530
Barnes, P. E. (*fl.* 1853), II, 872
Barnes, Thomas (*fl.* 1624), I, 803
Barnes, Thomas (1747–1810), educationalist, II, 19, 108
Barnes, Thomas (1785–1841), editor of 'The Times', III, 645, 798
Barnes, William (1801–1886), III, **278** f.

Barnes, William George (*fl.* 1727), II, 124, 600
Barnett, C. Z. (*fl.* 1838), III, 441
Barnett, Morris (1800–1856), III, **599**
Barnfield, Richard (1574–1627), I, 404, **427**
Baron, Richard (d. 1766), II, 913
Baron, Robert (1593?–1639), divine, I, 906
Baron, Robert (*fl.* 1630–after 1655), poet and dramatist, I, 474, 640, 658, 731
Baron, Samuel (*fl.* 1732), II, 750
Baron-Wilson, M. (*fl.* 1839), III, 406
Baronius, Caesar, I, 858
Barr, R. (*fl.* 1892), III, 831
Barr, T. B. (*fl.* 1766), II, 154
Barratt, Alfred (1844–1881), III, **862**
Barré, Isaac (1726–1802), II, 632
Barret, Robert (*fl.* 1603–6), I, 390, 474
Barret, W. (*fl.* 1639), I, 799
Barrett, B. (*fl.* 1812), II, 20
Barrett, C. F. (*fl.* 1802), II, 553; III, 667
Barrett, Eaton Stannard (1786–1820), III, **388**
Barrett, Henry (*fl.* 1796), II, 56
Barrett (or Baret), John (d. 1580?), I, 375
Barrett, John (1753–1821), II, 593
Barrett, Stephen (1718–1801), II, 767
Barrie, Alexander, II, 235
Barrie, Sir James Matthew (1860–1937), III, **623** f.
Barrière, Théodore, III, 548
Barriffe, William (*fl.* 1635), I, 390
Barrington, Daines (1727–1800), II, 79, 148, 823, 962
Barrington, George (b. 1755), II, 154
Barrington, Sir Jonah (1760–1834), II, 159
Barrough, Philip (*fl.* 1583), I, 889
Barrow Evening Echo, The (1894), III, 806
Barrow, Isaac (1630–1677), I, 861; II, 55, **846**, 960
Barrow, John (*fl.* 1749–56), II, 741, 927
Barrow, Sir John (1764–1848), explorer, III, 988–9, 1090
Barrow, John (*fl.* 1847–63), anglo-catholic, I, 701; II, 847; III, 126, 856 (2)
Barrow, William (1754–1836), III, 107
'Barrowcliffe, A. J.', i.e. Albert Julius Mott (*fl.* 1856), III, **473**
Barruel, Augustin, II, 770
Barry, David, Lord [wrongly designated Lodowick Barry] (1585–1610), I, 640
Barry, George (1748–1805), I, 773
Barry, H. B. (*fl.* 1854), III, 126
Barry, James (1741–1806), II, 19, 30 f., 635
Barry, Lodowick (1585–1610), I, 640. See also David, Lord Barry
Barry, Martin (1802–1855), III, 777, 956
Barry, William (*fl.* 1871), III, 771
Barrymore, William (d. 1845), III, **586** f.
Barstow, C. M. (*fl.* 1872), III, 760
Barter, W. B. (*fl.* 1846), III, 691
Barth, C. G. (*fl.* 1840), III, 572
Barth, William (*fl.* 1840), III, 585

Barthélemy, Jean Jacques, II, 770
Bartholomaeus Anglicus (*fl.* 1230), I, **291**, 765
Bartlet, J. (*fl.* 1754), II, 816
Bartlet, John (*fl.* 1606), I, 485
Bartlett, A. D. (*fl.* 1850), III, 379
Bartlett, John (*fl.* 1790), II, 743
Bartlett, T. (*fl.* 1850), III, 971
Bartley, Sir G. C. T. (*fl.* 1874), III, 976
Bartley, Nehemiah (*fl.* 1802), III, 969
Bartoli, Daniello, II, 808
Bartolozzi, Francesco (1727–1815), III, 90
Barton, Bernard (1784–1849), III, **227**, 577
Barton, J. (*fl.* 1820), III, 970
Barton, Lucy (*fl.* 1831–49), III, 227 (4)
Barton, Maria, later Hack (1777–1844), III, 566
Barton, R. C. (*fl.* 1820), III, 572
Barton, William (1598?–1678), I, 376–7, 679
Bartram, John (*fl.* 1751), II, 754
Barwell, Louisa Mary (1800–1885), III, 107, 572
Basak, Radhanath (*fl.* 1886), III, 1082
Basanier, Martin, I, 787
Bascom, J. (*fl.* 1859), III, 983
Basia Joannis Secundi (18 cent.), II, 201
Basia of Bonefonius, The (18 cent.), II, 196
Basileona (1900), III, 836
Basille, Theodore (Thomas Becon) (1512–1567), I, 677
Basire, Isaac (1607–1676), I, 386
Baskerville, Thomas (1630–1720), II, 139
Basnage de Beauval, Jacques, II, 33, 770
Basse, William (d. 1653?), I, 474, 592
Basset, Francis, Baron de Dunstanville (1757–1835), I, 826
Bassett, Thomas (*fl.* 1671), II, 96
Bastable, C. F. (*fl.* 1892), II, 984
Bastard, Thomas (1566–1618), I, 480
Bastian, Henry Charlton (1837–1915), III, 964, 966
Bastile, Or History of Charles Townly, The (18 cent.), II, 549
Baston, Thomas (*fl.* 1716), II, 143
Batchelor, The (1766), II, 665
Bate, Sir Henry, later Dudley (1745–1824), II, **465**, 695, 709 (2), 711 (2), 719
Bateman, Joseph (*fl.* 1838), III, 985
Bates, Henry Walter (1825–1892), III, 957
Bates, Isaac (*fl.* 1727), II, 104
Bates, Thomas (*fl.* 1641–6), I, 752, 757
Bateson, Mary (1856–1906), III, **928**
Bateson, Thomas (*c.* 1570–*c.* 1630), I, 484
Bateson, William (1861–1926), III, 955
BATH
  Magazines, II, 684 (1776)
  Newspapers, II, 720
Bath Advertiser, The (1755), II, 720
Bath and Bristol Chronicle, The (1768), II, 720
Bath and Bristol Magazine, The (1776), II, 684
Bath Argus, The (1900), III, 804
Bath Argus Evening Telegram, The (1875), III, 804

Bath, Bristol, Tunbridge and Epsom Miscellany, The (18 cent.), II, 204
Bath, Chartularies of (M.E.), I, 121
Bath Chronicle, The (1770), II, 720
Bath Chronicle and Herald, The (1925), II, 720
Bath Chronicle or Universal Register, The (1761), II, 720
Bath Contest, The (18 cent.), II, 225
Bath Courant, The (1773), II, 720
Bath Daily Chronicle, The (1883), III, 805
Bath Evening Chronicle, The (1877), III, 805
Bath Gazette, The (1778), II, 720
Bath Harmonic Society Glees [etc.] (19 cent.), II, 255
Bath Herald, The (1800), II, 720
Bath Herald and General Advertiser, The (1792), II, 720
Bath Herald and Register, The (1793), II, 720
Bath Journal, The (1744), II, 720
Bath Journal, The (1773), II, 720
Bath Miscellany, The (18 cent.), II, 209 (2)
Bath Register and Western Advertiser, The (1792), II, 720
Bath, William Pulteney, Earl of (1684–1764), II, 662
Bathe, William (1564–1614), I, 375
Bathoe, William (*fl.* 1743–56), II, 99
Bathurst, Charles (*fl.* 1857), I, 17
Bathurst, Richard (d. 1762), II, 544
Bathurst, Theodore (d. 1651), I, 417
Batman, Stephen (*fl.* 1582), I, 880
Batt, Antony (d. 1651), I, 684, 810
Battely (or Batteley), Nicholas (1648–1704), I, 843
Batten, William (*fl.* 1839), III, 963
Batteux, Charles, II, 28, 770
Battie, John (*fl.* 1644), I, 847
Battine, William (1765–1836), III, 200
Battle Abbey, Custumals of (M.E.), I, 120
Battle of Brunanburh (O.E.), I, **84**
Battle of Maldon (O.E.), I, 27, **83** f.
Battle of the Authors, The (18 cent.), II, 537
Battle of the Quills, The (18 cent.), II, 225
Batty, Beatrice, née Stebbing (*fl.* 1873), III, 573
Baudelaire, Charles, III, **21**
Baudelocque, Jean Louis, II, 770
Baudier, Michel, I, 785
Baumgarten, Martin von, II, 805
Bavande, William (*fl.* 1559), I, 508
'Bavius, Mr' (1732), II, 202
'Bavius Jun., Mr' (1731), II, 201
Bawbee, The [Edinburgh] (1857), III, **807**
Bax, E. Belfort (*fl.* 1890), III, 831, 977
Baxter, Andrew (1686–1750), II, 945
Baxter, G. R. Wythen (*fl.* 1839), III, 199, 976
Baxter, George (1804–1867), III, 90
Baxter, John (1781–1858), III, 71
Baxter, Langley (*fl.* 19 cent.), III, 802
Baxter, Nathaniel (*fl.* 1575–1606), I, 415

Baxter, Richard (1615–1691), I, **695**; II, 55, 108, 147, 846 (2), 857, 863
Baxter, Robert Dudley (1827–1875), III, 979
Baxter, S. S. (*fl.* 1831), III, 975
Baxter, William (1650–1723), II, 760, **935**
Bayle, Pierre, II, 33, 35, 204 (2), 205–6, 207 (2), 209, 541, 770
Bayley, Sir John (1763–1841), II, 962
Baylie, Simon (*fl.* 1603–25), I, 640
Bayly, Ada Ellen ('Edna Lyall') (1857–1903), III, **552**
Bayly, Anselm (d. 1794), II, 17, 932
Bayly, Lewis (d. 1631), I, 385, 684
Bayly, Mrs T. H. (*fl.* 1844), III, 227
Bayly, Thomas (d. 1657?), I, 731
Bayly, Thomas Haynes (1797–1839), III, **227**
Bayne, Peter (1830–1896), III, 721–2, **733**f.
Baynes, Thomas Spencer (1823–1887), III, **863**, 868
Bazin, René, III, 556
Beacon and Christian Times, The (1858), III, 819
Beaconsfield, Benjamin Disraeli, Earl of (1804–1881), III, **423**f.
Beadnell, H. (*fl.* 1859), III, 77
Beale, Dorothea (1831–1906), III, 141
Beames, John (*fl.* 1867), III, 1074
Bear University Magazine, The (1858), III, 834
Bear, W. E. (*fl.* 1888), III, 972
Bearblock (or Bereblock), John (*fl.* 1566), I, 519
Bearcroft, Philip (1697–1761), I, 372
Beard, Charles (1827–1888), III, 125, 830, 847
Beard, John (*fl.* 1813), III, 759
Beard, Thomas (d. 1632), I, 730
Beardsley, Aubrey Vincent (1872–1898), III, 90, **330**, 834
Beare, John Isaac (1857–1918), III, **1004**
Beare, Philip O'Sullivan (1590?–1660), III, 1047
Beasley, E. C. (*fl.* 1853), III, 33
Beatson, Alexander (1759–1833), III, 1075
Beatson, Benjamin Wrigglesworth (1803–1874), II, 935
Beattie, J. (*fl.* 1838), III, 135
Beattie, James (1735–1803), II, 19, 24, 108, 221, **352**f., 915
Beattie, James Hay (1768–1790), II, 353
Beattie, William (1793–1875), III, 184, 783
Beatty, Charles (*fl.* 1768), II, 755
Beatty-Kingston, William (1837–1900), III, 783
Beau's Academy, The (17 cent.), II, 184
Beau's Miscellany, The (18 cent.), II, 201, 205
Beauchamp, Lewis (*fl.* 1541), I, 816
Beaufain, Charles Random de Bérenger, Baron de (*fl.* 1835), III, 762
Beaufort, Margaret, Countess of Richmond and Derby (1443–1509), I, 266
Beaulieu, Augustin, II, 770
Beaulieu, Charles de Sainte-Maure de, II, 798
Beaumarchais, Pierre Auguste Caron de, II, 40, 774

Beaumont, Augustus H. (*fl.* 1834–40), III, 816
Beaumont, C. (*fl.* 1702), I, 474
Beaumont, Elie de, II, 141
Beaumont, Francis (1585?–1616), I, 211, **632**f., 805
Beaumont, Jeanne Marie le Prince de, II, 47, 566, 677, 788
Beaumont, Sir John (1583–1627), I, 474, 718, 800–1, 803 (2), 804, 806, 809
Beaumont, Joseph (1616–1699), I, 474
Beaumont, W. (*fl.* 1798), II, 770
Beaumont, William (1785–1853), III, 963
Beaumont de Péréfixe, Hardouin de, II, 770
Beausobre, Isaac de, II, 770
Beauties in Prose and Verse (18 cent.), II, 236
Beauties of all the Magazines Selected, The (1762), II, 678
Beauties of Ancient Poetry, The (18 cent.), II, 249
Beauties of English Poesy, The (18 cent.), II, 224
Beauties of Fables (18 cent.), II, 234
Beauties of Literature (18 cent.), II, 245
Beauties of Modern Dramatists, The (1800), II, 392
Beauties of Music and Poetry, The (18 cent.), II, 236, **243**
Beauties of Poetry, The (18 cent.), II, 231
Beauties of Poetry Display'd, The (18 cent.), II, 217
Beauties of the Anti-Jacobin, The (18 cent.), II, 254
Beauties of the English Stage, The (18 cent.), II, 206
Beauties of the Magazines (1775), II, 685
Beauties of the Poets, The (18 cent.), II, 232, 241, 243, 246, 254–5
Beauties of the Spectators, Tatlers, and Guardians, The (18 cent.), II, 217, 221, 240
Beauties of Thought in Prose and Verse, The (18 cent.), II, 248
BEAUTY (treatises on), II, 14f. (17, 18 cents.)
Beauvais, Guillaume, II, 770
Beauvoir, R. de, III, 598
Beauvoir, W. (*fl.* 1706), II, 780
Beaver, John (*fl.* 1724), II, 780
Beawes, William (*fl.* 1745), II, 750
Beazley, Samuel (1786–1851), III, **587**
Beccadelli, Lodovico, II, 808
Beccaria, Cesare Bonesana, II, 808
Beccaria, Giovanni Battista, II, 808
Bechstein, Ludwig (*fl.* 1854), III, 576
Beck, Jacob Sigismund, II, 52
Becke, Edmonde (*fl.* 1550), I, 665
Becke, George Louis (1848–1913), III, **1096**f.
Becker, Lydia Ernestine (1827–1890), III, 830
Becker, W. A., III, 50
Becket, Andrew (*fl.* 1786), II, 747, **916**
Becket, T. (*fl.* 1764), II, 883
Becket, Thomas (d. 1170), I, 116, **287**
Beckford, Peter (1740–1811), II, 821
Beckford, Richard (*fl.* 1755), II, 664

Beckford, William (d. 1799), historian, II, 757
Beckford, William (1760–1844), author of 'Vathek', II, 103, **528**f.
Beckingham, Charles (1699–1731), II, **434**
Beckington (or Bekynton), Thomas (1390?–1465), I, 265
Becon, Thomas (1512–1567), I, 677, 681, 684
Beddoe, John (1826–1911), III, 968
Beddoes, Thomas (1760–1808), II, 593; III, 167
Beddoes, Thomas Lovell (1803–1849), III, **248**f.
Bede (d. 735), I, 36–7, 80, 86f., **104**f., 126, 773, 811
'Bede, Cuthbert', i.e. Edward Bradley (1827–1889), III, **473**f.
Bedell, William (1571–1642), the elder, I, 818
Bedell, William (1613–1670), the younger, II, **871**
Bedford, Arthur (1668–1745), II, 30, 938
Bedford, Grosvenor Charles (*fl.* 1797), II, 666, 762
Bedford, H. (*fl.* 1870), III, 603
Bedford, H. A. Russell, Duke of (*fl.* 1897), III, 972
Bedford, J. H. (*fl.* 1825), III, 193
Bedford, P. J. (*fl.* 1864), III, 580
Bedford, Thomas (*fl.* 1635), I, 742
Bedingfield, Lady (*fl.* 1780–1843), III, 151
Bedingfield, Thomas (d. 1613), I, 393, 812, 816
Bedingfield Papers (17, 18 cents.), I, 383
Bedwell, William (d. 1632), I, 776, 785
Bee, The (1715), II, 192
Bee, The (1759), II, 664
Bee, The (1795), II, 250–2
Bee and Sketchley's Weekly Advertiser, The (1777), II, 722
Bee; Or, Literary Weekly Intelligencer, The (1790), II, 686
Bee; Or, Universal Weekly Pamphlet, The (1733), II, 714
Bee Revived, The (1750), II, 677
Bee Reviv'd; Or, Universal Weekly Pamphlet, The (1733), II, 714
Beeching, Henry Charles (1859–1919), III, **330**f.
Beechey, Henry William (d. 1870?), II, 629
Beeckman, Daniel (*fl.* 1718), II, 750
Beedome, Thomas (d. 1641?), I, 474
Beehive, The (1861), III, 817
Beer, Mrs F. A. (*fl.* 1894), III, 810–1
Beesly, Edward Spencer (1831–1915), III, **863**
Beeton, H. R. (*fl.* 1894), III, 974
Beeton, S. O. (*fl.* 1855), III, 577, 578 (3)
Beeton's Annual (1866), III, 578
Beeton's Boys' Own Magazine (1888), III, 831
Beever, John (*fl.* 1849), III, 770
Beeverele, James (*fl.* 1707), II, 139
Begg, James (1808–1883), III, 976
Béguin, Jean, II, 770

Behn, Aphra (1640–1689), I, 458; II, 15, 179–80, **417**f., 530 (2), 531 (3), 532, 794, 801
Behrens, J. (*fl.* 1868), III, 120
Beisley, Sidney (*fl.* 1864), I, 545
Beith, William (*fl.* 1480), I, **306**
Bek, Thomas (*fl.* 1270), of Castleford, I, 165
Beke, C. T. (*fl.* 1853), I, 769
Bekinson (or Bekinsau), John de (1496?–1559), I, 849
Bekker, Balthasar, II, 770
Bekynton (or Beckington), Thomas (1390?–1465), I, 265
Bel-Vedere Or The Garden of the Muses (17 cent.), I, 404
Belcher, J. (*fl.* 1834), III, 827
Belchier, Daubridgecourt (1580?–1621), I, 640
BELFAST
    Magazines, II, 688 (1753–99)
    Newspapers, II, 736; III, 808
    Printing, II, 90
Belfast Daily Mercury, The (1854), III, 808
Belfast Daily Times, The (1872), III, 808
Belfast Evening Star, The (1890), III, 808
Belfast Evening Telegraph, The (1870), III, 808
Belfast Mercury, The (1851), III, 808
Belfast Mercury; Or, Freeman's Chronicle, The, II, 736
Belfast Monthly Magazine, The (1808), III, 825
Belfast Morning News, The (1872), III, 808
Belfast News-Letter, The (1855), 808
Belfast Newsletter and General Advertiser, The (1737), II, 736
Belfast Times, The (1872), III, 808
Belges, Jean le Marie de, I, 331
Belgravia (1866), III, 830
Beling (or Bellings), Richard (d. 1677), I, 731, 840
Bell, A. H. H. (*fl.* 1884), III, 1089
Bell, A. W. (*fl.* 1877), III, 812
'Bell, Acton', i.e. Anne Brontë (1820–1849), III, **462**f.
Bell, Andrew (1753–1832), II, 108; III, 107
Bell, Benjamin (1749–1806), III, 969
Bell, Sir Charles (1774–1842), II, 956; III, **962**, 965
Bell, Charles Dent (1818–1898), III, **279**
'Bell, Currer', i.e. Charlotte Brontë (1816–1855), III, **461**f.
Bell, E. (*fl.* 1868), III, 1077
'Bell, Ellis', i.e. Emily Jane Brontë (1818–1848), III, **462**f.
Bell, Francis Jeffery (1773–1846), III, 962
Bell, G. M. (*fl.* 1841), III, 972
Bell, George (1814–1900), III, 98
Bell, Henry Thomas Mackenzie (*fl.* 1879–1927), III, **331**
Bell, J. W. (*fl.* 1855), III, 812
Bell, James (*fl.* 1551–96), I, 384, 815
Bell, John (1691–1780), traveller, II, 750, 999

Bell, John (1745–1831), publisher, II, 94, 259, 689, 694, 709, 711, 716 (2); III, 810

Bell, John Browne (1779–1855), III, 783, 810, 812 (3), 819

Bell, Robert (*fl.* 1801–20), journalist, II, 160; III, 810, 811 (2)

Bell, Robert (1800–1867), editor and miscellaneous writer, I, 210, 272, 387, 412 (2), 529; II, 258, 260; III, 181, 811

Bell, Thomas (*fl.* 1573–1610), I, 845

Bell, Thomas (*fl.* 1672–92), theologian, II, 992

Bell, Thomas (*fl.* 1692), librarian, II, 105

Bell, Thomas (1792–1880), III, 956

Bell, William (1731–1816), II, 787

Bell, Sir William James (*fl.* 1877–86), III, 812, 985

Bell's British Theatre (1776), II, 392

Bell's Classical Arrangement of Fugitive Poetry (18 cent.), II, 242–3, 245–6, 248–9, 251–2

Bell's Life in London and Sporting Chronicle (1882), III, 811

Bell's New Weekly Messenger (1832), III, 812

Bell's News (1855), III, 812

Bell's Penny Dispatch and Penny Sunday Chronicle (1840), III, 812

Bell's Penny Life in London (1859), III, 799

Bell's Sunday Dispatch (1815), III, 811

Bell's Weekly Messenger (1796), III, 810

Bellamy, Daniel, the elder (b. 1687), II, 130, 310, 799

Bellamy, Daniel, the younger (d. 1788), II, 353, 793

Bellamy, Edward (*fl.* 1698), II, 109

Bellamy, Henry (b. 1604), I, 655

Bellamy, James (*fl.* 1660), II, 766

Bellamy, Thomas (1745–1800), II, 408

Bellamy's Picturesque Magazine and Literary Museum (1793), II, 682

Belle Dame Sans Mercy, La (M.E.), I, 254

Bellefond, Nicolas Villaut, Sieur de, II, 802

Belleforest, François de, I, 334, 732

Bellegarde, Jean Baptiste Morvan de, II, 120, 792

Bellemare, L. de, III, 503

Bellendent (Ballenden or Ballentyne), John (*fl.* 1533–87), I, 258, 803, 901

Bellers, John (1654–1725), II, 111, 856, 958

Bellew, Henry Walter (1834–1892), III, 1077

Bellew, R. (*fl.* 1808), III, 969

Bellicard, Jérome Charles, II, 776

Bellingham, Thomas (*fl.* 1688), II, 151

Bellings (or Beling), Richard (d. 1677), I, 731, 840

Belloc, Hilaire (b. 1870), III, 570

Bellon, Peter (*fl.* 1689), II, 771, 773

Bellot, Jacques (*fl.* 1580), I, 44, 391

Belloy, P. L. Buirette de, II, 359

Beloe, William (1756–1817), II, 760; III, 1021f.

Belsham, Thomas (1750–1829), II, 20; III, 847

Belsham, William (1752–1827), II, 20, 23, 635

Belshis, A. (*fl.* 1776), II, 686

Belson, Mary, later Elliott (*fl.* 1812), III, 566

Belt, Thomas (1832–1878), III, 958

Beltaine (1899), III, 834

Belzoni, Giovanni Baptista (1778–1823), III, 989

BEMROSE & Co., III, 86

Ben, John (*fl.* 1529), I, 773

Ben Johnson's Jests (18 cent.), II, 214 (2), 218, 220

Ben Johnson's Last Legacy (18 cent.), II, 217

Benbow, W. (*fl.* 1825), III, 182

Bendall, Cecil (1856–1906), III, 1017

Bendyshe, T. (*fl.* 1863), III, 818, 966

Benedict, D. (*fl.* 1813), II, 862

Benedict, O. (*fl.* 1862), III, 600

Benedict, The [Cambridge] (1888), III, 835

Benedictine Office (O.E.), I, 94

Benedictine Rule
    Old English, I, 35, 93f.
    Middle English, I, 39

Benett, Etheldred (1776–1845), III, 950

Benger, Elizabeth Ogilvy (1778–1827), III, 239, 398, 597, 882

Benjamin, Judah Philip (1811–1884), III, 985

Benlowes, Edward (1603?–1676), I, 474

Bennet, Benjamin (1674–1726), II, 863

Bennet, James (*fl.* 1761), II, 914

Bennet, John (*fl.* 1599), I, 484

Bennet, John (*fl.* 1774), II, 353

Bennett, Agnes Maria (c. 1750–1808), III, 388

Bennett, Edward (*fl.* 1620?), I, 718

Bennett, Edward Turner (1797–1836), II, 841

Bennett, Elizabeth (*fl.* 1816), III, 388

Bennett, James (*fl.* 1808), II, 861

Bennett, John (*fl.* 1782), II, 130, 143

Bennett, John (*fl.* 1857), III, 577

Bennett, Joseph (1831–1911), III, 734, 777

Bennett, Mary (*fl.* 1857), III, 577

Bennett, Samuel (*fl.* 1867), Australian historian, III, 1097

Bennett, Samuel (*fl.* 1880), journalist, III, 818

Bennett, William Cox (1820–1895), III, 279f.

Benskin, T. (*fl.* 1681), II, 704

Bensley, Thomas (d. 1833), III, 86

Bensly, Robert Lubbock (1831–1893), III, 1011

Benson, Arthur Christopher (1862–1925), III, 734f.

Benson, E. F. (1867–1940), III, 832

Benson, Edward White (*fl.* 1824), III, 572

Benson, George (1699–1762), II, 863

Benson, Joseph (1749–1821), III, 823

Benson, Thomas (1679–1734), I, 843; II, 920, 928

Benson, William (1682–1754), II, 26, 768

Bent, James Theodore (1852–1897), III, 989

Bent, Robert (*fl.* 1824–39), III, 100–1

Bent, William (*fl.* 1799–1822), II, 94; III, 100

Bent's Literary Advertiser (1829), III, 101

Bent's Monthly Literary Advertiser (1832), II, 717

Bentham, Edward (1707–1776), II, 117
Bentham, George (1800–1884), III, **863**, 960
Bentham, J. (*fl.* 1774), II, 804
Bentham, Jeremy (1748–1832), II, 85, 635, 953 f.; III, 107, 143
Bentinck, William Henry Cavendish, Duke of Portland (1738–1809), II, 632
Bentivoglio, Guido, I, **780**; II, 808
Bentley, Edwin (*fl.* 1806), III, 666
Bentley, Henry (*fl.* 1823), II, 824
Bentley, Richard (1662–1742), classical scholar, II, 850, **933** f.
Bentley, Richard, the younger (1708–1782), II, **459**
Bentley, Richard (*fl.* 1692–6), publisher, II, 705
Bentley, Richard (1794–1871), publisher, III, 98
Bentley, Robert (1821–1893), III, 961
Bentley's Miscellany (1837), III, 827
Bentley's Monthly Review or Literary Argus (1853)**,** 829
Bentley's Quarterly Review (1859), III, 833
Benzon, Ernest (*fl.* 1898), III, 764
Beowulf (O.E.), I, 25, 27, 31, 35, **62** f.
Berdmore, Samuel (1740–1802), II, 20
Bereblock (or Bearblock), John (*fl.* 1566), I, 519
Berengarius of Capri, I, 891
Berenger, Richard (d. 1782), I, 393; II, 764, 816
Berens, E. (*fl.* 1849), III, 238
Beresford, James (1764–1840), II, 101, 666, 768, 773
Beresford, William (*fl.* 1789), II, 742
Bergerac, Hercule Savinien de Cyrano de, II, 777
Bergier, Nicolas, II, 771
Berguer, L. T. (*fl.* 1819), III, 815
Berington, Joseph (1746–1827), II, 17
Berington, Simon (*fl.* 1735), II, 540
Berkeley, George, Earl of (1628–1698), I, 455
Berkeley, George (1685–1753), philosopher, II, 135, **944** f.
Berkeley, George (1712–1767), letter-writer, II, 135
Berkeley, George Charles Grantley Fitz-hardinge (1800–1881), III, 14, 760
Berkeley, George Monck (1763–1793), II, 415
Berkeley Hall; or, The Pupil of Experience (18 cent.), II, 550
Berkeley, John, Baron (d. 1678), I, 842
Berkeley, Joseph Miles (1803–1889), III, 960
Berkeley, Sir William (1609–1677), I, 641; II, 751
Berkenhead (or Birkenhead), Sir John (1616–1679), I, 748, 754, 758
Berkenhout, John (1730?–1791), II, 923
Berkshire Chronicle, The (1771), II, 729
Berkshire Chronicle, The (1798), II, 684
Berkshire Repository, The (1797), II, 252
Berlioz, Hector, III, 711
Bermondsey, Annals of (15 cent.), I, 115
Bernard, Catherine, II, 46, 534, 771

Bernard, Charles de, III, 397
Bernard, Edward (1638–1696), II, 103, 908
Bernard, Herman Hedwig (1785–1857), III, 1013
Bernard, J. A. (*fl.* 1841), III, 400
Bernard, Jacques (*fl. c.* 1700), II, 676
Bernard, Jacques, II, 771
Bernard, John (1756–1828), II, 405
Bernard, John Peter (d. 1750), II, 921
Bernard, Nicholas (d. 1661), I, 686
Bernard, P. (*fl.* 1793), II, 771
Bernard, Richard (1568–1641), I, 661, 731, 771, 808, 894
Bernard, Samuel (1591–1657), I, 655
Bernard, Sir Thomas (1750–1818), II, 85; III, 107, 129, 970
Bernard, Thomas Dehaney (1815–1904), III, 853
Bernard, William Bayle (1807–1875), III, **599**, 604
Bernard of Gordon (d. *c.* 1305), I, **311**
Bernard de Saint-Pierre, Jacques Henri, II, 35, 46, 553, 771
Berners, Juliana (d. 1388?), I, 127, 266
Bernher, Augustine (*fl.* 1552), I, 669
Bernier, François, II, 771
Berquin, Arnaud, II, 47, 552 (2), 566
Berri, D. G. (*fl.* 1864), III, 83
Berrie, J. (*fl.* 1682), II, 801
Berrington, B. (*fl.* 1709), II, 710
Berrington, E. (*fl.* 1709), II, 710
Berrows Worcester Journal (1753), II, 729
Berry, Agnes (*fl.* 1791), II, 138 f.
Berry, Sir Edward (1768–1831), II, 748
Berry, Mary (1763–1852), II, 138 f., 836, 839–40
Bert, Edmund (*fl.* 1619), I, 394
Berthelet, Thomas (*fl.* 16 cent.), I, 351
Bertie, Willoughby, Earl of Abingdon (1740–1799), II, 634
Bertin, Joseph (*fl.* 1735), II, 826
Bertius, Petrus, I, 767, 811
Bertram, Charles (1723–1765), I, 44; II, 881
Bertram, James Glass (*fl.* 1858–90), III, 583, 764, 767, 783, 807
Berwick
    Printing, II, 89
    Magazines, II, 687 (1785)
Berwick, Edward (b. 1750), I, 386; II, 593
Berwick Museum; Or, Monthly Literary Intelligencer, The (1785), II, 687
Beryn, The Tale of (M.E.), I, 254
Besant, Annie (b. 1847), III, 155, 818, 831, 976–7, 1082
Besant, Sir Walter (1836–1901), III, **537** f., 831
Besse, Joseph (1683?–1757), II, 855–6
Best and Compleatest Academy of Compliments yet Extant, The (18 cent.), II, 213
Best and Most Perfect Intelligencer, The (1650), I, 761
Best, George (d. 1584?), I, 787
Best, Henry (*fl.* 1641), I, 387, 846
Best, Thomas (1570?–1638?), I, 783

Best, Thomas (*fl.* 1737), II, 822
Best, William Mawdesley (*fl.* 1849), III, 985
BESTIARIES (M.E.), I, 39
Bestiary (M.E.), I, **182**f.
Betagh, William (*fl.* 1723), II, 741
Betham-Edwards, Matilda Barbara (d. 1919), III, 573
Bethel, Augusta (*fl.* 1863), III, 573
Bethell, Richard, Baron Westbury (1800–1873), III, 152
Bethune, Alexander (1804–1843), III, **280**
Bethune, C. R. D. (*fl.* 1847), I, 788
Bethune, G. (*fl.* 1817), II, 971
Bethune, G. W. (*fl.* 1848), III, 307
Bethune, John (*fl.* 1770), II, 18, 665
Bethune, John (1812–1839), III, 280 (2)
Béthune, Maximilien de, Duc de Sully, II, 771
Betson, A. (*fl.* 1751), II, 399
Betson, Thomas (*fl. c.* 1500), I, 684
Betterton, Thomas (1635?–1710), I, 209; II, **418**, 794
Bettesworth, W. A. (*fl.* 1900), III, 774
Bettie, W. (*fl.* 1636), I, 731
Beues of Hamtoun (M.E.), I, **150**
Beuvius, Adam, II, 805
Bevan, Favell Lee, later Mortimer (1802–1878), III, 567
Beven, Thomas (*fl.* 1889), III, 985
Beveridge, H. (*fl.* 1876), III, 1077
Beveridge, William (1637–1708), II, **846**, **938**
Beverley, Charlotte (*fl.* 1792), II, 247
Beverley, John (1743–1827), II, 115
Beverley Town Documents (M.E.), I, **121**
Beverly, Robert (1705), II, 753
Beville, William (*fl.* 1782), II, 627
Bevington, Louisa Sarah, later Guggenberger (b. 1845), III, **331**
Beware the Beare (17 cent.), I, 731
Bewcastle Cross (O.E.), I, 59f.
Bewick, Thomas (1753–1828), II, 106, 827; III, 90
Bèze, Théodore de (Beza), I, 333, 678, 811
Bhandarkar, R. G. (*fl.* 1838), III, 1074
Bhattacharyya, J. N. (*fl.* 1896), III, 1085
BI-WEEKLY NEWSPAPERS, III, 810
Biber, George Edward (1801–1874), III, 107, 140, 993
BIBLE (translations of)
    Old English, I, 90f.
    Middle English, I, 187f., 204f. (Wycliffite)
    Renaissance to Restoration, I, 672f.
    Nineteenth Century, III, 1002, 1009
    See also PSALMS, GOSPELS
BIBLICAL SCHOLARS
    Middle English Period. See under WRITINGS IN LATIN, I, **280**f.
    Renaissance to Restoration, I, 855f.
    Restoration to Romantic Revival, II, 928 (concordances)
    Nineteenth Century, III, 1011f.

Biblington, Mary F. (*fl.* 1895), III, 1085
BIBLIOGRAPHIES (GENERAL), I, 3 f.
    Anglo-Saxon Period, I, 53
    Middle English Period, I, 113
    Renaissance to Restoration, I, 317f., 359f.
    Restoration to Romantic Revival, II, 3f.
    Nineteenth Century, III, 3f.
    See also CATALOGUES
BIBLIOGRAPHIES (SPECIAL)
    Bibliographies of Bibliographies, I, 3
    Current Lists of English Studies, I, 3
    Current Lists of New Books, I, 3
    English Universities and Provinces, I, 8f.
    Fiction, II, 488
    Irish Books, I, 8
    Law, I, 848f.
    Periodicals, I, 746, 750f. (1500–1660); II, 669f., 699f. (1660–1800); III, 794f. (19 cent.)
    Plays and Dramatists, I, 487 (1500–1660); II, **393**f. (1660–1800); III, 581 (19 cent.)
    Religious Bodies, I, 9
    Romances (M.E.), I, 128
    Scottish Books, I, 7
    Social Life, II, 132f.
    Travel, I, 798 (16, 17 cents.)
    Welsh Books, I, 7
    See also CATALOGUES
Bibliotheca Annua (1699), II, **717**
Bibliotheca Litteraria (1722), II, 675
Bibliotheca Universalis (1688), II, 675
Bibliothèque Angloise; Ou, Histoire Littéraire de la Grande Bretagne (1717), II, 688
Bibliothèque Britannique (1796), II, 688
Bibliothèque Britannique; Ou, Histoire des Ouvrages des Savans de la Grande Bretagne (1733), II, 673, 688
Bibliothèque Universelle des Sciences [etc.] (1816), II, 688
'Bickerstaff the Younger' (1738), II, 302
Bickerstaffe, Isaac (d. 1812?), II, **459**f., 794
Bickersteth, Edward (1786–1850), III, 853
Bickersteth, Edward Henry (1825–1906), III, **280**
Bickerton, T. (*fl.* 1719), II, 713
Bickham, George, the elder (d. 1769), II, 82, 129
Bickham, George, the younger (d. 1758), II, 148
Bickham, John (*fl.* 1731), II, 201, 206
Bicknell, Alexander (d. 1796), II, 408, 547
Bicycling Times, The (1877), III, 820
Biddle, John (*fl.* 1634), I, 803, 809
Biddulph, William (*fl.* 1600–12), I, 769
Bidpai, I, 811
Bielfeld, Jacob Frederick Baron de, II, 28, 141
Big Ben (1892), III, 814
Bigandet, P. (*fl.* 1858), III, 1081
Bigg, J. (*fl.* 1852), III, 102
Bigg, John Stanyan (1828–1865), III, **280**

Biggar, Emerson Bristol (*fl.* 1892), III, 1088
Bigge, Thomas (*fl.* 1798), II, 685
Bigges, Walter (*fl.* 1589), I, 739
Biggs, W. (*fl.* 1849), III, 107
Biggs, Walter (*fl.* 1587), I, 788
Bignold, T. F. (*fl.* 1888), III, 1069
Bignon, Jean Paul, II, 542
Billet, J. (*fl.* 1849), III, 982
BILLIARDS (books on), III, 777
Billinge's Liverpool Advertiser (1792), II, 725
Billingsley, Sir Henry (d. 1606), I, 377, 801, 880
Billingsley, Martin (*fl.* 1618–37), I, 346
Billingsley, Nicholas (*fl.* 1657), I, 175
Billington, or, Town and Country Songster, The (1790), II, 243
Billington: Or, Vocal Enchantress, The (1790), II, 243
Bilson, Thomas (1547–1616), I, 681, 687, 858
BINDING. See BOOK-BINDING
Bindley, Charles ('Harry Hieover') (1795–1859), III, 766
Bindley, James (1737–1818), II, 904
Bindon, D. (*fl.* 1738), II, 791
Bingham, John (*fl.* 1616), I, 799, 809
Bingham, Joseph (1668–1723), II, **851**
Bingham, Peregrine (1788–1864), II, 954
Bingham, Richard (1798–1872), II, 851
Bingham, W. (*fl.* 1859), III, 722
Bingley, Thomas (*fl.* 1840), III, 572
Bingley, William (d. 1799), bookseller, II, 100, 694, 711, 715
Bingley, William (1774–1823), miscellaneous writer, III, 570
Bingley's Journal (1771), II, 664, 715
Bingley's Journal; Or, The Universal Gazette (1770), II, 715
Bingley's London Journal (1772), II, 715
Binnell, Robert (*fl.* 1758), II, 820
Binney, Edward William (1812–1881), III, 952
Binney, Thomas (1798–1874), III, 107
Binning, Hugh (1627–1653), I, 906
Binstead, Arthur M. (d. 1914), III, 767
Binyon, Robert Laurence (b. 1869), III, 331 f.
Biographical and Imperial Magazine, The (1789), II, 681
Biographical Magazine, The (1773), II, 679
Biographical Magazine, The (1794), II, 682
BIOGRAPHIES
   Anglo-Saxon Period. See LIVES OF SAINTS, I, 89, 93, and under WRITINGS IN LATIN, I, 98 f.
   Middle English Period, I, 115 f. (royal lives), and under WRITINGS IN LATIN, I, 280 f.
   Renaissance to Restoration, I, 381 f., 823 f., 748 f. (journalists)
   Restoration to Romantic Revival, II, 133 f. (contemporary ·memoirs), 162 f. (1660–1714), 164 f. (1714–1800), 670 f. and 694 f.

(lives of journalists), 864 f. (principal biographers), 921 f. (biographical dictionaries and collections)
   Nineteenth Century, III, **14** f. (literary), 136 f. (educationalists), 145 f. (political), 580 f. (theatrical), 782 f. (journalists), 843 (biographical year books), 854 f. (high churchmen), 877 f. (principal biographers), 1074 f. (Anglo-Indians), 1087 (Canadians), 1090 (South Africa), 1097 f. (Australia, New Zealand)
Bion, II, 760
Biondi, Giovanni Francesco, I, 732
Birbeck, C. H. (*fl.* 1880), III, 805
Birch, E. (*fl.* 1839), III, 977
Birch, John (1616–1691), I, 386
Birch, S. (*fl.* 1834), III, 971
Birch, Samuel (1813–1885), III, **1014** f.
Birch, Timothy (*fl.* 1730), II, 714
Birch, Thomas (1705–1766), II, **874** f., **896**
Birckbek, Simon (1584–1656), I, 858
Bird, The (18 cent.), II, 234–5
Bird, H. E. (*fl.* 1890), III, 777
Bird, Isabella Lucy, later Bishop (1831–1904), III, **989**
Bird, J. (*fl.* 1888), III, 1091
Bird, John (*fl.* 1795), II, 550
Birdwood, Sir George (*fl.* 1880), III, 1084
Birgitta, The Revelations of Saint (15 cent.), I, 266
Birkbeck, W. J. (*fl.* 1900), III, 136
Birkenhead (or Berkenhead), Sir John (1616–1679), I, 748, 754, 758
Birket, James (*fl.* 1750), II, 754
Birks, Thomas Rawson (1810–1883), III, 853
Birley, W. (*fl.* 1851), III, 118
BIRMINGHAM
   Magazines, II, 684 (1764–71)
   Newspapers, II, 720 f.
   Printing, II, 86
   Schools, I, 372
   University, III, **123**
Birmingham and Wolverhampton Chronicle, The (1769), 721
Birmingham Chronicle and Warwickshire Journal, The (1770), II, 721
Birmingham Daily Gazette, The (1862), III, 803
Birmingham Daily Mail, The (1870), III, 804
Birmingham Daily Mercury, The (1855), III, 802
Birmingham Daily Post, The (1857), III, 792, 802
Birmingham Daily Press, The (1855), III, 802
Birmingham Daily Times, The (1885), III, 806
Birmingham Evening News, The (1875), III, 804
Birmingham Gazette, The (1741), III, 803
Birmingham Gazette and Express, The (1904), III, 803
Birmingham Gazette; or, The General Correspondent, The (1741), II, 721
Birmingham Journal, The (1732), II, 721

Birmingham Mazagine; Or, Lady's and Gentle-men's Weekly Amusements, The (1770), II, 684

Birmingham Morning News, The (1871), III, 804

Birmingham Register; Or, Entertaining Museum, The (1764), II, 684

BIRR, II, 736 (newspaper)

Birr Weekly Journal, The (1774), II, 736

Birrell, Augustine (1850–1933), III, **735** f.

Birrell, C. M. (*fl.* 1853), II, 493

Birrell (or Birrel), Robert (1532–1605), I, 901

Birth of Merlin, The (17 cent.), I, 579

Birthday Present; or, Conversation Between a Mother and Daughter, A (18 cent.), II, 563

Birthe of Hercules, The (17 cent.), I, 661

Bisaccioni, Hieronimo, I, 340

Bischoff, James (1776–1845), III, 970

Bishop, Isabella Lucy, née Bird (1831–1904), III, **989**

Bishop, James (*fl.* 1855), III, 573

Bishop, Nicholas (*fl.* 1432), I, 45

Bishop, Samuel (1731–1795), II, **224**, 337, **353**

Bishop, William (*fl.* 1619), I, 9

Bishopric Garland, The (18 cent.), II, 237, 246

Bispham, Thomas (*fl.* 1658), I, 773

Biss, E. (*fl.* 1654), I, 843

Bisset, James (1762–1832), II, 560

Bisset, John (*fl.* 1699), II, 731

Bisset, Robert (1759–1805), II, 603, 609, 635, 683 (2)

Blachford, Mary, later Tighe (1772–1810), III, 245

Black, Adam (1784–1874), III, 98, 118

Black, James (1788–1861), III, 963

Black, John (1783–1855), III, 34, 198, 798

Black, John (*fl.* 1798), II, 757

Black, Joseph (1728–1799), III, **945**

Black, Robert (*fl.* 1891), III, 764

Black, William (*fl.* 1706), II, 500

Black, William (1841–1898), III, **538**

Black, William Henry (1808–1872), I, 5, 6, 174

Black and White (1891), III, 815

Black Dwarf, The (1817), III, 816

Blackader (or Blackadder), John (1615–1686), the elder, II, 156

Blackader (or Blackadder), John (1664–1729), the younger, II, 151, 156

Blackbird, The (1764), II, 222, 228, 236

Blackbird, The (1777), II, 232

Blackbird, Being a Collection of Favourite Songs, The (18 cent.), II, 243

Blackbourne, John (1683–1741), II, 910

Blackbourne, Richard (b. 1652), I, 872

Blackburn, D. ('Sarel Erasmus') (*fl.* 1899), III, **1089**

Blackburn Evening Express, The (1887), III, 806

Blackburn, S. (*fl.* 1824), II, 994

Blackburn Times, The (19 cent.), III, 792

Blackburne, Francis (1705–1787), II, 913

Blacke Tom His Speech to the House (17 cent.), I, 719

Blacker, W. (*fl.* 1842), III, 769

'Blackford, Martha', i.e. Isabella Stoddart (*fl.* 1819), III, 571

Blackguardiana (18 cent.), II, 248

Blackie, John (1782–1874), III, 98

Blackie, John Stuart (1809–1895), III, **280** f.

Blacklock, Thomas (1721–1791), II, 219, 221, **990**

Blackmore, Sir Richard (d. 1729), II, 21, 75, **279**, 767

Blackmore, Richard Doddridge (1825–1900), III, **474**

Blackstone, Sir William (1723–1780), II, 303, 962

Blackwall, Anthony (1674–1730), II, 25

Blackwell, Henry (*fl.* 1702), II, 823

Blackwell, Thomas, the elder† (1660?–1728), II, **994**

Blackwell, Thomas, the younger (1701–1757), II, 25, **997**

Blackwood, Frederick Temple Hamilton-Temple, Marquis of Dufferin (1826–1902), III, 989

Blackwood, Hariot G., Marchioness of Dufferin and Ava (*fl.* 1889), III, 1078

Blackwood, Helen Selina, Baroness Dufferin, née Sheridan (1807–1867), III, **1052**

Blackwood, John (1818–1879), III, 825

Blackwood, William (1776–1834), III, 98, 825

Blackwood's Edinburgh Magazine (1817), III, 825

Blackwood's Lady's Magazine and Gazette of the Fashionable World (1836), III, 827

Blacman, John (*fl.* 1457), I, **313**

Blacow, Richard (*fl.* 1755), II, 117

Bladen, Martin (1680–1746), II, 764, 774

Blades, William (1824–1890), III, **1029**

Blaeu, Willem Janszoon, I, 779

Blagdon, Francis William (1778–1819), II, 614; III, 798, 816, 823

Blage, Thomas (*fl.* 1578), I, 715

Blagrave, John (d. 1611), I, 377, 881, 883

Blagrave, Joseph (1610–1682), II, 818

Blaicklock, Laurence (*fl.* 1643), I, 755

Blaikie, Thomas (*fl.* 1775), II, 747

Blaikie, William Garden (1820–1899), III, 830

Blaine, Delabere Pritchett (*fl.* 1840), II, 822; III, 758

Blair, Hugh (1718–1800), II, 19, 26, 914, 952, 999

Blair, James (1656–1743), II, 753

Blair, Robert (1593–1666), divine, I, 385, 841

Blair, Robert (1690–1746), poet, II, **310**

Blair, T. S. (*fl.* 1896), III, 985

Blair, William (1766–1822), II, 683

Blake, Charles W. (*fl.* 1874), III, 800

Blake, E. (*fl.* 1897), III, 979

Blake, W. (*fl.* 1810), economist, III, 973

Blake, William (1757–1827), II, **347** f.

Blakesley, Joseph Williams (1808–1885), III, 121, **996**

Blakey, Robert (1795–1878), III, 769
Blamire, Susanna (1747–1794), II, **354**
Blancard, Stephen (*fl.* 1702), II, 927
Blanchard, Edmund Forster (*fl.* 1857), III, 199
Blanchard, Edward Litt Leman (Laman) (1820–1889), III, **599**f.
Blanchard, Samuel Laman (1804–1845), III, **281**, 294, 471, 799, 800, 827
Blanco, José Maria, later Joseph Blanco White (1775–1841), III, **847**
Bland (later Bland-Tucker), Edith, née Nesbit (1858–1924), III, **350**f., 570
Bland, Edward (*fl.* 1650), I, 793
Bland, John (*fl.* 1787), II, 240 (2)
Bland, Robert (1779?–1825), III, 239
Bland, W. (*fl.* 1864), III, 971
Blandie, William (*fl.* 1576), I, 817
Blane, Sir Gilbert (1749–1834), III, 970
Blane, W. (*fl.* 1903), III, 1089
Blane, William (*fl.* 1781–8), II, 764, 816, 821
Blaneford, Henry (*fl.* 1330), I, 115
Blanford, William Thomas (1832–1905), III, 1080
BLANK VERSE. See PROSODY, I, 15f.
Blanket (or Blankett), John (*fl.* 1777), II, 746
Blaquiere, Edward (*fl.* 1825), III, 206
Blatchford, Robert (b. 1851), III, 783, 818
Blavatsky, H. P. (*fl.* 1890), III, 831, 1080
Blaxton, John (*fl.* 1625–34), I, 845
Blaydes, Frederick Henry Marvell (1818–1908), III, **996**f.
Blayds, Charles Stuart, later Calverley (1831–1884), II, **335**
Bleek, Wilhelm Heinrich Immanuel (1827–1875), III, **1092**
Blencowe, John (b. 1609), I, 655
Blenerhasset, Thomas (1550?–1625?), I, 413
Blessington, Marguerite, Countess of, née Power (1789–1849), III, **388**
Blew, William Charles Arlington (*fl.* 1899), III, 761
Blickling Homilies (O.E.), I, 27, 35–6, **92**
Bligh, William (1754–1817), II, 757
Blin de Sainmore, Adrien Michel Hyacinthe, II, 771
Blind, Harry. See Henry the Minstrel, I, 29
Blind, Mathilde (1841–1896), III, **332**
'Blinkhoolie' (1880), III, 767
Bliss, H. (*fl.* 1833), III, 981
Bliss, James (*fl.* 1848–60), I, 698; II, 846
Bliss, Philip (1787–1857), I, 409, 433, 661, 722; III, 867
Bliss, W. D. P. (*fl.* 1895), III, 978
Blith, Walter (*fl.* 1649), I, 846
Blizard, Sir William (1743–1835), II, 155
Blome, Richard (d. 1705), I, 879; II, 120, 787, 800, 819
Blomefield, Francis (1705–1752), II, **881**
Blomefield, Leonard, earlier Jenyns (1800–1893), III, 138, 956

Blomfield, A. (*fl.* 1863), III, 854
Blomfield, Charles James (1786–1857), III, **993**
Blondel, François, II, 28
Bloodie Banquet, The (17 cent.), I, 651
Bloom, J. H. (*fl.* 1831), I, 694
Bloomfield, Robert (1766–1823), III, **227**f., 571
Blount, Charles (1654–1693), II, 84, 270, 575, 941
Blount, Edward (*fl.* 1600), I, 352, 524, 812
Blount, Sir Henry (1602–1682), traveller, I, 772
Blount, Henry (*fl.* 1650), translator, I, 479
Blount, Thomas (1618–1679), II, 926, 962
Blount, Sir Thomas Pope (1649–1697), II, 15, 21
Blowitz, Henri Stephen de (1832–1903), III, 783
Blue Dwarf, The [Yarmouth] (1820), III, 816
Blue 'Un, The [Cambridge] (1884), III, 835
BLUESTOCKINGS, THE, II, 841f.
Bluet, George (*fl.* 1725), II, 600
Blumenfeld, Ralph David (b. 1864), III, 783
Blundell, H. (*fl.* 1642), I, 754
Blundell, James (1790–1877), I, 17
Blundell, William (1620–1698), II, 147
Blunden, Humphrey (*fl.* 1642–8), I, 752–3; II, 860–1
Blundeville (or Blundevile), Thomas (*fl.* 1580), I, 378, 393, 806, 813–4, 880, 883, 885
Blunt, Lady Anne (*fl.* 1881), III, 989
Blunt, Henry (1794–1843), III, 853
Blunt, John (*fl.* 1773), II, 817
Blunt, John Henry (1823–1884), I, 677
Blunt, John James (1794–1855), II, 937; III, 234, 853
'Blunt Spurs' (1870), III, 760
Blunt, W. (*fl.* 1820), III, 248
Blunt, Wilfrid Scawen (1840–1922), III, **332**f.
Blyth, Edward (1810–1873), II, 841
Boade, W. (*fl.* 1832), III, 117
Boaden, James (1762–1839), I, 581; II, 694, 709; III, **587**
Boaistuau, Pierre, I, 334
Boake, Barcroft Henry (*fl.* 1897), III, 1095
Boardman, J. (*fl.* 1790), II, 789
Boase, Henry (1763–1827), III, 972
Boate, Gerard (1604–1650), I, 776
Boaz, Herman (*fl.* 1789), II, 822
Boccaccio, Giovanni, I, 264, 326, 341, 662, 811 (2); II, 67, 808; III, 39, 353
Boddely's Bath Journal (1756), II, 720
Boden, Nicholas (*fl.* 1769), II, 721
Boden, Samuel S. (*fl.* 1851), III, 777
Bodenham, John (*fl.* 1597), I, 404, 715; II, 129
Bodens, Charles (*fl.* 1732), II, 518
Bodham, Charles (*fl.* 1846), I, 588
Bodin, Jean, I, 331, 844
Bodkin, M. M'D. (b. 1850), III, 783
BODLEIAN LIBRARY, II, 104
Bodley Homilies (M.E.), I, 170
Bodley New Testament Verse Passages (M.E.), I, 190

Bodley, Sir Thomas (1545–1613), I, 366, 384
Bodmer, Johann Jakob, II, 56, 805
Body and the Soul, The (M.E.), I, **177** f.
Boehme, Jacob, I, 336 f., 811; II, 54, **860** f.
Boemus, Joannes, I, 765
BOETHIUS
    O.E. Version, I, 87
    Chaucer's Version, I, 228
    Translations 1500–1800, I, 811; II, 764
Boethius, Hector (Boece) (1465?–1536), I, 773, 901
Bogan, Zachariah (*fl.* 1662), I, 780
Bogle, George (1746–1781), II, 750
Bogue, David (1750–1825), II, 861
Bohn, Henry George (1796–1884), I, 4; II, 647, 825; III, 34, 73, 84, 94, 103, 669
Bohun, Edmund (1645–1699), I, 381; II, 85, 134, 148, 921
Bohun, Ralph (b. 1639?), II, 960
Bohun, William (*fl.* 1702), II, 962
Boiardo, Matteo Maria, I, 340, 811; II, 39, 605
Boig, Adam (*fl.* 1705), II, 731
Boileau, A. H. E. (*fl.* 1845), III, 1083
Boileau, Daniel (*fl.* 1795–1811), II, 63; III, 980
Boileau-Despréaux, Nicolas, II, 28, 39, 44–5, 771
Boindin, Nicolas, II, 771
Bois, John (1561–1644), I, 856
Bois-Guillebert, Pierre le Pesant, Sieur de, II, 788
Boislebeau de la Chappelle, Armand, II, 688
Boisrobert, François le Metel de, I, 732
Boissier, J. L. (*fl.* 1787), II, 771
Boissy, Louis de, II, 771
Boke of Kervynge (15 cent.), I, 264
Bokenam (or Bokenham), Osbern (1393–1447?), I, 39, 253
Bolas, Thomas (*fl.* 1889), III, 818
Bold, Henry (1627–1683), II, **279**
Bold, M. (*fl.* 1702), I, 466
Bold, Samuel (1649–1737), II, 941
Bold, William (*fl.* 1685), II, 179
Boldon Buke, The (M.E.), I, 121
'Boldrewood, Rolf', i.e. Thomas Alexander Browne (1826–1915), III, **1096**
Boletarium (18 cent.), II, 239, 241
Bolger, John (*fl.* 1853?), III, 821
Bolingbroke, Henry St John, Viscount (1678–1751), II, 17, 39, 111, **612** f.
Bolland, William (*fl.* 1851), III, 774
Bolton, Edmund (1575?–1633?), I, 801, **837**, 865; II, 120
BOLTON, II, 86 (printing)
Bolton, M. P. W. (*fl.* 1867), III, 868
Bolton, Robert (1697–1763), II, 826
Bolton Daily Chronicle, The (1870), III, 804
Bolton Evening Guardian, The (1871), III, 804
Bolton Evening News, The (1867), III, 803
Bolton Morning News, The (1870), III, 804

Bolts, William (1740?–1808), III, 1075
Bon, Ottaviano, I, 779
Bon Ton Magazine, The (1791), II, 681
Bona, Joannes, II, 808
Bonar, A. A. (*fl.* 1863–85), I, 909 (2)
Bonar, Horatius (1808–1889), III, **281** f., 853
Bonar, J. (*fl.* 1885), III, 984
Bonarelli, G. de, I, 655
Bonatus, Guido, II, 808
Bonaventura, II, 808
Bond, A. E. [misprint for Sir E. A. Bond], II, 456
Bond, Sir Edward Augustus (1815–1898), III, **898** f.
Bond, John (1550–1612) [misprinted J. A. Bond], I, 860
Bond, John (*fl.* 1642), journalist, I, 752
Bond, John (*fl.* 1685), lawyer, II, 962
Bond, William (d. 1735), II, 506, 661–2, 814
Boner, Charles (1815–1870), III, 576
Bonhote, Elizabeth (1744–1818), II, 547
Boniface or Wynfrith (d. 755), I, **105** f.
Bonnac, Adolphus (pseud.?) (1756), II, 545
Bonner, Edmund (1500?–1569), I, 365
Bonner, G. (*fl.* 1833), III, 234
Bonner and Middleton's Bristol Journal (1774), II, 721
Bonnerjee, R. C. (*fl.* 1897), III, 1072
Bonnet, Charles (*fl.* 1766), II, 771
Bonney, Thomas George (1833–1923), III, **953**
Bonnor, Charles (*fl.* 1777–1829?), II, 692
Bonnot de Mably, Gabriel, II, 771
Bonstetten, Charles-Victor de, II, 335
Bonwick, James (1817–1906), III, **1097**
Bonwicke, Ambrose, the elder (1652–1722), II, 153
Bonze, or, Chinese Anchorite, The (18 cent.), II, 552
Book Exchange, The (1863), III, 103
Book of Cupid (M.E.), I, **187**
Book of Fun, The (18 cent.), II, 219
Book of Hawking, Hunting [etc.], *The*, I, 266
Book of Oddities, The (18 cent.), II, 243, 245
Book of Quinte Essence, The (15 cent.), I, 266
Book of Trades, The (19 cent.), III, 575
BOOK PLATES, II, 101
BOOK PRODUCTION AND DISTRIBUTION, I, 345 f. (1500–1660); II, 81 f. (1660–1800); III, 70 f. (19 cent.)
BOOK TRADE, REGULATION OF, I, 355 f. (1500–1660); II, 83 f. (1660–1800)
BOOK-BINDING, I, 347 f. (1500–1660), II, 107 (1660–1800); III, 92 f. (19 cent.)
BOOK-COLLECTING, I, 360 f. (14–17 cents.); II, 100 f. (17, 18 cents.); III, 103 f. (19 cent.)
Book-Finisher's Friendly Circular, The (1845), III, 92
BOOK-ILLUSTRATION, I, 348 (1500–1660); II, 106 (1660–1800), 160 f. (18 cent.); III, 89 f. (19 cent.), 577 (children's books)
Bookbinder's Trade Circular, The (1850), III, 92

Bookbuyer's Guide, The (1869), III, 101
Booke of Curtasye, The (15 cent.), I, 264
Booke of Demeanor, The (17 cent.), I, 264
Booke of the Common Prayer, The (16 cent.), I, 45
Booker, Thomas William (*fl.* 1842), III, 168
Bookman, The (1891), III, 831
Books of the Month, The (1861), III, 101
Bookseller, The (1858), III, 101
BOOKSELLERS, I, 350f. (1500–1660); II, 86f. (1660–1800); III, 102f. (19 cent.)
    Antiquarian and second-hand, III, 103
Bookseller's Record, The (1859), III, 101
Boole, George (1815–1864), III, **863, 942**
Boon, John (1859–1928), III, 783
Boone, James Shergold (1799–1859), III, 107, 126, 833
Boorde, Andrew (1490?–1859), I, 396, 713, 773, 777, 883, 888
Boosey, Thomas (*fl.* 1835), III, 769, 772
Boote, Richard (*fl.* 1766), II, 963
Booth, Miss A. E. (*fl.* 1794), II, 63
Booth, Abraham (1734–1806), II, 769
Booth, Barton (1681–1733), II, **311**f.
Booth, Charles (1840–1916), III, 976, 984
Booth, David (*fl.* 1817–23), accountant, III, 975
Booth, George (*fl.* 1700), II, 760, 963
Booth, James (1806–1878), III, 107, 141, 941
Booth, Richard (*fl.* 1646), I, 786
Booth, W. (*fl.* 1785), II, 756
Booth, William (1829–1912), III, 976
Boothby, Sir Brooke (1743–1824), II, 635
Boothby, Guy Newell (1867–1905), III, 1097
Boothby, Richard (*fl.* 1646), I, 786
Boothly, Miss Hill [misprint for Boothby (1708–1756)], II, 617
Bo-peep (1882), III, 578
Boquet, The (18 cent.), II, 237
Borcherds, P. B. (*fl.* 1861), III, 1090
Borck, K. W. von, II, 71
Bordeaux, Huon de, I, 333–4
Bordelon, Laurent, II, 541
Border, Daniel (*fl.* 1648), I, 755 (2), 758–9, 760 (2), 761 (2), 763 (2)
Bordley, Simon (*fl.* 1787), II, 129
Boreham, W. (*fl.* 1717), II, 712
Boreman (or Bourman), Robert (d. 1675), I, 367
Boreman, Thomas (*fl.* 1730), II, 560
Borlase, William (1695–1772), II, **890**
Borough (or Burroughes), Sir John (d. 1643), I, 846
Borough, William (1536–1599), I, 885
Borri, Cristoforo, I, 785
Borrow, George Henry (1803–1881), III, **421**f.
Borthwick, Algernon, Baron Glenesk (1830–1908), 783, 798
Borthwick, Peter (1804–1852), III, 798
Borton, William, II, 786
'Bos' (1839), III, 440

Bosan-Almogaver, Juan, 345
Bosanquet, Bernard (1848–1923), III, **863**f.
Bosanquet, Charles (1769–1850), III, 973
Bosanquet, Frederick Albert (1837–1923), III, 986
Bosanquet, W. H. F. (*fl.* 1860), I, 73
Boscawen, William (1752–1811), II, 24, **766**
Bose, P. N. (*fl.* 1894), III, 1085
Bose, S. S. (*fl.* 1903), III, 1085
Bose, Shib Chunder (*fl.* 1881), III, 1084
Bosse, A., II, 828
Bossewell, John (*fl.* 1572), I, 395
Bossuet, Jacques Bénigne, II, 35, 772
Bostock, John (1773–1846), III, 962
Bostock, R. (*fl.* 1644), I, 756
Boston, Thomas (1676–1732), II, **994**
Boswell, Sir Alexander (1775–1822), I, 427, 903 (2); III, **228**
Boswell, James, the elder (1740–1795), II, 55, 92, **650**f., 903
Boswell, James, the younger (1778–1822), II, 625; III, **1022**
Boswell, John (1698–1757), II, 101, 874
Bosworth, Joseph (1789–1876), III, **1022**
Bosworth, T. (*fl.* 1855), III, 71
Bosworth, William (1607–1650), I, 474
Bosworth, William (*fl.* 1830), III, 1022
Bosworth-Field (18 cent.), II, 189
Botanical Magazine; Or, Flower Garden Displayed, The (1787), II, 673, 681; III, 823
BOTANY (writings on), III, 959f. (19 cent.). For 1660–1800 see under LITERATURE OF SCIENCE, II, 959f.
Boteler, W. C. (*fl.* 1827), III, 92
Botero, Giovanni, I, 766, 847
Botfield, Beriah (1807–1863), III, **901**
Both Sides of the Gutter (18 cent.), II, 242 (2)
Botham, Mary, later Howitt (1799–1888), III, 43, 271, 486, 576, **672**f., 711
Bott, Edmund (*fl.* 1771), II, 963
Bottarelli, F. (*fl.* 1770), II, 810
Bottarelli, Giovanni Goalberto (*fl.* 1763–70), II, 808, 810
Bottle Companions, The (18 cent.), II, 188
Bottomley, Horatio (*fl.* 1896–1920), III, 800
Boucicault, Dionysius Lardner (1822–1890), III, 427, 456, **600**, 605
Bougainville, Louis Antoine de, II, 772
Bouhours, Dominique, II, 28, 40, 772
Bouilly, Jean-Nicoloas, II, 469
Boulainvilliers, Henri de, II, 772
Boulanger, N. A. (*fl.* 1795), II, 783
Boulter, Hugh (1672–1742), II, 158
Bouquet, A Selection of Poems from the Most Celebrated Authors, The (18 cent.), II, 240
Bouquet, or Blossoms of Fancy, The (18 cent.), II, 251
Bourchier, John, Baron Berners (1467–1533), I, 30, **263**, 813, 814 (3)
Bourdaloue, Louis, II, 772

Bourdeilles, Pierre de, Seigneur de Brantôme, II, 46, 772

Bourdillon, Francis William (1852–1921), III, 333

Boureau Deslandes, André François, II, 772

Bourgelat, Claude, II, 816

Bourget, J, II, 886

Bourguignon d'Anville, Jean Baptiste, II, 772

Bourhill, Mrs E. J. (*fl.* 1908), III, 1093

Bourignon, Antoinette, II, 39

Bourinot, Sir John George (1837–1902), III, 1085, 1087

Bourke, Sir Richard (1777–1855), II, 633

Bourman (or Boreman), Robert (d. 1675), I, 367

Bourn (or Bourne), William (d. 1583), I, 390 (2), 885

Bourne, Henry (1696–1733), I, 279, II, 891

Bourne, Henry Richard Fox (1837–1909), I, 390, 420; III, 983, 1093

Bourne, Nicholas (*fl.* 1621), I, 743

Bourne, Stephen (*fl.* 1827–32), III, 819 (2)

Bourne, Vincent (1695–1747), II, 204, 229, **935**

Bourne (or Bourn), William (d. 1583), I, 390 (2), 885

Bourryau, J. (*fl.* 1759), II, 773

Boursault, Edme, II, 40, 46

Boutigny, Rolland le Vayer de, II, 534

Bouyer, Reynold Gideon A. (d. 1826), III, 108

Bovill, Mai (*fl.* 1897), III, 764

Bovinian, The most Pleasant History of (17 cent.), I, 732

Bow Bells (1865), III, 830

Bow Bells Weekly (1888), III, 830

Bowden, Charles Topham (*fl.* 1791), II, 159

Bowden, J. E. (*fl.* 1866), III, 287 (2)

Bowden, James [misprint for James Boaden (1762–1839)], II, 81

Bowden, John William (1798–1844), III, **856**

Bowden, Samuel (*fl.* 1733–61), II, 22, **354**

Bowdler, Thomas (1754–1825), I, 549; II, 747

Bowen, Edward Ernest (1836–1901), III, 109, 136

Bowen, Sir George Ferguson (1821–1899), III, 1098

Bowen, H. C. (*fl.* 1893), III, 108

Bower, Alexander (*fl.* 1804–30), II, 966

Bower, Archibald (1686–1766), II, 675, **878**

Bower, Frederick Orpen (b. 1855), III, 962

Bower, H. (*fl.* 1851), III, 1083

Bower, R. (*fl.* 1848), III, 833

Bower, S. (*fl.* 1838), III, 977

Bowers, Georgina (*fl.* 1873), III, 760

Bowes, J. B. (*fl.* 1896), III, 800

Bowes, Sir Jerome (d. 1616), I, 813

Bowes, Paul (d. 1702), I, 841

Bowes, Robert (1535?–1597), of Ashe, I, 384

Bowes, Thomas (*fl.* 1586), I, 815

Bowle, J. (*fl.* 1736), I, 408

Bowle, John (1725–1788), II, 18, 914

Bowles, Carington (*fl.* 1786), II, 145

Bowles, Caroline Anne, later Southey (1786–1854), III, **228**, 416

Bowles, Edward (1613–1662), I, 748–9, 756

Bowles, John (*fl.* 1793–1807), II, 85; III, 111

Bowles, Oliver (*fl.* 1649), I, 694

Bowles, T. Gibson (1842–1922), III, 814

Bowles, William Lisle (1762–1850), II, 295, 304, **354**; III, 134

Bowlker, Charles (*fl.* 1746), II, 820

Bowlker, Richard (*fl.* 1746), II, 320

Bowman, Anne (*fl.* 1855), III, **573**

Bowman, Henry (*fl.* 1677), II, 178

Bowman, John (*fl.* 1685–1740), II, 403

Bowman, Sir William (1816–1892), III, 963

Bownas, Samuel (1676–1753), II, 754

Bowrey, Thomas (*fl.* 1669), II, 744, 749

Bowring, E. A. (*fl.* 1851–8), III, 32, 34, 982

Bowring, Sir John (1792–1872), III, **228**, 257

Bowstead, William (*fl.* 1896), III, 985

Bowtell, John (1753–1813), II, 107

Bowtell, Stephen (*fl.* 1642), I, 754

Bowyer, William (1699–1777), II, 330

Box, Charles (*fl.* 1868), III, 774

Boxall, T. (*fl.* 1800), II, 824

BOXING (books on), II, 822 f. (1660–1800); III, 776 (19 cent.)

Boy's Comic Journal, The (1883), III, 578

Boy's Journal: A Magazine of Literature, Science, and Amusement, The (1863), III, 578

Boy's Monthly Magazine, The (1864), III, 578

Boy's Own Annual, The (1829), III, 578

Boy's Own Journal, The (1856), III, 577

Boy's Own Magazine, The (1885), III, 577

Boy's Own Paper, The (1879), III, 578

Boy's Penny Magazine, The (1863), III, 578

Boy's Yearly Book, The (1863), III, 578

Boyce, Samuel (d. 1775), II, **354**f.

Boyd, Mr (*fl.* 1715), II, 823

Boyd, Andrew Kennedy Hutchinson (1825–1899), III, **708**

Boyd, Archibald (*fl.* 1850), III, **474**

Boyd, Elizabeth (*fl.* 1732), II, 539

Boyd, Frank M. (b. 1863), III, 783, 814

Boyd, Henry (d. 1832), III, **229**

Boyd, Hugh (1746–1794), II, 631, 665 (2), 666

Boyd, Hugh Macauley (*fl.* 1793), III, 1082

Boyd, Palmer (*fl.* 1872), III, 1072

Boyd, Percy (*fl.* 1856?), III, 827

Boyd, Robert (1578–1627), I, 906

Boyd, W. (*fl.* 1801–28), III, 973, 978

Boyd, Zachary (1585?–1653), I, 679, 906 f.

Boyer, Abel (1667–1729), II, 694, **876**
  Educational works, II, 33, 120, 182
  Periodicals, II, 676, 683 (2), 706, 707 (2), 710
  Translations, II, 122, 126, 485, 535, 541, 778, 786, 788, 799

Boyer, Jean Baptiste de, Marquis d'Argens, II, 35, 543, 552, 772

Boyes, John Frederick (1811–1879), III, 435
Boylan, R. D. (*fl.* 1846), III, 34
Boyle, Charles, Earl of Orrery (1676–1731), II, 15
Boyle, Eleanor Vere (*fl.* 1852), III, 572
Boyle, Frederick (1841–1883), III, 783
Boyle, George David (1828–1901), III, 154
Boyle, John, Earl of Cork and Orrery (1707–1762), I, 841; II, 593, 767, 773
Boyle, John (*fl.* 1771), publisher, II, 732
Boyle, Richard, Earl of Cork (1566–1643), I, 385
Boyle, Robert (1627–1691), I, 878; II, 531, **960**
Boyle, Robert Whelan (*fl.* 1876), III, 799
Boyle, Roger, Earl of Orrery (1621–1679), I, 732; II, **425**f., 530
Boyle, William (b. 1853), III, **1065**
Boyne, John (d. 1810), II, 85
Boyne, William (*fl.* 1869), I, 9
Boys, Thomas Shotter (1803–1874), III, 90
Boys. See under CHILDREN and EDUCATION
Boys (1892), III, 578
Boys and Girls (1887), III, 578
Boys, John (1571–1625), I, 681
Boys of England (1866), III, 578, 820
Boys of England (c. 1900), III, 820
Boys of our Empire (c. 1900), III, 820
Boys of the Empire (c. 1900), III, 820
Boys of the United Kingdom (1887), III, 578
Boys' and Girls' Companion for Leisure Hours, The (1857), III, 577
Boys' Illustrated News, The (1881), III, 821
Boys' Magazine, The (after 1900), III, 578
Boys' Newspaper, The (1880), III, 821
Boys' Own Paper, The (1879), III, 821
Boys' Standard, The (1875), III, 821
Boys' World, The (1879), III, 821
Boyse, Samuel (1708–1749), II, **311**, 799
Bozon, Nicole (*fl. c.* 1320), I, **301**
Brabourne, Edward Hugessen Knatchbull-Hugessen, Baron (1829–1893), II, 573
'Brace of Cantabs, A' (1824), III, 123
Bracebridge, C. H. (*fl.* 1862), I, 542
Bracken, Henry (1697–1764), II, 816 (2)
Bracken, Thomas (1867–1905), III, **1094**
Brackenbury, Sir Henry (1837–1914), III, 155
Brackley, Lady Elizabeth (c. 1645), I, 641
Bracton, Henry of (d. 1268), I, 116, **300**
Bradbury, Henry (1831–1860), III, 78
Braddon, Sir Edward (1829–1904), III, 1084
Braddon, Laurence (d. 1724), II, 869
Braddon, Mary Elizabeth, later Maxwell (1837–1915), III, **538**f.
Bradford, John (1510?–1555), I, 681, 684, 816
Bradford, John (1750–1805), II, 917
Bradford, William (1590–1657), I, 791, 793
Bradford Chronicle, The (1872), III, 804
Bradford Daily Argus, The (19 cent.), III, 806
Bradford Daily Chronicle and Mail, The (1882), III, 804

Bradford Daily Telegraph, The (1868), III, 803
Bradford Daily Times, The (1868), III, 803
Bradford Evening Mail, The (1872), III, 804
Bradford Observer, The (1868), III, 803
Bradlaugh, Charles (1833–1891), III, 783, 977
Bradley, Cuthbert (*fl.* 1898), III, 761
Bradley, Edward (1827–1889), 'Cuthbert Bede', III, **473**f.
Bradley, Francis Herbert (1846–1924), III, **864**f.
Bradley, Henry (1845–1923), III, **1036**
Bradley, Katherine Harris (1846–1913), III, **340**
Bradley, Margaret Louisa, later Woods (b. 1856), III, **563**
Bradley, Richard (d. 1732), II, 704–5, 763, 818f.
Bradley, Thomas (d. 1491), I, 314
Bradley, Thomas (1751–1813), II, 683
Bradley, Tom (*fl.* 1889), III, 765
Bradshaw, Henry (d. 1513), I, **253**
Bradshaw, Henry (1831–1886), III, **1036**f.
Bradshaw, Thomas (*fl.* 1591), I, 808
Bradshaw, Thomas (*fl.* 1792), II, 761
Bradshaw, W. (*fl.* 1637), II, 811
Bradshaw's Journal (1842), III, 827
Bradshaw's Manchester Journal (1841), III, 827
Bradshaw's Railway Gazette (1845), III, 822
Bradstreet, Anne (1612–1672), I, 474
Bradwardine, Thomas (c. 1290–1349), I, **312**
Brady, Cheyne (*fl.* 1856), III, 827
Brady, Nicholas (1659–1726), II, 412, 429, 768
Brady, Robert (d. 1700), II, 926
Brady, T. J. B. (*fl.* 1867), III, 1010
Bragg, Benjamin (*fl.* 1699–1705), II, 706
Bragge, Francis (*fl.* 1710), II, 796
Brailsford, W. (*fl.* 1867), III, 508
Brain (1878), III, 833
Brainerd, David (*fl.* 1746), II, 754
Braithwaite, G. F. (*fl.* 1884), III, 771
Braithwaite, John (1700?–1768?), II, 748
Bramhall, John (1594–1663), I, 386, **877**; II, 847
Brampton, Sir Henry Hawkins, Baron (1817–1907), II, 153
Brampton, Thomas (*fl.* 1414), I, 264
Bramsen, J. (*fl.* 1820), III, 31
Bramston, James (1694?–1744), II, **311**
Bramston, Sir John (1611–1700), I, 386
Bramwell, George William Wilshere, Baron (1808–1892), III, 977
Brand, Barbarina, Lady Dacre (1768–1854), III, **229**
Brand, Hannah (d. 1821), II, **460**, 776
Brand, John (1744–1806), II, **891**
Brande, William Thomas (1788–1866), III, 947
Brandes, J. C., II, 805
Brandl, Alois, III, 713
Brandon, John (*fl.* 1644), I, 369

Brandon, Samuel (*fl.* 1598), I, 534
Bransby, James Hews (1783–1847), II, 346
Bransby, John (*fl.* 1799), II, 684
Bransley, Charles (*fl.* 1540?), I, 716
Brant, Sebastian, I, 336
Brantôme, Pierre de Bourdeilles, Seigneur de, II, 46, 772
Brasbridge, Joseph (1743–1832), II, 137
BRASENOSE COLLEGE (Oxford), I, 368
Brass Halo, The [Cambridge] (1893), III, 835
Brassey, Anna, Lady (1839–1887), III, 989
Brassey, Thomas, Earl (1836–1918), III, 983
Brathwaite, Richard (1588?–1673), I, 378, 379, 658, 679, 711 f., 718, 723, 725, 731, 867
Braunche, William (*fl.* 1596), I, 818
Bray, Anna Eliza, earlier Stothard, née Kempe, (1790–1883), III, 389
Bray, Charles (1811–1884), III, 847, 977
Bray, J. F. (*fl.* 1839), III, 977
Bray, Thomas (1656–1730), II, 102
Bray, William (1736–1832), II, 830; III, 882
Braybrooke, Richard Griffin Neville, Baron (1783–1858), I, 386; II, 831
Brayley, Edward Wedlake (1773–1854), III, 884 f.
Brayne, J. (*fl.* 1653), I, 884
Bremer, Fredrika, III, 43
Bremner, D. (*fl.* 1869), III, 983
Bremner, Robert (d. 1789), II, 218
Bremner, Robert (*fl.* 1839), III, 939
Brémond, Gabriel de, II, 533–4, 773
Brende, John (*fl.* 1553), I, 801
Brennan, Christopher John (*fl.* 1913), III, 1096
Brent, The (18 cent.), II, 223
Brent, Sir Nathaniel (1573?–1652), I, 818, 858; II, 813
Brent, W. (*fl.* 1676), II, 810
Brereton, J. le Gay (*fl.* 1908), III, 1096
Brereton, Thomas (1691–1722), II, 662, 675
Brereton, Sir William (1604–1661), I, 383, 772
Brerewood (or Bryerwood), Edward (1565?–1613), I, 766, 854, 883
Brerewood, Francis (*fl.* 1722), II, 29, 801
Brerewood, Thomas (d. 1748), II, 311
Bret, — (*fl.* 1706), II, 105
Bret, D. (*fl.* 1707), II, 798
Brethren in Iniquity (17 cent.), I, 719
Bretnor, T. (*fl.* 1618), I, 718
BRETON LAIS, I, 151 f.
Breton, Nicholas (1545–1626), I, 415 f., 716, 722, 725, 730
Brett, Edwin J. (*fl.* 1867–98), III, 820–1
Brett, John (d. 1785), II, 30, 68
Brett, Peter (*fl.* 1748), II, 663
Brett, Richard (1560?–1637), I, 785
Brett, Samuel (*fl.* 1655), I, 773
Brett, Thomas (1667–1743), II, 851, 853
Brett's Miscellany (1748), II, 663
BRETTON PRIORY, I, 361 (library)
Breunings von Buchenbach, H. J., I, 384

Breval, John Durant (1680?–1738), II, 193, 311
Brewer, Anthony (*fl.* 1655), I, 641
Brewer, John Sherren (1810–1879), I, 116, 290, 292–3, 696, 702, 835
Brewer, Robert Frederick (*fl.* 1869), I, 17
Brewer, Thomas (*fl.* 1624), I, 641, 731
Brewman, D. (*fl.* 1780), II, 711
Brewster, Sir David (1771–1868), II, 686; III, 824, 937
Brewster, Thomas (b. 1705), II, 767, 770
Brewyn, William (*fl.* 1470), I, 313
Brian, Thomas (*fl.* 1637), I, 890
Briani, G., II, 808
Briant (or Bryan), Sir Francis (d. 1550), I, 814
Brice & Co.'s Old Exeter Journal (1789), II, 723
Brice, Andrew (1692–1773), II, 694
Brice, Seward (*fl.* 1874), III, 985
Brice's Old Exeter Journal, Or, Western Advertiser (1789), II, 723
Brice's Weekly Collection of Intelligence (1736), II, 724
Brice's Weekly Journal (1725), II, 723
Brickell, John (*fl.* 1737), II, 754
Bricknell, W. S. (*fl.* 1844), III, 691, 854
Briddon, J. (*fl.* 1859), III, 466
Bridgen, E. (*fl.* 1786), II, 516
Bridges, Jeremiah (*fl.* 1751), II, 816
Bridges, John (d. 1618), I, 690
Bridges, John (1666–1724), II, 102, 880
Bridges, John Henry (1832–1906), III, 865
Bridges, Robert Seymour (1844–1930), III, 323 f.
Bridges, Thomas (*fl.* 1762–75), II, 355
Bridgman (or Bridgeman), Sir Orlando (1606?–1674), II, 963
Brief Anatomie of Women, A (17 cent.), I, 717
Brief Introduction to the Skill of Musick, A (17 cent.), II, 173
Briefe Description or Character of the Religion and Manners of the Phanatiques in General, A (17 cent.), I, 724
Briefe Relation of some affaires and transactions Civill and Military, both Forraigne and Domestique, A (1649), I, 760
Brierton, John (*fl.* 1602), I, 788
Brigges, Agnes (*fl.* 1574), I, 893
Briggs, H. G. (*fl.* 1852–61), III, 1076, 1081
Briggs, Henry (1561–1630), I, 881
Briggs, John (1785–1875), III, 1070
Bright, John (1811–1859), III, 144, 148, 153
Bright, Timothy (1551?–1615), I, 377, 888
Bright, William (1824–1901), III, 921 f.
Brightland, John (*fl.* 1711), II, 27
Brightly, C. (*fl.* 1809), III, 75
Brighton and Sussex Daily Post, The (1876), III, 804
Brighton and Sussex Evening Post, The (1885), III, 804
Brighton Daily News, The (1868), III, 803
Brightwell, Cecilia Lucy (1811–1875), III, 412

Brimelow, William (*fl.* 1867), III, 803
Brimley, George (1819–1857), III, 256, 443, 709, 834
Brimmer, G. (*fl.* 1835), III, 75
Brinkelow, Henry (d. 1546), I, 713
Brinley, Francis (*fl.* 1696), II, 752
Brinsley, John (1600–1665), I, 365, 375, 695, 799, 800–1, 803, 805, 808, 854, 860
Brisbane, T. (*fl.* 1869), III, 306
Briscoe, John (*fl.* 1696), II, 958
Briscoe, Sophia (*fl.* 1772), II, 547
Brisebarre, Édouard, III, 456, 608
Brissot de Warville, Jean Pierre (1759–1793), II, 694, 719, 773
BRISTOL
    Library, II, 105
    Magazines, II, 684 (1782–1800)
    Newspapers, II, 721 (1702–1800)
Bristol, George Digby, Earl of (1612–1677), II, 418 f.
Bristol, The Little Red Book of (M.E.), I, 121
Bristol and Bath Magazine, The (1782), II, 684
Bristol, Bath and Somersetshire Journal, The (1742), II, 721
Bristol Chronicle; Or, Universal Mercantile Register, The (1760), II, 721
Bristol Daily Mercury, The (1901), II, 722
Bristol Daily Post, The (1860), III, 802
Bristol Evening News, The (1877), III, 805
Bristol Gazette and Public Advertiser, The (1767), II, 721
Bristol Journal, The (1748), II, 721
Bristol Mercury, The (1747), II, 721
Bristol Mercury and Daily Post, The (1878), III, 802
Bristol Mercury and Universal Advertiser, The (1790), II, 722
Bristol Mirror, The (1811), II, 721
Bristol Oracle, The (1744), II, 721
Bristol Oracle and Country Intelligencer, The (1742), II, 721
Bristol Post-Boy, The (1702), II, 721
Bristol Presentments: Exports for the Year (1770), II, 719
Bristol Presentments; Imports for the Year (1770), II, 719
Bristol Times and Bath Advocate, The (1839), III, 803
Bristol Times and Felix Farley's Bristol Journal, The (1853), III, 803
Bristol Times and Mirror, The (1884), III, 793, 803
Bristol Weekly Intelligencer, The (1749), II, 721
Bristol Weekly Mercury, The (1715), II, 721
Bristow, Henry William (1817–1889), III, 971
Bristow, James (*fl.* 1793), II, 751
Bristow, W. (*fl.* 1759), II, 114
Britain (1713), II, 661
Britain's Genius; Or, The Weekly Correspondent, II, 713

Britain's Remembrancer of the most remarkable passages in both Kingdomes (1644), I, 756
Britanicus Vapulans; or, The Whipping of poor British Mercury by Mercurius Urbanus, younger brother to Aulicus (1643), I, 755
Britannia (1839), III, 814
Britannia Rediviva (17 cent.), II, 173
Britannia's Delight (19 cent.), II, 255
Britannic Magazine, The (1793), II, 682
'Britannicus' (1822), III, 200
Britcher, Samuel (*fl.* 1790), II, 824
Britische Bibliothek (1757), II, 688
British Album, The (18 cent.), II, 243 (3), 246, 248 (2)
British and American Intelligencer, The (1835), III, 812
British and Foreign Medical Review and Quarterly Journal of Practical Medicine and Surgery, The (1836), III, 833
British and Foreign Review, or European Quarterly Journal, The (1835), III, 833
British Antidote to Caledonian Poison, The (18 cent.), II, 221 (3), 223
British Apollo, The (18 cent.), II, 190, 198, 208
British Apollo; Or, Curious Amusements for the Ingenious, The (1708), II, 660
British Apollo or Songster's Magazine, The (18 cent.), II, 246
BRITISH CELTIC WRITERS, I, 99 f.
British Censor, The (1737), II, 663
British Champion; Or, The Impartial Advertiser, The (1743), II, 710
British Chronicle; Or, Pugh's Hereford Journal, The (1770), II, 724
British Chronicle; Or, Union Gazette, The (1784), II, 733
British Critic, The (1793), III, 823
British Critic, Quarterly Theological Review and Ecclesiastical Record, The (1827), III, 823, 833
British Drama, The (1804), II, 392
British Drama, The (1817), II, 393
British Drama, The (1824), II, 393
British Drama, The (1864), III, 585
British Drama, The (1866), III, 585
BRITISH EMPIRE
    Historians of, III, 886 f., 906 f., 930 f.
    Literatures of Dominions, III, 1045 f.
British Empire Review, The (1899), III, 832
British Freeholder and Saturday Evening Journal, The (1820), III, 813
British Gazette and Sunday Monitor, The (1780), II, 716
British Guardian and Protestant Advocate, The (1824), III, 813
British Harlequin, The (1720), II, 662
British Intelligencer; Or, Universal Advertiser, The (1743), II, 708
BRITISH ISLES, DESCRIPTIONS OF, I, 773 (16, 17 cents.)

British Journal, The (1722), II, 713
British Journal; Or, The Censor, The (1728), II, 713
British Journal; or, The Traveller, The (1731), II, 713
British Librarian, The (1737), II, 675
British Luminary, The (1818), III, 811
British Luminary and Weekly Intelligencer, The (1821), III, 811
British Lyre, The (18 cent.), II, 248
British Magazine, The (1746), II, 677
British Magazine, The (1747), II, 686
British Magazine (1761), II, 664
British Magazine, The (1800), II, 683
British Magazine, The (1830), III, 826
British Magazine, The (1832), III, 854
British Magazine and General Review of the Literature of the Times, The (1772), II, 679
British Magazine and Review, The (1782), II, 680
British Magazine; Or, Monthly Repository for Gentlemen and Ladies, The (1760), II, 678
British Medical Journal, The (1858), III, 821
British Melody (18 cent.), II, 207
British Merchant, The (1713), II, 660
British Mercury, The (18 cent.), II, 536
British Mercury and Evening Advertiser, The (1780), II, 711
British Mercury; Or, Annals of History [etc.], *The* (1787), II, 688
British Mercury; Or, Annals of History [etc.], *The* (1790), II, 715
British Mercury or Historical Views of the Present Times, The (1798), II, 683
British Mercury; or, The Welch Diurnall, The (1643), I, 755
British Mercury. Published by the Company of London Insurers, The (1710), II, 707
British Military Library Or Journal, The (1798), II, 683
British Miner and General Newsman, The (1862), III, 817
British Miscellany, The (1765?), II, 223
British Miscellany, The (1779), II, 680
British Monitor, The (1818), III, 811
British Mothers' Family Magazine, The (1864), III, 828
British Mothers' Journal, The (1856), III, 828
British Mothers' Magazine, The (1845), III, 828
British Muse, The (1738), II, 207
British Muse, The (1775), II, 230, 237
British Muse, The (19 cent.), II, 255
BRITISH MUSEUM, II, 103; III, 104
British Museum; Or, Universal Register of Literature, The (1771), II, 684
British Musical Miscellany, The, II, 204 (2), 205
British Neptune, The (1803), III, 810
British Orpheus, The (18 cent.), II, 211
British Parnassus, The (18 cent.), II, 191
British Phoenix, The (18 cent.), II, 221

British Poetical Miscellany, The (19 cent.), II, 255
British Poets, The (1773), II, 259
British Press, or Morning Literary Advertiser, The (1803), III, 798
British Public Characters (1799), II, 684
British Quarterly Review, The (1845), III, 833
British Queen and Statesman, The (1841), III, 812
British Review and London Critical Journal, The (1811), II, 825
British Songs sacred to Love and Virtue (18 cent.), II, 217
British Songster, The (1788), II, 241
British Songster; or, Dibdin's Delight, The (18 cent.), II, 243
British Songster; Or, Pocket Companion, The (18 cent.), II, 245, 249, 253–5
British Spouter, The (18 cent.), II, 229
British Spy; Or, Derby Postman, The (1726), II, 723
British Spy; Or, New Universal London Weekly Journal, The (1752), II, 715
British Spy; Or, Weekly Journal, The (1725), II, 713
British Statesman, The (1819), III, 799
British Statesman, The (1842), III, 817
British Telescope, The (1724), II, 684
British Theatre, The (1808), II, 392
British Theatre (Leipzig, 1828), II, 393
British Traveller, The (1821), III, 800
British Weekly, The (1886), III, 814
British Weekly Mercury, The (1715), II, 707, 712
Briton, The (1723), II, 662
Briton, The (1762), II, 664
Briton, The (1793), II, 685
Britton, John (1771–1857), III, 93, **884**f.
Brittons Bowre of Delights (16 cent.), I, 404
Broad Arrow, The (1868), III, 821
'Broadgrin, Godfrey' (1790), II, 244, 255
'Broadgrin, Sir Toby' (1790), II, 243, 245
Broadhurst, F. (*fl.* 1826), III, 141
Broadhurst, J. (*fl.* 1842), III, 982
Broadhurst, T. (*fl.* 1808), III, 142
Broadley, J. (*fl.* 1824), I, 382
BROADSIDE BALLADS, I, 720f. (16, 17 cents.)
Broadway, The (1867), III, 830
Brock, E. (*fl.* 1865), I, 179
Brockbank, Thomas (1671–1709), II, 112, 134
Brockie, W. (*fl.* 1872), III, 1081
Broderip, Frances Feeling, née Hood (1830–1878), III, 224–5
Brodie, Alexander (1617–1680), II, 995
Brodie, Sir Benjamin, the elder (1783–1862), III, 963, 965
Brodie, Sir Benjamin, the younger (1817–1880), III, 947
Brodie, Erasmus H. (*fl.* 1866–87), III, **333**
Brodie, James (*fl.* 1680), II, 156

Brodrick, George Charles (1831–1903), III, 137, 783, 972
Brodrick, William (*fl.* 1865), III, 778 (2)
Broke, Arthur (d. 1563), I, 434, 810
Brokesby, Francis (1637–1714), II, 108, 127, 847
Brome, Alexander (1620–1666), I, 474, 641; II, 175
Brome, Humphrey (*fl.* 1667), II, 717
Brome, James (d. 1719), I, 843; II, 139
Brome, Richard (d. 1652?), I, 641, 719; II, 264
Brome Abraham and Isaac (M.E.), I, 278f.
Bromehead, W. C. (*fl.* 1876), III, 1077
Bromhall, Thomas (*fl.* 1667), II, 716
Bromley, Beatrice (*fl.* 1912), III, 1089
Bromley, Sir George (*fl.* 1787), I, 381
Bromley, Robert Anthony (*fl.* 1793), II, 30
Bromley, Thomas (d. 1691), II, **859**
Bromley, William (1664–1732), II, 744
Bromwich, J. (*fl.* 1766), II, 778
Brontë, Anne (1820–1849), III, 23, **462**f.
Brontë, Charlotte, later Nicholls (1816–1855), III, **461**f.
   Translations from, III, 23, 35, 39, 43
Brontë, Emily Jane (1818–1848), III, **462**f.
Bronterre's National Reformer (1837), III, 816
'Brooke, Arthur', i.e. J. C. Claris (1797?–1866), III, 215
Brooke, Charlotte (d. 1793), II, 80
Brooke, Christopher (d. 1628), I, 446, 616
Brooke, Edward (*fl.* 1788), I, 849
Brooke, Frances, née Moore (1724–1789), II, 546–8, 552. 664, 791, 797; III, 1086
Brooke, Francis (*fl.* 1660), I, 785
Brooke, Henry (1703?–1783), II, 81, 124, **435**, 546–7, 822
Brooke, James (*fl.* 1762), II, 664
Brooke, John (d. 1582), I, 816
Brooke, N. (*fl.* 1793), II, 748
Brooke, R. S. (*fl.* 1852), II, 435
Brooke, Ralph (1553–1625), I, 396, 827
Brooke, Richard (*fl.* 1839), III, 985
Brooke, Sir Robert (d. 1558), I, 849
Brooke, Samuel (d. 1632), I, 655
Brooke, Stopford Augustus (1832–1916), III, **736**
Brooke, T. D. (*fl.* 1775), II, 782
Brookes, Ralph (*fl.* 1723), II, 542, 779
Brookes, Richard (*fl.* 1740–63), II, 641, 820
Brookesbuy, Francis (1637–1714). See Brokesby
Brookfield, Jane Octavia, née Elton (1821–1894), III, 154
Brooks, Charles William Shirley (1816–1874), III, **600**f., 724, 818
Brooks, E. (*fl.* 1682), II, 704
Broom, Herbert (1815–1882), III, 985
Brooman, R. A. (*fl.* 19 cent.), III, 822
Broome, Sir Frederick Napier (1842–1896), III, 1094

Broome, William (1689–1745), II, 22, 191, 312, 761 (2)
Brosse, Baron de, II, 773
Brosses, Charles de, Comte de Tournay, I, **773**
Brother's Gift, or The Naughty Girl reformed, The (18 cent.), II, 562
Brotherhood (1887), III, 818
Brothers, Richard (1757–1824), II, 525
Brothers; A Novel for Children, The, II, 564
Brothers; or, Treachery Punish'd, The (18 cent.), II, 539
Brough, Robert Barnabas (1828–1860), III, **601**
Brough, William (1826–1870), III, 601
Brougham, Henry Peter, Baron Brougham and Vaux (1778–1868), II, 956; III, 105, 108, 149, 191, 668, **895**f., 945, 979
Broughton, Hugh (1549–1612), I, 681
Broughton, James (*fl.* 1830), I, 532
Broughton, John (*fl.* 1703), philosopher, II, 941
Broughton, John (*fl.* 1778), editor of Chatterton, II, 344
Broughton, John Cam Hobhouse, Baron (1786–1869), III, 991
Broughton, Rhoda (1840–1920), III, **539**
Broughton, Richard (d. 1634), I, 384
Broughton, Thomas Duer (1778–1835), III, 1082
Broughton, Thomas (1704–1774), II, 912
Brouncker, William, Viscount (1620?–1684), I, 813
Brounsmith, J. (*fl.* 1767), II, 405
Brown, A. (*fl.* 1660), II, 810
Brown, Alexander (*fl.* 1776), II, 104
Brown, Alexander Crum (b. 1838), III, 948
Brown, Andrew (*fl.* 1691–5), II, 998–9
Brown, Charles Armitage (1786–1842), I, 581
Brown, David (*fl.* 1622), I, 346
Brown, Edward (*fl.* 1690–3), I, 280; II, 813
Brown, Ernest William (b. 1866), III, 945
Brown, Ford Madox (1821–1893), III, 154
Brown, George Douglas ('George Douglas') (1869–1902), III, **542**
Brown, J. B. (*fl.* 1813), III, 246
Brown, J. P. (*fl.* 1868), III, 1081
Brown, James (*fl.* 1735), II, 761
Brown, James Moray (*fl.* 1891), III, 775
Brown, John (1610?–1679), II, **992**
Brown, John (1715–1766), 'Estimate Brown', II, 14, 17–8, 108, 114, 130, **460**f.
Brown, John (1722–1787), of Haddington, II, 928, **994**
Brown, John (*fl.* 1789), II, 400
Brown, John (*fl.* 1805–43), Minister of Langton, III, 118
Brown, John (*fl.* 1823–32), of Little Bolton, III, 119
Brown, John (1810–1882), III, **709**
   Articles by, III, 435, 716
Brown, John A. Harvie (*fl.* 1898), III, 772
Brown, Oliver Madox (1855–1874), III, **539**
Brown, Peter (1784–1863), III, 817

Brown, Sir Ridyard (*fl.* 1830), III, 778
Brown, Robert (1757–1831), of Haddington, II, 687
Brown, Robert (*fl.* 1794–1816), farmer at Markle, III, 970
Brown, Robert (1773–1858), botanist, III, **959**
Brown, Robert (*fl.* 1808), advocate, II, 971
Brown, Samuel (1817–1856), III, 947
Brown, Thomas (1663–1704), satirist, II, 532, **572f.**
  Doubtful ascriptions, II, 271, 402, 535
  Minor writings, II, 24, 184, 187, 218, 658
  Translations by, II, 32, 533–4, 762, 785, 787, 790 (2), 800, 810
Brown, Thomas (1778–1820), metaphysician, III, **865**
Brown, Thomas (*fl.* 1830), captain, III, 763
Brown, Thomas (*fl.* 1833), natural historian, II, 841; III, 405
Brown, Thomas (1822–1882), III, 775
Brown, Thomas Edward (1830–1897), III, 126, **282**
Brown, Thomas N. (*fl.* 1858), III, 722
Brown, W. (*fl.* 1770), translator, II, 810
Brown, W. (*fl.* 1793), of Dundee, II, 687
Brown, William (*fl.* 1671), II, 963
Brown, William (*fl.* 1796), II, 732 (3)
Brown, William Keer (*fl.* 1847), III, 971
Browne (or Brown), Anthony Maria, Viscount Montague (d. 1629), I, 384
Browne, Charles T. (*fl.* 1854), III, 182
Browne, Edward (1644–1708), II, 139, 743
Browne, Edward Granville (1862–1925), III, 989
Browne, Frances (b. 1816), III, **475**
Browne, Sir Francis Gore (*fl.* 1866), III, 985
Browne, Frederick Gordon ('A. Nobody') (d. 1932), III, 574
Browne, G. F. (1833–1930), III, 777
Browne, George (*fl.* 1864), III, 985
Browne, Hablot K. (1815–1882), III, 90
Browne, Henry (1804–1875), III, 856
Browne, Humphry (*fl.* 1642), I, 723
Browne, Isaac Hawkins (1705–1760), II, 18, 20, 312, 370
Browne, J. H. Balfour (*fl.* 1881), III, 985
Browne, J. Hamilton (*fl.* 1823), III, 207
Browne, James (1793–1841), III, 807
Browne, Joseph (*fl.* 1706–14), II, 541
'Browne, Matthew', i.e. William Brighty Rands (1823–1882), III, 467
Browne, Moses (1704–1787), II, **312**, 820 (2), 912
Browne, Patrick (1720?–1790), II, 754
Browne, Peter (d. 1735), II, 945
Browne, R. C. (*fl.* 1866), I, 464
Browne, Sir Richard (1605–1683), I, 386
Browne, Simon (1680–1732), II, 662, 863
Browne, Thomas (1604?–1673), canon of Windsor, I, 827
Browne, Sir Thomas (1605–1682), I, **834f.**, 890; II, 53, 65, 69, 74, 920

Browne, Thomas Alexander ('Rolf Boldrewood') (1826–1915), III, **1096**
Browne, William (1590?–1645?), of Tavistock, I, **449**
Browne, William (*fl.* 1624) [misprinted T. Browne], I, 393
Browne, William (*fl.* 1714), II, 577
Browne, William (*fl.* 1769), II, 312
Browne, William George (1768–1813), II, 743
Browning, Elizabeth Barrett (1806–1861), I, 212; III, 23, 118, **249**
Browning, G. (*fl.* 1834), III, 978
Browning, Oscar (1837–1923), III, 155
Browning, Robert (1812–1889), III, 161, 249 (2), **258f.**
Brownlee, C. (*fl.* 1896), III, 1093
Brownless, W. Methuen (*fl.* 1887), III, 774
Brownlow, Richard (1553–1638), I, 849
Brownrig, Ralph (1592–1659), I, 695
Bruce, Alexander Balmain (1831–1899), III, **865**
Bruce, Carlton (*fl.* 1835), III, 572
Bruce, Charles, Viscount (*fl.* 1733), II, 102
Bruce, Gainsford (*fl.* 1868), III, 988
Bruce, George Wyndham Hamilton Knight-(1852–1896), III, 1092
Bruce, Henry Austin, Baron Aberdare (1815–1895), III, 108, 900
Bruce, James (1730–1794), II, 749
Bruce, John (1745–1826), historian, III, **880**
Bruce, John (1802–1869), antiquary, I, 265, 382–3, 385 (2), 386, 393, 512, 671, 682, 837, 842; III, 1080
Bruce, John Collingwood (1805–1892), III, **903**
Bruce, Michael (1746–1767), II, **990**
Bruce, Peter (*fl.* 1686–8), II, 694
Bruce, Peter Henry (1692–1757), II, 742
Bruce, Robert (1554–1631), I, 681, 907
Bruce, Thomas, Earl of Ailesbury (1655?–1741), II, 135
Bruce, W. D. (*fl.* 1855), III, 807
Brudenell, Thomas (*fl.* 17 cent.), I, 352
Brueggemann, L. W. (*fl.* 1797), II, 757
Brueys, David-Augustin de, II, 40
Brulart de Sillery, Stéphanie Félicité, Comtesse de Genlis, afterwards Marquise de Sillery, II, 36, 41, 47, 108, 552, 566, 773; III, 393, 405
Brumoy, Pierre, II, 773
Brunanburgh, The Battle of (O.E.), I, **84**
Brunck, Richard Franz Philip (*fl.* 1808), II, 900
Bruni, Leonardo (Aretino), I, 339, 811
Brunius, B., II, 72
Brunne, Robert of. See Robert Manning
Bruno, Giordano (1548–1600), I, 338, 883
Brunswick, or True Blue, The (1821), III, 811
Brunt, Samuel (pseud.?) (1727), II, 539
Brunton, Alexander (1772–1854), III, 389
Brunton, Mary, née Balfour (1778–1818), III, **389**

Brunton, Thomas (d. 1389), I, **313**
Brunton, Sir Thomas Lauder (1844–1916), III, 964
Brusasque, Elizabeth (*fl.* 1806), II, 30
Brusoni, Girolamo, II, 808
Brussels Cross Inscription (O.E.), I, **85**
Brut (M.E.), I, **165**
Bruton, William (*fl.* 1633), I, 784
Bruts, G. M. (*fl.* 1598), I, 379
Bry, Theodore de, I, 764
Bryan, — (*fl.* 1703), III, 333
Bryan (or Briant), Sir Francis (d. 1550), I, 814
Bryant, Jacob (1715–1804), II, 344
Bryant, John Frederick (1753–1791), II, **355**
Bryce, J. (*fl.* 1839), III, 1083
Bryce, James, Viscount (1838–1922), III, 989
Brydall, John (b. 1635?), II, 963
Bryden, H. A. (*fl.* 1893–6), III, 1089, 1092
Brydges, Grey (1579?–1621), I, 725
Brydges, Sir Samuel Egerton (1762–1837), I, 460; II, 879, 922; III, **662**f., 980
Brydone, Patrick (1736–1818), II, 746
Bryskett, Lodowick (*fl.* 1571–1611), I, 813
Bubble, The [Cambridge] (1898), III, 835
Buc (or Buck), Sir George (d. 1623), I, 838
Bucer, Martin (*fl.* 1530), I, 677
Buchan, Alexander (*fl.* 1727), II, 744
Buchan, David Steuart Erskine, Earl of (1742–1829), II, 307
Buchan, J., Baron Tweedsmuir (1875–1940), III, 1092
Buchan, Peter (1790–1854), I, 272; II, 257
Buchanan, David (1595?–1652), I, 776, 904
Buchanan, David (1779–1848), III, 807 (2), 978, 980
Buchanan, George (1506–1582), I, 328, 654, 765, 774, 844 (2), **901**f.; II, 801, 910; III, 247
Buchanan, J. (*fl.* 1790?), II, 738
Buchanan, James (*fl.* 1766), II, 18, 915, 930, 932
Buchanan, John Lanne (*fl.* 1780–1816), II, 747
Buchanan, John P. (*fl.* 1895), III, 777
Buchanan, Robert (1813–1866), III, 817 (2), 977
Buchanan, Robert Williams (1841–1901), III, **333**f.
Buchanan, William (1781–1863), III, 783, 807
Buchanan-Hamilton, F. (*fl.* 1807), III, 1079
Buck (or Buc), Sir George (d. 1623), I, 838
Buck's Bottle Companion, The (18 cent.), II, 230
Buck's Delight, The (1746), II, 211
Bucks Delight, The (1764), II, 222
Buck's Delight, or Feast for the Sons of Comus, The (18 cent.), II, 234
Buck's Delight, or, Merry Companion, The (18 cent.), II, 236, 239
Buck's Delight, or Merry Fellow's Companion (18 cent.), II, 254
Buck's Delight; or, Pills to purge Melancholy, The (18 cent.), II, 253–4

Buck's Delight, or Vocal Companion, The (18 cent.), II, 246, 248
Buck's Merry Companion, The (18 cent.), II, 222
Buck's Pocket Companion; Or, The Merry Fellow, The (18 cent.), II, 252
Bucke, Charles (1781–1846), III, **663**f.
Buckeridge (or Buckridge), John (1562?–1631), I, 680
Buckham, P. W. (*fl.* 1836), III, 997
Buckingham, George Villiers, Duke of (1628–1687), II, **419**
Buckingham, James Silk (1786–1855), III, 783, 801 (2), 812, 818, 826–7
BUCKINGHAMSHIRE, I, 8 (bibliography)
Buckinghamshire, John Sheffield, Duke of (1648–1721), II, 21, 44, 196, **283**
Buckland, Anne Walbank (*fl.* 1891), III, 968
Buckland, C. E. (*fl.* 1901), III, 1078
Buckland, C. T. (*fl.* 1884), III, 1084
Buckland, Francis Trevelyan (1826–1880), III, 771
Buckland, William (1784–1856), III, **950**
Buckle, E. (*fl.* 1852), III, 907
Buckle, G. E. (*fl.* 1884), III, 798
Buckle, Henry Thomas (1821–1862), III, **908**
  Translations from, III, 23, 35, 41, 45
Buckler, John (1770–1851), III, 129
Buckley, Sir Henry Burton (*fl.* 1873), III, 985
Buckley, Samuel (*fl.* 1714), II, 702, 708
Buckley, W. E. (*fl.* 1862), I, 829
Buckley, William (d. 1570?), I, 880
Buckman, James (1816–1884), III, 952
Bucknill, Sir John Charles (1817–1897), I, 545; III, 833
Buckstone, John Baldwin (1802–1879), III, 199, **601**
Budd, A. (*fl.* 1897), III, 775
Budd, Thomas (*fl.* 1648), editor of 'Mercurius Catholicus', I, 759
Budd, Thomas (*fl.* 1685), writer on Pennsylvania, II, 752
Budgell, Eustace (1686–1737), I, 209; II, 108, 661, 714, **878**
Buds of Genius (19 cent.), III, 575
Bülow, Baroness M. von (*fl.* 1855), III, 142
Buenting, Heinrich, I, 771
Bürger, Gottfried August, II, 55f., 805; III, 52, 244, 369, 605
Büschel, Johann Gabriel Bernhard, II, 141
Buffier, Claude, II, 773
Buffon, Georges Louis Leclerc, Comte de, II, 35, 786
Bugbears, The (16 cent.), I, 520
Builder, The (1842), III, 822
Builder's Magazine, The (1774), II, 679
Builder's Reporter and Engineering Times, The (1886), III, 822
Builder's Weekly Reporter, The (1856), III, 822
Building News, The (1857), III, 822

Buist, George (1805–1860), III, 900, 1076
Bulkeley, J. (*fl.* 1720), II, 326
Bulkeley, John (*fl.* 1743), II, 754
Bulkeley, William (d. 1760), II, 134
Bulkley, Charles (1719–1797), II, 948
Bull, Edward (*fl.* 1842), III, 96
Bull, George (1634–1710), II, **846**
Bull, Henry (d. 1575?), I, 684, 815
Bull, Josiah (*fl.* 1868), II, 342
Bull, Robert (*fl.* 1713), II, 846
Bull, Roger (*fl.* 1739), II, 32, 805
Bull-Finch, The (18 cent.), II, 212, 214–5, 218–22, 225, 228, 230, 234–5, 241
Bullar, John (*fl.* 1806–44), II, 257
Bullein, William (d. 1576), I, 888
Bullen, Arthur Henry (1857–1920), III, 822, **1037**
Bullen, Edward (*fl.* 1860), III, 985
Buller, A. (*fl.* 1833), III, 855
Buller, Charles (1806–1848), III, 982
Buller, Sir Francis (1746–1800), II, 963
Bullet, Jean Baptiste, II, 774
Bullinger, Heinrich, I, 716
Bullionist, The (1866), III, 820
Bullock, Christopher (1690?–1724), II, **435**
Bullock, William (*fl.* 1649), I, 796, 845
Bullokar, William (*fl.* 1586), I, 44, 376, 799, 800
Bulmer, William (1757–1830), III, 86
Bulstrode, Sir Richard (1610–1711), II, 133
Bulteel, John (*fl.* 1656–83), II, 533, 776, 780, 809, 811
Bulwer, John (*fl.* 1648), I, 365
Bulwer, William Henry Lytton Earle, Baron Dalling and Bulwer (1801–1872), III, 145, 187, 631
Bulwer-Lytton, Edward George Earle Lytton, Baron Lytton (1802–1873), III, **475**f., 597, 599, 636, 647, 827
    Translations from, III, 25, 30, 36, 40, 43, 45
Bulwer-Lytton, Rosina, Lady, née Wheeler (1804–1882), III, **478**f.
Bunbury, C. J. F. (*fl.* 1848), III, 1091
Bunbury, Sir Henry Edward (1778–1860), II, 610
Bunbury, Henry William ('Geoffrey Gambado') (1750–1811), II, 817
Bunbury, Selina (*fl.* 1847), III, 572
Bund, John William Willis (*fl.* 1869–85), I, 834; III, 771
Bundy, Richard (d. 1739), II, 775
Bungiana (18 cent.), II, 217
Bunn, Alfred (1796–1860), III, **587**f.
Bunny, Edmund (1540–1618), I, 684
Bunsen, Christian Carl Josias, III, **29**, 1014
Bunting, Edward (1773–1843), III, 1048
Bunting, Jabez (1779–1858), III, 823
Bunting, Sir Percy (1836–1911), III, 830
Bunyan, John (1628–1688), II, 39, 55, 68–9, 130, **490**f.

Bunyon, Charles John (*fl.* 1854), III, 985
Buonarrotti, Michael Angelo, III, 358
Burbidge, T. (*fl.* 1849), III, 265
Burbury, John (*fl.* 1671), II, 743
Burchell, William John (1782–1863), III, 989
Burchet, Guglielmo, I, 779
Burckhardt, John Lewis (1784–1817), III, 989
Burdekin, R. (*fl.* 1827), III, 103
Burden, Mrs (*fl.* 1850), III, **572**
Burder, George (1752–1832), II, 330, 917
Burder, Henry Forster (1783–1864), III, 577
Burdett, Sir Francis (1770–1844), III, 148
Burdon, William (*fl.* 1730), II, 816
Burdon, William (1764–1818), II, 373
Burdon-Sanderson, Sir John Scot (1828–1905), III, 964
Burdy, Samuel (1760?–1820), III, **886**
Burel, John (*fl.* 1590), I, 896
Burges, Francis (*fl.* 1701), II, 82
Burges, George (1786?–1864), III, 198
Burgess, Anthony (*fl.* 1656), I, 856
Burgess, Joseph (*fl.* 1891), III, 818
Burgess, Thomas (1756–1837), III, **993**
Burgh, Benedict (d. 1483), I, 185, **253**
Burgh, James (1714–1775), II, 108
Burgh, William (1741–1808), II, 371, 883
Burgon, John William (1813–1888), I, 399; III, **856**
Burgoyne, John (1722–1792), II, **461**, 801
Burial and Resurrection (Bodley) (M.E.), I, **279**
Burigny, Jean Lévesque de, II, 789
Burke, Mrs — (*fl.* 1788), II, 549
Burke, Edmund (1729–1797), II, 17, 37, 53, 65, 163, **632**f., 663
Burke, J. (*fl.* 1853), III, 185–6
Burke, J. F. (*fl.* 1834), III, 971
Burke, John (*fl.* 1776), II, 802
Burke, Peter (1811–1881), II, 635; III, 94
Burke, William (d. 1798), II, 633, 773
Burkhardt, C. B. (*fl.* 1849), III, 576
Burkhead, Henry (*fl.* 1645), I, 641
Burlamqui, Jean Jacques, II, 774
BURLESQUES, I, 714f. (early 17 cent.); II, 288 (1660–1700)
    Criticism of, II, 24 (17, 18 cents.), 170 (recent criticism)
Burlettas, Duets, Interludes, &c., The, in the Spa Gardens, Bermondsey (18 cent.), II, 238
Burley, Walter (d. *c.* 1345), I, **304**
Burman, Francis (*fl.* 1702), II, 113
Burn, James (*fl.* 1833), III, 769
Burn, John (1744?–1802), II, 926, 932
Burn, Richard (1709–1785), II, 926, 963
Burn, Robert (1829–1904), III, 1004
Burnaby, Andrew (1734?–1812), II, 756
Burnaby, Frederick Gustavus (1842–1885), III, 989

Burnaby, William (1672?–1706), II, **435**f., 534
Burnand, Sir Francis Cowley (1836–1917), III, 772, 783, 820
Burnby, John (*fl.* 1773), II, 825
Burne, Sir Owen Tudor (1837–1909), III, 155
Burne-Jones, Sir Edward (1833–1898), III, 706
Burnell, Arthur Coke (1840–1882), III, **1017**
Burnell, Henry (*fl.* 1641), I, 641
Burnell, John (*fl.* 1712), II, 750
Burnes, Sir Alexander (1805–1844), III, 1079
Burnes, James M. H. (1801–1862), III, 1079
Burnet, Alexander (*fl.* 1733), II, 302
Burnet, Gilbert (1643–1715), II, 15, 108, 801, **867**f.
Burnet, John (1784–1868), II, 630
Burnet, Thomas (1635?–1715), II, 111, 572, 801, 941
Burnet, Sir Thomas (1694–1753), II, 301, 537, 661
Burnett, Frances Hodgson (1849–1924), III, 569
Burnett, George (1776?–1811), I, 466; III, 633
Burnett, James, Lord Monboddo (1714–1799), II, 955
Burney, Charles (1726–1814), II, 30, 102, 137, 746, 798, 905
Burney, Charles, jun. (1757–1817), I, 469; II, 899, 933
Burney, Fanny Anne, later Wood (b. 1812), III, 153
Burney, Frances, later D'Arblay (1752–1840), II, 131, **527**f.; III, 576
Burney, James (1750–1821), II, 151, 739
Burney, Sarah Harriet (1770?–1844), II, 550
Burney, William (*fl.* 1815), II, 361
Burns, James Drummond (1823–1864), III, 282
Burns, Robert (1759–1796), II, **973**f.
Burns, Robert, the younger (*fl.* 1809), II, 984
BURNS AND OATES, III, 98
Burnyeat (or Burneyeat), John (1631–1690), II, 856
Burrage, E. Harcourt (*fl.* 1888), III, 821
Burrant, Robert (*fl.* 1553), I, 800
Burrard, T. (*fl.* 1817), III, 970
Burrell, Sophia, Lady (1790?–1802), II, 777
Burrell, Thomas (*fl.* 1679), II, 702 (2)
Burrell, Timothy (1643–1717), II, 135
Burrough, Edward (1634–1663), II, 490 (2), 856
Burroughes (or Borough), Sir John (d. 1643), I, 846
Burroughes, John (*fl.* 1642), publisher, I, 752
Burroughes, Robert (*fl.* 1696), II, 666
Burroughs, E. (*fl.* 1821), III, 970
Burrow, Sir James (1701–1782), II, 92
Burrowes, Robert (*fl.* 1878–95), II, 20, 627
Burrows, Montagu (1819–1905), III, 153
Burt, Edward (d. 1755), II, 157
Burtell, J. (*fl.* 1785), II, 822
Burthogge, Richard (1638?–1694?), II, 941

Burton, Annals of (15 cent.), I, 115
Burton, Thomas of (*fl.* 1396), I, 265
Burton, Edmund (*fl.* 1752), II, 767
Burton, Henry (1578–1648), I, **695**
Burton, John (1696–1771), classical scholar, II, 206, 866, 993
Burton, John (1710–1771), antiquary, II, 1003
Burton, John Hill (1809–1881), III, **905**, 977
Burton, Richard (*fl.* 1796), I, 769
Burton, Sir Richard Francis (1821–1890), III, 778, **989**
Burton, Robert (1577–1640), I, **829**f., 889
'Burton, Robert' (or 'Richard'), i.e. Nathaniel Crouch (1632?–1725?), II, 145, 532, 706
Burton, Thomas (*fl.* 1656–9), I, 388
Burton, William (d. 1616), translator of Erasmus, I, 665
Burton, William (1575–1645), author of 'Description of Leicestershire', I, 775
Burton, William (1609–1657), classical scholar and translator, I, 777, 799, 856
Bury, Catherine M., Countess of Charleville (*fl.* 1796), II, 804
Bury, Lady Charlotte Susan Maria, née Campbell (1775–1861), III, **389**f.
Bury, John (*fl.* 1557), I, 803
Bury, Richard d'Aungerville de (1281–1345), I, 361
Bury and Norwich Post, The (1787), II, 722
Bury Post; Or, Suffolk and Norfolk Advertiser, The (1782), II, 722
BURY ST EDMUNDS
    Libraries, I, 361–2
    Magazines, II, 684 (1790)
    Newspapers, II, 722 (1716–1800)
    Schools, I, 372
Bury St Edmunds Abbey, Memorials of (M.E.), I, 121
Bury St Edmunds Fragment (M.E. drama), I, 277
Bury Times, The, III, 793
Bury Wills and Inventories (15 cent.), I, 46
Busbecq, Ogier Ghiselin de, I, 773
Busby, Richard (1606–1695), I, 374, 860–1; II, 127 (2), 129
Busby, Thomas (1755–1838), II, 632
Bushbequius, A. G., II, 429
Bushby, H. J. (*fl.* 1855), III, 1083
Bushman, John Stevenson (1808?–1884), II, 821
Busk, George (1807–1888), III, 833
Buss, Frances Mary (*fl.* 1870?), III, 142
Bussey, H. Findlater (d. 1919), III, 783
Bussy, Roger de Rabutin, Comte de, II, 47, 542, 795
Bust, Matthew (*fl.* 1610), I, 856
Busteed, H. E. (*fl.* 1882), III, 1078
Bustus, Matthaeus (*fl.* 1610), I, 856
Busy Bee, The (18 cent.), II, 243
Busy Body, The (1759), II, 664

Busy Body, The (1787), II, 666
Butcher, Richard (1583–1665?), I, 776
Butcher, Samuel Henry (1850–1910), III, **1004**
Bute, Sophia Stuart, Marchioness of (*fl.* 1858), III, 149
Butler, Alban (1711–1773), II, 745
Butler, Arthur John (1844–1910), III, **736**, 830
Butler, Charles (d. 1647), I, 44, 376, 391, 893
Butler, Charles (1750–1832), II, 138, 773; III, 879
Butler, D. (*fl.* 1839), III, 1080
Butler, Lady Eleanor (1745?–1829), II, 138
Butler, Frances Anne, née Kemble (1809–1893), III, **293**
Butler, H. M. (*fl.* 1854), II, 635
Butler, Joseph (1692–1752), II, 108, **946**
Butler, Josephine Elizabeth, née Grey (1825–1906), III, **926**
Butler, Nathaniel (*fl.* 1609–22), I, 791
Butler, Samuel (1612–1680), author of 'Hudibras', I, 45; II, 44, 59, 109, **260**f.
Butler, Samuel (1774–1839), headmaster of Shrewsbury, III, 108, 123, 133, 137, **993**f.
Butler, Samuel (1835–1902), author of 'Erewhon', III, **728**f.
Butler, Sarah (*fl.* 1716), II, 537
Butler, Weeden, the elder (1742–1823), II, 154
Butler, William (*fl.* 1788), II, 125
Butler, William Archer (1814?–1848), III, **865**
Butler, Sir William Francis (1838–1910), III, 155, 989, 1088
BUTLER AND TANNER, III, 86
Butt, Isaac (1813–1879), III, 827
Butt, Lucy Lyttelton, later Cameron (1781–1858), III, 566
Butt, Mary Martha, later Sherwood (1775–1851), III, **416**f.
Butt, Streeten (*fl.* 1818), III, 417 (2)
Butter, Nathaniel (d. 1664), I, 744, 752 (2)
Butterfly, The (1893), III, 831
Butterworth, J. (*fl.* 1805), writer of schoolbooks, III, 135
Butterworth, John (1727–1803), baptist minister, II, 928
Buttes, Henry (*fl.* 1599), I, 396, 718
Button, Edward (*fl.* 1754), II, 541
Button, I. (or J.) (*fl.* 1621), I, 771
Button, John (*fl.* 1804), II, 99
Button, Joseph (*fl.* 1710), II, 726
Buyers, W. (*fl.* 1848), III, 1083
Byerley, Thomas (d. 1826), III, 815
Byfield, Nicholas (1579–1622), I, 684
Byles, Sir John Barnard (1801–1884), III, 972, 982, 985
Byles, W. P. (*fl.* 1834), III, 803
Byles, William (*fl.* 1834), III, 803
Bynneman, Henry (d. 1583), I, 352
Byrd, William (1543–1623), I, 482
Byrhtferth of Ramsey (*fl.* 1011), I, **97**
Byrne, — (*fl.* before 1817), III, 798
Byrne, Charlotte, née Dacre (*fl.* 1805), III, **392**

Byrne, Desmond (*fl.* 1896), III, 1093
Byrne, Edward (*fl.* 1884–91), III, 809 (2)
Byrom, John (1692–1763), II, 23, 129, 823, **859**
Byron, George Gordon, Baron (1788–1824), III, **187**f., 591
   Bibliographies, III, 187
   Biography, III, 206f.
   Byron in Poetry and Fiction, III, 209f.
   Collected Editions, III, 187
   Criticism of, III, 210f.
   Partial Collections, III, 188f.
   Poetical Pieces first Published in Periodicals, etc., III, 202 f.
   Prose Pieces first Published in Periodicals, etc., III, 203f.
   Prose Writings, III, 201f.
   Selections, III, 190f.
   Selections from Letters and Journals, III, 202
   Separate Works, III, 191f.
   Translations from, III, 23f., 35f., 39f., 41, 43, 44f., 45
   Works incorrectly ascribed, III, 205f.
Byron, Henry James (1834–1884), III, **625**, 820
Byron, Isabella, Lady (*fl.* 1830), III, 207
Byron, John (1723–1786), II, 741, 755
Byron, Mary (*fl.* 1913), III, 1089
Byssett, Habakkuk (*fl.* 15 cent.), I, 260
Bysshe, Edward (*fl.* 1712), I, 45; II, 27, 185–6, 188–9, 191 (2), 194, 197 (2), 206–7, 220, 763
Bystander (1880), III, 1088
Bystander, or Universal Weekly Expositor, The (1789), II, 666
Bythewood, W. M. (*fl.* 1829), III, 985
Bywater, Ingram (1840–1914), III, **1004**
Bywater, John (*fl.* 1819), III, 962

'C.' (1863), I, 420
C., A. (*fl.* 1776), II, 772
C., D. (*fl.* 1642), I, 753
C., E. (*fl.* 1595), I, 434
C., E. (*fl.* 1677), II, 786
C., E. (*fl.* 1758), II, 769
C., H. (*fl.* 1579), I, 729
C., H. (*fl.* 1686), II, 759
C., H. (*fl.* 1719), II, 194
C., H. (*fl.* 1783), II, 563
C., I. (*fl.* 1620), I, 653
C., J. (*fl.* 1547), I, 816
C., J. (*fl.* 1595), I, 434
C., J. (*fl.* 1604), I, 480
C., J. (*fl.* 1652), I, 761
C., J. (*fl.* 1705), II, 783
C., J. (*fl.* 1711), II, 190–2, 196, 208–9
C., J. (*fl.* 1818), III, 822
C., L. S. (*fl.* 1820), II, 304
C., L. W. (*fl.* 1601), I, 393
C., M. (*fl.* 1621), I, 791
C., M. (*fl.* 1709), II, 820
C., M. (*fl.* 1746), II, 212

C., N. (*fl.* 1634), I, 745
C., P. (*fl.* 1689), II, 181
C., R. (*fl.* 1612), I, 391
C., R. (*fl.* 1614), I, 481
C., R. (*fl.* 1685), II, 180
C., R. (*fl.* 1687), II, 180
C., R. (*fl.* 1688), II, 128
C., Ro. (*fl.* 1609), I, 779
C., S. (*fl.* 1673), II, 120
C., S. P. (*fl.* 1837), II, 647
C., T. (*fl.* 1560), I, 811
C., T. (*fl.* 1623), I, 794
C., W. (*fl.* 1578?), I, 742
C., W. (*fl.* 1585?), I, 729
C., W. (*fl.* 1641), I, 731
C., W. (*fl.* 1720), II, 195
Cabala, sive Scrinia sacra (17 cent.), I, 397
Cabinet, The (1792), II, 709
Cabinet, The (1794), II, 666
Cabinet, The (1795), II, 250
Cabinet, The (1807), III, 825
Cabinet for Wit, The (18 cent.), II, 214
Cabinet Magazine; Or, Literary Olio, The (1796), II, 683
Cabinet of Choice Jewels, A (17 cent.), II, 180
Cabinet of Curiosities, The (18 cent.), II, 231
Cabinet of Fancy (18 cent.), II, 245
Cabinet of Genius, The (18 cent.), II, 240, 246, 252
Cabinet of Love, The (18 cent.), II, 246
Cabinet of Momus, The (18 cent.), II, 239
Cabinet of Wit Containing Droll and Merry Stories in Prose and Verse, The (18 cent.), II, 252
CADELL AND DAVIES, III, 98
Cadell, Jessie Ellen (1844–1884), III, 1069
Cadett, Herbert (*fl.* 1900), III, 783
Cadman, Henry (*fl.* 1898), III, 772
Cadogan, William Bromley (*fl.* 1809), II, 853
CAEDMON SCHOOL, I, 25, 27–8, 31, 35–6, 73 f.
   Azarias, I, **75**
   Caedmon's Hymn, I, **73**
   Christ and Satan, I, **75**
   Daniel, I, **75**
   Exodus, I, **75** f.
   Genesis, I, **74**
Caesar, Caius Julius, I, 773, 800; II, 764
Caesar, M. Philip, I, 845
Caesar's Revenge, The Tragedie of (17 cent.), I, 661
Caffero, François, II, 401
Caffyn, William (*fl.* 1899), III, 774
Caian, The [Cambridge] (1891), III, 835
Caigniez, Louis Charles, III, 587, 593
Caine, Sir Thomas Henry Hall (1853–1931), III, **540**
Caine, William Sproston (1842–1903), III, 1080
Caiphas (M.E.), I, 277
Caird, Edward (1835–1908), III, **865**
Caird, Sir James (1816–1892), III, **971**, 1080

Caird, John (1820–1898), III, 850, **866**
Cairncross, D. (*fl.* 1862), III, 770
Cairnes, John Elliot (1823–1875), III, 698, 982
Caius, John (1510–1573), I, 365, **671**, 811, 888, 892
Caius (or Key), Thomas (d. 1572), I, 369, 683
Calamy, Edmund (1600–1666), Puritan divine, I, **695** f.
Calamy, Edmund (1671–1732), biographer, II, 135, 848, 863, 924
Calasius, Marius (*fl.* 1747), II, 928
Calcott, Wellins (*fl.* 1756–69), II, 218, 225, 229
Calcutta Review, The (1844), III, 1067
Caldecott, Randolph (1846–1886), III, 90
Caldecott, Thomas (1744–1833), II, 358, 903
Calder, John (1733–1815), II, 680
Calder, Robert (1658–1723), II, **994**
Calderón de la Barca, Pedro, II, 68; III, 41, 589, 605
Calderwood, David (1575–1650), I, 839
Calderwood, Henry (1830–1897), III, **866**
Calderwood, Margaret (1715–1774), II, 136, 745
Caldwell, Anne, later Marsh (1791–1874), III, **496**
Caldwell, Robert C. (1814–1891), III, 1068
Caledoniad, The (18 cent.), II, 230
Caledonian Bee, The (18 cent.), II, 250
Caledonian Chronicle, The (1792), II, 732
Caledonian Gazetteer, The (1776), II, 665, 732
Caledonian Magazine and Review, The (1783), II, 687
Caledonian Magazine; Or, Aberdeen Repository, The (1786), II, 687
Caledonian Magazine; Or, Aberdeen Repository, The (1788), II, 687
Caledonian Mercury, The (1720), II, 731
Caledonian Mercury, The [Edinburgh] (1855), III, 807
Caledonian Mercury and Daily Express, The (1859), II, 731
Caledonian Miscellany, The (18 cent.), II, 208, 221, 227
Caledonian Muse, The (18 cent.), II, 238
Caledonian Weekly Magazine; Or, Edinburgh Intelligencer, The (1773), II, 686
Caley, John (d. 1834), II, 864, 875
Caligula-Jesus Poems (M.E.), I, **182**
Calkley, T. W. [misprint for Thomas Walkley, *fl.* 1622], I, 815
Call, Wathen Mark Wilks (1817–1890), III, **282** f., 834
Call to Prayer (O.E.), I, **82**
Callanan, Jeremiah John (1795–1829), III, **1051**
Callander, John (d. 1789), II, 915, **1000**
Callaway, G. (*fl.* 1905), III, 1093
Callaway, Henry (1817–1890), III, 1093
Callcott, Maria, Lady, earlier Graham (1785–1842), III, 1079
Calle, Caleb (*fl.* 1683), II, 767

Callender, James Thomas (d. 1803), II, 627
Callender, W. R. (*fl.* 1858), III, 982
Callery, J. M., III, 605
Callière, Jacques de, III, 120
Callières, François de, II, 774
Callimachus, II, 760
Calliope; or, English Harmony (1739), II, 207, 210–11, 227, 234
Calliope; Or, The Agreeable Songster (1777), II, 232
Calliope: Or, The Musical Miscellany (1788), II, 241–2
Calliope: or the Vocal Enchantress (1788), II, 241
Callipaedia (1712), II, 190, 203, 220, 228
Callipaedia: Or, The Art of Getting Pretty Children (1710), II, 189, 195, 200, 231
Callis, Robert (*fl.* 1622–34), I, 849
Calmet, Augustin, II, 774
Calprenède, Gauthier de Costes, Seigneur de la, II, 777
Calsabigi, Ranieri de', II, 808
Calthrop, Mrs H. (*fl.* 1895), III, 1070
Calthrope, Charles (*fl.* 1635), I, 849
Calverley, Charles Stuart, earlier Blayds (1831–1884), III, **335**, 440
Calvert, Frederick, Baron Baltimore (1731–1771), II, 745
Calvin, Jean, I, 326, 811, 883; II, 774
Camberwell and Peckham Times (1868), III, 810
Cambini, Andrea, I, 777
Cambrian Daily Leader, The [Swansea] (1861), III, 803
Cambridge, Ada, later Cross (*fl.* 1891–1903), III, **1096**
Cambridge, G. O. (*fl.* 1803), II, 355
Cambridge, Richard Owen (1717–1802), II, 24, 355 f.
CAMBRIDGE, I, 8 (bibliographies)
  Middle English Period, I, 124–5 (University)
  Renaissance to Restoration, I, 352 f. (printers and booksellers), 362 (libraries), 370 f. (University)
  Restoration to Romantic Revival, II, 86 (printers and booksellers), 104 (libraries), 115 f. (University), 153 f. University), 722 (newspapers)
  Nineteenth Century, III, 123 f. (University), 834 f. (University and college magazines)
Cambridge A.B.C., The (1892), III, 835
Cambridge Chronicle, The (1744), II, 722
Cambridge Chronicle and Journal, The (1762), II, 722
Cambridge Chronicle and University Journal, The (1849), II, 722
Cambridge Daily News, The (1888), III, 806
Cambridge Essays contributed by Members of the University (1855), III, 834
Cambridge Fortnightly, The (1888), III, 835
Cambridge Gazette, The (1898), III, 835

Cambridge Intelligencer, The (1793), II, 722
Cambridge Journal, The (1744), II, 722
Cambridge Magazine, The (1899), III, 835
'Cambridge Master of Arts, A' (1812), III, 126
Cambridge Meteor, The (1882), III, 835
Cambridge Monthly Repository, The (1819), III, 834
Cambridge Observer, The (1892), III, 835
Cambridge Quarterly Review, The (1824), III, 834
Cambridge Quarterly Review, The (1833), III, 834
Cambridge Review, The (1879), III, 835
Cambridge Tatler, The (1877), III, 835
Cambridge Terminal Magazine, The (1858), III, 834
Cambridge Undergraduates' Journal, The (1868), III, 834
Cambridge University Gazette, The (1868), III, 834
Cambridge University Magazine, The (1835), III, 834
Cambridge University Magazine, The (1840), III, 834
Cambridge University Magazine, The (1886), III, 835
CAMBRIDGE UNIVERSITY PRESS, III, 87
Cambridge University Reporter, The (1870), III, 835
Cambuscan (18 cent.), II, 238
Camden, William (1551–1623), I, 375, 774 f. **827**, 844, 862; II, 177
CAMDEN SOCIETY, III, 86
Cameron, C. (*fl.* 1772), II, 812
Cameron, C. (*fl.* 1860), III, 566, 807
Cameron, Sir Ewen (1629–1719), of Lochiel, II, 156
Cameron, George Frederick (*fl.* 1887), III, 1086
Cameron, John (1579–1625), I, 907
Cameron, Lucy Lyttelton, née Butt (1781–1858), III, 566
Cameron, Verney Lovett (1844–1894), III, 989
Camoens, Luis de, I, 345, 784, 812; II, 68; III, 41
Campanella, Tommaso, I, 767; III, 358
Campbell, Alexander (*fl.* 1747), II, 754
Campbell, Alexander (1763–1824), II, 23, 253, 917, 968
Campbell, Archibald, Duke of Argyll (1682–1761), II, 102
Campbell, Archibald (1691–1756), II, **994**
Campbell, Archibald (1726?–1780), II, 626
Campbell, Lady Charlotte Susan Maria, later Bury (1775–1861), III, **398** f.
Campbell, Colin (d. 1729), II, 161
'Campbell, Donald' (S. C. Carpenter) (*fl.* 1795), II, 751
Campbell, Duncan (1824–1890), III, 783
Campbell, F. (*fl.* 1824), II, 257
Campbell, Sir G. E. (*fl.* 1890), III, 831

Campbell, George (1719–1796), II, 19, **1000**
Campbell, Sir George (1824–1892), III, 1078
Campbell, George Douglas, Duke of Argyll
    (1823–1900), III, 283, **862**, 954
Campbell, James (fl. 1773), II, 821
Campbell, John (1708–1775), II, 16, 157, **879**
Campbell, John (1766–1840), III, 1091
Campbell, John (fl. 1813), naval historian, III,
    395
Campbell, John, Baron (1779–1861), III, **900**
Campbell, John Douglas Sutherland, Duke of
    Argyll (1845–1914), III, 155
Campbell, John McLeod (1800–1872), III, 847
Campbell, Lawrence Duncan (fl. 1800), III,
    1082
Campbell, Lewis (1830–1908), III, **1004**f.
Campbell, Patrick (fl. 1793), II, 757
Campbell, Reginald John (b. 1867), III, 850
Campbell, Robert (fl. 1745), II, 164
Campbell, Theophila Carlile (fl. 1899), III, 783
Campbell, Thomas (fl. 1735), II, 894
Campbell, Thomas (1733–1795), miscellaneous
    writer, II, 141, 159, 625
Campbell, Thomas (fl. 1767), traveller, II, 755
Campbell, Thomas (1777–1844), poet, III, 24,
    36, 125, 157, 207, **183**f., 825
Campbell, W. H. (fl. 1841), botanist, III, 960
Campbell, W. H. P. (fl. 1884), reformer, III,
    977
Campe, Joachim Heinrich, II, 566, 805
Campensis, Johannes, I, 677
Campion, Edmund (fl. 1633), I, 776
Campion, Thomas (1567–1600), I, **425**f., 741,
    865
Campion, W. J. H. (fl. 1889), III, 851
Campion, W. M. (fl. 1858), III, 121
Camus, Jean Pierre, I, 732f.; II, 533, 744
Cana, F. R. (fl. 1909), III, 1090
CANADA (literature of, in English), III, 1085f.
Canadian Magazine (1823), III, 1088
Canadian Monthly (1872), III, 1088
Canape, I, 891
Canary Bird, The (18 cent.), II, 211, 219
Cancer: Comoedia (17 cent.), I, 661
Candid Disquisition of the Principles and
    Practices of the Society of Free and
    Accepted Masons, A (18 cent.), II, 225, 229
Candid Inquiry into the Principles of the Society
    of Bucks (18 cent.), II, 227
Candid Review and Literary Repository, The
    (1765), II, 679
Candlish, Robert Smith (1806–1873), I, 908;
    III, 853
Caninius, Angelus, I, 376
Cann, C. (fl. 1828), I, 469
Canne, John (d. 1667?), I, 760, 763
Canning, George (1770–1827), II, 61, **356**
Canon (M.E.), I, 192, 204
Canon, John (fl. 1320), I, **303**
Cant, J. (fl. 1774), I, 899

Cantab, The (1873), III, 835
Cantab, The (1899), III, 835
CANTERBURY
    Libraries of, I, 361, 362; II, 105
    Magazines, II, 684 (1792–5)
    Newspapers, II, 722
    Printing in, II, 86
    Schools, I, 372
Canterbury, Register of Abbey of (M.E.), I, 121
Canterbury Journal, The (1770), II, 722
Canterbury Tales of Chaucer, The (18 cent.),
    II, 206, 208
Canterbury Tales of Chaucer, Modernis'd by
    several hands, The (18 cent.), II, 209 (2)
Cantillon, Richard (d. 1734), II, 958
Canting Academy, The (17 cent.), II, 176
Canton, G. (fl. 1788), II, 799
Canton, William (1845–1926), III, **335**
Cantopher, W. E. (fl. 1878), III, 1069
Cantù, Cesare, III, 200
Cantuarienses, Epistolae (M.E.), I, 115
Cantus, Songs and Fancies (17 cent.), II, 174 (2),
    178
Caorsin, Gulielmus, I, 742, 777
Cap of Liberty, The (1819), III. 816
Capell, Edward (1713–1781), II, **897**f   929
Capella, Martianus, I, 125
Capes, E. J. (fl. 1890), III, 830
Capes, J. B. (fl. 1826), III, 798
Capgrave, John (1393–1464), I, 45, 115, **260**
Capitalist, The (1885), III, 820
Cappe, Catherine (fl. 1800), II, 138; III, 129
Capper, James (1743–1825), II, 750
Capps, E. (fl. 1857), III, 978
Capriata, Pietro Giovanni, II, 808
Caps Well Fit (18 cent.), II, 238
Car (or Carre), Thomas (alias Miles Pinkney)
    (1599–1674), I, 456
Caraccioli, Louis Antoine de, II, 774
Carcasse, J. (fl. 1679), II, 833
Cardale, J. S. (fl. 1829), I, 87
Cardano, Girolamo, I, 812; II, 809
Cardiff Times, The (19 cent.), III, 793
Cardonell, later Cardonell-Lawson, Adam de
    (d. 1820), I, 59
Cardonne, Denis Dominique, II, 774
Cardonnel, Philip de (d. 1667), II, 174
CARD GAMES (books on), II, 825f. (18 cent.);
    III, 776f. (19 cent.)
Carducci, Giosuè, III, 39
Cardwell, Edward (1787–1861), church his-
    torian, I, 676–7; II, 880
Cardwell, Edward, Viscount (1813–1886), III,
    889
Care, Henry (fl. 1678–89), I, 809, II, 120, 270,
    656, 657 (3), 658, 694, 702 (3), 704–5, 805
'Careless, John' (1821), III, 759
Carew, — (fl. 1729), II, 770
Carew, Bamfylde Moore (1693–1770?), II, 155
Carew, Sir George (d. 1612), I, 384, 779, 837

Carew, George, Baron Carew and Earl of Totnes (1555–1629), I, 385, 838
Carew, Richard (1555–1620), I, 775, 813, 814, 819, **826**, 865
Carew, Thomas (1598?–1639?), I, 453
Carey, David (1782–1824), III, 800
Carey, Eustace (1791–1855), III, 1017
Carey, George Savile (1743–1807), II, **356**
Carey, Henry, Earl of Monmouth (1596–1661), I, 455, 811; II, 808, 810
Carey, Henry (1687?–1743), II, **433**f.
Carey, John (1756–1826), III, 571
Carey, Robert, Earl of Monmouth (1560?–1639), I, 383, 841
Carey, Walter (*fl.* 1626), I, 714
Carey, William (1761–1834), III, **1017, 1073**
Carey's General Evening Post (1796), II, 736
Carey's Waterford Packet (1791), II, 738
Caribbeana (18 cent.), II, 209
CARICATURE, II, 160f. (18 cent.)
Caritat, Marie Jean Antoine Nicolas, Marquis de Condorcet, II, 774
Carleill, Christopher (1551?–1593), I, 787
Carlell, Lodowick (1602–1675), I, 642
Carlet de Chamblain de Marivaux, Pierre, II, 41, 47, 543 (2), 774
Carleton, George (1559–1628), I, 838, 884
Carleton, George (*fl.* 1728), II, 151
Carleton, John William (*fl.* 1839–47), III, 759, 762, 776
Carleton, Rowland (*fl.* 1679), II, 530
Carleton, Thomas (*fl.* 1619), I, 661
Carleton, William (1794–1869), III, **390**
Carli, Donigi, II, 809
Carlile, Mrs (*fl.* 1832), III, 816
Carlile, Richard (1790–1843), III, 783, 816 (5), 826, **866**
CARLISLE
  Magazines, II, 684 (1776–1800)
  Newspapers, II, 722 (1798)
Carlisle, Sir Anthony (1768–1840), III, 946
Carlisle, George Howard, Earl of (1802–1864), III, 152
Carlisle, Nicholas (1771–1847), I, 371
Carlisle Journal, The (1798), II, 722
Carlisle Museum, The (1776), II, 684
CARLOW, II, 737 (newspaper)
Carlow Journal or Leinster Chronicle, The (1773), II, 737
Carlton, Richard (1557?–1638?), I, 484
Carlton House Magazine, The (1792), II, 681
Carlyle, Alexander (1722–1805), II, **1000**
Carlyle, G. (*fl.* 1864), III, 853
Carlyle, John Aitken (1801–1879), III, 1025
Carlyle, Jane Welsh (1801–1866), III, 152, 654, 656
Carlyle, Thomas (1795–1881), III, **652**f.
  Translations from, III, 24f., 36, 40–1
Carlyon, Clement (1777–1864), III, 176
Carman, E. (*fl.* 1889), III, 984

Carmeni, Francesco, I, 733
Carmichael, Grace Jennings, later Mullis (*fl.* 1895), III, 1095
Carmichael, John (*fl.* 1772), II, 750
Carmina ad Nobilissimum Thomam Holles (18 cent.), II, 216
Carnegie, David W. (*fl.* 1898), III, 989
Carnegie, G. Fullerton (1799–1851), III, 775
Carnegie, James, Earl of Southesk (1827–1905), III, 989
Carnie, William (*fl.* 1900), III, 783
Caroline de Montmorenci (18 cent.), II, 550
CAROLINE DIVINES, I, 694f.
CAROLINE DRAMA, I, 609f. (major dramatists). 640f. (minor dramatists), 651f. (anonymous plays), 654f. (university plays)
CAROLINE POETRY, I, 440f. (criticism), 441f. (major poets), 473f. (minor verse)
CAROLS, I, 267f.
Caron de Beaumarchais, Pierre Augustin, II, 40, 774
Carové, Friedrich Wilhelm, III, 576
Carpenter, Edward (1844–1929), III, **736**f.
Carpenter, J. (*fl.* 1803), III, 969
Carpenter, James (1840–1899), III, 944
Carpenter, John (*fl.* 1636), I, 805
Carpenter, Joseph Estlin (1844–1928), III, 850
Carpenter, Lant (1780–1840), III, 113
Carpenter, Mary (1807–1877), III, 1080
Carpenter, Nathanael (1589–1628?), I, 766, 875
Carpenter, S. C. ('Donald Campbell') (*fl.* 1795), II, 751
Carpenter, William (1797–1874), III, 801, 811, 812 (2), 813, 816, 821
Carpenter, William Benjamin (1813–1885), III, 833, **866**, 957, 963, 965
Carr, Emsley (*fl.* 1891), III, 812
Carr, G. S. (*fl.* 1895), III, 978
Carr, J. (*fl.* 1687), II, 180
Carr, J. W. Comyns (*fl.* 1900), III, 831
Carr, John (1732–1807), II, 762
Carr, Lascelles (*fl.* 1869), III, 803
Carr, M. W. (*fl.* 1868), III, 1072
Carr, Philip (*fl.* 1900), III, 814
Carr, S. (*fl.* 1843), I, 682
Carré, Michel, III, 598, 605, 608
Carre (or Car), Thomas (*alias* Miles Pinkney) (1599–1674), I, 456
Carrington, Richard Christopher (1826–1865), III, 944
'Carroll, Lewis', i.e. Charles Lutwidge Dodgson (1832–1898), III, **513**f.
Carroll, Susanna, later Centlivre (1667?–1723), II, **432**f.
Carroll, W. (*fl.* 1818), III, 768
Carroll, William (*fl.* 1706), II, 942
Carruthers, J. (*fl.* 1883–94), III, 977, 983
Carruthers, Robert (1799–1878), III, **664**
Carstairs, R., III, 1084
Carte, Thomas (1686–1754), II, 91, 784, **878**f.

Carter, Edmund (*fl.* 1753), II, 116
Carter, Elizabeth (1717–1806), II, **842**
Carter, Francis (d. 1783), II, 746
Carter, George (1737–1794), II, 749; III, 1091
Carter, Matthew (*fl.* 1660), I, 843
Carter, T. F. (*fl.* 1882), III, 1092
Carter, Thomas (b. 1792), III, 151
Carteret, Philip (d. 1796), II, 741
Carthy, Charles (*fl.* 1731), II, 765
Cartier, Jacques, I, 787
Cartigny, Jean de, I, 733
Carton Dancourt, Florent, II, 774
Cartwright, Elizabeth, later Penrose ('Mrs Markham') (*fl.* 1850), III, 135
Cartwright, George (*fl.* 1661), I, 642
Cartwright, George (*fl.* 1792), II, 757
Cartwright, Mrs H. (*fl.* 1777), II, 130, 549
Cartwright, John (*fl.* 1611), I, 783
Cartwright, John (1740–1824), III, 149
Cartwright, R. (*fl.* 1864), I, 618
Cartwright, Thomas (1535–1603), puritan, I, 676, 687 (2)
Cartwright, Thomas (1634–1689), bishop of Chester, II, 134
Cartwright, W. (*fl.* 1854), III, 770
Cartwright, William (1611–1643), I, 655, 696
Carus, William (*fl.* 1847), III, 852
Carve, Thomas (1590–1672?), I, 772
Carver, Jonathan (1732–1780), II, 756
Carver, Thomas Gilbert (*fl.* 1885), III, 985
Cary, Amelia, Viscountess Falkland (*fl.* 1857), III, 989
Cary, Lady Elizabeth (1586–1639), I, 642
Cary, Henry (*fl.* 1826–68), historian, I, 400; III, 230
Cary, Henry Francis (1772–1844), translator of Dante, I, 464; II, 295; III, **229**f.
Cary, John (d. 1720?), II, 958
Cary, John (1756–1826), I, 17
Cary, Patrick (*fl.* 1651), I, 474
Cary, Walter (*fl.* 1552), I, 892
Caryll, John (1625–1711), II, **419**
Casa, Giovanni della, I, 338, 378, 812; II, 120f., 809
Casalis, E. (*fl.* 1861), III, 1092
Casas, Bartolomé de las, II, 67
Casaubon, Isaac (1559–1614), I, 858, 860, 862
Casaubon, Meric (1599–1671), I, 800–1, 852, 858, 860–2; II, 959
Case, John (d. 1600), I, 508, **874**
Case, Thomas (1844–1925), III, 774
CASHEL, I, 737 (newspaper)
Casimir, Mathias, I, 328
Casket; Or Hesperian Magazine, The (1797), II, 688
Casley, David (d. 1755?), II, **911**
Cassagnes, Jacques, II, 774
Cassandra (But I hope not) (1704), II, 659
Cassell, John (1817–1865), III, 98

CASSELL & Co., III, 87
Cassell's Family Magazine (1874), III, 829
Cassell's Illustrated Family Paper (1853), III, 815, 829
Cassell's Magazine (1867), III, 815, 829
Cassell's Saturday Journal (1883), III, 814
Cassels, Walter Richard (1826–1907), III, 848
Castaing, John (*fl.* 1697), II, 718
Castanheda, Fernão Lopes de, I, 782
Castel of Love (M.E.), I, **186**
Castell, William (d. 1645), I, 795
Castell of Perseverance, The (16 cent.), I, 514
Castelvetro, Ludovico, I, 338
Casti, Giovanni Battista, II, 809; III, 39
Castiglione, A. P. (*fl.* 1727), II, 809
Castiglione, Baldassare, I, 338, 378, 812; II, 120, 809
Castillo, John (1792–1845), III, **230**
Castillo Solorzano, Alonso del, II, 69, 532f.
Castleford, Thomas. See Thomas Bek, I, 39
Castlemaine, Roger Palmer, Earl of (d. 1705), II, 743
Castlereagh, Robert Stewart, Viscount (1769–1822), III, 150
'Castor' (1891), III, 761
Casuist, The (1719), II, 662
Caswall, Edward (1814–1878), III, **283**
Catalogue of Books Continued, A (1670), II, 717
CATALOGUES
　　Book-Trade Catalogues, I, 358f. (16, 17 cents.); II, 93f. (17, 18 cents.); III, 100f. (19 cent.)
　　Divinity, II, 95f. (17, 18 cents.)
　　Libraries (general), I, 4
　　Manuscripts, I, 4f., 113 (M.E.)
　　Printed Books, I, 6f.
　　See also BIBLIOGRAPHIES
Cataneo, Girolamo, I, 812
Catch Club, The (18 cent.), II, 240
Catch Club or Merry Companions, The (18 cent.), II, 186, 195, 221
Catch that Catch can (1663), II, 174
Catch that Catch can: Or The Musical Companion (1667), II, 175–7, 179, 180 (2), 185 (2), 188–9, 196–8, 208
Catcott, Alexander Stopford (1692–1749), II, 206, 762
CATECHISMS, I, 376
Caterer, The (1789), II, 685
Cates, Thomas (*fl.* 1589), I, 788
Catesby, Mark (1679?–1749), II, 753
Catharine Parr, Queen of England (1512–1548), I, 684
Catholic Advocate, The (1820), III, 819
Catholic Journal, The (1828), III, 819
Catholic Standard, The (1849), III, 819
Catholic Standard, The (1854), III, 860
Catholic Vindicator, The (1818), III, 819
Catholick Intelligence, The (1680), II, 703

Catholicon Anglicum (M.E.), I, 26

Catley, The (18 cent.), II, 228

Catlin, Zachary (*fl.* 1639), I, 805

Catling, Thomas (1838–1920), III, 783, 812

Catnach, James (1792–1841), III, 98

CATNACH PRESS, III, 87

'Cato' (1720), II, 662

Cato, Dionysius, I, 262, 375, 800

Caton, John, II, 856

Catrou, François, II, 774 f.

Cats, Jacob, I, 479

Cattermole, Richard (1795?–1858), I, 445 f., 852

Cattley, S. R. (*fl.* 1837), I, 824

Catuelan, Comte de, II, 72

Catullus, II, 187, 764; III, 298, 340, 359

Caulfeild, James, Earl of Charlemont (1728–1799), II, 158

Caulfield, James (1764–1826), I, 709; II, 248, 903

'Causidicus' (1791), II, 654

Caussin, Nicolas, I, 733; II, 775

Causton, William (*fl.* 1730), II, 764

Cave, Edward (1691–1754), II, 96, 671, 677, 695, 727

Cave, Jane, later Winscom (*fl.* 1786), II, 240, 243

Cave, Richard (*fl.* 1754–66), II, 677

Cave, William (1637–1713), I, 89

Cave-Brown, J. (*fl.* 1857–86), III, 1070, 1083

Cavendish, George (1500–1561?), I, 434, 824

Cavendish, Georgiana, Duchess of Devonshire (1757–1806), II, 548

Cavendish, Henry (1731–1810), natural philosopher, III, 936, **945**

Cavendish, Sir Henry (1732–1804), parliamentary reporter, II, 167

'Cavendish', i.e. Henry Jones (1831–1899), III, 774, 776 f.

Cavendish, Lady Jane (*c.* 1645), I, 641

Cavendish, Margaret, Duchess of Newcastle (1624?–1674), I, 380, 642, 732, 842; II, 14, 529 (2)

Cavendish, Michael (1565?–1628), I, 483

Cavendish, William, Duke of Newcastle (1592–1676), I, 642; II, 816

Cawdell, James (d. 1800), II, 356

Cawthorn, James (1719–1761), III, 356

Cawthorn's Minor British Theatre (1806), II, 392

Cawwood the Rooke, The Pleasant History of (17 cent.), I, 731

Caxton, William (1421–1491), I, 45, **261** ff., 351, 880, 887

Cayet, Pierre-Victor Palma, I, 334

Cayley, Arthur (d. 1848), biographer, I, 666, 829

Cayley, Arthur (1821–1895), mathematician, III, 942

Cayley, Charles Bagot (1823–1883), I, 21

Cayley, Cornelius (1729–1780?), II, 746

Cayley, George John (1826–1878), III, 989

Caylus, Anne Claude Philippe de Tubières de Grimoard de Pestels de Levis, Comte de, II, 802

Caylus, Marthe Marguerite Hippolyte de Tubières de Grimoard de Pestels de Levis, Marquise de, II, 802

Cazenove, J. (*fl.* 1822–9), III, 978, 980

Cazotte, Jacques, II, 775

Cebes, I, 800

'Cecil', i.e. Cornelius Tongue (*fl.* 1851), III, 766

Cecil, Edward, Viscount Wimbledon (1572–1638), I, 771

Cecil, Richard (1748–1810), III, 852

Cecil, Robert, Earl of Salisbury (1563?–1612), I, 384–5, 399

Cecil, Robert Arthur Talbot Gascoyne, Marquis of Salisbury (1830–1903), III, 149, 833

'Cecil, Sabina' (1815), III, 571

Cecil, William, Baron Burghley (1520–1598), I, 363, 383, 399; II, 121

Celenia; or, The History of Hyempsal (18 cent.), II, 540

Celesia, Dorothea, née Mallet (1738–1790), II, 485

Celestina, I, 812

Cellini, Benvenuto, II, 809; III, 358, 679

'Celt' (1900), III, 832

CELTIC

    British Celtic Writers (in Latin, Gildas, etc.), I, 99 f.

    Irish Writers (in Latin, 5–9 cents.), I, 101 f.

    Loan-Words from, I, 33

Celtic Magazine, The (1875), III, 830

Cely Papers, The (15 cent.), I, 45, 115

Censor, The (1715), II, 662

'Censor Dramaticus' (1793), II, 400

Censor; or Covent Garden Journal (1753), II, 664

Censor; or, Muster-Master-General of all Newspapers, The (1726), II, 713

Censor, or the Citizen's Journal, The (1749), II, 663

CENSORSHIP

    Renaissance to Restoration, I, 355 f. (book trade), 499 f. (theatrical), 746 (news)

Censura Temporum (1708), II, 660

Centinel, The (1757), II, 664

Centlivre, or Carroll, Susanna (1667?–1723), II, **432** f.

CENTRAL MIDLAND TEXTS (M.E.), I, 42

Century Guild Hobby Horse, The (1886), III, 834

'Cergiel' (1834), III, 176

Cerlol, Federico Furio, I, 342, 813

Ceriziers, René de, I, 733

Cerri, Urbano, II, 809

Certain Epigrams on the Dunciad (18 cent.), II, 202

Certain Passages of Every Dayes Intelligence (1654), I, 762

Certain Speciall and Remarkable Passages of the Proceedings in both Houses of Parliament (1642), I, 754

Certaine Informations (1643), I, 754

Certaine Speciall and Remarkable Passages from both Houses of Parliament (1642), I, 753

Cervantes Saavedra, Miguel de, I, 812; II, 68 f., 534, 542

Cespedes y Meneses, Gonzalo de, I, 344, 733; II, 534

Cessolis, J. de, I, 262

Chad, St (O.E.), I, **93**

Chadsworth, E. (*fl.* 1837), III, 826

Chadwell, W. (*fl.* 1680), II, 928

Chadwick, Sir Edwin (1800–1890), III, 983

Chadwick, W. (*fl.* 1859), II, 511

Chafin, William (*fl.* 1818), III, 765

Chaigneau, William (*fl.* 1752), II, 544

Chakrabarti, Khetrapal (*fl.* 1893–7), III, 1070, 1078, 1082

Chalkhill, John (*fl.* 1600), I, 475

Challis, H. W. (*fl.* 1882), III, 937

Challis, James (1803–1882), III, 941, 944

Challoner, Richard (1691–1781), II, 781

Chalmeriana (19 cent.), II, 255

Chalmers, Alexander (1759–1834), II, 666, 695; III, **1022**
  Newspapers edited by, II, 709 (2), 711
  Writings edited by, II, 609 (2), 651

Chalmers, George (1742–1825), I, 257; II, 511, 614, 634, 699, 700, **889** f. 916, 969; III, 979

Chalmers, James, the elder (*fl.* 1748), II, 732

Chalmers, James, the younger (1782–1853), newspaper proprietor, II, 732 (3)

Chalmers, James (1841–1901), missionary, III, 989

Chalmers, Patrick (1802–1854), III, 905

Chalmers, R. (*fl.* 1826), I, 699

Chalmers, Thomas (1780–1847), III, 852, 866, 976, 979

Chaloner, Sir Thomas (1521–1565), I, 665

Chambaud, Lewis (*fl.* 1762), II, 126, 794

Chamber, John (1546–1604), I, 884

Chamberlain, E. (*fl.* 1660), I, 720

Chamberlain, John (1553–1627), I, 384, 398

Chamberlain, Robert (1607?–1660), I, 475, 642, 715

Chamberland, — (*fl.* 1784), II, 771

Chamberlayne, — (*fl.* 1733), II, 591

Chamberlayne, Edward (1616–1703), II, 139

Chamberlayne, John (1666–1723), II, 69, 786, 800, 808, 810

Chamberlayne, Tankerville (*fl.* 1839), II, 849

Chamberlayne, William (1619–1689), I, 475; II, 530

Chamberlen, Hugh (*fl.* 1672–1720), II, 958

Chamberlen, Peter (1601–1683), I, 845

Chamberlen, Paul (*fl.* 1730), II, 537 f., 542

Chambers, Ephraim (d. 1740), II, 37, 671, 675

Chambers, J. (*fl.* 1846), III, 234

Chambers, R. (*fl.* 1831), of the British Museum, I, 62

Chambers, Robert (1571–1624?), I, 730

Chambers, Robert (1802–1871), III, 93, 163, 682, **709** f., 827 (3)

Chambers, Sir William (1726–1796), architect, II, 30, 148, 621

Chambers, William (*fl.* 1781–95), of Bengal, II, 240, 810

Chambers, William (1800–1883), publisher and author, III, 93, 783, 827 (3)

Chambers's Edinburgh Journal (1832), III, 827

Chambers's Historical Newspaper (1832), III, 827

Chambers's Journal of Popular Literature (1854), III, 827

Chambers's London Journal of History [etc.] (1841), II, 827

Chambers's Papers for the People (1850), III, 828

Chambers's Pocket Miscellany (1852), III, 829

Chambers's Repository of Instructive and Amusing Tracts (1852), III, 828

Chamier, Frederick (1796–1870), III, **391**, 881

Chamisso, Adelbert von, III, 229, 576, 674

Champion, The (1739), II, 663, 698

Champion, The (1763), II, 665

Champion, The (1814), III, 811

Champion, H. H. (*fl.* 1889), III, 818

Champion and Weekly Herald, The (1836), III, 812

Champion; or, British Mercury, The (1739), II, 707

Champion; Or, Evening Advertiser, The (1740), II, 710

Chance, W. (*fl.* 1895), III, 976

Chander, Bolanath (*fl.* 1869), III, 1080

Chandler, Edward (1668?–1750), II, 490, **851**

Chandler, Mary (1687–1745), II, **312**

Chandler, Richard (1738–1810), II, **935** f.

Chandler, Samuel (1693–1766), II, 124, 600, 663, 863

Chandos, The Herald of (*fl.* 14 cent.), I, 115

Chandra, B. L. (*fl.* 1870), III, 1081

Changy, Pierre de, I, 765

Channing, F. A. (*fl.* 1897), III, 972

Chanter, The (18 cent.), II, 215

Chanticleer, The [Cambridge] (1885), III, 835

Chantreau, Pierre Nicolas, II, 141

CHAPBOOKS, II, 105 f.

Chapelain, Jean, I, 331

Chaplet, The (18 cent.), II, 207

Chaplet of Chearfulness, The (18 cent.), II, 221 (2)

Chaplet: Or, Gentleman and Lady's Musical Companion, The (18 cent.), II, 221

Chapman, Mrs E. F. (*fl.* 1891), III, 1078

Chapman, George (1559?–1634), I, **609** f., 741, 802 (2), 803, 804 (2), 817, 865

Chapman, George (1723–1806), II, 108

Chapman, George (*fl.* 1861), III, 778
Chapman, J. K. (*fl.* 1849), III, 581
Chapman, James (*fl.* 1818), I, 17
Chapman, James (*fl.* 1868), traveller, III, 1091
Chapman, John (1704–1784), II, 116
Chapman, John (1822–1894), III, 833
Chapman, John W. (1822–1894), III, 98, 102
Chapman, Priscilla (*fl.* 1839), III, 1083
Chapman, Robert (*fl.* 1778), II, 733
Chapman, Robert, the younger (*fl.* 1788), II, 733
CHAPMAN AND HALL, III, 98
Chapone, Hester (1727–1801), II, **843**
Chappe d'Auteroche, Jean, II, 775
Chappell, Bartholomew (*fl.* 1595), I, 434
Chappell, F. P. (*fl.* 1863), III, 94
Chappell, William (1582–1649), I, 694
Chappell, William (1809–1888), I, 404, 407; III, **710**
Chappuys, Gabriel, I, 817
Character of a Phanatique, The (17 cent.), I, 724
Character of a Presbyter, The (17 cent.), I, 724
Character of an Agitator, The (17 cent.), I, 724
Character of an Anti-Malignant, A (17 cent.), I, 724
Character of an Oxford Incendiary, The (17 cent.), I, 724
CHARACTER-BOOKS AND ESSAYS, I, 721 f. (17 cent.)
Chard, Thomas (*fl.* 1583), I, 352
Chardin, Jean, II, 775
Charges and Regulations of the Free and Accepted Masons (18 cent.), II, 239
Charing-Cross Medley, The (18 cent.), II, 202
Charitable Mercury, The (1716), II, 662
Charitable Mercury, and Female Intelligence, The (1716), II, 712
Chariton, II, 760
Charke, Charlotte (d. 1760?), II, 136
CHARLEMAGNE ROMANCES, I, **140** f.
Charlemont, James Caulfeild, Earl of (1728–1799), II, 158
Charles I, King (1600–1649)
  Letters by, I, 386
  Pamphlets on, I, 719 f.
Charles I, The Famous Tragedie of King (17 cent.), I, 651
Charles, Elizabeth, née Rundle (1828–1896), III, **283** f.
Charles, Robert Henry (1855–1931), III, 850
Charles the Grete (M.E.), I, 142
Charlesworth, Maria Louisa (1819–1880), III, 567
Charleton, T. W. (*fl.* 1819), III, 768
Charleton, Walter (1619–1707), I, 732, 890; II, 15, 264
Charleville, Catherine M. Bury, Countess of (*fl.* 1796), II, 804
Charlevoix, Pierre François Xavier de, II, 775
Charlton, Mary (*fl.* 1794–1830), III, **391**
Charlton, W. (*fl.* 1716), II, 712

Charm, The (1852), III, 577
Charmer, The (1749), II, 213–5, 223, 236
Charmer, The (1790), II, 243
Charmer: or Entertaining Companion, The (18 cent.), II, 210
Charmer: Or The Lady's Garland, The (18 cent.), II, 222
CHARMS (O.E.), I, 98
Charms of Chearfulness, The (1778), II, 233
Charms of Chearfulness, The (1792), II, 246
Charms of Chearfulness. An elegant and polite Selection of English and Scotch Songs, The (1791), II, 245
Charms of Chearfulness; Or, Merry Songster's Companion, The (1783), II, 236, 242, 246
Charms of Liberty, The (18 cent.), II, 188
Charms of Melody, The (1776), II, 231 (2)
Charms of Melody; Or Siren Medley, The (1796), II, 251
Charnock, John (1756–1807), II, **890**
Charrière, Isabelle Agnès Élisabeth de, II, 775
Charron, Pierre, II, 775
Charter, The (1839), III, 812
CHARTERHOUSE SCHOOL, I, 372; III, 130
Charteris, Henry (1565–1628), I, 683
CHARTERS
  Old English, I, 36, 97
  Middle English, I, 40–1, 115, 119 f.
Charters of Christ (M.E.), I, **186**
Chartier, Alain, I, 262, 812
Chartist, The (1839), III, 817
Chartist Circular, The [Glasgow] (1839), III, 817
Chase, J. C. (*fl.* 1869), III, 1090
Chassebœuf, de Volney, Constantin François, II, 775
Chassepol, François, de, II, 775
Chastellux, François Jean de, II, 775
Chatelain (or Chatelaine), John Baptist (1710–1771), II, 145
Chatham, William Pitt, Earl of (1708–1778), II, 116, 164, 632 (2)
Chatrian, Alexandre, III, 603
'Chatter, Charly' (1777), II, 562
Chatterbox (1866), III, 578
Chatterjee, Mohinimohan (*fl.* 1887), III, 1072
Chatterton, Thomas (1752–1770), II, **344** f.
Chatto, William Andrew (1799–1864), III, 84 (2), 760, 769, 776
Chattopadhyay, Nisikanta (*fl.* 1882), III, 1072
Chaucer, Geoffrey (1340?–1400)
  Astrolabe, I, 232
  Bibliographies, I, 208
  Boethius, I, 228
  Canon, I, 213
  Canterbury Tales, I, 232 f. (general), 235 f. (individual fragments and tales)
  Chronology of works, I, 213
  Collected Works, I, 208
  Early Criticism and Scholarship, I, 211 f.

Chaucer (*cont.*)
General studies, I, 213 f.
History of Criticism, I, 211
Influence on successors, I, 215 f.
Language, I, 29, 32, 39, 217 f.
Legend of Good Women, I, 230 f.
Life, I, 218 f.
Minor poems, I, 220 f.
Miscellaneous studies, I, 214 f.
Modernisations and Translations, I, 209 f.
Romaunt of the Rose, I, 227 f.
Science in, I, 215
Selections, 209
Sources, I, 216 f.
Troilus and Criseyde, I, 228 f.
Versification, I, 218
Chaucer's Ghost (17 cent.), II, 288
Chaucer's Whims (18 cent.), II, 185
CHAUCERIANS
English, I, 250 f.
Pseudo-Chaucerian pieces, I, 254
Scottish, I, 254 f.
Chaudon, Louis Maïeul, II, 775
Chauliac, Guy de, I, 890
'Chaunter, Lyrick' (1766), II, 224
Chavigny de la Bretonnière, François de, II, 775
Chaytor, H. (*fl.* 1880), III, 972
Cheadle, Walter Butler (1835–1910), III, 990
'Cheakill, Sir Joseph', i.e. Watson Taylor (*fl.* 1815), II, 154
'Cheap, John' (1785), III, 555
Chear, Abraham (d. 1668), II, 556
Chearful Companion, The (1766), II, 223
Chearful Companion, The (1786), II, 239
Chearful Companion, A Collection of Favourite Scots and English Songs, Catches &c., The (1780), II, 234, 236 (2)
Chearful Companion; Or, Complete Modern Songster, The (1780), II, 234
Chearful Companion: Or, Songster's Delight, The (1770), II, 227, 229
Chearful Companion: Or, Songster's Pocket-Book, The (1768), II, 225
Chearful Companion; Or, Suffolk, Norfolk, and Essex Song-Book, The (1792), II, 246
Chearful Linnet, The (18 cent.), II, 228 (2)
Cheek, Thomas (*fl.* 1700), II, 803, 808
Cheeke (or Cheke), Henry (1548?–1586?), I, 523
Cheerful Companion, In his Hours of Leisure, The (1797), II, 252
Cheerful Ayres or Ballads (17 cent.), II, 173
Cheever, G. B. (*fl.* 1828), II, 493
Cheife Heads of Each Dayes Proceedings in Parliament (1644), I, 756
Cheke (or Cheeke), Henry (1548?–1586?), I, 523
Cheke, Sir John (1514–1557), I, 366, 379, 669
Chekhov, Anton, III, 44

CHELMSFORD
Magazine, II, 684 (1800)
Newspapers, II, 722 (1764–1800)
Chelmsford and Colchester Chronicle, The (1764), II, 722
Chelmsford Chronicle, The (1771), II, 722
Chelsum, James (1740?–1801), II, 883
CHELTENHAM COLLEGE, III, 839
'Cheltonian, A' (1885), III, 764
CHEMISTRY (writings on), I, 885 f. (16, 17 cents.); III, 945 f. For 1660–1800 see LITERATURE OF SCIENCE, II, 959 f.
Chenery, Thomas (1826–1884), III, 798
Chénier, Marie Joseph de, II, 374
Cheny, John (*fl.* 1729), II, 718
Chepman and Myllar Prints, The (M.E.), I, 260
Chertsey Cartulary (M.E.), I, 41
Cherub, The (18 cent.), II, 253
CHESHIRE, I, 8 (bibliography)
Cheshire Daily Echo, The (1895), III, 805
Cheshire Echo, The (1889), III, 805
Cheshire Evening Echo, The (1893), III, 805
Chesney, Sir George Tomkyns (1830–1895), III, **1069**, 1077
CHESS (treatises on), II, 825 f. (18 cent.), III, 777 (19 cent.)
Chesshyre, E. (*fl.* 1837), III, 769
Chesshyre, Sir John (1662–1738), II, 105
Chesson, F. W. (*fl.* 1872), III, 1077
Chesson, Nora, née Hopper (1871–1906), III, **1059**
Chester, Sir Robert (1566?–1640), I, 475
Chester, Thomas (*fl.* 15 cent.), I, 152
CHESTER
Booksellers and Printers of, I, 353 (1500–1660), II, 86 (1660–1800)
Newspapers, II, 722 (1721–1800)
Chester Chronicle, The (1775), II, 722
Chester Courant, The (1730), II, 722
Chester Courant and Advertiser for North Wales, The (1831), II, 722
Chester Courant and Anglo-Welsh Gazette, The (1825), II, 722
Chester Miscellany, The (18 cent.), II, 214
Chester Plays (M.E.), I, **277**
Chester Weekly Journal, The (1721), II, 722
Chesterfield, Philip Stanhope, Earl of (1633–1713), II, 134
Chesterfield, Philip Dormer Stanhope, Earl of (1694–1773), II, 121, 196, 229, 437, 632, 663, **835** f.
Chesterton, George Laval (*fl.* 1853), III, 989
Chetham, James (1640–1692), II, 819
Chettle, Henry (1560?–1607?), I, 534, 730, 740
Chetwood, Knightly (1650–1720), II, 22, 269, 286, 790
Chetwood, William Rufus (d. 1766), II, 213, 537–8 f., 543, 663, 913, 923
Chetwynd, Sir George (*fl.* 1891), III, 764
Chevalere Assigne (M.E.), I, **146**

Chevreau, Urbain, II, 534, 775
Cheyne, George (1671–1743), II, **859**
Cheyne, James (d. 1602), I, 883
Cheyne, Thomas Kelly (1841–1915), III, 850, 1012
Cheynell, Francis (1608–1665), I, 357, 696
Chicken, George (*fl.* 1725), II, 753
Chifney, Samuel (1753?–1807), II, 817
Child, Gilbert William (*fl.* 1868), III, 963
Child, Sir Josiah (1630–1699), II, 942, 958
Child of Bristowe (M.E.), I, **163**
Child's Companion and Juvenile Instructor, The (1846), III, 577
Child's Companion; or Sunday Scholars Reward, The (1824), III, 577
Child's Own Annual, The (1843), III, 577
Child's New Play-Thing, The (18 cent.), II, 561
Childers, Robert Cæsar (1838–1876), III, 1017
Childhood of Christ (M.E.), I, **176**
CHILDREN
    Books for, II, 106, 130, 553 f.; III, 135 f., **564** f.
    Education of, I, 377
    Juvenile annuals, III, 842
    Juvenile papers, III, 820 f.
Children's Friend, The (1826), III, 577
Children's Magazine, The (1799), II, 564
Children's Miscellany, The (18 cent.), II, 243, 252, 563
Children's Prize, The (1864), III, 578
Children's Treasury, The (1868), III, 578
Childrey, Joshua (1623–1670), I, 777
Chillingworth, William (1602–1643), I, 696, 857
Chilmead, Edmund (1610–1654), I, 767, 862
Chilton, Edward (*fl.* 1727), II, 753
Chilton, William (*fl.* 1843), III, 817
CHINESE SCHOLARS, III, 1019 f.
Ching-Ching's Own (1888), III, 821
Chisholm, — (*fl.* 1859), II, 986
Chisholm, Hugh (1866–1924), III, 801
Chishull, Edmund (1671–1733), II, 745
CHISWICK PRESS, III, 88
Chit-Chat (1716), II, 662
Chitty, Joseph, the elder (1776–1841), II, 963; III, 986
Chitty, Joseph, the younger (d. 1838), III, 986
Chitty, Thomas (1802–1878), III, 986
Chloe, or the Musical Magazine (18 cent.), II, 219
Chloe Surpriz'd [etc.] (18 cent.), II, 202
Choice Collection of Comic and Serious Scots Poems both Ancient and Modern, A (18 cent.), II, 187–8, 190 (2), 193, 195
Choice Collection of Favorite Hunting Songs, A (18 cent.), II, 227
Choice Collection of Favourite New Songs, A (18 cent.) II, 252
Choice Collection of Hymns and Moral Songs, A (18 cent.), II, 235

Choice Collection of 120 [180] Loyal Songs, A (17 cent.), II, 179 (2), 182
Choice Collection of Masons Songs, A (18 cent.), II, 217
Choice Collection of New Songs, A (18 cent.), II, 238
Choice Collection of Poetry, A (18 cent.), II, 207
Choice Collection of Scotch and English Songs, A (18 cent.), II, 222
Choice Collection of Scots Poems, A (18 cent.), II, 224
Choice Collection of Songs, compos'd by Purcell [etc.], *A* (18 cent.), II, 224, 230
Choice Collection of Songs [on Freemasonry], *A* (1785), II, 238
Choice Compendium, A (17 cent.), II, 178
Choice Emblems (18 cent.), II, 202
Choice Of the best Poetical Pieces (18 cent.), II, 236, 238–9
Choice Selection of Ancient & Modern Scots Songs, A (18 cent.), II, 250
Choice Scraps (18 cent.), II, 564
Choice Songs and Ayres (17 cent.), II, 176, 177 (2), 178 (2), 179 (2)
Choice Spirit's Chaplet, The (18 cent.), II, 228
Choice Spirits Delight (18 cent.), II, 228
Choice Spirit's Pocket Companion, The (18 cent.), II, 229
Choice Tales; consisting of Little Pieces for Young Persons (18 cent.), II, 564
Choice, The (18 cent.), II, 200, 202, 203 (3), 206
Choir of Anacreon, The (18 cent.), II, 243
Choisy, François Timoléon de, II, 776
Cholmley, Sir Hugh (1600–1657), I, 842
Cholmondeley, Mary (d. 1925), III, **540**
Cholmondeley-Pennell, Harry (1836–1915), III, **335**
Chomel, Noel (*fl.* 1725), II, 819
Chorley, Henry Fothergill (1808–1872), III, 706, **710** f.
Chorley, Josiah (d. 1719?), II, 928
Chorus Poetarum (17 cent.), II, 182–4
Choyce Drollery (17 cent.), I, 405
Choyce Poems (17 cent.), II, 173
Christ and Satan (O.E.), I, **75**
CHRIST CHURCH (Oxford), I, 368
CHRIST'S COLLEGE (Cambridge), I, 370
Christ's College Magazine, The (1886), III, 835
CHRIST'S HOSPITAL, I, 372; III, 130
Christian, The (1870), III, 819
Christian, Edmund Brown Viney (b. 1864), III, 336, 774 (2)
Christian, J. (*fl.* 1891), III, 1072
Christian Advocate, The (1830), III, 819
Christian Commonwealth, The (1881), III, 819
Christian Herald, The (1814), II, 686
Christian Lady's Magazine, The (1834), III, 827
Christian Magazine; Or, Evangelical Repository, The (1797), II, 686

Christian Miscellany; Or, Religious and Moral Magazine, The (1792), II, 681
Christian Monitor and Religious Register, The (1821), II, 686
Christian Monthly History, The (1743), II, 686
Christian Observer, The (1802), III, 824
Christian Observer and Advocate, The (1875), III, 824
Christian Poet, The (1728), II, 199
Christian Poet, The (1735), II, 204
Christian Remembrancer, The (1841), III, 854
Christian Reporter, The (1820), III, 813
Christian Socialist, The (1850), III, 817
Christian Times, The (1848), III, 819
Christian World, The (1857), III, 793, 819
Christian's Amusement, The (1740), II, 714
Christian's Gazette, The, II, 660
Christian's Magazine, The (1760), II, 678
Christian's Magazine; Or, Gospel Repository, The (1790), II, 681
'Christianus' (1828), III, 125
Christie, James (1730–1803), auctioneer, II, 695
Christie, James (*fl.* 1817), sportsman, III, 765
Christie, Richard Copley (1830–1901), III, **927**
Christie, Robert (*fl.* 1848), III, 1087
Christie, Thomas (1761–1796), II, 635, 671, 681
Christie, William Dougal (1816–1874), III, 94, 121, **899**
Christine de Pisan, I, 733
Christmas, Henry, afterwards Noel-Fearn (1811–1868), I, 670; III, 818, 848
Christmas Box, The (1828), III, 577
Christmas Prince, The (17 cent.), I, 661
Christmas Treat, The (18 cent.), II, 224
Christoforo, Armeno, II, 542, 809
Christopher, St (O.E.), I, **93**
Christopherson, John (d. 1558), I, 655
Christy, Henry (1810–1865), III, 967
Chromolithograph, The (1867), III, 79
Chronicle, The (Waterford, 1844), II, 738
CHRONICLES
    Anglo-Saxon Period, I, 27, 29, 35–6, 40, 42 (linguistic), 84 (poems in O.E.), **88**f.
    Middle English Period, I, 115f. (mainly Latin), 132f. (Arthurian matter), **163**f. (English), 265 (15 cent., English and Latin)
Chronicles of England (M.E.), I, **165**
Chronicon Angliae (M.E.), I, 116
Chrystal, George (1851–1911), III, 943
Chubb, Thomas (1679–1747), II, 946
Chubbe, John (*fl.* 1765), II, 152
Chuckerbutty, Goodeve S. (*fl.* 1870), III, 1084
Chudleigh, Mary, Lady (1656–1710), II, **280**
Chums (1892), III, 821
Church, Alfred John (1829–1912), III, 568
Church, Florence, née Marryat (*fl.* 1868), III, 1069
Church, Herbert (*fl.* 1904), III, 1096

Church, Ralph (d. 1787), II, 915
Church, Richard William (1815–1890), I, 686; III, 39, **856**f.
Church and Household (1896), III, 824
CHURCH HISTORY, I, 119 (M.E.); III, 920f. See also under RELIGION
CHURCH LANGTON LIBRARY, II, 105
Church of England Quarterly Review, The (1837), III, 833
Church Quarterly Review, The (1875), III, 833
Church Times, The (1863), III, 819
Churchill, Awnsham (d. 1728), I, 764
Churchill, Charles (1731–1764), II, **339**f.
Churchill, John (1650–1722), I, 764
Churchill, Lord Randolph (1849–1894), III, 149
Churchill, Lady Randolph S. (*fl.* 1899), III, 834
Churchill, Sarah, Duchess of Marlborough (1660–1744), II, 135, 149
Churchill, T. O. (*fl.* 1800–23), II, 52
Church-Man, The (1718), II, 712
Churchman; Or, Loyalist's Weekly Journal, The (1720), II, 713
Churchman's Last Shift, The (1720), II, 713
Churchyard, Thomas (1520?–1604), I, 413, **434**f., 724, 738 (2), 769, 775, 787, 805
Churton, Edward (1800–1874), I, 699 (2); III, 96, 854
Chute, Anthony (d. 1595), I, 718
Chute, Francis (*fl.* 1716), II, 311
Cibber, Colley (1671–1757), II, 44, 61, 220, **430**f. 444, 485 (2), 536, 659, 794
Cibber, Susannah Maria (1714–1766), II, 459
Cibber, Theophilus (1703–1758), II, **436**, 708
Cibber and Sheridan (18 cent.), II, 210
Cicero, Marcus Tullius, I, 262, 800; II, 764
Cicero, Marcus Tullius (17 cent.), I, 651
Cid, III, 41
Cinthio, Gianbattista Giraldi, I, 338, 340, 813; II, 810
Circle, The (17 cent.), I, 177 (2)
Circle, The (1874), III, 799
Circular to Bankers, The (1828), III, 820
CIRCULATING LIBRARIES, II, 99 (18 cent.)
CIRCUMNAVIGATIONS, II, 741f.
CIRENCESTER
    Booksellers and printers of, II, 86
    Newspapers, II, 722f. (1718–44)
Cirencester Flying Post and Weekly Miscellany, The (1740), II, 723
Cirencester Post; Or, Gloucestershire Mercury, The (1718), II, 722
Citie Matrons, The (17 cent.), I, 717
Citizen, The (1716), II, 662
Citizen, The (1727), II, 663
Citizen, The (1788), II, 666
Citizen, The (1878), III, 814
Citizen and Weekly Register, The (1776), II, 715
Citizen; or, General Advertiser, The (1757), II, 709

Citizen; or, Morning Post, The (1756), II, 708–9
Cittíes Weekly Post, The (1645), I, 757
City and Country Mercury, The (1667), II, 716
City Intelligencer, The (1709), II, 707
City Mercury, The (1667), II, 716
City Mercury, The (1680), II, 716
City Mercury; Or Advertisements concerning Trade, The (1675), II, 716
City Mercury; Or Advertisements concerning Trade, The (1680), II, 716
City Mercury. Published for the Promotion of Trade, The (1692), II, 717
City Press, The (1857), III, 793, 810
City Scout, The (1645), I, 756
City-Dame's petition in the behalfe of the Cavaliers, The (17 cent.), I, 716
City-Hermit, The [etc.] (18 cent.), II, 209
Civil Service Gazette, The (1853), III, 821
CIVIL WARS, I, 720 (tracts on)
Clack, F. H. (*fl.* 1845), II, 635
Clag, J. (*fl.* 1864), III, 777
Claget (or Clagett), William (1646–1688), II, 95
Clairville, Louis-François, III, 598
Clancy, Michael (*fl.* 1750), II, 745, 783
Clapham, David (d. 1551), I, 809
Clapham, John (*fl.* 1589), I, 806
Clapperton, Hugh (1788–1827), III, 990 (2)
Clapwell, Richard (*fl.* 1286), I, **296**
Clare, G. (*fl.* 1891), III, 974
Clare, J. M. (*fl.* 1732), II, 794
Clare, John (1793–1864), III, **218**f., 636
Clare, Thomas (*fl.* 1796), II, 353
CLARE COLLEGE (Cambridge), I, 370
Clare Journal, The (1777), II, 737
Clarendon, Edward Hyde, Earl of (1609–1674), II, **864**f.
Clarendon, John Charles Villiers, Earl of (1757–1838), II, 747
Clarges, Sir (M.E.), I, 158
Clariodus (M.E.), I, 39
Clarion, The (1891), III, 818
Claris, John Chalk (1797?–1866), III, 215
Claris, de Florian, Jean Pierre, II, 553, 776
Clark, Bracy (*fl.* 1835), III, 763
Clark, Charles (1806–1880), III, 198
Clark, Emily (*fl.* 1817), III, 571
Clark, Ewan (*fl.* 1779), II, 356
Clark, George (*fl.* 1786), II, 822
Clark, George Thomas (1809–1898), III, **927**
Clark (or Clarke), H. (*fl.* 1774), II, 759
Clark, H. (*fl.* 1863), III, 35
Clark, James (d. 1724), II, **992**
Clark, James (*fl.* 1770–1806), II, 817
Clark, John Willis (1833–1910), III, **927**f.
Clark, Robert (*fl.* 1806), journalist, III, 800
Clark, Robert (*fl.* 1875), golfer, III, 775
Clark (or Clarke), Samuel (1626–1701), annotator of the Bible, II, 928
Clark, Samuel (1810–1875), educationalist, III, 567

Clark, Samuel (*fl.* 1758), mathematician, II, 826
CLARK, T. AND T., III, 98
Clark, William (*fl.* 1663–89), Scottish poet, II, 968
Clark, William (*fl.* 1815), of Somerset, III, 975
Clark, William George (1821–1878), III, 709, 990, 1043–4
Clarke, Adam (1762?–1832), II, 95, 875, 935
Clarke, A. W. (*fl.* 1879), III, 1071
Clarke, Adrian (*fl.* 1621), I, 743
Clarke, Charles (*fl.* 1863–71), III, **479**
Clarke, Charles Baron (1832–1906), III, 984
Clarke, Charles Cowden (1787–1877), III, 223, **664**
Clarke, Edward (*fl.* 1690), friend of John Locke, II, 941
Clarke, Edward (1730–1786), II, 745
Clarke, Edward Daniel (1769–1822), II, 159; III, 137, 203, 990
Clarke, Sir Edward George (*fl.* 1881–1919), III, 972
Clarke, Frances Elisabeth, later MacFall ('Sarah Grand') (b. 1862), III, **546**f.
Clarke, George (*fl.* 1703), II, 753
Clarke, George Somers (*fl.* 1790), II, 763
Clarke, H. (*fl.* 1859), genealogist, I, 471
Clarke, H. (*fl.* 1865), economist, III, 974
Clarke, H. G. (*fl.* 1844), I, 449
Clarke, Henry Butler (1863–1904), III, **935**
Clarke, Herbert Edwin (b. 1852), III, **336**
Clarke, Hewson (1787–1832?), III, 205
Clarke, J. (*fl.* 1742), II, 854
Clarke, J. Erskine (*fl.* 1858–66), III, 119, 578 (2)
Clarke, James (*fl.* 1788), philologist, II, 928
Clarke, James (*fl.* 1860–88), editor of 'The Christian World', III, 819
Clarke, James G. (*fl.* 1890), editor of 'The Christian World', III, 819
Clarke, James Stanier (1765?–1834), II, 361, 683
Clarke, John (*fl.* 1633), headmaster of Lincoln Grammar School, I, 376, 854
Clarke, John (d. 1730), moral philosopher, II, 946
Clarke, John (1682–1757), dean of Salisbury, II, 946
Clarke, John (1687–1734), schoolmaster at Hull, II, 16, 108, 127 (2), 128, 767 (2), 768
Clarke, John (*fl.* 1819), legal bibliographer, I, 848
Clarke, Joseph (d. 1749), II, 946
Clarke, Laurence (*fl.* 1737), II, 714
Clarke, Marcus Andrew Hislop (1846–1881), III, **1096**
Clarke, Mary Victoria Cowden, née Novello (1809–1897), II, **711**
Clarke, Samuel (1599–1683), divine and biographer, I, 767; II, 743, **870**, 924
Clarke, Samuel (1625–1669), orientalist, I, 786

Clarke (or Clark), Samuel (1626–1701), anno-
tator of the Bible, II, 928
Clarke, Samuel (1675–1729), metaphysician,
II, 32 (2), 53, **851, 946**
Clarke, W. (*fl.* 1742), translator from Latin, II,
330
Clarke, Sir William (1623?–1666), I, 387
Clarke, William (*fl.* 1819), author of 'Reper-
torium Bibliographicum', II, 103
Clarke, William (*fl.* 1889), of 'The Manchester
Guardian', III, 783, 977
Clarke Papers (17 cent.), I, 400
Clarkson, E. (*fl.* 1830), III, 300
Clarkson, Thomas (1760–1846), II, 773; III,
678, **880**
Clarkson, W. (*fl.* 1816), III, 975
Classical Arrangement of Fugitive Poetry, A
(18 cent.), II, 251
CLASSICS (Greek and Latin)
    Ancient historians, III, 894f., 913f.
    Classical metres in English. See under
    PROSODY, I, 15f.
    Classical scholars, I, 852f. (16 cent.); II, 933f.
    (17, 18 cents.), 993f.
    Influence of, III, 49f. See also under
    Chaucer's SOURCES, I, 216f. and WRITINGS
    IN LATIN, I, 280f.
    Translations from, I, 799f. (1500–1660); II,
    757f. (1660–1800). For 19 cent. see under
    particular writers
Clater, Francis (1756–1823), II, 817
Claude, Isaac, II, 534, 776
Claude, Jean, II, 776
Claudian, I, 801; II, 765
*Claudius Tiberius Nero, Rome's greatest Tyrant,
The Tragedie of* (17 cent.), I, 651
Clavel, Robert (d. 1711), II, 93
Clavell, John (1603–1642), I, 717
Claver, Morris (*fl.* 1684–1726), II, 135
Clavigero, Francesco Saverio, II, 809
Clay, W. L. (*fl.* 1868), III, 932
Clay, William Keatinge (1797–1867), I, 684
Clayton, Charlotte, Viscountess Sundon (d.
1742), II, 135
Clayton, John (*fl.* 1646), I, 849
Clayton, John (*fl.* 1694), II, 752
Clayton, Robert (1695–1758), II, 951
Cleanness (Purity) (M.E.), I, 202f.
Cleave's London Satirist and Gazette of Variety
(1837), III, 812
Cleave's Penny Gazette of Variety (1837), III,
812
Cleaveland Revived, J. (17 cent.), II, 173–5, 180,
184, 209
Cleaver, William (1742–1815), II, 900, 934
Cleges, Sir (M.E.), I, **158**
Cleghorn, George (1716–1789), II, 745
Cleghorn, Hugh (*fl.* 1795), II, 751
Cleghorn, James (1778–1838), III, 970
Cleghorn, William (*fl.* 1817), III, 825

Cleland, James (*fl.* 1607), I, 378
Cleland, John (1709–1789), II, 544 (2)
Cleland, William (1661?–1689), II, 968
Clemens Scottus (*fl.* 826), I, 108
Clément, Félix, III, 598
Clement, F. (*fl.* 1587), I, 376
Clement, John (d. 1572), I, 363
Clement, Simon (*fl.* 1695), II, 958
Clement of Llanthony (d. *c.* 1190), I, **289**
Clements, H. G. J. (*fl.* 1860), III, 685
Clements, Henry (*fl.* 1700), II, 127
Clements, J. (*fl.* 1851), III, 117
Clemons, Mrs (*fl.* 1841), III, 1083
Clenche, John (*fl.* 1675), II, 743
Clencock, John (d. 1352), I, **312**
'Cleophil' (1691), II, 531
CLERGY, II, 152 (17, 18 cents.), 924 (biographical
    collections of)
Clerk, Sir John (1684–1755), II, 156, 997
Clerk, John F. (*fl.* 1889), III, 986
Clerk, William (*fl.* 1677), II, 823
Clerk Who Would See the Virgin, The (M.E.),
I, **162**
Clerke, Agnes Mary (1842–1907), III, 944
Clerke, Ellen Mary (1840–1906), III, 944
Clerke, Gilbert (1626–1697?), I, 871
Clerke, William (*fl.* 1595), I, 713
Clerkenwell News and General Advertiser, The
(1855), III, 799
Clerkenwell News and London Daily Chronicle
(1869), III, 799
Clerkenwell News and London Times (1866), III,
799
Clermont, Thomas Fortescue, Lord (*fl.* 1869),
I, 261
Cleve, C. (*fl.* 1700), I, 458
Cleveland, John (1613–1658), I, 475, 720, 723,
747 (2), 748, 757; II, 173–5, 180, 184, 209
Cliffe, J. H. (*fl.* 1860), III, 770
Clifford, Lady Anne (1590–1676), I, 385
Clifford, Arthur (1778–1830), I, 397; II, 257
Clifford, Christopher (*fl.* 1585), I, 393
Clifford, H. I. (*fl.* 1818), III, 670
Clifford, Lucy (*fl.* 1882), III, 569
Clifford, Martin (d. 1677), II, 271, 419
Clifford, R. (*fl.* 1797), II, 770
Clifford, William Kingdon (1845–1879), III,
573, 943f., 966
Clifton, F. (*fl.* 1718), II, 712
CLIFTON COLLEGE, III, 130, 839
CLIMBING (books on), III, 777
Clinton, Charles John Fynes (1799–1872), III,
151, 997
Clinton, George (*fl.* 1825), III, 206
Clinton, H. (*fl.* 1857), III, 982
Clinton, Henry Fynes (1781–1852), III, **997**
Clio and Euterpe (18 cent.), II, 218, 219 (2), 221,
225, 233
Clio and Strephon (18 cent.), II, 202
Clipperton, John (*fl.* 1764), II, 741

Clissold, Augustus (1797?–1882), III, 126
Clive, Caroline, née Meysey-Wigley (1801–1873), III, **479**
Clive, Catharine (1711–1785), II, **461**f.
Clodd, Edward (1840–1930), III, 905, **968**
Clogie (or Clogy), Alexander (1614–1698), II, **871**
CLONMEL, II, 737 (newspapers)
Clonmel Gazette, The (1790), II, 737 (2)
Cloria and Narcissus (17 cent.), I, 732
Close, Francis (1797–1882), III, 118, 133, 853
Clough, Anne Jemima (1820–1892), III, 142
Clough, Arthur Hugh (1819–1861), III, 137, 264f., 269
Clowes, J. (*fl.* 1653), I, 762
Clowes, John (1743–1831), II, 33 (3), 800
Clowes, William (1540?–1604), I, 891
Clowes, Sir William Laird (1856–1905), III, **925**
Club Law (16 cent.), I, 661
Clubbe, William (1745–1814), II, 748, 766
CLUBS, II, 693f.
Cluny, Alexander (*fl.* 1770), II, 755
Clutterbuck, Henry (1767–1896), II, 682
Clutterbuck, Robert (1772–1831), III, **885**
Cluverius, Philippus, I, 767
Clyomon and Clamydes, The Historie of (16 cent.), I, 520
Clytophon (17 cent.), I, 661
COACHING (books on), III, 765
Coad, J. (*fl.* 1803–24), III, 768, 978
Coal-Hole of Cupid, The (18 cent.), II, 225
Coape, H. C. (*fl. c.* 1850), III, 602
Coates, Henry (*fl.* 1823), III, 199
Coates, John (*fl.* 1770), II, 227, 826
Coates, T. (*fl.* 1838), III, 129
Cobb, James (1756–1818), II, 456, **462**
Cobb, James Francis (*fl.* 1871), III, 573
Cobb, Samuel (1675–1713), II, 15, 22, 76, 312f., 771
Cobbe, Frances Power (1822–1904), III, 67, 142, **866**
Cobbes Prophecies (17 cent.), I, 715
Cobbett, James P. (*fl.* 1835), III, 629–30
Cobbett, John M. (*fl.* 1835), III, 629, 631
Cobbett, Richard, III,.812
Cobbett, T. G. (*fl.* 1860), III, 77
Cobbett, William (1762–1835), III, **629**f.
Cobbett, William, the younger (*fl.* 1836), III, 816
Cobbett's Evening Post (1820), III, 800
Cobbett's Political Register (1802), III, 816
Cobbin, Ingram (1777–1851), III, 135
Cobbold, Richard (1797–1877), III, **391**
Cobden, Edward (1684–1764), II, 606, 826
Cobden, Richard (1804–1865), III, 148
Cobham, S. (*fl.* 1848), III, 978
Cobler of Caunterburie, The (16 cent.), I, 714, 729
Cobler, Stick to your Last (19 cent.), III, 574
Cocchi, Antonio Celestino, II, 809

Cochin, Charles Nicolas, II, 776
Cochois, Barbe, II, 776
Cochrane, Alfred (*fl.* 1896), III, 774
Cochrane, G. (*fl.* 1845), III, 976
Cochrane, John George (1781–1852), I, 671, 906; III, 375, 807, 833
Cochrane, Thomas, Earl of Dundonald (1775–1860), III, 150, 990
Cock, S. (*fl.* 1810), III, 973
Cockaine (or Cokayne), Sir Thomas (1519?–1592), I, 394
Cockayne, Oswald (1807–1873), I, 85, 97
Cockburn, Catharine, later Trotter (1679–1749), II, **444**f., 946
Cockburn, Sir George (1772–1853), III, 150
Cockburn, Henry Thomas, Lord (1779–1854), III, **904**
Cockburn, John (1652–1729), II, 39, 120, 675, 869, **996**
Cockburn, John (1652–1729), of Ormistoun, II, 156
Cockburn, John (*fl.* 1735), voyager, II, 754
Cocke Lorelles Bote (16 cent.), I, 713
Cocker, Edward (1631–1676), I, 346; II, 125, 127, 926
Cocking, Matthew (*fl.* 1772), II, 755
Cockle, Mary (*fl.* 1807), III, 195, 571
Cockman, Thomas (*fl.* 1699), II, 764
Cocks, Richard (*fl.* 1615–22), I, 784
Cockton, Henry (1807–1853), III, **479**
Codex Wintoniensis (M.E.), I, 39
Codrington, Robert (d. 1665), I, 659, 808; II, 121, 765
Coe, Andrew (*fl.* 1641–9), I, 753, 755–6, 759
Coe, Jane (*fl.* 1646), I, 756
Coello, Antonio, II, 68
Coetlogon, Charles Edward de (1746?–1820), II, 671, 680
Coffee House, The (1781), II, 666
Coffee-House Evening Post, The (1729), II, 710
Coffee House Mercury, The (1690), II, 705
Coffee-House Morning Post, The (1729), II, 698, 708
COFFEE HOUSES, II, 693f.
Coffey, Charles (d. 1745), II, **436**
Coffin, Paul (*fl.* 1760), II, 755
Coffin, Richard (*fl.* 1687–97), II, 101
Coffin, Robert Aston (1819–1885), III, 856
Cogan, Henry (*fl.* 1653), I, 781, 784, 801, 819
Cogan, Thomas (1545?–1607), I, 391, 860, 889
Cogan, Thomas (1736–1818), II, 747
Coggeshall, William Turner (*fl.* 1856), III, 797
Cogniard, Hippolyte, III, 599
Cohen, B. (*fl.* 1822), III, 978
Coignet, Matthieu, I, 812
Cokayne, Sir Aston (1608–1684), I, 642f.
Cokayne (or Cockaine), Sir Thomas (1519?–1592), I, 394
Coke, Sir Edward (1552–1634), judge, I, 508, **849**

Coke, Edward (*fl.* 1645), colonel, I, 842
Coke, J. (*fl.* 1550), I, 844
Coke, Sir John (1563–1644), I, 400
Coke, Kinloch (*fl.* 1870), III, 810
Coke, Lady Mary (1756–1779), II, 137
Coke, Roger (*fl.* 1670–96), II, 958
Coke, Thomas (1747–1814), II, 757
Coke, William (*fl.* 1785), II, 108
Colburn, Zerah (*fl.* 1859), III, 822 (2)
Colburn's United Service Magazine (1843), III, 826
COLCHESTER, II, 723 (newspaper)
Colchester, Cartulary of (M.E.), I, 121
Colchester, Charles Abbot, Baron (1757–1829), III, 149
Colchester Spie, The (1648), I, 759
Colden, Cadwallader (1688–1776), II, 753
Cole, A. W. (*fl.* 1852–96), III, 1090–1
Cole, C. A. (*fl.* 1858), I, 116
Cole, Charles Nalson (1723–1804), II, 319, 864
Cole, Christian (*fl.* 1733), II, 166
Cole, H. H. (*fl.* 1883), III, 1084
Cole, Sir Henry (1808–1882), I, 115; III, 576
Cole, J. W. (*fl.* 1859), III, 581
Cole, John (1792–1848), II, 843
Cole, Ralph (*fl.* 1795), II, 822
Cole, Thomas (d. 1571), I, 681
Cole, William (*fl.* 1659), I, 718
Cole, William (1714–1782), I, 124; II, 132, 136, 745, 837
Colebrooke, Henry Thomas (1765–1837), III, **1017**, 1073
Coleman, C. (*fl.* 1832), III, 1081
Coleman, Edward (*fl.* 1798), II, 817
Coleman, J. (*fl.* 1851), II, 337
Colenso, Frances Ellen (1849–1887), III, 1093
Colenso, John William (1814–1863), III, 848, 1091
Coleraine, George Hanger, Baron (*fl.* 1801), III, 765
Coleraine, Hugh Hare, Baron (1606?–1667), II, 811
Coleridge, Christabel R. (*fl.* 1882), III, 574, 828
Coleridge, Derwent (1800–1883), III, 173, 175 (3), 230 (3), 240, 247
Coleridge, Hartley (1796–1849), III, **230**
Coleridge, Henry Nelson (1798–1843), III, **664**
    Reviews by, III, 230, 239, 284, 302, 307, 479, 636, 784
Coleridge, Herbert (1830–1861), I, 114
Coleridge, John (1719–1781), II, 127
Coleridge, John Duke, Baron (1820–1894), III, 126
Coleridge, Sir John Taylor (1790–1876), III, 131, 832, 858
Coleridge, Mary Elizabeth (1861–1907), III, **336**
Coleridge, Samuel Taylor (1772–1834), III, **172f.**, 181
Coleridge, Sara (1802–1852), III, 173–5, **284**

Coles, Elisha (1640?–1680), II, 125, 127, 926
Coles, F. (*fl.* 1642), I, 753 (2), 754 (2), 755
Coles, Henry (*fl.* 1864), III, 669
Coles, W. (*fl.* 1657), I, 892
Colet, John (1467?–1519), I, **666**, 684
Coley, Henry (1633–1695?), II, 809
Colgan, John (d. 1657?), III, 1047
Colin Blowbols Testament (16 cent.), I, 713
Collection and Selection of English Prologues and Epilogues, A (18 cent.), II, 233
Collection for the Improvement of Husbandry and Trade, A (1692), II, 675, 705
Collection from the Spectator, A [etc.] (18 cent.), II, 215, 220, 223
Collection of All the New Songs Sung at Vauxhall, Ranelagh (18 cent.), II, 218
Collection of Bacchanalian Songs, A (1729), II, 200
Collection of Bacchanalian Songs, A (1763), II, 222
Collection of Catches, A (1764), II, 222, 224
Collection of Catches, Canons and Glees, A (1763), II, 222
Collection of Catches, Canons, Glees, Duettos &c., A (1780), II, 234
Collection of Catches, Glees, A (1771), II, 228
Collection of Choice Pieces Composed on Different Persons, A (18 cent.), II, 237
Collection of Comic Songs, by H— R—, A (18 cent.), II, 218
Collection of Constitutional Songs, A (18 cent.), II, 254–5
Collection of Diverting Songs, A (18 cent.), II, 207
Collection of 86 Loyal Poems, A (17 cent.), II, 179
Collection of English Prose and Verse for Schools, A (18 cent.), II, 235
Collection of English Songs, A (18 cent.), II, 251
Collection of Epigrams, A (18 cent.), II, 198, 204, 206
Collection of Farces, A (1809), II, 392
Collection of Favourite English, Scotch, Irish, & French Songs, A (18 cent.), II, 233
Collection of Favorite Glees [etc.], *A* (19 cent.), II, 255
Collection of Favourite Songs Sung at the Beef Steak Club, A (18 cent.), II, 245
Collection of Hymns for the October Club, A (18 cent.), II, 190
Collection of Interesting Anecdotes, A (18 cent.), II, 248
Collection of Letters and Essays, A (1729), II, 200
Collection of Letters for the Improvement of Husbandry and Trade (1681), II, 704
Collection of Loyal Songs (1744), II, 210
Collection of Loyal Songs, A (1749), II, 213, 220, 227

Collection of Loyal Songs, A (1750), II, 214

Collection of Loyal Songs, as sung at all the Orange Lodges in Ireland, A (1798), II, 253

Collection of Masonic Songs (18 cent.), II, 250

Collection of Merry Poems, A (18 cent.), II, 205

Collection of Miscellany Poems, Letters, &c., A (17 cent.), II, 184 (2)

Collection of Miscellany Poems, never before Publish'd, A (18 cent.), II, 206

Collection of Modern Fables, A (18 cent.), II, 228

Collection of Modern Poems, A (18 cent.), II, 221

Collection of Moral and Sacred Poems, A (18 cent.), II, 210

Collection of more than eight hundred Prologues and Epilogues, A (18 cent.), II, 233

Collection of New Plays, A (1774), II, 392

Collection of New Songs, A (1696), II, 183, 184

Collection of New Songs, A (1712), II, 190

Collection of New Songs, Compos'd by Mr Morgan, A (1697), II, 183

Collection of New Songs Compos'd by Several Masters, A (1715), II, 192

Collection of New Songs, Sett by Mr Gillier, A (1698), II, 184

Collection of New Songs set by Mr Wm Morley and Mr John Isum, A (1710), II, 189

Collection of New State Songs, A (18 cent.), II, 202

Collection of Odes, Songs, and Epigrams against the Whigs, A (18 cent.), II, 243-4

Collection of Old Ballads, A (18 cent.), II, 197 (4), 198 (2), 207

Collection of One Hundred and Fifty Scots Songs, A (18 cent.), II, 225

Collection of Original Miscellaneous Poems, A (1770), II, 227

Collection of Original Poems, A (1714), II, 191

Collection of Original Poems, A (1724), II, 197

Collection of Original Poems, and Translations, A (1745), II, 211

Collection of Original Poems. By Mr Blacklock [etc.], A (1760), II, 219, 221

Collection of Original Scotch Songs, A (1732?), II, 202

Collection of Original Scots Songs, Poems, etc., A (1772), II, 229

Collection of Pieces in Verse and Prose on the Dunciad (18 cent.), II, 202 (2)

Collection of Plays by Eminent Hands, A (1719), II, 392

Collection of Poems, A (1672), II, 176 (2), 182, 183, 185 (2), 192

Collection of Poems, A [pbd by R. Dodsley] (1748), II, 212 (2), 213, 214 (2), 216, 218-9 222-4, 227, 230, 236

Collection of Poems. By Beattie Langhorne [etc.], A (1779), II, 233

Collection of Poems. By John Whaley, A (1732), II, 202

Collection of Poems, A. By Several Hands (1744), II, 210

Collection of Poems. By Several Hands, A (Paris, 1779), II, 233

Collection of Poems, by the Author of the Cambridge Ladies, A (1733), II, 203

Collection of Poems. By Pope [etc.], A (1777), II, 232

Collection of Poems, For and Against Dr Sacheverell, A (18 cent.), II, 189 (4), 190

Collections of Poems, from the best Authors. By James Elphinston, A (18 cent.), II, 222

Collection of Poems in Two Volumes, A (1768), II, 225, 227, 230, 236

Collection of Poems, Mostly Original, By Several Hands, A (1789), II, 242, 244

Collection of Poems on Affairs of State, A (17 cent.), II, 181 (3)

Collection of Poems on Divine and Moral Subjects, A (18 cent.), II, 230

Collection of Poems, On Religious and Moral Subjects, A (18 cent.), II, 252

Collection of Poems on Several Occasions Publish'd in The Craftsman, A (1731), II, 201

Collection of Poems on Several Occasions Written in the Last Century, A (1747), II, 212

Collection of Poems on State-Affairs, A (1712), II, 190

Collection of Poems, on Various Subjects, A [Ed. Samuel Whyte] (1792), II, 247, 251

Collection of Poems upon the Victories of Blenheim and Ramilies, A (18 cent.), II, 188

Collection of Political and Humorous Letters, A (18 cent.), II, 212

Collection of Pretty Poems, A (18 cent.), II, 218-9, 227, 230, 233

Collection of Pretty Poems for the Amusement of Children Three Feet High, A (18 cent.), II, 232

Collection of Scarce, Curious and Valuable Pieces, A (18 cent.), II, 229, 238

Collection of Scots Poems on Several Occasions, A (18 cent.), II, 217, 226, 240

Collection of Scots Songs, A (1782), II, 236

Collection of Sea Songs, A (18 cent.), II, 197

Collection of Select Epigrams, A (18 cent.), II, 218

Collection of Several Pamphlets [on] Admiral Byng, A (18 cent.), II, 217

Collection of Songs, A (1762), II, 221

Collection of Songs, Chiefly such as are Eminent for Poetical Merit, A (1782), II, 236

Collection of Songs Compos'd by Mr John Eccles, A (1704), II, 186

Collection of Songs Compos'd by Mr John Sheeles, A (1725), II, 197

Collection of Songs for Two or Three Voices, A (1745), II, 211, 214

Collection of Songs on Various Subjects, A (1720), II, 195

Collection of Songs, Selected from the Works of Mr Dibdin, A [etc.] (1799), II, 254

Collection of Songs set by Purcell & Eccles, A (1696), II, 183

Collection of Songs set to Musick by Mr James Graves, A (1717), II, 193

Collection of Songs set to Musick by Mr Pixell, A (1759), II, 219

Collection of Speciall Passages, A (1642), I, 754

Collection of Spiritual Songs, A (18 cent.), II, 245

Collection of State Songs, A (18 cent.), II, 192, 194

Collection of the best English Plays, A (1712), II, 392

Collection of the Best English Poetry, A (18 cent.), II, 193

Collection Of the best Modern Poems, A (18 cent.), II, 228

Collection of the Best old Scotch and English Songs, A (18 cent.), II, 221

Collection of the Choycest and newest Songs, A (17 cent.), II, 180

Collection of the Choicest Songs & Dialogues, A (1704), II, 186, 189, 192

Collection of the Choicest Songs and Dialogues Compos'd by the most Eminent Masters of the Age, A (1710), II, 189

Collection of the English Poets, A (1776), II, 259

Collection of the Most Celebrated Prologues, A (18 cent.), II, 199

Collection of the most celebrated Songs set by Several Authors adapted for the Guitar, A (18 cent.), II, 227

Collection of the most esteemed Farces, A (1786), II, 392

Collection of the Most esteemed Pieces of Poetry By the Late Moses Mendez [etc.], *A* (18 cent.), II, 224, 227

Collection of the most favourite new songs, A (1795), II, 250

Collection of the most favorite Scots Songs, A (18 cent.), II, 233

Collection of The Newest and Most Ingenious Poems against Popery, A (17 cent.), II, 181 (3)

Collection of the Songs composed by Henry Purcell (18 cent.), II, 186

Collection of Twenty Four Songs, A (17 cent.), II, 179

Collection of vocal harmony, A (18 cent.), II, 234

COLLECTIONS
Anglo-Saxon Period, I, 62 (verse), 85 (prose), 98 (Latin writings)
Middle English Period, I, 115 and 119f. (official documents), 129f. (romances), 272f. (ballads)

Renaissance to Restoration, I, 317f., 403f. (verse), 480f. (epigrams and satires), 487f. (plays), 763f. (travel books)
Restoration to Romantic Revival, II, 14 (criticism), II, 257f. (verse), II, 392f. (plays, prologues and epilogues), II, 740f. (voyages)
Nineteenth Century, III, 7f. (essays), III, 585 (plays)
See also ANTHOLOGIES, MISCELLANIES and READERS

Collectors (book-), I, 360f. (14–17 cents.); II, 100f. (1660–1800); III, 103f. (19 cent.)

Colles, Ramsay (1862–1919), III, 784

Colley Cibber's Jests (18 cent.), II, 220

Collier, Arthur (1680–1732), II, 947

Collier, Jeremy (1650–1726), II, 15, 44, 400, 759, 777, 826, 875

Collier, John (1708–1786), II, 927

Collier, John Payne (1789–1883), I, 541; III, 647, **1022**f.

COLLIER CONTROVERSY, THE, II, 400f.

Colliery Guardian, The (1858), III, 822

Collingridge, W. H. (*fl.* 1857), III, 810

Collings, Richard (*fl.* 1643), I, 754 (2), 761, 763

Collins, Anne (*fl.* 1653), I, 475

Collins, Anthony (1676–1729), II, 16, 940, 947

Collins, Arthur (1690–1760), II, **879**

Collins, Charles Alston (1828–1873), III, **479**

Collins, Charles James (1820–1864), III, 820

Collins, David (1756–1810), II, 751

Collins, H. G. (*fl.* 1860), III, 75

Collins, J. P. (*fl.* 1870), III, 830

Collins, John (1741–1797), Shakespearian scholar, II, 898, 901

Collins, John (1742–1808), actor and poet, II, **357**

Collins, John Churton (1848–1908), III, **737**f.

Collins, Joshua (*fl.* 1802), II, 101

Collins, Mabel (*fl.* 1890?), III, 831

Collins, Mortimer (1827–1876), III, **479**f.

Collins, Ruth (*fl.* 1732), II, 663, 677

Collins, Samuel (1619–1670), II, 743

Collins, Thomas (*fl.* 1615), I, 475

'Collins, Tom', i.e. Joseph Furphy (*fl.* 1903), III, 1097

Collins, William (1721–1759), poet, II, **335**f.

Collins, William (*fl.* 1787), editor of 'New Vocal Miscellany', II, 240

Collins, William Edward (1867–1911), III, **924**

Collins, William Lucas (1817–1887), I, 372

Collins, William Wilkie (1824–1889), III, 445 (4), 446–8, **480**f.

COLLINS, WILLIAM, SONS & CO., III, 98

Collin's Weekly Journal (1723), II, 713

Collinson, John (1757?–1793), II, **891**

Collinson, Sir Richard (1811–1883), I, 787 (2)

Collop, John (*fl.* 1660), I, 475, 687

Collyer, Joseph (d. 1766), II, 56 (2), 543, 806 (2)

Collyer, Mary (d. 1763), II, 56 (2), 543 (2), 805

Collyer, N. (*fl.* 1812), III, 111
Collyer, William Bengo (1782–1854), III, 240
Collyns, Charles Palk (*fl.* 1862), III, 763
Colman, George, the elder (1732–1794), II, 108, 116, **451**f., 485, 767, 898, 915
Colman, George, the younger (1762–1836), II, **462**f.
Colnett, James (*fl.* 1793), II, 757
Colom, Jacob, I, 780
Colonial and Asiatic Review, The (1852), III, 828
Colonial Magazine and East India Review, The (1849), III, 828
COLONIES (writings on), I, 845 (16, 17 cents.)
Colonist and Commercial Weekly Advertiser, The (1824), III, 811
Colonist and Weekly Courier, The (1824), III, 811
Colonna, Francesco, I, 733
Colonne, Guido Delle, I, 733
COLOUR PRINTING, III, 79f.
Coloured News, The (1855), III, 815
Colquhoun, A. R. (*fl.* 1893), III, 1092
Colquhoun, John (1805–1885), sporting writer, III, 770
Colquhoun, John Campbell (1803–1870), miscellaneous writer, III, 108, 117
Colquhoun, Patrick (1745–1820), II, 114, 145, 155; III, 108, 975, 980
Colquhoun, William (*fl.* 1858), III, 762
Colse, Peter (*fl.* 1596), I, 435, 802
Colson, John (1680–1760), II, 774
Colsoni, F. (*fl.* 1695), II, 145
Colt, Sir Henry (*fl.* 1631), I, 792
Colton, Charles Caleb (1780?–1832), III, 198
Colum, Padraic (b. 1881), III, **1065**
Columba (or Colum-cille) (d. 597), I, **101**
Columbanus (d. 615), I, **102**
Columbian Songster, The (18 cent.), II, 254
Columbine, P. (*fl.* 1795), II, 61
Coluthus (*fl.* 1586), I, 431
Colvil, Samuel (*fl.* 1681), II, 288
Colvile, George (*fl.* 1556), I, 811
Colvill, Robert (d. 1788), II, **990**
Colville, F. L. (*fl.* 1870), III, 640, 674
Colvin, I. D. (*fl.* 1905–12), III, 1089, 1090–1
Colvin, Sir Sidney (1845–1927), III, **738**
Comazzi, Giovanni Battista, II, 809
Combe, A. A. (*fl.* 1824), III, 976
Combe, E. (*fl.* 1725), II, 772, 780, 783
Combe, George (1788–1858), II, 987; III, 108, **866**, 965, 974
Combe, William (1741–1823), II, 24, 235, **357**f., 548 (2); III, 798
Comber, Thomas (1645–1699), II, 823
Comber, W. T. (*fl.* 1808), III, 969
Comberbach, Roger (*fl.* 1755), II, 23
Comedian's Tales, The (18 cent.), II, 200
COMEDIES, I, 517f. (16 cent.)
  Comedy of manners, II, 395
  Recent works on comedy, II, 395f.
  See also under DRAMA

Comenius (or Komensky), Johannes Amos, I, 326, 365, 375 (2)
Comer, John (*fl.* 1705), II, 753
Comes Amoris (17 cent.), II, 180 (2), 181, 182 (2)
Comet, The (1791), II, 711
Comfort, Bessie, née Marchant (b. 1862), III, 574
Comic Adventures of Old Mother Hubbard, The (19 cent.), III, 575
Comic Conviviality (18 cent.), II, 252
Comic Cuts (1890), III, 821
Comic Miscellany, The (18 cent.), II, 217
Comic Muse, The (18 cent.), II, 229
Comic News, The (1863), III, 820
Comic Pictorial Nuggets (1892), III, 821
Comic Songster, The (18 cent.), II, 242, 249
Comical Adventures of a Little White Mouse, The (18 cent.), II, 563
Comical Pilgrim, The (18 cent.), II, 538
Comical Observator, The (1704), II, 659
Comick Magazine, The (18 cent.), II, 251
Comick Magazine; Or Library of Mirth [etc.], *The* (1796), II, 682
Comines (or Commines), Philippe de, Seigneur d'Argenton, I, 331, 812; II, 776
Comitia Westmonasteriensium (18 cent.), II, 199 (2)
Commendatio Lamentabilis Edward I (M.E.), I, 115
Commendatory Verses (17 cent.), II, 185 (2)
Commentator, The (1720), II, 662
Commercial and Agricultural Magazine, The (1799), II, 683
COMMERCIAL PAPERS, III, 820
COMMERCIAL YEAR BOOKS, III, 845
Commercial World, The (1874), III, 820
Common Condicions (16 cent.), I, 520
Common Prayer, The Booke of (16 cent.), I, 45
Common Sense (1737), II, 663
Common Sense (1824), III, 811
Common Sense and Weekly Globe (1825), III, 811
Common Sense; or, The Englishman's Journal (1737), II, 714 (2)
Commonweal, The (1885), III, 818
Commonwealth, The (1866), III, 817
COMPANIES (theatrical), I, 501f. (16, 17 cents.)
Companion, The (18 cent.), II, 244–5
Companion, The (1828), III, 818
Companion for a Leisure Hour, A (18 cent.), II, 226
Companion for the Fire-Side, A (18 cent.), II, 229
Companion for Youth, The (1858), III, 577
Companion in a Post-Chaise, A (18 cent.), II, 229
Companion to the Newspaper, The (1834), III, 827
Company Keeper's Assistant, The (18 cent.), II, 227

COMPARATIVE LITERATURE, I, 325
  See also CONTINENT (LITERARY RELATIONS
    WITH)
Compassio Mariae (M.E.), I, 39
Compendio Mercuriale (1691), II, 719
Compendious Library, The (1751), II, 687
Complaint of the Ploughman (M.E.), I, **201**
Complaynt of Scotland, The (16 cent.), I, 902
Compleat Academy of Complements, The (18
    cent.), II, 186
*Compleat Academy Of Complements; Or,
    Lover's Magazine, The* (18 cent.), II, 200
*Compleat Collection Of All The Poems Wrote By
    Alexander Pennecuik, A* [etc.], II, 214
*Compleat Collection Of all the Verses occasioned
    by Pope and Company, A* (18 cent.), II, 199
*Compleat Collection Of Prologues and Epilogues,
    A* (18 cent.), II, 228
Compleat Courtier, The (1683), II, 179
*Compleat Courtier; Or, The Morals of Tacitus,
    The* (1700), II, 659
Compleat English Secretary, The (18 cent.), II,
    191
Compleat French-Master, The (17 cent.), II, 182,
    184, 189, 193, 196, 200
Compleat Library, The (1692), II, 675
Compleat Mendicant or Unhappy Beggar, The
    (17 cent.), II, 532
*Compleat Mercury; Or, The Haerlem Courant,
    The* (1682), II, 704
Compleat Tutor For the Guitar, A (18 cent.), II,
    216
Compleat Universal Jester, The (18 cent.), II,
    226
Compleate Intelligencer and Resolver, The (1643),
    I, 755
Complementum Fortunatarum Insularum (17
    cent.), II, 174
Complete Art of Poetry, The (18 cent.), II, 194
Complete Art of Writing Letters, The (18 cent.),
    II, 227
*Complete Collection of all the Papers in the
    present Contest for Members for Northum-
    berland, A* (18 cent.), II, 230
*Complete Collection of Old and New English
    and Scotch Songs, A* (18 cent.), II, 204, 205
Complete English Songster, The (18 cent.), II,
    221
Complete Fabulist, The (18 cent.), II, 234, 236
Complete Free Mason, The (18 cent.), II, 222,
    226
*Complete Historical Detail of the most Remark-
    able Public Occurrences, A* (1796), II, 716
Complete London and Dublin Jester, The (18
    cent.), II, 240
Complete London Jester, The (18 cent.), II,
    222-5, 228, 233-5, 237-8
Complete Magazine, The (1764), II, 679
Compositor's Chronicle, The (1840), III, 88
Compton, Henry (1632–1713), II, **846**f.

Compton, Sir Herbert Abingdon Draper
    (1770–1846), III, 800
Compton, Samuel (*fl.* 1694), II, 774
Comptroller, in English and French, The (1759),
    II, 719
Comte, Auguste, III, **21**
Concanen, Matthew (1701–1749), II, 201, **313**,
    713 (2)
Concanen, Matthew (*fl.* 1816), II, 458
Concerts of Antient Music (18 cent.), II, 242,
    244-5, 247-53
Conceyts and Jeasts, Certaine (17 cent.), I, 715
Conciliade, The (18 cent.), II, 226
CONCORDANCES, II, 928
Condell, Henry (d. 1627), I, 546
Conder, Claude Reignier (1848–1910), III, 990
Conder, Eustace R. (*fl.* 1857), III, 231 (2)
Conder, Josiah (1789–1855), III, **230**f., 241,
    781, 819, 824
Condillac, Étienne de, II, 28
Condorcet, Marie Jean Antoine Nicolas
    Caritat, Marquis de, II, 774
Conestaggio, Girolamo, I, 778
Confession of Richard Brandon, The (17 cent.),
    I, 719
Congleton, Sir Henry Parnell, Baron (1776–
    1842), II, 972, 978
CONGREGATIONAL WRITERS, II, 862
Congreve, F. A. (*fl.* 1798), II, 407
Congreve, Richard (1818–1899), III, 21, **866**
Congreve, William (1670–1729), II, 21, 61,
    414f., 531, 589
Coningsby, Sir Harry (*fl.* 1664), II, 764
Coningsby, Sir Thomas (d. 1625), I, 384
Conington, John (1825–1869), III, 108, **284**
Conjurer, The (1735), II, 663
*Conjurer's Magazine; Or, Magical and Physio-
    gnomical Mirror, The* (1791), II, 681
Connaught Gazette, The (1797), II, 738
*Connaught Mercury; Or, Universal Register,
    The* (1769), II, 738
Connoisseur, The (1754), II, 664
Connor (or O'Connor), Bernard (1666?–1689),
    II, 744
Conolly, John (1794–1866), III, 833
Conolly, M. F. (*fl.* 1861), III, 244
Conscience, Hendrik, III, 573
Conservative, The [Edinburgh] (1837), III, 807
*Conservative Journal and Church of England
    Gazette, The* (1839), III, 813
Consett, Matthew (*fl.* 1789), II, 747
Const, Francis (1751–1839), II, 963
Constable, Archibald (1774–1827), III, 98
Constable, Henry (1562–1613), I, 431
Constable, John (1676?–1744), II, 16
Constitution, The (1812), III, 811
Constitution; or, Anti-Union Evening Post, The
    (Dublin, 1799), II, 736
Constitutional and Public Ledger, The (1836),
    III, 799

Constitutional Chronicle, The (1780), II, 722
CONSTITUTIONAL HISTORY, I, 118 (M.E.), 401 f.
    (16, 17 cents.); II, 167 f. (17, 18 cents.)
Constitutional Magazine, The (1768), II, 679
Constitutional Songs (18 cent.), II, 254
Constitutions of the Free and Accepted Masons,
    The (18 cent.), II, 247
Constitutions of the Free-Masons, The (18 cent.),
    II, 197, 201, 207, 212, 214, 217, 220, 223–4,
    226, 237, 247
Contarini, Gasparo, I, 778, 812
Contemporary Review, The (1866), III, 830
Contest, The (1734), II, 204
Contest, The (1756), II, 664
Contest, The (1768), II, 225
Contest, The (1800), II, 255
Conti, Antonio, II, 73
Conti, Armand de Bourbon, Prince of, II, 769
CONTINENT
    English printing on, I, 355 (15–17 cents.)
    Literary relations with, I, 216 f. (Chaucer),
    325 f. (1500–1660); II, 31 f. (1660–1800);
    III, 17 f., 54 f.
    See also EUROPE
Continental Times, The (1878), III, 799
Continuation of a journall of passages of the
    Parliament and other papers, A (1646), I,
    757
Continuation of Certaine Speciall and Remark-
    able Passages, A (1642), I, 753, 754 (5)
Continuation of Certain Speciall and Remark-
    able Passages, A (1644), I, 755–6
Continuation of Certaine Speciall and Remark-
    able Passages, A (1645), I, 757
Continuation of Certaine Speciall and Remark-
    able Passages, A (1647), I, 757
Continuation of our Weekly Intelligence from
    His Majesties Army, A (1642), I, 754
Continuation of Papers, A (1646), I, 757
Continuation of the most remarkable Passages in
    both Houses of Parliament, by G. H. (1642),
    I, 754
Continuation of the Narrative of the Tryal of
    the King, A (1649), I, 759
Continuation of the Politicks of Europe, A
    (1690), II, 705
Continuation of the Proceedings of the Meeting
    of the Estates in Scotland, A (1690), II,
    705
Continuation of the true Diurnall Occurrences in
    Parliament, A (1642), I, 752
Continuation of the true Diurnall Occurrences
    and passages in both Houses of Parliament,
    A (1642), I, 753
Continuation of the true Diurnall, of all the
    Passages in Parliament, A (1642), I, 752
Continuation of the True Diurnal of Passages in
    Parliament, A (1642), I, 752 (3), 753
Continuation of the true Diurnall of Proceedings
    in Parliament, A (1642), I, 752

Continuation of the Weekly Occurrences in
    Parliament, A (1642), I, 753
Continuation of True and Special Passages, A
    (1642), I, 754
Continuation of True Intelligence from the Earl
    of Manchester's Army, A (1644), I, 756
Continued Heads of Perfect Passages (1649), I,
    759
Controller, The (1714), II, 661
Conventicle Courant, The (1682), II, 704
Conversations Moral and Entertaining, between
    an English Gentleman and a Knight of
    Malta (18 cent.), II, 543
Convivial Companion: or the Delights of Har-
    mony, The (18 cent.), II, 252
Convivial Harmony (19 cent.), II, 255
Convivial Jester, Or Bane of Melancholy, The
    (18 cent.), II, 244, 255
Convivial Magazine and Polite Intelligencer,
    The (1775), II, 680
Convivial Songster, The (18 cent.), II, 236 (2),
    241, 244
Conway, Anne, Viscountess (d. 1679), I, 387
Conway, Edward, Viscount (d. 1631), I, 364
Conway, F. W. (*fl.* 1821), II, 735
Conway, Gilbert (*fl.* 1878), I, 18
Conway, Henry Seymour (1721–1795), II, 771
'Conway, Hugh', i.e. Frederick John Fargus
    (1847–1885), III, **540**
Conway, James (*fl.* 1859), III, 770
Conway, Sir Martin (1856–1937), III, 990
Conway, Roger (*fl.* 1357), I, **305**
Conway, W. Martin, Baron (b. 1856), III, 777,
    830
Conybeare, John (*fl.* 1580–94), I, 371
Conybeare, John Josias (1779–1824), I, 60, 62
Conybeare, William Daniell (1787–1857), III,
    950
Conybeare, William John (1815–1857), III, 853
Cook, Charles Henry (*fl.* 1887), III, 772
Cook, Sir E. T. (1857–1919), III, 784, 799,
    801 (2)
Cook, Eben (*fl.* 1708), II, 753
Cook, Edward Dutton (1829–1883), II, 405,
    407; III, 704, 829
Cook, Eliza (1812–1889), III, **284**
Cook, G. H. (*fl.* 1856), III, 974
Cook, George (1772–1845), III, **886**
Cook, J. [misprint for James Cooke (*fl.* 1655–
    62), physician], I, 890
Cook, James (1728–1779), II, 741 f.
Cook, John (d. 1660) [misprinted Sir J. Cooke],
    I, 845
Cook, John (*fl.* 1770), II, 750
Cook, John (*fl.* 1826), III, 759
Cook, John Douglas (1808?–1868), III, 798, 814
Cook, Sir Theodore Andrea (*fl.* 1896), III, 779
Cook (or Cooke), Thomas (*fl.* 1642), I, 753 (2)
Cook (or Cooke), Walter (*fl.* 1642), I, 753 (3),
    754

Cook (or Cooke), William (*fl.* 1642), I, 752 (2), 753 (3), 754 (4)
Cooke, Anne, Lady Bacon (1528–1610), I, 817 (2)
Cooke, Douglas (*fl.* 1859), III, 833
Cooke, E. (*fl.* 1596), I, 376
Cooke, E. (*fl.* 1676), II, 787
Cooke, Edward (*fl.* 1712), II, 741
Cooke, George Wingrove (1814–1865), II, 441
Cooke, J. (*fl.* 1840), author of 'The Stage', III, 581
Cooke, James (*fl.* 1655–62), physician, I, 890 [misprinted Cook], 891
Cooke, John (*fl.* 1577), sailor, I, 787
Cooke, John (*fl.* 1612), dramatist, I, 643
Cooke, John (*fl.* 1783), rector of Ventnor, II, 96
Cooke, Kenningale (*fl.* 1877), III, 827
Cooke, Kinloch (*fl.* 1892), III, 801
Cooke, M. (*fl.* 1852), I, 186
Cooke, Thomas (1703–1756), II, 17, 24, 302, 313f., 695, 761
Cooke, W. H. (*fl.* 1866), III, 883
Cooke, William (*fl.* 1746), translator of Sallust, II, 767
Cooke, William (*fl.* 1775–1804), dramatic critic, II, 295, 400, 407–8, 624, 647
Cooke's Pocket Edition of Select British Poets (1794), II, 260
COOKERY BOOKS, I, 396 (16, 17 cents.)
Cookworthy, William (1705–1780), II, 33
Cooley, William Desborough (d. 1883), I, 788
Coolidge, W. A. B. (1850–1926), III, 777, 830
Co-operative News, The (1871), III, 817
CO-OPERATIVE PRINTING SOCIETY, III, 87
Co-operator, The [Manchester] (1860), III, 817
Cooper, A. W. (*fl.* 1878), III, 770
Cooper, Anthony Ashley, First Earl of Shaftesbury (1621–1683), politician, I, 387
Cooper, Anthony Ashley, Third Earl of Shaftesbury (1671–1713), philosopher, II, 39, 54, 117, **948**
Cooper, Anthony Ashley, Seventh Earl of Shaftesbury (1801–1885), philanthropist, III, 119
Cooper, Sir Astley Paston (1768–1841), III, 962
Cooper, C. (*fl.* 1685), I, 44; II, 931
Cooper, Charles (*fl.* 1880), III, 807
Cooper, Charles A. (1829–1916), III, 784
Cooper, Charles Henry (1808–1866), III, **904**
Cooper, Charles Purton (1793–1873), III, 896
Cooper, Edith Emma (1862–1914), III, **340**
Cooper, Elizabeth (*fl.* 1737), II, 206, 923
Cooper, F. (*fl.* 1866), editor of Praed, III, 247
Cooper, Frederick Fox (*fl.* 1840), III, 442
Cooper, George (*fl.* 1799), II, 159
Cooper, H. F. (*fl.* 1840), III, 811
Cooper, J. (*fl.* 1790), II, 565
Cooper (or Coprario), John (1580?–*c.* 1650?), I, 485

Cooper, John (*fl.* 1795), III, 760
Cooper, John Gilbert (1723–1769), II, 17, 303, 782
'Cooper, Margaret' (1584), I, 893
Cooper, Maria Susanna (*fl.* 1775), II, 547
Cooper, S. (*fl.* 1787), II, 566
Cooper, T. (*fl.* 1741), publisher, II, 715
Cooper (or Couper), Thomas (1517?–1594), bishop of Winchester, I, 375, 670, 691, 824
Cooper, Thomas (*fl.* 1598–1626), divine and pamphleteer, I, 894
Cooper, Thomas (1759–1840), natural philosopher and lawyer, II, 757
Cooper, Thomas (1805–1892), chartist poet, III, **284f.**, 817
Cooper, W. D. (*fl.* 1789), II, 558, 560, 566
Cooper, William (*fl.* 1673–86), bookseller, II, 96–7
Cooper, William Durrant (1812–1875), I, 523
Cooper's Journal (1850), III, 817
Coote, Charles (1761–1835), II, 889 (2), 932
Coote, Edmund (*fl.* 1596), I, 44
Coote, Henry Charles (1815–1885), III, 986
Coote, Richard Holmes (*fl.* 1821), III, 986
Cope, Sir Anthony (d. 1551), I, 803
Cope, Edward Meredith (1818–1873), III, 888, **997**
Cope's Tobacco Plant (1870), III, 830
Copeland, William John (1797–1868), III, 687 (2), 856 (2)
Copernicus, Nicolas, I, 882
Copinger, Walter Arthur (1847–1910), III, 95
Copland, Robert (*fl.* 1508–47), I, 351, 395, 716, 719, 884, 887, 890
Copland, S. (*fl.* 1866), III, 971
Copland, William (*fl.* 1556–69), I, 819
Copleston, Edward (1776–1849), III, 126, **664**
Copleston, W. J. (*fl.* 1851), III, 665
Coplestone, — (*fl.* 1884), III, 801
Copley, Anthony (1567–1607?), I, 435
Copley, Esther, née Hewlett (*fl.* 1824–59), III, 572
Copper Plate Magazine, The (1774), II, 679
Copperplate Magazine; Or, Monthly Cabinet of Picturesque Prints, The (1792), II, 681
Coppinger, Matthew (*fl.* 1682), II, **280**
Coprario (or Cooper), John (1580?–*c.* 1650?), I, 485
COPYRIGHT, II, 91f. (1660–1800), III, 93f. (19 cent.)
Coranto from Beyond the Sea, A (1643), I, 755
CORANTOS, I, 743
Corbet, Henry (*fl.* 1864), III, 766
Corbet, John (1603–1641), I, 907
Corbet, Richard (1582–1635), I, 475
Corbet, T. (*fl.* 1841), III, 982
Corbett, Edward (*fl.* 1890), III, 765
Corbett, Thomas (*fl.* 1792), II, 736
Cordell, Charles (1720–1791), II, 780
Cordemoy, Géraud de, II, 776

Cordery, A. (*fl.* 1878), III, 986
Cordier, Maturin, I, 375; II, 127
Cordonnier de Saint Hyacinthe, Hyacinthe, II, 776
Corelli, Marie (1864–1924), III, 540 f.
'Corinna' (1719), II, 398
Cork, Richard Boyle, Earl of (1566–1643), I, 385
Cork and Orrery, John Boyle, Earl of (1707–1762), I, 841; II, 593, 767, 773
CORK
    Magazines, II, 688 (1779–97)
    Newspapers, II, 737; III, 808
    Printing in, I, 354 (17, 18 cents.)
Cork Advertiser, The (1799), II, 737
Cork Chronicle; Or Free Intelligencer, The (1765), II, 737
Cork Chronicle; Or Universal Register, The (1763), II, 737
Cork Constitution, The (1860), III, 808
Cork Courier, The (1794), II, 737
Cork Daily Advertiser, The (1836), III, 808
Cork Daily Herald, The (1860), III, 808
Cork Evening Post, The (1754), II, 737
Cork Examiner, The (1861), III, 808
Cork Gazette; Or General Advertiser, The (1789), II, 737
Cork General Advertiser, The (1776), II, 737
Cork Herald, The (1856), III, 808
Cork Herald; Or Munster Advertiser, The (1798), II, 737
Cork Journal, The (1778), II, 737
Cork News Letter, The (1717), II, 737
Cork Packet, The (1793), II, 737
Cork Weekly Journal, The (1779), II, 737
Corkine, William (*fl.* 1610), I, 485
Corkran, Alice (d. 1916), III, 574
Corlett, John (*fl.* after 1865), III, 820
Cormack, Sir John Rose (1815–1882), III, 821
Cormon, E., III, 605
Corn Trade Circular, The (1825), III, 819
Corn-Cutter's Journal, The (1733), II, 714
Cornand de la Crose, Jean, II, 672, 674, 675 (3), 776
Cornaro, Ludovico, I, 338
Cornaro, Luigi, I, 452; II, 809
Corneille, Pierre, I, 333, 812; II, 40, 485, 776
Corneille, Thomas, II, 41, 776
Cornelius, Arnold (1711–1757), II, 309
Corner, Julia (1798–1875), III, 567, 1076
Corney, Bolton (1784–1870), I, 663, 783; II, 637, 895; III, 822
Cornhill Magazine, The (1860), III, 829
Cornish, C. L. (*fl.* 1847–54), III, 856
Cornish, Charles John (1859–1906), III, 763
Cornish, H. Warre (*fl.* 1892), III, 835
Cornish, Joseph (1750–1823), II, 108
Cornish, Sidney William (*fl.* 1842), II, 846
Cornish Plays (M.E.), I, 279

'Cornwall, Barry', i.e. Bryan Waller Procter (1787–1874), III, 241, 248, 636, 643
Cornwall, Henry (*fl.* 1720), II, 750
CORNWALL
    Bibliography, I, 8
Cornwallis, Caroline Frances (1786–1858), III, 866
Cornwallis, Jane, Lady (1581–1659), I, 386
Cornwallis, Sir William (d. 1631), I, 725
CORPUS CHRISTI COLLEGE (Cambridge), I, 370
    Library, I, 362; II, 104
CORPUS CHRISTI COLLEGE (Oxford), I, 368
Corpus Glossary (O.E.), I, 36
Corral, G. (*fl.* 1776), II, 709
Corraro, Angelo, II, 809
Correspondance Française (1793), II, 719
Correspondance Politique; Ou, Tableau de L'Europe (1793), II, 719
Correspondents, The (18 cent.), II, 547
Corri, Domenico (1746–1825), II, 234, 241, 244–5
Corrie, George Elwes (1793–1885), I, 669 (2)
Corrigan, Sir Dominic John (1802–1880), III, 125
Corrozet, Gilles (*fl.* 1602), I, 714
Corser, Thomas (1793–1876), I, 4
Corsicans, The (18 cent.), II, 486
Corte, Claudio, I, 812
Cortés, Martín, I, 812
Cory, Sir G. E. (*fl.* 1910), III, 1091
Cory, William, earlier Johnson (1823–1892), III, 292
Coryat, George (*fl. c.* 1600?), I, 775
Coryat, Thomas (1577?–1617), I, 769, 783
Cosin, John (1594–1672), I, 386, 696, 856
Cosmopolitan, The (1788), II, 681
Cosmopolite, The (1832), III, 816
Costeker, John Littleton (*fl.* 1731), II, 119, 539
Costello, Louisa Stuart (1799–1870), III, 231
Costes, Gauthier de, Seigneur de la Calprenède, II, 777
Costigan, Arthur (*fl.* 1737), II, 747
Costlie Whore, The (17 cent.), I, 651
COSTUME, I, 393 (16, 17 cents.); II, 160 (17, 18 cents.), 405 f. (theatrical, 17, 18 cents.)
Cotes, D. (*fl.* 1725), II, 779
Cotes's Weekly Journal; or, The English Stage Player (1734), II, 714
Cotgrave, John (*fl.* 1644–55), I, 405, 756 (2); II, 174
Cotgrave, Randle (d. 1634?), I, 376
Cotsforde, Thomas (*fl.* 1555), I, 820
Cotta, John (1575?–1650?), I, 886, 889, 893
Cottager, The (1761), II, 664
Cotterell, Sir Charles (1612?–1702), I, 815; II, 284
Cotterill, C. F. (*fl.* 1831–50), III, 971, 981
Cotterill, T. (*fl.* 1819), III, 240
Cottin, Sophie, III, 576
Cottle, Amos Simon (1768?–1800), II, 81

Cottle, Joseph (1770–1853), II, 344; III, 198, 231
Cotton, Bartholomew (d. 1298?), I, 116
Cotton, Charles (1630–1687), II, **261** f.
Cotton, Frederick Henry (*fl.* 1888), III, 761
Cotton, Henry (1789–1879), I, 352, 672
Cotton, Sir Henry (b. 1868), III, 1085
Cotton, J. S. (*fl.* 1875), III, 818
Cotton, Nathaniel (1705–1788), II, **314**
Cotton, Nathaniel, the younger (*fl.* 1791), II, 314
Cotton, Sir Robert Bruce (1571–1631), I, 720, 726, 832–3, 837, 847
Cotton, Roger (*fl.* 1596), I, 435
Cotton, William (*fl.* 1859), II, 630
Cotton Vespasian Homilies (M.E.), I, **172**
Cottoni Posthuma (17 cent.), I, 726
Cottrell, C. H. (*fl.* 1867), III, 1014
Coule, I. (*fl.* 1642), I, 754
Coules, F. (*fl.* 1641), I, 752 (2)
Couling, S. (*fl.* 1851), III, 119
Coulson, H. J. W. (*fl.* 1880), III, 986
Coulson, Walter (1794?–1860), III, 800
Coulton, David Trevenna (1810–1857), III, 814 (2)
COUNCIL, THE, I, 402 (16, 17 cents.); II, 168 (17, 18 cents.)
Counsellor, The (1861), III, 817
Count D'Soissons, The (17 cent.), II, 534
Count Piper's Packet (18 cent.), II, 202
Countess of Salisbury, The (17 cent.), II, 534
COUNTIES, ENGLISH
  Bibliographies, I, 8 f.
  Dialects of, I, 45; II, 927 f.
  Magazines, II, 684 f.
  Newspapers, II, 720 f. (1701–1800); III, 801 f. (19 cent.)
  Printers and Booksellers in, I, 352 f. (1500–1660); II, 86 f. (1660–1800)
  Stage and theatres in, II, 404 f.
Countrey Foot-post, The (1644), I, 756
Countrey Messenger, The (1664), I, 756
Countrey Messenger; or, The Faithfull Foot Post, The (1644), I, 756
Country Curate, The (1782), II, 666
Country Gentleman, The (1726), II, 662
Country Gentleman, The (Dublin, 1726), II, 662
Country Gentleman's Courant, The (1706), II, 712
Country Journal or the Craftsman, The (1726), II, 662
Country Journal; Or, The Craftsman, The (1727), II, 713
Country Journal; Or, The Craftsman, The (1750), II, 715
COUNTRY LIFE, II, 147 f. (17, 18 cents.). See also under AGRICULTURE and SPORT
Country Life (1897), III, 815
Country Life Illustrated (1897), III, 759

Country Literary Chronicle and Weekly Review, The (1819), III, 818
Country Magazine, Calculated for the Gentleman, The (1763), II, 678
Country Magazine or, The Gentleman and Lady's Pocket Companion, The (1736), II, 677
Country Mercury, The (1667), II, 716
Country Oracle, The (1741), II, 715
'Country Schoolmaster' (1848), III, 127
Country Spectator, The (1792), II, 666
Country Sport and Messenger of Agriculture (1896), III, 810
Country Times, The (1830), III, 813
Country-mans New Commonwealth, The (17 cent.), I, 716
County Chronicle [etc.], *The* (1787), II, 715
County Chronicle and Weekly Advertiser, The (1787), III, 813
County Gentleman, The (1861), III, 759
County Gentleman, The (1880), III, 820
County Herald and Weekly Advertiser, The (1791), III, 813
County Journal, The (Dublin, 1735), II, 735
County Magazine, The (1786), II, 685
Couper, Archibald Scott (1831–1892), III, 948
Couper, J. R. (*fl.* 1896), III, 1089
Couper (or Cooper), Thomas (1517?–1594), I, 375, 670, 691, 824
Couperus, Louis, III, 339
Courier, The (1792), III, 800
Courier and Argus, The [Dundee] (1899), III, 807
Courier and Evening Gazette, The (1792), II, 711
Courier de L'Europe (1776), II, 698, 719
Courier de Londres (1787), II, 719
Courier de Londres (1808), II, 719
Courier de Londres; ou Mercure Universel de L'Europe (1805), II, 719
Courier Politique et Littéraire (1777), II, 719
Courrier Politique et Littéraire; Or, French Evening Post (1777), II, 711
Course of the Exchange, The (1697), II, 718
COURSING (books on), I, 393 f. (16, 17 cents.); II, 818 f. (1660–1800)
Court, John (*fl.* 1733), II, 761
COURT
  Education at, I, 127 (M.E.)
  Life at, II, 149 f. (17, 18 cents.)
  Plays at, I, 500, 503 (16, 17 cents.)
Court and City Magazine, The (1763), II, 678
Court and City Magazine, The (1770), II, 679
Court and City Medley, The (18 cent.), II, 223
Court Circular, The (1829), III, 813
Court, City and Country Magazine, The (1764), II, 678
Court, City and Country Magazine; The (1788), II, 681

Court Gazette, The (1838), III, 813
Court Jester, The (18 cent.), II, 228, 240, 244
Court Journal, The (1829), III, 813
Court Magazine and Belle Assemblée, The (1832), III, 824
Court Magazine and Monthly Critic, The (1837), III, 824
Court Magazine and Monthly Critic, The (1838), II, 679
Court Magazine and Monthly Critic and Ladies' Magazine and Museum of Belles Lettres, The (1838), III, 823
Court Magazine; Or, Royal Chronicle, The (1761), II, 678
Court Mercurie communicating the most remarkable passages of the Kings Armie, The (1644), I, 756
Court Miscellany, The (1719), II, 195
Court Miscellany, The (1731), II, 201
Court Miscellany; Or, Gentleman and Lady's New Magazine, The (1766), II, 679
Court Miscellany; Or, Ladies New Magazine, The (1765), II, 679
Court of Apollo, Containing Songs, sung at Ranelagh, The (18 cent.), II, 234
Court of Atalantis, The (18 cent.), II, 191, 193, 195, 202
Court of Comus, The (18 cent.), II, 222
Court of Curiosities, The (17 cent.), II, 181
Court of Love, The (M.E.), I, **254**
Court of Oberon, The (19 cent.), III, 576
Court of Thespis, The (18 cent.), II, 226
Court Oracle, The (18 cent.), II, 204
Court Parrot, The (18 cent.), II, 201, 203
Court Poems (18 cent.), II, 192 (2), 193, 195, 198
Court Tales (18 cent.), II, 193
Court Whispers (18 cent.), II, 210
Courte of Venus, The (16 cent.), I, 403
Courtenay, Edward (Earl of Devonshire) (1526?–1556), I, 817
Courtenay, John (1741–1816), II, 624, 654, 665
Courtenay, Thomas Peregrine (1782–1841), I, 597; II, 570; III, 975, 978
Courtesy Literature, I, 378f. (16, 17 cents.); II, 119f. (17, 18 cents.)
Courteville, Ralph (or Raphael) (d. 1772), II, 708
Courthop, Sir George (1616–1685), I, 386
Courthope, William John (1842–1917), III, **738**f., 831
Courtilz de Sandras, Gatien de, II, 535, 676, 777
Courtin, Antoine de, II, 121
Courtney, L. H., Baron (1832–1918), III, 784, 978
Courtney, W. L. (1850–1928), III, 784, 830–1
Cousin, Victor, III, **21**, 110
Cousins, Samuel (1801–1887), III, 90

Cousonages of John West [etc.], *The* (17 cent.), I, 717
Coustard de Massi, Anne Pierre, II, 777
Coutts-Nevill, Francis Burdett Thomas, Baron Latymer (1852–1923), III, **345**, 353
Coutures, Jacques Parrain, Baron des, II, 792
Couvray, Jean Baptiste Louvet de, II, 795
Couvreur, Jessie Catherine ('Tasma') (*fl.* 1889), III, 1096
Covel, John (1638–1722), II, 749
Covell, William (d. 1614?), I, 687, 884
Covenant (16 cent.), I, 907
Covent Garden Drolery (17 cent.), II, 176 (2)
Covent Garden Theatrical Gazette, The (1816), III, 585
Covent-Garden Journal, The (1752), II, 664
Covent-Garden Journal Extraordinary, The (1752), II, 664
Covent-Garden Journal; or, The Censor, The (1752), II, 664
Covent Garden Magazine, The (1772), II, 679
Covent Garden Monthly Recorder, The (1792), II, 682
Coventriae, Ludus (M.E.), I, 39, 277
Coventry, Andrew (1764–1832), III, 970
Coventry, Francis (d. 1759?), II, 544
Coventry, G. (*fl.* 1825), II, 632
Coventry, Henry (d. 1752), II, 16
Coventry
  Library, I, 361
  Magazines, II, 684 (1764–5)
  Newspapers, II, 723 (1741–65)
Coventry, Birmingham and Worcester Chronicle, The (1762), II, 723
Coventry Leet Book (M.E.), I, 42, 121
Coventry Mercury, The (1787), II, 723
Coventry Museum; Or, The Universal Entertainer, The (1764), II, 684
Coventry Plays (M.E.), I, **277**
Coventry Standard, The (1836), II, 723
Coverdale, Myles (1488–1568), I, 45, 665, **669**, 675 (2), 677, 716, 811
Coverte, Robert (*fl.* 1612), I, 783
Cowan, Charlotte Elizabeth Lawson, later Mrs J. H. Riddell (1832–1906), III, **557**f.
Coward, William (1657?–1725), II, 22
Cowdroy's Manchester Gazette and Weekly Advertiser (1797), II, 726
Cowell, Edward Byles (1826–1903), III, 906, **1018**, 1019, 1071
Cowell, J. W. (*fl.* 1843), III, 974
Cowell, John (1554–1611), I, 659, 844, 849
Cowell, John (*fl.* 1672), II, 926
Cowell, S. H. (*fl.* 1851), III, 83
Cowen, Joseph (1831–1900), III, 784, 802
Cowie, G. (*fl.* 1829), III, 77, 92
Cowley, — (*fl.* 1699), captain, II, 741
Cowley, Abraham (1618–1667), I, 365, **458**f., 867; II, 440, 759
Cowley, Hannah (1743–1809), II, **463**f.

Cowley, William (*fl.* 1840), III, 199
Cowley's History of Plants (18 cent.), II, 250
Cowper, Judith, later Madan (*fl.* 1731), II, 27, 296, 302
Cowper, Mary, Countess of (1685–1724), II, 135, 150
Cowper, William (1568–1619), I, 681, 684
Cowper, William (1731–1800), II, 317, **341**f.
Cowper, William, Earl (d. 1723), II, 163
Cowton, Robert (*fl.* 1300), I, **303**
Cox, George Valentine (1786–1875), II, 153
Cox, George William (1827–1902), III, **914**
Cox, I. E. B. (*fl.* 1864), III, 770
Cox, J. E. (*fl.* 1846), I, 669 (2)
Cox, Joseph (*fl.* 1796), II, 155
Cox, Leonard (*fl.* 1524–72), I, 376, 864
Cox, Nicholas (*fl.* 1674), II, 818
Cox, P. S. (*fl.* 1861), III, 815
Cox, Robert (d. 1655), I, 643
Cox, Robert (1810–1872), I, 852; II, 987; III, 950
Cox, Samuel (1826–1893), III, 819, 848
Cox, Thomas (d. 1734), II, **880**
Coxe, Daniel (*fl.* 1722), II, 740, 753
Coxe, Francis (*fl.* 1561), I, 883
Coxe, Henry Octavius (1811–1881), I, 5 (2), 116
Coxe, William (1747–1828), III, **877**f.
Coxeter, Thomas (1689–1747), II, **911**
Coxon, Henry (*fl.* 1896), III, 772
Coxwell, Henry (*fl.* 1718), II, 765
Coyer, Gabriel François, II, 141, 777
Coyne, Joseph Stirling (1803–1868), III, **601**f.
Cozens, Zechariah (*fl.* 1793–1802), II, 858
Crabb, George (1778–1851), II, 51
Crabb, Habakkuk (1750–1794), II, 790
Crabbe, George (1754–1832), II, 138, **345**f.; III, 24
Crabbe, George, the younger (*fl.* 1832), II, 346
Crab-Tree, The (1757), II, 664
Crabhouse Nunnery, The Register of (M.E.), I, 121
Crackanthorpe, Hubert (d. 1897), III, **541**
Crackelt (or Crakelt), William (1741–1812), II, 931
Craddock, T. (*fl.* 1867), III, 634
Cradle of Security, The (16 cent.), I, 517
Cradock, Joseph (1742–1826), II, **464**, 485
Craft of Deyng (M.E.), I, 260
Craftsman, The (1726), II, 698, 713
Craftsman; Or, Say's Weekly Journal, The (1758), II, 715
Crafty Whore, The (17 cent.), I, 717
Craggs, James (1686–1721), II, 761
Craig, Alexander (1567?–1627), of Rosecraig, I, 899
Craig, Isa, later Knox (1831–1903), III, **336**
Craig, John (1512?–1600), Scottish divine, I, 902f.
Craig, John (*fl.* 1814), Glasgow economist, III, 980

Craig, Sir Thomas (1538–1608), I, 910
Craig, William, Lord Craig (1745–1813), II, 108, 114
Craigie, P. G. (*fl.* 1878), III, 979
Craigie, Pearl Mary Teresa ('John Oliver Hobbes') (1867–1906), III, **549**
Craik, Dinah Maria, née Mulock (1826–1887), III, **498**f.
Craik, George Lillie (1798–1866), III, **665**
Craik, Sir Henry (1846–1927), III, **739**
Crakanthorp, Richard (1567–1624), I, 857–8, 875
Crakelt (or Crackelt), William (1741–1812), II, 931
Cramer, John Anthony (1793–1848), III, **994**
Cramer, K. G., II, 805
Cramp, W. (*fl.* 1821), II, 632
Crane, Ralph (*fl.* 1625), I, 475
Crane, Walter (1845–1915), III, 90
Cranley, Thomas (*fl.* 1635), I, 475
Cranmer, George (1563–1600), I, 687
Cranmer, J. A. (*fl.* 1841), I, 383
Cranmer, Thomas (1489–1556), I, **669**f., 675
Cranwell, John (d. 1793), II, 33, 312, 814
Crapelet, Georges Adrien, II, 142
Crashaw, Richard (1612 or 1613–1649), I, **456**f., 679
Crashawe, William (1572–1626), I, 508
Craster, T. (*fl.* 1841), III, 982
Crathorn (*fl.* 1341), I, **306**
Crauford (or Craufurd), Quintin (1743–1819), II, 751
Craufurd (or Crawford), David (1665–1726), II, 576, 996
Craufurd, G. (*fl.* 1803), III, 973
Craven, Elizabeth, Baroness, later Margravine of Anspach (1750–1828), II, **464**
'Craven, Henry Thornton', i.e. Henry Thornton (1818–1905), III, **602**
Craven, Keppel Richard (1779–1851), II, 486
Craven, William George (*fl.* 1870), III, 764
Crawford (or Craufurd), David (1665–1726), II, 576, 996
Crawford, H. (*fl.* 1828), III, **777**
Crawford, Isabella Valancy (*fl.* 1884), III, 1086
Crawford, J. (*fl.* 1836–46), economist, III, 978, 982
Crawford (or Crawfurd), John (1783–1868), III, 1083
Crawford, M. (*fl.* 1732), I, 904
Crawford, William Sharman (1781–1861), III, 971
Crawford and Balcarres, Alexander William C. Lindsay, Earl of (1812–1880), I, 898
Crawfurd, George (d. 1748), II, **876**
Crawfurd, John (1783–1868), III, 790, 990
Crawfurd, Oswald John Frederick (d. 1909), III, 767, 815, 833
Crawfurd, Thomas (d. 1662), I, 910
Crawhall, Joseph (*fl.* 1859), III, 770

'Crawley, Captain' (1866), III, 777

Crealock, Henry Hope (1831–1891), III, 763

Creasy, Sir Edward Shepherd (1812–1878), I, 125; III, 131

Crébillon, Claude Prosper Jolyot de, the younger, II, 47, 542, 544, 783

Crébillon, Prosper Jolyot de, the elder, II, 41, 544, 783

Crediton, a Boy who was entertained by the Devill about (17 cent.), I, 719

Creech, Thomas (1659–1700), II, 29, 763, 765, 766 (2), **936**

Creech, William (1745–1815), II, 671, 695

Creed (O.E.), I, 81

Creevey, Thomas (1768–1838), III, 150

Creichton, John (*fl.* 1731), II, 587

Creighton, Mandell (1843–1901), III, 834, **912**f.

Cremer, John (1700–1774), II, 136

Cresswell, Beatrix F. (*fl.* 1889), III, 570

Cresswell, F. S. (*fl.* 1889), III, 775

Cresswell, Nicholas (*fl.* 1774), II, 756

Cresswick, Mr (*fl.* 1789), II, 242, 245, 247

Cressy, Hugh Paulin [Serenus] (1605–1674), I, 695, **696**

Cressy, R. F. S. [misprint for Hugh P. Cressy], I, 195

Creswell, S. F. (*fl.* 1863), I, 8

Creswell and Burbage's Nottingham Journal (1775), II, 727

Creswell's Nottingham Journal (1756), II, 727

Crèvecœur, Michel Guillaume Jean de (1731–1813), II, 961

Crew of kind London Gossips, A (17 cent.), II, 174

Crewdson, Jane (1808–1863), III, 572

Crewe, Sir G. (*fl.* 1843), III, 976

Crewe, Thomas (*fl.* 1580), I, 715

Crichett, G. A. (*fl.* 1868), III, 834

Crichton, Andrew (1790–1855), II, 151; III, 886

Crichton, Arthur (*fl.* 1818), III, 571

Crichton-Browne, Sir J. (*fl.* 1900), III, 833

CRICKET (books on), II, 824f. (18 cent.); III, 772f. (19 cent.)

Cricket (1882), III, 773

Cricket Field, The (1892), III, 773

Cricketers' Annual (1872), III, 773

CRIME, II, 155f. (17, 18 cents.)

Cripps, — (*fl.* 1587), Lieutenant, I, 788

Cripps, Arthur Shearly (b. 1869), III, 1089–90

Cripps, Sir C. A., Baron Parmoor (*fl.* 1881), III, 986

Cripps, Henry William (*fl.* 1845), III, 986

Crisis, The (1775), II, 665

Crisis, The (1792), II, 666

Crisis, The (1832), III, 816

Crisp, Samuel (d. 1783), II, 61, 138, 154

Crisp, Stephen (1628–1692), II, 134

Crisp, W. F. (*fl.* 1866), III, 77

Crispin, Gilbert (d. 1117), I, **283**f.

Crist (O.E.), I, **76**

Critchett, B. (*fl.* 1804–39), III, 797

Critical Memoirs of the Times (1769), II, 679

Critical Review, Or, Annals of Literature, The (1756), II, 678

CRITICAL TERMS AND THEORIES, II, 10f. (17, 18 cents.)

CRITICISM, LITERARY, I, 863f. (16, 17 cents.); II, 9f. (17, 18 cents.), 39f. (17, 18 cents., French-English); III, 7f. (critical essays, 19 cent.), 70 (influence of), 157f. (of poetry)

Criticisms on the Rolliad (18 cent.), II, 237, 238 (6), 240–1, 244 (2), 245

Critick, The (1718), II, 662

Critick; A Review of Authors and their Productions, The (1718), II, 675

Criticks, The (1719), II, 662, 675

Croal, David (*fl.* 1832–59), III, 784

Crockett, Samuel Rutherford (1860–1914), III, **541**f.

Crosse, G. (*fl.* 1696), II, 854

Croft, George (1747–1809), II, 108, 363

Croft, Sir Herbert (1751–1816), II, 345, 548, 627, 665

Croft, James (*fl.* 1825), II, 341

Croft, John (1732–1820), II, 247 (2)

Crofts, Robert (*fl.* 1638), I, 731

Croghan, George (d. 1782), II, 755

Crokatt, J. (*fl.* 1745), II, 211, 677

Croke, Sir Alexander (1758–1842), I, 677

Croke, Sir John (1553–1620), I, 677

Croker, John Wilson (1780–1857), III, **665**f. Reviews by, III, 223, 257, 300, 368, 494, 686 Works edited by, II, 295, 625, 837, 879

Croker, Richard (*fl.* 1799), II, 748

Croker, Temple Henry (1730?–1790?), II, 808

Croker, Thomas Crofton (1798–1854), I, 387, 449, 631; III, 83, 186, **576**, 577 (2), 890, 892 (2), 1050

Crole (or Crowley), Robert (1518?–1588), I, 677, 719, 824

Croll, James (1821–1890), III, **944**, 952

Croly, George (1780–1860), II, 295, 635; III, **231**f., 648

Cromarty, George Mackenzie, Viscount Tarbat, Earl of (1630–1714), II, **869**

Crombie, Alexander (1762–1840), III, 970, 972

Cromek, Robert Hartley (1770–1812), II, 257, 974

Crompton, Hugh (*fl.* 1657), I, 475, 809

Crompton, Richard (*fl.* 1573–99), I, 849

Crompton, Sarah (*fl.* 1853), III, 572

Cromwell, Oliver (1599–1658), I, 386, 400

Crooke, Helkiah (1576–1635) I, 891

Crookes, Sir William (1832–1919), III, 940, **948**

Crookshank, William (1712?–1769), II, 994

CROQUET (books on), III, 774f.

Crosby, Thomas (*fl.* 1740), II, 125, 862

Crosby's Modern Songster (18 cent.), II, 249

Crosfield, Thomas (b. 1602), I, 386
Crosland, Thomas William Hodgson (1865–1924), III, 336 f.
Cross, Ada, earlier Cambridge (*fl.* 1891–1903), III, 1096
Cross, John C. (*fl.* 1809), III, 588
Cross, Mary Ann, née Evans ('George Eliot') (1819–1880), III, 465 f.
  Reviews and articles by, III, 27, 32, 654, 848
  Translations from, III, 24, 36
Cross, M. (*fl.* 1833), III, 832
Cross, R. (*fl.* 1747), II, 212
Cross, Thomas (*fl.* 1861), III, 765
Crosse, William (*fl.* 1629), I, 807
CROSSES, RUNIC
  Bewcastle, I, 59 f.
  Brussels, I, 85
  Ruthwell, I, 59 f.
Crossgrove, Henry (1663–1744), II, 695
Crossley, James (1800–1883), I, 386, 420, 703, 886
Crossman, Samuel (1624?–1684), I, 475; II, 119
Crosthwaite, J. C. (*fl.* 1846), III, 691
Crouch, E. H. (*fl.* 1907–17), III, 1089
Crouch, Humphrey (*fl.* 1635–71), I, 732
Crouch, John (*fl.* 1648–81), I, 759 (2), 761 (3), 762 (2), 763; II, 701–2
Crouch, Nathaniel ('R. Burton') (1632?–1725?), II, 145, 532, 706
Crousaz, Jean Pierre de, II, 302, 777
Crow (or Crowe), William (1616–1675), I, 359, 854; II, 95
Crowe, Catherine, née Stevens (1800?–1876), III, 482 f., 505
Crowe, Eyre Evans (1799–1866), III, 799
Crowe, Sir Joseph (1825–1896), III, 784
Crowe (or Crow), William (1616–1675), I, 359, 854; II, 95
Crowe, William (1745–1829), II, 358
Crowfoot, John Rustat (1817–1875), I, 699
Crowley (or Crole), Robert (1518?–1588), I, 677, 719, 824
Crown, The (1838), III, 812
Crowne-Garland of Goulden Roses, A (17 cent.), I, 404; II, 174, 179, 182
Crowne, John (d. 1703), II, 61, 419 f., 485, 529
Crowne, William (*fl.* 1637), I, 739, 772
Crowned King (M.E.), I, 200
Crowther, Joseph (*fl.* 1630), I, 655
Croxall, Samuel (d. 1752), II, 24, 314, 759
Croxton Play of the Sacrament (M.E.), I, 279
Croyland Abbey, The Chronicles of (15 cent.), I, 265
Croyser, William (*fl.* 1434), I, 302
Cruden, Alexander (1701–1770), II, 100, 928, 994
Cruickshanks, S. (*fl.* 1881), III, 1089
Cruikshank, George (*fl.* 1734–75), II, 963
Cruikshank, George (1792–1878), III, 91, 453, 576

Cruindmelus (*fl.* 1st half of 9 cent.), I, 108
Cruise, William (d. 1824), II, 963
Crump, A. (*fl.* 1866–89), III, 973–4, 983
Crump, Basil (*fl.* 1843?), III, 821
Crumpe, Samuel (1766–1796), II, 160
Crusius, Lewis (1701–1775), II, 25
Cruso, Aquila (*fl.* 1614–8), I, 655
Cruso, John (d. 1681), I, 390
Cruso, T. (*fl.* 1640), I, 800
Cruttwell, Clement (1743–1808), II, 140
Cruttwell's Sherborne Journal (1764), II, 728
Crutwell, Richard (1776–1846), III, 972
Cry from the Wilderness, The (1712), II, 661
Cubières de Palmézeaux, Michel de, II, 777
Cubitt, G. (*fl.* 1850?), III, 823
Cuckold's Miscellany, The (18 cent.), II, 204
Cuckoo and Nightingale (M.E.), I, 187
Cudworth, Ralph (1617–1688), I, 877
Culbertson, Robert (1765–1823), II, 687
Cullen, Charles (*fl.* 1789), II, 53, 809
Cullen, Stephen (*fl.* 1796), II, 550
Cullinan, M. C. (*fl.* 1867), III, 1010
Culmann, Leonhard, I, 375
Culpeper, Nicholas (1616–1654), I, 890, 892; II, 797
Culpeper (or Culpepper), Sir Thomas (1578–1662), I, 845
Culpeper, Sir Thomas, the younger (1626–1697), I, 726
Culverwel, Ezekiel (*fl.* 1634), I, 725
Culverwel, Nathanael (d. 1651?), I, 878
Cumberland, George (*fl.* 1771–84), II, 112
Cumberland, John (*fl.* 1826), III, 585 (2)
Cumberland, Richard, the elder (1632–1718), I, 872; II, 942
Cumberland, Richard, the younger (1732–1811), II, 108, 452 f., 549–50; III, 825
Cumberland, Richard Denison (*fl.* 1771–84), II, 112
Cumberland Chronicle, The (1776), II, 729
Cumberland Magazine, The (1778), II, 685
Cumberland Packet, The (1898), II, 729
Cumberland Packet and Ware's Whitehaven Advertiser, The (1774), II, 729
Cumberland's British Theatre (1826), III, 585
Cumberland's Minor Theatre (1828), III, 585
Cuming (or Cumming), Sir Alexander (1690?–1775), II, 753
Cuming, E. D. (*fl.* 1897), III, 1085
Cumming, G. (*fl.* 1840), I, 904
Cumming, J. (*fl.* 1806), I, 725
Cummings, R. (*fl.* 1791), II, 972
Cummins, John (*fl.* 1743), II, 754
Cummins, Maria S. (*fl.* 1857), III, 428
Cummyng, Susannah (*fl.* 1798), II, 776
Cunaeus, Petrus, I, 781
Cundall, Joseph (*fl.* 1849), III, 576–7
Cunningham, Alexander (1655?–1730), II, 1000
Cunningham, Allan (1784–1842), II, 306, 977 (3), 984, 986; III, 163, 187, 391 f.

Cunningham, Francis (1820–1875), I, 630

Cunningham, G. (*fl.* 1797), II, 252

Cunningham, Sir Harry Stewart (*fl.* 1875), III, 1069

Cunningham, James (d. 1709?), II, 750

Cunningham, John (1729–1773), II, 358

Cunningham, John William (1780–1861), II, 341; III, 824

Cunningham, Joseph Davey (1812–1851), III, 1076

Cunningham, Peter (*fl.* 1800?), compiler, II, 256

Cunningham, Peter (1816–1869), critic and scholar, III, **1029** f.

　　Editions by, I, 445, 497, 501, 533; II, 295; III, 183, 243, 392 (2)

Cunningham, Thomas Mounsey (1776–1834), III, 232

Cunningham, Timothy (d. 1789), II, 926

Cunningham, W. (1849–1919), III, 974, **983**

Cunningham, William (*fl.* 1559), I, 378, 765, 884

Cunningham, William (*fl.* 1673), of Craigends, II, 156

Cunningham, William (1805–1861), I, 681, 907

Cunningham-Graham, Robert Bontine (1852–1936), III, 990

Cup of Sweets, A (19 cent.), III, 574

Cupid, The (18 cent.), II, 205–7

Cupid and Bacchus (18 cent.), II, 227

Cupid and Hymen (1742), II, 209, 211 (2), 212 (2)

Cupid and Hymen (1772), II, 229

Cupid Triumphant (18 cent.), II, 212

Cupid's Bee-Hive (18 cent.), II, 196

Cupids Garland Set Round about with Gilded Roses (17 cent.), II, 177

Cupid's Masterpiece (17 cent.), II, 179

Cupid's Metamorphoses (18 cent.), II, 199

Cupids Posies (17 cent.), II, 177

Cupid's Soliciter of Love (17 cent.), II, 178

'Curate, Jacob' (1692), II, 994

Cure for a Cuckold, A (17 cent.), I, 651

Cure for the Spleen, The (18 cent.), II, 226

Cure for the State, A (17 cent.), I, 720

Cureau de la Chambre, Marin, II, 777

Cureton, William (1808–1864), III, **1012**

Curiosity, The (18 cent.), II, 207 (2)

Curiosity; Or, Gentlemen and Ladies Repository, The (1740), II, 685

Curious Collection of Songs in Honour of Masonry, A (18 cent.), II, 201

Curious Collection of Scots Poems (18 cent.), II, 224

Curlewis, Ethel, née Turner (b. 1872), III, 570

Curli, — de, II, 533

Curling (books on), III, 777 f.

Curll, Edmund (1683?–1747), II, 100, 202, 293, 296; 301, 403, 407 (2), 611, 820

Curran, W. H. (*fl.* 1840?), III, 595

Currant Intelligence, The (1681), II, 704

Currant Intelligence; Or An Account of Transactions both foreign and domestick, The (1680), II, 703

Currant Intelligence; Or, An Impartial Account of Transactions, The (1680), II, 703

Current, A (1642), I, 753

Current Intelligence, The (1666), II, 702

Current Lists

　　English Studies, I, 3

　　New Books, I, 3

Currey, Frederick (1819–1881), III, 833

Curriculum (educational), II, 110 f.

Currie, A. E. (*fl.* 1906), III, 1093

Currie, J. (*fl.* 1857), III, 108

Currie, James (1756–1805), II, 985

Currie, Mary Montgomerie, Lady, née Lamb, later Singleton (pseudonym 'Violet Fane') (1843–1905), III, **345**

Cursor Mundi (M.E.), I, 32, 39, **182**

Cursus, The. See under Prose Rhythm, I, 23 f.

Curtasye, The Boke of (15 cent.), I, 43, 264

Curteis, Thomas (*fl.* 1725), II, 152

Curties, T. J. Horsley (*fl.* 1801–7), III, **392**

Curtis, G. B. (*fl.* 1900), III, 799

Curtis, Samuel (1779–1860), III, 823

Curtis, William (1746–1799), II, 671; III, 823

Curtis's Botanical Magazine (1801), III, 823

Curtiss, Langley (*fl.* 1682), I, 704

Curtius, Quintus, I, 801

Curwen, Henry (1845–1892), III, 1070

Curwen, John Christian (*fl.* 1818), II, 159

Curwen, Samuel (*fl.* 1775–84), II, 138

Curwers, J. C. (*fl.* 1808), III, 969

Curzon, George Nathaniel, Marquess (1859–1925), III, 990

Curzon, Robert (1810–1873), III, 990

Cussans, John Edwin (1837–1899), III, **928**

Cust, H. J. C. (1861–1917), III, 801

Cust, Robert Needham (1821–1909), III, 1074

Custance, Henry (1842–1908), III, 764

Custance, Olive, later Lady Douglas, III, **337**

Cutcliffe, H. C. (*fl.* 1813), III, 768

Cuthbertson, The Misses (*fl.* 1803–30), III, **392**

Cuthbertson, C. (*fl.* 1896), III, 975

Cuthbertson, James Lister (*fl.* 1893), III, 1095

Cutpell, E. E. (*fl.* 1893), III, 1084

Cutts, H. W. (*fl.* 1874), III, 815

Cutts, John, Baron (1661?–1707), II, **280**

Cutwode, Thomas (*fl.* 1599), I, 436

Cyclic Romances (M.E.), I, 130 f.

　　Alexander Romances, I, 142 f.

　　Arthurian Romances, I, 130 f.

　　Charlemagne Romances, I, 140 f.

　　Godfrey of Bouillon Cycle, I, 146

　　Thebes Cycle, I, 146

　　Troy Romances, I, 144 f.

Cycling (books on), III, 778

Cycling Times (1884), III, 820

Cyder, With the Splendid Shilling, Paradise Lost [etc.] (18 cent.), II, 188 (2)
CYNEWULF SCHOOL, I, 25, 27, 28, 31 f., 35 (linguistic), **75** f.
  Andreas, I, 77
  Crist, I, 76
  Dream of the Rood, I, 78
  Elene, I, 76
  Fates of the Apostles, I, 77
  Guðlac, I, 78
  Harrowing of Hell, I, 78
  Juliana, I, 76 f.
  Phoenix, I, 77
  Physiologus, I, 78
Cynthia: with the Loves of Almerin and Desdemona (17 cent.), II, 531
Cyprian Cabinet, The (18 cent.), II, 203
Cyprian Conqueror, The (17 cent.), I, 651
Cyrano de Bergerac, Hercule Savinien, I, 813; II, 47, 777
Cythereia (18 cent.), II, 197
CZECHO-SLOVAKIA
  Literary Relations with, II, 71 f. (1660–1800), III, 43 (19 cent.)

D., A. (*fl.* 1699), II, 401
D., B. (*fl.* 1648–9), I, 758
D., B. (*fl.* 1651–5), I, 761
D., B. (*fl.* 1662), II, 174
D., G. (*fl.* 1642), I, 753
D., H. (1702), II, 185
D., I. (*fl.* 1598), I, 800
D., I. (*fl.* 1632), I, 795
D., J. (*fl.* 1562), I, 741
D., J. (*fl.* 1640), I, 652
D., J., Gent. (*fl.* 1674), II, 811
D., J. (*fl.* 1686), II, 428
D., J. (*fl.* 1692), II, 28
D., J. (*fl.* 1744), II, 765
D., J. (*fl.* 1779), I, 898
D., J. M. (*fl.* 1752), II, 783
D., L. (*fl.* 1781), II, 785
D., M. (*fl.* 1689), II, 181
D., N. (*fl.* 1661), II, 173
D., R. K. (*fl.* 1831), III, 789
D., T. (*fl.* 1587), I, 738
D., T. (*fl.* 1620?), I, 651
D., T. (*fl.* 1671), II, 816
D., T. (*fl.* 1676), II, 530
D., W. (*fl.* 1657), I, 732
Daborne, Robert (d. 1628), I, 643
Dacier, André, II, 27–8, 777
Dacre, Barbarina Brand, Lady (1768–1854), III, **229**
Dacre, Charlotte, later Byrne (*fl.* 1805), III, **392**
Dacres, Edward (*fl.* 1636–61), I, 816; II, 811
Dafforne, Richard (*fl.* 1640), I, 366
Daft, Richard (1835–1900), III, 774
D'Aguilar, Rose (*fl.* 1799), II, 59

Daily Advertiser, The (1730), II, 698, 708, 717
Daily Advertiser (1751), II, 664
Daily Advertiser, The (1847), III, 799
Daily Advertiser and Oracle, The (1802), III, 798
Daily Argus, The [Birmingham] (1891), III, 806
Daily Argus, The [Dundee] (1859), III, 807
Daily Benefactor, The (1715), II, 662
Daily Bristol Times, The (1865), III, 803
Daily Bulletin [Glasgow] (1855), III, 807
Daily Bullionist, The (1866), III, 820
Daily Chronicle, The (1872), III, 799
Daily Chronicle, The [Newcastle] (1858), III, 802
Daily Courant, The (1702), II, 707–8
Daily Courant, The [Edinburgh] (1860), III, 807
Daily Courier, The (1896), III, 800
Daily Examiner, The [Belfast] (1870), III, 808
Daily Express, The (1877), III, 799
Daily Express, The (1900), III, 800
Daily Express, The [Dublin] (1851), III, 809
Daily Express, The [Edinburgh] (1855), III, 807
Daily Express and Morning Journal [Glasgow] (1870), III, 807
Daily Free Press, The [Aberdeen], III, 806
Daily Gazette, The [Derby] (1860), III, 802
Daily Gazette for Middlesbrough, The (1872), III, 804
Daily Gazetteer, The (1735), II, 708
Daily Gazetteer and London Advertiser, The (1735), II, 698
Daily Gazetteer; Or, London Advertiser, The (1746), II, 708
Daily Graphic, The (1890), III, 793, 815
Daily Guardian, The [Warrington] (1891), III, 806
Daily Herald, The [Ipswich] (1897), III, 806
Daily Independent Press, The [Cambridge] (1892), III, 806
Daily Intelligencer of Court, City and Countrey, The (1643), I, 754
Daily Journal, The (1720), II, 708
Daily Mail, The (1896), III, 793, 800
Daily Mail [Glasgow] (1848), III, 807
Daily Mail, The (Hull) (1896), III, 805
Daily Messenger, The (1896), III, 800
Daily Midland Echo, The [Wolverhampton] (1877), III, 805
Daily Nation, The [Dublin] (1897), III, 809
Daily News, The (1846), III, 793, 799
DAILY NEWSPAPERS, II, 708 f. (1660–1800); III, 798 f. (19 cent.)
Daily Oracle, The (1715), II, 660, 708
Daily Oracle, The (1889), III, 800
Daily Packet; Or, The New London Daily Post, The (1721), II, 708
Daily Politician, The (1836), III, 799
Daily Post, The (1719), II, 708
Daily Post, The [Liverpool] (1853), III, 801
Daily Post, The [Liverpool], III, 802

Daily Post-Boy, The (1728), II, 706, 708
Daily Proceedings, The (1653), I, 762
Daily Record, The [Glasgow] (1895), III, 808
Daily Recorder (of Commerce), The (1866), III, 801
Daily Review, The [Edinburgh] (1861), III, 807
Daily Scotsman, The [Edinburgh] (1855), III, 807
Daily Statement of the Packet Boats (1798), II, 698
Daily Telegram, The [Wisbech] (1877), III, 805
Daily Telegraph, The (1855), III, 793, 799
Daily Telegraph [Manchester] (1855), III, 802
Daily Times, The [Liverpool] (1860), III, 802
Daily Universal Register, The (1785), II, 709
Daily War Telegraph, The [Manchester] (1854), III, 802
Daily Western Mercury, The [Plymouth] (1860), III, 802
Daines, Simon (*fl.* 1640), I, 44, 376
Dairymaid, The (18 cent.), II, 237
Dalby, W. (*fl.* 1834), III, 122
Dale, Henry (*fl.* 1863), III, 948
Dale, Robert William (1829–1895), III, 848
Dale, Sir Thomas (d. 1619), I, 790
Dale, Thomas (*fl.* 1737), II, 302
Dale, Thomas F. (*fl.* 1896), III, 761, 775
Dale's Collection of Sixty Favorite Scotch Songs (18 cent.), II, 249, 250
Daley, Victor James (1858–1905), III, 1095
Dalgairns, John Dobrée [Bernard] (1818–1876), III, 857
Dallam, Thomas (*fl.* 1599), I, 769
Dallas, Alexander Robert Charles (1791–1869), III, 201, 393
Dallas, Eneas Sweetland (1828–1879), I, 17; III, 711f.
Dallas, Robert Charles (1754–1824), III, **392**f.
Dallaway, James (1763–1834), I, 396 [misprinted Dalloway]; II, 748, 835, 838
Dallin, T. F. (*fl.* 1870), III, 1002
Dallington, Sir Robert (1561–1637), I, 778f., 814
Dalrymple, Alexander (1737–1808), II, 251, 741, 749, 915
Dalrymple, David, Lord Hailes (1726–1792), II, **888**, **997**
    Ed. by, I, 697, 878; II, 217, 832, 915
    Minor writings, II, 114, 883, 929
Dalrymple, David (*fl.* 1800), II, 927
Dalrymple, James, Viscount Stair (1619–1695), II, 963, 996, 998
Dalrymple, Sir John (1726–1810), II, **888**
Dalrymple, William (*fl.* 1777), II, 746
Dalta, Harachandra (*fl.* 1871), III, 1068
Dalton, John (1766–1844), III, 135, **946**
D'Alton, John (1792–1867), II, 891
Dalton, Michael (d. 1648?), I, 849
Dalton, Michael (*fl.* 1670), II, 963

Dalton, Regina Maria, later Roche (1764?–1845), III, **415**
Dalton, W. (*fl.* 1860), III, 1069
Dalton's Dublin Impartial News Letter (1734), II, 735
Daly, J. B. (*fl.* 1896), III, 1080
Daly, John (1800–1878), III, 1048
Daly, Robert (1783–1872), II, 108, 1047
Dalyell, Sir John Graham (1775–1851), I, 255, 901; II, 814; III, 955
Dalzel, A. (*fl.* 1862), III, 124
Dalzel, Archibald (*fl.* 1793), II, 749
Dalziel, Charles (*fl.* 1878), III, 820
Dalziel, Edward (1817–1905), III, 91
Dalziel, George (1815–1902), III, 91
Dalziel, J. H. (*fl.* 1894), III, 807
Dame and her Donkeys Five, The (19 cent.), III, 575
Dame Partlet's Farm (19 cent.), III, 575
Dame Siriz (M.E.), I, **161**
Dame Trot and her Comical Cat (19 cent.), III, 575
Damiano da Odemira, I, 395
Dampier, Henry (*fl.* 1779), II, 899
Dampier, William (1652–1715), II, 741, 749
Dance, Charles (1794–1863), III, **588**, 593
Dance, James, later Love (1722–1774), II, 447, 825
Dancer, John (*fl.* 1660–75), I, 819; II, 29, 485, 795, 814
Dancer, N. (*fl.* 1704), II, 186
Dancey, John (*fl.* 1662), II, 532
DANCING (books on), I, 395 (16, 17 cents.); II, 825 (18 cent.); III, 778 (19 cent.)
Dancourt, Florent Carton, II, 41, 774
Daneau, Lambert, I, 713
Danett, Thomas (*fl.* 1566–1601), I, 812, 814
Danican, François André, later Philidor (1726–1795), II, 826
Daniel (O.E.), I, **75**
Daniel of Morley (*fl.* 1175), I, **288**
Daniel, Gabriel, II, 777
Daniel, George (1616–1657), I, 475
Daniel, George (1798–1864), III, **666**
Daniel, H. J. (*fl.* 1849), II, 199
Daniel, Henry (*fl.* 1379), I, **306**
Daniel, Peter Augustin (*fl.* 1870–1904), III, 1030
Daniel, Samuel (1562–1619), I, **422**f., 534, 655, 740, 837, 865
Daniel, Thomas (*fl.* 1795–1810), II, 1079 (2)
Daniel, William (1769–1837), III, 1069, 1079
Daniel, William Barker (1753?–1833), III, 758
DANIEL PRESS, III, 86
Daniell, Edmund Robert (*fl.* 1837), III, 986
Daniell, J. (*fl.* 1655), I, 793
Daniell, John Frederick (1790–1845), III, 947
Daniell, William (*fl.* 1702), II, 749
D'Annunzio, Gabriele, III, 359
Dansey, William (1792–1856), II, 818

Dansie, John (*fl.* 1627), I, 377
Danson, J. T. (*fl.* 1886), III, 984
Dant, J. M. (*fl.* 1800), II, 784
Dante Alighieri, I, 340; II, 67, 809f.; III, **39**, 229 (2), 298, 310, 724
D'Anvers, Alicia (*fl.* 1691), II, 117
'D'Anvers, Caleb' (1731), II, 201
Danvers, Henry (d. 1687), II, 491
Danyel, John (1564?–1625?), I, 485
Daphnis [etc.] (18 cent.), II, 188
d'Après de Mannevillette, J. B. N. D. (*fl.* 1781), III, 1079
D'Arblay, Frances, née Burney (1752–1840), II, **527**f.
Darby, Jonathan George N. (*fl.* 1867), III, 691, 986
Darby, S. (*fl.* 1785), I, 469
Darcie (or Darcy), Abraham (*fl.* 1625), I, 827
Dare, Josiah (*fl.* 1673), II, 121
Darell, John (*fl.* 1652), I, 786
Dares Phrygius, I, 801
Dariot, Claude, I, 883
Darley, George (1795–1846), III, **219**f., 241, 248
DARLINGTON, II, 723 (newspaper)
Darlington Mercury, The (1772), II, 723
Darlington Pamphlet; or, County of Durham Intelligencer, The (1772), II, 723
Darmesteter, Agnes Mary Frances, née Robinson, later Duclaux (b. 1857), III, **355**f.
Darmesteter, James, III, 356
Darnell, William Nicholas (1776–1865), I, 852
Darrell, John (*fl.* 1562–1602), I, 741, 893
Darrell, William (1651–1721), II, 121
Dart, John (d. 1730), II, 22, **314**f.
Dart, Joseph Henry (1817–1887), III, 986
Darton, William (1755–1819), II, 558
Darwell, Elizabeth (*fl.* 1764), II, **385**
Darwin, Charles Robert (1809–1882), III, 24, 36, **952**, **953**f., **956**f., **960**f., 965
Darwin, Erasmus (1731–1802), II, 20, **358**f.
Darwin, Sir Francis (1848–1925), III, 962
Darwin, Sir George Howard (1845–1912), III, 940, 945
Darwin, L. (*fl.* 1897), III, 975
DARWINISM, III, 66f.
Das, Devendranath (*fl.* 1887), III, 1084
Dasent, Sir George Webbe (1817–1896), III, 576–7
D'Assigny, Marius (*fl.* 1671), II, 778, 781
Daston, John (*fl.* 1320), I, **311**
Datta, Harachandra (*fl.* 1853), III, 1083
Datta, Narendranath ('Swami Vivekananda') (*fl.* 1896), III, 1082
Datta, Sasichandra (*fl.* 1848–64), III, 1068, 1083
Daubeny, Charles (1795–1867), III, 947, 951
Daudet, Alphonse, III, **21**
Daunce, Edward (*fl.* 1585), I, 724

Dauncey (or Dauncy), John (*fl.* 1663), II, 770
Dauncey, W. (*fl.* 1838), II, 968
Daus, John (*fl.* 1560), I, 817
D'Auvergne, Edward (1660–1737), II, 124
Davall, P. (*fl.* 1723), II, 781
Davanzati Bostichi, Bernardo, I, 846
Davenant (or D'Avenant), Charles (1656–1714), II, 268, 958
Davenant (or D'Avenant), Sir William (1606–1668), I, 453ff., 866
Davenant (or D'Avenant), William, the younger (d. 1681), II, 785
Davenport, John (1597–1670), I, 894
Davenport, Richard Alfred (1777?–1852), II, 257, 260, 881
Davenport, Robert (*fl.* 1623), I, 643f.
Davenport, S. T. (*fl.* 1869), III, 81
Davenport, Selina (*fl.* 1814–34), III, **393**
Davenport, William Bromley (*fl.* 1885), III, 767
Davey, William (*fl.* 1865), III, 773
Davidson, Andrew Bruce (1831–1902), III, 850, **1012**
Davidson, C. J. S. (*fl.* 1851), Anglo-Indian dramatist, III, 1068
Davidson, Charles (*fl.* 1855), lawyer, III, 986
Davidson, James (1793–1864), I, 8
Davidson, John (1549?–1604), I, 903
Davidson, John (1857–1909), III, **337**
Davidson, Joseph (*fl.* 1746), II, 767–8
Davidson, Samuel (1806–1898), III, 848
Davidson, Thomas (1838–1870), Scottish poet, III, 337
Davidson, Thomas (1840–1900), philosopher, III, **866**f.
Davies, Augusta, later Webster (1837–1894), III, **362**f.
Davies, Christian (1667–1739), II, 151
Davies, Clement (*fl.* 1886), III, 777
Davies, D. (*fl.* 1896–1901), III, 824
Davies, David (d. 1819?), II, 148
Davies, Edward W. L. (*fl.* 1878), III, 761
Davies, Emily (1830–1921), III, 142
Davies, F. (*fl.* 1774), II, 847
Davies, G. (*fl.* 1840), III, 117
Davies, G. C. (*fl.* 1876), III, 771
Davies, G. S. (*fl.* 1871), III, 835
Davies, J. (*fl.* 1882), Sanskrit translator, III, 1072
Davies, James (*fl.* 1607), I, 789
Davies, John (1565?–1618), of Hereford, poet and writing-master, I, 346, 377, **425**, 446, 679
Davies, Sir John (1569–1626), poet and lawyer, I, **426**f., 837, 844, 874
Davies, John (1627?–1693), of Kidwelly, translator, I, 476, 819 (3); II, 69, 532–3, 759–60, 777 (2), 796, 800 (2)
Davies, John (o Fallwyd) (*fl.* 1710), II, 77
Davies, John (1679–1732), classical scholar, II, **936**

Davies, John Llewellyn (1826–1916), III, 850
Davies, Miles (1662–1715?), II, 101, 908
Davies, R. (*fl.* 1889), Persian scholar, III, 1071
Davies, Richard (1635–1708), Welsh quaker, II, 856
Davies, Richard (d. 1762), physician, II, 115
Davies, Robert (1793–1875), I, 9; II, 864
Davies, Rowland (1649–1721), II, 135
Davies, Thomas (1712?–1785), II, 449, 895, **913**
    Ed. by, I, 453; II, 229, 230 (2), 237, 440, 614, 913
Davies, William (*fl.* 1614), traveller, I, 770
Davies, William (1830–1896), III, **285**
D'Avignon, E. H. (*fl.* 1882), III, 761
Davila, Enrico Caterino, II, 810
Davin, Nicholas Flood (*fl.* 1889), III, 1086
Davis, A. (*fl.* 1898), Australian novelist, III, 1089, 1093
Davis, Alexander (*fl.* 1869), writer on cycling, III, 778
Davis, Emily, later Pfeiffer (1827–1890), III, **303**f.
Davis, Henry Edwards (*fl.* 1778), II, 883
Davis, J. E. (*fl.* 1858), historian of Windsor, I, 826
Davis, Jo. (*fl.* 1687), translator of Bossuet, II, 772
Davis (or Davys), John (1550?–1605), I, 390, 794
Davis, Sir John Francis (1795–1890), III, **1019**
Davis, Joseph Barnard (1801–1881), III, 967
Davis, Nathan (1812–1882), III, **895**
Davis, Nathaniel (*fl.* 1702), II, 753
Davis, Thomas Osborne (1814–1845), III, **1052**
Davis, W. (*fl.* 1728), II, 708
Davis, William (*fl.* 1825), II, 526
Davison, James William (1813–1885), III, 712
Davison, John (1777–1834), III, 126, 847
Davison, William (1541?–1608), I, 384
Davitt, Michael (1846–1906), III, 818
Davy, Adam (*fl.* 1308?), I, 167
Davy, Sir Humphry (1778–1829), III, 769, 945, **946**
Davy, John (1790–1868), III, 770, 946, 990
Davy, William (*fl.* before 1783), III, 1070
Davy du Perron, Jacques, II, 777
Davys (or Davis), John (1550?–1605), I, 390, 794
Davys, Mary (*fl.* 1724–56), II, 538 (2), 539
Dawes, Richard (1708–1768), Greek scholar, II, 936
Dawes, Richard (1793–1867), dean of Hereford, III, 108f.
Dawkins, Sir William Boyd (1837–1929), III, 968
Dawks, Ichabod (1661–1731), II, 695
Dawks, J. (*fl.* 1697), II, 706
Dawks's News Letter (1696), II, 692, 710
Dawson, George (1821–1876), III, 804, 853

Dawson, James (*fl.* 1865), III, 581
Dawson, John (*fl.* 1761), II, 151
Dawson, Sir John William (1820–1899), III, 952, 967
Dawson, Thomas (*fl.* 1587), I, 396
Dawson, Thomas (*fl.* 1732), II, 758
Dawson, William James (1854–1928), III, **338**
Day, Angel (*fl.* 1586), I, 804
Day, Isaac (*fl.* 1807), III, 571
Day, James, (*fl.* 1637), I, 475
Day, John (*c.* 1574–*c.* 1640), I, 351, 534f.
Day, Sir John C. F. S. (1826–1908), III, 986
Day, Richard (1552–1607?), I, 684, 824
Day, Thomas (1748–1789), II, 49, 112, 243, 548, 557, 563
Day, W. J. (*fl.* 1841), III, 77
Day, William (1823–1908), III, 764
Day, The (1809), III, 798
Day, The [Glasgow] (1832), III, 807
Day, The (1867), III, 799
Day and New Times, The (1817), III, 799
Daylight [Norwich] (1878), III, 818
De, Amritalal (*fl.* 1889), III, 1078
De, Nandalal (*fl.* 1899), III, 1080
Deacon, John (*fl.* 1616), I, 718
Deacon, Thomas (1697–1753), II, 788, **852**
Deacon, William Frederick (1799–1845), III, 193, 800
'Deadfall' (1868), III, 762
Dean, Jasper (*fl.* 1711), II, 753
Dear Variety (18 cent.), II, 236
Dearden, W. (*fl.* 1859), III, 240
Death and Liffe (M.E.), I, **200**f.
De Beauchesne, John (*fl.* 1570), I, 346
De Beck, A. M. (*fl.* 1900), III, 831
Deborah Dent and her Donkey (19 cent.), III, 575
De Cardonell, later Cardonell-Lawson, Adam (d. 1820), I, 59
Deceyte of Women, The (16 cent.), I, 716, 728
de Chatelain, Catherine (*fl.* 1847), III, 572, 576
Decker, Sir Matthew (1679–1749), II, 958
Declaration collected out of the Journals of both Houses of Parliament, A (1648), I, 759
Decoisnon, D. (*fl.* 1676), II, 775
De Colyar, Henry Anselm (*fl.* 1894), III, 986
Decremps, Henri, II, 145
De Crespigny, Sir Claude Champion (1847–1935), III, 767
Dedekind, Friedrich, I, 328, 813; II, 32
Dee, John (1527–1608), I, 363, 384, 801, 880 (2), 883, 885–6
DEER-STALKING (books on), III, 763
Deffand, Marie, Marquise du, II, 46; III, 409
Defoe, B. N. (*fl.* 1735), II, 713
Defoe, Daniel (1660–1731), II, **495**f.
    Authenticated writings, II, 496f.
    Bibliographies, II, 495f.
    Biography and criticism of, II, 511f.

Defoe (*cont.*)
  Conjectural attributions, II, 151, 532, 536, 538, 692, 783, 792
  Periodicals ed. by, II, 510, 659–61, 676 (2), 706–8, 710, 712, 731
  Translations from, II, 48–9, 64
Degare, Sir (M.E.), I, **153**
Degge, Sir Simon (1612–1704), II, 963
Degrevant, Sir (M.E.), I, **158**
'Dehan, Richard', i.e. Clotilda Inez Mary Graves (*fl.* 1910), III, 1090
De Imitatione Christi, I, 266
Deist or Moral Philosopher, The (1819), III, 816
Dekker, Thomas (1572?–1632), I, **619**f., 715, 730, 740, 889
De la Beche, Sir Henry Thomas (1776–1855), III, **951**
Delacoste, J. (*fl.* 1719), II, 799
Delacour, A., III, 625–6
De la Faye, Charles (*fl.* 1702), II, 702
Delamaine, Richard (*fl.* 1631), I, 882
De la Mare, William (d. 1298), I, **295**
De la Mothe, G. (*fl.* 1595), I, 377
De la Motte, P. (*fl.* 1847), III, 83
Delane, John Thaddeus (1817–1879), III, 784, 798
De la Pryme, Abraham (1672–1704), II, 134
Delavigne, Casimir, III, 209, 590, 604
Delavigne, Germain, III, 591
Delany, Mary (1700–1788), II, **842**
Delany, Patrick (1685?–1768), II, 232, 234 (2), 593 (2), 663
Delap, John (1725–1812), II, **464**f.
Deletanville, Thomas (*fl.* 1796), II, 126
Delicate Jester, The (18 cent.), II, 234, 256
Delicate Songster, The (1767), II, 224
Delicate Songster, Or, Ladies Vocal Repository, The (1795), II, 250
Deliciae Musicae (17 cent.), II, 183 (7)
Deliciae Poeticae (18 cent.), II, 187, 188 (2), 192
Delight and Pastime (17 cent.), II, 183
Delightful and Ingenious Novels (17 cent.), II, 531
Delightful New Academy of Compliments, The (18 cent.), II, 223
Delightful Vocal Companion, The (18 cent.), II, 230
Delights for the Ingenious (1684), II, 179
Delights for the Ingenious (1711), II, 190, 676
Delights of the Muses, The (18 cent.), II, 207
Delille, Jacques, II, 45
Delineator, The (1779), II, 665
De Laune, Thomas (d. 1685), II, 145, 499, 693
Delectable Demaundes and Pleasant Questions (16 cent.), I, 716
Dell, Henry (*fl.* 1766), II, 90, 224
Dell, William (d. 1664), I, 367, **696**
Della Casa, Giovanni, I, 338, 378, 812
DELLA CRUSCANS, THE, II, 390f.
della Porta, G. B., I, 655, 657 (2), 659, 660

Delle Colonne, Guido, I, 812
Del Mar, A. (*fl.* 1885), III, 974
De Lolme, Jean Louis (1740?–1807), II, 632, **889**
Deloney, Thomas (1543?–1607?), I, 404 (2), 721, 730, 738; II, 177
Delphick Oracle, The (1719), II, 675
Delusseux, J. (*fl.* 1729), II, 772
de M., D. F. R. (*fl.* 1589), I, 739
Demaundes Joyous, The (16 cent.), I, 716
Demaus, Robert (1829?–1874), I, 669
Demeanor, The Booke of (17 cent.), I, 264
De Mille, James (*fl.* 1869), III, 1087
Democrat, The (1884), III, 818
Democratic Recorder and Reformer's Guide, The (1819), III, 816
Democratic Review, The (1849), III, 828
'Democraticus' (1779), II, 665
Democritus (18 cent.), II, 228, 237
'Democritus Junior' (*fl.* 1679), II, 178
Democritus Ridens; Or, Comus and Momus (1681), II, 657
De Moivre, Abraham (1667–1754), II, 960–1
Demolins, E. (*fl.* 1897), III, 109
De Morgan, Augustus (1806–1871), I, 880; III, 105, 125, **867**, **942**
Demosthenes, I, 801; II, 760
Dempster, George (1732–1818), II, 650
Dempster, Thomas (1579?–1625), I, 10, 860, 898
Dendy, Walter Cooper (1794–1871), III, 221
Denham, Dixon (1786–1828), III, 990
Denham, Henry (*fl.* 1591), I, 352
Denham, Sir James Steuart (1712–1780), II, 956; III, 972, 979
Denham, Sir John (1615–1669), I, **457**f., 809, 866; II, 199
Deniehy, Daniel Henry (*fl.* before 1884), III, 1097
Denina, Carlo Giovanni Maria, II, 810
Denis (or Dennis), Charles (d. 1772), II, **359**, 551
Denison, George Anthony (1805–1896), III, 117–8, 137
Denison, John (d. 1629), I, 681
Denison, John Evelyn, Viscount Ossington (1800–1873), III, 152
Denison, W. (*fl.* 1846), III, 774
Denman, Thomas Baron (1779–1854), III, 443
DENMARK
  Literary Relations with, II, 70f. (1660–1800), III, 42f. (19 cent.)
  Loan-Words from Danish, I, 33
Denne, J. (*fl.* 1673), II, 491 (2)
Denney, James (1856–1917), III, 850
Dennis (or Denis), Charles (d. 1772), **359**, II, 551
Dennis, John (1657–1734), II, 44, **571**f., 771
Dennis, John (*fl.* 1863), III, 818
Denny, Sir William (d. 1676), I, 644
Dennys, John (d. 1609), I, 394
Denson, J. (*fl.* 1829), III, 826

Dent, C. T. (*fl.* 1892), III, 777
Dent, J. M. (1849–1926), III, 98
Dent, John (*fl.* 1785?), II, 457
Dent, John Charles (*fl.* 1881), III, 1087
Denton, Daniel (*fl.* 1670), II, 752
Denton, William (1605–1691), II, 813
Deor (O.E.), I, **68**f.
De Peyster, J. F. (*fl.* 1866), III, 105
De Pisan, Christine [du Castel], I, 262 (2)
De Prati, J. (*fl.* 1829), III, 112
De Principis Institutione (M.E.), I, 127
De Quincey, Thomas (1785–1859), III, **648**f.
  Articles by, I, 212, 471; II, 934; III, 47, 49,
    50, 57, 109, 132, 157, 636
  Translations from, III, 24, 45
Derby, Edward George Geoffrey Smith
  Stanley, Earl of (1799–1869), III, **306**f.
Derby, Edward Henry Stanley, Earl of (1826–
  1893), III, 149
Derby, Ferdinando Stanley, Earl of (1559?–
  1594), I, 546
Derby, II, 723 (newspapers)
Derby and Burton Evening Gazette, The (1880),
  III, **805**
Derby and Burton Gazette (1881), III, 805
Derby and Derbyshire Gazette, The (1866), III,
  802
Derby Daily Telegraph and Reporter, The
  (1879), III, 805
Derby Evening Gazette, The (1879), III, 805
Derby Evening Gazette, The (1884), III, 805
Derby Exchange Gazette, The (1860), III, 802
*Derby Herald; Or, Derby, Nottingham and
  Leicester Advertiser, The* (1792), II, 723
Derby Mercury, The (1733), II, 723
Derby Mercury, The (1789), II, 723
Derby Morning Post, The (1885), III, 806
Derby Postman, The (1719), II, 723
DERBYSHIRE, II, 86 (printing)
Derham, Enid (*fl.* 1912), III, 1096
Derham, William (1657–1735), II, 927, 947
Dering, Edward (1540?–1576), I, 681
Dermody, Thomas (1775–1803), III, **232**
Dermott, Laurence (1720–1791), II, 217, 222,
  233, 235, 240, 250
Derodon, David, II, 777
Derozio, Henry Louis Vivian (*fl.* 1827), III,
  1068
Derrick, Samuel (1724–1769), II, 139, 159, **359**
Derrick's Jests (18 cent.), II, 226
Derricke, John (*fl.* 1578), I, 774
Derry Journal, The (1880), II, 738
Derzhavin, G. R., III, 228
Desaguliers, John Theophilus (1683–1744), II,
  114, 197, 327, 960
Desainliens, Claude, i.e. Claudius Hollyband,
  (*fl.* 1575), I, 377, 814
Descartes, René, I, 331, 813; II, 35, 777
Deschamps, François Michel Chrétien, II, 41,
  778

*Description of the Round-Head and Rattle Head,
  A* (17 cent.), I, 723
DESCRIPTIONS, GEOGRAPHICAL, I, 765f. (16, 17
  cents.)
Deserres de la Tour, M., II, 719 (2)
Desfontaines, Pierre François Guyot, II, 542
Desiderata Curiosa (18 cent.), II, 202, 204, 233
Desjardins, Marie Catherine Hortense, II, 778
Des Maizeaux, Pierre (1673?–1745), I, 826; II,
  688, 770, 799, **909**
Desmarets de Saint Sorlin, Jean, I, 733
Despairing Lover, The (18 cent.), II, 188
Despairing Shepherd, The (18 cent.), II, 188
Des Periers, Jean Bonaventure, II, 778
Desportes, Philippe, I, 332, 334, 813
Destouches, Philippe Néricault, II, 41, 792
Destruction of Jerusalem (couplet version) (M.E.),
  I, **157**f.
Destructive and Poor Man's Conservative, The
  (1833), III, 816
Desvoeux, V. (*fl.* 1751), II, 687
Detector, The (Dublin, 1800), II, 736
Detrosier, Rowland (1800?–1834), III, 816
Devas, C. S. (*fl.* 1883), III, 984
De Veil, Hans (*fl.* 1737), II, 543
Devenish, Anne D. (*fl.* 1747), II, 431
De Vere, Sir Aubrey, originally Hunt (1788–
  1846), III, **232**
De Vere, Aubrey Thomas (1814–1902), III,
  1052f.
Deverell, earlier Pedley, Robert (1760–1841),
  II, 685
Devereux, Robert, Earl of Essex (1566–1601),
  I, 436
Devereux, Walter, Earl of Essex (1541?–1576),
  I, 436
Devereux, W. B. (*fl.* 1853), I, 382
Devil, The (1755), II, 664
Devil, The (1786), II, 666
Devil upon Crutches in England, The (18 cent.),
  II, 545, 664
Devil's Pocket-book, The (1786), II, 666
Devils Cabinet Broke Open, The (17 cent.), I, 718
Devon and Exeter Daily Gazette, The (19 cent.),
  III, 793
Devon Evening Express, The (1873), III, 803
DEVONSHIRE
  Bibliographies, I, 8
  Booksellers of, I, 353 (17, 18 cents.)
Devonshire, Georgiana Cavendish, Duchess of
  (1757–1806), II, 548
Devonshire, John (*fl.* 1794), II, 250
DEVOTIONAL WRITINGS. See RELIGIOUS AND
  DEVOTIONAL WRITINGS
Dewar, George Albemarle Bertie (b. 1862),
  III, 772
Dewar, Sir James (1842–1923), III, 940
D'Ewes, Sir Simonds (1602–1650), I, 386
Dewey, William (*fl.* 1673), II, 766
De Worde, Wynkyn (d. 1534?), I, 351

Dewsbury, William (1621–1688), II, 857
Dey, Lal Behari (*fl.* 1874), III, 1068, 1072
Deyverdun, Georges (*fl.* 1768), II, 34, 684
Dhanakoti Raju, W. E. (*fl.* 1887), III, 1078
Dharmapala, H. (*fl.* 1900), III, 1078
Dial, The (1858), III, 814
DIALECTS
    Old English, I, 34f.
    Middle English, I, 38f.
    Modern English, I, 45f.; II, 927f. (glossaries)
Dialogue between Mistris Macquerella [etc.], *A*
    (17 cent.), I, 717
Dialogue between the Hangman and Death, A
    (17 cent.), I, 720
Dialogue betweene Prince Ruperts Dogge [etc.]
    (17 cent.), I, 719
Dialogue concerning the present Revolution, A
    (1689), II, 658
DIALOGUE PAPERS, II, 656f. (1676–1718)
DIALOGUES, COMIC, I, 714f. (16, 17 cents.)
Dialogus de Scaccario (M.E.), I, 117
Diamond Magazine, The (1831), III, 826
Diaper, William (1686?–1717), II, **315**
Diarian Miscellany, The (18 cent.), II, 230
Diarie or an Exact Journall of the Proceedings
    of the Treaty betwixt the Parliament and
    the Army, A (1647), I, 757
DIARIES, I, 381f. (16, 17 cents.); II, 133f. (17,
    18 cents.), 156 (17, 18 cents. Scottish),
    158f. (17, 18 cents. Irish), 827f. (Evelyn,
    Pepys, etc.); III, 149f. (19 cent.)
Diary, The (1651), I, 761
Diary, or an Exact Journal, A (1646), I, 756
Diary of the Royal Tour, A (18 cent.), II, 242
Diary; Or, Woodfall's Register, The (1789), III,
    709
Dibben, Thomas (d. 1741), II, 289
Dibdin, Charles (1745–1814), II, 226, 254,
    465, 800, 822, 916; III, 763
Dibdin, Charles Isaac Mungo (1768–1833), III,
    588f.
Dibdin, Thomas Frognall (1776–1847), I, 667;
    II, 666; III, 818, **1023**f.
Dibdin, Thomas John (1771–1841), II, 392,
    486; III, 585, 587, **589**
Dibdin, The (18 cent.), II, 250
Dibdin's Charms of Melody (18 cent.), II, 252
Diceto, Ralph de (d. 1202?), I, 116
Dicey, Albert Venn (1835–1922), III, 986
Dicey, Edward (1832–1911), III, 799, 810
Dick of Devonshire (17 cent.), I, 651
Dick, Sir Alexander (1703–1785), II, 745
Dick, H. St John (*fl.* 1873), III, 771
Dick, Robert (*fl.* 1776), Edinburgh journalist,
    II, 686
Dick, Robert (1811–1866), geologist, III, 977
Dickens, Charles (1812–1870), III, **435**f.
    Articles or reviews by, III, 109, 581, 596, 640
    Dramatisations from, III, 599, 608
    Translations from, III, 24, 36, 40, 41, 43, 45

Dickens, Charles (1837–1896), III, 818
Dickens, Mamie (*fl.* 1880), III, 449
Dickenson, John (*fl.* 1594), I, 436, 730
Dickenson, Mary, née Hamilton (*fl.* 1756–
    1816), II, 137, 150
Dickes, William (1815–1892), III, 91
Dickinson, F. H. (*fl.* 1854), III, 908
Dickinson, G. (*fl.* 1835), III, 978
Dickinson, G. L. (1862–1932), III, 984
Dickinson, James (1659–1741), II, 754
Dicks, John (*fl.* 1866), III, 585 (2)
Dick's Standard Plays (1875), III, 585
Dickson, David (1583–1663), I, 907
Dickson, R. W. (*fl.* 1805), III, 969
Dickson, William (*fl.* 1789–97), II, 757, 790
Dickson, William Purdie (1823–1901), III, 33
Dickson's News Letter (1727), II, 734
DICTION, I, 30f.; II, 172 (poetry, 17, 18 cents.)
DICTIONARIES, I, 25f. (English), 114f. (M.E.),
    375 (Latin, etc., 1500–1660); II, 926f.
    (technical terms, dialects, concordances,
    glossaries, etc., 1660–1800)
    Biographical dictionaries, II, 921f. (1660–
    1800)
Dictionary of Love, The (19 cent.), II, 255
Dicuil (d. *c.* 825), I, **108**
DIDACTIC WRITINGS, I, 78f. (O.E. poems), 94
    (O.E. prose), 177f. (M.E.). See also under
    EDUCATION and RELIGION
Diderot, Denis, II, 41, 552, 778; III, 22, 405
Dieulafoi, Joseph Marie Armand Michel, III,
    590
Digby, Everard (*fl.* 1579–95), I, 395, 873
Digby, Francis (*fl.* 1635), II, 763
Digby, George, Earl of Bristol (1612–1677), I,
    815; II, **418**f.
Digby, John (*fl.* 1712–6), II, 760–1, 765, 779, 804
Digby, Sir Kenelm (1603–1665), I, 396, 834,
    842, 866, 877, 887
Digby, William (*fl.* 1776), II, 152
Digby Plays (M.E.), I, **279**
Digges, Sir Dudley (1583–1639), judge, I, 398,
    794, 847
Digges, Dudley (1613–1643), political writer,
    I, 725
Digges, Leonard (d. 1559?), mathematician, I,
    378, 880, 882
Digges, Leonard (1588–1635), poet and trans-
    lator, I, 592, 801
Digges, Thomas (1545–1595), I, 378, 725, 880,
    882–3
Digges, West (1720–1786), II, 971
Dilke, Ashton Wentworth (1850–1883), III, 810
Dilke, Charles Wentworth (1789–1864), III,
    449, **666**f., 818
Dilke, Sir Charles Wentworth (1810–1869),
    III, 970
Dilke, Thomas (*fl.* 1696), II, **420**
Dillingham, John (*fl.* 1643–9), I, 748, 755 (2),
    756, 760–1

Dillingham, William (1617?–1689), I, 370, 827, 878 (2); II, 901
Dillon, Sir John Talbot (1740?–1805), II, 746
Dillon, Peter (1785?–1847), III, 990
Dillon, Wentworth, Earl of Roscommon (1633?–1685), II, 21, **285**f.
Dilucidator; Or, Reflections upon Modern Transactions, The (1689), II, 658, 705
Dilworth, Thomas (*fl.* 1740), II, 931
Dilworth, W. A. (*fl.* 1760), II, 803
Dilworth, W. H. (*fl.* 1758), II, 593
Dimock, James Francis (1810–1876), I, 290
Dimock, Nathaniel (1825–1909), III, 853
Dimond, William (1780?–1836?), III, 194, **589**
Dimsdale, Joshua (*fl.* 1782), II, 761
Dineley, Thomas (*fl.* 1681), II, 159
Ding, L. (*fl.* 1785), II, 239
Dingley, Francis (*fl.* 1578), I, 413
Dio Cassius, II, 760
Diodati, John (or Giovanni) (*fl.* 1643–56), I, 856 (2)
Diodorus Siculus, I, 409, 767, 801; II, 760
Diogenes Laertius, II, 760
Dionysius of Halicarnassus, II, 760
Dionysius Periegetes, I, 765, 801
Diplomatic Review, The (1866), III, 829
Dircks, Henry (1806–1873), I, 852; III, 75
Director, The (1720), II, 662
Director, The (1807), III, 818
DIRECTORIES, III, 73 (paper trade)
Dirty Dogs for Dirty Puddings (18 cent.), II, 202
Disloyal Favourite, The (17 cent.), I, 651
Disney, John (1746–1816), II, 895
Disraeli, Benjamin, Earl of Beaconsfield (1804–1881), III, 125, **423**f.
    Translations from, III, 24, 36
D'Israeli, Isaac (1766–1848), II, 20, **908**; III, 201, **667**
Diss, Walter (*fl.* 1404), I, **313**
DISSENTERS
    Admission to Universities, III, 122
    Dissenting Academies, II, 118 f.
    Literature of Dissent, I, 9 (bibliographies); II, 861 f. (1660–1800)
Dissenting Gentleman's Magazine, The (1750) II, 677
Distichs of Cato (O.E.), I, **94**
Distichs of Cato (M.E.), I, **185**
Distracted Emperor, The (17 cent.), I, 652
Distructio Jerusalem (alliterative version) (M.E.), I, **158**
Ditters von Dittersdorf, C., II, 805
Diurnal Occurrances, Touching the dayly Proceedings in Parliament (1641), I, 752
Diurnal Occurrences, or Proceedings in the Parliament the last weeke, The (1642), I, 752
Diurnal Occurrences or, The Heads of Proceedings in both Houses of Parliament (1642), I, 752

Diurnal Occurrences, Touching the dailie Proceedings in Parliament, The (1642), II, 730
Diurnal of Remarkable Occurrents (16 cent.), I, 903
Diurnall and Particular of the last weekes daily Occurrents, A (1642), I, 753
Diurnall Occurrances in Parliament, The (1642), I, 752
Diurnall Occurrances: or, The Heads of Proceedings in Parliament, The (1641), I, 752
Diurnall Occurrences in Parliament (1642), I, 752
Diurnall Ocurrences in Parliament (1642), I, 753
Diurnall Occurrences, or, The Heads of Severall Proceedings in both Houses of Parliament (1641), I, 752
Diurnall of Some Passages and Affairs, A (1652), II, 730
Diurnall, or, The Heads of All the Proceedings in Parliament, The (1641), I, 752
Diutinus Britanicus (1646), I, 757
Divell a Married Man, The (17 cent.), I, **716**
Diverting Muse, The (18 cent.), II, 187
Diverting Post, The (1704), II, 186–7, 676
Diverting Post, The (Dublin, 1709), II, **734**
Diverting Post (1725), II, 734
Dives et Pauper (15 cent.), I, 266
Divine Hymns and Poems (1704), II, 186, 188, 195
Divine Hymns and Poems (1708), II, 188
Divine, Moral, and Historical Miscellanies (18 cent.), II, 220–2
DIVINITY. See RELIGIOUS AND DEVOTIONAL WRITINGS. See also PHILOSOPHY
    Catalogues, II, 95 f. (1660–1800)
Dix, John (1800?–1865?), II, 345; III, 168
Dixie, Lady Florence Caroline (1857–1905), III, 990
Dixon, Charles (*fl.* 1893), III, 763
Dixon, George (d. 1800?), II, 742
Dixon, H. (*fl.* 1854), III, 299
Dixon, Henry Hall (1822–1870), III, 763
Dixon, J. H. (*fl.* 1845), I, 272
Dixon, Richard Watson (1833–1900), III, **338**
Dixon, Robert (d. 1688), II, 288
Dixon, Thomas (*fl.* 1744), II, 827
Dixon, W. Willmott (*fl.* 1898), III, 767, 776, 784
Dixon, William Hepworth (1821–1879), III, 818, **899**, 990
Dixon, William Scarth (*fl.* 1889–1900), III, 761
Dobbs, Arthur (1689–1765), II, 754
Dobell, Bertram (1842–1914), III, 103
Dobell, Sydney Thompson (1824–1874), III, **285**f. 464 (review)
Doble, C. E., III, 818
Dobree, Peter Paul (1782–1825), III, **994**
Dobson, George (*fl.* 1607), I, 730
Dobson, Henry Austin (1840–1921), III, **739**f.
Dobson, Susanna (d. 1795), II, 784, 798, 812

Dobson, W. S. (*fl.* 1825), editor of Hooker, I, 685
Dobson, William (*fl.* 1734–50), classical scholar, I, 466; II, 289
Dobson, William (*fl.* 1814), sporting writer, III, 762
Docking, Thomas (d. *c.* 1270), I, **293**
Dockwra (or Dockwray), William (d. 1716), II, 692
Doctor, The (1718), II, 662
DR WILLIAMS'S LIBRARY, II, 104
Doctor's Miscellany, The (18 cent.), II, 201
Dod, Henry (1550?–1630?), I, 678
'Dodd, Charles', i.e. Hugh Tootell (1672–1743), II, 95
Dodd, James Solas (1721–1805), II, 227, 784
Dodd, James William (*fl.* 1818), III, 776
Dodd, William (1729–1777), II, **359**f., 623, 678, 680, 762, 790, 915
Doddington, George Bubb, Baron Melcombe (1691–1762), II, 135
Doddridge, Philip (1702–1751), II, 330, 862, 1002
Dodgson, Charles Lutwidge ('Lewis Carroll') (1832–1898), III, **513**f.
Dodoens, Rembert, I, 892
Dodridge (Doddridge or Doderidge), Sir John (1555–1628), I, 776, 849, 851
Dodsley, Robert (1703–1764), II, 96, 108, 307, **436**f., 715, 759, 912
Dodsworth, Roger (1585–1654), I, 843; II, 864
Dodwell, Edward (1767–1832), III, **994**
Dodwell, Henry (1641–1711), II, **847, 936**
Dodwell, Henry, the younger (d. 1784), II, 947
Doe, C. (*fl.* 1692), II, 493
Doggett, Thomas (d. 1721), II, **420**
Doherty, Hugh (*fl.* 1840), III, 817, 977
Doherty, J. (*fl.* 1831), III, 816
Dolben, Digby Mackworth (1848–1867), III, 338
Dolby, Thomas (*fl.* 1823), III, 585
Dolby's British Theatre (1823), III, 585
Dolce, Ludovico, I, 340; II, 810
D'Olier Isaac (*fl.* 1816), II, 435
Dolling, Robert William Radclyffe (1851–1902), III, 155
Dolman, John (*fl.* 1561), I, 801
Dolman, Richard (*fl.* 1601), I, 815
Domat, Jean, II, 778
Dome, The (1897), III, 834
Domesday Book (M.E.), I, 119
Domestick Intelligence, The (1679), II, 702
Domestick Intelligence for Promoting Trade (1683), II, 716
Domestick Intelligence; Or, News both from City and Country, The (1679), II, 702
Domestick Intelligence; Or, News from City and Country, The (1681), II, 704
Domett, Alfred (1811–1887), III, **286**
Domiduca Oxoniensis (17 cent.), II, 174

'Domina' (1813), III, 142
DOMINICANS
Writings by English, I, 295f. (13 cent.), 305 (14 and 15 cents.)
DOMINIONS, BRITISH
Anglo-Indian Literature, III, 1067f.
Anglo-Irish Literature, III, 1045f.
English-Canadian Literature, III, 1085f.
English-South African Literature, III, 1088f.
Literature of Australia and New Zealand, III, 1093f.
Don, David (1800–1840), III, 960
Don, George (1798–1856), III, 960
Don Tomazo (17 cent.), II, 530
Donaldson, Alexander (*fl.* 1770), II, 92, 731
Donaldson, James (*fl.* 1696–1713), miscellaneous writer, II, 731 (3), 998f.
Donaldson, James (1751–1830), journalist, II, 695, 731
Donaldson, John (*fl.* 1780), aesthetician, II, 19
Donaldson, John (1799–1876), author of 'Agricultural Biography', III, 971
Donaldson, John William (1811–1861), philologist, III, 57, **997**
Donaldson, W. A. (*fl.* 1865), III, 581
Donatus, I, 808
DONCASTER, II, 723 (newspaper)
Doncaster Gazette, The (1882), II, 723
Doncaster Journal, The (1792), II, 723
Doncaster, Nottingham and Lincoln Gazette, The (1786), II, 723
Doni, Antonio Francesco, I, 338
Donisthorpe, W. (*fl.* 1888), III, 977, 983
Donne, J. M. (*fl.* 1898), III, 772
Donne, John (1573–1631), poet, I, **441**f., 681, 725
Donne, John (*fl.* 1633), translator, I, 862
Donne, John, the younger (1604–1662), III, 173
Donne, William Bodham (1807–1882), III, **997**
Donneau de Visé, Jean, II, 778
Doran, John (1807–1878), II, 839; III, **712**, 818
Dorchester and Sherborne Journal and Western Advertiser, The (1794), II, 728
Doré, Gustav (1833–1883), III, 91
Dorrington, C. W. (*fl.* 1866), III, 782
Dorrington, Theophilus (d. 1715), II, 744
Dorrington, W. (*fl.* 1863–6), III, 88 (2)
DORSET, I, 8 (bibliography)
Dorset, Catherine Anne, née Turner (1750?–1817?), III, 566
Dorset, Charles Sackville, Earl of (1638–1706), II, **280**
Dosabhai, Framji (*fl.* 1858), III, 1076
Dossie, Robert (*fl.* 1768), II, 148
Dostoïevski, Fiodor, III, 44
Doubleday, Thomas (1790–1870), III, **232**, 770, 976
Douce, Francis (1757–1834), I, 4, 277; II, 917; III, **1024**

Dougall, James Dalziell (*fl.* 1857), III, 766
Doughty, Charles Montagu (1843–1926), III, 338 f.
Douglas, A. (*fl.* 1796), II, 748
Douglas, Lord Alfred (b. 1870), III, **339**
Douglas, D. (*fl.* 1846), II, 862
Douglas, Francis (1710?–1790?), II, 157, 251, 732, 973, 1003
Douglas, G. (*fl.* 1772), II, 738
Douglas, Gavin (1475?–1522), I, 45, **259** f.
'Douglas, George', i.e. George Douglas Brown (1869–1902), III, **542**
Douglas, Sir George (*fl.* 1891), II, 258
Douglas, James (1753–1819), II, 746, 782
Douglas, John (1721–1807), I, 469; II, 745, 878, 951, 961
Douglas, Olive, Lady, née Custance (*fl.* 1897–1911), III, **337**
Douglas, Sylvester, Baron Colenbervie (1743–1823), II, 1000
Douglas, Thomas, Earl of Selkirk (1771–1820), II, 158
Douglas, William (*fl.* 1659), I, 907
Douglas Jerrold's Shilling Magazine (1845), III, 828
Douglas Jerrold's Weekly News and Financial Economist (1849), II, 814
Douglas Jerrold's Weekly Newspaper (1846), III, 814
D'Ouvilly, George Gerbier (*fl.* 1661), I, 644
Dove, J. (*fl.* 1832), I, 461
Dover, George James Welbore Agar-Ellis, Baron (1797–1833), II, 837
Doves Press, III, 86
Dovey, Frank G. (*fl.* 1886), III, 798
Dow, Alexander (d. 1779), II, **465**
Dowden, Edward (1843–1913), III, 160, **740** f.
Dowel, John (*fl.* 1683), I, 879
Dowell, Stephen (1833–1898), III, 979, 986
Dowland, John (1563–1626), I, 483
Dowland, Robert (*fl.* 1610), I, 485
Dowling, Frank Lewis (1823–1867), II, 822; III, 776, 811
Dowling, G. D. (*fl.* 1840), II, 822
Dowling, Vincent George (1785–1852), III, 811
Downame, George (d. 1634), I, 696
Downes, Andrew (1549?–1628), I, 862
Downes, Bartholomew (*fl.* 1622), I, 744
Downes, John (*fl.* 1662–1710), II, 403
Downey, Edmund (b. 1856), III, 784
Downing, Clement (*fl.* 1737), II, 750
Downing, S. (*fl.* 1889), III, 799
Downman, Hugh (1740–1809), II, 23, **360**
'Downright, Sir Daniel' (*fl.* 1764), II, 223
Downside School, I, 772
Dowsett, C. F. (*fl.* 1892), III, 972
Dowsing, William (1596?–1679?), I, 387
Dowson, Ernest Christopher (1867–1900), III, **339** f.

Dowson, John (*fl.* 1861), M.D., II, 359
Dowson, John (1810–1881), orientalist, III, 1018
Doyle, Andrew (*fl.* 1843–8), III, 798
Doyle, Sir Arthur Conan (1859–1930), III, **542** f.
Doyle, Sir Francis Hastings Charles (1810–1888), III, **286**
Doyle, John Andrew (1844–1907), III, **933**
Doyle, Matthew (*fl.* 1765), II, 738
Doyley, Edward (1617–1675), I, 793
D'Oyly, Sir Charles (1781–1845), III, 1079
D'Oyly, George (1778–1846), I, 700
D'Oyly, Samuel (*fl.* 1718–32), II, 774, 781
Doyne, P. (*fl.* 1761), II, 814
Draco Normannicus (M.E.), I, 116
Drage, Theodore S. (*fl.* 1748), II, 743
Drakard's Paper (1813), III, 811
Drake, Edward C. (*fl.* 1768), II, 741
Drake, Sir Francis (1540?–1596), I, 791 f.
Drake, Frank (*fl.* 1754), II, 821
Drake, Mrs J. B. (*fl.* 1903), III, 1093
Drake, James (1667–1707), II, 401, 498–9, 660, 790
Drake, Judith (*fl.* 1696), II, 121
Drake, Nathan (1766–1836), III, **667** f.
Drake, Roger (1608–1669), I, 684 (2)
Drake, Samuel (1686?–1753), I, 671
Drama, I, 11 (general histories), 13 (general collections)
Medieval Drama, I, **274** f.
Renaissance to Restoration, I, 487 f. For details see Renaissance to Restoration (Drama of)
Restoration to Romantic Revival, II, 392 f. For details see Restoration to Romantic Revival (Drama of)
Nineteenth Century, III, 580 f. For details see Nineteenth-Century Drama. See also Dramatists of the Irish Revival, III, 1063 f.
Drama; or Theatrical Pocket Magazine, The (1821), III, 826
Dramatic Budget, The (19 cent.), II, 255
Dramatic Dialogues (18 cent.), II, 253
Dramatic Miscellanies (18 cent.), II, 237 (2), 238
Dramatic Muse, The (18 cent.), II, 226
Dramatic Theory and Criticism, II, 397 f. (1660–1800); III, 580 f. (19 cent.)
'Dramaticus' (1816), III, 582
Drant, Thomas (d. 1578?), I, 681, 802
Draper, W. H. (*fl.* 1751), II, 215
Draper, Sir William (1721–1787), II, 630
Draper's Record, The (1887), III, 822
Draughts (books on), II, 825 f. (18 cent.); III, 777 (19 cent.)
Drawing-Room Verse, III, 159
Drayton, Michael (1563–1631), I, **423** f., 535, 775, 865; II, 366

'Dreadnought, D.' (1826), III, 379
Dream of the Rood (O.E.), I, 59f., **78**
Dreamer, The (1776), II, 665
Dregs of Drollery (17 cent.), II, 173
Drelincourt, Charles (*fl.* 1706), II, 499, 778
Drelincourt, Laurent (*fl.* 1783), II, 126
Drewry's Derby Mercury (1769), II, 723
Drift, A. (*fl.* 1741), II, 776
Driver, H. A. (*fl.* 1835), III, 210
Driver, Samuel Rolles (1846–1914), III, **1012**
DROGHEDA, II, 737 (newspapers)
Drogheda Journal; Or, Meath and Louth Advertiser, The (1775), II, 737
Drogheda Newsletter, The (1800), II, 737
Droll Miscellany, The (18 cent.), II, 219
Droz, Jean Pierre (*fl.* 1744), II, 687
'Drub, Timothy' (1717), II, 580
Drue (or Drew), Thomas (*fl.* 1623), I, 644
'Druid, The', i.e. Henry Hall Dixon (1822–1870), III, 763
Drumfries Mercury, The (1721), II, 732
Drummond, Alexander (*fl.* 1754), II, 742
Drummond, Henry (1786–1860), III, 971
Drummond, Henry (1851–1897), III, 850
Drummond, James (1835–1918), III, 850
Drummond, John (*fl.* 1718), II, 820
Drummond, Thomas (*fl.* 1756), II, 23
Drummond, William (1585–1649), of Hawthorden, I, 363, 434, **444**f.
Drummond, Sir William (1770?–1828), II, 767
Drummond, William Henry (1854–1907), III, 1086
Drury, Dru (1725–1803), III, 973
Drury, Robert (*fl.* 1729), II, 748
Dryander, Jonas (1748–1810), II, 103
Drybrough, T. B. (*fl.* 1898), III, 775
DRYDEN, John (1631–1700), II, **262**f.
    Biography and Criticism, II, 272f.
    Collected Works, II, 262
    Dramatic works, II, 266f.
    Drydeniana, II, 270f.
    Miscellany Poems, II, 263
    Poems, II, 263f.
    Prologues and Epilogues, II, 267f.
    Prose, II, 268f.
    Translations, II, 265f., 786, 808
    Translations from, II, 59, 61
Dryden, John, the younger (1668–1701), II, 268, 746
Drysdale, C. R. (*fl.* 1878), III, 976
Du Bail, Louis Moreau, II, 778
Du Bartas, Guillaume de Saluste, Seigneur, I, 818; II, 45
Du Bec-Crispin, Jean, I, 785
Du Bellay, Guillaume, I, 813
Du Bellay, Joachim, I, 331, 332, 813
DUBLIN
    Libraries, I, 362
    Magazines, II, 687f. (1734–1800)

Newspapers, II, 733f. (1660–1800), III, 808f. (19 cent.)
Printing, I, 354 (16, 17 cents.); II, 90 (17 cent.)
University, II, 117; III, 124, 838 (magazines)
Dublin Abraham and Isaac (M.E.), I, 279
Dublin and London Magazine, The (1825), III, 826
Dublin Castle, The (1708), II, 734
Dublin Chronicle (1762), II, 735
Dublin Chronicle, The (1787), II, 736
Dublin Courant, The (1740), II, 735
Dublin Courant, The (1744), II, 735
Dublin Courant, containing news both foreign and domestick, The (1716), II, 734
Dublin Courier, The (1758), II, 735
Dublin Daily Advertiser, The (1736), II, 735
Dublin Evening Journal, The (1778), II, 736
Dublin Evening Mail, The (1861), III, 809
Dublin Evening Packet, The (1770), II, 735
Dublin Evening Post, The (1771), II, 735
Dublin Evening Post, The (1732), II, 735
Dublin Evening Post, The (1778), II, 736
Dublin Evening Post, The (1865), III, 809
Dublin Gazette, The (1689), II, 733
Dublin Gazette, The (1705), II, 734
Dublin Gazette, The (1750), II, 735
Dublin Gazette; Or, Weekly Courant, The (1703), II, 733
Dublin Impartial News Letter (1734), II, 734
Dublin Intelligence (1690), II, 733
Dublin Intelligence, containing a full account of foreign and domestick news (1703), II, 733
Dublin Intelligence, containing a full and impartial account of news (1724), II, 734
Dublin Intelligence, giving a true Account of the Killing of several Rapparees in Ireland (1691), II, 731
Dublin Intelligence, Published by Authority (1690), II, 733
Dublin Intelligencer, The (1756), II, 735
Dublin Journal (1725), II, 662
Dublin Journal, The (1725), II, 734
Dublin Journal with Advices Foreign and Domestick, The (1729), II, 734
Dublin list of Imports and Exports (1800), II, 719
Dublin Literary Gazette, The (1830), III, 826
Dublin Literary Journal, The (1734), II, 687
Dublin Magazine, The (1733), II, 203
Dublin Magazine, The (1762), II, 687
Dublin Magazine and Irish Monthly Register, The (1788), II, 687
Dublin Mercury, The (1704), II, 733
Dublin Mercury, The (1723), II, 734
Dublin Mercury, The (1742), II, 735
Dublin Mercury, The (1766), II, 735
Dublin News-Letter, The (1737), II, 735
Dublin Packet, The (1730), II, 735
Dublin Penny Journal, The (1832), III, 827
Dublin Post Boy, The (1732), II, 734

Dublin Post Boy, Being a Supplement to the Dublin Journal, The (1729), II, 734
Dublin Postman, Being the most Impartial Advices, The (1726), II, 734
Dublin Post-Man, Containing foreign and domestick news, The (1724), II, 734
Dublin Quarterly Maske, The (18 cent.), II, 199
Dublin Review, The (1836), III, 827
Dublin Songster, The (18 cent.), II, 230
Dublin Sporting News, The (1889), III, 809
Dublin, Spy, The (1753), II, 664
Dublin University Magazine, The (1833), III, 827
Dublin University Review, The (1833), III, 827
Dublin Weekly Intelligence (1710), II, 734
Dublin Weekly Journal, The (1725), II, 734
Dublin Weekly Magazine, The (1778), II, 687
Dubois, Edward (1774–1850), II, 763
Du Bois, N. (*fl.* 1715), II, 812
Du Bois, P. B. (*fl.* 1726), II, 1726
'Dubois de la Cour', i.e. Jean Filleau de la Chaise, II, 778
Dubois-Fontanelle, Jean Gaspard, II, 778
Dubos, Jean Baptiste, II, 778
Ducange, Victor, III, 591
Ducarel, Andrew Coltee (1713–1785), II, 96, **891**
Du Cerceau, Jean Antoine, II, 778
Du Chaillu, Paul B. (1835–1903), III, 990
Duchal, James (1697–1761), II, 863
Duchesne, Joseph (*fl.* 1605), I, 886
Ducis, Jean François, II, 72
Duck, Sir Arthur (1580–1648), I, 850
Duck, Stephen (1705–1756), II, **315**
Duckett, George (d. 1732), II, 662
Duckworth, Wynfrid Lawrence (b. 1870), III, 968
Duclaux, Agnes Mary Frances, née Robinson, later Darmesteter (b. 1857), III, 355f.
Du Clos, Charles Pinot, II, 778
Dudley, Edmund (1462?–1510), I, 844
Dudley, Sir Henry Bate, earlier Bate (1745–1824), II, **465**, 695, 709 (2), 711 (2), 719
Dudley, Robert, Earl of Leicester (1532?–1588), I, 398
Dudley, Thomas (*fl.* 1631), I, 792
DUELLING (books on), I, 394f. (16, 17 cents.); II, 120 (17, 18 cents.), 822f. (1660–1800)
Duff, Alexander (1806–1878), III, 1076
Duff, James, Earl of Fife (1729–1809), II, 1000
Duff, James Grant (1789–1858), III, **887**
Duff, Sir Mountstuart Elphinstone Grant (1829–1906), III, 123, **917**
Duff, William (*fl.* 1750), historian, II, 997
Duff, William (1732–1815), miscellaneous writer, II, 18, 143, 547
Duff-Gordon, Lucy, Lady (1821–1869), III, 1091
Dufferin, Frederick Temple Hamilton-Temple Blackwood, Marquis of (1826–1902), III, 989

Dufferin, Helen Selina Blackwood, née Sheridan, Baroness (1807–1867), III, **1052**
Dufferin and Ava, Hariot G., Marchioness of (*fl.* 1889), III, 1078
Duffett, Thomas (*fl.* 1673), II, 280, **420**
Duffy, Sir Charles Gavan (1816–1903), III, 809, 1046, 1052 (2)
Duffy's Hibernian Magazine (1860), III, 829
Du Four de Longuerne, Louis, II, 779
du Fresnoy, Charles Alphonse, II, 32, 506, 779
Dufresny, Charles Rivière, II, 573
Dufton, J. (*fl.* 1847), III, 109
Dugard, William (1602–1662), II, 127 (2)
Dugdale, Gilbert (*fl.* 1604), I, 740
Dugdale, Sir William (1605–1686), I, 776, 851 (3); II, **864**
Dugmore, F. S. (*fl.* 1871), III, **778**
du Halde, Jean Baptiste, II, 779
Du Jon, François (1589–1677) (Franciscus Junius), I, 855; II, 918
Duke, Richard (1658–1711), II, 194, **280**
Duke Rowlande and Sir Ottuell (M.E.), I, **141**
Dukes, C. (*fl.* 1887), III, 109
Dukes, Nicholas (*fl.* 1752), II, 825
Dulcken, H. W. (*fl.* 1866), III, 576
DULWICH SCHOOL, I, 372
Dumas, Alexandre, III, **22**
Dumas, Alexandre, fils, III, 22
Du Mats de Montmartin, Esau (*fl.* 1624), I, 737
Du Maurier, George Louis Palmella Busson (1834–1896), III, **543**
Dumbeley, John (*fl.* 1386), I, **313**
DUMFRIES
  Magazine, II, 687 (1773)
  Newspapers, II, 732
  Printing, II, 89 (18 cent.)
Dumfries Weekly Journal, The (1777), II, 732
Dumfries Weekly Magazine, The (1773), II, 687, 732
Dumont, Étienne, II, 953–4
Dumont, Jean, II, 676, 779
du Moulin, Pierre, the elder, II, 779
du Moulin, Pierre, the younger, II, 779
Dunbar, William (1460?–1520?), I, 39, **258**f.
Dunbar, William (*fl.* 1681), I, 259
DUNBAR, II, 89 (printing)
Duncan, Andrew (1744–1828), II, 651, 686; III, 228
Duncan, Henry (1774–1846), I, 59
Duncan, Philip Bury (1772–1863), II, 321
Duncan, Robert (*fl.* 1789), II, 764
Duncan, William (1717–1760), II, 764–5
Dunckley, Henry (1823–1896), III, 802
Duncombe, Giles (*fl.* 1765), II, 963
Duncombe, John (1729–1786), miscellaneous writer, II, 114, 218–9, 225, **360**f.
Duncombe, John (*fl.* 1821), publisher, III, 585 (3)
Duncombe, T. H. (*fl.* 1868), III, 14

Duncombe, Thomas Slingsby (1796–1861), III, 14
Duncombe, William (1690–1769), II, 218–9, 225, 318 (2), 485, 766
Duncombe's British Theatre (1828), III, 585
Duncombe's New Acting Drama (1821), III, 585
Duncon, John (*fl.* 1648), I, 385
Duncumb, John (1765–1839), III, **883**
Dundas, G. (*fl.* 1829), I, 260
DUNDEE
  Magazines, II, 687 (1775–99)
  Newspapers, II, 732; III, 807
Dundee Advertiser, The (1861), III, 793, 807
Dundee Advertiser and Courier, The (1926), III, 807
Dundee Courier, The (1861), III, 793, 807
Dundee Herald, The (1842), III, 817
Dundee Magazine, The (1775), II, 687
Dundee Magazine and Journal of the Times, The (1799), II, 687
Dundee Mail, The (1798), II, 732
Dundee Repository of Political and Miscellaneous Information, The (1793), II, 687
Dundee Weekly Courier, The (1816), III, 807
Dundee Weekly Intelligencer, The (1755), II, 732
Dundee Weekly Magazine, The (1775), II, 687
Dundonald, Thomas Cochraine, Earl of (1775–1860), III, 150, 990
Dundrennan, Thomas Maitland, Lord (1792–1851), I, 445, 449, 453, 901
Dungal (*fl.* 787), I, **107**
DUNGANNON, II, 688 (magazine)
Dungannon Weekly Magazine, The (1800), II, 688
Dunkin, William (1709?–1765), II, 591
Dunlap, William (*fl.* 1813), II, 60, 408
Dunlop, Andrew (*fl.* 1911), III, 784
Dunlop, Durham (*fl.* 1854?), III, 827
Dunlop, John Colin (d. 1842), III, **668**
Dunn, D. (*fl.* 1761), II, 781
Dunn, H. (*fl.* 1837), III, 109
Dunn, H. A. C. (*fl.* 1889), III, 778
Dunn, J. (*fl.* 1844), Scottish antiquary, I, 899
Dunn, J. N. (*fl.* 1897–1905), editor of 'The Morning Post', III, 798
Dunniad, The (18 cent.), II, 225
Dunning, John, Baron Ashburton (1731–1783), II, 631
Dunning, R. (*fl.* 1856), III, 109
Dunning, T. J. (*fl.* 1850), III, 92 (2)
Dunraven, Windham Thomas Wyndham Quin, Earl of (1841–1926), III, 992
Duns Scotus, John (d. 1308), I, **302**f.
Dunsany, Edward John Moreton Drax Plunkett, Baron (b. 1878), III, **1067**
Dunstable, Annals of (15 cent.), I, 115
Dunstanville, Francis Basset, Baron de (1757–1835), I, 826
Dunster, Charles (1750–1816), II, 759, **917**
Dunster, Samuel (1675–1754), II, 765
Dunton, John (*fl.* 1637), I, 772

Dunton, John (1628–1676), II, 530
Dunton, John (1659–1733)
  Books by, II, 90, 100, 159
  Periodicals ed. by, II, 186, 187 (4), 189 (2), 199, 658 (3), 660 (3), 675–6, 689, 706
Dunton's Ghost (1716), II, 660
Dunton's Whipping-Post (18 cent.), II, 187
Dupérier-Dumouriez, Charles François, II, 779
Duperron de Castera, Louis Adrien, II, 779
Du Pin, Louis Ellies, II, 779
du Plessis, J. (*fl.* 1911), III, 1093
Duplessis, P. C. T. M. (*fl.* 1863), III, 1068
Dupont de Nemours, Pierre Samuel, II, 779
Duport, James (1606–1679), I, 451, 862
Duppa, B. F. (*fl.* 1837), III, 109, 115, 117, 129, 142
Duppa, Brian (1588–1662), I, 617
Duppa, Richard (1770–1831), III, 93, 317, 617
Dupuy, P. S. (*fl.* 1795), III, 633
Du Quesne, Abraham, the elder, II, 779
Du Quesne, Abraham, the younger, II, 788, 779
Durand, David (1680–1763), II, 876
Durand de Villegagnon, Nicolas, II, 779
Durant, Gilles, I, 332
Durante, Castore, II, 810
Du Refuge, Eustache, II, 121
Durette, François Parrain de, II, 792
D'Urfey, Thomas (1653–1723), II, 195, **420**f., 530, 803
'D'Urfey, Young' (1766), II, 224
DURHAM
  Library, I, 361, 362
  Newspapers, II, 723 (1735)
  University, III, 124
Durham, James (1622–1658), I, 907
Durham, John George Lambton, Earl of (1792–1840), III, 151
Durham, Simeon of (*fl.* 1130), I, 116
Durham County Advertiser, The (1814), II, 726
Durham Courant, The (1735), II, 723
Durham Household Book, The (16 cent.), I, 383
Durham Poem (O.E.), I, **84**
Durham Register of (M.E.), I, 121
Durham Ritual (M.E.), I, 25, 35, 37
Durie, John (*fl.* 1650), I, 363
Durnford, Richard (*fl.* 1809), III, 768
Du Rondel, Jacques, II, 779
Du Roveray, F. J. (*fl.* 1804), II, 295
Dury, Giles (*fl.* 1659), II, 701 (2)
Dury, John (*fl.* 1649), I, 365, 854
Dusautoy, J. A. (*fl.* 1805), III, 72
DUTCH
  Loan-Words from, I, 33. See also HOLLAND
Dutch Intelligencer, The (1652), I, 761
Dutch Prophet; Or, The Devil of a Conjurer, The (1700), II, 659
Dutch Rogue, The (17 cent.), II, 530
Dutch Spy, The (1652), I, 761
Dutens, Louis (1730–1812), II, 141, 779
Dutt, Govind Chandra (*fl.* 1887), III, 1069

Dutt, J. C. (*fl.* 1879), III, 1072
Dutt, Manmathanath (Sastri) (*fl.* 1891), III, 1073
Dutt, Michael Madhu Sudan (*fl.* 1849–71), III, 1068, 1071
Dutt, Romes Chandra (1848–1909), III, 1070, 1073, 1077, 1080, 1084
Dutt, Torulata (*fl.* 1876), III, 1069
Dutta, Sitanath (*fl.* 1897), III, 1073
Dutton, Anne (*fl.* 1761), II, 220
Dutton, C. (*fl.* 1882), III, 1084
Dutton, R. (*fl.* 1806), III, 135
Dutton, Thomas (*fl.* 1798), II, 60, 63, 373, 486
Du Vair, Guillaume, II, 780
Duval, J. (*fl.* 1767), II, 126
Du Wes or Duwes, Giles (*fl.* 1532), I, 44, 377
Dux Moraud (M.E.), I, 277
Dyalogus betwixt Salomon and Marcolphus (15 cent.), I, 266
Dyce, Alexander (1798–1869), III, 194, **1024**
Dyce, William (1806–1864), III, 694
Dyche, Thomas (*fl.* 1707–19), II, 931
Dyer, Sir Edward (d. 1607), I, 436
Dyer, George (1755–1841), I, 659; III, **232**f., 636
Dyer, John (1700?–1758), II, 221, **315**
Dyer, R. (*fl.* 1833), III, 582
Dyke, Daniel (d. 1614), I, 337
Dykes, T. (*fl.* 1881), III, 767
Dymmok, John (*fl. c.* 1600), I, 775
Dymock, Edward (*fl.* 1602), I, 814
Dymock, Roger (*fl.* 1395), I, **306**
Dyott, William (1761–1847), II, 152
Dyson, Humfrey (*fl.* 1640), I, 363
Dyson, Humphrey (*fl.* 1618–33), I, 380, 825
Dyson, Jeremiah (1722–1776), II, 350

'E.' (1819), III, 677
E., B. (*fl.* 1690), II, 930
E., B. (*fl.* 1850), I, 407
E., I. (*fl.* 1602), I, 739
E., J. (*fl.* 1684), II, 785
E., J. (*fl.* 1670), II, 127
E. Johnson's British Gazette and Sunday Monitor (1784), II, 716
E. Johnson's Sunday Monitor and British Gazette (1780), III, 810
E., R. (*fl.* 1653), I, 762
E., R. B. (*fl.* 1843), III, 653
Each Side of the Gutter (18 cent.), II, 242
Eachard, John (1636?–1697), II, **847**
Eachard, Laurence (1670?–1730). See Echard
Eadmer (d. *c.* 1124), I, **284**
Eagle, William (*fl.* 1830), III, 986
Eagle, The [Cambridge] (1858), III, 835
Eagles, John (1783–1855), III, 825
Earbery, Mathias (*fl.* 1722), II, 676, 802
Eardley-Wilmot, Sir John Eardley (1810–1892), III, 760
Earl of Toulous (M.E.), I, **153**
Earle, John (1601?–1665), I, **722**

Earle, John (1824–1903), III, **1030**
Earle, William (*fl.* 1800–59), II, 458
Earsden, John (*fl.* 1618), I, 486
East (or Este), Michael (1580?–1640), I, 484
East, Thomas (1540?–1608?), I, 352
East Anglian Daily Times, The (1874), III, 804
East End News, The (1859), III, 810
East Indian, The (18 cent.), II, 487
EAST INDIES, II, 749f. (voyages to). See also INDIA
EAST MIDLAND ENGLISH
  Dialect (M.E.), I, 38
  Texts (M.E.), I, 42
Easter Gift, or The Way to be Very Good, The (18 cent.), II, 563
Eastern Counties Daily Press, The (1870), III, 804
Eastern Daily Press, The (1871), III, 804
Eastern Daily Telegraph, The [Grimsby] (1897), III, 806
Eastern Evening News, The [Hull] (1864), III, 803
Eastern Evening News (Norwich), The (1882), III, 805
Eastern Morning News, The [Hull] (1863), III, 803
Eastern Post, The (1868), III, 817
Eastlake, Sir Charles Lock (1793–1865), III, 712
Eastlake, Elizabeth, Lady, née Rigby (1809–1893), III, 435, **712**f.
Eastward Ho! (1884), III, 831
Eastwick, Edward Backhouse (1814–1883), III, 1083
Eastwood, Jonathan (1824–1864), III, 1043
Eaton, Daniel Isaac (d. 1814), II, 85, 682
Ebert, Johann Arnold (*fl.* 1751), II, 58
Ebrietatis Encomium (18 cent.), II, 197, 210
Ebrington, Hugh Fortescue, Viscount (*fl.* 1896), III, 761
Ebsworth, Joseph Woodfall (1824–1908), II, 258
Eburne, Richard (*fl.* 1624), I, 794
Eccles, Ambrose (d. 1809), II, 917
ECCLESIASTICAL HISTORY, I, 119 (M.E.); III, 920f. (19 cent.). See also under RELIGION
'Eccletus' (1806), III, 111
Echard, Laurence (1670?–1730), I, 828; II, 127, 767–8, **876**
Echo, The (1868), III, 793, 799, 801
Echo, Or Edinburgh Weekly Journal, The (1729), II, 663, 731
Eckerman, J. P., III, 605
Eclectic Review, The (1805), III, 824
Eclipses, The (18 cent.), II, 250
ECLOGUE, THE, II, 170 (18 cent.)
ECONOMIC HISTORY
  Middle English Period, I, 118f.
  Nineteenth Century, III, 147f., 925f. (social and economic historians)

ECONOMICS (writings on), I, 843f. (1500–1660); II, 957f. (1660–1800); III, 969f. (19 cent.)

Economist, The (1843), III, 820

Economist: a periodical paper explanatory of Robert Owen, The (1821), III, 816

Eddis, William (*fl.* 1792), II, 757

Eddius Stephanus (*fl.* 711–31), I, 103

Eden, Charles Page (1807–1885), I, 701, 828; III, 855

Eden, Emily (1797–1869), III, 393 .

Eden, Sir Frederick Morton (1766–1809), II, 112; III, 975

Eden, Richard (1521?–1576), I, 812, 884

Eden, Robert (1804–1886), I, 687

Eden, William, Baron Auckland (1744–1814), II, 138, 963

Edgar, Sir James David (*fl.* 1885), III, 1086

Edgar, Matilda, Lady, née Ridout (*fl.* 1805–15), III, 1087

Edgcumbe, Sir R. P. (*fl.* 1895), III, 975

Edgeworth, F. A. (*fl.* 1867), III, 368

Edgeworth, Francis Ysidro (1845–1926), III, 983

Edgeworth, Maria (1767–1849), III, 137, 366f.

Edgeworth, Richard Lovell (1744–1817), III, 109, 135, 137, 367 (2), 368 (4)

Edie, George (*fl.* 1760), II, 821

EDINBURGH
Libraries, II, 104
Magazines, II, 686f. (1739–1800)
Newspapers, II, 730f. (1642–1800); III, 807
Printing in, I, 354 (16, 17 cents.); II, 89 (18 cent.)
Schools, III, 130
University, II, 117; III, 124, 837 (magazines)

Edinburgh Advertiser, The (1764), II, 731

Edinburgh Christian Instructor, The (1810), III, 825

Edinburgh Chronicle, The (1759), II, 731

Edinburgh Courant, The (1705), II, 731

Edinburgh Courant, The (1871), III, 807

Edinburgh Courant Reviewed, The (1707), II, 731

Edinburgh Courant, with the freshest advices, Forreign and Domestick, The (1710), II, 731

Edinburgh Eighth Day Magazine, The (1779), II, 686, 732

Edinburgh Entertainer, The (18 cent.), II, 214

Edinburgh Evening Courant, The (1860), III, 807

Edinburgh Evening Dispatch, The (1886), III, 807

Edinburgh Evening News, The (1873), III, 793, 807

Edinburgh Evening Post, The (1780), II, 732

Edinburgh Evening Telephone, The (1878), III, 807

Edinburgh Flying Post, The (1707), II, 731

Edinburgh Flying Post, The (1708), II, 731

Edinburgh Fugitive Pieces (18 cent.), II, 245

Edinburgh Gazette, The (1680), II, 730

Edinburgh Gazette, The (1699), II, 731

Edinburgh Gazette, The (1707), II, 731

Edinburgh Gazette, The (1709), II, 731

Edinburgh Gazette, The (1780), II, 732

Edinburgh Gazette, The (1793), II, 732

Edinburgh Gazette, Or Scots Postman, The (1714), II, 731

Edinburgh Gazetteer, The (1792), II, 732

Edinburgh Herald, The (1790), II, 732

Edinburgh Magazine, The (1762), II, 686

Edinburgh Magazine, The (1817), II, 686

Edinburgh Magazine and Literary Miscellany, The (1817), III, 822

Edinburgh Magazine and Review, The (1773), II, 673

Edinburgh Magazine and Review, The (1776), II, 686

Edinburgh Magazine; Or, Literary Amusement, The (1779), II, 686

Edinburgh Magazine; Or, Literary Miscellany, The (1785), II, 686

Edinburgh Medical and Surgical Journal, The (1805), II, 686

Edinburgh Miscellany, The (18 cent.), II, 195

Edinburgh Monthly Magazine, The (1817), III, 825

Edinburgh Monthly Review, The (1819), III, 825

Edinburgh Museum, The (1763), II, 686

Edinburgh Musical Miscellany, The (18 cent.), II, 247–8

Edinburgh Quarterly Magazine, The (1798), II, 687

Edinburgh Repository for Polite Literature, The (1792), II, 686

Edinburgh Repository; Or, Fortnight's Magazine, The (1774), II, 686

Edinburgh Review, The (1755), II, 686

Edinburgh Review, The (1756), II, 673

Edinburgh Review, or Critical Journal, The (1802), III, 832

Edinburgh Syren, The (18 cent.), II, 247

Edinburgh Theological Magazine, The (1826), II, 686

EDINBURGH UNIVERSITY PRESS, III, 87

Edinburgh Weekly Journal, The (1798), II, 732

Edinburgh Weekly Magazine, The (1784), II, 686

Edith Vernon's Life Work (19 cent.), III, 575

Edkins, Joshua (*fl.* 1789–1801), II, 242, 244

Edler, K. E., III, 347

Edmond's Weekly Register [Birmingham] (1819), III, 816

Edmondes, Sir Clement (1564?–1622), I, 800

Edmondes, Sir Thomas (1563?–1639), I, 385

Edmonds, Charles (*fl.* 1852–81), II, 390

Edmonds, Cyrus R. (*fl.* 1837–63), II, 947

Edmonds, E. (*fl.* 1819), III, 816

Edmonds, T. R. (*fl.* 1832), III, 975

Edmonston, Arthur (1776?–1841), III, 970

Edmund Ironside (17 cent.), I, 539

Edmunds, L. (b. 1860), III, 814

Edmundson, Henry (d. 1659), I, 861
Edmundson, William (1627–1712), II, 753
EDUCATION
  Old and Middle English Periods, I, 124f.
  Renaissance to Restoration, I, 364f.
  Restoration to Romantic Revival, II, 107f.
    See also PHILOSOPHY
  Nineteenth Century, III, 106f., 844f. (year
    books)
Edward VI, King (1537–1553), I, 383, 399
Edward the Third (16 cent.), I, 577
Edward Waters' Dublin Intelligence (1708), II,
  734
Edwardes, Charles (*fl.* 1895), III, 574
Edwardes, Sir Herbert Benjamin (1819–1868),
  III, 1080
Edwards, Amelia Blandford (1831–1892), III,
  990
Edwards, Bryan (1743–1800), II, 757
Edwards, D. (*fl.* 1891), III, 802, 806
Edwards, E. J. (*fl.* 1897), III, 1092
Edwards, Edward (*fl.* 1773–1801), vicar of
  Llanarmon, II, 880
Edwards, Edward (1812–1886), librarian, I,
  122, 384; III, 104, 105 (3), 125
Edwards, George (1752–1823), III, 969, 976,
  979
Edwards, H. (*fl.* 1844), III, 109
Edwards, H. Sutherland (1828–1906), III, 784,
  815
Edwards, J. Passmore (1823–1911), III, 784, 801
Edwards, John (1637–1716), II, 24, 942
Edwards, Richard (1523?–1566), I, 403, 519,
  523, 728, 864
Edwards, T. R. (*fl.* 1828), III, 981
Edwards, Thomas (*fl.* 1595), poet, I, 436
Edwards, Thomas (1599–1647), puritan divine,
  I, 696, 720
Edwards, Thomas (1699–1757), critic, II, 315f.,
  912
Edwards, Thomas (*fl.* 1790–1810), Cambridge
  divine, I, 883, 934
Eelbeck, Henry (*fl.* 1720), II, 764, 767
Eeles, R. (*fl.* 1653), I, 762
*Effects of Vanity; or, Mary Meanwell and Kitty
  Pertly, The* (18 cent.), II, 563
Effendi, Khojah, I, 781
Egan, Pierce (1772–1849), III, 592, **668**, 811–2
Eger, Sir, Sir Grime, and Sir Graysteele (M.E.),
  I, **160**
Egerton, A. G., Earl of Wilton (*fl.* 1868), III,
  766
Egerton, Hugh Edward (1855–1927), III, 985
'Egerton, William.' (1731), II, 407
Egerton-Warburton, Rowland Eyles (1804–
  1891), III, **286**
Eglamour of Artois, Sir (M.E.), I, **157**
Egmont, John Perceval, Earl of (1683–1748),
  II, 136
EGYPTOLOGISTS, III, 1014f.

EIGHTEENTH CENTURY. See RESTORATION TO
  ROMANTIC REVIVAL, II, 3f.
'Eireneus, Philalethes' (b. 1622), I, 887
Eisdell, J. S. (*fl.* 1839), III, 982
Ekins, Jeffery (d. 1791), II, 759
Elder, John (*fl.* 1555), I, 738
Elderton, William (d. 1592?), I, 721, 741
Eldon, John Scott, Earl of (1751–1838), III, 149
Election Magazine, The (18 cent.), II, 237
*Election Magazine; Or the Oxfordshire Register,
  The* (18 cent.), II, 215
Elector, The (1860), III, 817
ELECTROTYPE, III, 75
Elegiac and other Poems (18 cent.), II, 226
ELEGIAC POEMS (O.E.), I, 70ff.
ELEGIAC POETRY, I, 20f. (O.E.)
Elegies (18 cent.), II, 253
Elene (O.E.), I, **76**
'Eleutherius' (1669), II, 778
Eleven pains of Hell (M.E.), I, **176**f.
Elger, Thomas Gwyn (*fl.* 1895), III, 945
'Eliot, George', i.e. Mary Ann Evans, later
  Cross (1819–1880), III, **465**f.
  Reviews and articles by, III, 27, 32, 654, 848
  Translations from, III, 24, 36
Eliot, John (*fl.* 1592), I, 778, 818
Eliot, Sir John (1592–1632), I, 385
Eliot's Court Printing House, I, 352
Elixir, The (1706), II, 660
Elizabeth, Electress Palatine, Queen of Bo-
  hemia (1596–1662), I, 386
Elizabeth, Queen (1533–1603), I, 47, 811
ELIZABETHAN PERIOD. See under RENAISSANCE
  TO RESTORATION
Ellacombe, Henry Noel (*fl.* 1883), III, 771
Ellerton, John (1826–1893), III, **286**
Ellicott, Charles John (1819–1905), III, **1012**f.
Ellingsale, T. (*fl.* 1832), III, 768
Elliot, A. R. D. (1846–1923), III, 832
Elliot, Lady Charlotte (1839–1880), III, 340
Elliot, Sir Gilbert, Earl of Minto (1751–1814),
  II, 137, 166
Elliot, Sir Henry Miers (1808–1853), III, 1074,
  1077
Elliot, J. (*fl.* 1870), III, 106
Elliot, Robert (*fl.* 1822–33), III, 1079
Elliot, T. J. (*fl.* 1834), III, 972
Elliot-Murray-Kynynmound, W. H., Earl of
  Minto (*fl.* 1863), III, 770
Elliott, Charlotte (1789–1871), III, **233**
Elliott, Ebenezer (1781–1849), III, **233**
Elliott, G. P. (*fl.* 1853), I, 388
Elliott, Henry Venn (1792–1865), III, 233
Elliott, Mary, née Belson (*fl.* 1812), III, 566
Elliott, Thomas (*fl.* 1846), III, 801
Ellis, III, 103
Ellis, Mrs (*fl.* 1843), III, 577
Ellis, Alexander John (1814–1890), III, **1030**
Ellis, Arthur (*fl.* 1878), III, 820
Ellis, Clement (1630–1700), I, 724

Ellis, George (1753–1815), II, 245, **361**
   Reviews by, III, 192–3, 194 (2)
Ellis, Havelock. See Henry Havelock Ellis
Ellis, Henry (1721–1806), traveller, II, 743
Ellis, Sir Henry (1777–1869), antiquary, I, 62,
   349; III, 768, **881**f., 1024
Ellis, Henry Havelock (1859–1939), critic, III,
   741
Ellis, Hercules (*fl.* 1850), III, 1051
Ellis, James (1763?–1830), III, 372
Ellis, John (1643?–1738), II, 134, 153
Ellis, Joseph (*fl.* 1869), III, **340**
Ellis, Lady M. (*fl.* 1838), III, 142
Ellis, Robert (1820?–1885), classical scholar,
   III, **997**
Ellis, Robert Leslie (1817–1859), editor of
   Bacon, I, 871
Ellis, Robinson (1834–1913), III, 340
Ellis, Sarah, née Stickney (1810?–1872), III,
   240, **483**
Ellis, Thomas (*fl.* 1578), I, 787
Ellis, Thomas Flower (1796–1861), III, 684
Ellis, William (*fl.* 1759–82), miscellaneous
   writer, II, 742, 759, 765, 816, 935
Ellis, William (1794–1872), missionary, III,
   967, 982
Ellison, Henry (1811–1880), III, **286**
Elliston, Robert William (1774–1831), II, 459
Ellistone, John (*fl.* 1649), II, 860–1
Ellwood, Thomas (1639–1713), II, **280**, 855–6
Ellyot, George (*fl.* 1581), I, 737
Elmes, James (1782–1862), III, 825
Elmham, Thomas (d. 1440?), I, 265
Elmhirst, Edward Pennell (*fl.* 1878), III, 760
Elmsley, Peter (1773–1825), III, **994**
Eloisa to Abelard [etc.] (18 cent.), II, 195
Elphinston, James (1721–1809), I, 44; II, 222,
   615, 766, 772, 799
Elphinstone, Sir Howard Warburton (*fl.* 1878),
   III, 987
Elphinstone, Mountstuart (1779–1859), III, **906**
Elrington, Charles Richard (1787–1850), I, 702
Elrington, John Battersby (*fl.* 1803), II, 63
Elstob, Elizabeth (1683–1756), II, 77, **919**
Elstob, William (1673–1715), II, 909, **919**
Elsum, John (*fl.* 1700–5), II, 272
Elton, Sir Charles Abraham (1778–1853), I,
   453; III, 219, 636
Elton, Charles Isaac (1839–1900), III, 986
Elton, Richard (*fl.* 1650), I, 390
Elwes, F. (*fl.* 1831), III, 680
Elwin, Whitwell (1816–1900), III, 190, **713**, 832
Ely Inquisition (M.E.), I, 121
Elyot, Sir Thomas (1490?–1546), I, 375, 378,
   670, 684, 716, 803–4, 806 (2), 811, 888
Elys, Edmund (1634?–1707?), I, 475, 876; II,
   764
Elzevir Miscellany, The (18 cent.), II, 192
Emare (M.E.), I, **152**
Emaricdulfe (16 cent.), I, 434

*Emblems for the Improvement and Entertain-
   ment of Youth* (18 cent.), II, 560
Emerson, Ralph Waldo, III, 47f.
Emery, T. (*fl.* 1849), III, 109
Emery, William (1825–1910), III, 121
Emily Herbert; or, Perfidy Punished (18 cent.),
   II, 549
Emin, Joseph (*fl.* 1792), II, 635
Emlyn, Thomas (1663–1741), II, 863
EMMANUEL COLLEGE (Cambridge), I, 370
Emmanuel College Magazine, The (1889), III,
   835
Emmert, J. H. (*fl.* 1793), II, 515 (2)
Emmet, Lewis, E. (*fl.* 1875), III, 986
Emmett, W. L. (*fl.* 1869), III, 821 (2)
Emonson, William (*fl.* 1760), II, 616
EMPIRE, BRITISH
   Historians of, III, 886f., 906f., 930f.
   Literatures of Dominions, III, 1045f.
Empson, William (1791–1852), III, 832
Enciso, Martin Fernández de, I, 794
ENCLOSURE CONTROVERSY, II, 148f. (18 cent.)
Enderby, C. (*fl.* 1872), III, 983
Enfield, W. (*fl.* 1809), political economist, III,
   980
Enfield, William (1741–1797), divine and
   miscellaneous writer, II, 92, 111, 126, 230,
   234, 666 (2), 922
Engel, J. J., III, 396
Engineer, The (1856), III, 822
Engineering (1866), III, 822
England (1880), III, 814
ENGLAND, DESCRIPTIONS OF, I, 381, 773f.; II,
   140f. (by foreigners)
England's Genius (18 cent.), II, 204
England's Glory, A Collection of Loyal Songs
   (18 cent.), II, 221
Englands Helicon (17 cent.), I, 404
Englands Memorable Accidents (1642), I, 754
England's Merry Jester (17 cent.), II, 182
England's Moderate Messenger (1649), I, 760
England's Monitor (1682), II, 657
*England's Monitor; Or, The History of Separa-
   tion* (1682), II, 704
Englands Parnassus (17 cent.), I, 404
England's Remembrancer of London's Integritie
   (1647), I, 757
England's Witty and Ingenious Jester (18 cent.),
   II, 192, 194 (2)
English and French Journal, The (1723), II, 713,
   719
English and French News Journal, The (1723),
   II, 713, 719
English Anthology, The (18 cent.), II, 248–9
English Chartist Circular, The (1841), III, 817
English Chronicle, The (1779), II, 711
*English Chronicle and Universal Evening-Post,
   The* (1781), II, 711
*English Chronicle and Whitehall Evening Post,
   The* (1802), II, 711

English Churchman, The (1843), III, 819
English Comedy (1810), II, 392
◆ *English Courant, The* (1688), II, 704
English Courant, The (1695), II, 706
English Currant, The (1679), II, 702
English Freeholder, The (1791), II, 666
English Gazette, The (1680), II, 703
English Gentleman, The (1824), III, 811
English Gentleman, The (1845), III, 811
English Gratitude (18 cent.), II, 190
English Guilds (M.E.), I, 39
English Guzman, The (1683), II, 657
English Guzman; Or, Captain Hilton's Memoirs, The (1683), II, 704
ENGLISH HEROES, ROMANCES OF (M.E.), I, 147 f.
English Historical Review, The (1886), III, 834
English Illustrated Magazine, The (1883), III, 831
English Independent, The (1867), III, 810, 819
English Intelligencer, The (1679), II, 702
English Labourers' Chronicle, The (1877), III, 818
English Leader, The (1864), III, 817
English Lucian, The (1698), II, 658
English Lyceum, The (18 cent.), II, 240–1, 688
English Magazine, The (1779), II, 688
English Magazine and Commercial Repository, The (1796), II, 683
English Martial, The (1699), II, 659
English Miscellanies (18 cent.), II, 206
English Nobleman, The (18 cent.), II, 540
English Orpheus (17 cent.), II, 210
English Parnassus, The (17 cent.), II, 177
English Poems on the Death of Frederick Prince of Wales, The (18 cent.), II, 214
English Post, Giving an Authentick Account of the Transactions of the World, The (1700), II, 706
English Post; with News, Foreign and Domestick, The (1700), II, 706
English Review of Literature [etc.], *The* (1796), II, 680
English Review; Or, An Abstract of English and Foreign Literature, The (1783), II, 680
English Review, or Quarterly Journal of Ecclesiastical and General Literature, The (1844), III, 833
English Roscius, The (18 cent.), II, 226
English Spy; Or, The Weekly Observator, The (1699), II, 659, 711
ENGLISH STUDIES. See LITERARY HISTORIANS, II, 892 f. (1660–1800), ENGLISH SCHOLARSHIP, III, 1021 f. (19 cent.) and LITERARY HISTORIES *passim.*
ENGLISH, TEXTBOOKS OF, II, 125 (17, 18 cents.)
Englishman, The (1713), II, 661
Englishman, The (1738), II, 714
Englishman, The (1768), II, 665
Englishman, The (1779), II, 665
Englishman, The (1803), III, 810
Englishman; Or, Sunday Express, The (1803), II, 716

Englishman's Evening Post, The (1740), II, 710
Englishman's Journal, The (1722), II, 713
Englishman's Miscellany, The (18 cent.), II, 209
Englishwoman's Domestic Magazine, The (1852) III, 829
Engraver's Present, The (18 cent.), II, 563
ENGRAVING, I, 392 (16, 17 cents.); III, 80 f. (19 cent.)
Ennemoser, J., III, 674
Ennery, Adolphe d', III, 598 (3)
ENNIS, II, 737 (newspapers)
Ennis Journal and Clare Advertiser, The (1917), II, 737
Enniss Chronicle and Clare Advertiser, The (1784), II, 737
Enquirer, The (1796), II, 666
Ensor, George (1769–1843), III, 109, 819, 975, 977, 980
Enterlude of Welth, and Helth, An (16 cent.), I, 515
Entertainer, The (1717), II, 662
Entertainer, The (1746), II, 211
Entertainer, The (1754), II, 664
Entertainer Being the Third Volume of The Merry-Fellow, The (1765), II, 223
Entertainer, Collected by Charles Telltruth, The (1766), II, 224
Entertaining Companion, The (18 cent.), II, 224
Entertaining Extracts (18 cent.), II, 250
Entertaining History of William Watling, The [etc.] (18 cent.), II, 242
Entertaining Medley, The (18 cent.), II, 224 (2)
Entertainment of His Most Excellent Majestie Charles II, The (17 cent.), II, 174
Entick, John (1703?–1773), II, 664 (misspelt Entinck), 912, 931
Entinck, John. See Entick
Entire New Collection of Humourous Songs, An (18 cent.), II, 214
Entire Set of The Monitors, An, II, 190, 192
Entr'acte (1872), III, 821
'Ephelia' (*fl.* 1679) [Joan Philips?], II, 178, **280**
EPIC
  Adaptations and Translations, II, 45 f. (French-English, English-French), 56 f. (German-English, English-German), 66 f. (Italian-English, English-Italian)
  Criticism, II, 21 f. (1660–1800), 169 (recent works); III, 159 (19 cent.)
  Old English epic, I, 61 f.
Epicedia Academiae Oxoniensis (1660), II, 173 (2)
Epicedia Cantabrigiensia (1671), II, 175
Epicedia Oxoniensia In Obitum Frederici Principis Walliae (18 cent.), II, 215
Epictetus, I, 801; II, 760; III, 1000
Epicurus, II, 760
EPIGRAMMATISTS, I, 479 f. (16, 17 cents.)
Epigrammes (Paris, *c.* 1630), I, 481

Epigrammes, mirrour of New Reformation (17 cent.), I, 481
Epigrams or Humours Lottery (17 cent.), I, 481
EPILOGUES, COLLECTIONS OF, II, 393
Epinal Glossary (O.E.), I, 36
Epinay, Louise Florence Petronille de la Live d', II, 784
Epithalamia Oxoniensia (18 cent.), II, 204
Epithalamia Oxoniensia sive Gratulationes in Georgii III et Sophiae Charlottae Nuptias (18 cent.), II, 220
Epithalamium in Desideratissimis Nuptiis [of William III and Mary] (17 cent.), II, 178
Epitome of the Weekly News, The (1682), II, 704
Era, The (1838), III, 821
ERAGNY PRESS, III, 86
Erasmus, Desiderius, I, **326**f., 375, 395, **664**f., 666, 680; II, 32, 128
Erckmann, Émile, III, 603
Erdeswicke, Sampson (d. 1603), I, 775, 826
Eremyte and the Outelawe (M.E.), I, **163**
Erfurt Glossary (O.E.), I, 35
Erigena, Johannes Scotus (d. 860), I, **109**f.
Erkenwald (M.E.), I, **203**
Erndtel, C. H., II, 805
Ernle, R. E. Prothero, Baron (*fl.* 1888), III, 832, 972
Eromena; or the Noble Stranger (17 cent.), II, 530
Erondelle, Pierre (*fl.* 1609), I, 794
Erskine, Andrew (*fl.* 1763–73), II, 24, 650
Erskine, David Steuart, Earl of Buchan (1742–1829), II, 307
Erskine, Ebenezer (1680–1754), II, 994
Erskine, Francis Robert St Clair, Earl of Rosslyn (1833–1890), III, **340**
Erskine, John (*fl.* 1683–7), diarist, II, 156
Erskine, John, Earl of Mar (1675–1732), II, 121
Erskine, Ralph (1685–1752), II, 994f.
Erskine, Thomas, Baron (1750–1823), II, 85 (2); III, **668**f.
Erskine, Thomas (1788–1870), III, **847**, 848
Erskine, William (*fl.* 1736–43), II, 795, 814
Ervine, St John Greer (b. 1883), III, **1066**
Escalante, Bernardino de, I, 782
Eschenburg, Johann Joachim, II, 71
Escott, T. H. S. (1844–1924), III, 784, 830
Esdall, James (*fl.* 1744–9), II, 663, 735
Esdall's News-Letter (1746), II, 735
Esher, Reginald Baliol, 2nd Viscount (1852–1930), III, 144
'Esmond, Henry Vernon', i.e. Henry Vernon Jack (1869–1922), III, **625**f.
Espejo, Antonio de, I, 787
Espinasse, Francis (*fl.* 1864–93), III, 784, 807
Esprit, Jacques, II, 780
Essay on Poetry, An [etc.] (17 cent.), II, 183
ESSAYS, I, 724f. (1500–1660); II, 567f. (1660–1800), 660f. (periodical, 1697–1800); III, 7f. (collections of critical essays, 19 cent.), 629f. (principal 19 cent. essayists)

Essays after the Manner of Goldsmith (1800), II, 667
Essays and Poems by J. S. Dodd [etc.] (18 cent.), II, 227
Essays, By a Society of Gentlemen, at Exeter (18 cent.), II, 251
Essays in Prose and Verse (19 cent.), II, 255
Essays on Several Subjects (1775), II, 665
Essays on Song-Writing (18 cent.), II, 229–30, 232
Essays on the Vices and Follies of the Times (1726), II, 663
Essays Serious and Comical (18 cent.), II, 187, 189
Essence of Theatrical Wit, The (18 cent.), II, 225
Essex, James (1722–1784), II, 746
Essex, John (*fl.* 1710–22), II, 131, 825
ESSEX
    Dialect, I, 41
    Printers and booksellers, II, 86
Essex Chronicle, The (1920), II, 722
Essex County Chronicle, The (1884), II, 722
Essex Harmony, The (18 cent.), II, 216, 224, 226, 230, 232, 239, 245, 248
Essex Herald, The (1800), II, 722
ESSEX HOUSE PRESS, III, 86
Essex, Lives and Letters of Devereux, Earls of (1540–1646), I, 382
Essex Mercury; Or, Colchester Weekly Journal, The (1733), II, 723
Est (or East), Thomas (1540?–1608?), I, 352
Estcourt, Richard (1668–1712), II, **437**
Este, Charles (*fl.* 1785–1800), II, 408, 695, 709, 748
Estella, Diegode, I, 343, 685
Estienne, Charles, I, 662, 706
Estienne, Henri, I, 733, 813, 854; II, 780
Estrades, Godefroi d', II, 780
État Present de L'Europe, L' (1682), II, 719
Etches, James M. (*fl.* 1884), III, 761
Etherege, Sir George (1635?–1691), II, **410**
Etheridge, Robert (1819–1903), III, 952
Etherington's York Chronicle (1774), II, 730
Ethic Tales and Fables (18 cent.), II, 230
ETHICS. See PHILOSOPHY
ETON, II, 723 (newspaper)
Eton, William (*fl.* 1798), II, 748
ETON COLLEGE, I, 372; II, 87 (printing); III, 130f., 838f. (magazines)
Eton Journal; or, Early Intelligencer, The (1745), II, 723
'Etonensis' (1830), III, 131
Eucherius, I, 461
Euclid, I, 801
Eudes de Mézeray, François, II, 780
Eulenspiegl, II, 805
Eulogium Historiarum (M.E.), I, 116
Eunapius Sardianus, I, 801
Euordanus, Prince of Denmark (17 cent.), I, 730

'Euphrosyne' (1763), II, 221 (2)
Euripides, I, 801; II, 760; III, 260, 353, 362, 888, 926, 1010
EUROPE
    Descriptions of, I, 777f.
    English historians of, III, 887, 907f., 933f.
    Voyages to, I, 767f. (16, 17 cents.); II, 743f. (1661–1800)
    See also CONTINENT
European Magazine, The (1782), II, 666 (2), 673
European Magazine (1788), II, 666
European Magazine (1798), II, 666
European Magazine (1799), II, 666
European Magazine (1800), II, 667
European Magazine and London Review, The (1782), II, 680
European Repertory, The (1800), II, 688
Eusden, Laurence (1688–1730), II, 191, **316**, 762
Eusebius (or Hwaetberht) (*fl.* 730), I, **104**
Eustace, John Chetwode (1762?–1815), III, 878
Eutropius, I, 801
Evangelical Magazine, The (1777), II, 685
Evangelical Magazine, The (1793), II, 673, 682
Evangelical Magazine and Missionary Chronicle, The (1813), III, 823
EVANGELICALS (writings by), III, 851f.
Evans, Abel (1679–1737), II, **316**
Evans, Anne (1820–1870), III, 287
Evans, Sir Arthur John (b. 1851), III, **1005**
Evans, C. (*fl.* 1780), II, 381
Evans, Daniel Silvan (1818–1903), I, 7
Evans, David Morier (1819–1874), III, 790, 820
Evans, Evan (1731–1789), II, 79
Evans, George Essex (1863–1909), III, **1095**
Evans, Howard (*fl.* after 1868), III, 801
Evans, John (1767–1827), baptist minister, II, 559, 647
Evans, John (*fl.* 1792–1812), miscellaneous writer, II, 306; III, 135
Evans, John (1774–1828), printer, III, 77
Evans, Sir John (1823–1908), archaeologist, III, **914**
Evans, Lewis (*fl.* 1561), I, 716, 803
Evans, M. S. (*fl.* 1911), III, 1093
Evans, Mary Ann, later Cross ('George Eliot') (1819–1880), III, **465**f.
    Reviews and articles by, III, 27, 32, 654, 848
    Translations from, III, 24, 36
Evans, Robert Harding (1778–1857), II, 232, 237; III, 890
Evans, Robert Wilson (1789–1866), I, 17
Evans, Sebastian (1830–1909), III, **287**, 803, 813
Evans, Thomas (1739–1803), bookseller, II, 695
Evans, Thomas (1742–1784), bookseller and editor, II, 232, 237, 289, 428
Evans, Thomas Saunders (1816–1889), III, **998**
Evans and Ruffy's Farmer's Journal (1809), III, 819

Evans's Edition, Old Ballads (18 cent.), II, 232, 237
Eve, H. W. (*fl.* 1883), III, 109
Evelin, Robert (*fl.* 1641–8), I, 795
Evelyn, John (1620–1706), diarist, II, **827**f.
Evelyn, John, the younger (1655–1699), II, 831
Evelyn, John (*fl.* 1830), author of 'Co-operation', III, 981
Evelyn, Mrs John (*fl.* 1655), II, 134
Evelyn, Mary (*fl.* 1690), II, 831
Evelyn, William Glanville (*fl.* 1775), II, 151
Evening Advertiser, The (1754), II, 710
Evening Argus, The [Bath] (1876), III, 804
Evening Argus, The [Brighton] (1896), III, 805
Evening Chronicle, The (1824), III, 801
Evening Chronicle, The (1835), III, 809
Evening Chronicle, The [Dublin] (1783), II, 736
Evening Chronicle, The [Newcastle on Tyne] (1885), III, 806
Evening Chronicle, The [Oldham] (1880), III, 805
Evening Citizen [Glasgow] (1864), III, 808
Evening Courant, The (1711), II, 710
Evening Echo, The (1875), III, 801
Evening Echo, The [Cork] (1893), III, 808
Evening Entertainment, The (1727), II, 710
Evening Express, The (1871), III, 804
Evening Express [Aberdeen] (1879), III, 806
Evening Express, The [Edinburgh] (1880), III, 807
Evening Express, The [Wolverhampton] (1876), III, 804
Evening Express and Star, The [Wolverhampton] (1884), III, 804
Evening Express of the Devon Weekly Times [Exeter] (1866), III, 803
Evening Express Telegram, The [Cheltenham] (1874), III, 804
Evening Freeman, The [Dublin] (1859), III, 809
Evening Gazette [Aberdeen] (1882), III, 807
Evening Gazette for Middlesbrough, The (1869), III, 804
Evening General Post, The (1716), II, 710
Evening Herald, The (1857), III, 801
Evening Herald, The [Dublin] (1891), III, 809
Evening Herald, The [Ipswich] (1897), III, 806
Evening Herald, The [Northampton] (1880), III, 805
Evening Herald; Or, General Advertiser, The (1786), II, 736
Evening Irish Times, The [Dublin] (1865), III, 809
Evening Journal, The (1727), II, 710
Evening Journal, The (1851), III, 801
Evening Journal, The [Glasgow] (1869), III, 808
Evening Mail, The (1789), II, 711
Evening Mail, The (1896), III, 801
Evening Mail, The [Portsmouth], III, 805
Evening News, The (1881), III, 801
Evening News, The (1889), III, 801
Evening News [Dundee] (1876), III, 807

Evening News [Greenock] (1866), III, 808
Evening News, The [Hull] (1870), III, 804
Evening News, The [Norwich] (1882), III, 805
Evening News, The [Portsmouth] (1877), III, 805
Evening News, The [Waterford] (1898), III, 809
Evening News and Post, The (1889), III, 801
Evening News and Star [Glasgow] (1875), III, 808
EVENING NEWSPAPERS, II, 710 f. (1660–1800), III, 800 f. (19 cent.)
Evening Post, The (1709), II, 710
Evening Post, The (1887), III, 801
Evening Post [Dundee] (1900), III, 807
Evening Post, The [Exeter] (1885), III, 806
Evening Post, The [Warrington] (1878), III, 805
Evening Post, The [Worcester] (1877), III, 805
Evening Post or The New Edinburgh Gazette, The (1710), II, 731
Evening Post, with the Historical Account, &c., The (1706), II, 710
Evening Press, The [Belfast] (1871), III, 808
Evening Press, The [York] (1882), III, 805
Evening Standard, The (1860), III, 801
Evening Star, The (1842), III, 801
Evening Star, The (1856), III, 801
Evening Star [Glasgow] (1872), III, 808
Evening Star, The [Wolverhampton] (1880), III, 805
Evening Star, And Grand Weekly Advertiser, The (1788), II, 715
Evening Star of Gwent and South Wales Times, The (1877), III, 805
Evening Telegram, The [Cheltenham] (1875), III, 804
Evening Telegram, The [Newport] (1870), III, 804
Evening Telegraph, The [Dublin] (1871), III, 809
Evening Telegraph [Dundee] (1877), III, 807
Evening Telegraph, The [Dundee] (19 cent.), III, 793
Evening Telegraph, The [Newport] (1891), III, 804
Evening Telegraph and Star, The [Sheffield] (1888), III, 806
Evening Times, The (1825), III, 801
Evening Times, The [Liverpool] (1883), III, 805
Evening Weekly Pacquet, The (1716), II, 710
Ever Green, The (18 cent.), II, 197, 220
Everard, E. (fl. 1680), II, 801
Everard, E. C. (fl. 1818), II, 408
Everard, John (1575?–1650?), I, 862
Everard, Robert (fl. 1732), II, 748
Everard, William (fl. 1765), II, 725
Everett, A. H. (fl. 1823), III, 975
Everett, James (1784–1872), III, 240
Everett W. (fl. 1866), III, 123
Everie Woman in her Humor (17 cent.), I, 652
Everingham, E. (fl. 1707), II, 717
Eversfield, C. (fl. 1784), II, 751

Eversley, C. G. Lefevre, Viscount (1794–1888), III, 971
Eversley, William Pinder (fl. 1885), III, 986
Everts, W. W. (fl. 1868), III, 669
Every Lady's own Valentine Writer (18 cent.), II, 249, 253
Everyday (1915), III, 578
Everyman, The Summoning of (15 cent.), I, 515
Everyman's Journal [Dublin] (1765), II, 735
Everyman's Magazine; Or Monthly Repository of Science (1771), II, 679
Evesham, Monk of (fl. 1400), I, 116
EVOLUTION (writings on), III, 953 f.
Ewald, Johannes, III, 422
Ewen, James (fl. 1787), II, 767
Ewes, Sir Simonds d' (1602–1650), I, 841
Ewing, Alexander (1814–1873), III, 848
Ewing, Greville (1767–1841), II, 686
Ewing, Juliana Horatia (1841–1885), III, **543 f.**, 578
Exact Accompt of the Daily Proceedings in Parliament, An (1660), I, 763
Exact and True Collection of the Weekly Passages, An (1646), I, 757
Exact and True Diurnall of the Proceedings in Parliament, An (1642), I, 753
Exact Collection of many Wonderful Prophesies Relating to the Government of England, An (17 cent.), II, 181, 182, 191
Exact Diurnall, An (1644), I, 756
Examen Miscellaneum (18 cent.), II, 185
Examiner, The (1710), II, 661
Examiner, The (Dublin, 1710), II, 661
Examiner, The (1808), III, 793, 810
Excellent and pleasant Comedie, termed Common Condicions, An (16 cent.), I, 520
Exchange Evening Post, The (1721), II, 710
Exchange Intelligencer, The (1645), I, 756
Exercises for Improvement in Elocution (18 cent.), II, 232
Exercises in Elocution (18 cent.), II, 234, 245
Exercises Performed at Bristol, The (18 cent.), II, 206
EXETER
    Booksellers, I, 353 (17 cent.)
    Newspapers, II, 723 f. (1701–1800)
Exeter and Plymouth Gazette Daily Telegrams, The (1863), III, 803
Exeter Book, The (O.E.), I, 62
EXETER COLLEGE (Oxford), I, 368
Exeter Evening Post, The (1765), II, 724
Exeter Evening Post; Or, Plymouth and Cornish Advertiser, The (1767), II, 724
Exeter Gazette, The (1772), II, 724
Exeter Journal, The (1792), II, 724
Exeter Mercury, The (1714), II, 723
Exeter Mercury; Or, Weekly Intelligence, The (1715), II, 723
Exeter Mercury; Or, West-Country Advertiser, The (1763), II, 724

Exeter Weekly Times (1827), III, 803
Exiles, Antoine François Prévost d', II, 33, 48, 72, 140, 542–3, 795
Exley, Dimsdale and Hopkinson's Corn Exchange Circular (1824), III, 819
Exodus (O.E.), I, 75 f.
Exposition on the Common Prayer (1737), II, 714
Express, The (1846), III, 801
Express and Evening Chronicle, The (1794), II, 711
Express and Star, The [Wolverhampton] (1889), III, 804
Express and the London Herald, The (1799), II, 711
Exshaw's Magazine (1741), II, 687
Extract of Letters (1644), I, 756
EXTRACTS, BOOKS OF. See ANTHOLOGIES, MISCELLANIES, and READERS
Extracts, Elegant, Instructive, and Entertaining, in Poetry (18 cent.), II, 245, 251
Extracts from the Album at Streatham (18 cent.), II, 241 (2)
Extracts from the Works of Italian Poets (18 cent.), II, 253
Extraordinary North Briton, The (1768), II, 665
Extravagant Shepherd, The (17 cent.), I, 652
Eynsham Cartulary, The (M.E.), I, 121
Eyre, — (*fl.* 1743), II, 105
Eyre, Adam (*fl.* 1646–8), I, 382
Eyre, Edward John (1815–1901), III, 990
Eyre, Sir Vincent (1811–1881), III, 1076
Eyres' Weekly Journal, or Warrington Advertiser (1756), II, 729
Eyton, Robert William (1815–1881), III, **904**
Eyton, Thomas Campbell (1809–1880), III, 957
Eyzat, Edward (*fl.* 1695), II, 999

F. (*fl.* 1833), III, 379
F., A. (*fl.* 1587), I, 787
F., C. (*fl.* 1674), II, 177
F., C. (*fl.* 1748), II, 213–4
F., C. (*fl.* 1790), II, 243
F., E. (*fl.* 1747), II, 447
F., E. M. (*fl.* 1800), II, 551
F., G. (*fl.* 1682), II, 965
F., G. T. (*fl.* 1852), I, 449
F., N. (*fl.* 1604), I, 391
F., R. (*fl.* 1605), I, 813
F., R. (*fl.* 1668), II, 270
F., T. (*fl.* 1585), I, 509
F., T. (*fl.* 1642), I, 753
F. Farley's Bristol Journal (1743), II, 721
Fabb, J. A. (*fl.* 1882), III, 835
Faber, F. A. (*fl.* 1869), III, 287
Faber, Frederick William (1814–1863), III, **287**
'Fabius' (1823), III, 201
Fables and other Short Poems (18 cent.), II, 201, 206
Fabyan, Robert (d. 1513), I, 116, 823
Faden, W. (*fl.* 1758), II, 715

Fagan, Christophe Barthélemie, II, 780
Fage, Robert (*fl.* 1658), I, 767
Fagnan, Marie Antoinette, II, 780
Fair Hibernian, The (18 cent.), II, 549
Fairbairn, Andrew Martin (1838–1912), III, 850
Fairbridge, Dorothea (*fl.* 1910), III, 1090
Fairbridge, Kingsley (1885–1924), III, 1089
Faire Em, A pleasant commodie of (17 cent.), I, 579
Faire Maide of Bristow, The (17 cent.), I, 652
Fairfax, Brian, the elder (1633–1711), II, 871
Fairfax, Brian, the younger (1676–1749), II, 102
Fairfax, Edward (d. 1635), I, 819, 894
Fairfax, Ferdinando, Baron Fairfax (1584–1648), I, 387
Fairfax, John (1623–1700), II, 928
Fairfax, Mary, later Somerville (1780–1872), III, 937
Fairfax, Thomas, Baron Fairfax (1612–1671), I, 387; II, 121, 871
Fairfax, Thomas (*fl.* 1760), II, 815
Fairholt, Frederick William (1814–1866), I, 267, 411; III, **904**
Fairies, The (18 cent.), II, 217 (2)
Fairing, or, A Golden Toy for Children, The (18 cent.), II, 563
'Fairless, Michael', i.e. Margaret Fairless Barber (1869–1901), III, **544**
FAIRY TALES, III, 575 f.
Fairy Tatler, The (1722), II, 662
Faithful Friends, The (17 cent.), I, 652
Faithful Memoirs of the Grubstreet Society (18 cent.), II, 202
Faithful Post, The (1653), I, 762 (2)
Faithful Post, The (1660), II, 701
Faithful Scout, The (1659), I, 763
Faithfull, Emily (*fl.* 1867), III, 87, 829
Faithfull Intelligencer from the Parliament's Army in Scotland, The (1659), II, 730
Faithfull Mercury, The (1679), II, 702
Faithfull Relation of the late Occurrences and Proceedings of the Scotish Army, A (1644), I, 756
Faithfull Scout, The (1651), I, 761
Faithfull Scout, The (1653), I, 761
Fajardo, Diego de Saavedra, I, 478
Falconbridge, Alexander (d. 1792), II, 749
Falconbridge, Anna Maria (*fl.* 1794), II, 749
Falconer, David (*fl.* 1753), II, 750
'Falconer, Lanoe', i.e. Mary Elizabeth Hawker (1848–1908), III, **544**
Falconer, Thomas (1772–1839), II, 779
Falconer, William (1732–1769), II, **361**
Falconet, Étienne Maurice, II, 780
FALCONRY (books on), I, 394 (1500–1660); II, 818 f. (1660–1800); III, 778 (19 cent.)
Fale, Thomas (*fl.* 1593), I, 881
Falkiner, Caesar Litton (1863–1908), III, **930**
Falkirk Herald, The, III, 793

Falkland, Amelia Cary, Viscountess (*fl.* 1857), III, 989
Falkner, G. (*fl.* 1841), III, 827
Falkner, Thomas (1707–1784), II, 756
Falla, John (*fl.* 1799), II, 800
Fallam, Robert (*fl.* 1671), II, 752
Fallaw, L. (*fl.* 1906), III, 1089
Fallon S. W. (*fl.* 1852), III, 1074
Fallowfield, John (*fl.* 1790–5), II, 250
False Alarms (18 cent.), II, 562
Falseness of Men (O.E.), I, **82**
Familiar Letters (17 cent.), II, 183 (2), 184, 186
Familiar Letters of Love (18 cent.), II, 194, 197
Family Friend, The (1849), III, 828
Family Magazine, The (1788), II, 681
Family Magazine, The (1834), III, 827
Family Times, The (1846), III, 812
Famous Historye of Captaine Thomas Stukeley, The (17 cent.), I, 539
Famous Tragedie of King Charles I, The (17 cent.), I, 651
Famous Victories of Henry the fifth, The (16 cent.), I, 538, 563
Fancourt, Samuel (1678–1768), II, 99
Fane, Sir Francis (d. 1689?), II, **422**
Fane, Julian Henry Charles (1827–1870), III, **287**
Fane, Mildmay, Earl of Westmorland (*c.* 1600–1665), I, 644
Fane, Priscilla Anne, Countess of Westmorland (1793–1879), III, 152
'Fane, Violet', i.e. Mary Montgomerie Lamb, later Singleton, later Lady Currie (1843–1905), III, **345**
Fanshawe, Anne, Lady (1625–1680), II, 133
Fanshawe, Catherine Maria (1765–1834), III, **233**
Fanshawe, Sir Richard (1608–1666), I, 644, 803, 809, 812, 814
Fanthorne, J. F. (*fl.* 1896), III, 1070
Fantosme, Jordan (*fl.* 12 cent.), I, 116
Faraday, Michael (1791–1867), III, 937, **947**
Faret, Nicolas, II, 780
Farewell, Christopher (*fl.* 1633), I, 784
Farewell, James (*fl.* 1689), II, 288
Farey, John (1766–1826), III, 949
Fargus, Frederick John ('Hugh Conway') (1847–1885), III, **540**
Faria y Sousa, Manuel de, II, 68
FARINGDON, II, 684 (magazine)
Farington, Joseph (1747–1821), II, 161, 629
Farish, William (1759–1837), II, 116
Farjeon, Benjamin Leopold (1838–1903), III, **544**f.
Farley, A. (*fl.* 1783), I, 115
Farley (or Farlie), Robert (*fl.* 1638), I, 478–9
Farley's Bath Journal (1756), II, 720
Farley's Bristol Advertiser (1743), II, 721
Farley's Bristol Journal (1748), II, 721
Farley's Bristol Newspaper (1725), II, 721
Farley's Exeter Journal (1723), II, 724

Farmer, John (1565?–1605?), I, 484
Farmer, Richard (1735–1797), II, **900**f.
Farmer, William (*fl.* 1614), I, 837
Farmer, The (1865), III, 819
Farmer and Stockbreeder, The (1889), III, 819
Farmer's Journal, The (1807), III, 819
Farmer's Journal, The (1839), III, 819
Farmer's Magazine, The (1800), II, 687
Farmer's Magazine and Useful Family Companion, The (1776), II, 680
FARMING (treatises on), I, 391f. and 845f. (16, 17 cents.); III, 969f. See also AGRICULTURE
Farnaby, Giles (1560?–1600), I, 484
Farnaby, Thomas J. (1575?–1647), I, 374, 376, 861–2
Farnborough, Sir Thomas Erskine, Baron (1815–1886), III, **901**
Farneworth, Ellis (d. 1763), II, 810–1
Farnie, — (*fl.* 1857), III, 775
Farnie, Henry Brougham (*fl.* 1870), III, 628
Farquhar, George (1678–1707), II, 61, **416**f., 532
Farr, Edward (*fl.* 1845), I, 405; III, 300
Farrant, Richard (*fl.* 1564–80), I, 538
Farrar, Adam Storey (1826–1905), II, 939
Farrar, Frederic William (1831–1903), III, 109, 119, 128, **545**, 848
Farrell, John (1851–1904), III, **1095**
Farrell, Sarah (*fl.* 1792), II, 63
Farrer, J. A. (*fl.* 1879), III, 1093
Farrer, Richard Ridley (*fl.* 1880), III, 990
Farrer, T. C. (*fl.* 1889), III, 984
Farrer, Thomas Henry, Baron (1819–1899), III, 984
FARRIERY (books on), I, 393 (16, 17 cents.); II, 815f. (1660–1800)
Farrington, J. (*fl.* 1754), II, 769
Farroe, Daniel (*fl.* 1754), II, 932
Farrow, George Edward (*fl.* 1895), III, 574
Farther Hue and Cry after Dr Sw - - - t, A (18 cent.), II, 191 (2)
Farwell, Sir George (1845–1915), III, 986
Fary Knight, The (17 cent.), I, 652
Fasciculi Zizaniorum (M.E.), I, 120
Fashionable Magazine; Or, Lady and Gentleman's Recorder of Fashions, The (1786), II, 681
Fashions of London and Paris (1795), II, 682
Fatall Maryage, The (17 cent.), I, 652
Fates of Men (O.E.), I, **82**
Fates of the Apostles (O.E.), I, **77**
Father William's Stories (1866), III, 578
Father's Instruction, A (O.E.), I, **81**
Fatum Vortigerni Seu (17 cent.), I, 661
Fauconpret, Auguste Jean Baptiste de, II, 142
Faujas de St Fond, Barthélemi, II, 141
Faulkner, George (1699?–1775), II, 734
Faulkner, Thomas Todd (*fl.* 1775), II, 734
Faulkner's Dublin Post Boy (1725), II, 734

Faussett, Bryan (1720–1776), III, 903
Faust, II, 805
Faust Cycle, I, 335
Favart, Charles Simon, II, 780
Favorite New Glees, The (18 cent.), II, 247
Favourite Collection of the most Admir'd Glees and Catches, A (18 cent.), II, 233
Favyn, André (*fl.* 1623), I, 395
Fawcett, Benjamin (1808–1893), III, 91
Fawcett, Henry (1833–1884), III, 142, 149, 976, 983
Fawcett, Joseph (d. 1804), II, 27
Fawcett, Millicent Garrett (1847–1929), III, 109, 983
Fawconer, Thomas (*fl.* 1769–70), II, 718, 817
Fawkes, Francis (1720–1777), II, 222, **361**f., 914
Fay, Eliza (*fl.* 1821), III, 1079
Fayre Mayde of the Exchange, The (17 cent.), I, 652
Fayrer, Sir Joseph (1824–1907), III, 1082
Fea, James (*fl.* 1775), II, 157
Feales, William (*fl.* 1732), II, 96
Fearn, David (*fl.* 1707), II, 731
Fearne, Charles (1742–1794), II, 963
Feast of Apollo, The (18 cent.), II, 241
Featley, Daniel (1582–1645), I, 682, 747, 755, 857
Federici, Cesare, I, 782; II, 810
Feelings of the Heart, The (18 cent.), II, 547
Feeny, R. (*fl.* 1845), III, 77
Fees, Book of (M.E.), I, 120
Feilde, John (d. 1588). See Field
Feilde, M. H. (*fl.* 1858), III, 105
Felbermann, Heinrich (1850–1925), III, 784, 814
Félibien, André, II, 780
Felicius, C., I, 807
Felipe, Bartolomé, I, 342
Felissa, or, The Life and Opinions of a Kitten of Sentiment (19 cent.), III, 575
Felix, Monk of Croyland (*fl.* 730), I, **103**
Felix Farley's Bristol Journal (1752), II, 721
Fell, Isaac (*fl.* 1769), II, 711
Fell, John (1625–1686), I, 852, 862; II, 846, **847**
Fell, John (1735–1797), II, 932
Fell, R. C. (*fl.* 1856), III, 99
Fell, Sarah (1673–8), II, 134
Fellow, The [Cambridge] (1836), III, 834
Fellowes, R. (*fl.* 1817), writer on Ceylon, II, 870
Fellowes, Robert (1771–1847), philanthropist and translator of Milton, I, 467
Fellows, Sir Charles (1799–1860), III, **998**
FELSTED SCHOOL, I, 372
Feltham, John (*fl.* 1797–1821), II, 145
Feltham (or Felltham), Owen (1602?–1668), I, 475, 725, 780
Felton, Henry (1679–1740), II, 16
Felton, Samuel (*fl.* 1732–7), I, 593; II, 916

Female American, The (18 cent.), II, 546
Female Inconstancy [etc.] (18 cent.), II, 202
Female Jester, The (18 cent.), II, 233
Female Poems On Several Occasions (17 cent.), II, 178
Female Politician, The (18 cent.) II, 539
Female Reader, The (18 cent.), II, 242, 245
Female Rebellion, The (17 cent.), I, 652
Female Spectator, The (1744), II, 663
Female Tatler, The (1709), II, 661
FENCING (books on), I, 394f. (16, 17 cents.); II, 882f. (1660–1800); III, 778 (19 cent.)
Fénelon, François de Salignac de la Mothe, II, 28, 35, 39, 40, 47, 535, 798f.; III, 22
Fenley and Shephard's Bristol Journal (1804), II, 721
Fenn, Lady Ellenor, née Frere (1743–1813), II, 557
Fenn, George Manville (1831–1909), III, **569**
Fenn, John (d. 1615), I, 817
Fenn, Sir John (1739–1794), II, 901
Fennell, James (*fl.* 1792), II, 666, 747
Fennell, John Greville (1807–1885), III, 771
Fenner, Dudley (1558?–1587), I, 690
Fenning, Daniel (*fl.* 1756–75), II, 125–7, 129
Fennor, William (*fl.* 1612–9), I, 416, 715, 717
Fenton, Elijah (1683–1730), II, 188, 196, **316**, 485, 910
Fenton, Sir Geoffrey (1539?–1608), I, 508, 810, 814 (2)
Fenton, Roger (1565–1616), I, 845
Fenton, T. (*fl.* 1713), II, 779
Fenwich, Thomas J. (*fl.* 1870), III, 101
Fenwick, — (*fl.* 1798), II, 469
Fenwick, Miss — (*fl.* 1843), III, 166
Fenwick, C. A. (*fl.* 1828), III, 1075
Fenwick, Eliza (*fl.* 1805), III, 571
Fenwick, John (*fl.* 1794–1807), II, 779; III, 800
Ferguson, Adam (1723–1816), II, 53, 471, **955**, **1000**
Ferguson, J. C. (*fl.* 1856), III, 210
Ferguson, James (1710–1776), II, 129
Ferguson, Sir Samuel (1810–1886), III, 1049, 1052
Fergusson, Hary (*fl.* 1767), II, 823
Fergusson, James (1621–1667), I, 907f.
Fergusson, James (1808–1886), III, 1076
Fergusson, R. (*fl.* 1851), III, 1080
Fergusson, Robert (1750–1774), II, **990**f.
Feriae Poeticae (18 cent.), II, 224
Fernandez, Jeronimo, I, 344
Fernandez de Navarette, M., III, 679
Ferne, Sir John (d. 1610?), I, 378, 396
Ferrabosco, Alfonso, the younger (1580?–1628), I, 485
Ferrar, John (*fl.* 1767–96), II, 159
Ferrar, Nicholas (1592–1637), I, 385, 452, **696**, 856
Ferrare Dutot, Charles de, II, 780
Ferrarius Montanus, Joannes, I, 508

Ferrers, George (1500?–1579), I, 413
Ferrers, Richard (*fl.* 1622), I, 716
Ferrey, Benjamin (1810–1880), III, 724
Ferri di San Costante, Giovanni L., II, 142
Ferriar, John (1761–1815), I, 630; II, 26
Ferrier, Auger, I, 884
Ferrier, Sir David (1843–1925), III, 964
Ferrier, James Frederick (1808–1864), III, 176, 682, **867**
Ferrier, John (*fl.* 1833), II, 732
Ferrier, Richard (*fl.* 1687), II, 744
Ferrier, Susan Edmonstone (1782–1854), III, **393**
Ferris, Richard (*fl.* 1590), I, 714, 768
Festival of Anacreon, The (18 cent.), II, 241, 242 (4), 247
Festival of Humour, The (19 cent.), II, 255
Festival of Love, or a Collection of Cytherean Poems, The (18 cent.), II, 242, 248, 251
Festival of Mirth, The (19 cent.), II, 255
Festival of Momus, The (18 cent.), II, 239–40, 247, 251, 255
Festival of Wit, The (18 cent.), II, 236 (2), 242, 245 (2), 248, 250, 255
Festoon, The (18 cent.), II, 224 (3)
Fetherstone, Christopher (*fl.* 1585), I, 812
Fetherstone, T. (*fl.* 1688), II, 760
Feuducci, G. F. (*fl.* 1784), II, 808
Feuerbach, Ludwig, III, 29
Feuillet, Raoul Auger, II, 825 (2)
Fevrier, D. (*fl.* 1900?), III, 833
Fewtrell, Thomas (*fl.* 1790), II, 823
Feyjoo y Montenegro, Benito Gerónimo, II, 30, 68
Fialetti, Odoardo, II, 810
Fichte, Johann Gottlieb, III, 29, 46 f.
Ficino, Marsilio, I, 327
FICTION, PROSE, I, 11 (general histories)
  Middle English period, I, 161 f.
  Renaissance to Restoration, I, 726 f.
  Restoration to Romantic Revival, II, 488 f. (recent criticism), 490 f. (principal novelists), 529 f. (minor fiction and translation), 553 f. (children's books)
  Nineteenth Century, III, 364 f. (bibliographies, histories, studies), 366 f. (Edgeworth-Marryat), 387 f. (minor, fiction, 1800–35), 421 f. (Borrow-Meredith), 471 f. (minor fiction, 1835–70), 513 f. (Carroll-Kipling), 534 f. (minor fiction, 1870–1900), 564 f. (children's books), 1069 f. (Anglo-Indian), 1086 f. (Canadian), 1089 f. (South African), 1096 f. (Australian-New Zealand)
Fiddes, Richard (1671–1725), II, 301, 600
Fidge, George (*fl.* 1652), I, 718, 732
Fidler, Peter (*fl.* 1791), II, 757
Field, Barrow (1786–1846), I, 539, 622; III, 636, 1094
Field, Frederick (1801–1885), III, **1013**

Field, J. (*fl.* 1642), publisher, I, 754
Field (or Feild), John (1525?–1587), astronomer, I, 882
Field (or Feilde), John (d. 1588), puritan divine, I, 687, 816
Field, Kate (*fl.* 1867), III, 582
Field, Louise Frances (*fl.* 1890), III, 574
Field, M. B. (*fl.* 1852), III, 403
'Field, Michael', i.e. Katherine Harris Bradley (1846–1913) and Edith Emma Cooper (1862–1914), III, **340**
Field, Nathaniel (1587–1633), I, 507, **644** f.
Field, Richard (*fl.* 1579–1624), I, 352, 858
Field, William (1768–1851), II, 937
Field, The (1853), III, 815
Fieldhouse, H. (*fl.* 1892), III, 806
Fielding, Anna Maria, later Hall (1800–1881), III, **485** f., 577, 711
  Articles by, III, 368, 400, 414
Fielding, D. (*fl.* 1853), III, 77
Fielding, Henry (1707–1754), II, 49, 61, 64, 69, 70–1, 121, **517** f., 663 (3), 664, 794, 796
Fielding, Sir John (d. 1780), II, 155, 228, 519
Fielding, Sarah (1710–1763), II, 24, 130, 543, 544 (2), 545 (3), 556, 763
Fielding, Theodore Henry (1781–1851), III, 81
Fiennes, Celia (*fl.* 1690), II, 139
Fiennes, Nathaniel (1608?–1669), I, 839
Fiest, Henry (*fl.* 1859), III, 800
Fieux, Charles de, Chevalier de Mouhy, II, 551, 780
Fiévée, Joseph, II, 142
Fife, James Duff, Earl of (1729–1809), II, 137
FIFTEENTH CENTURY, LITERATURE OF
  English Chaucerians, I, 250 f.
  English Prose (Capgrave to Berners), I, 260 f.
  Middle Scots Writers, I, 254 f.
  Miscellaneous and Anonymous Verse and Prose, I, 264 f.
Figaro (1870), III, 814
Figaro in London (1831), III, 820
Fight at Finnsburg, The (O.E.), I, 63 ff.
Filangieri, Gaetano, II, 810
Filberd, The (18 cent.), II, 244
Fildes, Sir Luke (1844–1927), III, 91
Filial Duty recommended by stories of children (18 cent.), II, 564
Fillingham Otuel and Firumbras (M.E.), I, **141**
Filmer, — (*fl.* 1662), II, 275
Filmer, Edward (*fl.* 1707), II, 402
Filmer, Sir Robert (d. 1653), I, 845, 877 f., 894
FINANCE, III, 820 (periodicals), 978 f. (treatises on)
Financial and Mining News, The (1884), III, 800
Financial Chronicle, The (1883), III, 820
Financial News, The (1884), III, 793, 800
Financial Times, The (1888), III, 800
Financial World, The (1886), III, 820
Financier, The (1870), III, 799

Finch, Anne, Countess of Winchilsea (1666–1720), II, **333**

Finch, Heneage, Earl of Winchilsea (d. 1689), II, 743

Finch, Sir Henry (1558–1625), I, 850

Findlay, Sir George (1829–1893), III, 984

FINE ARTS, I, 392f. (treatises on, 16, 17 cents.); II, 13–4f. (influence on literature), 30f. (treatises on, 18 cent.)

Fine Arts Quarterly Review, The (1863), III, 833

Finett (or Finet), Sir John (1571–1641), I, 381

Finlason, F. W. (*fl.* 1869), I, 848

Finlay, Francis Dalzell (1793–1857), III, 808

Finlay, George (1799–1875), III, **889**

Finlay, Hugh (*fl.* 1773), II, 756

Finlay, J. (*fl.* 1859), III, 302

Finlay, J. W. (*fl.* 1855), III, 807

Finlay, John (1782–1810), I, 272

Finlayson, John (1770–1854), III, 970

Finn's Leinster Journal (1766), II, 737

Finnerty, Peter (1766?–1822), II, 736

Finnsburg, The Fight at (O.E.), I, **63**f.

Fioravanti, Leonardo, I, 891

Fiquet du Boccage, Marie Anne, II, 141

Fiquet du Boccage, P. J., II, 44

Firebrace, Henry (1619–1691), I, 842

Firminger, T. A. C. (*fl.* 1864), III, 1084

First Part of Jeronimo, The (17 cent.), I, 539

First part of Sir John Oldcastle, The (17 cent.), I, 580

First Part of the Contention betwixt Yorke and Lancaster, The (16 cent.), I, 552–3

Firumbras, Sir (M.E.), I, **141**

Fischer, Kuno, III, 605

Fish, Simon (d. 1531), I, 670, 845

Fishacre, Richard (d. 1248), I, **295**

Fisher, Arthur T. (*fl.* 1892), III, 772

Fisher, Daniel (1731–1807), II, 754

Fisher, Hawkins (*fl.* 1871), III, 778

Fisher, Jasper (*fl.* 1639), I, 656

Fisher, John (1459?–1535), I, 681f., 684

Fisher, John (*fl.* 1796), compiler of biblical concordance, II, 928

Fisher, John Abraham (1744–1806), violinist, II, 81

Fisher, Jonathan (d. 1812), II, 159

Fisher, P. (*fl.* 1890?), III, 814

Fisher, Payne (1616–1693), I, 833

Fisher, Samuel (1605–1665), II, 857

Fisher, Thomas (*fl.* 1643), I, 390

Fisher, W. H. (*fl.* 1899), III, 799

Fisher, William Richard (*fl.* 1856), III, 986

Fisher's Juvenile Scrap-Book (1836), III, 577

FISHERIES (writings on), I, 845f. (16, 17 cents.); III, 969f. (19 cent.)

FISHING (books on), I, 393f. (16, 17 cents.); II, 818f. (1660–1800); III, 768f. (19 cent.)

Fishing Gazette, The (1877), III, 820

Fitch, Sir Joshua Girling (1824–1903), III, 109

Fitch, R. (*fl.* 1830–56), I, 279, 527

Fitch, Ralph (*fl.* 1583–1606), III, 1079

Fitch, Tobias (*fl.* 1725), III, 753

Fitt, J. Nevil (*fl.* 1869), II, 766

Fitton, William Henry (1780–1861), III, 950

Fitzball, Edward, earlier Ball (1792–1873), III, **586**, 607

Fitz-Cook, H. (*fl.* 1865), III, 84

Fitz-Geffry (1575?–1638), I, 475f.

Fitzgerald, — (*fl.* 1815), III, 850

Fitzgerald, Lord Edward (1763–1798), II, 757

FitzGerald, Edward (1809–1883), III, **251**f., 834

FitzGerald, Edward Arthur (1871–1931), III, 990

Fitzgerald, Francis (*fl.* 1785), II, 681

Fitzgerald, George Francis (1851–1901), III, 940

Fitzgerald, Gerald (*fl.* 1773), II, 821

Fitzgerald, Percy Hetherington (1834–1925), **545**f.

Fitzgerald, R. A. (*fl.* 1866), III, 774 (2)

Fitzgerald, Thomas (1695?–1752), II, **316**

Fitzgibbon, Edward (1803–1857), III, 769

Fitzherbert, Sir Anthony (1470–1538), I, 845–6, 850

Fitzherbert, John (*fl.* 1523), I, 391, 845

Fitzjames, Richard (d. 1522), I, 682

Fitzmaurice, George (*fl.* 1903–17), III, **1065**

Fitzneal (or Fitznigel), Richard (d. 1198), I, **289**

Fitzpatrick, Sir J. P. (*fl.* 1897), III, 1089

Fitzpatrick, P. (*fl.* 1899), III, 1092

Fitzpatrick, Thomas (*fl.* 1760), II, 448

Fitzpatrick, William John (1830–1895), III, 379, 412, 682

Fitzralph, Richard (d. 1360), I, **312**

Fitzroy, Augustus Henry, Duke of Grafton (1735–1811), II, 165

FitzSimons, F. W. (b. 1875), III, 1088

Fitzthomas, — (*fl.* 1781), II, 626

Fitzwilliam, Charles William Wentworth, Earl (1787–1857), II, 633

Fitzwilliam, William Charles de Meuron Wentworth, Viscount Milton (1839–1877), III, 970

Fitzwygram, J. (*fl.* 1859), III, 109

Five Love-Letters from a Nun to a Cavalier (17 cent.), II, 533

FIVES (books on), III, 775

Flagel; or A Ramble of Fancy through the Land of Electioneering (18 cent.), II, 546

Flagellant, The (1792), II, 666

Flammenberg, Lorenz, II, 805

Flamsteed, John (1646–1719), II, 960

Flanders New Garland, The (18 cent.), II, 188

Flapper, The (1796), II, 666

Flatman, Thomas (1637–1688), II, **281**

Fleay, Frederick Gard (1831–1909), III, **1037**

Fléchère, Jean Guillaume de la (or John William Fletcher) (1729–1785), II, **852**

Fléchier, Valentin Esprit, II, 780

Flecknoe, Richard (c. 1620–1678?), I, 723 f., 772; II, **422**
Fleet, A Terrier of (M.E.), I, 121
Fleet Street Gazette, The (1874), III, 782
Fleetwood, Edward (fl. 1652), I, 717, 809
Fleetwood, William (1656–1723), III, 783
Fleming, Abraham (1552?–1607), I, 671, 741, 799, 801, 803, 806, 808, 811, 883
Fleming, Caleb (1698–1779), II, 863
Fleming, F. (fl. 1771), II, 154
Fleming, G. A. (fl. 1834), III, 816
Fleming, John (1785–1857), III, 956
Fleming, William (fl. 1779), II, 756
Fleming's British Farmer's Chronicle (1826), III, 819
Fleming's Weekly Express (1823), III, 819
Flemings in Oxford, The (17 cent.), I, 387
Flesher, Thomas (fl. 1685), II, 120
Fleta (M.E.), I, 300
Fletcher, Alfred Ewen (fl. 1889), III, 799
Fletcher, Alfred H. (fl. 1889), III, 804
Fletcher, Andrew, of Saltoun (1655–1716), II, 999
Fletcher, Ebenezer (fl. 1774), II, 848
Fletcher, Eliza (1770–1858), III, 150
Fletcher, Francis (fl. 1580), I, 787
Fletcher, Giles, the elder (1549–1611), I, 366, 430, 778, 804
Fletcher, Giles, the younger (1588?–1623), I, 445 f.
Fletcher, John (1579–1625), I, **632 f.**
Fletcher, John (1754–1835), Chester journalist, II, 695, 776
Fletcher, John (1793–1836), medical writer, III, 963
Fletcher, John William (or Jean Guillaume de la Fléchère) (1729–1785), II, **852**
Fletcher, Joseph (1816–1876), II, 862
Fletcher, Phineas (1582–1650), I, 444, 656, 679
Fletcher, R. (fl. 1656), I, 804
Fletcher, R. (fl. 1833), I, 463, 466
Fletcher, Robert (fl. 1586), I, 476
Fletcher, Thomas (1666–1713), II, **281**
Fleur-de Lys [Cambridge] (1871), III, 835
Fleury, Claude, II, 780; III, 688–9
Flinders, Matthew (1774–1814), III, 990
Flint, George (fl. 1716), II, 712
Flint, Robert (1838–1910), III, **867**
Flioris, Peter, I, 783
Flloyd, Thomas (fl. 1743–62), II, 622, 783, 788, 922
Flora's Fair Garland (17 cent.), II, 180
Florence of Worcester (d. 1118), I, 116
Florence Miscellany, The (18 cent.), II, 238
Flores Historiarum (M.E.), I, 116
Flores, Juan de, I, 344, 733
Florian, Jean Pierre Claris de, II, 553, 776
Florimene, The Argument of the Pastorall of (17 cent.), I, 652

Florio, Giovanni (or John) (1553?–1625), I, 377, 715, 787, 811, 816
Floris and Blauncheflur (M.E.), I, 42, **153 f.**
Florus, I, 801
Flower, Benjamin (1755–1829), II, 695
Flower, Sarah Fuller, later Adams (1805–1848), III, **275**, 636
Flower, Sir William (1831–1899), III, 958, 968
Flower and the Leaf, The (M.E.), I, **254**
Flower-Piece, The (1731), II, 201
Flower-Piece, The (1780), II, 234
Flowers of Epigrammes (16 cent.), I, 403
Flowers of Harmony, The (18 cent.), II, 252
Flowers of Parnassus, The (18 cent.), II, 205–6
Floyd, Ann (fl. 1722), II, 792
Floyd, John (1572–1649), I, 810
Floyd, William (fl. 1821), III, 762
Fludd, Robert (1754–1637), I, 874, 886
Flügel, Johann Gottfried, III, 606
Flying Eagle, The (1652), I, 761
Flying Post, The (1644), I, 756
Flying Post, The (1714), II, 707
Flying Post, The (1727), II, 707
Flying Post, The (Dublin, 1722), II, 734
Flying Post, The (Dublin, 1729), II, 735
Flying Post, The (Dublin, 1744), II, 735
Flying Post and Medley, The (1714), II, 707
Flying Post; Or, The Post-Master, The (1659), II, 706
Flying Post; Or the Post Master, The (1699), II, 733
Flying Post; or The Postmaster's News, The (Dublin, 1708), II, 734
Flying Post; Or, The Weekly Medley, The (1728), II, 713, 719
Flying Postman; Or The Dublin Postman, The (1729), II, 734
Fog's Weekly Journal (1728), II, 712
Fogg, Peter Walkden (fl. 1796), I, 16
Foigny, Gabriel de, II, 534
Folkard, Henry Coleman (fl. 1853–76), III, 762, 778, 986
Folkingham, William (fl. 1620), I, 377
FOLKLORE, GERMANIC. See under GERMANIC BACKGROUND, I, 54 f.
Folklore (1890), III, 834
Folks at Home (1896), III, 821
Fonblanque, Albany (1793–1872), III, 784, 810, 982
Fonblanque, E. B. de (fl. 1786), II, 461
Fonetic Frend, The (1849), III, 1030
'Fontaines, Louis' (Zacharie de Lisieux), II, 781
Fontanier, V. (fl. 1844), III, 1076
Fontanieu, Gaspard Moïse, II, 542, 781
Fontenelle, Bernard le Bovier, Sieur de, II, 28, 35 f., 40, 111, 786
Fonvive, John de (fl. 1730), II, 706
Fool, The (1746), II, 663
'Foot, Ferdinando' (1751), II, 215

FOOTBALL (books on), III, 775
Foote, G. W. (*fl.* 1883), III, 819, 831
Foote, Samuel (1720–1777), II, **449**f., 485
Forbes, Alexander, Baron Forbes of Pitsligo (1678–1762), II, 16, 785
Forbes, Alexander Penrose (1817–1875), III, **857**
Forbes, Archibald (1838–1900), III, 784
Forbes, Edward (1815–1854), III, 952, **957**, 1002
Forbes, Eli (*fl.* 1762), II, 755
Forbes, G. H. (*fl.* 1854–64), III, 686, 857
Forbes, Henry Ogg (1851–1932), III, 990
Forbes, James (1749–1819), III, 1079
Forbes, James David (1809–1893), III, 938, 990
Forbes, John (1593–1648), I, 908
Forbes, John (*fl.* 1666), II, 174
Forbes, Sir John (1787–1861), III, 833
Forbes, Patrick (1564–1635), I, 908
Forbes, Patrick (*fl.* 1740), I, 398
Forbes, Robert (1708–1775), II, 1003
Forbes, Urquhart A. (*fl.* 1880), III, 986
Forbes, William Henry (1851–1914), III, 1005
Force, Peter (*fl.* 1836), I, 764
Force of Example, or the History of Henry and Caroline, The (18 cent.), II, 564
Ford, A. (*fl.* 1649), I, 760
Ford, A. L. (*fl.* 1897), III, 774
Ford, Charles (*fl.* 1712), II, 702
Ford, E. (*fl.* 1660), I, 715
Ford, Ford H. Madox, earlier Hueffer (b. 1873), III, 574
Ford, Horace Alfred (*fl.* 1856), III, 776
Ford, J. J. (*fl.* 1788), II, 801
Ford, John (1586–1639), I, **637**f.
Ford, Sir Richard (*fl.* 1790), II, 460
Ford, Richard (1796–1858), III, 423, **990**
Ford, Simon (1619?–1699), II, 820
Ford, T. (*fl.* 1834), III, 77
Ford, Thomas (1580?–1648), I, 485
Ford, William Justice (1853–1904), III, 774 (2)
Forde, Emanuel (*fl.* 1600), I, 730
Forde, Thomas (*fl.* 1660), I, 720, 723, 726
Forde, William (1771–1832), I, 17
Fordyce, David (1711–1751), II, 24, 108
Fordyce, James (1720–1796), II, 119, **362**
Foreign and Colonial Quarterly Review, The (1843), III, 833
Foreign and Domestick News; With the Pacquet Boat from Holland (1695), II, 706
FOREIGN IMPRESSIONS (of England), II, 140f. (17, 18 cents.)
Foreign Medical Review, The (1779), II, 680
FOREIGN NEWSPAPERS, II, 719
Foreign Post, The (1697), II, 706
Foreign Post; or, Historical Narrative, The (1697), II, 706
Foreign Quarterly Review, The (1827), III, 833
Foreign Review and Continental Miscellany, The (1828), III, 833

Foreman, Sloper (*fl.* 1766), II, 28
Forester, T. (*fl.* before 1863), III, 892
Forestus, Petrus, I, 889
Forman, Charles (*fl.* 1725–41), II, 302, 772, 798
Forman, Harry Buxton (1842–1917), III, **1037**f.
Forman, J. R. (*fl.* 1905), III, 803
Forman, S. (*fl.* 1766), II, 781
Forman, Simon (1552–1611), I, 384
Formby, C. W. (*fl.* 1896), III, 109
Formey, Jean Henri Samuel, II, 781
Forrest, Ebenezer (*fl.* 1729), II, 787
Forrest, Sir G. W. (1845–1926), III, 1078
Forrest, Thomas (*fl.* 1580), I, 803
Forrest, Thomas (1739?–1802?), II, 750
Forrest, William (*fl.* 1581), I, 436
Forrester, Charles Robert (1803–1850), III, **288**
Forrester, James (*fl.* 1734), II, 121
Forrester, Thomas (1635?–1706), II, 992
Forrester, William (*fl.* 1788), II, 817
Forset (or Forsett), Edward (1553–1630), I, 656, 847 (misprinted Edwin Forset)
Forshall, Josiah (1795–1863), I, 204; III, 1034
Forster, C. L. (*fl.* 1834), III, 858
Forster, George (d. 1792), II, 751
Forster, Johann Georg Adam (1754–1794), II, 141, 742
Forster, Johann Reinhold (*fl.* 1771–1801), II, 742, 772
Forster, John (1812–1876), II, 830; III, 249, 259, 449–50, 636, **713**, 799, 810, 833
Forster, Nathaniel (1726?–1790), II, 148
Forster, Thomas Ignatius Maria (1789–1860), II, 940
Forsyth, Andrew Russell (b. 1858), III, 943
Forsyth, Joseph (1763–1815), III, 990
Forsyth, Peter Taylor (1848–1927), III, 850
Forsyth, Robert (1766–1846), III, 969
Forsyth, William (1737–1804), III, 959
Forsyth, William (1812–1899), III, **713**f., 784, 806
Fortescue, G. (*fl.* 1859), III, 361
Fortescue, Hugh, Viscount Ebrington (1818–1905), III, 761
Fortescue, James (1716–1777), I, 16; II, 17
Fortescue, Sir John (1394?–1476?), I, 261, 313, 844
Fortescue, Sir John William (1859–1934), III, 761
Fortescue, Thomas (*fl.* 1571), I, 816
Fortescue, Thomas, Lord Clermont (*fl.* 1869), I, 261
Fortescue-Aland, John, Baron Fortescue (1670–1746), II, 920
Fortiguerra, N., III, 239
Fortnight's Register; Or, A Chronicle of Interesting Events, The (1762), II, 678, 715
Fortnightly Review, The (1865), III, 830
Fortnum, Sophia (*fl.* 1798), II, 551
Fortrey, Samuel (1622–1681), II, 958

Fortunate Blue-Coat Boy, The (18 cent.), II, 547
Fortunate Shepherdess, The [etc.] (18 cent.), II, 251
Fortunatus (in German), I, 336; II, 805
Fosbroke, Thomas Dudley (1770–1842), III, **883**
Foscolo, Ugo, III, 203, 230
Foss, Edward (1787–1870), I, 261
Foster, B. F. (*fl.* 1837), III, 115
Foster, David (*fl.* 1882), III, 771
Foster, Ernest (1852–1919), III, 784, 814, 821
Foster, James (1697–1753), II, 863
Foster, John (1731–1774), Eton master, I, 16
Foster, John (1770–1843), essayist, III, 368, **669**
Foster, Sir Michael (1689–1763), II, 963
Foster, Sir Michael (1836–1907), III, **964**
Foster, Samuel (d. 1652), I, 881
Foster, William (1591–1643), I, 886
Fotherbie, Robert (*fl.* 1613), I, 770
Fotherby, Martin (1549?–1619), I, 875
Fothergill, John (1712–1780), II, 754
Foucher D'Osbornville, —, II, 469
Fougasses, Thomas de, I, 779
Foulis, Sir John, of Ravelston, II, 156
Foulkes, J. (*fl.* 1876), III, 1072
Foulkes, W. D. I. (*fl.* 1879–90), III, 821
Foundation of the Chapel of Walsingham, The (15 cent.), I, 264
Foundling Hospital for Wit, The (18 cent.), II, 210 (3), 212 (3), 213 (2), 222 (2)
Foundling, or, The History of Lucius Stanhope, The (18 cent.), II, 563
Fountainhall, Sir John Lauder, Lord (1646–1722), II, **997**f.
Fouqué, Friedrich Heinrich Karl de la Motte, III, **29**
Four Poems (18 cent.), II, 229
Foure Sonnes of Aymon (M.E.), I, **142**
Fowldes, William (*fl.* 1603), I, 803
Fowle, Thomas Welbank (1835–1903), III, 976
Fowler, Alfred (b. 1868), III, 945
Fowler, Edward (1632–1714), II, 491, **847**
Fowler, Thomas (1832–1904), III, **867**
Fowler, William (*fl.* 1597), of Hawick, I, 896
Fowler, William (*fl.* 1603), Scottish sonneteer, I, 432
Fowler, William Warde (1847–1921), III, **1005**
FOWLING (books on), III, 818f.
Fownes, George (1815–1849), III, 947
Fox, Augustus Henry Lane, later Pitt-Rivers (1827–1900), III, **915**
Fox, Caroline (1819–1871), III, 153
Fox, Charles (*fl.* 1875), III, 821
Fox, Charles James (1749–1806), II, 165
Fox, George (1624–1691), I, 377; II, **855**
Fox, H. (*fl.* 1778), II, 791
Fox, Henry, Baron Holland (1705–1774), II, 136, 664–5
Fox, Henry Edward, Baron Holland (1802–1859), III, 152

Fox, Henry Richard Vassall, Baron Holland (1773–1840), II, 165, 837 (2)
Fox, J. (*fl.* 1808), educationalist, III, 111
Fox, John (1516–1587). See Foxe
Fox, John (1686?–after 1723), essayist, II, 537, 662
Fox, Luke (1586–1635), I, 792
Fox, Richard (1486–1527), I, 383
Fox, S. (*fl.* 1830–64), I, 79, 87
Fox, William (*fl.* 1796), II, 666
Fox, William Johnson (1786–1864), III, 117, 275 (2), 784, 790, 801, 812, 824, 847
Fox, William Tilbury (1836–1879), III, 821
Foxcroft, A. B. (*fl.* 1911), III, 1093
Foxe, John (1516–1587), I, 668, 682, **824**f.
Foxton, Thomas (*fl.* 1721–36), II, 196, 556
Foxwell, E. (*fl.* 1889), III, 984
Foxwell, H. S. (*fl.* 1886–95), III, 973, 975
Foyle, Oxenbridge (*fl.* 1659), I, 793
Fracastoro, Girolamo, II, 810
Fragments and Links, and their Order (M.E.), I, 234
Fragments of Printed Alexander (M.E.), I, 144
Frame, Richard (*fl.* 1692), II, 752
Frampton, John (*fl.* 1577–96), I, 765, 782, 794, 816, 818, 892
Frampton, Mary (1773–1846), II, 138
FRANCE
Literary relations with, I, 330f. (1500–1660); II, **33**f. (1660–1800); III, **18**f. (19 cent.), 54f.
See also FRENCH
Francis, Francis (1822–1886), III, 770
Francis, G. H. (*fl.* 1852), III, 426, 798 (2), 809, 811
Francis, John (1811–1882), II, 506; III, 98, 784, 972
Francis, P. (*fl.* 1857), II, 651
Francis, Philip (1708?–1773), II, **317**, 632, 664
Francis, Sir Philip (1740–1818), II, 137, 165, **631**f., 665
Francis, W. (*fl.* 1890), III, 824
FRANCISCANS
Writings by English, I, **291**f. (13 cent.), **302** (14, 15 cents.)
Franck, Johann Wolffgang (*fl.* 1690), II, 182
Franck, Richard (1624?–1708), I, 777; II, 535, 819
Francke, August Hermann, II, 54
Francklin, Richard (*fl.* 1730), II, 695
Francklin, Thomas (1721–1784), II, **466**, 485, 762–4, 784, 804 (3)
Francklin, William (1763–1839), II, 751; III, 1075
François de Sales, II, 781
Frank, Joseph (*fl.* 1804–5), of Germany, II, 142
Frank, Joseph (*fl.* 1825–33), Joseph Ritson's nephew, II, 906 (4), 907
Frank, Mark (1613–1664), I, 696
Frankland, Edward (1829–1899), III, **948**

Frankland, Sir Thomas (1717?–1784), II, 822
Franklin, Benjamin (1706–1790), II, 696
Franklin, Lady Jane (1792–1875), III, 151
Franklin, Sir John (1786–1847), III, 990
Franks, Sir Augustus Wollaston (1826–1897), I, 60, 898
Franks Casket (O.E.), I, 60
Frankz, Thomas, II, 745
Fraser, Alexander Campbell (1819–1914), III, **867**
Fraser, D. (*fl.* 1831), II, 994
Fraser, Duncan (*fl.* 1895), III, 772
Fraser, Hastings (*fl.* 1865), III, 1077
Fraser, James (1818–1885), III, 121
Fraser, James Baillie (1783–1856), III, **393** f.
Fraser, Lydia Falconer, later Miller ('Harriet Myrtle') (1811?–1876), III, 572, 721
Fraser, R. (*fl.* 1802), III, 969
Fraser, S. (*fl.* 1729), II, 774
Fraser, William (*fl.* 1771), II, 702
Fraser's Magazine for Town and Country (1830), III, 826
Frasier, J. (*fl.* 1689), II, 705
Fraud Detected [etc.] (18 cent.), II, 197
Fraunce, Abraham (*fl.* 1587–1633), I, 376, 436, 678, 729, 802 (2), 808, 819 (2), 864
Fraus Pia (17 cent.), I, 661
Frazer, Sir James George (b. 1854), III, 968
Freake, J. (*fl.* 1651), I, 809, 887
Freake, W. (*fl.* 1629), I, 838
Fréart, Roland (Sieur de Chambray), II, 829–30
Frederica: or The Memoirs of a Young Lady (18 cent.), II, 550
Frederick II, King of Prussia, II, 805
Free (or Phreas), John (d. 1465), I, **313**
Free, John (*fl.* 1749), II, 17, 23
Free Briton, The (1729), II, 663
Free Enquirer, The (1761), II, 664
Free Masonry, For the Ladies (18 cent.), II, 246
Free Masons Songs, The (18 cent.), II, **219**
Free Press, The (1855), III, 829
Free Review, The (1893), III, 831
Free Thinker, The (18 cent.), II, 537
Freebairn, J. (*fl.* 1725), II, 788
Freebairn, Robert (*fl.* 1706), II, 731
Freehold Land Times and Building News, The (1854), III, 822
Free-Holder, The (1715), II, 604
Freeholder, The (Cork, 1716), II, 737
Freeholder and the Weekly Packet, The (1716), II, 731
Freeholder; or, Political Essays, The (1715), II, 662
Freeholder's Journal, The (1721), II, 662
Freeholder's Journal, The (1722), II, 713
Freeholder's Magazine; Or, Monthly Chronicle of Liberty, The (1769), II, 679
Freeland, William (*fl.* 1872), III, **340**
Freeman, Edward Augustus (1823–1892), III, 893, **908** f.

Freeman, Gage Earle (1820–1903), III, 778 (3)
Freeman, Harriot (*fl.* 1797), II, 791
Freeman, Sir Ralph (1590?–1655), I, 645, 807
Freeman, Thomas (*fl.* 1614), I, 481
Freeman, The (1855), III, 819
Freeman's Journal, The (1807), II, 735
Freeman's Journal, The [Dublin] (before 1820), III, 809
Freeman-Mitford, John Thomas, Earl of Redesdale (1805–1886), I, 17
Freemason's Magazine; Or, General and Compleat Library, The (1793), II, 682
Freemason's Monthly Magazine, The (1855), III, 833
Free-Mason's Pocket Companion, The (18 cent.), II, 215◆
Freemason's Quarterly Magazine, The (1853), III, 833
Freemason's Quarterly Magazine and Review, The (1850), III, 833
Freemason's Quarterly Review, The (1834), III, 833
Freemasonry Stripped Naked (18 cent.), II, 223
Freemen's Magazine, The (1774), II, 685
Freethinker, The (1711), II, 661
Freethinker, The (1718), II, 662
Freethinker, The (1881), III, 818
Fréjus, Roland, II, 781
Freke, Mrs E. (1641–1714), II, 158
Freke, John (*fl.* 1710?), II, 718
Freke (or Freeke), William (1662–1744), II, 108
Fremantle, H. E. S. (*fl.* 1909), III, 1092
FRENCH
      Loan-Words from, I, 33
      Textbooks of, I, 377 (16, 17 cents.); II, 126 (17, 18 cents.)
      Translations from, I, 809 f. (16, 17 cents.); II, 28 f. (literary criticism), 769 f. (1660–1800)
      See also FRANCE
French, George Russell (1803–1881), I, 542
French, Gilbert James (1804–1866), III, 379
French, Samuel (*fl.* 1891), III, 585
French, Sydney (*fl.* 1856), III, 810
French Convert, The (17 cent.), II, 532
French Intelligencer, The (1651), I, 761
French Occurrences, The (1652), I, 761
FRENCH REVOLUTION
      Literary influence of, III, 158
French Rogue, The (17 cent.), II, 530
French's Acting Edition (1890), III, 585
Frend, William (1757–1841), II, 85, 115; III, 109, 941
Freoul, J. B. de (*fl.* 1737), II, 799
Fresh Whip for all Scandalous Lyers, A (17 cent.), I, 723
Frere, Sir Henry Bartle Edward (1815–1884), II, 362; III, 577
Frere, John Hookham (1769–1846), II, 61, **362**

Frere, Mary Eliza Isabella (1845–1911), III, 577, 1073
Frere, Mary (*fl.* 1868), III, 577
Freshfield, Douglas W. (1845–1934), III, 777, 830, 990
Freshman, The [Cambridge] (1836), III, 834
Fresnoy, Nicolas Lenglet du, II, 788
Freval, J. B. de (*fl.* 1740), II, 793
Frew, J. J. (*fl.* 1855), III, 687
Frewen, Moreton (*fl.* 1888), III, 974
Freytag, Gustav, III, 29
Friar Daw Thopias, Reply of (M.E.), I, 200
Fridegodus (or Frithegode) (*fl.* 950), I, 107
Friend, The (1755), II, 664
Friend, A Weekly Essay, The (1796), II, 666
Friend of the People, The (1850), III, 817
Friend of the People, The (1860), III, 817
Friends' Quarterly Examiner, The (1867), III, 833
Friendly Couriere, The (1711), II, 660, 712
Friendly Debate upon the next elections of Parliament, A (1687), II, 657
Friendly Instructor, The (18 cent.), II, 560
Friendly Intelligence, The (1679), II, 702
Friendly Writer and Register of Truth, The (1732), II, 663, 677
Frier Rush, The Historie of (17 cent.), I, 714
Frisky Songster, The (18 cent.), II, 227, 231
Frisky Songster, The (19 cent.), II, 255 (2)
Frith, John (1503–1533), I, 667
Frith, William Powell (1819–1909), III, 153
Frithegode (or Fridegodus) (*fl.* 950), I, 107
Frobisher's New Select Collection of Epitaphs (18 cent.), 244
Froebel, Friedrich Wilhelm August (1782–1852), III, 29, 109
Froger, François, II, 781
Frogges of Egypt (17 cent.), I, 718
Froissart, Jean, I, 116, 813
From The Mercury Office. For Buying and selling of Estates [etc.] (1685), II, 717
From the Office. For Buying and selling of Estates [etc.] (1685), II, 717
Frontinus, I, 802
Frost, John (*fl.* 1816), III, 776
Frost, Thomas (1821–1908), III, 785
Frost, Walter (*fl.* 1649), I, 748, 760
Froude, James Anthony (1818–1894), III, 35, 826, **892**f.
    Articles by, III, 48, 50f., 53, 58, 63f., 65
Froude, Richard Hurrell (1803–1836), III, 856, **857**
Frowde, Philip (d. 1738), II, **437**
Fruitless Repentance, The (18 cent.), II, 547
Fry, A. (*fl.* 1838), III, 130
Fry, Caroline, later Wilson (1787–1846), III, 852
Fry, Charles Burgess (b. 1872), III, 774
Fry, Sir Edward (1827–1918), III, 986
Fry, Elizabeth (1780–1845), III, 151
Fry, Francis (1803–1886), I, 673, 675 (2)
Fry, H. J. (*fl.* 1845), III, 33

Fry, John (1792–1822), I, 407, 453; II, 257
Fry, Roger (1866–1934), III, 835
Fryer, George (*fl.* 1798), II, 254
Fryer, John (d. 1733), III, 1079
Fryer Bacon, The Famous Historie of (17 cent.), I, 731
Fuessli (or Fuseli), Johann Heinrich (1741–1825), II, 31, 52–3, 806, 951
Fugger News-Letters, The (16 cent.), I, 383
Fugitive Miscellany, The (18 cent.), II, 230 (2)
Fugitive Pieces (18 cent.), II, 252
Fulbecke, William (1560–1603?), I, 848, 850
Fulford, W. (*fl.* 1856), III, 271
Fulke, William (1538–1589), I, 672, 676, 690, 882–3
Full Collection of all Poems upon Charles, Prince of Wales, A (18 cent.), II, 211
Fullarton, John (1780–1849), III, 974
Fullarton, William (1754–1808), III, 969
Fuller, Anne (*fl.* 1789), II, 549
Fuller, J. G. (*fl.* 1843), II, 862
Fuller, Nicholas (1557?–1626), I, 856
Fuller, Sir Thomas Ekins (1831–1910), III, 1090
Fuller, Thomas (1608–1661), I, 371, 683, 723, 732, 780, **835**f.
Fullerton, Lady Georgiana Charlotte (1812–1885), III, **483**f.
Fulman, William (1632–1688), I, 697; II, 117
Fulwel, Ulpian (*fl.* 1586), I, 516
Fun (1861), III, 820
Funnell, William (*fl.* 1707), II, 741
'Funny, Ferdinando' (1760), II, 219
Furetière, Antoine, II, 533
Furley (or Furly), Benjamin (1636–1714), I, 377
Furneaux, Henry (1829–1900), III, 1005
Furniss, Harry (1854–1925), III, 91, 774
Furnivall, Frederick James (1825–1910), III, **1030**f.
Furphy, Joseph ['Tom Collins'] (*fl.* 1903), III, 1097
Fuseli (or Fuessli), Henry (1741–1825), II, 31, 52–3, 806, 951
Fuzelier, Louis, II, 781, 787
Fyffe, Charles Alan (1845–1892), III, **935**
Fysher, Robert (*fl.* 1738), II, 104
Fytton, Anne (*fl.* 1574–1618), I, 384
Fytton, Mary (*fl.* 1574–1618), I, 384
Fyvie, Isabella, later Mayo ('Edward Garrett') (*fl.* 1877), III, 573

G., A. (*fl.* 1682), I, 785
G., C. (*fl.* 1705), II, 819
G., F. (*fl.* 1653), I, 819
G., F. (*fl.* 1690), II, 800
G., G. (*fl.* 1561), I, 883
G., H. (*fl.* 1618). Author of 'The Mirrour of Majestie' incorrectly ascribed to Henry Peacham, I, 479

G., H. (*fl.* 1648), I, 810
G., H. (*fl.* 1854), III, 186
G., H. S. (b. 1829), III, 154
G., I. (*fl.* 1589), I, 692
G., I. H. (*fl.* 1885), III, 761
G., J. (*fl.* 1642), I, 753
G., J. (*fl.* 1661), II, 173
G., J. (*fl.* 1605), I, 716
G., R. (*fl.* 1653), I, 869
G., R. (*fl.* 1662), II, 751
G., T. (*fl.* 1736), II, 205–6
G., W. (*fl.* 1745), II, 272
G., W. (*fl.* 1789), II, 337
Gaboriau, Émile, III, 22
Gace, William (*fl.* 1578), I, 815
Gadfly, The [Cambridge] (1888), III, 835
Gaelic Journal, The (1882), III, 1051
GAELIC SOURCES (of Anglo-Irish literature), III, 1047f.
Gage, Thomas (d. 1656), I, 793
Gager, William (*fl.* 1580–1609), I, 507, 513, 656–7
Gailhard, Jean, II, 121
Gainsforde (or Gainsford), Thomas (d. 1624), I, 508, 731, 739, 775
Gairdner, C. (*fl.* 1873), III, 973
Gairdner, James (1828–1912), III, **922**
Gaisford, Thomas (1779–1855), I, 106; II, 936; III, **994**f.
Gale, Charles James (*fl.* 1839), III, 986
Gale, Fred (*fl.* 1853), III, 774
Gale, John (1680–1721), II, 863
Gale, Norman Rowland (b. 1862), III, **341**
Gale, Roger (1672–1744), I, 122
Gale, Samuel (*fl.* 1784), II, 958
Gale, Theophilus (1628–1678), I, 878
Gale, Thomas (1507–1587), surgeon, I, 802, 891
Gale, Thomas (1635?–1702), dean of York, II, 783
Gale, Walter, II, 148
Galen, I, 802, 887
Galignani's Messenger (1890), III, 800
Galileo, II, 810
Gall, Richard (1776–1801), II, 991
Galland, Antoine, II, 540
Gallenga, Antonio (1810–1895), III, 785
Gallery of Fashion (1794), II, 682
Gallery of Poets (18 cent.), II, 244, 246–7–8
Gallimaufry, The (18 cent.), II, 251
Galloway, Sir Archibald (1780?–1850), III, 1075
Galloway, Randolph Stewart, Earl of (*fl.* 1854), III, 132
Galloway, Thomas (1796–1851), III, 941
Gally, Henry (1696–1769), II, 25, 763
Galt, John (1779–1839), III, 187, 207, **394**f., 800
Galton, Sir Francis (1822–1911), III, 777, **867**, 954, 965, 990

Galvam, Antonio, I, 764
Galvanist, The [Cambridge] (1804), III, 834
GALWAY, II, 737 (newspapers)
Gamba, Pietro (*fl.* 1825), III, 206
 Gambado, Geoffrey' (Henry William Bunbury), II, 817
Gambart, E. (*fl.* 1863), III, 94
Gamble, J. (*fl.* 1857), III, 71
Gamble, John (d. 1687), I, 486
Gamelyn (M.E.), I, **151**
GAMES (books on), I, 393f. (16, 17 cents.); II, 825f. (1660–1800)
Gamgee, Arthur (1841–1909), III, 964
Gammage, Robert George (1815–1888), III, 815
Gammer Gurton's Garland (18 cent.), II, 255, 554
Gandy, later Deering, John Peter (1787–1850), III, 995
Gangopadhayay, Jagatchandra (*fl.* 1860), III, 1081
Garbett, Edward (1817–1887), III, 818
Garbett, James (1802–1879), III, 126
Garcia, Carlos, I, 733
Garcie, Pierre, I, 777
Garden, Francis, Lord Gardenstone (1721–1793), II, 400, 747
Garden, Francis (1810–1884), theologian, III, 854
Garden, George (1649–1733), II, 39 (2)
Gardener, Lion (*fl.* 1660), I, 796
Gardener's Chronicle, The (1841), III, 821
Gardener's Gazette, The (1837), III, 821
Gardener's Magazine, The (1826), III, 826
GARDENING (books on), I, 391f. (16, 17 cents.); II, 30 (18 cent. landscape gardening), 148 (17, 18 cents.)
Gardenstone, Francis Garden, Lord (1721–1793), II, 400, 747
Gardiner, Allen Francis (1794–1851), III, 1091
Gardiner, Edmund (*fl.* 1610), I, 718
Gardiner, H. (*fl.* 1845), I, 834
Gardiner, J. (*fl.* 1803), III, 979
Gardiner, J. S. (*fl.* 1750), II, 821
Gardiner, James, the younger (d. 1732), II, 796
Gardiner, R. (*fl.* 1655), I, 894
Gardiner, Richard (*fl.* 1603), I, 391
Gardiner, Richard (1723–1781), II, 755
Gardiner, S. J. (*fl.* 1786), II, 825
Gardiner, Samuel Rawson (1829–1902), III, 834, **910**f.
Gardiner, Stephen (1483?–1555), I, **668**f.
Gardiner, W. (*fl.* 1715), II, 786
Gardiner, William (1770–1853), musical composer, I, 17
Gardiner, William Nelson (1766–1814), engraver and bookseller, II, 100
Gardner, James Anthony (*fl.* 1775–1814), II, 150
Gardner, Percy (b. 1846), III, 850

Gardnor, John (1729–1808), II, 747
Gardyne, Alexander (1585?–1634?), I, 899
Gardyner, George (*fl.* 1651), I, 796
Garfield, John (*fl.* 1660), II, 702
Garfit, A. (*fl.* 1862), III, 110
Garland, John (d. *c.* 1258), I, **299** f.
Garland of Good Will, The (17 cent.), I, 404
Garle, Hubert (*fl.* 1896), III, 761
Garnett, Jeremiah (1793–1870), III, 802
Garnett, Richard (1835–1906), III, **742**
Garnett, Thomas (1766–1802), II, 157
Garnier, — (*fl.* 1855), III, 82
Garnier, R. M. (*fl.* 1892), III, 972
Garnier, Robert, I, 333 f.
Garrard, William (*fl.* 1591), I, 390
Garrett, Edmund W. (*fl.* 1890), III, 986
'Garrett, Edward', i.e. Isabella Fyvie, later
    Mayo (*fl.* 1877), III, 573
Garrett, Fydell Edmund (1865–1907), III, 785,
    1092
Garrick, David (1717–1779), II, 323, **445** f.,
    615, 745, 780 (2)
Garrick, H. B. W. (*fl.* 1889), III, 1069
Garrick's Jests (18 cent.), II, 244
Garter, Bernard (*fl.* 1570), I, 436, 740
Garter, Thomas (*fl.* 1578), I, 516
Garth, Sir Samuel (1661–1718), II, 193, 200,
    210, **281**, 766
Garvie, Alfred Ernest (b. 1861), III, 850
Garzoni, T., I, 713
Gascoigne, G. T. (*fl.* 1896), III, 1080
Gascoigne, George (1542–1577), I, **414** f., 521,
    523, 678, 728, 742, 801, 810, 864
Gascoigne, H. B. (*fl.* 1818), III, 975
Gascoigne, Thomas (1403–1458), I, **313**
Gaskell, Elizabeth Cleghorn, née Stevenson
    (1810–1865), III, 24 f., 41, **427** f.
Gaskell, Frank (*fl.* 1890), III, 87
Gaskell, P. (*fl.* 1833), III, 981
Gaskell, Walter Holbrook (1847–1914), III, 964
Gaskell, William (1805–1884), III, 427–8
Gaspey, Thomas (1788–1871), III, **395** f., 811
Gassendi, Pierre, II, 781
Gast of Gy, The (M.E.), I, **162**
Gataker, Thomas (1574–1654), I, 862
Gateshead and Tyneside Echo, The (1879), III,
    805
Gatherer, J. (*fl.* 1703), I, 910
Gatonbe, John (*fl.* 1612), I, 790
Gatty, H. K. F. (*fl.* 1874), III, 578
Gatty, Margaret (1807–1873), III, **484**, 578
Gau, John (1493?–1553?), I, 260
Gauden, John (1605–1662), I, 686, 688, **696** f.
Gaudry, Richard (*fl.* 1795), II, 250
Gaule, John (*fl.* 1646), I, 894
Gaultier, A. E. C. (*fl.* 1800), III, 135
Gauntlet, The (1833), III, 816
Gauthier de Metz (or Gossouin de Metz), I,
    765
Gautruche, Pierre, II, 781

GAWAIN LEGEND, I, 131
Gawane and the Carle of Carelyle (M.E.), I, **138**
Gawayne and the Grene Knight (M.E.), I, **135** f.,
    203
Gawdy, Philip (*fl.* 1579–1616), I, 384
Gay, Florence (*fl.* 1912), III, 1093
Gay, John (1685–1732), II, 67, **292** f., 301, 351
Gay, William (*fl.* 1894), III, **1095**
Gaylard, Dr — (*fl.* 1722), II, 713
Gayton, Edmund (1608–1666), I, 715, 718, 724
Gazette-a-la-Mode, The (1709), II, 660
Gazette de Londres (1673), II, 719
Gazette: The Accurate Intelligencer, The (1706),
    II, 727
Gazetteer and London Daily Advertiser, The
    (1755), II, 709
Gazetteer and New Daily Advertiser, The
    (1764), II, 709
Gedde, Walter (*fl.* 1615), I, 886
Geddes, Alexander (1737–1802), II, 761
Geddes, James (d. 1748?), II, 26
Geddes, Patrick (b. 1854), III, 955
Geddes, William (1600?–1694), II, 992
Geddes, Sir William Duguid (1828–1900), III,
    1005
Gee, Edward (1657–1730), II, 95
Gee, John (*fl.* 1749), I, 474
Gee, Joshua (*fl.* 1729), II, 958
Geffe, N. (*fl.* 1607), I, 893
Geikie, Sir Archibald (1835–1924), III, **953**
Geisweiler, Constantine (*fl.* 1800), II, 51, 60
Geisweiler, Maria (*fl.* 1799), II, 59, 60 (2), 486
Gell, Sir William (1777–1836), III, **995**
Gellert, Christian Fürchtegott, II, 62, 805
Gelli, Giovanni Battista, I, 813; II, 810
Gellibrand, Henry (1597–1636), I, 792, 882,
    885
Gellibrand, S. (*fl.* 1644), I, 756
Gemelli-Careri, Giovanni Francesco, II, 810
Geminus, Thomas (1500?–1570), I, 890
General Account, The (1645), I, 756
General Advertiser, The (1744), II, 708
General Advertiser, The (1754), II, 735
General Advertiser, The (1765), II, 725
General Advertiser, The (1784), II, 709
*General Advertiser and Morning Intelligencer,
    The* (1776), II, 709
General Baptist Magazine, The (1798), II, 683
*General Baptist Magazine, Repository and
    Missionary Observer, The* (1854), III, 824
General Baptist Repository, The (1802), III, 824
*General Baptist Repository and Missionary
    Observer, The* (1822), III, 824
General Correspondent, The (1740), II, 735
General Dictionary, A (18 cent.), II, 204 (2),
    205–6, 207 (2), 209
General Election, The (18 cent.), II, 547
General Evening Post, The (1733), II, 698, 710
General Evening Post, The (Dublin, 1781), II,
    736

General History of the Principal Discoveries in Useful Arts, A (1726), II, 675

General History of the Stage [etc.], *A* (18 cent.), II, 213

General History of Trade, The (1713), II, 676

General London Evening Mercury, The (1743), II, 710

General Magazine, The (1764), II, 679

General Magazine and Impartial Review, The (1787), II, 681

General Magazine of Arts and Sciences, The (1755), II, 677

General Magazine; Or, Compleat Repository of Arts [etc.], *The* (1776), II, 680

General Magazine; Or, Epitome of Useful Knowledge, The (1793), II, 682

General News-Letter, The (Dublin, 1744), II, 735 (2)

General Post, The (1711), II, 710

General Post, The (1716), II, 710, 712

General Post Office (1798), II, 718

General Post Office Advertiser, The (1739), II, 735

General Postscript, The (1709), II, 707

General Remark on Trade, The (1705), II, 707

General Remark on Trade: With An Extract of Foreign News, The (1707), II, 707

General Remark: Or, Miscellanies, The (1708), II, 707

General Review, The (1752), II, 677

General Review of Foreign Literature, The (1775), II, 680

General Songster, The (18 cent.), II, 238, 240, 248

Generall News from All Parts of Christendome (1646), I, 757

Generous Advertiser, Or, Weekly Information of Trade and Business, The (1707), II, 717

Generous London Morning Advertiser, The (1742), II, 707

Generydes (M.E.), I, **159**

Genesis (O.E.), I, **74**

Genesis and Exodus (M.E.), I, **187** f.

Genest, Charles Claude, II, 781

Genest, John (1764–1839), III, 1024

GENIUS (treatises on), II, 14 f. (17, 18 cents.)

Genius, The (1761), II, 664

Genius of Albion, The (1790), II, 681

Genius of Kent, The (1792), II, 684

Genlis, Stéphanie Félicité Ducrest, Comtesse de, later Brulart de Sillery, II, 36, 41, 47, 108, 552, 566, 773; III, 393, 405

Gent, J. B. [misprint for I. B., gent., *fl.* 1657], I, 378

Gent, Thomas (1693–1778), printer and topographer, II, 88, 135, 671, 696

Gent, Thomas (*fl.* 1816), author of 'Monody to Sheridan', II, 458

Gentiles, D. (*fl.* 1899), I, 510

Gentilis, Albericus (1552–1608), I, 850

Gentilis, Robert (1590–1654?), I, 818; II, 813

Gentillet, Innocent, I, 813

Gentleman, Francis (1728–1784), II, **466**, 546, 711

Gentleman, Tobias (*fl.* 1614), I, 846

Gentleman, The (1775), II, 665

Gentleman and Ladies Polite Songster, The (18 cent.), II, 234

Gentleman and Lady's Museum, The (1777), II, 680

Gentleman and Lady's Pocket Register, The (1780), II, 686

Gentleman and Lady's Weekly Magazine, The (1774), II, 686

'Gentleman of the University, A' (1811), III, 128

Gentleman's and London Magazine, The (1752), II, 687

Gentleman's Collection of Catches, The (18 cent.), II, 240

Gentleman's Journal, The (1692), II, 35, 531, 673, 676

Gentleman's Journal, The (1734), II, 714

Gentleman's Journal, The (1869), III, 821

Gentleman's Journal And Tradesman's Companion, The (1721), II, 713

Gentleman's Journal for the War, The (1693), II, 658, 706

Gentleman's Journal, or, Weekly register of news [etc.], *The* (1768), II, 715

Gentleman's Journal, or Weekly Register of News [etc.], *The* (1769), II, 679

Gentleman's Magazine, The (1731), II, 665–6, 673, 676; III, 822

Gentleman's Magazine And Monthly Oracle, The (1736), II, 677

Gentleman's Magazine Extraordinary, The (18 cent.), II, 204

Gentleman's Miscellany, The (18 cent.), II, 250, 252

Gentleman's Miscellany, in Verse and Prose, The (18 cent.), II, 200 (2), 201

Gentleman's Museum, The (1763), II, 678

Gentleman's Museum And Grand Imperial Magazine, The (1770), II, 679

Gentleman's Musical Magazine, The (1788), II, 241, 681

Genuine Collection of all the New Songs at Vaux-Hall Garden, A (18 cent.), II, 224

Genuine Collection of the Several Pieces of Political Intelligence, A (18 cent.), II, 224

Geoffrey de Vinsauf (*fl.* 1200), I, **290**

Geoffrey of Monmouth (d. *c.* 1152), I, 133, **285**

Geoffrey the Grammarian, of Lynn (*fl.* 1440), I, **306**

Geographical Intelligence for the better understanding of foreign news (1689), II, 705

Geographical Intelligence for understanding foreign news (1689), II, 658

Geographical Magazine; Or, The Universe Displayed, The (1790), II, 688

GEOGRAPHY

Geographical descriptions, I, 765f., 773f., 777f., 785f., 794f. (1500–1660); III, 1079f. (India). See also under TRAVEL

Textbooks, I, 884f. (1500–1660); II, 126f. (1660–1800)

Geohst, The (1858), III, 829

GEOLOGY (writings on), III, 949f.

George III, King (1738–1820), II, 102, 165

George IV, King (1762–1830), III, 144

George, Hereford Brooke (1838–1910), III, 830

George, John (*fl.* 1812), II, 85

George a Greene (16 cent.), I, 538

George Faulkner. The Dublin Journal (1745), II, 734

George Lord Fauconbridge, The Famous History of (17 cent.), I, 731

George Swiney's Corke Journal (1754), II, 737

GEORGIC, THE, II, 170 (18 cent.)

Georgievitz, Bartholomaeus, I, 777

Gerard, — (*fl.* 1734), II, 302

Gerard, Alexander (1728–1795), II, 17, 29, 769, **1000**

Gerard, Gilbert (1760–1815), II, 1000

Gerard, John (1545–1612), herbalist, I, 892

Gerard, John (1564–1637), Jesuit, I, 385, 840

Gerardus, Andreas, I, 680

Gerbier, Sir Balthazar (1591?–1667), I, 378f., 796; II, 120

Gerbier, Charles (*fl.* 1651), I, 717

Geree, John (1601?–1649), I, 724, 884

Gerfaut, — (French novelist), III, 397

Geritszoon, Cornelis, I, 782

Germ, The (1850), III, 833

Germain, George Sackville, Viscount Sackville (1716–1785), II, 632 (2)

German Museum; Or, Monthly Repository of the Literature of Germany, The (1800), II, 683

GERMANIC BACKGROUND (to O.E. literature), I, 54ff.

GERMANY

Literary Relations with, I, 335f. (1500–1660); II, **50**f. (1660–1800); III, **26**f. (19 cent.), 55

Translations from German, II, **804**f. (1660–1800)

Gerrard, John (*fl.* 1769), II, **362**

Gervase of Canterbury (*fl.* 1188), I, 115

Gervase of Melkley (*fl.* 1213), I, **298**

Gervase of Tilbury (*fl.* 1180), I, **289**

Gervinus, G. G., I, 594

Gery, Peter (*fl.* 1659), I, 346

Gesner, Conrad, I, 813

Gessner, Salomon, II, 56, 805

Gest Historiale of the Destruction of Troy (M.E.), I, **144**f.

Gesta Abbatum (15 cent.), I, 265

Gesta Edwardi de Carnarvon (M.E.), I, 115

Gesta Romanorum (15 cent.), I, 266, 301

Gesta Stephani (M.E.), I, 116

Gething, Richard (1585?–1652?), I, 346, 377

Ghose, Jogendrachandra (*fl.* 1884), III, 1082

Ghose, Kasi Prasad (*fl.* 1830), III, 1068

Ghose, Loka Nath (*fl.* 1873), III, 1084

Ghose, Nagendra Nath ('N. N.') (*fl.* 1877), III, 1077

Ghose, Nanda Lal (*fl.* 1896), III, 1085

Ghose, Ram Chandra (*fl.* 1881), III, 1078

Ghose, Shishir Kumar (*fl.* 1897), III, 1082

Ghost, The (1796), II, 666

Ghost, Or The Woman wears the Breeches, The (17 cent.), I, 652

Giannone, Pietro, II, 810

Gibb, Elias John Wilkinson (1857–1901), III, **1021**

Gibbes, Phebe (*fl.* 1764), II, 546

Gibbon, A. (*fl.* 1851), III, 978

Gibbon, Charles (1843–1890), III, 606

Gibbon, Edward (1737–1794), II, 37, 53, 65, 632 (2), **882**f.

Gibbon, Percival (*fl.* 1905), III, 1089–90

Gibbons, Alfred (*fl.* 1881), III, 815

Gibbons, Orlando (1583–1625), I, 485

Gibbons, Richard (1550?–1632), I, 815

Gibbs, H. C., Baron Hunsdon (*fl.* 1894), III, 974

Gibbs, Henry Hucks, Baron Aldenham (1819–1907), I, 146, 974

Gibbs, Philip (*fl.* 1729–40), II, 621

Gibbs, T. M. (*fl.* 1721), II, 788

Giberne, Agnes (*fl.* 1874), III, 573

Giblet Pye, The (19 cent.), II, 255

Gibson, A. H. (*fl.* 1900), III, 985

Gibson, Edmund (1669–1748), I, 843 (3); II, 77, 102, **852**, **880**, 920

Gibson, J. Y. (*fl.* 1903), III, 1093

Gibson, Kennet (1730–1772), II, 882

Gibson, R. (*fl.* 17 cent.), II, 150

Gibson, William (*fl.* 1720), II, 816

Gichtel, J. G. (*fl.* 1722), II, 857

Giddal, David (*fl.* 1763), II, 733

Giffard, John (*fl.* 1793), II, 734

Giffard, Martha, Lady (1664–1722), II, 135, 570

Giffard, Stanley Lees (1788–1858), III, 785, 798, 801, 809

Giffen, Sir Robert (1837–1910), III, 820, 974

Gifford, Edwin Hamilton (1820–1905), III, **1005**

Gifford, George (d. 1620), I, 893

Gifford, Humphrey (*fl.* 1580), I, 436, 729

Gifford, John, earlier John Richards Green (1758–1818), II, 63, 165, 552, 671, 683, 696, 710

Gifford, Nathaniel (*fl.* 1736), II, 799

Gifford, William (1756–1826), II, 138, **362**f.; III, 203, 832
GIFT-BOOKS, III, **839**f.
Gifts of Men (O.E.), I, **81**
Γιγαντομαχια (17 cent.), II, 288
Gilbart, James William (1794–1863), III, 972
Gilbert (called the 'Universal') (d. 1134), I, **284**
Gilbert of the Haye (*fl.* 1456), I, 260
Gilbert the Englishman (*fl.* 1250), I, **300**
Gilbert, Ann, née Taylor (1782–1866), III, 565 (3)
Gilbert, earlier Giddy, Davies (1767–1839), I, 279
Gilbert, Sir Geoffrey (1674–1726), II, **963**
Gilbert, George (*fl.* 1776), II, 756
Gilbert, Sir Humfrey (1539?–1583), I, 379, 742, 794
Gilbert, Sir John Thomas (1829–1898), III, **929**f.
Gilbert, Sir Joseph Henry (1817–1901), III, 961
Gilbert, Richard (1794–1852), III, 128
Gilbert, Thomas (d. 1747), poet, II, **317**
Gilbert, Thomas (*fl.* 1789), traveller, II, 751
Gilbert, William (1540–1603), scientist, I, 885
Gilbert, William, the younger (*fl.* 1651), I, 885
Gilbert, William (*fl.* 1676), angler, II, 818
Gilbert, William (1760?–1825?), poet, III, **233**
Gilbert, William (1804–1890), novelist, III, 573
Gilbert, Sir William Schwenck (1836–1911), III, **610**f.
Gilbey, Tresham (*fl.* 1896), III, 761
Gilbie, Anthony (*fl.* 1581–90), I, 678
Gilby (or Gylby), Goddred (*fl.* 1561), I, 801
Gilchrist, Alexander (1828–1861), II, 349
Gilchrist, John (*fl.* 1815), II, 257
Gilchrist, John Borthwick (1759–1841), III, 1073, 1079
Gilchrist, Octavius Graham (1779–1823), I, 618; II, 304, 903; III, 201, 218
Gildas (d. *c.* 570), I, **99**f.
Gildon, Charles (1665–1724), II, **575**f.
    Miscellanies ed. by, II, 182 (2), 185 (3), 192, 194, 196
    Minor writings, II, 15, 401, 535–6, 707
    Translations by, II, 763, 777
Gilead (1866), III, 830
Giles, John Allen (1808–1884), I, 85, 89, 103–5, 116 (2), 282, 287–8, 671
Giles, Joseph (*fl.* 1771), II, 308
Giles, William (*fl.* 1775), II, 230
Gilfillan, George (1813–1878), III, **714**
Gilfillan, Robert (1798–1850), III, 233
Gilks, T. (*fl.* 1866), III, 84
Gill, Alexander (1565–1635), I, 44
Gill, Sir David (1843–1914), III, 945
Gill, J. (*fl.* 1863), III, 110
Gill, John (1697–1771), II, 863
Gill, Thomas Hornblower (b. 1819), III, **288**
Gill, William John (1843–1882), III, 991
Gill, William Wyatt (1829–1896), III, 968

Gilles, Pierre, II, 781
Gillespie, George (1613–1648), I, 908
Gillet, Robert, II, 781
Gillies, John (1712–1796), II, 759, 761, 913
Gillies, Robert Pearce (1788–1858), I, 897; III, 151, 193, 374
Gillies, T. B. (*fl.* 1871), III, 807
Gilliland, Thomas (*fl.* 1804–16), II, 394
Gillman, J. (*fl.* 1838), III, 176
Gillmore, Parker (*fl.* 1869–78), III, 766, 1092
Gillray, James (1757–1815), III, 91
Gillum, W. (d. 1797), II, **363**
Gilpin, Bernard (1517–1583), I, 682
Gilpin, S. (*fl.* 1866), II, 354
Gilpin, William (1724–1804), I, 682; II, 30, 822
Ginsburg, Christian David (1831–1914), III, **1013**
Giovanni 'Fiorentino', II, 810
Giraffi, Alessandro, I, 833
Giraldi, Giovanni Battista (Cinthio), I, 813
Giraldus Cambrensis (1146?–1220), I, 116, **290**, 768
Girdlestone, Thomas (1758–1822), II, 631
Girl's Own Paper, The (1880), III, 578
Girl's Realm, The (1898), III, 579
GIRLS
    Education of, I, 127 (M.E.), 379f. (16, 17 cents.); II, 130f. (17, 18 cents.); III, 141f. (19 cent.)
    See also under Children
Girton Review, The (1882), III, 835
Gisbert, Blaise, II, 781
Gisborne, Thomas, the elder (1758–1846), II, 143, **363**
Gisborne, Thomas, the younger (1794–1852), III, 978
Gissing, George Robert (1857–1903), III, **525**f.
Gist, Christopher (*fl.* 1751), II, 754
Gladstone, G. (*fl.* 1774), III, 830
Gladstone, John Hall (1827–1902), III, 948
Gladstone, Mary (1847–1927), III, 155
Gladstone, William Ewart (1809–1898), III, 143, **714**f.
    Reviews by, III, 257, 716
Gladwin, Francis (d. 1813?), III, 1070, 1073
Glances at Life (1795), II, 666
Glanvill, John (1664?–1735), II, **281**, 786
Glanvill, Joseph (1636–1680), II, **942**
Glanvill, Ranulf de (d. 1190), I, 117, **289**
Glanville, E. (*fl.* 1892), III, 1089
Glanville, Sir John (1586–1661), I, 771
Glapthorne, Henry (*fl.* 1639), I, 645
Glas, John (1695–1773), II, 995
Glascock, William Nugent (1787?–1847), III, **396**
GLASGOW
    Libraries, II, 105
    Magazines, II, 687 (1770–95)
    Newspapers, II, 732f.; III, 807f.
    Printing in, I, 354 (17 cent.); II, 89 (18 cent.)
    University, II, 117; III, 125, 838 (magazines)

Glasgow, Geraldine (*fl.* 1889), III, 1070
Glasgow Advertiser, The (1783), II, 733; III, 808
Glasgow Advertiser, The (1794), II, 733
Glasgow Advertiser and Evening Intelligencer, The (1789), II, 733
Glasgow Citizen, The (1842), III, 808
Glasgow Courant, The (1745), II, 733
Glasgow Courant, Containing the Occurrences both at Home and Abroad, The (1715), II, 733
Glasgow Courier, The (1791), II, 733
Glasgow Daily Mail (1901), III, 807
Glasgow Daily News, The (1855), III, 807
Glasgow Evening Herald, The (1865), III, 808
Glasgow Evening Mail, The (1865), III, 808
Glasgow Evening News (1888), III, 808
Glasgow Evening Post, The (1866), III, 808
Glasgow Herald, The (1805), II, 733
Glasgow Herald, The (1859), III, 793, 808
Glasgow Journal, The (1741), II, 733
Glasgow Magazine, The (1770), II, 687
Glasgow Magazine, The (1795), II, 687
Glasgow Magazine and Review; Or, Universal Miscellany, The (1783), II, 687
Glasgow Mercury, The (1778), II, 733
Glasgow Miscellany, The (18 cent.), II, 247
Glasgow Miscellany, The (19 cent.), II, 255
Glasgow Morning Journal, The (1858), III, 807
Glasgow Museum; Or, Weekly Instructor, The (1773), II, 687
Glasgow News, The (1873), III, 808
Glasgow Times, The (1855), III, 807
Glasgow Universal Magazine, The (1772), II, 687
GLASGOW UNIVERSITY PRESS, III, 87
Glasgow Weekly Chronicle, The (1766), II, 733
Glass, A. H. (*fl.* 1856), III, 96
Glasse, Samuel (1735–1812), II, 120
Glasse of Godly Love, The (17 cent.), I, 713
Glauber, Jean-Rodolphe, I, 887
Glazebrook, Sir Richard Tetley (b. 1854), III, **940**
Gleaner, The (1795), II, 686
Gleig, George (1753–1840), bishop of Brechin, II, 614, 882, 984
Gleig, George Robert (1796–1888), novelist and biographer, III, **396**, 676
Glen, W. Cunningham (*fl.* 1858), III, 986
Glen, William (1787–1826), III, 234
Glenbervie, Sylvester Douglas, Baron (1743–1823), II, 1000
Glenelg, Charles Grant, Baron (1778–1866), III, 234
Glenesk, Algernon Borthwick, Baron (1830–1908), III, 783
'Glenfin' (1860), III, 770
Glenny, George (1793–1874), III, 811, 821
Gliddon, George Robins (1809–1857), III, **1015**
Gl' Ingannati, I, 662
Glisson, Francis (1597–1677), I, 890–1; II, 942

Globe, The (1803), III, 793, 800
Globe and Traveller, The (1822), III, 800
GLOSSARIES, I, 25 f., 35–6; II, 926 f.
Glosses (O.E.), I, 35, 36
GLOUCESTER, II, 724 (newspapers)
Gloucester, Robert of (*fl.* 1260–1300), I, 40
Gloucester, Cartulary of (M.E.), I, 121
Gloucester Gazette; And South Wales, Worcester and Wiltshire Advertiser, The (1782), II, 724
Gloucester Journal, The (1722), II, 724
GLOUCESTERSHIRE
    Bibliographies, I, 8
    Printing in, II, 87
Glover, — (*fl.* 1774), II, 646
Glover, John (*fl.* 1863), III, 1043
Glover, Joseph (*fl.* 1884), III, 764
Glover, Richard (1712–1785), II, 45, 57, **317**
Glover, Thomas (*fl.* 1676), II, 752
Glow-worm, The (1865), III, 801
Gnaphaeus, Gulielmus, I, 328
GNOMIC POEMS (O.E.), I, **83**
Goadby, Edwin N. (*fl.* 1874), III, 802, 804
Godard, J. G. (*fl.* 1892), III, 977
Godart de Beauchamps, Pierre Francois, II, 781
Goddard, A. P. (*fl.* 1753), II, 811
Goddard, Edward (*fl.* 1726), II, 753
Goddard, John Leybourn (*fl.* 1871), III, 986
Goddard, Thomas (*fl.* 1706), II, 727
Goddard, William (*fl.* 1599–1616), I, 480
Godeau, Antoine, II, 781
Godefroi, Henry (*fl.* 1879), III, 986
Godefroy of Boloyne (M.E.), I, 146
Godefroy, D. (*fl.* 1674), II, 776
Godfrey of Cambrai (d. 1107), I, **282**
Godfrey, D. W. (*fl.* 1843), III, 819
Godfrey, John (*fl.* 1747), II, 823
GODFREY OF BOUILLON, ROMANCES OF, I, 146
Godfridus, astronomer, I, 883
Godham (or Wodham), Adam (d. *c.* 1358), I, **305**
Godman, Frederick du Cane (*fl.* 1879), III, 958
Godolphin, John (1617–1678), II, 963
Godolphin, Sidney (1610–1643), I, 476
Godolphin, Sidney, Earl of (1645–1712), II, 275
Godric (1065?–1170), I, 271
Godson, R. (*fl.* 1823), III, 93
Godstowe Nunnery, English Register of (15 cent.), I, 46
Godwin (*fl.* 1120), I, **284**
Godwin, Francis (1562–1633), I, 731, 838
Godwin, George (1815–1888), II, 491; III, 822
Godwin, M. (*fl.* 1620), I, 838
Godwin, Mary, née Wollstonecraft (1759–1797), II, 39, 551, 558, 566, **656**, 792
Godwin, Mary Wollstonecraft, later Shelley (1797–1851), III, **416**

Godwin, William (1756–1836), II, 20, 109, 551, **655**f.; III, 641, 975–6
Godwyn (or Godwin), Thomas (d. 1642), I, 779
Goede, Christian August Gottlieb, II, 142
Goes, Damianus de, I, 781
Goethe, Johann Wolfgang von
  18th-century translations and adaptations, II, 56, 59, 63, 71, 343, 486, 552, 805
  19th-century translations, III, 30f., 48, 49f., 225, 281, 298, 369, 605, 670
Goeurot, Jehan, I, 888
Goffe, Thomas (1591–1629), I, 646
Goggin's Ulster Magazine (1798), II, 688, 738
Gogol, Nikolai Vasilievich, III, 44
Goguet, Antoine Yves, II, 781
Gokin, Thomas (*fl.* 1623), I, 801
Golagrus and Gawain (M.E.), I, **139**
Goldborne, Sophia (*fl.* 1789), II, 549
Golden Garland of Princely Delight, The (17 cent.), II, 181
Golden Garland of Princely Pleasures, The (17 cent.), I, 404
Golden Hours (1864), III, 578
Goldfinch, The (18 cent.), II, 214, 216, 221, 232, 236 (2), 237, 238 (2), 241, 256
Golding, Arthur (1536?–1605?), I, 741, 885
  * Translations by, I, 678, 800, 804–5, 807–8, 811 (2), 814, 816–7, 819
Golding, Peter (*fl.* 1608), I, 813
Goldingham, William (d. 1589), I, 656
Goldoni, Carlo, II, 66, 810; III, 39
Goldsmid, Edmund M. (*fl.* 1885), II, 258
Goldsmith, Francis (1613–1655), I, 376, 646
Goldsmith, Lewis (1763?–1846), III, 811
Goldsmith, Oliver (1730?–1774), II, 37, 45, 49, 64, 224–5, 227, 239, **636**f.; III, 609
Goldwel, Henry (*fl.* 1581), I, 740
Goldwin, William (*fl.* 1706), II, 825
GOLF (books on), III, 775
Gollancz, Sir Israel (1863–1930), III, **1038**
Golsworthy, Arnold (*fl.* 1900), III, 831
Gómara, Francisco López de, I, 787
Gombaud, Antoine, Chevalier de Méré, II, 781
Gombauld, Jean Ogier de, I, 733; II, 781
Gomberville, Marin Leroy, Sieur de, I, 334, 733; II, 788
Gomersal, Robert (1602–1646?), I, 476
Gomez, Madeleine Angelique Poisson de, II, 542 (2), 793
Gomme, Sir G. L. (*fl.* 1888), III, 834
Goncourt, Edmond de, III, 339
Gondi, Jean François Paul de (Cardinal de Retz), II, 781
Gongoray Argote, Luis de, I, 345
Gonner, Sir Edward Carter Kersey (*fl.* 1888), III, 978, 984
Gonsalvius Montanus, Reginaldus, I, 813
GONVILLE AND CAIUS COLLEGE (Cambridge), I, 370
Gooch, Richard (*fl.* 1823), III, 124

Good, John Mason (1764–1827), II, 631
Good, William (*fl.* 1644), I, 756
Good Man and the Devil, The (M.E.), I, **186**
Good Things Annual (1873), III, 578
Good Words (1860), III, 829
Good Words for the Young (1869), III, 578
Goodale, John (*fl.* 1550?), I, 816
Goodall (or Goodal), Walter (1706?–1766), II, 104, **887**
Goode, William (1801–1868), III, 691, 853
Goodere, Sir Henry (*fl.* 1618). See Peacham (Henry)
Goodeve, Louis Arthur (*fl.* 1883), III, 986
Goodhall, Walter (*fl. c.* 1770), II, 821
Goodhugh, William (1799?–1842), III, 104
Goodlake, Thomas (*fl.* 1828), III, 765
Goodman, C. W. (*fl.* 1862), III, 818 (2)
Goodman, Christopher (1520?–1603), I, 844
Goodman, Godfrey (1583–1656), I, 840
Goodman, Nicholas (*fl.* 1632), I, 731
Goodridge, Richard (*fl.* 1634), I, 679
Goodwin, Charles Wycliffe (1817–1878), I, 93 (2); III, 848
Goodwin, John (1594?–1665), I, 357
Goodwin, Thomas Pope (*fl.* 1595), I, 730
Googe, Barnabe (1540–1594), I, 391, 394, 437, 816–7
Gookin, Daniel (1612?–1687), II, 752
Gorcock, Jeffrey (*fl.* 1827), III, 762
Gordon, Lord Adam (1726?–1801), II, 755
Gordon, Adam Lindsay (1833–1870), III, **1094**
Gordon, Alexander (d. 1752), biographer, II, 997
Gordon, Alexander (1692?–1754?), antiquary, I, 59; II, 811
Gordon, Charles Gedge (1833–1885), III, 155
Gordon, Sir Cosmo (*fl.* 1824), III, 187, 206
Gordon, Daniel M. (*fl.* 1880), III, 991
Gordon, Harry (*fl.* 1766), II, 755
Gordon, James (1615?–1686), I, 776, 910
Gordon, John (*fl.* 1762), II, 26, 109
Gordon, Mary (*fl.* 1862), III, 650
Gordon, Patrick (*fl.* 1614–50), poet, I, 899
Gordon, Patrick (1635–1699), general, II, 911
Gordon, Pryse Lockhart (*fl.* 1830–4), III, 207
Gordon, Sir Robert (1580–1656), I, 795
Gordon, S. (*fl.* 1836), III, 978
Gordon, Thomas (d. 1750), II, 16, 91, 433, 662 (2), 696, 713 (2), 765, 767–8 (2)
Gordon, William (*fl.* 1726), historian of Gordon family, II, 997
Gordon, William (1728–1807), independent minister, II, 756
Gordon, William (*fl.* 1738), translator of Voltaire, II, 803
Gore, Catherine Grace Frances, née Moody (1799–1861), III, **396**f.
Gore, Charles (*fl.* 1889), III, 851
Gore, George (1826–1908), III, 948
Gore, John Ellard (1845–1910), III, 945

Gore, Thomas (1632–1684), I, 359
Gore's General Advertiser (1797), II, 725
Gorges, Sir Arthur (d. 1625), I, 804, 828, 870 (2)
Gorges, Sir Ferdinando (1566?–1647), I, 793
Gorgon, The (1818), III, 816
Gorham, George Cornelius (1787–1857), I, 93
Gorst, Sir John (1835–1916), III, 799, 801
Gorrell, James (fl. 1761), II, 755
Goscelin (d. c. 1099), I, 282
Goschen, George Joachim, Viscount (1831–1907), III, 973
Gospel Magazine and Theological Review, The (1796), III, 824
Gospel Magazine; Or, Spiritual Library, The (1766), II, 679
Gospel Magazine; Or, Treasury of Divine Knowledge, The (1774), II, 679
Gospel of Nicodemus (O.E.), I, 93
Gospel of Nicodemus (M.E.), I, 188 f.
GOSPELS
    Middle English, I, 39, 187 f. and 204 f.
    Old English, I, 26, 28, 35–7, 95
Gosse, Sir Edmund William (1845–1928), III, 742 f.
Gosse, Philip Henry (1810–1888), III, 957
Gossip, G. H. D. (fl. 1875), III, 777
Gossip's Braule, The (17 cent.), I, 652
Gosson, Stephen (1555–1624), I, 508 f.
Gosynhill, Edward (fl. 1542?), I, 380, 716
Gott, Samuel (fl. 1648), I, 861, 866
Goudanus, G. H., I, 799
Gouge, William (1578–1653), I, 682
Gough, H. (fl. 1855), I, 317
Gough, Hugh (fl. 1570), I, 777
Gough, John (fl. 1528–56), I, 200
Gough, John (fl. 1640), I, 646
Gough, John (1721–1791), II, 855
Gough, Richard (1735–1809), II, 97, 882
Gough, Strickland (d. 1752), II, 714
Goujet, Claude-Pierre, II, 34
Goulart, Simon, I, 331, 733
Goulburn, Edward Meyrick (1818–1897), III, 133
Gould, J. B. (fl. 1871), III, 830
Gould, Martha (fl. 1709), II, 281
Gould Nathaniel (1857–1919), III, 759, 764
Gould, Robert (d. 1709?), II, 281
Gouldman, Francis (d. 1688?), I, 856, 861
Gouldsbury, C. (fl. 1912), III, 1089
Goulston (or Gulston), Theodore (1572–1632), I, 862
Goussault, Jacques, II, 781
Gover, Charles E. (d. 1872), III, 1072
Governor, The (17 cent.), I, 652
Gower, Charles (fl. 1788), II, 666
Gower, John (1330?–1408?), I, 205 f.
    Language of, I, 29, 32, 39, 313
Gower, John (fl. 1640), I, 805
Gowers, Sir William Richard (1845–1915), III, 964

Gownsman, The [Cambridge] (1829), III, 834
Gowther, Sir (Robert the Devil) (M.E.), I, 153
Gozzi, Carlo, III, 358
Grabe, John Ernest (1666–1711), II, 846
Grace, William Gilbert (1848–1915), III, 774 (2)
Gracey, H. K. (fl. 1892), III, 1069
Gracián Dantisco, Lucas, II, 121
Gracián y Morales, Baltasar, II, 121
Gracie, J. B. (fl. 1836), I, 277
'Graduate, A' (1824), III, 121
'Graduate, A' (1833), III, 126
Graeme, James (1749–1772), II, 762
Graffanio-Mastix (18 cent.), II, 200
Graffigny, Françoise d'Issembourg d'Happoncourt, II, 552
Grafton, Henry Augustus Fitzroy, Duke of (1735–1811), II, 165
Grafton, Richard (d. 1572?), I, 351, 825
Graham, earlier Macaulay, Catherine (1731–1791), II, 92, 131, 634, 888
Graham, Dougal (1724–1779), II, 991, 1002
Graham, G. F. G. (fl. 1815), III, 1075
Graham, Sir Gerald (1831–1899), III, 155
Graham, J. (fl. 1848), III, 77
Graham, James, Marquis of Montrose (1612–1650), I, 900
Graham, James (fl. 1795), II, 686
Graham, Sir James Robert George (1792–1861), III, 151, 974
Graham, Maria, later Lady Callcott (1785–1842), III, 1079
Graham, P. A. (fl. 1892), III, 972
Graham, Richard, Viscount Preston (1648–1695), II, 121, 764
Graham, Thomas (1803–1858), III, 947
Graham, William (1839–1911), III, 868
Grahame, J. (fl. 1817), Glasgow critic, III, 379
Grahame, James (1765–1811), Scottish poet, II, 991; III, 239
Grahame, James (fl. 1816), advocate and writer on population, III, 975
Grahame, Simion (1570?–1614), I, 889, 899
GRAIL, HOLY (Legend of), I, 132
Grainger, James (1721?–1766), II, 337, 363, 773
Grammar and Rhetorick (13 cent.), II, 232
GRAMMAR, ENGLISH
    General, I, 24 f.
    Middle English, I, 37 f.
    Modern English. See under PHONOLOGY, I, 43 f.
    Old English, I, 34 f.
    Textbooks of, I, 376 f. (1500–1660); II, 931 f. (1660–1800)
GRAMMAR SCHOOLS. See SCHOOLS
GRAMMARIANS
    Anglo-Saxon Period, I, 98 f.
    Renaissance to Restoration, I, 43 f., 374 f.
    See also under SCHOLARS AND SCHOLARSHIP, I, 852 f.

Grammarians (*cont.*)
  Restoration to Romantic Revival, II, 931f.
    See also under SCHOOL- AND TEXT-BOOKS,
    II, 125f. and CLASSICAL AND ORIENTAL
    SCHOLARS, II, 933f.
  Nineteenth Century. See under SCHOOL- AND
    TEXT-BOOKS, III, 135, CLASSICAL, BIBLICAL
    AND ORIENTAL SCHOLARSHIP, III, 993f.,
    ANGLO-IRISH LITERATURE, III, 1047f. and
    ANGLO-INDIAN LITERATURE, III, 1067f.
Grammatical Drollery (17 cent.), II, 178
Granada, Luis de, I, 343
Granan, Edward (*fl.* 1771), II, 33
'Grand, Sarah', i.e. Frances Elizabeth Mac-
  Fall, née Clarke (b. 1862), III, **546**f.
*Grand Diurnall of the Passages in Parliament,
  A* (1642), I, 754
Grand Magazine of Magazines, The (1759), II,
  678
Grand Magazine of Universal Intelligence, The
  (1758), II, 678
Grand Politique Post, The (1654), I, 762
Grange, John (*fl.* 1577), I, 728
Granger, James (1723–1776), II, **888**, 922
Grant, Sir Alexander (1826–1884), III, 867,
  998
Grant, Anne (1755–1838), II, 156, **991**
Grant, Charles, Baron Glenelg (1778–1866),
  II, 234
Grant, Sir Charles (1836–1903), III, 1084
Grant (or Graunt), Edward (1540?–1601) I,
  376, 806
Grant, Edward (*fl.* 1703), II, 909
Grant, Edward (*fl.* 1850), III, 606
Grant, Elizabeth (1745?–1814?), II, 156
Grant, G. (*fl.* 1849), III, 375
Grant, George Monro (1835–1902), III, 1088
Grant, Harding (*fl.* 1830), III, 200
Grant, James (*fl.* 1736–45), Scottish journalist,
  II, 731
Grant, James (1802–1879), journalist, III 97,
  100, 631, 790, 798, 983
Grant, James (*fl.* 1856), lawyer, III, 986
Grant, James (1822–1887), novelist, III, **484**f.
Grant, John Peter (*fl.* 1844), writer to the
  signet, III, 149
Grant, Patrick (*fl.* 1832), III, 794, 800–1, 812
Grant, Sir Robert (1779–1838), hymn-writer,
  III, **234**
Grant, Robert (1814–1892), astronomer, III,
  944
Grant, Robert Edmond(1793–1874), anatomist,
  III, 953, 956
Grant, W. (*fl.* 1720), II, 799
Grant-Duff, James (1789–1858), III, 1075
Granta, The [Cambridge] (1889), III, 835
Grantham (or Granthan), Henry (*fl.* 1571–87),
  I, 811–2
Grantham, Thomas (d. 1664), schoolmaster, I,
  803

Grantham, Sir Thomas (*fl.* 1673–84), naval
  commander, II, 753
Granville, Denis (*fl.* 1665–*c.* 1702), II, 152
Granville, George, Baron Lansdowne (1667–
  1735), II, 21, **438**
Granville, Sir Richard (*fl.* 1627), I, 771
Graphic, The (1869), III, 815
Graphic and Historical Illustrator, The (1832),
  III, 885
GRAPHIC PROCESSES, III, 80f.
Gratiae Ludentes (17 cent.), I, 715
Grattan, C. J. (*fl.* 1860), III, 790
Grattan, Henry (1746–1820), III, 148
Grattan, Henry, the younger (*fl.* 1822), III, 148
Grattan, Thomas Colley (1792–1864), III, **398**
Gratton, John (1641–1712), II, 857
*Gratulatio Academiae Cantabrigiensis de reditu
  Georgii II* (18 cent.), II, 212
*Gratulatio Academiae Cantabrigiensis Frederici
  Walliae Principis et Augustae Principissae
  Saxo-Gothae Nuptias Celebrantis* (18 cent.),
  II, 205
*Gratulatio Academiae Cantabrigiensis Georgii III
  et Charlottae Nuptias Celebrantis* (18
  cent.), II, 220
*Gratulatio Academiae Cantabrigiensis Gulielmi
  Principis Auriaci et Annae Georgii II Filiae
  Nuptias Celebrantis* (18 cent.), II, 203
*Gratulatio Academiae Oxoniensis in Nuptias
  Frederici Principis Walliae et Augustae
  Principissae de Saxo-Gotha* (18 cent.), II,
  205
*Gratulatio Academiae Cantabrigiensis in Pacem
  Georgii III* (18 cent.), II, 222
*Gratulatio Academiae Cantabrigiensis Natales
  Georgii Walliae Principis Celebrantis* (18
  cent.), II, 221
*Gratulatio Solennis Universitatis Oxoniensis ob
  Georgium Fred. Aug. Walliae Principem
  Natum* (18 cent.), II, 221
Gratulationes Juventutis Academiae Dubliniensis
  (1761), II, 220
Graunt (or Grant), Edward (1540?–1601), I,
  376, 806
Graunt, John (1620–1674), II, 958
Grave, Jean de (*fl.* 1633), I, 375
Graves, Alfred Perceval (1846–1932), III, **1055**f.
Graves, Charles Edward (1839–1920), III, **1005**
Graves, Clotilda Inez Mary ('Richard Dehan')
  (*fl.* 1900), III, 1090
Graves, John Woodcock (1794–1886), III, 762
Graves, Richard (1715–1804), II, 25, 224,
  547–8 (2), **628**f., 805
Graves, Robert James (1796–1853), I, 664
Gray, Andrew (1633–1656), I, 908
Gray, C. (*fl.* 1876), III, 1090
Gray, David (1838–1861), III, **341**
Gray, Dionis (*fl.* 1577), I, 377
Gray, Edmund Dwyer (1845–1888), III, 809
Gray, Gilbert (d. 1616), I, 911

Gray, J. H. (*fl.* 1834), writer on Oxford University, III, 122
Gray, James (*fl.* 1886), Burmese scholar, III, 1072
Gray, John (*fl.* 1831–48), political economist, III, 974, 976
Gray, Sir John (1816–1875), journalist, III, 809
Gray, John (*fl.* 1893–1930), poet, III, **341**
Gray, John A. (*fl.* 1895), writer on Afghanistan, III, 1085
Gray, Joshua (*fl.* 1836), educationalist, III, 110
Gray, Robert (*fl.* 1794), II, 748
Gray, Simon ('George Purves') (*fl.* 1815), III, 980
Gray, Thomas (1716–1771), II, 67, 109, 221, **333** f., 364, 914
Gray, W. (*fl.* 1649), I, 776
Gray, William (*fl.* 1535–51), I, 721
Gray, William (*fl.* 1772), II, 99
Gray, William (1802?–1835), I, 11, 419
Gray's-Inn Journal, The (1753), II, 664
Graydon, A. (*fl.* 1822), III, 395
Graziani, Antonio Maria, II, 810
Grazzini, Antonio Francesco, I, 340
Great Britain's Weekly Pacquet (1716), II, 712
Great Britain's Post (1653), I, 762
Great Britaines Paine-full Messenger Affording true notice of all affaires (1649), I, 760
Greathead, Bertie (1759–1826), II, **363**
Greatheed, S. (*fl.* 1805–14), II, 342; III, 824
Greatrex, C. B. (*fl.* 1866), III, 760
Greaves, John (1602–1652), I, 779, 786, 862
Greaves, Paul (*fl.* 1594), I, 376
Greaves, Thomas (*fl.* 1604), I, 484
Greaves, W. (*fl.* 1814), III, 970
GREECE (modern)
    Literary Relations with, II, 71 (1660–1800); III, 45 (19 cent.)
GREEK
    Influences, III, 49 f.
    Scholarship, I, 861 f. (16, 17 cents.); II, 933 f. (18 cent.); III, 993 f. (19 cent.)
    Text-books, I, 375 f. (16, 17 cents.); II, 127 (17, 18 cents.)
    Translations, I, 799 f. (16, 17 cents.); II, 27 f. (literary criticism), 758 f.
Greek Anthology, I, 802; III, 239, 1008
Green, Alice Stopford (Mrs J. R.) (1847–1929), III, 984
Green, B. H. (*fl.* 1869), III, 702
Green, C. F. (*fl.* 1857), I, 542
Green, Evelyn Everett (*fl.* 1885), III, **574**
Green, G. (*fl.* 1894), III, 976
Green, George (1793–1841), III, 938, 941
Green, Henry (1801–1873), I, 479 (2); III, 428
Green, J. H. (*fl.* 1801), III, 82
Green, John (*fl.* 1736), traveller in Syria, II, 750
Green, John (*fl.* 1756), poet, II, 17
Green, John (1706?–1779), bishop of Lincoln, II, 116

Green, John Richard (1837–1883), III, **911**
    Translations from, III, 25, 36, 40, 45
Green, John Richards, later John Gifford (1758–1818), II, 63, 165, 552, 671, 683, 696, 710
Green, Joseph Henry (1791–1863), III, 48
Green, Joseph Reynolds (1848–1914), III, 962
Green, M. (*fl.* 1795), II, 654
Green, Mary Anne Everett, née Wood (1818–1895), III, **899**
Green, Matthew (1696–1737), II, **317**
Green, Sarah (*fl.* 1806–13), III, **398**
Green, Thomas Hill (1836–1882), III, 848, **868**
Green, William (*fl.* 1783), II, 762, 766–7
Green, William Charles (1832–1914), III, **1005** f.
Green Room Songster, The (18 cent.), II, 250
Green's Nursery Annual (1847), III, 577
Greenaway, Catherine (Kate) (1846–1901), III, 569
Greene, C. (*fl.* 1868), III, 834
Greene, Edward Burnaby (d. 1788), II, 23, 26, **363** f., 766
Greene, John (*fl.* 1615), I, 509
Greene, Robert (1568–1592), I, 335, 529 f., 729
Greener, W. W. (*fl.* 1876), III, 763
Greenham, Richard (1535?–1594?), I. 682, 725
GREENOCK
    Newspapers, II, 733; III, 808
Greenock Advertiser, The (1799), II, 733
Greenock Daily Press (1867), III, 808
Greenock News (1868), III, 808
Greenock Telegraph, The (1863), III, 808
Greenough, George Bellas (1778–1855), III, 950
Greensmith, John (*fl.* 1641), I, 752
Greenwell, Dora (1821–1882), III, **288**
Greenwell, W. (1820–1918), I, 121
Greenwood, Frederick (1830–1909), III, 428, 785, 801 (2), 829
Greenwood, George (*fl.* 1839), III, 760
Greenwood, J. (*fl.* 1802), III, 135
Greenwood, James (d. 1737), II, 128, 194, 931
Greenwood, William (*fl.* 1657), I, 830
Greenwood, William (*fl.* 1787), II, 822
Greepe, Thomas (*fl.* 1587), I, 788
Greg, William Rathbone (1809–1881), III, 8, 429, 848
Gregg, T. H. (*fl.* 1866–78), III, 830
Grego, Joseph (1843–1908), III, 434, 778
Gregory I, Pope, I, 813
Gregory the Englishman (*fl.* 13 cent.), I, **289**
Gregory, Barnard (1796–1852), III, 812–3
Gregory, David (1661–1708), II, 961
Gregory, Duncan Farquharson (1813–1844), III, 942
Gregory, Francis (1625?–1707), I, 375–6; II, 84
Gregory, George (1754–1808), I, 17; II, 345; III, 824

'Gregory Griffin' (1786), II, 123

Gregory, Isabella Augusta, Lady (1859–1932), III, **1063**f.

Gregory, James (1638–1675), II, 961

Gregory, John (1724–1773), physician, II, 18, 121, 131

Gregory, John (*fl.* 1753–80), publisher, II, 725

Gregory, Sir Richard Arman (b. 1864), III, 945

Gregory, Robert (1819–1911), III, 110, 138

Gregory, Timothy (*fl.* 1720), II, 846

Gregory, William (d. 1467), I, 116

Gregory, William (*fl.* 1765), traveller in North America, II, 755

Gregory, William (*fl.* 1799), missionary in Paraguay, II, 743

Gregory, William (1803–1858), chemist, III, 947

Gregory's Dialogues (O.E.), I, 88

Gregory's Pastoral Care (O.E.), I, **86**

Greig, A. (*fl.* 1844), III, 110

Grein, J. T. (*fl.* 1896), III, 831

Grene Knight (M.E.), I, **139**

Grenewey, Richard (*fl.* 1598), I, 807

Grenfell, H. R. (*fl.* 1875), III, 973

Grenfell, W. H. (*fl.* 1898), III, 779

Grenville, Sir Bevil (1596–1643), I, 385

Grenville, George (1712–1770), II, 164

Grenville, Richard Temple, Earl Temple (1711–1779), II, 164, 632

Grenville, T. (*fl.* 1800), II, 934

Grenville, William Wyndham, Baron (1759–1834), II, 136, 166; III, 978

Gresham, James (*fl.* 1626), I, 805

Gresham, Thomas (1519?–1579), I, 383

Gresley, William (1801–1876), III, 572

Gresset, Jean Baptiste Louis, II, 44, 782

Greswell, W. H. P. (*fl.* 1885), III, 1090

Gretton, F. E. (*fl.* 1808–58), III, 138, 994

Greville, Charles Cavendish Fulke (1794–1865), III, 145

Greville, Fulke, Baron Brooke (1554–1628), I, **421**

Greville, Fulke (*fl.* 1756), II, 17, 654

Greville, Henry William (1801–1872), III, 152

Greville, Robert, Baron Brooke (1608–1643), I, 875

Greville, Robert Fulke (*fl.* 1781–94), II, 150

Greville, Robert Kaye (1794–1866), III, 960

Grew, Nehemiah (1641–1712), II, 961

Grey, Anchitel (d. 1702), II, 167

Grey, Charles, Earl (1764–1845), III, 144

Grey, G. (*fl.* 1780), II, 234, 236

Grey, Edward, Viscount (d. 1933), III, 772

Grey, Henry, Earl (1802–1894), III, 144

Grey, Josephine Elizabeth, later Butler (1828–1906), III, **926**

Grey, Maria Georgina, née Shirreff (*fl.* 1850–74), III, 110, 142

Grey, Nicholas (1590?–1660), I, 376

Grey, Richard (1694–1771), II, 129, 312

Grey, Zachary (1688–1766), II, 877, **892**f.

Gribble, F. H. (b. 1862), III, 777

Gribble, Samuel (*fl.* 1829), III, 765

Grierson, Constantia (1706–1733), II, **317**f.

Grierson, Sir G. A. (b. 1851), III, 1072, **1074** (2)

Grieve, G. (*fl.* 1780), II, 775

Griffin, Bartholomew (d. 1602), I, 433

Griffin, Benjamin (1680–1740), II, **438**

Griffin, Daniel (*fl.* 1843), III, 485

Griffin, Gerald (1803–1840), III, **485**

GRIFFIN, CHARLES, & Co., III, 98

Griffith, A. F. (*fl.* 1815), I, 360

Griffith, Elizabeth (1720?–1793), II, **466**, 534, 545, 547 (3), 560, 637, 778, 790, 802

Griffith, J. M. (*fl.* 1856), III, 961

Griffith, John (*fl.* 1779), II, 756

Griffith, M. (*fl.* 1894), III, 1078

Griffith, Ralph Thomas Hotchkin (1826–1906), III, 1018, 1071

Griffith, Richard (1714?–1788), II, 233, 466, 545–7

Griffith, T. A. (*fl.* 1876), III, 760

Griffith, William (1810–1845), III, 961

Griffith's Iron Trade Exchange (1873), III, 822

Griffiths, Arthur Broer (*fl.* 1891–1927), III, 964

Griffiths, George Edward (d. 1829), III, 823

Griffiths, John (1806–1885), III, 121

Griffiths, Ralph (1720–1803), II, 671, 677, 709, 1002

Griffiths, Roger (fl. 1746), II, 820

Griffiths, William (*fl.* 1784), II, 817

Grillet, Jean, II, 782

Grillparzer, Franz, III, **31**

Grimald, Nicholas (1519?–1562?), I, 403, **437**, 800

Grimalkin, or the Rebel Cat (17 cent.), II, 530

Grimble, Augustus (*fl.* 1886), III, 767

Grimeston (or Grimstone), Edward (*fl.* 1604–33), I, 779, 785, 794, 806, 816, 819

Grimm, Jacob Ludwig Carl, III, 576

Grimm, Wilhelm Carl, III, 576

Grimsal, Richard (*fl.* 1680), II, 178

Grimsby Daily Telegraph, The (1899), III, 806

Grimsby Express, The (1878), III, 805

Grimshawe, Thomas Shuttleworth (1778–1850), II, 341

Grimston, William, Viscount (1683–1756), II, 434

Grimston, 3rd Viscount (*fl.* 1768), II, 139

Grimstone, Edward (*fl.* 1604–33). See Grimeston

Grindal, Edmund (1519–1583), I, 682

Gringoire, Pierre (Vaudemont), I, 331, 813

Grisone, Federico, I, 814

Grobiana's Nuptialls (17 cent.), I, 661

Grocer, The (1862), III, 822

Gronow, Rees Howell (1794–1865), III, 207

Groome, Francis Hindes (1851–1902), III, **744**

Groot, Hugo de. See Grotius

Grosart, Alexander Balloch (1835–1899), III, **1038**

Grose, Francis (1731?–1791), II, 143, 152, 155, 247–8, 252, **891**, 928
Grose, John Henry (*fl.* 1750–83), II, 750
Groser, Albert (*fl.* 1878), III, 802
Groser, William (*fl.* 1839–56), III, 825
Grosley, Pierre Jean, II, 141, 782
Grosse, Carl, Marquis von Pharnusa, II, 63, 553
Grosseteste, Robert (d. 1253), I, **299**, 845
'Grosvenor' (1733), I, 209
Grote, George (1794–1871), III, **888**
Grote, John (1813–1866), III, **868**, 1002
Grotius, Hugo (de Groot), I, 327, 376, 394, 780, 844; II, 787
Groto, Luigi, I, 655, 662
Grouler, The (1711), II, 661
Grouse, F. S. (*fl.* 1877), III, 1072
Grout, L. (*fl.* 1863), III, 1092
Grove, Archibald (*fl.* 1889), III, 831
Grove, Sir George (1820–1900), III, **715**f., 829
Grove, Joseph (d. 1764), I, 824; II, 913
Grove, Matthew (*fl.* 1587), I, 437
Grove, William (*fl.* 1782), II, 811
Grove, Sir William Robert (1811–1896), III, 938
Grove, The (18 cent.), II, 196, 203
Grover, Henry Montague (1791–1866), III, 234
Grub, G. (*fl.* 1853), II, 997
Grub, George (1812–1892), III, **906**
Grub-Street Journal, The (1730), II, 663, 698, 714
Grub-Street Miscellany, The (18 cent.), II, 201–2
Grubiana (18 cent.), II, 202
Gruget, Claude, I, 816
Grumble, T. (*fl.* 1671), I, 400
Grumbler, The (1715), II, 661
Grundy, Sydney (1848–1914), III, **626**
Grymeston, Elizabeth (d. 1603), I, 678, 725
Gryndall, William (*fl.* 1596), I, 394
Gualdo-Priorato, Galeazzo, II, 810
Guardian, The (17 cent.), II, 35, 52, 69, 109
Guardian, The (1713), II, 609
Guardian, The (1819), III, 811
Guardian, The (1846), III, 819
Guarini, Giovanni Battista, I, 340, 662, 814; II, 810f.
Guarna, Andrea, I, 376, 657
Guazzo, Steffano, I, 338, 379, 814; II, 121
Gude and Godlie Ballatis (16 cent.), I, 903
Guénée, Antoine, II, 782
Gueret, Gabriel, II, 537
Guest, Edwin (1800–1880), I, 17
Guest, R. (*fl.* 1828), III, 981
Gueullette, Thomas Simon, II, 542–3, 782
Guevara, Antonio de, I, **342**f., **814**
Guez, Jean Louis, Sieur de Balzac, I, 810; II, 35, 782
Guggenberger, Louisa Sarah, née Bevington (b. 1845), III, **331**
Gui, Joly, II, 783
Guibert, Jacques Antoine Hippolyte de, II, 782

Guicciardini, Francesco, I, 337, 814; II, 811
Guicciardini, Lodovico, I, 778, 814; II, 811
Guide for Malt-Worms, A (18 cent.), II, 195
Guidott, Thomas (*fl.* 1669–98), I, 889
Guild, R. A. (*fl.* 1858), III, 106
Guild, William (1586–1657), I, 908
GUILDFORD SCHOOL, I, 372
Guilford, Francis North, Baron (1637–1685), II, 30
Guilford, Frederick North, Earl of (1732–1792) II, 165
Guilleraques, Gabriel Joseph de Lavergne de, II, 533
Guillim, John (1565–1621), I, 396; II, 120
Guilpin, Edward (*fl.* 1598), I, 480
Guimps, R. de, III, 112
Guisborough, Cartulary of (M.E.), I, 121
Guizot, François, I, 594
Gulich, J. T. (*fl.* 1888), III, 955
'Gulliver, Lilliputius' (1782), II, 563
Gulliveriana (18 cent.), II, 199
Gulston (or Goulston), Theodore (1572–1632), I, 862
'Gundy, Sir Solomon' (1745), II, 211
Gunn, Jeannie (*fl.* 1907), III, 1097
Gunn, W. M. (*fl.* 1844), I, 683
Gunning, Elizabeth (1769–1823), II, 782
Gunning, Henry (1768–1854), III, 123, 150
Gunning, Peter (1614–1684), I, 697
Gunning, Susannah, née Minifie (1740?–1800), II, 546–7, 550 (2)
Gunston, Daniel (*fl.* 1770), II, 227, 234
Gunter, Edmund (1581–1626), I, 881
Gurdon, P. R. (b. 1863), III, 1073
Gurney, Archer Thompson (1820–1887), III, 32
Gurney, Anna (1795–1857), I, 89
Gurney, Edmund (1847–1888), III, **744**
Gurney, Hudson (1775–1864), II, 764
Gurney, M. (1872), III, 142
Gurwood, John (1790–1845), III, 144
Gutch, John (1746–1831), II, 162, 867 (2)
Gutch, John Mathew (1776–1861), I, 272, 446; III, 634, 799
Guthlac, St (O.E.)
   In prose, I, **93**
   In verse, I, 28, 31, 35, **78**
Guthrie, C. (*fl.* 1864), III, 972
Guthrie, Thomas (1803–1873), III, 129, 830, 853
Guthrie, Thomas Anstey ('F. Anstey') (1856–1934), III, **535**, 835
Guthrie, W. M. (*fl.* 1888), III, 835
Guthrie, William (1620–1665), II, 992
Guthrie, William (1708–1770), II, 28, 127, 447, 545, 696, 710, 715, 764, 767, **887**
Guthry, Henry (1600?–1676), I, 840
Guy of Southwick (d. 1217), I, **297**
Guy of Warwick (M.E.), I, 39, **149**f.
Guy, E. (*fl.* 1869), I, 194
Guy, Thomas (1645?–1724), II, 100

Guy, Earl of Warwick (17 cent.), I, 652
Guyon, Madame Jeanne-Marie Bouvier de la Mothe, II, 39, 782
Guyot Desfontaines, Pierre François, II, 782
Gwinne (or Gwynne), Matthew (1558?–1627), I, 656, 886
Gwynn, Edward (d. 1645?), I, 364
Gwynn (or Gwin), John (d. 1786), II, 17, 622 (2)
Gwynne (or Gwinne), Matthew (1558?–1627), I, 656, 886
Gylby (or Gilby), Goddred (*fl.* 1561), I, 801
Gyles, John (*fl.* 1736), III, 754

H., A. (*fl.* 1848), III, 34
H., A. W. (*fl.* 1791), II, 797
H., B. (*fl.* 1716), II, 565
H., C. (*fl.* 1660), II, 801
H., C. (*fl.* 1800), II, 774
H., E. (*fl.* 1780), II, 785
H., E. (*fl.* 1855), I, 824
H., G. (*fl.* 1642), I, 754
H., G. (*fl.* 1660), II, 532
H., H. (*fl.* 1701), II, 808
H., I. (*fl.* 1642), I, 716
H., J. (*fl.* 1602), I, 718
H., J. (*fl.* 1659), I, 887
H., M. (*fl.* 1818), III, 575
H., N. (*fl.* 1694), II, 182
H., P. (*fl.* 1739), II, 593
H., R. (*fl.* 1709), II, 827
H., S. (*fl.* 1610), I, 862
H., S. J. (*fl.* 1847), III, 300
H., T. (*fl.* 1560), I, 437
H., T. (*fl.* 1594), I, 592
H., T. (*fl.* 1647), I, 720
H., T. (*fl.* 1656), I, 732
H., T. (*fl.* 1835–40), III, 96
H., V. (*fl.* 1681), II, 178
H., W. (*fl.* 1764), II, 780
H., W. (*fl.* 1799), II, 666
H. his Devises (16 cent.), I, 404
Haak, Theodore (1605–1690), I, 856
Haberkorn, John, II, 55
Habert, Philippe, II, 283
Habington, Thomas (1560–1647), I, 453, 843, 854
Habington, William (1605–1654), I, 453, 724
Hack, Maria, née Barton (1777–1844), III, 566
Hacke, William (*fl.* 1699), II, 740
Hacket, John (1592–1670), I, 366, 657
Hackett, John (*fl.* 1757), II, 218 (2)
Hackluyt, John (*fl.* 1647–8), I, 747–8, 757, 759 (2), 760
Hackman, Alfred (1811–1874), I, 5
Hackney and Kingsland Gazette, The (1864), III, 809
Haddan, Arthur West (1816–1873), I, 702; III, 910
Hadden, James Murray (d. 1817), II, 152
HADDINGTON, II, 89 (printing)

Haddington, T. H. (*fl.* 1761), II, 786
Haddington, Thomas Hamilton, Earl of (1680–1735), II, 499
Haddon, Alfred Cort (1855–1940), III, 969
Haddon, Walter (1516–1572), I, 672
Haden, Sir Frank Seymour (1818–1910), III, 91
Hadfield, Joseph (*fl.* 1785), II, 756
HADLEIGH SCHOOL, I, 372
Hadow, James (1670?–1764), II, 995
Hadow, Sir William Henry (1859–1937), III, 744
Hadwen, E. C. (*fl.* 1856), III, 135
Haeckel, Ernst, III, 32
Haeften, Benedictus von, I, 478
Haerlem Courant Truly Rendered into English, The (1679), II, 703
Haerlem Courant, Truly Rendred into English, The (1682), II, 704
Haggard, A. (*fl.* 1876), III, 1081
Haggard, Ella (*fl.* 1857), III, 1068
Haggard, Sir Henry Rider (1856–1925), III, 547f.
Hagthorpe, John (*fl.* 1627), I, 476, 795
Haigh, Arthur Elam (1855–1905), III, 1006
Haigh, Daniel Henry (1819–1879), I, 56, 59, 60
Hailes, David Dalrymple, Lord (1726–1792), II, 888, 997
    Ed. by, I, 697, 878; II, 217, 832, 915
    Minor writings, II, 114, 883, 929
HAILEYBURY SCHOOL, III, 839
Haine, William (*fl.* 1611), I, 801
Haines, E. N. (*fl.* 1862), III, 72
Haines, John Thomas (1799?–1843), III, 589
Haiton of Armenia, I, 785
Hake, A. E. (*fl.* 1895), III, 978
Hake, Edward (*fl.* 1574–9), I, 365, 665, 713
Hake, Thomas Gordon (1809–1895), III, 288f.
Hakewill, George (1578–1649), I, 697, 866, 875
Hakluyt, Richard (1552?–1616), I, 764, 787, 788–9, 794
Hal's Looking-Glass (18 cent.), II, 237
Haldane, John Scott (1860–1935), III, 964
Haldenstone, James (d. 1443), I, 313
Hale, Sir Matthew (1609–1676), I, 834, 850; II, 121, 960, 964, 965
Hale, Thomas (*fl.* 1763), II, 222
Hale, William Hale (1795–1870), I, 121–2
Hales, Job (*fl.* 1543), I, 806
Hales, John (*fl.* 1581), I, 391
Hales, John (1584–1656), I, 376, 697, 846, 854, 867
Hales, John Wesley (1836–1914), III, 109, 1039
Hales, Stephen (1677–1761), II, 961
Halévy, Ludovic, III, 610, 612
Halford, Frederic M. (*fl.* 1889), III, 772
Halfpenny, John (*fl.* 1671), II, 816
Halfpenny, William (*fl.* 1750), II, 148
Halfpenny London Journal, The (1724), II, 713
'*Halfpenny Marvel*' *Library, The* (1893), III, 578

Halfpenny Picture Magazine for Little Children, The (1854), III, 577
Halfpenny Surprise, The (1894), III, 579
Halhed, Nathaniel Brassey (1751–1830), II, 457; III, 1073
Hali Meidenhad (M.E.), I, **168**
Haliburton, Thomas Chandler ('Sam Slick') (1796–1865), III, 1086–7
HALIFAX
  Newspapers, II, 724 (1759)
  Printing in, II, 87
Halifax, Charles Montagu, Earl of (1661–1715), II, **282**
Halifax, Charles Wood, Viscount (1800–1885), III, 684, 1077
Halifax, George Savile, Marquis of (1633–1695), II, **570**f.
Halifax, S. See Hallifax
Halifax (or Hallifax), William (1655?–1722), II, 749
Halifax Evening Courier, The (1892), III, 806
Halkett, Anne, Lady (1622–1699), I, 386
Hall, — (*fl.* 1655), of Gray's Inn, I, 444
Hall, A. Vine (b. 1862), III, 1089
Hall, Anna Maria, née Fielding (1800–1881), III, **485**f., 577, 711
  Articles by, III, 368, 400, 414
Hall, Anthony (1679–1723), I, 6, 837; II, 139
Hall, Arthur (*fl.* 1563–1604), I, 802
Hall, Basil (1788–1844), III, **670**
Hall, Charles (1745?–1825?), III, 969, 975–6
Hall, Edward (d. 1547), I, **823**
Hall, F. (*fl.* 1731), II, 753
Hall, Fitz-Edward (1825–1901), I, 897; III, 1071, 1081
Hall, G. W. (*fl.* 1815), III, 970
Hall, Herbert Byng (*fl.* 1847), III, 766
Hall, James (d. 1612), I, 789
Hall (or Halle), John (1529?–1566?), poet and medical writer, I, 678, 891
Hall, John (1575–1635), physician, I, 890
Hall, John (1627–1656), poet and pamphleteer
  Essays, I, 726
  Pamphlets, I, 367
  Poems, I, 476, 479
  Periodicals ed. by, I, 748, 758 (2), 760
  Translations, I, 476, 804
Hall, John (1739–1797), line-engraver, I, 593
Hall, Joseph (1574–1656), I, **697, 841**
  Poems, I, 480, 678
  Religious and controversial writings, I, 333, 337, 468, 722, 725, 874; II, 55
  Writings in Latin, I, 329, 733, 847, 858
Hall, Marshall (1790–1857), III, 963, 965
Hall, Peter (1802–1849), I, 677, 697, 897
Hall, R. N. (*fl.* 1902), III, 1091
Hall, Robert (1764–1831), II, **955**; III, 669
Hall, Robert Gream (*fl.* 1830), III, 986
Hall, Mrs S. C. See Anna Maria Hall
Hall, Samuel (*fl.* 1785), II, 19

Hall, Samuel Carter (1800–1889), III, 634
  Articles by, III, 368, 392, 400, 412
Hall, Thomas (1610?–1665), I, 369, 697, 714, 805
Hall, W. H. (*fl.* 1789), II, 56
Hall, William (b. 1838), III, **341**
Hall, William Clarke (*fl.* 1894), III, 986
Hallam, Arthur Henry (1811–1833), III, **716**f.
Hallam, Henry (1777–1859), III, 25, 36, 716, **880**
Hallam, Isaac (*fl.* 1742), II, 827
Halle, John (1529?–1566?). See Hall
Haller, Albrecht von, II, 56, 63
Hallett (or Hallet), Joseph (1691?–1744), II, 863
Halley, Edmund (1656–1742), I, 881; II, 129, 961 (2)
Halliburton, William Dobson (b. 1860), III, 964
Halliday, Andrew (1830–1877), III, 598
Hallifax, Samuel (1733–1790), II, 946 (misprinted Halifax)
Hallifax (or Halifax), William (1655?–1722), II, 749
Halliwell, James Orchard, later Halliwell-Phillipps (1820–1889), III, 891, **1032**f.
  Reprints ed. by, III, 898, 903–4, 916 (2)
Hallmann, Johann Christian, II, 62
Halloran, Henry (*fl.* 1887), III, 1095
Hallywell, H. (*fl.* 1686), II, 943
Halm, K., III, 1007, 1011
Halpin, Nicholas John (1790–1850), I, 524
HALTON LIBRARY, II, 105
Ham, John (*fl.* 1738), II, 577
Hamber, Thomas (*fl.* 1857–76), III, 798 (2), 799 (2), 801
Hamerton, Philip Gilbert (1834–1894), III, 19, **744**f.
Hamilton, Alexander (d. 1732?), traveller in East Indies, II, 750
Hamilton, Alexander (*fl.* 1744), traveller in America, II, 754
Hamilton, Anthony (1646–1720), II, 46, 149, 406, 541, 782
Hamilton, Caroline (*fl.* 1790), II, 138
Hamilton, Charles (1753?–1792), II, 812; III, 1075
Hamilton, Edward, III, 771
Hamilton, Elizabeth (1758–1816), III, **398**
Hamilton, Lord Frederic (*fl.* 1893), III, 831
Hamilton, Gavin (d. 1766), II, 696
Hamilton, George (*fl.* 1793), II, 742
Hamilton, H. (*fl.* 1849), dramatist, III, 602
Hamilton, H. C. (*fl.* 1848), I, 116
Hamilton, Hugh (*fl.* 1851), of Dublin, II, 937
Hamilton, J. (*fl.* 1815), III, 976
Hamilton, James, Duke of Hamilton (1606–1649), I, 387
Hamilton, James (*fl.* 1742), II, 768
Hamilton, James (*fl.* 1869), III, 282
Hamilton, Janet (1795–1873), III, 234

Hamilton, John (1511?–1571), I, 903
Hamilton, John Potter (*fl.* 1860), III, 766
Hamilton, Mary, later Dickenson (*fl.* 1756–1816), II, 137, 150
Hamilton, Patrick (1504?–1528), I, 903
Hamilton, R. (*fl.* 1863), III, 983
Hamilton, Richard Winter (1794–1848), III, 110
Hamilton, Robert (1743–1829), economist, III, 978, 981
Hamilton, Robert (1749–1830), physician, II, 152
Hamilton, Thomas, Earl of Haddington (1680–1735), II, 499
Hamilton, Thomas (1789–1842), III, 242, **399**
Hamilton, W. (*fl.* 1784), journalist, II, 680
Hamilton, W. D. (*fl.* 1859), I, 468
Hamilton, Walter (*fl.* 1820), III, 1079
Hamilton, William (*fl.* 1661), translator, II, 792
Hamilton, William, of Gilbertfield (1665?–1751), II, 973
Hamilton, William, of Bangour (1704–1754), II, 973
Hamilton, Sir William (1730–1803), diplomatist and archaeologist, II, 746
Hamilton, Sir William (1788–1856), metaphysician, III, 21, 122, **868**, 957
Hamilton, William Gerard (1729–1796), II, 617
Hamilton, Sir William Rowan (1805–1868), mathematician, III, **941**
Hamlain, or The Hermit of the Beach (18 cent.), II, 564
Hamley, Sir Edward (1824–1893), III, 695
Hammick, James T. (*fl.* 1887), III, 986
Hammond, Anthony (1668–1738), II, 195
Hammond, Henry (1605–1660), I, **697**
Hammond, J. L. (b. 1872), III, 814
Hammond, James (1710–1742), II, **318**
Hammond, John (*fl.* 1642), publisher, I, 752 (2)
Hammond, John (*fl.* 1656), writer on America, I, 796
Hammond, Lawrence (*fl.* 1677), II, 752
Hammond, Thomas (*fl.* 1605), I, 739
Hammond, William (b. 1614), I, 476
Hamond, Walter (*fl.* 1643), I, 785
Hamor, Ralph (*fl.* 1614), I, 790
Hampden, R. (*fl.* 1682), II, 801
Hampden, Renn Dickson (1793–1868), III, 848
Hamper, William (1776–1831), II, 864
HAMPSHIRE
    Bibliography, I, 8
    Printing, II, 87
Hampshire Advertiser, The, III, 793
Hampshire Chronicle and Portsmouth and Chichester Journal, The (1785), II, 729
Hampshire Chronicle; Or, Portsmouth, Winchester and Southampton Gazette, The (1778), II, 729

Hampshire Chronicle; Or, Portsmouth, Winchester and Southampton Gazette, The (1780), II, 727
Hampshire Chronicle; Or, Southampton, Winchester and Portsmouth Mercury, The (1772), II, 728
Hampshire Chronicle; Or Southampton, Winchester and Portsmouth Mercury, The (1778), II, 729
Hampshire Journal, The (1792), II, 729
Hampshire Telegraph and Sussex Chronicle, The (1802), II, 727
Hampson, John (1760–1817?), II, 814
Hampson, R. T. (*fl.* 1859), I, 87
Hampton, Benjamin (*fl.* 1704–11), II, 128, 942
Hampton, James (1721–1778), II, 763
Hampton, W. (*fl.* 1763), II, 337
Hanbury, Benjamin (1778–1864), I, 685; II, 862
Hanbury, William (*fl.* 1760), II, 105
Hanchet, Daniel (*fl.* 1717), II, 537, 662
Hancock, Jasper (*fl.* 1680), II, 703
Hancock, W. N. (*fl.* 1850), III, 971
Handefull of Pleasant Delites, A (16 cent.), I, 404
Handlo, Robert (*fl.* 1326), I, **311**
Handson, Raphe (*fl.* 1614), I, 881
HANDWRITING, I, 346f. (1500–1660), 586 (Shakespeare's); II, 82 (1660–1800)
Hane, Joachim (*fl.* 1653), I, 772f.
Hanger, George, Baron Coleraine (1751?–1824), III, 765
Hangman's Joy, The (17 cent.), I, 715
Hankey, Thomson (1805–1893), III, 972–3
Hankin, Edward (1747–1835), III, 789
Hanmer, Sir John, afterwards Baron (1809–1881), III, **289**
Hanmer, Sir Thomas (1677–1746), II, 148, **610**, **910**, 929
Hanna, J. (*fl.* 1738), II, 803
Hanna, William (1808–1882), III, 852
Hannah, John (1818–1888), I, 405
Hannay, James (1827–1873), III, **717**, 724, 807
    Articles by, III, 603, 720, 785
Hannay, James (*fl.* 1879), barrister, III, 1087
Hannay, Patrick (d. 1629?), I, 476
Hannes, Sir Edward (d. 1710), II, 574
Hannett, John (*fl.* 1835), II, 107
Hannington, James (1847–1885), III, 155
Hansard, George Agar (*fl.* 1834–40), III, 776
Hansard, J. (*fl.* 1829), III, 87
Hansard, L. G. (*fl.* 1829), III, 87
Hansard, Luke (1752–1828), III, 87
Hansard, Thomas Curson (1776–1833), III, 74, 76 (2)
Hanshall, T. H. (*fl.* 1775), II, 722
Hanson, Alfred (*fl.* 1865), III, 986
Hanson, C. H. (*fl.* 1890?), III, 807
Hanson, Sir Richard Davies (1805–1876), III, 800

Hanway, Jonas (1712–1786), II, 124, 139, 146, 150, 237, 750, 765
Hanway, Mary Anne (*fl.* 1776–95), II, 550, 626
Harangues, The (18 cent.), II, 221 (2)
Harcourt, Mrs (*fl.* 18 cent.), II, 150
Harcourt, Leveson Vernon (1788–1860), III, 149
Harcourt, Robert (1574?–1631), I, 790
Harcourt, Simon (1684–1720), II, 196
Hardcastle, Thomas (d. 1678?), II, 928
Hardiman, James (1790?–1855), III, 1047–8
Harding, Samuel (1618?–1642?), I, 646
Harding, Silvester (1745–1809), II, 922
Harding's Dublin Impartial News Letter (1724), II, 734
Harding's Weekly Impartial News Letter (1723), II, 734
Hardinge, George (1743–1816), II, 255 ('Owen Junior'), 634, 887, 903
Hardman, Frederick (1814–1874), III, 399
Hardman, Sir William (1828–1890), III, 154, 785, 798
Hardouin, Jean, II, 782
Hardwick, Charles (1821–1859), I, 95, 169, 265
Hardwicke, Philip Yorke, Earl of (1720–1790), II, 164, **887**
Hardwicke State Papers (16, 17 cents.), I, 397
Hardy, A. E. Gathorne (*fl.* 1900), III, 772
Hardy, Frances. [Misprint for Francis Hardy, 1751–1812], II, 635
Hardy, Nathaniel (1618–1670), I, **697**
Hardy, P. D. (*fl.* 1831), III, 826–7
Hardy, Thomas (1752–1832), radical journalist, II, 683
Hardy, Thomas (1840–1928), novelist and poet, III, **516**f.
Hardy, Sir Thomas Duffus (1804–1878), III, **898**
Hardyng, John (1378–1465?), I, 265
Hare, Augustus John Cuthbert (1834–1903), III, **745**
Hare, Augustus William (1792–1834), III, 670
Hare, Francis (1671–1740), II, 592
Hare, Hugh, Baron Coleraine (1606?–1667), II, 811
Hare, Hugh (1668–1707), II, 811
Hare, John (1668–1720), II, 909
Hare, Julius Charles (1795–1855), III, 110, **670**, 691
Hare, Robert (d. 1611), I, 124
Hare, Thomas (*fl.* 1737), II, 765
'Harewood, Henry' (1835), III, 758
Harflete, Henry (*fl.* 1653), I, 726, 859
Harford, John Scandrett (1785–1866), III, 993
Hargrave, Dr (*fl.* 1787), II, 738
Hargrave, Francis (1741?–1821), II, 92
'Hargrave, Jasper' (1800), i.e. George Hardinge (1743–1816), II, 255
Hargrove, Ely (1741–1818), II, 824
Hargrove, W. Wallace (*fl.* 1846), III, 804

Hargrove, William (1788–1862), III, 804
Harington, Henry (1755–1791), II, 917
Harington, John (*fl.* 1550), I, 800
Harington, Sir John (1561–1612), I, **705**, 810, 815, 889
Harington, John (1627?–1700?), II, **282**
Harington, Sir John (*fl.* 1769), II, 226, 231, 234, 247
Hariot (or Harriot), Thomas (1560–1621), I, 794, 845, 881
Harison, William (1685–1713), II, **318**, 661
Harkness, James (*fl.* 1893), II, 943
Harkon, J. M. (*fl.* 1867), III, 376
Harlan, J. (*fl.* 1842), III, 1076
Harland, John (1806–1868), I, 121, 384; II, 258; III, 885
Harleian Gloss (O.E.), I, 36
Harleian Miscellany (18 cent.), II, 210–2, 216, 881
Harlem's Courant, The (1695), II, 711
Harlequin, The (1773), II, 665
Harley, Lady Brilliana (1600?–1643), I, 386
Harley, Edward, Earl of Oxford (1689–1741), II, 102, 139
Harley, George (1829–1896), III, 963
Harley, Mrs M. *fl.* 1786), II, 549
Harman, Thomas (*fl.* 1567), I, 717, 845
Harmar (or Harmer), John (1594?–1670), I, 374, 856
Harmer, James (1777–1853), III, 810
Harmer, Thomas (1714–1788), II, 775
Harmon, David Williams (*fl.* 1820), III, 1087
Harmonia Anglicana (18 cent.), II, 219
Harmonia Anglicana or English Harmony Reviv'd (18 cent.), II, 223 (2)
Harmonia Sacra (1688), II, 180, 182, 185–6, 191 (2), 198
Harmonia Sacra (1790), II, 244
Harmonia Sacra, Or Divine and Moral Songs (1780), II, 234
Harmsworth, Alfred C. W., Viscount Northcliffe (1865–1922), III, 787
Harmsworth Magazine, The (1900), III, 832
Harmsworth Monthly Pictorial Magazine, The (1898), III, 832
Harness, William (1790–1869), I, 549; III, 200
Harney, G. J. (*fl.* 1839–52), III, 817 (3), 828
Harp, The (18 cent.), II, 214
Harp of Erin, The (1798), II, 737
Harper, — (*fl.* 1757), II, 471
Harper, A. (*fl.* 1856), III, 130
Harper, Charles George (b. 1863), III, 765
Harper, F. (*fl.* 1879), III, 830
Harper, F. W. (*fl.* 1842), III, 691
Harper, Richard (*fl.* 1645), I, 756
Harper, Thomas Norton (1821–1893), III, **868**
Harpsfield, John (1516–1578), I, 682
Harpsfield, Nicholas (1519?–1575), I, 824
Harpur, Charles (1817–1868), III, **1094**
Harpur, John (*fl.* 1617), I, 377

Harpur, Joseph (1773–1821), II, 21
Harraden, Beatrice (b. 1864), III, **548**
Harrington (or Harington), James (1611–
1677), I, 732, 847, **878**; II, 53
Harrington, Sir John (*fl.* 1658), I, 809, 865
Harrington, Leicester Fitzgerald Charles
Stanhope, Earl of (1784–1862), III, 206
Harriot (or Hariot), Thomas (1560–1621), I,
794, 845, 881
Harriott, John (1745–1817), II, 138
Harris, A. (*fl.* 1621), I, 717
Harris, Benjamin (*fl.* 1673–1708?), II, 696, 702,
703 (2), 706 (2), 716
Harris, Frank (*c.* 1855–1931), III, 785, 801,
814 (2), 830
Harris, Furlong Elizabeth Skipton (*fl.* 1847),
III, 857
Harris, George (*fl.* 1752), II, 17
Harris, George (1809–1890), III, 153
Harris, James (1709–1780), II, 16, 955
Harris, James, Earl of Malmesbury (1746–
1820), II, 138
Harris, James Edward, Earl of Malmesbury,
III, 763
Harris, James Howard, Earl of Malmesbury
(1807–1889), III, 146, 149
Harris, John (*fl.* 1648), journalist, I, 747 (2),
748, 757 (2), 759 (2)
Harris, John (1667?–1719), II, 661, 740, 926,
961
Harris, Joseph (*c.* 1650–*c.* 1715), II, **423**
Harris, Joseph (1702–1764), II, 958
Harris, Stanley (*fl.* 1882), III, 765
Harris, Thaddeus Mason (*fl.* 1792), II, 247
Harris, Walter (1647–1732), II, 744, 788
Harris, Walter (1686–1761), I, 838
Harris, Walter Burton (*fl.* 1889), III, 991
Harris, William (1675?–1740), II, 863
Harris, Sir William Cornwallis (1807–1848),
III, **1091**
Harrison, Benjamin (1808–1887), III, 855
Harrison, C. (*fl.* 1879–1902), journalist, III,
820
Harrison, C. (*fl.* 1890), publisher, III, 98
Harrison, Frederic (1831–1923), III, 110, **745**f.
Harrison, G. (*fl.* 1802), III, 110
Harrison, J. (*fl.* 1845), I, 877
Harrison, John (*fl.* 1619), I, 737
Harrison, Mary St Leger, née Kingsley
('Lucas Malet') (d. 1931), III, 553f.
Harrison, Ralph (1748–1810), II, 119, 932; III,
134
Harrison, Robert (d. 1585?), I, 893
Harrison, Stephen (*fl.* 1604), I, 622
Harrison, W. (*fl.* 1813), III, 134
Harrison, W. (*fl.* 1890), III, 803
Harrison, William (1534–1593), I, 773–4, 846
HARRISON AND SONS, III, 87
Harrison's Amusing Picture and Poetry Book
(18 cent.), II, 563

*Harrison's Derby and Nottingham Journal; Or,
Midland Advertiser* (1776), II, 723
Harrison's Derby Journal (1776), II, 723
Harrllum Courant, The (1689), II, 705
Harrod, William (d. 1819), II, 871
Harrop's Manchester Mercury (1752), II, 726
HARROW SCHOOL, I, 372; III, 132, 839
Harrowby, Dudley Ryder, Earl (1762–1847),
148
Harrower, John (*fl.* 1773), II, 756
Harrowing of Hell (O.E.), I, **78**
Harrowing of Hell (M.E.), I, **188**
Harry, Blind. See Henry the Minstrel
Harsnet, Samuel (1561–1631), I, 893
Harston, Edward (*fl.* 1845–64), III, 291
Hart, Mrs E. A. (*fl.* 1868), III, 305
Hart, Ernest Abraham (1835–1898), III, 821
Hart, J. (*fl.* 1749), II, 760
Hart, James (b. 1580–1590), I, 889
Hart, John (d. 1574), I, 44, 376
Hart, W. (*fl.* 1863), I, 121
Hart, W. H. (*fl.* 1895), III, 1080
Harte, Walter (1709–1774), II, **318**, 321
Hartford, Robert (*fl.* 1679), II, 702
Hartford Mercury, The (1772), II, 724
Hartgill, George (*fl.* 1594), I, 883
Harthill, John (*fl.* 1833), II, 732
Hartland, Edwin Sidney (b. 1848), III, 968
Hartlay, Mrs James (*fl.* 1840), III, 1069
HARTLEBURY SCHOOL, I, 372
Hartley, David (1705–1757), II, 955
Hartley, John (*fl.* 1699–1709), II, 103
Hartley, Thomas (*fl.* 1737–70), II, 33
Hartley, Walter Noel (1846–1913), III, 963
Hartlib, Samuel (d. 1670), I, 365–6, 375, 776,
846, 875; II, 112
Hartopp, E. C. C. (*fl.* 1894), III, 767
Hartshorne, Charles Henry (1802–1865), I,
114; II, 103
Hartshorne, N. C. (*fl.* 1843), I, 672
Hartson, Hall (d. 1773), II, **466**f.
Hartwell, Abraham, the elder (*fl.* 1565), I, 519
Hartwell, Abraham, the younger (*fl.* 1595–
1603), I, 778, 782, 816
Hartwell, Henry (*fl.* 1727), II, 753
Harvey, Alexander (*fl.* 1774), II, 756
Harvey, Christopher (1597–1663), I, 476, 478
Harvey, Daniel Whittle (1786–1863), III, 785,
799, 801, 811–2 (2)
Harvey, G. (*fl.* 1867), III, 1069
Harvey, Gabriel (1545?–1630?), I, 693, **704**f.,
864
Harvey, James (*fl.* 1752), II, 111
Harvey, John (1563?–1592), I, 884
Harvey, John (*fl.* 1726,) II, 973
Harvey, P. W. (*fl.* 1891), III, 809
Harvey, Richard (d. 1623?), I, 693, 884
Harvey, Thomas (*fl.* 1656–77), I, 819, 859
Harvey, William (1578–1657), I, 854, 889
Harvey, William Henry (1811–1866), III, **961**

Harward, Simon (*fl.* 1623), I, 391
Harwood, Edward (1729–1794), II, 936
Harwood, Isabella (1840–1888), III, **341** f.
Harwood, Philip (1809–1887), III, 785, 814
Harwood, Thomas (1767–1842), I, 826
Hasan Ali, Mir (*fl.* 1832), III, 1083
Haslerig and Vain (17 cent.), I, 719
Hasleton, Richard (*fl.* 1595), I, 769
Haslewood, Joseph (1769–1833), I, 433, 520;
    II, 404, 407, 906; III, **1024**
Haslop, Henry (*fl.* 1587), I, 768
Hassell, John (d. 1825), III, 82
Hasted, Edward (1732–1812), II, **891**
Hastie, William (1842–1893), III, 342
Hastings, Francis Rawdon-Hastings, Marquis
    of (1754–1826), III, 149
Hastings, J. D. (*fl.* 1880), II, 346
Hastings, James (1852–1922), III, 850
Hastings, Warren (1732–1818), II, 750
Hatch, Edwin (1835–1889), III, 848
HATCHARD & CO., III, 98
Hatchett, Charles (1765?–1847), III, 973
Hatchett, William (*fl.* 1729–33), II, 438, 542,
    784, 809
Hatfield, John (1758?–1803), II, 154
Hatton, Sir Christopher (1540–1591), I, 384,
    523
Hatton, Christopher, Viscount (1601–1704), I,
    386
Hatton, Edward (*fl.* 1696–1733), II, 145, 926
Hatton, Joseph (1841–1907), III, **548**, 811, 813,
    822
Hatton, Richard (*fl.* 1627), I, 805
Hau-Kiou-Choaan, or, the Pleasing History
    (18 cent.), II, 552
Hauboys, John (*fl.* 1470), I, **313**
Hauff, W. (*fl.* 1839), III, 410
Haughton, A. (*fl.* 1657), I, 882
Haughton, Sir Graves Champney (1788–1849),
    III, 1073
Haughton, John Colpoys (1817–1887), III, 1077
Haughton, William (*c.* 1575–1605), I, 535
Haugwitz, Adolf von, II, 62
Hauksbee, Francis (d. 1713?), II, 961
Hausted, Peter (d. 1645), I, 657, 663
Havard, William (1710?–1778), II, **438**
Have at You All (1752), II, 664
Havelock, Sir Henry (1795–1857), III, 1075
Havelok, Lay of (M.E.), I, 29, 39, 42, **148** f.
Haverfield, Eleanor Louisa (b. 1870), III, 574
Havergal, Frances Ridley (1836–1879), III, **342**,
    573
Havers, George (*fl.* 1661–70), I, 819; II, 811,
    814
Haward, Nicholas (*fl.* 1569), I, 801
Haweis, H. R. (*fl.* 1858), III, 834
Haweis, J. O. W., I, 680
Hawes, J. (*fl.* 1754), II, 216
Hawes, Stephen (*c.* 1475–1530), I, 46, **253** f.
Hawes, William (*fl.* 1709), II, 95

Hawes, William (1785–1846), musical com-
    poser, I, 484
Hawes, William (1736–1808), physician, II, 646
HAWICK, II, 87 (printing)
Hawke, Martin (*fl.* 1794–1835), II, 666; III, 760
Hawke, Michael (*fl.* 1657), I, 850
Hawker, Mary Elizabeth ('Lanoe Falconer')
    (1848–1908), III, **544**
Hawker, Peter (1786–1853), III, 762
Hawker, Robert Stephen (1803–1875), III, **289**
Hawkes, John (1767–1834), III, 759
Hawkesworth, John (1715?–1773), II, **467**,
    544 (2), 799
Hawkesworth, Walter (d. 1606), I, 657
Hawkey, John (1703–1759), II, 912
HAWKING (books on), I, 394 (16, 17 cents.);
    II, 818 f. (1660–1800); III, 778 (19 cent.)
Hawkins, Sir Anthony Hope ('Anthony Hope')
    (1863–1933), III, **549**
Hawkins, Edward (1789–1882), I, 464
Hawkins, Ernest (1802–1868), I, 253
Hawkins, F. W. (*fl.* 1869), III, 582
Hawkins, Francis (1628–1681), I, 812; II, 121
Hawkins, Henry (1572?–1646), I, 479
Hawkins, Sir Henry, Baron Brampton (1817–
    1907), III, 153
Hawkins, Sir John (1532–1595), I, 786
Hawkins, John (*fl.* 1635), I, 679
Hawkins, John (d. 1692), II, 124
Hawkins, Sir John (1719–1789), II, **898** f.
Hawkins, Laetitia (*fl.* 1822), II, 625, 841
Hawkins, Richard (*fl.* 1658), I, 777
Hawkins, Sir Richard (1562?–1622), I, 788
Hawkins, Sir Thomas (d. 1640), I, 766, 803
Hawkins, Thomas (1729–1772), II, 915
Hawkins, William (1605?–1637), I, 646
Hawkins, William (*fl.* 1721), II, 848
Hawkins, William (1722–1801), II, **467**
Hawkshaw, Mrs (*fl.* 1852), III, 567
Hawkshaw, Benjamin (d. 1738), II, **282**
Haworth, B. (*fl.* 1829), III, 975
Haworth, Martin E. (*fl.* 1882), III, 765
Haws, W. (*fl.* 1701), II, 711
Hawtrey, M. (*fl.* 1896), III, 110
Hawtrey, S. T. (*fl.* 1859), III, 110
Hay, D. (*fl.* 1704), II, 788
Hay, Sir Gilbert (*fl.* 1456), I, 144, 260
Hay, J. B. (*fl.* 1839), III, 125
Hay, William (1695–1755), II, 217, 250, 312,
    766
Haydn, Joseph T. (d. 1856), II, 809
Haydocke, Richard (*fl.* 1598), I, 392, 815
Haydon, Benjamin Robert (1786–1846), III, **671**
Haydon, Frank Scott (1822–1887), I, 116
Hayes, Alfred (b. 1857), III, **342**
Hayes, Christopher (*fl.* 1718), II, 604
Hayes, J. (*fl.* 1744), II, 766
Hayes, Samuel (*fl.* 1789), II, 617
Hayes, Thomas (*fl.* 1685), II, 534
Haygarth, A. (*fl.* 1862 or later), III, 773

Hayley, William (1745–1820), I, 464; II, 342, **364**f., 916
Hayman, Henry (1823–1904), III, 1006
Hayman, Robert (*fl.* 1628), I, 481
Hayman, Robert (d. 1631?), I, 795, 859
Hayman, Samuel (1818–1886), II, 415
Haynes, James (*fl.* 1821–40), III, **589**f.
Haynes, Samuel (d. 1752), I, 399
Haynie, Henry (*fl.* 1905), III, 785
Hayter, Thomas (1702–1762), II, 84, 887, 952
Hayward, Abraham (1801–1884), III, 368, **717**f.
Hayward, J. (*fl.* 1825), III, 970
Hayward, Sir John (1564?–1627), I, 837, 844
Hayward, Thomas (d. 1779?), II, 913
Haywood, Eliza (1693?–1756), II, **438**
    Fiction, II, 515, 537, 538 (3), 539 (2), 540, 542, 543f., 544 (2), 545, 551
    Translation, II, 795
Haywood, Francis (1796–1858), III, 32
Hazlitt, William (1778–1830), III, **640**f.
    Articles and reviews by, III, 192, 201, 218, 668, 789
Hazlitt, William, the younger (*fl.* 1836–48), III, 33 (2), 410, 641–2, 887
Hazlitt, William Carew (1834–1913), III, **1039**
    Editions by, I, 460; III, 641–3
Head, Barclay Vincent (1844–1914), III, **1006**
Head, Sir Francis Bond (1793–1875), III, 991
Head, H. (*fl.* 1900?), III, 833
Head, Richard (1637?–1686?), I, 718; II, 24, 155, 176, 529 (2), 530, 930
Head, W. W. (*fl.* 1867), III, 87
Headlam, Walter George (1866–1908), III, **1006**
Headley, Henry (1765–1788), II, 241, **365**
Heads of a Diarie (1648), I, 759
Heads of all the Proceedings in both Houses of Parliament, The (1642), I, 753
Heads of Chiefe Passages in Parliament (1648), I, 758
Heads of Severall proceedings in both Houses of Parliament, The (1641), I, 752
Heads of Severall Proceedings in this Present Parliament, The (1641), I, 752
Heads of Some Notes of the Citie Scout (1645), I, 756
Heale, William (1581?–1627), I, 716
Healey, John (d. 1610), I, 801, 810, 857, 862
Healey, T. P. (*fl.* 1839?), III, 821
Healy, Christopher (*fl.* 1904), III, 785
Heaphy, Thomas (1813–1873), III, 449
Hearn, William Edward (1826–1888), III, 983
Hearne, Mary (*fl.* 1718), II, 537
Hearne, Samuel (1745–1792), II, 743, 756
Hearne, Thomas (1678–1735), II, 117, **873**f., 910, 919, 928–9
Heath, Benjamin (1704–1766), II, 912
Heath, F. G. (*fl.* 1872), III, 971
Heath, J. (*fl.* 1790), II, 770
Heath, James (1629–1664), I, 400

Heath, James Dunbar (*fl.* 1874), III, 775
Heath, John (*fl.* 1610), I, 481
Heath, John (*fl.* 1615), I, 724
Heath, R. (*fl.* 1893), III, 972
Heath, Sir Robert (1575–1649), I, 847
Heath, Robert (*fl.* 1650), I, 476, 726
Heathcote, Ralph (1721–1795), II, 895, 922, 951
Heathcote, W. (*fl.* 1717), II, 707, 712
Heathfield, R. (*fl.* 1851), III, 978
Heavysege, Charles (*fl.* 1857), III, 1086
Heber, A. (*fl.* 1827), III, 234 (5)
Heber, Mary (*fl.* 1765–1806), II, 137
Heber, Reginald (*fl.* 1752), writer on racing, II, 718
Heber, Reginald (1783–1826), poet, I, 701; III, 199 (2), **234**, 847
Heber, Richard (1773–1833), I, 4
Heberd, J. (*fl.* 1834), II, 862
Heberden, William, the younger (1767–1845), II, 116; III, 110
Hedderwick, Edwin C. (*fl.* 1897), III, 808
Hedderwick, James (1814–1897), III, 341, 785, 808
Hédelin, François (Abbé d'Aubignac), II, 39, 782
Hedge, Mary Ann (*fl.* 1819), III, 571
Hedgeland, Isabella, née Kelly (*fl.* 1794–1813), III, **404**
Hedges, Sir William (1632–1701), II, 749
Heely, Joseph (*fl.* 1777), II, 30
Hegel, Georg Wilhelm Friedrich, III, **32**, 47
Hegge Plays (M.E.), I, **277**
Heiberg, T. C., III, 397
Heidegger, John James (1659?–1749), II, 805
Heideloff, Nikolaus (*fl.* 1794), II, 160
Heine, Heinrich, III, **32**, 47, 287, 354
Heinemann, William (1863–1920), III, 98
Heinse, Johann Jacob Wilhelm, II, 63
Heinsius, Daniel, I, 327
Heliodorus, I, 802; II, 760
Hellowes, Edward (*fl.* 1574–1600), I, 814, 885
Helm, E. (*fl.* 1899), III, 974
Helme, Elizabeth (d. 1816), II, 549–50, 560, 566; III, **399**
Helmont, Jean-Baptiste van, I, 890
Help to Discourse, A (17 cent.), II, 174, 175, 178
Help to History, A (1709), II, 676
Helps, Sir Arthur (1813–1875), III, 95, **718**
Helvétius, Claude Adrien, II, 36, 782; III, 411
Hely, James (*fl.* 1793), III, 1047
Hely-Hutchinson, John (1724–1794), II, 159
Helyas, The Knight of the Swan (M.E.), I, 146
Hemans, Felicia Dorothea, née Browne (1793–1835), III, **235**
'Hemery, Wilfred', i.e. T. le B. Roscoe (*fl.* 1912), III, 1090
'Heming, Bracebridge' (1893), III, 578 (2)
Heming, John (d. 1630), I, 546
Heming, William (1602?–after 1637), I, 646

Hemingburgh (or Hemingford), Walter of (*fl.* 1300), I, 116
Hemmingsen, Niel (*fl.* 1569–80), I, 845
Hempel, C. J., III, 298
Hénault, Charles Jean François, II, 782
Henchman, William (*fl.* 1681), II, 703
Henderson, Alexander (1583?–1646), I, 908
Henderson, Andrew (*fl.* 1734–75), II, 526, 626, 803, 1002
Henderson, H. B. (*fl.* 1843), III, 1083
Henderson, James (*fl.* 1871–97), III, 821
Henderson, Sir James (*fl.* 1890), III, 808
Henderson, James A. (*fl.* 1845), III, 808
Henderson, John Scott (*fl.* 1867), III, 807, 820
Henderson, William (*fl.* 1796), II, 252
Henderson, William (*fl.* 1876), III, 771
Hendley, William (1691?–1724), II, 124
Henfrey, Arthur (1819–1859), III, 961
Henley, Anthony (d. 1711), II. 661
Henley, John (1692–1756), II, 16, 302, 663, 677, 769, 789, 791, 920
Henley, Samuel (1740–1815), II, 528, 768
Henley, Walter of (*fl.* 13 cent.), I, 120, 845
Henley, William Ernest (1849–1903), III, **342**f., 814, 831 (2)
Hennell, Charles Christian (1809–1850), III, 61, 848
Hennell, Mrs Charles, III, 465
Hennell, Henry (d. 1842), III, 947
Hennell, Mary (1802–1843), III, 977
Hennepin, Louis, II, 782
Hennequin, A., III, 625
Hennessy, William Maunsell (1829–1889), III, 1047
Henning, F. W. J. (*fl.* 1889), III, 776
Henrici Quinti Angliae Regis Gesta (15 cent.), I, 116
Henrietta Maria, Queen (1609–1669), I, 386
Henry V, King (1387–1422), I, 116
Henry, Prince of Wales (1594–1612), I, 385
Henry de Bracton (d. 1268), I, **300**
Henry of Harclay (*fl.* 1312), I, **311**
Henry of Huntingdon (d. 1155), I, **286**
Henry the Minstrel (*fl.* 1470–92), I, 29
Henry, Alexander (1739–1824), III, 1087–8
Henry, David (*fl.* 1754–73), II, 677, 741
Henry, Matthew (1662–1714), II, 863
Henry, Philip (1631–1696), I, 387
Henry, Robert (1718–1790), II, 38, **887**, 921
Henry, Thomas (1734–1816), II, 20
Henry, W. (*fl.* 1894), III, 776
Henry, W. C. (*fl.* 1854–67), III, 137, 946
Henry, William (1774–1836), III, 946
Henry of Northumberland; or The Hermit's Cell (1800), II, 551
Henry's Winchester Journal (1746), II, 728
Henryson, Robert (1425?–1500?), I, **257**f.
Henshall, Samuel (1764?–1807), II, 921
Henshaw, Joseph (1603–1679), I, 725
Henslow, George (1835–1925), III, 962

Henslow, John Stevens (1796–1861), III, **960**
Henslowe, Philip (d. 1616), I, 498
Henty, George Alfred (1832–1902), III, **569**, 578, 831
Hentzner, Paulus, I, 381
Hepburn, George (*fl.* 1695), II, 999
Hepburn, Robert (1690?–1712), II, 661, 823
Heraclitus and Democritus, The Riddles of (16 cent.), I, 716
Heraclitus Ridens (1681), II, 657
Heraclitus Ridens : A Discourse between Jest and Earnest (1718), II, 660
Heraclitus Ridens in a Dialogue between Jest and Earnest (1703), II, 659
Heraclitus Ridens; Or, A Discourse between Jest and Earnest (1681), II, 703
Herald, The (Clonmel, 1800), II, 737
Herald and Advertiser, The (1802), II, 733
Herald and Chronicle, The (1796), II, 732
HERALDRY (books on), I, 395f. (16, 17 cents.); II, 120 (17 cent.)
Heraud, John Abraham (1799–1887), III, **235**f., 582, 824
HERBALS, I, 891f. (16, 17 cents.)
Herbart, J. F. (*fl.* 1892), III, 110
Herbert de Losinga (d. 1119), I, **284**
Herbert, Algernon (1792–1855), III, 1034f.
Herbert, Auberon Edward William Molyneux (1838–1906), III, **868**
Herbert, Dorothea (*fl.* 1770–89), II, 159
Herbert, Edward, Baron Herbert of Cherbury (1583–1648), I, 476, 772, 841f., 875
Herbert, George (1593–1633), I, **451**f., 679, 724
Herbert, George Robert Charles, Earl of Pembroke (1850–1895), III, 977, 991
Herbert, H. (*fl.* 1727), II, 780
Herbert, Sir Percy (*fl.* 1652), I, 720, 726
Herbert, Philip, 5th Earl of Pembroke (1619–1669), II, 173
Herbert, Sidney, Baron Herbert of Lea (1810–1861), III, 148
Herbert, Sir Thomas (1606–1682), I, 784, 842
Herbert, Thomas Martin (1835–1877), III, **868**
Herbert (or Herebert), William (d. 1333), I, 42, 271
Herbert, William (1778–1847), I, 20; III, **236**, 885 (2)
Herd, David (1732–1810), I, 836, 902; II, 79, 225, 231, 245, 927
Herder, Johann Gottfried von, II, 52, 71; III, 46
Here Prophecy (M.E.), I, 167
Herebert (or Herbert), William (d. 1333), I, 42, 271
HEREFORD
    Library, II, 105
    Newspapers, II, 724 (1713–1800)
Hereford Journal, The (1713), II, 724
Hereford Journal, The (1803), II, 724

Hereford Journal, with The History of the World, The (1739), II, 724
HEREFORDSHIRE, II, 87 (bibliography)
Herford, Charles Harold (1853–1931), III, **746**
Herford, William Henry (1820–1908), III, 110
Heriot, George (*fl.* 1804), III, 1087 (2)
Heriot, John (1760–1833), II, 696; III, 798, 800
Herklots, G. A. (*fl.* 1863), III, 1084
Hermanni, Philippus, I, 888
Hermes Straticus, or a Scourge for Elencticus (1648), I, 759
Hermit, The (1711), II, 661
Hernandez de San Pedro, Diego, I, 814
Herne, John (*fl.* 1657–60), I, 850
Herodian, I, 802; II, 760
Herodotus, I, 658, 778, 802; II, 760
HEROIC PLAY, THE, II, 396
HEROIC POEMS (O.E.), I, 63 ff.
Heroicall Adventures of the Knight of the Sea, The (17 cent.), I, 730
Heron, Robert (1764–1807), II, 157, 306, 486, 631, 666, 985; III, 798, 800, 809–10
Herrick, Robert (1591–1674), I, 449 f.
Herries, John (*fl.* 1773), I, 16
Herring, R. (*fl.* 1853–61), III, 71, 72 (2), 231
Herring, Thomas (1693–1747), II, **852**
Herschel, Caroline Lucretia (1750–1848), III, 943
Herschel, Sir John Frederick William (1792–1871), III, 868, **938**, 941, 943 (2)
Herschel, Sir William (1738–1822), III, **943**
HERTFORD, II, **724** (newspapers)
Hertford Mercury and Reformer, The (1844), II, 724
Hertfordshire Mercury and County Press, The (1872), II, 724
Hertz, Henrik, III, 298
Hervet, Gentian (*fl.* 1532), I, 396, 809
Hervey, A. (*fl.* 1850), III, 1076
Hervey, Christopher (*fl.* 1785), II, 747
Hervey, Elizabeth (*fl.* 1788), II, 549, 551
Hervey, James (1714–1758), II, 45, 947
Hervey, John, Earl of Bristol (1665–1751), II, 135
Hervey, John, Baron (1696–1743), II, 600, **879**
Hervey, Thomas Kibble (1799–1859), III, 818
Hesiod, I, 802; II, 761
Heslop, Luke (1738–1825), III, 969
Hesse, E. (*fl.* 1793), II, 51
Hester, John (d. 1593), I, 888, 891
Hetherington, Henry (1792–1849), III, 785, 816
Hetherington, William Maxwell (1803–1865), I, 908; II, 995
Hetherington's Twopenny Dispatch and People's Police Register (1834), III, 816
Hewerdine, — (*fl.* 1790), II, 243–4
Hewes, John (*fl.* 1624), I, 376
Hewitt, John (1807–1878), I, 390
Hewlett, Esther, later Copley (*fl.* 1824–59), III, 572

Hewlett, Henry G. (*fl.* 1873), III, 785
Hewlett, James Philip (*fl.* 1848), II, 848
Hewlett, Joseph Thomas James (1800–1847), III, 400
HEXAMETERS, ENGLISH
  See under PROSODY, I, 15 f.
Hexham, Henry (1585?–1650?), I, 390, 885
Hexham, The Priory of (M.E.), I, 121
Hey Hoe for a Husband (17 cent.), I, 717
Heydon, Sir Christopher (d. 1623), I, 884
Heylin (or Heylyn), Peter (1600–1662), I, 754, 766, 781, **839**, 854
Heylyn, H. (*fl.* 1668), I, 839
Heyrick, Thomas (1650?–1694), II, 282, 819
Heytesbury, William (*fl.* 1340–72), I, **312**
HEYWOOD (Lancs.), II, 87 (bibliography)
Heywood, J. (*fl.* 1850), III, 891 (2)
Heywood, Jasper (1535?–1598), I, 522, 807
Heywood, John (1497?–1580?), I, **518**
Heywood, Oliver (1630–1702), I, 367, 387
Heywood, Samuel (1753–1828), II, 964; III, **880**
Heywood, Thomas (1574?–1641), I, **622** f., 723, 739–40, 804, 805, 865, 874
Hibbard, J. (*fl.* 1804), III, 979
Hibbert, George (1757–1837), I, 263
Hibbert, H. G. (*fl.* 1916), III, 785
Hibernian Chronicle, The (1763), II, 737
Hibernian Chronicle (1770), II, 665
Hibernian Gazette, or Universal Advertiser, The (1772), II, 737
Hibernian Journal; Or, Chronicle of Liberty, The (1773), II, 736
Hibernian Magazine; Or, Compendium of Entertaining Knowledge, The (1771), II, 687
Hibernian Morning Post; Or Literary Chronicle, The (1776), II, 737
Hibernian Patriot [etc.], *The* (18 cent.), II, 200
Hibernian Telegraph; Or, Morning Star, The (1798), II, 736
'Hibernicus' (1725), II, 662
Hibernicus's Letters (1734), II, 204
Hichcock, Robert (*fl.* 1590), I, 818
Hickeringill, Edmund (1631–1708), II, 271, 751
Hickes, Francis (1566–1631), I, 804
Hickes, George (1642–1715), I, 462; II, 77, 131, 798, **847**, **918**
Hickey, Emily Henrietta (1845–1924), III, **343**
Hickey, William (1749–1809), II, 138
Hickford, R. (*fl.* 1782), II, 345
Hickman, Spencer (*fl.* 1680), II, 785
Hickok, Thomas (*fl.* 1582), I, 782
Hicks, C. (*fl.* 1837), III, 209
Hicks, Robert (*fl.* 1713), II, 764
Hicks, William (*fl.* 1671), II, 175–6, 178
Hickson, Samuel (*fl.* 1847), I, 555, 576, 578
Hickson, Sydney John (b. 1859), III, 959
Hickson, William Edward (1803–1870), III, 833

'Hieover, Harry', i.e. Charles Bindley (1795–1859), III, 766
Hieronymus von Braunschweig, I, 890, 892
Hiffernan, Paul (1719–1777), II, 400, 448, 663–4, 784
Higden, Henry (*fl.* 1686), II, **282**
Higden, Ranulf (d. 1364), I, 116, 167, **302**, 765, 773
Higford, William (1581?–1657), II, 122
Higgie, T. H. (*fl.* 1854), III, 442 (2)
Higginbotham, J. J. (*fl.* 1874), III, 1077
Higgins, Francis (1746–1802), III, 809
Higgins, John (*fl.* 1570–1602), I, 413 (2), 808
Higgins, Matthew James (1810–1868), III, 131, 785
Higgins, William (d. 1825), III, 945
Higginson, Francis (1587–1630), I, 792
Higginson, Nesta, later Skrine ['Moira O'Neill'] (*fl.* 1900–24), III, **1057**
Higgons, Bevil (1670–1735), II, **318**
Higgs, Griffin (*fl.* 1607), I, 661
Higgs, Henry (b. 1864), III, 985
Higgs, Henry (*fl.* 1767), II, 546
HIGH CHURCH MOVEMENT, III, 854f.
High-German Doctor, The (1714), II, 661
'HIGHER CRITICISM', III, 58f.
Highmore, John (*fl.* 1782), II, 779
Highmore, Joseph (1692–1780), II, 18
Hilaria (18 cent.), II, 253
Hilary (*fl.* 1125), I, **284**
Hildesham (Hildersam or Hildersham), Arthur (1563–1632), I, 697, 856
Hildrop, John (d. 1756), II, 152
Hill, Aaron (1685–1750), II, 22, 191, **438**f., 485, 662, 707
Hill, Abraham (1635–1721), II, 846
Hill, Arthur (*fl.* 1833–57), III, 110, 115, 132
Hill, Benson E. (*fl.* 1841), III, 824
Hill, Brian (*fl.* 1792), II, 747
Hill, F. D. (*fl.* 1868), III, 110
Hill, Frank Harrison (1830–1910), III, 799
Hill, Frederic (1803–1896), III, 110, 132, 138, 142, 152
Hill, George (1716–1808), II, 963
Hill, George Birkbeck Norman (1835–1903), III, 138, **1039**f.
Hill, H. (*fl.* 1845), III, 180
Hill, J. (*fl.* 1760), II, 522
Hill, John (*fl.* 1659), author of 'A Penny Post', II, 692
Hill, Sir John (1716?–1775), quack doctor and miscellaneous writer, II, 409, 448, 544, 664, 671, 677, 709
Hill, John (*fl.* 1764), translator of Theophrastus, II, 763
Hill, John (*fl.* 1788), of the Royal Society, Edinburgh, II, 25
Hill, Sir John (*fl.* 1801), M.R.C.S.L., III, 975
Hill, Leonard Erskine (b. 1866), III, 964

Hill, Matthew Davenport (1792–1872), III, 132, 138
Hill, N. (*fl.* 1858), II, 493
Hill, Richard (1655–1727), II, 166
Hill, Sir Rowland (1795–1879), III, 132, 971
Hill, Thomas (*fl.* 1590), I, 377, 391, 713, 846, 882
Hill, Thomas (*fl.* 1799), II, 757
Hill, Thomas Ford (d. 1795), II, 80, 747
Hill, Thomas Wright (1763–1851), II, 132, 138
Hill, W. A. (*fl.* 1851), III, 183 (2)
Hill, William (*fl.* 1839–52), III, 817
Hillary, John (*fl.* 1776), II, 733
Hillern, Wilhelmine von, III, 535
Hillier, A. P. (*fl.* 1897), III, 1092
Hillier, J. (*fl.* 1687), II, 748
Hills, Henry (d. 1713), II, 100
Hilton, Arthur Clement (1851–1877), III, **343**, 835
Hilton, John, the younger (1599–1657), I, 486
Hilton, John (*fl.* 1663), II, 174, 704
Hilton, W. (*fl.* 1797), II, 684
Hilton, Walter (d. 1395–6?), I, 194f.
Hilton, William (*fl.* 1664), II, 751
Hinckley, John (*fl.* 1800), II, 63
Hinoks, Edward (1792–1866), III, **1015**f.
Hind, C. L. (*fl.* 1893), III, 814, 818
Hind, Henry Youle (1823–1908), III, 1088
Hind, John Russell (1823–1895), III, 944
Hind Horn (Ballad) (M.E.), I, **148**
Hinde, John (*fl.* 1644), I, 698
Hinde, William (1569?–1629), I, 683 (2)
Hinderwell, Thomas (1744–1825), II, 154
Hindmarsh, Robert (1759–1835), II, 682
Hinds, J. (*fl.* 1830), II, 816 (2)
Hinds, Richard Brinsley (*fl.* 1843), III, 956
Hinds Elder Brother (17 cent.), I, 718
Hine, J. (*fl.* 1831), III, 166
Hingeston, F. C. (*fl.* 1858), I, 260
Hingston, E. P. (*fl.* 1856), III, 582
Hinkson, Katharine, née Tynan (1861–1931), III, **1057**
Hinton, James (1822–1875), III, **868**
Hinton, Sir John (1603?–1682), I, 387
Hinton, John (*fl.* 1745), II, 708
Hinton, John Howard (1791–1873), III, 110, 118
Hippisley, J. H. (*fl.* 1837), I, 212
Hippisley, John (d. 1748), II, 430
Hippisley, John (d. 1767), II, 399
Hippocrates, I, 802; II, 761
Hippocrates Ridens (1686), II, 657
Hircarrah (1793), II, 666
Hirschfeld, Christian Cayus Lorenz, II, 148
Hirst, W. (*fl.* 1844), III, 982
Hispanus (16 cent.), I, 662
Hisperica Famina (O.E.), I, **100**f.
Historia Anglicana (15 cent.), I, 265
Historia Britonum (O.E.), I, **100**
Historia Croylandensis (15 cent.), I, 265

Historia Litteraria (1730), II, 675
Historia Monasterii S. Augustini [at Canterbury] (M.E.), I, 265
Historia Vitae et Regni Ricardi II (14 cent.), I, 116
Historian, The (1712), II, 661
HISTORIANS. See HISTORICAL WRITINGS
Historic Times, The (1849), III, 815
Historical Account of the Publick Transactions, An (1694), II, 706
Historical Account of the Publick Transactions in Christendom, An (1695), II, 706
Historical and Poetical Medley, The (18 cent.) II, 207
Historical and Political Mercury, The (1759), II, 678
HISTORICAL BACKGROUND
  Anglo-Saxon Period. See ARCHAEOLOGY AND HISTORY, I, 56f.
  Middle English Period. See POLITICAL BACKGROUND, I, 115f. and SOCIAL BACKGROUND, I, 119f.
  Renaissance to Restoration. See POLITICAL BACKGROUND, I, 396f.
  Restoration to Romantic Revival. See POLITICAL BACKGROUND, II, 161f.
  Nineteenth Century. See POLITICAL AND SOCIAL BACKGROUND, III, 143f.
Historical, Biographical, Literary and Scientific Magazine, The (1799), II, 683
Historical Chronicle, The (1785), II, 680
Historical Detail of Public Occurrences for the Fortnight Past, An (1763), II, 678
Historical Detail of the most remarkable Public occurrences, An (1796), II, 716
Historical Journal, The (1732), II, 714
Historical Journal; or an account in English and French of occurrences in Europe, An (1697), II, 719
Historical List of Horse Matches [etc.], *An* (1770), II, 718
Historical List of horse matches [and]*cockmatches, An* (1729), II, 718
Historical List of Horse Matches, Cock Matches, An (1752), II, 718
Historical List of Horse Races, An (1729), II, 718
Historical Magazine; Or, Classical Library of Public Events, The (1788), II, 681
Historical Register, The (1716), II, 676
Historical Register of Public Occurrences, The (1772), II, 679
Historical Register; Or, Edinburgh Monthly, The (1791), II, 686
HISTORICAL WRITINGS
  Anglo-Saxon Period. See HISTORICAL POEMS, I, 83f., CHRONICLES, I, 88f. and under WRITINGS IN LATIN, I, 98f.
  Middle English Period. See CHRONICLES, I, 115f. (mainly Latin), 132f. (Arthurian

matter), 163f. (in English), 265 (15 cent.). See also under WRITINGS IN LATIN, I, 280f.
  Renaissance to Restoration, I, 823f., 909f. (Scottish). See also under POLITICAL BACKGROUND, I, 396f.
  Restoration to Romantic Revival, II, 864f., 995f. (Scottish). See also POLITICAL BACKGROUND, II, 161f.
  Nineteenth Century, III, 877f. (principal writers), 1074f. (Anglo-Indians), 1087 (Canada), 1090f. (South Africa), 1087f. (Australia, New Zealand). See also POLITICAL AND SOCIAL BACKGROUND, III, 143f.
Historie of Clyomon and Clamydes, The (16 cent.), I, 520
Historie of the Arrival of Edward IV (15 cent.), I, 265
HISTORIES, LINGUISTIC, I, 24f., 30
HISTORIES, LITERARY. See LITERARY HISTORIES
History and Adventures of Frank Hammond, The (18 cent.), II, 545
History of a Schoolboy, The (18 cent.), II, 563
History of Adolphus, Prince of Russia, The (17 cent.), II, 182
History of Autonous, The (18 cent.), II, 540
History of Charlotte Summers (18 cent.), II, 544
History of Cradle-Convulsions, The (1701), II, 659
History of Jasper Banks, The (18 cent.), II, 545
History of John Bull, The [etc.] (18 cent.), II, 214
History of Learning, The (1691), II, 675
History of Learning, Giving a Succinct Account of New Books, The (1694), II, 675
History of Little Dick, The (18 cent.), II, 563
History of Little Goody Twoshoes, The (18 cent.), II, 546
History of Little Henry, The (19 cent.), III, 575
History of Lord Belford and Miss Sophia Woodley, The (18 cent.), II, 548
History of Lord Stanton, The (18 cent.), II, 547
History of Mademoiselle de St Phale, The (17 cent.), II, 534
History of Masonry, The (18 cent.), II, 229
History of Miss Delia Stanhope, The (18 cent.), II, 546
History of Our Own Times, The (1741), II, 677
History of Prince Mirabel's Infancy, The (18 cent.), II, 536
History of the Reformation, The (1681), II, 657
History of the Reign of Queen Anne Digested into Annals, The (1702), II, 683
History of the tryall of Chevalry, The (17 cent.), I, 653
History of Sixteen Wonderful Old Women, The (19 cent.), III, 575
History of the Westminster Election (18 cent.), II, 237, 238

History of the Works of the Learned, The (1699), II, 675
History of the Works of the Learned, The (1737), II, 675
History of Tom Jones in his Married State, The (18 cent.), II, 544
History of Young Edwin and Little Jessy, The (18 cent.), II, 564
Histrio-Mastix (17 cent.), I, 652
Hitchcock, Robert (*fl.* 1580–91), I, 846
Hitchcock, Robert (d. 1809), II, **467**
Hitchin, Charles (*fl.* 1718), II, 155
Hitchman, Francis (*fl.* 1890?), III, 803
Hitchman, S. F. (*fl.* 1865), II, 340
Hive, The (1724), II, 197 (5), 198–200, 202 (2), 203 (2)
Hive, The (1789), II, 666, 681
Hive, The (1797), II, 252
Hive of Modern Literature, The (18 cent.), II, 254, 256
Hive, Or, A Collection of Thoughts, The (18 cent.), II, 250–1
Hoadly, Benjamin (1676–1761), bishop, II, 809, 847, 851, **852**
Hoadly, Benjamin (1706–1757), physician, II, 61, **439**, 713
Hoadly, John (1711–1776), II, 440–1, 485, 852
Hoare, L. (*fl.* 1822), III, 110
Hoare, Prince (1755–1834), II, 60, 460, **467**f., 486
Hoare, Sir Richard Colt (1758–1838), III, **878**f.
Hobart, John, Earl of Buckinghamshire (1723–1793), II, 166
'Hobbes, John Oliver', i.e. Pearl Mary Teresa Craigie (1867–1906), III, **549**
Hobbes, Thomas (1588–1679), I, **871**f.
    Foreign influence of, II, 38, 53
    Literary criticism by, I, 867
    Minor reprints, I, 808, 844; II, 759, 761
Hobby Horse, The (1893), III, 834
Hobhouse, Sir Benjamin (1757–1831), II, 748
Hobhouse, Edmund (1817–1904), I, 125
Hobhouse, John Cam, Baron Broughton (1786–1869), III, 192, 203, 206
Hobhouse, Thomas (*fl.* 1785), II, 624
Hobler, J. Paul (*fl.* 1794), II, 250
Hoblyn, Robert (1710–1756), II, 102
Hobson, J. (*fl.* 1838), III, 977
Hobson, J. A. (1858–1940), III, 984
Hobson, J. H. (*fl.* 1889), III, 984
Hoby, Sir Edward (1560–1617), I, 390, 812, 816
Hoby, Lady Margaret (1599–1605), I, 385
Hoby, Sir Thomas (1530–1566), I, 383, 767, 812
Hoccleve (or Occleve), Thomas (1368?–1450?), I, 39, **252**f.
HOCKEY (books on), III, 775
Hocking, Silas K. (*fl.* 1896), III, 831
Hockley, William Browne (1792–1860), III, 399

Hodder, George (d. 1870), III, 785
Hoddesdon, John (*fl.* 1650), II, 264
Hodge, D. (*fl.* 1894), III, 772
Hodge, H. (*fl.* 1899?), III, 814
Hodges, Anthony (*fl.* 1638), I, 799, 862
Hodges, Richard (*fl.* 1644), I, 44
Hodges, William (1744–1797), III, 1079
Hodgkin, Thomas (*fl.* 1848), III, 799
Hodgkin, Thomas (1831–1913), III, **934**
Hodgskin, Thomas (*fl.* 1825–43), III, 978, 981
Hodgson, Brian Houghton (1800–1894), III, 1083
Hodgson, Francis (1781–1852), III, 192
Hodgson, John (d. 1684), I, 387
Hodgson, Shadworth Hollway (1832–1912), I, 18; III, **868**f.
Hodgson, Thomas (*fl.* 1820), of Newcastle, II, 83
Hodgson, Thomas (*fl.* 1844–60), publisher, III, 100f., 101
Hodgson, William Ballantyne (1815–1880), III, 110, 138, 142, 983
Hodson, J. W. (*fl.* 1861), II, 890
Hodson, W. (*fl.* 1780), II, 400
Hodson, W. H. (*fl.* 1855), III, 93
Hody, Humphrey (1659–1707), II, **847**f.
Hoernle, A. F. R. (*fl.* 1880), III, 1074
Hoey, John Cashel (*fl.* 1858–65), III, 148
Hoey, James, the younger (*fl.* 1766), II, 735
Hoey, William (*fl.* 1882), III, 1081
Hoffman, Francis (*fl.* 1711), II, 661
Hoffman, Heinrich, III, 576
Hoffmann, Ernst Theodore Amadeus, III, **32**
Hoffmann, Friedrich (*fl.* 1746), II, 813
Hoffmeister, W. (*fl.* 1848), III, 1080
Hofland, Barbara, née Wreaks, later Hoole (1770–1844), III, 142, **400**f., 566
Hofland, T. C. (*fl.* 1839), III, 769
Hofmeyr, J. H. (b. 1894), III, 1090
Hog, James (1658?–1734), II, **995**
Hog, W. (*fl.* 1690), I, 466
Hog's Wash (1793), II, 682
Hog's Wash; Or, A Salmagundy for Swine (1793), II, 682
Hog's Wash; Or, Politics for the People (1793), II, 682
Hogan, — (*fl.* 1815?), III, 798
Hogan-Moganides (17 cent.), II, 288
Hogarth, David George (1862–1928), III, 991
Hogarth, George (1783–1870), III, 582, 809
Hogarth, Georgina (*fl.* 1880), III, 449
Hogarth, William (1697–1764), II, 30, 160
Hogg, Mrs, née Lyte (*fl.* 1850), III, 238
Hogg, James (1770–1835), III, **164**f., 413
Hogg, James (*fl.* 1895), III, 777
Hogg, Thomas Jefferson (1792–1862), III, 215
Hogg, W. T. M. (*fl.* 1896), III, 775
Hogg's Weekly Instructor (1845), III, 828
Holbach, Paul Heinrich Dietrich von, II, 783
Holberg, Ludwig, II, 140, 153, 552

Holborn-Drollery (17 cent.), II, 176

Holbrook, Ann Catherine (1780–1837), III, 583

Holbrooke, F. (*fl.* 1869?), II, 875

Holcot, Robert (d. 1347), I, **301**

Holcroft, Sir Henry (*fl.* 1653), I, 781

Holcroft, Thomas (1745–1809), II, 52, 58 (2), 61 (2), 70, **468**f., 548, 550 (2), 552 (2), 566, 665, 680–1, 688

Holden, Hubert Ashton (1822–1896), III, **998**

Holdich, Sir T. H. (1843–1929), III, 1078

Holdsworth, Edward (1684–1746), II, 312, 896 (2)

Holdsworth, Philip Joseph (1849–1902), III, 1095

Hole, J. (*fl.* 1853), promoter of free library movement, III, 105

Hole, J. (*fl.* 1893), writer on railways, III, 984

Hole, Richard (1746–1803), I, 594; II, **76**

Hole, Samuel Reynolds (1819–1904), III, 153

Holiday, Barten (1593–1661), I, 657

Holinshed, Raphael (d. 1580?), I, 825

Hollams, Sir John (1820–1910), III, 154

HOLLAND

    Literary Relations with, I, 345 (1500–1660); II, 69f. (1660–1800); III, 45

Holland, Abraham (d. 1626), I, 425

Holland, H. Scott (1847–1918), III, 851

Holland, Henry (d. 1604), divine, I, 616, 725, 893

Holland, Henry (1583–1650?), compiler and publisher, I, 396

Holland, Sir Henry (1788–1873), III, 965

Holland, Henry Edward Fox, Baron (1802–1859), III, 152

Holland, Henry Fox, Baron (1705–1774), II, 136, 664–5

Holland, Henry Richard Vassall Fox, Baron (1773–1840), II, 165, 837 (2)

Holland, Hugh (d. 1633), I, 592

Holland, John (1794–1872), III, 240, 785

Holland, Philemon (1552–1637), I, 804, 806 (2), 807, 809, 827, 837, 861, 880

Holland, Robert (1557–1622?), I, 437

Holland, Saba, Lady, née Smith (d. 1866), III, 680

Holland, Samuel (*fl.* 1656), I, 732

Holland, Sir Thomas Erskine (1835–1926), III, 986

Holland Packet Boat, The (1695), II, 706

Holles, Lord Denzil (1599–1680), II, **870**

Hollings, W. (*fl.* 1867), III, 1072

Hollingshead, John (1827–1904), III, 785

Hollingsworth, N. J. (*fl.* 1812), III, 107

Hollingsworth, S. (*fl.* 1786), II, 756

Hollis, Thomas (1720–1774), II, 102

'Hollyband, Claudius', i.e. Claude Desainliens (*fl.* 1575), I, 377, 814

Holman, Joseph George (1764–1817), II, **470**, 486

Holme, Benjamin (1683–1749), II, 742

Holme, C. Geoffrey (b. 1887), III, 831

Holme, Charles (1848–1923), III, 831

Holme, Randle (1571–1655), II, 815

Holmes, Arthur (1837–1875), III, **998**

Holmes, Edmond Gore Alexander (b. 1850), III, **343**

Holmes, George (1662–1749), antiquary, III, 875

Holmes, George (*fl.* 1797), writer on Ireland, II, 159

Holmes, J. (*fl.* 1852), I, 824

Holmes, John (*fl.* 1738), II, 27, 124

Holmes, Nathaniel (1599–1678), I, 720, 845, 884

Holmes, Samuel (*fl.* 1793), II, 751

Holmes, T. R. E. (*fl.* 1885), III, 1078

Holroyd, J. J. (*fl.* 1838), III, 33

Holroyd, John Baker, Earl of Sheffield (1735–1821), II, 884; III, 975

Holt, Daniel (*fl.* 1794), II, 696

Holt, Francis Ludlow (1780–1844), II, 85; III, 810

Holt, John (*fl.* 1510), I, 374

Holt, John (*fl.* 1749), II, 913

Holt, Joseph (1756–1826), II, 159

Holt, T. L. (*fl.* 1846–61), III, 798–9, 829

Holwell, John Zephaniah (1711–1798), III, 1074

HOLY GRAIL LEGEND, I, 132

Holyday, Barten (1593–1661), I, 697, 803, 805; II, 766

Holyoake, George Jacob (1817–1906), III, 98, 285, 783, 785 (2), 817 (3), 982

Holyoake, Thomas (1616?–1675), I, 861; II, 128

Holyoke (or Holyoake), Francis (1567–1653), I, 861

Holywood, John (*fl.* 1230), I, **298**

Home, Henry, Lord Kames (1696–1782), II, 18, 53, 109, 952, **955**, **1000**

Home, John (1722–1808), II, 111, **470**f.

Home and Foreign Review, The (1862), III, 828

Home Chat (1895), III, 822

Homer, I, **802**; II, **761**, 893; III, 243, 281, 363, 1004–5

Homer, Henry (*fl.* 1789), II, 104

Homer A la Mode (17 cent.), II, 288

Homer A La Mode, The Second Part (17 cent.), II, 288

HOMILIES

    Latin (5–10 cents.). See under WRITINGS IN LATIN, I, 98f.

    Middle English, I, 170f.

    Old English, I, 89f., 92f.

Hone, Richard Brindley (*fl.* 1834), II, 848

Hone, William (1780–1842), I, 275; II, 891; III, 194, 198 (2), 631, **671**f., 816

Honest Amusement (18 cent.), II, 193

Honest Fellow, The (1763), II, 222, 224
Honest Fellow, or Buck's necessary Companion, The (1794), II, 249
Honest Gentleman, The (1718), II, 662
Honest Lawyer, The (17 cent.), I, 652
Honey-Moon (18 cent.), II, 198
Honeysuckle, a curious Collection of Poems, The (1731), II, 201
Honey-suckle, The (1734), II, 204
Honyman, Andrew (d. 1676), II, 992
Honywood, Sir Robert (1601–1686), II, 812
Hood, Edwin Paxton (1820–1885), III, 170, 219, 629, 830
'Hood, Eu.', i.e. Joseph Haslewood, I, 501
Hood, H. J. (*fl.* 1882), III, 987
Hood, Jane (*fl.* 1840?), III, 225
Hood, Thomas (*fl.* 1588–98), I, 881
Hood, Thomas (1799–1845), III, 93, 219, **224**f., 401
Hood, Thomas, the younger (1835–1874), I, 17; III, 224 (3), 225, 354, 820
Hood's Magazine and Comic Miscellany (1844), III, 828
Hook, James (1771–1828), III, 399
Hook (or Hooke), John (1655–1712), sergeant-at-law, II, 132
Hook, Theodore Edward (1788–1841), III, **399**f.
Hook, Thomas (*fl.* 1837–42), III, 825
Hook, Walter Farquhar (1798–1875), III, 110, 291, **857**
Hooke, D. B. (*fl.* 1891–1904), III, 823
Hooke, Nathaniel (d. 1763), II, **879**
Hooke, Robert (1635–1703), II, 134, 674, 961 (2)
Hooke, Thomas (*fl.* 1738), II, 814
Hooker, John, *alias* Vowel(l) (1526?–1601), I, 774
Hooker, Sir Joseph Dalton (1817–1911), III, 823, **961**, 991
Hooker, Richard (1554–1600), I, **685**f.
Hooker, Sir William Jackson (1785–1865), III, 823 (2), **959**f.
Hookes, Nicholas (1628–1712), I, 476
Hoole, Barbara, later Hofland, née Wreaks (1770–1844), III, 142, **400**f., 566
Hoole, Charles (1610–1667), educational writer, I, 366, 375, 800, 854; II, 127 (2), 759, 768
Hoole, John (1727–1803), II, **471**, 625
Hoole, Samuel (*fl.* 1781), II, **365**
Hooper, John (d. 1555), I, 682
Hooper, R. (*fl.* 1857), I, 610 (3)
Hooper, Robert (*fl.* 1798), II, 927
Hooper, Samuel (*fl.* 1777), II, 103
Hooper, William (*fl.* 1770), II, 28, 56, 778, 782
Hooson, William (*fl.* 1747), II, 927
'Hope, Anthony', i.e. Sir Anthony Hope Hawkins (1863–1933), III, **549**
'Hope, Ascott', i.e. A. R. Hope-Moncrieff (1846–1927), III, **569**

Hope, C. D. (*fl.* 1909), III, 1090
Hope, Thomas (1770–1831), III, **401**
Hope, Sir William (*fl.* 1687–96), II, 816, 823
Hope-Moncrieff, A. R. ('Ascott Hope') (1846–1927), III, **569**
Hope-Scott, James Robert (1812–1873), III, 153
Hopkins, Charles (1664–1700), II, **423**
Hopkins, E. W. (*fl.* 1890), III, 1082
Hopkins, F. Powell (*fl.* 1893), III, 772
Hopkins, Gerard Manley (1844–1889), III, 325f.
Hopkins, J. B. (*fl.* 1850), III, 811
Hopkins, John (d. 1570), I, 678
Hopkins, John (*fl.* 1698), II, **282**
Hopkins, John Castell (*fl.* 1898), III, 1085
Hopkins, Mathew (d. 1647), I, 894
Hopkins, Richard (d. 1594?), I, 815
Hopkins, T. (*fl.* 1822–8), III, 980
Hopkins, William (1793–1866), III, 951
Hopper, Clarence (*fl.* 1863), I, 251, 768, 824
Hopper, Nora, later Chesson (1871–1906), III, 1059
Hoppus, John (1789–1875), III, 110
Hopton, Sir Ralph, Baron Hopton (1598–1652), I, 387, 842
Horace, I, **803**; II, 28, 201, **765**; III, 247, 284, 298, 353, 476, 511, 1006, 1011
Hore, John Philip (*fl.* 1886), III, 767
Horlock, K. W. (*fl.* 1852), III, 760
Horman, William (d. 1535), I, 374
Horn. See *Childe Horn, King Horn*
Horn Childe and Maiden Rimnild (M.E.), I, **148**
Hornamus, H. Junius, I, 801
Horne, George (1730–1792), II, 131, 625, 952
Horne, H. P. (*fl.* 1900), III, 834
Horne, later Horne Tooke, John (1736–1812), II, 630–1, 932, 937, 957
Horne, Nathaniel Freebody (*fl.* 1768), II, 665
Horne, Richard Henry (or Hengist) (1803–1884), II, 250, **290**, 824
Horne, Robert (*fl.* 1666), II, 751
Horne, Thomas (1610–1654), I, 375, 855
Horne, Thomas Hartwell (1780–1862), I, 672; II, 846
Horneck, Anthony (1641–1697), II, **848**
Horneck, Philip (*fl.* 1714), II, 661
Horner, Leonard (1785–1864), III, 110
Hornsey, John (*fl.* 1793), II, 932
Hornsuch, Jerome, I, 348
Horrocks, Jeremiah (1617–1641), I, 883
Horse and Hound (1884), III, 820
Horseman (or Horsman), Nicholas (*fl.* 1662–89), II, 560
HORSEMANSHIP (books on), I, 393 (16, 17 cents.); II, 815f. (1660–1800); III, 765f. (19 cent.). See also HUNTING and RACING
Horsey, Sir Jerome (*fl.* 1573–1627), I, 768
Horsfield, Thomas Walker (d. 1837), III, **903**
Horsley, Fanny (*fl.* 1833–6), III, 152
Horsley, H. (*fl.* 1810), II, 955

Horsley, John (1685–1732), II, **880**
Horsley, Samuel (1733–1806), I, 17; II, 937, **955**, 961
Horsley, Sophy (*fl.* 1833–6), III, 152
Horsman, Edward (1807–1876), III, 148
Hort, Fenton John Anthony (1828–1892), III, 848
Horton, George (*fl.* 1652), I, 761 (2), 762 (10), 763 (2)
Horton, H. H. (*fl.* 1838), III, 977
Horton, Sir Robert John Wilmot (1784–1841), III, 975, 981
Hortop, Job (*fl.* 1591), I, 788
Horwood, Thomas (*fl.* 1820), I, 775
Hosack, John (d. 1887), III, **929**
Hoskins, John (1566–1638), I, 865
Hospitall of Incurable Fools, The (17 cent.), I, 713
Hotham, Charles (1615–1672?), II, 860–1
Hotham, Durant (or Durand) (1617?–1691), I, 756; II, 860–1
Hothby, John (d. 1487), I, **314**
Hotman, François, I, 742; II, 783
Hotten, John Camden (1832–1873), III, 434, 447, 654
Houdart de la Motte, Antoine, II, 783
Hough, James (*fl.* 1829), III, 1079
Hough, William (*fl.* 1853), III, 1076
Houghton, Arthur Boyd (1836–1875), III, 91
Houghton, John (d. 1705), II, 674–5, 704–5, 818, 958
Houghton, Richard Monckton Milnes, Baron (1809–1885), III, 220, 221 (2), **299**
  Reviews, prefaces, etc. by, III, 257, 332, 341, 429
Houghton, R. (*fl.* 1771), II, 799
Houghton, T. S. (*fl.* 1841), III, 77
Hour, The (1873), III, 799
Household Narrative of Current Events for the Year 1850, The (1850), III, 828
Household Words (1850), III, 818
Housman, Alfred Edward (1859–1936), III, **326**
Housman, Laurence (b. 1865), III, **343**f.
Houston, John (1802–1845), II, 595
Houston, T. (*fl.* 1848), II, 993
Houstun, James (*fl.* 1725), II, 748
Houtman, Frederik de, I, 785
Houtteville, Claude François, II, 783
Houy, George (*fl.* 1826), III, 807
How, John (*fl.* 1680), II, 703
How, William (1620–1656), I, 892
How, William Walsham (1823–1897), III, **290**
How a man may chuse a good Wife from a bad (17 cent.), I, 623
How do You Do? (1796), II, 666
How the Psalter of Our Lady Was Made (M.E.), I, **161**
Howard, Alfred (*fl.* 1826–33), II, 614, 976; III, 190 (2), 668
Howard, Edward (1624–*c.* 1700), II, **423**

Howard, Edward George Granville (d. 1841), III, **401**
Howard, Frank (1805?–1866), I, 420
Howard, George, Earl of Carlisle (1802–1864), III, 152
Howard, Gorges [misprinted George] Edmund (1715–1786), II, 81
Howard, H. (*fl.* 1801), I, 59
Howard, Henry, Earl of Surrey (1517?–1547), I, **412**f., 677, 808
Howard, H. M. P., Earl of Suffolk (*fl.* 1886), III, 764
Howard, Henrietta, Countess of Suffolk (1681–1767), II, 135
Howard, Henry Newman (b. 1861), III, **344**
Howard, James (b. 1630?), II, **423**
Howard, John, Duke of Norfolk (1430?–1485), I, 120
Howard, John (*fl.* 1726–89), II, 137, 155, 747
Howard, Leonard (1699?–1767), II, 223 (2), 314
Howard, M. F. (*fl.* 1711), I, 876
Howard, Sir Robert (1626–1698), I, 807, 809; II, **423**f., 768
Howard, Thomas, Duke of Norfolk (1443–1524), I, 120
Howard, Thomas (*fl.* 1663), II, 529
Howe, John (1630–1705), II, **848**, 862
Howe, Joseph (1804–1873), III, 1086–7
Howel, Thomas (*fl.* 1739), II, 751
Howell, James (1594?–1666), I, 719, 726, **731**, 747, 776, 780, **832**f., 855, 866
Howell, M. S. (*fl.* 1880), III, 1074
Howell, Thomas (*fl.* 1568), I, 437, 805
Howell, Thomas Bayly (1768–1815), I, 380; III, 144
Howell, Thomas Jones (d. 1858), III, 144
Howes, John (16 cent.), I, 372
Howes, R. (*fl.* 1642), I, 754
Howes, Thomas (1729–1814), II, 19
Howgill, Francis (*fl.* 1828), II, 857
Howgrave's Stamford Mercury (1732), II, **729**
Howie, John (1735–1793), II, 925, 995 (2)
Howitt, F. E. (*fl.* 1849), III, 77
Howitt, Mary, née Botham (1799–1888), III, 43, 271, 486, 576, **672**f., 711
Howitt, Samuel (1765?–1822), III, 768, 822
Howitt, William (1792–1879), III, 576, **673**f.
Howkins, Thomas (*fl.* 1692), II, 717
Howleglas, A Merye Jest of (16 cent.), I, 714
Howlett, John (1731–1804), II, 149; III, 969
Howlett, Robert (*fl.* 1684–1709), II, 815, 819, 827
Howley, William (1766–1848), II, 378
Howorth, Mrs J. (*fl.* 1794), II, 56
Howson, John Saul (1816–1885), III, 853
Hoy, Thomas (1659–1718?), II, 182, 762, 766
Hoyland, Francis (b. 1727), II, **365**
Hoyle, Edmond (1672–1769), II, 826
Hoyle, Joshua (d. 1654), I, 698

Huarte Navarro, Juan de Dios, I, 814
Huartes, Juan, I, 343; II, 109
Hubback, Catherine (*fl.* 1850), III, 382
Hubbard, John Gellibrand, Baron Addington (1805–1889), III, 979
Hubberley, William (*fl.* 1786), II, 751
Huber, Marie, II, 783
Huber, V. A. (*fl.* 1843), III, 121
Huby, William (*fl.* 1650), I, 761
Huchown (*fl.* 14 cent.), I, 137
Hucks, J. (*fl.* 1795), II, 140
Huddersfield Daily Chronicle, The (1871), III, 804
Huddersfield Daily Examiner, The (1871), III, 804
Huddersfield Examiner, The, III, 793
Huddesford, George (1749–1809), II, **365**f., 825
Huddesford, William (1732–1772), I, 823; II, 104, 867
Hudgebutt, J. (*fl.* 1693), II, 182
Hudson, Alfred A. (*fl.* 1891), III, 987
Hudson, J. W. (*fl.* 1851), III, 117
Hudson, John (1662–1719), I, 786
Hudson, Thomas (*fl.* 1584–1610) I, 818
Hudson, William Henry (1841–1922), III, **549**f.
Hue and Cry and Police Gazette, The (1791), II, 717
Hueffer, Ford H. Madox, later Ford (b. 1873), III, 574
Hueffer, Francis (1845–1889), III, 833
Hügel, Carl A. A. von, Baron (*fl.* 1845), III, 1080
Huet, Pierre Daniel, II, 36, 47, 783
Huffumbourghausen, 'Baron', II, 805
Huges, Michael (*fl.* 1746), II, 1002
Huggins, William (1696–1761), II, 808, 814, 899
Huggins, Sir William (1824–1910), III, 944
Hugh of Newcastle (*fl.* 1322), I, 304
Hugh Peters last Will and Testament (17 cent.), I, 719
Hughes, Mrs, née Browne (*fl.* 1839), III, 235
Hughes, Charles (*fl.* 1772), II, 817
Hughes, Griffith (*fl.* 1750), II, 754
Hughes, Jabez (1685?–1731), II, **318**, 765, 768
Hughes, John (1677–1720), I, 838; II, 22, 28, 240, 241, **318**f., 541, 661, 808, 910
Hughes, Lewis (*fl.* 1615–21), I, 790
Hughes, Thomas (*fl.* 1587), I, 523
Hughes, Thomas (1822–1896), author of 'Tom Brown's Schooldays', III, 119, **486**f., 781
Hughes, Thomas Smart (1786–1847), miscellaneous writer, I, 397; II, 853, 950
Hughes, William (*fl.* 1657), I, 818; II, 964
Hughes, William (1803–1861), III, 769
Hughlings-Jackson, J. (*fl.* 1900?), III, 833
Hughs, Mary, née Robson (*fl.* 1813), III, 566
Hughson, David (*fl.* 1817), II, 404
Hugo, Herman (*fl.* 1690), I, 479

Hugo, Thomas (1820–1876), III, 90
Hugo, Victor, III, **22**, 504 (2), 608
Huguet de Graffigny, Françoise, II, 783
Huish, Marcus (*fl.* 1849), III, 828
Huish, R. (*fl.* 1795), II, 807
Huish, Robert (1777–1850), III, 631
Hulbert, Charles (1778–1857), III, 190
Hull
    Booksellers and printers, II, 87
    Newspapers, II, 724
Hull, J. (*fl.* 1835), III, 110
Hull, Thomas (1728–1808), II, 233, **471**f., 547
Hull Advertiser, The (1794), II, 724
Hull Courant, The (1739), II, 724
Hull Daily Mail, The (1885), III, 805
Hull Express, The (1876), III, 804
Hull Morning Telegraph, The (1855), III, 802
Hull Packet, The (1787), II, 724
Hullmandel, Charles Joseph (1789–1850), III, 83
Hulsius, Levinus, I, 764
Hulton, Sir Edward (1869–1925), III, 804
Hulton, Henry (*fl.* 1772), II, 755
Hulton, William Adam (1802–1887), I, 122
HUMANISM, III, 48f., 67f.
Humanist, The (1757), II, 664
HUMANISTS AND REFORMERS, I, 664f. (16 cent.)
HUMANITARIANISM, III, 48f., 59f., 65f.
Hume, A. (*fl.* 1658), of Edinburgh, I, 657
Hume, A. (*fl.* 1766), translator, II, 801
Hume, Abraham (1814–1884), III, 85
Hume, Alexander (1560?–1609), I, 896, 911
Hume, Anna (*fl.* 1644), I, 817, 899
Hume, David, of Godscroft (1560?–1630), I, 910
Hume, David, Lord Crossrigg (1643–1707), II, 156
Hume, David (1711–1776), philosopher and historian, II, 38, 53, 65, 913, 927, **949**f., 1002
Hume, Hugh, Earl of Marchmont (1708–1794), II, 710
Hume, Joseph (1777–1855), III, 1083
Hume, Martin Andrew Sharp (1843–1910), III, **934**f.
Hume, Sir Patrick of Polwart (*fl.* 1580), I, 897
Hume, Patrick (*fl.* 1695), I, 464; II, 908
Hume, Tobias (d. 1645), I, 485
Humfrey (or Humphrey), Richard (*fl.* 1637), I, 857
Humming Bird, The (18 cent.), II, 231, 238
HUMOROUS PAPERS, III, 820
Humourist, The (Manchester, 1750), II, 685
Humourist's Magazine, The (1787), II, 681
Humours of a Coffee House, The (1707), II, 660
Humours of a Country Election, The (18 cent.), II, 204, 209
Humours of London, The (18 cent.), II, 221
Humours of New Tunbridge Wells, The (18 cent.), II, 204
Humours of the Times, The (18 cent.), II, 228

Humphrey, Laurence (1527?–1590), I, 379
Humphrey (or Humfrey), Richard (*fl.* 1637), I, 857
Humphreys, Cecil Frances, afterwards Alexander (1818–1895), III, **291**
Humphreys, David (1689–1740), II, 791
Humphreys, J. (*fl.* 1733), II, 793
Humphreys, R. (*fl.* 1824), II, 408
Humphreys (or Humphries), Samuel (1698?–1738), II, 205, 221, 289, 542, 782–4, 813
Hundred Mery Tales, A (16 cent.), I, 714
Hundred Riddles, The Boke of A (16 cent.), I, 716
Hundreth sundrie Flowres, A (16 cent.), I, 403
HUNGARY
　Literary Relations with, II, 71 (1660–1800)
Hunnis, William (d. 1597), I, 521, 678
Hunsdon, H. C. Gibbs, Baron (*fl.* 1894), III, 975
Hunt, Arthur Joseph (*fl.* 1866), III, 987
Hunt, Frederick Knight (1814–1854), III, 790, 799
Hunt, Henry (1773–1835), III, 150
Hunt, Henry Higgs (*fl.* 1807), III, 191
Hunt, J. (*fl.* 1810), editor of John Howe's 'Works', II, 848
Hunt, James (1833–1869), III, 968
Hunt, John (1775–1848), III, 646, 800, 810 (2), 816
Hunt, John Higgs (1780–1859), translator of Tasso, III, 39
Hunt, Leigh (1784–1859), III, **643** f.
　Articles and reviews by, I, 210; III, 194, 199, 203, 218 (4), 223 (3), 257, 636
Hunt, Robert (*fl.* 1650), I, 786
Hunt, Thomas (1627?–1688), II, 271
Hunt, Thorton Leigh (1810–1873), III, 215, 644–7, 799, 814
Hunt, William (*fl.* 1837–87), III, 785, 803, 971
Hunt, William Holman (1827–1910), III, 154
Hunter, Alexander (1729–1809), II, 828
Hunter, Anne (1742–1821), II, 991
Hunter, David (*fl.* 1857), III, 88
Hunter, Henry (1741–1802), II, 52, 553, 771
Hunter, James (*fl.* 1796), II, 815, 927
Hunter, John (1738–1821), admiral, II, 751, 756
Hunter, John (1728–1793), surgeon, II, 961; III, 955
Hunter, Joseph (1783–1861), I, 6, 277, 346, 415; III, 636, **1024** f.
Hunter, R. (*fl.* after 1790), II, 815
Hunter, Samuel (1769–1839), III, 808
Hunter, Sylvester (*fl.* 1861), III, 1025
Hunter, W. (*fl.* 1832), I, 260
Hunter, William (1718–1783), anatomist, II, 961
Hunter, William (*fl.* 1764), editor of 'The Blackbird', II, 222
Hunter, William (1755–1812), orientalist, II, 751; III, 1073

Hunter, William (*fl.* 1792–1812), traveller in Near East, II, 748
Hunter, Sir William Wilson (1840–1900), Indian historian, III, **933**, 1074
HUNTING (books on), I, 393 f. (16, 17 cents.); II, 818 f. (1660–1800); III, 759 f. (19 cent.)
Hunting of the Hare, The (17 cent.), I, 714
Huntingford, George Isaac (1748–1832), II, 934
Huntington, — (*fl.* 1650?), major, I, 842
Huntley, R. W. (*fl.* 1869), I, 589
Huon of Bordeaux, I, **142**, 814
Hurault, Jaques, I, 814
Hurd, Richard (1720–1808), I, 459; II, 17, 23, 26, 120, 399, 601, **852** f., 914, 949, 952
Hurdis, James (1763–1801), II, **366**
Hurry, Mrs Ives, née Mitchell (*fl.* 1803), III, **570**
Hurst, — (*fl.* 1721), captain, II, 438
Hurt, William (*fl.* 1714), II, 696
Hurtado, Luis, I, 344
Hurtado de Mendoza, Antonio, II, 68
Hurwitz, Hyman, III, 174
Husband's Message, The (O.E.), I, **71**
Husbands, John (1706–1732), II, 74
Husenbeth, Frederick Charles (1798–1872), III, 133
Huskisson, William (1770–1830), III, 148, 973
Hutcheon, William, III, 785
Hutcheson, Francis (1694–1747), II, 38, 600, 759, **947**
Hutchins, John (1698–1773), II, **890**
Hutchins, Thomas (*fl.* 1778), II, 756
Hutchinson, Benjamin (*fl.* 1789), II, 925
Hutchinson, Francis (1660–1739), II, 850
Hutchinson, George Andrew (*fl.* 1879–1912), III, 578
Hutchinson, H. (*fl.* 1885), socialist, III, 977
Hutchinson, Horace G. (*fl.* 1894), sporting writer, III, 763, 772, 774–5
Hutchinson, J. (*fl.* 1806), editor of Lucy Hutchinson's 'Memoirs', II, 871
Hutchinson, James (*fl.* 1838), Anglo-Indian poet, III, 1068
Hutchinson, Lucy (b. 1620), II, **871**
Hutchinson, Roger (d. 1555), I, 682
Hutchinson, Thomas (1698–1769), scholar, II, 934
Hutchinson, Thomas (1711–1780), governor of Massachusetts, II, 141
Hutchinson, William (1732–1814), II, 139, **891**
Huth, Henry (1815–1878), I, 406
Huth, Henry (*fl.* 1867), I, 720
Hutten, Leonard (1557?–1632), I, 657
Hutten, Ulrich von, I, 887
Hutton, Alfred (1840–1910), III, 778
Hutton, Catherine (1756–1846), III, **674**
Hutton, Charles (1737–1823), II, 230; III, 941
Hutton, George (*fl.* 1642), I, 752
Hutton, Henry (*fl.* 1619), I, 481

Hutton, James (1726–1797), III, **949**
Hutton, John (1740?–1806), II, 928
Hutton, Luke (d. 1598), I, 717
Hutton, Matthew (1529–1606), I, 383
Hutton, R. N. (*fl.* 1848), III, 133
Hutton, Richard Holt (1826–1897), III, 305, **719**, 813, 833
Hutton, William (1723–1815), II, 139, 154
Hutton, William (1798–1860), III, 951
Huxley, Leonard (*fl.* 1900–30), III, 829
Huxley, Thomas Henry (1825–1895), III, 110, **869**, **954**, **958**, 963, 968
Huygens, Christian, II, 576f.
Hwaetberht (or Eusebius) (*fl.* 730), I, **104**
Hyckescorner (16 cent.), I, 515
Hyde, Douglas (b. 1860), III, **1052** (2), **1056**f.
Hyde, Edward, Earl of Clarendon (1609–1674), II, **864**f.
Hyde, Frederick Augustus (*fl.* 1796), II, 251, 253
Hyde, Henry, Viscount Cornbury (1710–1753), II, 839
Hyde, Thomas (1636–1703), II, 104, 826, 938
Hyland, Inez K. (1863–1892), III, 1095
Hylton, John Scott (*fl.* 1784), II, 366
Hymenæus (16 cent.), I, 662
Hymenaeus Cantabrigiensis (17 cent.), II, 179
Hymers, John (1803–1887), I, 681
HYMNS
  Latin (Irish), I, 101 (5–7 cents.)
  Old English, I, 26, 80f.
Hynd, John (*fl.* 1603–6), I, 725, 730
Hyndman, H. M. (*fl.* 1884), III, 818, 977
Hyne, Charles John Cutcliffe Wright (b. 1866), III, 574
Hyp-Doctor, The (1730), II, 663
Hypochondriack, The (1777), II, 665
Hyrde, Richard (*fl.* 1529), I, 819
Hyslop, James (1798–1827), III, 236

I., H. (1674), II, 533
I., W. (*fl.* 1595), I, 814
I., Z. (*fl.* 1596), I, 417
Ibbotson, I. (*fl.* 1675), I, 703
Ibis, The (1859), III, 829
Ibn al-Tuphail, II, 533
Ibsen, Henrik, III, **43**, 613
ICELAND
  Influence of Sagas, III, 42, 52
Iddesleigh, Sir Stafford Northcote, Earl of (1818–1887), III, 153
Idea of Christian Love, The (17 cent.), II, 180
IDEAS (literary influence of), I, 321f. (16, 17 cents.); II, 5f. (17, 18 cents.), 171f. (poetry, 1660–1800); III, 6f. (19 cent.), 46f., 157f. (poetry, 19 cent.)
Iden, Henry (*fl.* 1557), I, 813
'Idle, Christopher' (1855), III, 766
Idler, The (1758), II, 664
Idler, The (1892), III, 831
Idley, Peter (*fl.* 15 cent.), I, 264

Iffland, August Wilhelm, II, 59
Ignatius, St, II, 994
Ilbert, Sir Courtenay Peregrine (1841–1924), III, 1078
Iley, Matthew (*fl.* 1825), III, 206
Illegal Lovers, The (18 cent.), II, 539
Illingworth, J. R. (*fl.* 1889), III, 851
Illingworth, William (1764–1845), I, 120
Illuminated Magazine, The (1843), III, 828
Illustrated Book of Rural Sports, The (1844), III, 759
Illustrated Historic Times, The (1849), III, 815
Illustrated Household Journal and Englishwoman's Domestic Magazine, The (1880), III, 829
Illustrated London Life (1843), III, 815
Illustrated London Magazine, The (1853), III, 829
Illustrated London News, The (1842), III, 815
Illustrated Mail, The (1899), III, 815
Illustrated Midland News, The [Birmingham] (1869), III, 815
Illustrated News of the World, The (1858), III, 815
Illustrated Newspaper, The (1869), III, 815
ILLUSTRATED PAPERS, III, 814f.
Illustrated Sporting and Dramatic News, The (1874), III, 815
Illustrated Sporting and Theatrical News, The (1864), III, 815
Illustrated Sporting News, The (1862), III, 815
Illustrated Times, The (1855), III, 815
Illustrated Weekly News, The (1861), III, 815
Illustrated Weekly Times, The (1843), III, 815
ILLUSTRATION OF BOOKS, I, 348 (1500–1660); II, 106 (1660–1800), 160f. (18 cent.); III, 89f. (19 cent.), 577 (children's books)
Illustrations of Masonry (18 cent.), II, 229–30, 235, 241, 247, 251
Illustrious History of Women, The (17 cent.), II, 180
Illustrissimi Principis Ducis Cornubiae Genethliacon (17 cent.), II, 180
Il Pastor Fido (17 cent.), I, 539
Image, Selwyn (1849–1930), III, **344**
Image of Idlenesse, A lyttle treatyse called the (16 cent.), I, 728
IMAGINATION (treatises on), II, 14f. (17, 18 cents.)
Impacient Poverte, A new enterlude of (16 cent.), I, 515
Impartial History of the Life of Mr John Barber, An (18 cent.), II, 209
Impartial London Intelligence, The (1681), II, 703
Impartial Occurrences, Foreign and Domestick (1703), II, 733
Impartial Protestant Mercury, The (1681), II, 704
Impartial Review; Or, Literary Journal, The (1759), II, 678

Impartial Scout, The (1650), i, 760
Impartiall Intelligencer, The (1649), i, 759
'Impecuniosus' (1872), iii, 760
Imperial and Colonial Magazine, The (1900), iii, 832
Imperial Magazine; Or, Complete Monthly Intelligencer, The (1760), ii, 678
Imperial Review, The (1804), iii, 824
Imperial Weekly Gazette and Westminster Journal, The(1818), iii, 813
Impey, E. B. (*fl.* 1846), iii, 685
IMPORT LISTS (newspaper advertising), ii, 718f.
Inchbald, Elizabeth (1753–1821), ii, 460, **472f.**, 486, 791–2
Inchbold, John William (1830–1888), iii, 291
Indagine, Joannes A. B., i, 883
Independent, The (1890), iii, 819
Independent Chronicle And Universal Advertiser, The (Dublin, 1777), ii, 736
Independent Chronicle; Or, The Freeholder's Evening Post, The (1769), ii, 711
Independent Irishman, The (1770), ii, 735
Independent London Journal, The (1735), ii, 714
Independent London Journalist, The (1735), ii, 714
Independent Observer, The (1821), iii, 811
Independent Whig, The (1720), ii, 662
Independent Whig, The (1806), iii, 810
Inderwick, Frederick Andrew (1836–1904), iii, **918**
Index to Current Literature (1859), iii, 101
INDIA (literature of, in English)
  Fiction, iii, 1069f.
  Geography, Topography and Travel, iii, 1079f.
  History, Biography and Politics, iii, 1074f.
  Philology, iii, 1017f., 1073f.
  Poetry and Drama, iii, 1068f.
  Religion and Philosophy, iii, 1080f.
  Social and Miscellaneous, iii, 1082f.
  Translations, iii, 1070f.
  Works of Reference, iii, 1067f.
Indian Observer, The (1793), ii, 666
Indicator, The (1819), iii, 818
INDIES, EAST
  Voyages to, ii, 749f.
Individual, The [Cambridge] (1836), iii, 834
INDOOR GAMES (books on), i, 393f. (1500–1660); ii, 825f. (1660–1800); iii, 776f. (19 cent.)
Industrial Review, The (1877), iii, 817
Infallible Astrologer, The (1700), ii, 659
Infant's Library, The (18 cent.), ii, 564
Infant's Magazine, The (1866), iii, 578
Infernal Congress, The (18 cent.), ii, 536
INFLUENCES
  Continental influences. See CONTINENT
  Influence of Earlier English poets, 1660–1800, ii, 171

Influences on the drama, ii, 396 (native influences), 396f. (foreign influences)
Intellectual influences, iii, **46f.** (19 cent.). See also IDEAS
  Medieval influences, ii, 73f. (1660–1800), iii, 52f. (19 cent.)
Informator Rusticus; or, The Country Intelligencer (1643), i, 755
Inge, William Ralph (b. 1860), iii, 850
Ingelend, Thomas (*fl.* 1560), i, 520–1
Ingelo, Nathaniel (1621?–1683), i, 698; ii, 24, 529
Ingelow, Jean (1820–1897), iii, **291f.**
Ingleby, Clement Mansfield (1823–1886), iii, **1034**
Inglefield, John Nicholson (1748–1828), ii, 756
Ingler, William (*fl.* 1643–4), i, 754
Inglis, Sir Robert Harry (1786–1855), iii, 118, 852, 880
Ingram, Bruce S. (b. 1877), iii, 815
Ingram, James (1774–1850), i, 88; ii, 918; iii, 126
Ingram, J. F. (*fl.* 1893), iii, 1089
Ingram, John Kells (1823–1907), iii, 983, **1053f.**
Ingram, Robert Acklom (1763–1809), ii, 116, 124; iii, 110, 129
Ingram, Thomas Dunbar (1826–1901), iii, **929**
Ingram, Sir William (*fl.* 1900?), iii, 831
Ingulf (or Ingulph) (d. 1109), i, 265
INK, iii, 73f.
Innes, Alexander (*fl.* 1709–28), ii, 600
Innes, Arthur (*fl.* after 1851), iii, 828
Innes, Cosmo (1798–1874), iii, 766, **904f.**
Innes, J. (*fl.* 1681), ii, 800
Innes, Thomas (1662–1744), ii, 997
Innocui Sales (17 cent.), ii, 182
Inquisitor, The (1711), ii, 661
Inquisitor, The (1724), ii, 662
Inquisitor, The (1808), iii, 810
Inscriptions upon the Tombs near Bunhill-Fields, The (18 cent.), ii, 193
Inspector, The (1751), ii, 664
Institoris, Henricus (or Krämer), i, 328
Institutions of Freemasonry, The (18 cent.), ii, 241
Instructor, The (1724), ii, 662
Insurance Record, The (1863), iii, 820
INTELLECTUAL BACKGROUND
  Anglo-Saxon Period. See under ARCHAEOLOGY AND HISTORY, i, 56f., WRITINGS IN LATIN, i, 98f. and EDUCATION, i, 124f.
  Middle English Period. See under INTRODUCTION, i, 113f. (especially Education, i, 124f.) and WRITINGS IN LATIN, i, 280f.
  Renaissance to Restoration. See WORKS ON SPECIAL SUBJECTS IN THE HISTORY OF ENGLISH LITERATURE, i, 321f. See also PHILOSOPHY, i, 868f.
  Restoration to Romantic Revival, ii, 5f., 171f. (poetry)
  Nineteenth Century, iii, 6f., 46f.

Intelligence Domestick and Foreign (1695), II, 706

Intelligence Domestick and Foreign, With the Flying Post-Boy from the Camp in Flanders (1695), II, 706

Intelligence from the Scottish Army (1644), I, 756

Intelligence from the South Borders of Scotland (1644), I, 756

Intelligencer, The (1663), II, 702

Intelligencer, The (1728), II, 663

Intelligencer for Publishers and Booksellers, The (1854), III, 101

Intelligencer For Publishers and Booksellers, The (1855), III, 102

Interesting and affecting history of Prince Lee Boo, The (18 cent.), II, 563

Interesting Anecdotes, Memoirs, Allegories, Essays, and Poetical Fragments (18 cent.), II, 249, 250–2

Interesting Tales from the German (18 cent.), II, 553

Interesting Walks of Henry and his Tutor (19 cent.), III, 575

Interlude of Johan the Evangelyst, The (16 cent.), I, 515

Interludium de Clerico et Puella (M.E.), I, 277

International Herald, The (1872), III, 817

Intrepid Magazine, The (1784), II, 680

Introduction to Singing, An (18 cent.), II, 211, 215, 227, 239

Introduction to the History of Poetry in Scotland, An [etc.] (18 cent.), II, 253

Introduction to the London Mercury, The (1692), II, 658

Invective against the Pride of Women, An (17 cent.), I, 717

Investigator, The (1762), II, 665

Investigator, The (1822), III, 811

Investor's Guardian, The (1863), III, 820

Investor's Chronicle and Money Market Review (1922), III, 820

Ipomedon (M.E.), I, **155**

IPSWICH
  Library, II, 105
  Magazines, II, 684 (1799)
  Newspapers, II, 724
  Printing in, I, 353 (16 cent.)

Ipswich Express, The (1839), III, 804

Ipswich Gazette, The (1733), II, 724

Ipswich Journal, The (1720), II, 724

Ipswich Journal, The (1739), II, 724

Ipswich Journal, The (1774), II, 724

Ipswich Magazine, The (1799), II, 684

Ipswich Times, The (1864), III, 803

Irby, Adelina Paulina (*fl.* 1862), III, 991

Irby, Charles Leonard (1789–1845), III, 991

Ireland, Alexander (1810–1894), III, 631, 647, 802

Ireland, John (*fl.* 1475–1490), I, 260, 313

Ireland, John (d. 1808), biographer, II, 408

Ireland, John (1761–1842), dean of Westminster, III, 108

Ireland, Samuel (d. 1800), II, 747, 903

Ireland, William Henry (1777–1835), III, **236**, 403

IRELAND, II, 158f. (social background, 1660–1800); III, 125 (University of). See also under next entry

IRELAND, LITERATURE OF
  Bibliographies, I, 8
  Dramatists of the Irish Revival, III, 1063f.
  Gaelic Sources, III, 1047f.
  Historical Writings, III, 886, 906, 928f.
  Magazines, II, 687f. (1734–1800)
  Newspapers, II, 733f. (1660–1800); III, 808f. (19 cent.)
  Poets of the Irish Revival, III, 1051f.
  Printing in, I, 354 (16, 17 cents.); II, 90 (18 cent.)
  Writers in Latin, I, 101f. (5–7 cents.), 107f. (8 and 9 cents.)
  Yeats and Synge, III, 1059f.

Iris Oofisiúil (1922), II, 734

Iris; Or, Sheffield Advertiser, The (1792), II, 728

Irish Agricultural Magazine, The (1798), II, 688

Irish Daily Independent, The [Dublin] (1891), III, 809

Irish Daily Telegraph, The [Cork] (1871), III, 808

Irish Garland, The (17 cent.), II, 181

Irish Harp, The (18 cent.), II, 253

IRISH LITERATURE. See IRELAND

Irish Miscellany, The (18 cent.), II, 213, 214

Irish Monthly, The (1875), III, 830

Irish Monthly Magazine, The (1873), III, 830

Irish News, The [Belfast] (1891), III, 808

Irish Quarterly Review, The (1851), III, 833

Irish Rogue, The (17 cent.), II, 531

Irish Times, The [Dublin] (1859), III, 809

Irlandia, Johannes de (*fl.* 1475–1490), I, 260. See John Ireland

Iron (1873), III, 822

Iron and Steel Trades Journal and Mining Engineer, The (1877), III, 822

Iron Times, The (1845), III, 799

Irons, William Josiah (1812–1883), III, **292**, 691

Irvine, Alexander (*fl.* 1802), II, 157

Irvine, Christopher (*fl.* 1638–85), II, 996

Irving, David (1778–1860), I, 10, 445; II, 991; III, **1025**

Irving, Edward (1792–1834), III, 853

Irving, Joseph (1830–1891), II, 525

Irwin, Eyles (1751?–1817), II, 750

Isaac, Mr — (*fl.* 1706), II, 825

Isaacs, Mrs — (*fl.* 1801–20), III, **402**

Isaeus, II, 761

Isham, Sir John (*fl.* 1626), I, 386

Isham, Sir Thomas (1657–1681), I, 386

Isidore of Seville, I, 125
Isis, The (1832), III, 816
Isle of Man Daily Times, The (1897), III, 806
Isle of Man Times, The (1861), III, 793
Isocrates, I, 803; II, 761
Isola, Agostino (*fl.* 1778), II, 233
Isselt, Michael ab, I, 815
Isumbras, Sir (M.E.), I, **156** f.
Iswarā Dās (*fl.* 1860), III, 1084
'Isys, Cotswold' (1883), III, 771
ITALIAN
    Translations from, I, 337 f., 809 f. (16, 17
        cents.); II, 29 f. (18 cent. literary criticism),
        807 f. (general, 1660–1800). For 19 cent.
        see under LITERARY RELATIONS WITH
        CONTINENT or particular authors
Italian Magazine, The (1795), II, 682
Italian Magazine, The (1796), II, 682
ITALY
    Literary Relations with, I, 337 f. (1500–
        1660); II, **65** f. (1660–1800); III, **38** f. (19
        cent.), 54
Itinerarium Peregrinorum et Gesta Regis Ricardi
    (M.E.), I, 115
Ive, Paul (*fl.* 1589), I, 813
Ives, Chester (*fl.* 1900), III, 800
Ives, Edward (d. 1786), II, 750
Ivimey, Joseph (1773–1834), I, 469; II, 493, 862
Ivory, Sir James (1765–1842), III, 941

J., B. (*fl.* 1656), I, 405
J., B. (*fl.* 1661), I, 652
J., C. (*fl.* 1656), I, 405
J., C. (*fl.* 1660), II, 801
J., F. (*fl.* 1651), I, 658
J., H. (*fl.* 1676), II, 802
J., R. (*fl.* 1786), II, 563
J., W. (*fl.* 1695), II, 786
J. Wisden's Cricketers' Almanack (1864), III, 773
Jachin and Boaz (18 cent.), II, 224, 231, 234,
    239, 244, 248, 252
Jack, Henry Vernon ('Henry Vernon Esmond')
    (1869–1922), III, **625** f.
Jack, T. C. (*fl.* 1855), III, 797
Jack, William (*fl.* before 1887), III, 808
Jack and the Beanstalk (19 cent.), II, 553
Jack Harkaway's Journal for Boys (1893), III,
    578
Jack in a Box, Here's (17 cent.), I, 715
Jack Sprit-Sail's Frolic (18 cent.), II, 242, 246,
    248
Jack the Giant Killer (18 cent.), II, 553
Jack Upland (M.E.), I, **200**
Jack Upland, Rejoinder of (M.E.), I, **200**
Jacke Drums Entertainment (16 cent.), I, 539
Jacke Jugeler (16 cent.), I, 521
Jacke of Dover (17 cent.), I, 714, 730
Jacke Straw (16 cent.), I, 538
Jacks, Lawrence Pearsall (b. 1860), III, 850
Jackson, — (*fl.* 1714), II, 763

Jackson, Andrew (*fl.* 1750), I, 209
Jackson, Charles (*fl.* 1803), II, 826
Jackson, Sir George (1785–1861), III, 151
Jackson, Henry (1586–1662), editor of Hooker,
    I, 686, 861
Jackson, Henry (*fl.* 1644), surgeon in South-
    wark, I, 891
Jackson, Henry (*fl.* 1736), II, 761
Jackson, J. (*fl.* 1833), agriculturist, III, 971
Jackson, J. L. (*fl.* 1765), equestrian, II, 817
Jackson, John (*fl.* 1668), compiler of biblical
    concordance, II, 928
Jackson, John (*fl.* 1708), traveller, II, 759
Jackson, John (1686–1763), theologian, II, 947
Jackson, John (*fl.* 1761–1809), actor, II, 404
Jackson, John (d. 1807), traveller and excavator,
    II, 751
Jackson, John (1801–1848), wood-engraver,
    III, 84
Jackson, John (*fl.* 1854), angler, III, 770
Jackson, John Edward (1805–1891), antiquary,
    III, 884
Jackson, Maria (*fl.* 1838–43), III, 153
Jackson, Robert (*fl.* 1777), II, 732
Jackson, Thomas (1579–1640), I, 698
Jackson, Thomas (1783–1873), III, 823
Jackson, W. (*fl.* 1795), of Oxford, II, 104
Jackson, William (*fl.* 1642–5), I, 793
Jackson, William (1730–1803), of Exeter, II, 19
Jackson, William (*fl.* 1780), editor of 'The
    Morning Post', II, 709
Jackson's Oxford Journal (1753), II, 727
Jacob, Edward (1710?–1788), II, 913
Jacob, G. A. (*fl.* 1881), III, 1072
Jacob, Giles (1686–1744), II, 394, 605, 820, 923,
    926, **964**
Jacob, Sir Hildebrand (1693–1739), II, 16, 290,
    319, 745
Jacob, John (*fl.* 1734), I, 860
Jacob, William (1762?–1851), III, 970
Jacob and Esau (16 cent.), I, 521
Jacob and Josep (M.E.), I, 39, 188
Jacob's Well (15 cent.), I, 266
JACOBEAN DRAMA, I, 609 f. (major dramatist),
    640 f. (minor dramatists), 651 f. (anony-
    mous plays), 654 f. (university plays)
JACOBEAN POETRY, I, 440 f. (criticism), 441 f.
    (major poets), 473 f. (minor verse)
Jacobi, Johann Christian, II, 55
JACOBITE LITERATURE, II, 1001
Jacobite's Journal, The (1747), II, 663, 715
Jacobs, F. C. W., III, 605
Jacobs, Joseph (*fl.* 1890), III, 576
Jacobson, William (1803–1884), I, 700; III, 860
Jacobus de Voragine, I, 262
Jacomb, F. (*fl.* 1863), III, 1071
Jacottet, E. (*fl.* 1908), III, 1093
Jacox, Francis (*fl.* 1855), III, 651
Jacquemont, Victor (*fl.* 1834), III, 1080
Jacques, John (*fl.* 1843), II, 632

Jaffray, Alexander (1614–1673), II, 996
Jaffray, Sir John (*fl.* 1871), III, 804
Jaggard, William (*fl.* 1620), I, 352, 358
Jago, Richard (1715–1781), II, **366**
James I, King of Scotland (1394–1437), I, **256**f.
James VI of Scotland and I of England, King
  (1566–1625), I, 363, 844, 883, **911**
  Poems, I, 679, 818, **897**
  Reprints, I, 718, 893; II, 122
James II, King of England (1633–1701), II, 163
James, Bartholomew (1752–1827), II, 150–1
James, Charles (d. 1821), II, 774
James, Charles Canniff (*fl.* 1899), III, 1085
James, Eleanor (*fl.* 1689–1715), II, 84
James, George (1683–1735), II, 706–7
James, George Payne Rainsford (1799–1860),
  III, 97, **402**f.
James, Sir Henry Evan Murchison (d. 1923),
  III, 991
James, John (d. 1746), architect, II, 793
James, John (1729–1785), schoolmaster, II, 113
James, John (1811–1867), III, 240, 244
James, Richard (1592–1638), I, 863
James, Robert (1705–1776), II, 621, 654, 927
James, Silas (*fl.* 1797), II, 751
James, T. (*fl.* 1862), III, 219
James, Thomas (1573?–1629), of the Bodleian
  Library, I, 359, 361, 384
James, Thomas (1593?–1635?), navigator, I,
  792
James, Thomas (*fl.* 1771), II, 746
James, William (1635?–1663), I, 861
James, William (d. 1827), III, **881**
Jameson, Anna Brownell, née Murphy (1794–
  1860), III, **674**f., 1088
Jameson, Robert (1774–1854), III, 950
Jameson, William, II, 992
Jamieson, John (1759–1838), III, **1025**
Jamieson, Robert (1780?–1844), II, 257; III,
  1028
Jamnes and Mambres (O.E.), I, 93
Janes, Thomas (*fl.* 1777), II, 232, 241, 243, 246,
  254–5
Janet, P. (*fl.* 1858), II, 939
Janeway, James (1636?–1674), II, 556
Janeway, Richard, the younger (*fl.* 1700), II,
  706
Jansen, née Cumberland, Frances Marianne,
  II, 454
Janssen, Sir Stephen Theodore (*fl.* 1742–72),
  II, 155
Januaries Account (1645), I, 756
Japp, Alexander Hay (1837–1905), III, 8
Jaques, Francis (*fl.* 1642), I, 646
Jardine, Alexander (d. 1799), II, 743
Jardine, George (1742–1827), III, 111
Jardine, Sir William (1800–1874), II, 841, 997;
  III, 956–7
Jarman, Thomas (*fl.* 1829–41), III, 985, 987
Jarrett, H. S. (*fl.* 1891), III, 1073

Jarrett, Thomas (1805–1882), III, 1069
JARROLD & Co., III, 99
Jarvis (or Jervas), Charles (1675?–1739), II, 69
Jeaffreson, Christopher (*fl.* 1676–86), II, 134,
  752
Jeaffreson, John Cordy (1831–1891), III, **918**
Jeans, A. G. (*fl.* 1879), III, 805
Jeans, Thomas (*fl.* 1860), III, 762
Jeaste of Syr Gawayne (M.E.), I, **139**
Jebb, John (1736–1786), II, 115
Jebb, Sir Richard Claverhouse (1841–1905),
  III, 257, **1006**f.
Jebb, S. (*fl.* 1722), II, 675
Jefferies, Richard (1848–1887), III, **550**f.
Jeffery, John (1647–1720), I, 879 (2); II, 897
Jeffrey, Edward (*fl.* 1822), II, 332
Jeffrey, Francis, Lord (1773–1850), III, **675**,
  832, 949
  Reviews by, III, 132, 164, 172, 184, 186,
    192–6, 199 (2), 200, 223, 226, 232, 234–5,
    240–1, 243, 368, 395, 635
Jeffreys, George (1678–1755), II, **319**
Jeffreys, H. (*fl.* 1839), III, 856
Jeffreys, John Gwyn (1809–1885), III, 957
Jelf, Richard William (1798–1871), I, 682; III,
  126
Jellett, John Hewitt (1817–1888), III, 378, 942
Jemmat, Catharine (*fl.* 1766), II, **366**
Jemmy Carson's Collections (18 cent.), II, 240
Jemmy Twitcher's Jests (18 cent.), II, 227, 231,
  253
Je-ne-scai-quoy, The (18 cent.), II, 204
Jeninges, Edward (*fl.* 1590), I, 846
Jenkin, Fleming (*fl.* 1883), I, 21; III, 979
Jenkin, Robert (1656–1727), II, 788
Jenkins, Robert (*fl.* 1826), II, 404
Jenkins, Tobias (*fl.* 1727), II, 813
Jenkinson, Robert Banks, Earl of Liverpool
  (1770–1828), III, 973
Jenkinson, T. B. (*fl.* 1882), III, 1093
Jenks, Edward (b. 1861), III, 984
Jenkyn (or Jenkyns), Pathericke (*fl.* 1661), I,
  476
Jenkyns, H. (*fl.* 1833), I, 669
Jennens, Charles (1700–1773), II, **912**
Jenner, Charles (1736–1774), II, 146, **366**f., 547
Jenner, Edward (1749–1823), II, 961–2
Jennings, David (1691–1762), II, 330
Jennings, Henry Constantine (1731–1819), II,
  810
Jennings, J. (*fl.* 1767), poet, II, 18
Jennings, John (*fl.* 1766), traveller, II, 755
Jennings, Louis John (1836–1893), III, 814
Jennings, Theodore (*fl.* 1647), I, 720, 759
Jenour, Matthew (*fl.* 1791), II, 708, 751
Jenyns, Leonard, later Blomefield (1800–1893),
  III, 138, **956**
Jenyns, Soame (1704–1787), II, 143, **319**f.
Jephson, H. (*fl.* 1892), III, 984
Jephson, J. M. (*fl.* 1858), III, 818

Jephson, Robert (1736–1803), II, **473**, 665
Jerdan, William (1782–1869), I, 382; III, 97, 413, 452, 636, 798, 800, 818
Jerment, G. (*fl.* 1814), I, 698
Jerningham, —, Lady (*fl.* 1780–1843), III, 151
Jerningham, Edward (1727–1812), II, **367**
Jerome, Jerome Klapka (1859–1927), III, **551**, 814, 831
Jeronimo (17 cent.), I, 539
Jerram, Jane Elizabeth (*fl.* 1837), III, 567
Jerrard, George B. (d. 1863), III, 942
Jerrold, Douglas William (1803–1857), III, **602**f., 812, 828 (2), 834
Jerrold, William Blanchard (1826–1884), III, 602–3, 812
Jervas (or Jarvis), Charles (1675?–1739), II, 69
Jervis, Sir John (1802–1856), III, 821, 987
Jervis, T. B. (*fl.* 1845), III, 1080
Jesse, Edward (1780–1868), II, 841; III, 765, 769 (2)
Jesse, John Heneage (1815–1874), III, **899**
Jessey, Henry (1601–1663), II, 556
Jessopp, Augustus (1823–1914), III, **916**
JEST-BOOKS, I, 714f. (1500–1660). For 1660–1800 see under POETICAL MISCELLANIES, II, 173f.
Jester's Magazine; Or, The Monthly Merry-maker, The (1765), II, 679
Jesting Astrologer, The (1701), II, 659
Jesuit, The (1783), II, 666
Jesuite. With Political Reflections on material occurrences, The (1719), II, 713
Jeune, Margaret Dyne (b. 1818), III, 153
Jevons, William Stanley (1835–1882), III, **869**, 974, 979, **983**
Jewel, John (1522–1571), I, 682
Jewish Chronicle, The (1841), III, 819
Jewish Quarterly Review, The (1888), III, 834
Jewitt, Llewellyn Frederick William (1816–1888), III, **927**
'Jews-Trump, Jeremiah van' (1732), II, 202
Jewsbury, Geraldine Endsor (1812–1880), III, 412, **487**
Jeyes, Samuel Henry (1857–1911), III, 786
JIGS, I, 721 (16, 17 cents.)
Joanereidos...With...several Copies of Verses (17 cent.), II, 177
Joannes de Mediolano, I, 815
Joannes Secundus, I, 478
Jobson, Richard (*fl.* 1623), I, 784
Jockey, The (1890), III, 820
Jockey's Intelligencer, The (1683), II, 718
Joe Miller's Jests (18 cent.), II, 209, 210 (2), 211, 212 (2), 215, 216, 218, 221, 225–6, 229, 234, 244
Joersson, S. A. (*fl.* 1796), II, 953
Johan the Evangelyst, The Interlude of (16 cent.), I, 515
John XXI (Petrus Hispanus), Pope, I, 815
John de Bromyard (*fl.* 1390), I, **302**

John de Burgo (d. 1386), I, **313**
John de Hanville (*fl.* 1184), I, **289**
John de Ridevaus (or Rideval or Redovallensis) (*fl.* 1330), I, **304**
John de Sheppey (d. 1360), I, **312**
John of Basingstoke (d. 1252), I, **299**
John of Cornwall (*fl.* 1170), I, **288**
John of Gaddesden (d. 1361), I, **312**
John of Hoveden (d. 1275), I, **300**
John of Mirfield (*fl. c.* 1370), I, **302**
John of Reading (*fl.* 1320), I, **303**
John of Rodington (d. *c.* 1348), I, **304**
John of St Giles (*fl.* 1230), I, **295**
John of Salisbury (d. 1180), I, **288**
John of Tynemouth (d. 1366), I, **302**
John of Wales (*fl.* 1260–83), I, **293**
John Bull (1820), III, 811
John Bull's British Journal (1821), III, 811
John Hillary's Pue's Occurrences (1788), II, 733
John Lillywhite's Cricketers' Companion (1865), III, 773
John Roe's Pue's Occurrences (1763), II, 733
'John-the-Giant-Killer' (1758), II, 561
Johns, Claude Hermann Walter (1857–1920), III, **1016**
Johns, Thomas (*fl.* 1798), II, 718
Johnson, Anthony (*fl.* 1730), II, 95
Johnson, Charles (1679–1748), dramatist, II, **439**f., 485
Johnson, Charles (*fl.* 1724–36), captain, II, 151, 155, 742
Johnson, Charles (*fl.* 1770), grammarian, II, 126, 227
Johnson, Cuthbert William (1799–1878), III, 971
Johnson, E. (*fl.* 1788), II, 715
Johnson, Edward (1599?–1672), I, 793
Johnson, Emily Pauline ('Tekahionwake') (*fl.* 1895), III, 1086
Johnson, Francis (1796?–1876), III, 1071
Johnson, George William (1802–1886), II, 148; III, 1083
Johnson, Henry (1698?–1760), II, 783, 790
Johnson, J. (*fl.* 1762), lexicographer, II, 932
Johnson, J. (*fl.* 1763), translator of Voltaire, II, 804
Johnson, J. (*fl.* 1850), author of 'Laws and Canons of Church of England', I, 96
Johnson, J. G. W. (*fl.* 1848), editor of Fairfax correspondence, I, 387
Johnson, J. R. (*fl.* 1873), typographer, III, 74
Johnson, James (d. 1811), engraver and publisher, II, 80, 241, 782
Johnson, James (1777–1845), physician, III, 1079
Johnson, John (*fl.* 1641), I, 731
Johnson, John (1662–1725), II, **853**
Johnson, John (d. 1833), friend of Cowper, 341–2, 365
Johnson, John (*fl.* 1818), colonel, III, 1079

Johnson, John (1777–1848), printer, II, 82
Johnson, John Noble (1787–1823), biographer of Linacre, I, 664
Johnson, Laurence (*fl.* 1577), I, 521
Johnson, Lionel Pigot (1867–1902), III, **344**
Johnson, Richard (1573–1659?), I, 404 (2), 713f., 715, 729f.
Johnson, Richard (d. 1721), II, 128, 931
Johnson, Robert (*fl.* 1601–9), I, 725, 766, 789
Johnson, Samuel (1649–1703), Whig divine, II, 942
Johnson, Samuel (1709–1784), lexicographer, II, 49, 51, 111, **613**f., 671, 678, 689, 897, 920
Johnson, Samuel (1754–1778), Sir Joshua Reynolds's nephew, II, 138
'Johnson, T.' (1740), II, 303
Johnson, Thomas (d. 1644), I, 891, 892 (2)
Johnson, Thomas Burgeland (d. 1840), III, 765
Johnson, W. M. (*fl.* 1795), II, 783
Johnson, William (1534–1614), I, 657
Johnson, William (1784–1864), educationalist, II, 922
Johnson, William, later Cory (1823–1892), III, **292**
Johnson's Lottery Song Book (18 cent.), II, 227, 232 (2)
Johnson's Sunday Monitor and British Gazette (1805), III, 810
Johnston, A. G. (*fl.* 1816), II, 632
Johnston, Arthur (1587–1641), I, 900
Johnston, George (*fl.* 1772), II, 687
Johnston, George (1797–1855), III, 956
Johnston, Sir Harry Hamilton (1858–1927), III, 991
Johnston, James (d. 1798). See Johnstone
Johnston, Joseph (*fl.* 1686), II, 772
Johnston, Robert (1567–1639), I, 910
JOHNSTON, W. AND A. K., III, 99
Johnston, William (*fl.* 1764–1800), of Tunbridge Wells, II, 256, 931
Johnston, William (*fl.* 1792), editor of 'The Edinburgh Gazetteer', II, 732
Johnston, William (*fl.* 1851–7), barrister and friend of Wordsworth, III, 242
Johnstone, Charles (1719?–1800), II, 545–6, 547 (2)
Johnstone, Christian Isobel (1781–1857), III, 403f., 827
Johnstone, James (d. 1798), II, 70, 80, 486
Johnstone, Sir James (*fl.* 1896), III, 1080
Johnstone, John (*fl.* 1828), II, 936
Johnstone, P. de Lacy (*fl.* 1902), III, 1073
Johnstone, W. S. (*fl.* 1893), III, 801
Joke upon Joke (19 cent.), II, 256
Jole, William (*fl.* 1660–1710), II, 556
Jolly (or Jollie), Thomas (1629–1703), II, 134
Jolly Companion; or, a Cure for Care, The, II, 242

Jolyot de Crébillon, Claude Prosper (the younger), II, 783
Jolyot de Crébillon, Prosper (the elder), II, 783
Joncourt, Elie de, II, 688
Jones, A. (*fl.* 1773), II, 827
Jones, Basset (*fl.* 1634–59), I, 861
Jones, C. (*fl.* 1841), economist, III, 974
Jones, Charles (*fl.* 1803), writer on whist, II, 826
Jones, David (*fl.* 1759), writer in Welsh, II, 79
Jones, David (*fl.* 1774), traveller in North America, II, 756
Jones, Ebenezer (1820–1860), III, **292**
Jones, Edward (*fl.* 1776), translator of Cicero, II, 765
Jones, Edward (1752–1824), editor of song-collections, II, 80, 233, 237, 249, 256 (2)
Jones, Ernest Charles (1819–1868), III, **293**, 817, 977
Jones, F. M. (*fl.* 1834), III, 583
Jones, Giles (*fl.* 1766), II, 546, 561 (2)
Jones, Griffiths (1722–1786), II, 696, 709
Jones, H. B. (*fl.* 1870), biographer of Faraday, III, 947
Jones, Harry Longueville (1806–1870), III, 890
Jones, Henry (1721–1770), II, **367**f.
Jones, Henry (Cavendish) (1831–1899), writer on whist, III, 774, 776f.
Jones, Sir Henry (1852–1922), philosopher, III, **869**
Jones, Henry Arthur (1851–1929), dramatist, III, **613**f.
Jones, Hugh (*fl.* 1724), II, 753
Jones, Hugh (Bardd Llangwm) (*fl.* 1759), II, 79
Jones, J. (*fl.* 1765), editor of Dugdale's 'Antiquities of Warwickshire', II, 864
Jones, James (*fl.* 1727), II, 199
Jones, Jeremiah (1693–1724), II, 862
Jones, John (*fl.* 1635), dramatist, I, 646
Jones, John (*fl.* 1651), lawyer, I, 850
Jones, John (d. 1660), regicide, I, 718
Jones, John (*fl.* 1658), translator, I, 805
Jones, John (*fl.* 1701), teacher of pronunciation, I, 44
Jones, John (1693–1752), classical scholar, II, 315
Jones, John (*fl.* 1826), curate of Cradley, I, 697
Jones, John (*fl.* 1827), poet, III, 182
Jones, John Gale (1769–1838), II, 689
Jones, John Winter (1805–1881), I, 787
Jones, Kennedy (1865–1921), III, 786, 801
Jones, M. A. (*fl.* 1826), III, 135
Jones, Mary (*fl.* 1740), II, **368**
Jones, Owen (Owain Myvyr) (1741–1814), II, 80
Jones, Owen Glynne (*fl.* 1897), III, 777
Jones, R. (*fl.* 1689), icelandic scholar, II, 918
Jones, Richard (1790–1855), III, 981
Jones, Robert, the younger (b. *c.* 1575), I, 484

Jones, Robert (*fl.* 1772), II, 827
Jones, Stephen (1763–1827), I, 829; II, 96, 252, 334, 624, 682–4, 689, 710 (2), 922; III, 809
Jones, T. E. (*fl.* 1849–71), III, 778, 884
Jones, Theophilus (*fl.* 1732), II, 735
Jones, Thomas (*fl.* 1816), III, 759
Jones, W. (*fl.* 1704), II, 809
Jones, William (*fl.* 1595), translator from Italian, I, 417
Jones, William (*fl.* 1607), pamphleteer, I, 742
Jones, Sir William (1746–1794), II, 240, **368**, 827; III, 1070, 1073
Jones, William (*fl.* 1777), traveller, II, 746
Jones, William (1777–1821), diarist, II, 138
Jones, William (*fl.* 1852–5), secretary to Russell Institute, III, 828
Jones, William Basil (1822–1897), III, 908
Jones's British Theatre (1795), II, 392
Jones's Coventry and Warwick Ledger (1765), II, 723
Jones's Coventry, Warwick and Birmingham Magazine (1764), II, 684
Jones's Evening News Letter (1716), II, 692, 710
Jonghe, Ellert de, I, 782
Jonson, Ben (1572–1637), I, **613**f., 726, 746, 803, 866, 870
Jonson, Broer (*fl.* 1621), I, 743
Jonson, John (*fl.* 1642), I, 753
Joplin, Thomas (1790?–1847), III, 972, 974, 980
Jopson's Coventry and Northampton Mercury (1743), II, 723
Jopson's Coventry and Warwick Mercury (1743), II, 723
Jopson's Coventry Mercury; Or, The Weekly Country Journal (1741), II, 723
Jordan, C. J. (*fl.* 1839–53), III, 75, **83**
Jordan, Denham (*fl.* 1889–98), III, **747**
Jordan, Dorothy (1762–1816), II, 460
Jordan, John (1746–1809), II, 916
Jordan, Thomas (1612?–1685), I, 646, 720, 723, 747; II, 146
Jordan, W. L. (*fl.* 1888), III, 974
Jordan's Elixir of Life (18 cent.), II, 242
Jorden, Edward (1569–1632), I, 889, 893
Jortin, John (1698–1770), II, **895**
Jortin, Rogers (*fl.* 1790), II, 895
Jos. Bliss's Exeter Post-Boy (1709), II, 723
Jose, Arthur W. (*fl.* 1911), III, 1098
Joseph, De Sancto (M.E.), I, 140
Joseph of Arimathie (M.E.), I, **134**
Joseph of Exeter (*fl.* 1190), I, **289**
Joseph, Prose Life of (M.E.), I, 140
Josephus, Flavius, I, 778, 803; II, 761
Josephus Scottus (d. after 791), I, **107**
Josselin, Ralph (*fl.* 1616–83), I, 385
Josselyn, John (*fl.* 1672), II, 752
Joubert, Joseph, III, 22
Joule, James Prescott (1818–1890), III, 938
Jourdain, John (d. 1619), I, 783

Jourdan (or Jourdain), Silvester (d. 1650), I, 790
Journal, The (1886), III, 800
Journal Britannique (1750), II, 688
Journal de L'Europe (1789), II, 719
Journal de Middlesex (1791), II, 719
Journal d'un Bourgeois de Paris (15 cent.), I, 116
Journal Étranger de Littérature (1777), II, 680
Journal of Natural Philosophy, A (1797), II, 683
Journal of Philology, The (1868), III, 1044
Journal of the Typographic Arts (1860), III, 88
JOURNALISM. See under NEWSPAPERS. Technique of, III, 781 f.
Journalism (1887), III, 782
Journalist, The (1879), III, 782
Journalist, The (1886), III, 782
JOURNALISTS
Biographies of, II, 670f., 694f. (1660–1800); III, 782f. (19 cent.)
JOURNALS. See PERIODICAL PUBLICATIONS
Jovial Companion, The (18 cent.), II, 219
Jovial Companion, or the Alive and Merry Fellow, The (18 cent.), II, 217
Jovial Companions, The (18 cent.), II, 189
Jovial Garland, A (17 cent.), II, 175
Jovial Mercury, The (1693), II, 658
Jovial Sailor's Chearful Companion (19 cent.), II, 256
Jovial Songster, The (18 cent.), II, 237, 239, 242
Jovis et Junonis Nuptiae (17 cent.), I, 662
Jovius, Paulus, I, 777
Jowett, Benjamin (1817–1893), III, 126, 684, 848, **998**
Joyce, Heath (*fl.* 1895?), III, 815
Joyce, Jeremiah (1763–1816), III, 113, 135
Joyce, Patrick Weston (1827–1914), III, 1049
Joyce, Robert Dwyer (1830–1883), III, **1054**
Joye, George (d. 1553), I, 675 (2), 677
Joyful Cuckoldom (17 cent.), II, 183
Judas, Leo, I, 677
Judd, J. (*fl.* 1856), III, 96
Judgement Poems (O.E.), I, **79**
Judith (O.E.), I, 28, **78**f.
Judy, or the London Serio-Comic Journal (1867), III, 820
Jugurtha, or the Faithless Cosen German (17 cent.), I, 652
Jukes, Andrew (1810–1901), III, 853
Julian, II, 361
Juliana (O.E.), I, **76**f.
Juliana (M.E.), I, **169**
'Junius' (1768), II, **630**f.
Junius, Franciscus (François du Jon) (1589–1677), I, 855; II, 918
JUNIUS MS, THE, I, 62f.
Junius, Patricius (Patrick Young) (1584–1652), I, 857, 859
Junod, H. A. (*fl.* 1912), III, 1093
Jurieu, Pierre, II, 783
Jurist, The (1837), III, 821

Justamond, J. O. (*fl.* 1777), ii, 835
Justice (1884), iii, 818
Justice, Alexander (*fl.* 1710), ii, 707
Justice, Elizabeth (*fl.* 1739), ii, 745
Juta, Sir H. H. (*fl.* 1912), iii, 1090
Juvenal, i, 803; ii, 182, 184–5, 190 (2), 198, 203, 205, 216, 766
'Juvenal (Pindar)' (1827), iii, 1094
Juvenal de Carlenças, Felix de, ii, 784
Juvenile. A Penny Magazine for Children, The (1852), iii, 577
Juvenile Encyclopedia, The (1801), ii, 683
Juvenile Forget Me Not, The (1829), iii, 577
Juvenile Library, The (1800), ii, 565, 683
JUVENILE LITERATURE, i, 377 (1500–1660); ii, 106, 130, **553**f. (1660–1800); iii, 135f., 564f., 820f. (weekly papers), 842 (annuals)
Juvenile Magazine, The (1788), ii, 681
Juvenile Miscellany of Facts and Fiction, The (1844), iii, 577
Juvenile Olio, or Monthly Medley, The (1796), ii, 682
Juvenile Review, The, ii, 554
Juvenile Scrap Book, The (1850), iii, 577
Juvenile Speaker, The (18 cent.), ii, 240

K., H. (*fl.* 1682), ii, 178
K., J. A. C. (*fl.* 1892), iii, 775
K., M. (*fl.* 1674), ii, 811
'*K. P.*' *Illustrated, The* [Cambridge] (1893), iii, 835
Kalm, Pehr, ii, 141
Kames, Henry Home, Lord (1696–1782), ii, 955, 1000
Kane, Paul (*fl.* 1859), iii, 1088
Kane, Sir Robert John (1809–1890), iii, 824
Kant, Immanuel, ii, 52; iii, **32**f., 46
Kapelion; Or, Poetical Ordinary, The (1750), ii, 677
Karr, J. B. A., iii, 601
Kater, Henry (1777–1835), iii, 941
Katherine (M.E.), i, 39, **169**
KATHERINE GROUP (ALLITERATIVE)
 Hali Meidenhad, i, **168**
 Juliana, i, **169**
 Katherine, i, **169**
 Sawles Warde, i, **168**f.
 Seinte Master, etc., i, **170**
Kaufmann, M. (*fl.* 1874), iii, 977
Kavanagh, Julia (1824–1877), iii, **487**
Kay, D. (*fl.* 1883), iii, 111
Kay, John (*fl.* 1490), i, 777
Kay, Joseph (1821–1878), iii, 111, 119
Kay, S. (*fl.* 1833), iii, 1091
Kay-Shuttleworth, Sir J. P. (1804–1877), iii, 111, 116
Kaye, John (1783–1853), iii, 234
Kaye, Sir John William (1814–1876), iii, **907**
Keach, Benjamin (1640–1704), ii, **282**, 530
Keally, Joseph (*fl.* 1700), ii, 415

Kean, Charles John (1811?–1868), ii, 456; iii, 199
Keane, Henry Augustus (b. 1833), iii, 968
Kearsley, George (*fl.* 1785), ii, 447, 614
Kearton, Richard (*fl.* 1900), iii, 574
Keary, Annie (1825–1879), iii, 568
Keary, Eliza (*fl.* 1857), iii, 568
Keary, Peter (*fl.* 1898?), iii, 831
Keate, George (1729–1797), ii, **368**f., 548, 751, 756
Keating, Geoffrey (1570?–1644?), iii, 1047
Keats, John (1795–1821), iii, 40, 45, **220**f.
Kebbel, T. E. (*fl.* 1861–70), iii, 651, 658, 971
Keble, John (1792–1866), i, 685; iii, 231, 291, 687, 856 (2), **857**f.
Keble, Thomas (1793–1875), iii, 858
Keddie, Henrietta ('Sarah Tytler') (*fl.* 1868–77), ii, 554; iii, 573
Keeling, W. (*fl.* 1842), i, 677
Keene, Charles (1823–1891), iii, 91
Keene, Henry George (1781–1864), iii, 577, **1068**, 1077
Keene, J. H. (*fl.* 1881), iii, 771
Keene's Bath Journal (1824), ii, 720
Keightley, Thomas (1789–1872), ii, 520; iii, **894**
Keill, James (1673–1719), ii, 820
Keill, John (1671–1721), ii, 942
Keimer, Samuel (1690?–1742), ii, 696, 712
Keir, James (1735–1820), ii, 26
Keir, Susanna Harvey (*fl.* 1787), ii, 549
Keith, Charles (d. 1807), ii, 251, 991
Keith, George (1639?–1716), ii, 533, 753, **992**
Keith, George Skene (1752–1823), ii, 1000
Keith, James Francis Edward (1696–1758), ii, 1003
Keith, Robert (1681–1757), ii, 997
Keith, Sir William (1680–1749), ii, 997
Keith-Falconer, Ion Grant Neville (1856–1887), iii, 1020
Kelland, Phillip (1808–1879), iii, 938, 942
Kelley, Edward (1555–1595), i, 886
Kelley, Samuel (*fl.* 1764–95), ii, 743, 757
Kellwaye, Simon (*fl.* 1593), i, 889
Kelly, Charles Arthur (*fl.* 1864), iii, 1068
Kelly, Hugh (1739–1777), ii, 43, 50, 61, **473**f., 546, 671, 678 (2), 679, 790
Kelly, Isabella, later Hedgeland (*fl.* 1794–1813), iii, **404**
Kelly, John (1680?–1751), ii, **440**, 542–3, 789, 793, 796, 799
Kelly, Matthew (1814–1858), iii, 1047
Kelly, Michael (1764?–1826), iii, 149
Kelly, P. (*fl.* 1826), ii, 635
Kelly, Sophia (*fl.* 1854), iii, 417
Kelly, Thomas (1772–1855), iii, 99
Kelly, W. (*fl.* 1865), ii, 404
KELMSCOTT PRESS, iii, 86
Kelsall, T. F. (*fl.* 1851), iii, 248–9
Kelsey, Henry (*fl.* 1691), ii, 752

KELSO
  Newspapers, II, 733
  Printing, II, 89
Kelso Chronicle, The (1783), II, 733
Kelso Mail, The (1797), II, 733
Keltie, John Scott (*fl.* 1870), I, 630
Kelty, Mary Ann (1789–1873), III, 572
Kelvin, Sir William Thomson, Baron (1824–1907), III, **939**
Kelway, Thomas (*fl.* 1593), I, 884
Kemble, Charles (1775–1854), III, **590**
Kemble, Frances Anne, later Butler (1809–1893), III, **293**
Kemble, John Mitchell (1807–1857), I, 59, 843; II, 918; III, **898**
Kemble, John Philip (1757–1823), II, **474**
Kemble, W. F. (*fl.* 1858), I, 95
Kemmish's Annual-Harmonist (18 cent.), II, 248, 250–1
Kemp, William (*fl.* 1600), I, 714, 769
Kempe, Anna Eliza, later Stothard, later Bray (1790–1883), III, **389**
Kempe, Alfred John (1785?–1846), I, 382
Kempe, William (*fl.* 1587), I, 366
Kemys (or Keymis), Lawrence (d. 1618), I, 788
Ken, Thomas (1637–1711), II, **848**
KENDAL
  Magazine, II, 684 (1749)
  Newspapers, II, 724
Kendal Courant, The (1731), II, 724
Kendal Weekly Mercury, The (1733), II, **724**
Kendall, Abram (*fl.* 1594), I, 788
Kendall, Edward Augustus (1776?–1842), II, 559 f.
Kendall, George (1610–1663), I, 368
Kendall, Henry Clarence (1841–1882), III, **1094**
Kendall, John (1726–1815), II, 114, 800, 856
Kendall, May (b. 1861), III, **344 f.**
Kendall, R. A. (*fl.* 1791), II, 771
Kendall, Timothy (*fl.* 1577), I, **403**, 800, 802, 804
Kendall, William (1768–1832), II, **369**
Kendrew, J. (*fl.* 1803), of York, II, 555
Kendrick, W. (*fl.* 1775), II, 786
Kenealy, Edward Vaughan Hyde (1819–1880), III, 677
Kennard, Mary E. (*fl.* 1883), III, 767
Kennedy, Benjamin Hall (1804–1889), III, **998 f.**
Kennedy, Charles Rann (1808–1867), III, **293**, 999
Kennedy, Edward Shirley (*fl.* 1862), III, 991
Kennedy, G. J. (*fl.* 1877?), III, 999
Kennedy, James (1793?–1827), III, 207
Kennedy, John (*fl.* 1626), I, 731
Kennedy, John (1698–1782), II, 622
Kennedy, Patrick (1801–1873), III, 1050
Kennedy, Quintin (1520–1564), I, 903

Kennedy, Vans (1784–1846), III, 1073
Kennett (or Kennet), Basil (1674–1715), II, 32, 781–2, 793, 796
Kennett (or Kennet), White (1660–1728), I, 843; II, 32, 104, 767, **853**, **875 f.**
Kenney, J. H. (*fl.* 1808), II, 983
Kenney, James (1780–1849), III, **590**
KENNINGS. See under VOCABULARY (O.E.), I, 30 f. and POETRY (O.E.), I, 61 f.
Kenny, James (*fl.* 1758), II, 755
Kenrick, Daniel (*fl.* 1685–1700), II, 272
Kenrick, W. S. (*fl.* 1775), II, 679, 822
Kenrick, William (1725?–1779), II, 92, **474 f.**, 552, 678–9, 931–2
KENT
  Bibliography, I, 8
Kent, Charles (1823–1902), III, 477, 647, 800
Kent, E. (*fl.* 1823), III, 647
Kent, George (*fl.* 1815), III, 810
Kent, John (*fl.* 1892), III, 764
Kent, Nathaniel (1737–1810), II, 148
Kent Herald, The (1824), II, 722
Kent's Weekly Dispatch and Sporting Mercury (1816), III, 820
Kentish Chronicle and Canterbury Journal, The (1788), II, 722
KENTISH DIALECT
  Dialect (M.E.), I, 38
  Texts, I, 36 (O.E.), 41 (M.E.)
Kentish Express and Ashford News, The (1855), III, 793
Kentish Gazette, The (1768), II, 722
Kentish Glosses (O.E.), I, 35, 36
Kentish Herald, The (1802), II, 722
Kentish Herald, and Universal Register, The (1792), II, 722
Kentish Post and Canterbury Journal, The (1769), II, 722
Kentish Post; Or, Canterbury News-Letter, The (1717), II, 722
Kentish Register, The (1793), II, 684
Kentish Sermons (M.E.), I, **171 f.**
Kentish Songster, The (18 cent.), II, 230, 233, 237, 247
KENTISH TEXTS (O.E.), I, 36
Kentish Weekly Post; Or, Canterbury Journal, The (1768), II, 722
Kenworthy, J. C. (*fl.* 1893), III, 977
Kenyon, John (1784–1856), III, 237
Kepers, John (*fl.* 1598), I, 379, 818
Keppel, George Thomas, Earl of Albemarle (1799–1891), III, 152, 1079
Ker, David (*fl.* 1874), III, **569**
Ker, John (1673–1726), II, **876**
Ker, Patrick (*fl.* 1684), II, **282 f.**
Ker, William (*fl.* 1688), II, 744
Ker, William Paton (1855–1923), III, **747**
Kerly, Sir D. M. (1863–1938), III, 987
Kern, J. H. C. (*fl.* 1865), III, 1071
Kerner, A. J. C., III, 482

Kerr, J. (*fl.* 1865), III, 1084
Kerr, John (*fl.* 1896), III, 775, 778
Kerr, William Williamson (*fl.* 1867), III, 987
Kerry Evening Post, The (1774), II, 738
Kersey, John (1616–1690?), II, 125, 129, 930
Kershaw, Thomas (*fl.* 1785), II, 19
Kervynge, Boke of (16 cent.), I, 264
Kethe, William (d. 1608?), I, 678
Ketley, J. (*fl.* 1844), I, 676
Kett, Henry (1761–1825), II, 365
Kettlewell, John (1653–1695), II, **848**
Key (or Caius), Thomas (d. 1572), I, 369
Key, Thomas (*fl.* 1878), lawyer, III, 987
Key, Thomas Hewitt (1799–1875), Latin scholar, III, **999**
Key of Knowledg, The (1682), II, 178
Key of Knowledg for Children, The (18 cent.), II, 556
Keymis (or Kemys), Lawrence (d. 1618), I, 788
Keymor, John (*fl.* 1610–20), I, 846
Keynes, J. N. (b. 1852), III, 984
Keyssler, J. G., II, 806
Khayyam, Omar, III, 252, 353, 552
Kidd, Benjamin (1858–1916), III, 984
Kidd, Dudley (*fl.* 1904), III, 1093
Kidd, John (1775–1851), III, 950
Kidd, Samuel (1804–1843), III, 1020
Kidd, Thomas (1770–1850), III, **995**
Kidder, Richard (1633–1703), II, 848
Kidgell, John (*fl.* 1755–66), II, 545
Kielmansegg, Frederick, II, 141
Kilburne, Richard (1605–1678), I, 776
Kilburne, W. (*fl.* 1659), I, 673
Kildare Poems (M.E.), I, 39
Kilgour, Alexander (*fl.* 1825), III, 206
Kilham, Alexander (1762–1798), II, 684
KILKENNY
  Newspaper, II, 737
  Printing, II, 90 (17 cent.)
Kilkenny Journal and Leinster Commercial Advertiser, The (1830), II, 737
Killigrew, Anne (1660–1685), II, **283**
Killigrew, Ferdinando (*fl.* 1759), II, 216, 219, 226
Killigrew, Henry (1613–1700), I, 647; II, 766
Killigrew, Thomas, the elder (1612–1683), II, 49
Killigrew, Thomas, the younger (1657–1719), II, 195, **440**
'Killigrew, Tom, Junior' (1778), II, 233
Killigrew, Sir William (1606–1695), II, **424**
Killigrew's Jests (18 cent.), II, 219
Killmister, A. K. (*fl.* 1836), III, 762
Kilner, Dorothy (1755–1836), II, 557f.
Kilner, Mary Jane, née Maze (1753–?), II, 557–8
Kilwardby, Robert (d. 1279), I, **296**f.
Kimber, Edward (1719–1769), II, 544–5, 677, 696, 710, 754, 783
Kimber, Isaac (1692–1755), II, 671, 676–7, 846

Kimber, J. (1720) [Misprint for Isaac Kimber (1692–1755)], II, 846
Kimbolton, Papers at (17 cent.), I, 382
Kinaston. See Kynaston
Kind Words For Boys and Girls (1866), III, 578
Kindersley, Mrs Nathaniel E. (*fl.* 1777), II, 742, 801
King, Charles (*fl.* 1713–21), II, 660
King, Charles William (1818–1888), III, **999**
King, Gregory (1648–1712), II, 958
King, Harold (*fl.* 1863), III, 780
King, Harriet Eleanor Hamilton (1840–1920), III, **345**
King, Henry (1592–1669), I, **450**, 698
King, J. W. (*fl.* 1854), III, 233, 240
King, James (1750–1784), II, 742
King, John (*fl.* 1706), German teacher, II, 51
King, John (1696–1728), classical scholar, II, 936
King, Leonard William (1869–1919), III, **1016**
King, Peter, Baron (1669–1734), II, 863
King, Peter, Baron (1776–1833), II, 941; III, 972–3
King, Philip Gidley (1758–1808), II, 751
King, Mrs R. H. (*fl.* 1884), III, 1084
King, Thomas (1730–1805), II, **475**, 796
King, W. (*fl.* 1822–7), II, 632, 890
King, W. R. (*fl.* 1853), III, 1091
King, William (1650–1729), archbishop of Dublin, II, 159, 942, 947
King, William (1663–1712), miscellaneous writer, II, 25, 541, **574**f., 661, 702, 792
King, William (1685–1763), principal of St Mary Hall, Oxford, II, 117f., **320**f.
King and Queenes Entertainement at Richmond, The (17 cent.), I, 652
King Charles I, The Famous Tragedie of (17 cent.), I, 651
King Edward the Fourth (17 cent.), I, 539, 623
King Henry the Eighth, The Pleasant History of (17 cent.), I, 731
King Horn (M.E.), I, 29, 39, **147**
King of Tars (M.E.), I, **154**
King Pontus and the Fair Sidone (M.E.), I, **148**
KING'S COLLEGE (Cambridge), I, 370
King's College Literary and Scientific Magazine, The (1849), III, 836
King's College Magazine, The (1842), (1850), (1877), (1896), III, 836
King's Own, The (1890), III, 831
KING'S PRINTING OFFICE, III, 87
Kingdom's Weekly Post, The (1648), I, 758
Kingdome's Intelligencer, The (1659), II, 701
Kingdome's Faithfull and Impartiall Scout, The (1649), I, 759
Kingdomes Faithfull Scout, The (1649), I, 759
Kingdomes Intelligencer, The (1660), II, 702
Kingdomes Intelligencer, The (1663), I, 763
Kingdomes Scout, The (1645), I, 757

Kingdomes Weekly Intelligencer sent abroad to prevent misinformation, The (1643), I, 754
Kingdomes Weekly Post, The (1645), I, 757
Kingdomes Weekly Post with his packet of letters, publishing his message to the City and the Countrey, The (1643), I, 755
Kingdoms Intelligencer of the Affairs now in Agitation in Scotland [etc.], *The* (1664), II, 730
Kingdoms Weekly Account of Heads of Chiefe Passages in Parliament (1648), I, 758
Kinglake, Alexander William (1809–1891), III, 901
Kingscote, Adeline G. I. (*fl.* 1890), III, 1072
Kingsford, William (1819–1898), III, **930**
Kingsley, Charles (1819–1875), III, **487**f.
   Articles and reviews by, II, 987; III, 59, 210, 257, 302, 306, 675
Kingsley, George Henry (1827–1892), III, 991, 1031
Kingsley, Henry (1830–1876), III, **490**f., 807
Kingsley, John Sterling (*fl.* 1888), III, 958
Kingsley, Mary Henrietta (1862–1900), III, 991
Kingsley, Mary St Ledger, later Harrison ('Lucas Malet') (d. 1931), III, **553**f.
Kingsman, A. (*fl.* 1874), III, 979
Kingston, Richard (*fl.* 1682–1700), II, 573
Kingston, William Henry Giles (1814–1880), III, **491**, 578, 828
Kinloch, George Ritchie (1796?–1877), I, 272; II, 996
Kinnear, J. G. (*fl.* 1827), I, 259
Kinnear, T. (*fl.* 1823), I, 900
Kinwelmersh, Francis (d. 1580?), I, 523, 801
Kip, Johannes (1653–1722), II, 161
Kipling, Rudyard (1865–1936), III, **527**f.
Kippars, R. (*fl.* 1688), II, 760
Kippis, Andrew (1725–1795), II, 109, 441, 678, 684, 921
Kirby, Charles F. (*fl.* 1867), III, 1069
Kirby, Thomas (*fl.* 1758), II, 17
Kirby, William (1759–1850), entomologist, III, 955
Kirby, William (*fl.* 1877), Canadian novelist, III, 1087
Kirbye, George (1565?–1634), I, 483
Kirchmayer, Thomas, I, 328
Kirk, Robert (1641?–1692), II, 999
Kirkby, John (1705–1754), II, 540
Kirkcaldy, Sir William (d. 1573), of Grange, I, 903
Kirke, Edward (1553–1613), I, 864
Kirke, John (d. 1642?), I, 647
Kirke, Thomas (1650–1706), II, 157
Kirkes, William (1823–1864), III, 963
Kirkham, R. (*fl.* 1659), I, 647
Kirkman, Francis (*fl.* 1661–74), I, 810; II, 96, 176, 529–30
Kirkman, Jacob (*fl.* 1799), II, 407

Kirkman, Thomas Penyngton (1806–1895), III, **941**
Kirkpatrick, James (*fl.* 1750–72), II, 22, 801–2
Kirkpatrick, William (1754–1812), III, 1079
Kirkton, James (1620?–1699), II, 996
Kirkup, T. (*fl.* 1887), III, 977
Kirkwood, Daniel (b. 1814), III, 944
Kirkwood, James (*fl.* 1698), II, 103
Kitchin, George William (1827–1912), III, **922**
Kitchin, John (*fl.* 1579), I, 850
Kitto, John (1804–1854), III, 853
Klein, Augusta W. (*fl.* 1895), III, 1080
Klimius, Nicholas, II, 552
Klinger, Friedrich Maximilian, II, 59, 63; III, 422
Klopstock, Friedrich Gottlieb, II, 56, 59, 806; III, 409
Knacke to knowe a knave, A (16 cent.), I, 538
Knacke to know an honest Man, A (16 cent.), I, 538
Knaresborough Wills (16 cent.), I, 46
Knatchbull-Hugessen, Edward Hugessen, Baron Brabourne (1829–1893), III, 573
Knave in Graine, New Vampt, The (17 cent.), I, 652
Knel (or Knell), Thomas, the younger (*fl.* 1560–81), I, 741
Knevet, Ralph (1600–1671), I, 390, 647
Knigge, Adolf Franz Friedrich, II, 63
Knight, —, Lady (*fl.* 1799), II, 625
Knight, Charles (1791–1873), II, 641; III, 72, 151, 248, 497, 789–90, 825, 827, 832, 982, **1025**f.
Knight, E. F. (*fl.* 1893), III, 1080
Knight, Ellis Cornelia (1757–1837), II, 549; III, 164, 907
Knight, F. H. (*fl.* 1850), III, 982
Knight, Francis (*fl.* 1640), I, 772
Knight, Henrietta, Lady Luxborough (d. 1756), II, 136
Knight, J. (*fl.* 1786), II, 804
Knight, James (d. 1719?), II, 753
Knight, Joseph (1829–1907), III, **719**, 818, 822
Knight, Miriam S. (*fl.* 1884–95), III, 1072
Knight, Lady Philippina (*fl.* 1776), II, 748
Knight, Richard Payne (1750–1824), II, 20, 30, 934
Knight, Samuel (1675–1746), I, 666
Knight, Sarah K. (*fl.* 1704), II, 753
Knight, Thomas Andrew (1759–1838), III, 959
Knight of Curtesy (M.E.), I, **160**
Knight's Quarterly Magazine (1823), III, 832
Knight-Bruce, George Wyndham Hamilton (1852–1896), III, 1092
Knight-Errant, The (1729), II, 663
Knighton, Dorothea, Lady (*fl.* 1838), III, 150
Knighton, Henry (*fl.* 1363), I, 42, 116
Knighton, W. (*fl.* 1855), III, 1083
Knighton, Sir William (1776–1836), III, 150
Knolles, Richard (1550?–1610), I, 778

Knowler, W. (*fl.* 1739), I, 400
Knowles, Herbert (1798–1817), III, 237
Knowles, J. H. (*fl.* 1885), III, 1072
Knowles, James Sheridan (1784–1862), III, 374, **590**f., 834
Knowles, Sir James Thomas (1831–1908), III, 830 (2)
Knowles, Richard Brinsley (1820–1882), III, 829
Knowles, Thomas (1723–1802), II, 879
Knox, A. E. (*fl.* 1850), III, 762
Knox, Alexander (1757–1831), II, 666; III, 181, 858
Knox, Isa, née Craig (1831–1903), III, **336**
Knox, John (1505–1572), I, 716, **904**
Knox, John (*fl.* 1769), II, 741, 755
Knox, Robert (1641?–1720), II, 749, 870
Knox, Robert (1791–1862), ethnologist, III, 967
Knox, Robert (*fl.* 1846–57), journalist, III, 798, 801
Knox, Vicesimus (1752–1821), II, 19, 109, 111, 118, 131, 245, 251, 336; III, 129
Knyff, Leonard (1650–1721), II, 161
Knyveth, Sir H. (*fl.* 1596), I, 844
Knyvett, Sir Thomas (d. 1622), I, 390
Kock, Paul de, III, 504
Koenig, F., III, 78
Koenigsmarck, M. A., Countess of, II, 806
Kohl, J. G., III, 679
Kolbe, F. C. (*fl.* 1907), III, 1089
Komensky (or Comenius), Jan Amos, I, 326, 365, 375
Koops, M. (*fl.* 1800), III, 71
Kotzebue, August Friedrich Ferdinand, II, 60, 63, 486, 553, **806**; III, 406, 590, 596 (2), 597
Krafft, John Charles Philip von, II, 152
Kratter, Franz, II, 60
Krazinski, i.e. Jósef Ignacy Kraszewsk, III, 347
Kreysig, G. C. (*fl.* 1750), II, 818
Kuechelbecker, J. B., II, 140
Kuettner, C. G., II, 142, 159
Krüsi, H., III, 112f.
Kugler, F. T., III, 303, 712
Kunte, Mādhavarāva M. (*fl.* 1877), III, 1072
Kurzer Versuch den Character...Carolinä, Königin von Gross-Britannien, Ein (18 cent.), II, 207
Kyd, Stewart (d. 1811), II, 85, 964
Kyd, Thomas (1558–1594), I, 396, **525**f., 741, 819
Kyffin, Maurice (d. 1599), I, 808
Kyllour, Friar (*fl. c.* 1550), I, 904
Kymer, Gilbert (d. 1463), I, **313**
Kynaston (or Kinaston), Sir Francis (1587–1642), I, 379, 476, 861
Kynaston, Herbert (1809–1878), of St Paul's School, III, 133
Kynaston, Herbert, earlier Snow (1835–1910), Greek scholar, III, **1007**

Kyng Alisaunder, or Lyfe of Alisaunder (M.E.), I, **143**
Kyng Daryus, A Pretie new Enterlude of (16 cent.), I, 516
Kyrkham, W. (*fl.* 1570), I, 738

L., A. (*fl.* 1589), I, 692
L., A. (*fl.* 1677), II, 794
L., A. (*fl.* 1678), II 796
L., A. (*fl.* 1680), II, 791
L., C. (*fl.* 1835), III, 244
L., F. (*fl.* 1600), I, 805
L., F. B. (*fl.* 1767), II, 409
L., G. (*fl.* 1687), II, 816
L., H. (*fl.* 1799), II, 806
L., L. E. (Letitia Elizabeth Landon, later Maclean: 1802–1838), III, **294**, 478
L., M. D. S. D. (*fl.* 1788), II, 145
L., R. (1687), II, 534
L., S. (*fl.* 1670), II, 748
L., T. (*fl.* 1653), I, 762
L., W. (*fl.* 1642), I, 717
Labadie, Jean de, II, 784
La Barre, François Poulain de, II, 794
Labat, Jean Baptiste, II, 784
La Baume le Blanc de la Vallière, Louise Françoise, II, 784
L'Abbat (or Labat), II, 823
La Belle Assemblée; or Bell's Court and Fashionable Magazine (1806), III, 824
Labiche, Eugène M., III, 598, 626
La Boétie, Étienne de, II, 784
La Bouchere, Henry (1831–1912), III, 786, 814
Labour Elector, The (1888), III, 818
Labour Leader, The (1891), III, 818
Labour World, The (1890), III, 818
La Bruyère, Jean de, II, 36, 784
La Calprenède, Gautier de Costes, Seigneur de, I, 334, 815; II, 47, 532
Lacedemonian Mercury, The (1692), II, 658
Lacey, T. A. (*fl.* 1895?), III, 819
La Chaise, Jean Filleau de, i.e. 'Dubois de la Cour', II, 778
La Chappelle, Jean de, II, 41, 540, 784
Lachrymae Academiae Marischallanæ (17 cent.), I, 911
Lackington, James (1746–1815), II, 100, 138
Laclos, Pierre Choderlos de, III, 339
Lacombe, François (*fl.* 1784), II, 141
La Condamine, Charles Marie de, II, 784
La Coste, — de, II, 141
La Croix, Jacques Vincent de, II, 784
Lacrymae Cantabrigienses in Obitum Serenissimae Reginae Mariae (17 cent.), II, 183
Lactantius, II, 868
La Curne de Sainte-Palaye, Jean Baptiste de, II, 784
Lacy, Captain — (*fl.* 1842), III, 762
Lacy, G. (*fl.* 1888), III, 977
Lacy, John (*c.* 1615–1681), II, **424**

Lacy, Michael Rophino (1795–1867), III, **591**
Lacy, Thomas Hailes (1809–1873), III, 442, 585, 598
Lacy's Acting Edition of Plays (1849), III, 585
Ladies Amusement (18 cent.), II, 212
Ladies and Gentlemen's Musical Memorandum, The (18 cent.), II, 244
Ladies Collection of Catches, The, II, 240
Ladies Delight, The (1732), II, 202
Ladies Delight, The (1741), II, 209 (2)
Ladies Dictionary, The (17 cent.), II, 182
Ladies Journal, The (1727), II, 663
Ladies Mercury, The (1693), II, 658
Ladies Miscellany, The (1718), II, 194, 195
Ladies Miscellany, The (1730), II, 200, 201–2
Ladies Monthly Magazine. The World of Fashion, The (1852), III, 826
Ladies Most Elegant Lottery Pocket Book, The (18 cent.), II, 233
Ladies Polite Songster, The, II, 226–7
Ladies Tales, The (18 cent.), II, 536
Ladies' Cabinet of Fashion, Music, and Romance, The (1839), III, 827
Ladies' Companion at Home and Abroad, The (1850), III, 828
Ladies' Complete Pocket-Book, The (18 cent.), II, 235
Ladies' Magazine; Or, The Universal Entertainer, The (1749), II, 677
Ladies' Monthly Museum, The (1798), III, 824
Ladies' Museum, The (1798), III, 824
Ladies' Museum, The (1829), II, 683
Ladies' Own Memorandum-Book, The (18 cent.), II, 239
Ladies' Treasury, The (1857), III, 829
La Drévetière, Louis François Lisle de, II, 41, 789
Lady, The (1885), III, 815
Lady Alimony, or the Alimony Lady, I, 652
Lady and Gentleman's Scientifical Repository, The (1782), II, 685
Lady's Curiosity, The (1752), II, 677
Lady's Drawing Room, The (18 cent.), II, 543
Lady's Gazette and Evening Advertiser, The (1789), II, 711
Lady's Magazine and Museum of Belles Lettres, The (1832), III, 823
Lady's Magazine; Or, Entertaining Companion for the Fair Sex, The (1770), II, 679
Lady's Magazine; Or, Polite Companion for the Fair Sex, The (1759), II, 678
Lady's Miscellany; Or, Pleasing Essays, The (18 cent.), II, 248, 252
Lady's Monthly Museum (1798), II, 666
Lady's Musical Magazine, The (1788), II, 681
Lady's Museum, Consisting of a Course of Female Education, The (1760), II, 678
Lady's New and Elegant Pocket Magazine, The (1795), II, 682
Lady's Newspaper, The (1847), III, 815

Lady's Newspaper and Pictorial Times, The (1848), III, 815
Lady's Pictorial, The (1881), III, 815
Lady's Poetical Magazine, The (1781), II, 235–6, 246, 680
Lady's Preceptor, The (18 cent.), II, 247
Lady's Weekly Magazine, The (1747), II, 715
Laelia (16 cent.), I, 662
Laet, Joannes de, I, 775f.
La Fayette, Marie Madeleine Pioche de la Vergne de, II, 47, 533f., 792
Lafont, Joseph de, II, 41, 784
Lafontaine, August Heinrich, II, 63, 553, 806; III, 391
La Fontaine, Jean de, II, 44, 784; III, 413
La Fontaine, Jean Baptiste de, Seigneur de Savoy et de Fontenai, II, 784
La Force, Charlotte Rose de Caumont de, II, 784
La Fosse d'Aubigny, Antoine de, II, 41, 784
Lagden, Godfrey (*fl.* 1909), III, 1093
La Harpe, Jean François de, II, 784
Lahontan, Louis Armand de Lom D'Arce, Baron de, II, 789
Lai le Freine (M.E.), I, **151**
Laidlaw, William (1780–1845), III, 237
Laing, Alexander Gordon (1793–1826), III, 991
Laing, David (1793–1878), III, 1025, **1026**
  Editions by, I, 445, 528, 899 (2), 906; II, 984; III, 86 (2), 374, 905, 1025
Laing, J. (*fl.* 1867), III, 983
Laing, Malcolm (1762–1818), II, 343, 887; III, 886
Laing, Samuel (1780–1868), III, 991
LAIS, BRETON, I, **151**f.
Lake, E. (*fl.* 1825), III, 1075
Lake, Edward (1641–1704), II, 134
Lake, J. W. (*fl.* 1822–9), II, 462, 631; III, 184, 187, 190, 193–4, 206
Lake, John Neal (*fl.* 1781–1802), II, 29
Lake, Osmund (*fl.* 1612), I, 509
La Live d'Épinay, Louise Florence Pétronille de, II, 784
La Marche, Olivier de, I, 733
Lamartine, Alphonse de, III, 209
Lamb, Lady Caroline, née Ponsonby (1785–1828), III, **404**
Lamb, Charles (1775–1834), III, 244, 590, **631f.**
  Articles and reviews by, III, 172, 223, 227, 238, 241, 300, 647, 789
Lamb, John (1789–1850), I, 370
Lamb, Mary Ann (1764–1847), III, 633, **675f.**
Lamb, Mary Montgomerie, later Singleton, later Lady Currie, pseudonym 'Violet Fane' (1843–1905), III, **345**
Lamb, Roger (*fl.* 1776), II, 152
Lamb, William, Viscount Melbourne (1779–1848), III, 144–5
Lambard, William (1536–1601), I, 774, **825f.**, 850

Lambe, Charles (*fl.* 1711), II, 574
Lambe, Robert (1712–1795), II, 826
Lambert, Anne Thérèse de, II, 122, 784
Lambert, James (*fl.* 1700), II, 819
Lambert, William (*fl.* 1816), III, 773
Lambert's Monthly (1890), III, 831
Lambeth Homilies (M.E.), I, **170**
Lambewell, Sir (M.E.), I, **153**
Lambton, John George, Earl of Durham (1792–1840), III, 151
Lamentable and true tragedie of Arden of Faversham, The (16 cent.), I, 579
Lamentable Tragedie of Locrine, The (16 cent.), I, 579
La Mettrie, Julien Offray de, II, 792
Lamont, John (*fl.* 1649–71), II, 996
La Mothe, Marie Catherine de, Comtesse d'Aulnoy, II, 46, 149, 534, 541, 565, 785
La Mothe Langon, E. L. de, III, 677
La Mothe le Vayer, François de, II, 785
Lamotte, Charles (*fl.* 1730), II, 16
La Motte, Houdart de, II, 541
La Motte, Jeanne de, II, 785
La Motte, Philemon de, II, 785
La Motte Fouqué, Friedrich Heinrich Karl de, III, **29**
La Mottraye, Aubry de, II, 785
Lampadius, W. A. (*fl.* 1865), III, 711
Lampe, John Frederick (1703?–1751), II, 207
Lamphire, John (1614–1688), I, 684
Lampit, Juliana (Julian of Norwich) (1343?–1443?), I, 195
Lampman, Archibald (*fl.* 1888), III, 1086
Lampoons; Or, Reflections on Public News Letters (1690), II, 658
Lamwell, Sir (M.E.), I, **153**
Lamy, Bernard, II, 785
LANCASHIRE
    Bibliography, I, 8
    Printing in, II, 87 (to 1800)
Lancashire Daily Express and Standard, The (1895), III, 806
Lancashire Daily Post, The (1893), III, 806
Lancashire Evening Post, The (1886), III, 806
Lancashire Journal; with the History of the Holy Bible, The (1738), II, 726
Lancaster, Charles (*fl.* 1889), III, 763
Lancaster, Henry Hill (1829–1875), III, 111, 706
Lancaster, Joseph (1778–1838), III, 111, 139, 143
Lancaster, Nathaniel (1701–1775), II, 18, 447
Lancaster Guardian, The, III, 793
Lancelot, Claude, II, 785
LANCELOT, LEGEND, I, 131
Lancelot of the Laik (15 cent.), I, 43, **139**f.
Lancet, The (1823), III, 793, 821
Land and Building News, The (1855), III, 822
Land and Water (1866), III, 815
Land of Cockaygne (M.E.), I, **161**f.

Landells, E. (*fl.* 1858), III, 573
Lander, John (1807–1839), III, 991
Lander, Richard Lemon (1804–1834), III, 991
Landeval, Sir (M.E.), I, **152**
Landon, Letitia Elizabeth, later Maclean (1802–1838), III, **294**, 478
Landor, Owen (*fl.* 1894), III, 574
Landor, Robert Eyres (1781–1869), III, **237**
Landor, Walter Savage (1775–1864), III, 636, 637f.
LANDSCAPE GARDENING (treatises on), II, 30 (18 cent.)
Landseer, John (1769–1852), III, 82
Lane, A. (*fl.* 1700), II, 931
Lane, Edward William (1801–1876), III, **1020**
Lane, George (*fl.* 1803), III, 798, 800
Lane, John (*fl.* 1600–20), I, 713
Lane-Poole, S. (*fl.* 1863), III, 1020
Laneham, Robert (*fl.* 1575), I, 509, 740 ·
Lanfranc (d. 1089), I, **282**
Lanfranc of Milan, I, 266
Lang, Andrew (1844–1912), III, 576, **747**f.
Lang, David (*fl.* 1853), I, 509
Lang, John (*fl.* 1852–9), III, 1068–9
Lang, John Dunmore (1799–1878), III, 1094
Langbaine, Gerard, the elder (1609–1658), I, 369, 371, 858, 862
Langbaine, Gerard, the younger (1656–1692), II, **892**
Langcake, Thomas (*fl.* 1781), II, 54, 858
Langford, John Alfred (1823–1903), I, 718
Langham, William (*fl.* 1597), I, 892
Langhorne, J. T. (*fl.* 1804), II, 369
Langhorne, John (1735–1779), II, 337, **369**, 546 (2), 900
Langhorne, William (1721–1772), II, 763
Langlade, Jacques de, Baron de Saumières, II, 785
Langlade, Jean Louis Ignace de La Serre, Sieur de, II, 786
Langland, William (1330?–1400?). See *Piers Plowman*
Langley, Batty (1696–1751), II, 30
Langley, Samuel (*fl.* 1767), II, 761
Langlois de Motteville, Françoise, II, 785
Langston, John (1641?–1704), II, 128
Langton, Bennet (1737–1801), II, 108, 616
Langton, Robert (d. 1524), I, 767
Langton, Stephen (d. 1228), I, **298**
LANGUAGE (treatises on), II, 14f. (17, 18 cents.)
LANGUAGE, THE ENGLISH, I, 24f.
    Chaucer's language, I, 217f.
    Dictionaries and Glossaries, I, 25f.
    Phonology and Grammar, I, 34f. (O.E.), 37f. (M.E.), 43f. (Modern English)
    Place and Personal Names, I, 47f.
    Syntax, I, 26f.
    Vocabulary, Word-Formation, etc., I, 30f.
Langwith, Benjamin (1684?–1743), II, 580
Lanii Triumphantes (17 cent.), II, **288**

Lankester, Edwin (1814–1874), scientist, II, 962

Lankester, Sir Edwin Ray (1847–1929), III, 955, **958**

La Noue, François de, I, 331, 815

Lanquet (or Lanket), Thomas (1521–1545), I, 824

Lansdowne, George Granville, Baron (1667–1735), II, 21, **438**

Lantern, The (Dublin, 1799), II, 736

Lantern of the Cam, The (1871), III, 835

Lanterne of Light, The (15 cent.), I, 266

Lanzi, J. A., III, 629

La Peña, Juan Antonio de (*fl.* 1623), I, 741

La Pillonière, F. de (*fl.* 1718), II, 792

La Place, Pierre Antoine de, II, 44, 72

La Porte, Ortensia de, Duchesse de Mazarin, II, 785

Lappenberg, J. M., III, 1028

La Primaudaye, Pierre de, I, 331, 379, 815

Lapthorne, Richard (*fl.* 1687–97), II, 135

La Quintinie, Jean de, II, 785

Lar (O.E.), I, **82**

La Ramée, Marie Louise de ('Ouida') (1839–1908), III, 556

La Ramée, Pierre de (Ramus), I, 327f., 680, 800, 881

Larcom, Sir Thomas Aiskew (1801–1879), I, 846

Lardner, Dionysius (1793–1859), III, 827, 938, 941

Lardner, Nathaniel (1684–1768), II, 947

Lark, The (1740), II, 208, 209

Lark, The (1765), II, 223

Lark, The (1768), II, 225

Lark, Etc. Or, English Songster, The (1770), II, 227

Larkin, George (*fl.* 1696), II, 706

Larking, Lambert Blackwell (1797–1868), I, 843; III, 898

Larkins, John P. (*fl.* 1789), II, 751

Larminie, William (1849–1900), III, **1056**

Larmor, Sir Joseph (b. 1857), III, 940f.

La Roberdière, le Sieur de, II, 785

La Roche, Marie Sophie von, II, 141, 806

La Roche, Michel de, II, 672, 675 (3), 688 (2)

La Rochefoucauld, François de, II, 34, 36, 141, 785; III, 22

La Roche-Guilhem, Mlle de, II, 534, 786

La Sale, Antoine, II, 786

Las Casas, Bartolome de, I, 794

Lascelles, Robert (*fl.* 1813), III, 765

Las Coveras, Francisco de, I, 733

La Serre, Jean Louis Ignace de, Sieur de Langlade, II, 786

La Serre, Jean Puget de, II, 795

Lashley's York Miscellany (18 cent.), II, 204

Lassels, Richard (1603?–1668), II, 743

Lassenius, Johannes, II, 55

Lasso de la Vega, Garcia, II, 68

Last and Best Edition of New Songs, The (17 cent.), II, 178

Last & most Exact Edition of New Songs, The (17 cent.), II, 178

Last Will and Testament of P. Rupert, The [etc.] (17 cent.), I, 719

Late Proceedings of the Scottish Army, The (1644), I, 756

Late Will and Testament of the Doctors Commons, The (17 cent.), I, 719

Latest News, The (1869), III, 814

Latey, John (1842–1902), III, 815

Latey, John Lash (*fl.* 1853), III, 815

Latham, Henry (1821–1902), III, 111

Latham, Robert Gordon (1812–1888), I, 17; III, 898, **967**

Latham, Simon (*fl.* 1615–18), I, 394

Lathbury, John (*fl.* 1340), I, **305**

Lathbury, Thomas (1798–1865), II, 850, 875

Lathbury, W. H. (*fl.* 1896), III, 819

Lathcen (d. 661), I, 102

Lathom, Francis (1777–1832), III, **404f.**

Lathum, William (*fl.* 1634), I, 476

Lathy, Thomas Pike (*fl.* 1805–19), III, **405**

Latimer, Hugh (1485?–1555), I, **669**, 682

Latimer, Isaac (*fl.* 1860), III, 802

Latimer, Thomas (*fl.* 1835), III, 803

LATIN

   English writers in, I, 98f. (O.E. period), 115f. (chronicles), 280f. (M.E. period), 326f. (Renaissance), 654f. (university plays, 16, 17 cents.), 859f. (Renaissance scholars); II, 31f. (later 17 cent.)

   Loan-words from, I, 33

   Scholarship, I, 859f. (1500–1660); II, 933f. (1660–1800); III, 993f. (19 cent.)

   Text-books and grammars, I, 374f. (1500–1660); II, 127f. (1660–1800)

   Translations from, I, 799f. (1500–1660); II, 28 (literary criticism); 764f. (1660–1800). For 19 cent. see under particular authors

Latine Songs (17 cent.), II, 179

Latini, Bruno, I, 799

Latocnaye, Henri Marie de Bougrenet de, II, 142, 159

La Tour D'Auvergne, A. de, II, 778

La Tour Landry, G. de (*fl.* 1484), I, 262

Latrobe, Christian Ignatius (1758–1836), III, 1091

Latymer, Francis Burdett Thomas Coutts-Nevill, Baron (1852–1923), III, **345**, 353

Laud, William (1573–1645), I, 680, **698**, 841

Laud Troy-Book (M.E.), I, 32, **145**

Lauder, George (*fl.* 1629), I, 900

Lauder, Sir John, Lord Fountainhall (1646–1722), I, **997f.**

Lauder, Sir Thomas Dick (1784–1848), III, **405**

Lauder, William (1520?–1573), I, 897

Lauder, William (d. 1771), I, 469

Lauderdale, James Maitland, Earl of (1759–1839), III, 973, 978–9
Lauderdale, Richard Maitland, Earl of (1653–1695), II, 768
Laudonnière, René de, I, 788
Laugh and be Fat (1703), II, 186
Laugh and be Fat (1733), II, 203, 209, 216, 220
Laugh and be Fat, Or, The Merry Companion (1795), II, 250
Laugh and grow fat (18 cent.), II, 252
Laughing Mercury, The (1652), I, 761
Laughing Philosopher's Legacy to Dull Mortals, The (18 cent.), II, 254
Laughton, Sir John Knox (1830–1915), III, **924**
Launfal, Sir (M.E.), I, **152**
Lauphier, W. H. (*fl.* 1816), III, 134
Laurence of Durham (d. 1154), I, **285** f.
Laurence of Lindores (d. 1437), I, 302
Laurence of Somercote (*fl.* 1254), I, **300**
Laurence, Edward (d. 1740?), II, 148
Laurence, French (1757–1809), II, **369**, 632
Laurence, T. B. (*fl.* 1866), III, 1068
Laurie, Simon Somerville (1829–1909), III, 111, **869**
Laurie, W. A. (*fl.* 1850), III, 1076
Laurie, W. F. B. (*fl.* 1850), III, 1076
Laval, Étienne Abel, II, 786
Lavater, Johann Kaspar, II, 52
La Vega, Garcilasso de, III, 246
La Verne de Tressan, Abbé de, II, 786
La Vieuville, D'Orville, Adrien de, II, 792
LAW. See LEGAL LITERATURE
Law, Edmund (1703–1787), II, 92, 947
Law, James (*fl.* 1845), III, 807
Law, John, of Lauriston (1671–1729), II, 999
Law, Robert (d. 1690?), II, 996
Law, Thomas Graves (1836–1904), III, **923**
Law, William (1686–1761), II, 109, 118, **858**
Law, William John (1786–1869), III, **999**
Law Chronicle and Estate Advertiser, The (1815), III, 821
Law Gazette, The (1822), III, 821
Law Journal, The (1866), III, 821
Law Magazine and Law Review, The (1856), III, 833
Law Magazine and Review, The (1872), III, 833
Law Magazine, or Quarterly Journal of Jurisprudence, The (1829), III, 833
Law Quarterly Review, The (1885), III, 834
Law Review, and Quarterly Journal of British and Foreign Jurisprudence, The (1845), III, 833
Law Times, The (1843), III, 821
Lawes, Henry (1595–1662), I, 486
Lawless, Emily (1845–1913), III, **1055**
Lawn, Buxton (*fl.* 1801), III, 969
LAWN TENNIS (books on), III, 775
Lawrence, A. (*fl.* 1900), III, 831
Lawrence, F. W., III, 985
Lawrence, Frederick (1821–1867), II, 520

Lawrence, George Alfred (1827–1876), III, **491**
Lawrence, Sir Henry Montgomery L. (1806–1857), III, 1083
Lawrence, Herbert (*fl.* 1769), II, 291, 547 (2)
Lawrence, James (*fl.* 1800), translator of Kotzebue, II, 60
Lawrence, James (*fl.* 1813–28), knight of Malta, III, 131, 583
Lawrence, John (1753–1839), II, 817; III, 765
Lawrence, Leonard (*fl.* 1639), I, 476, 814
Lawrence, Rose (*fl.* 1799), II, 486
Lawrence, T. B. (*fl.* 1869), III, 1067
Lawrence, Sir William (1783–1867), III, 963, 966
Laws of Poetry, The (18 cent.), II, 196
Lawson, E. L. (*fl.* 1890?), III, 799
Lawson, George (d. 1678), I, 878
Lawson, Henry Hertzberg (1867–1922), III, **1095**
Lawson, J. A. (*fl.* 1880), captain, III, 1080
Lawson, James Anthony (1817–1887), Irish judge, III, 982
Lawson, John (d. 1712), II, 753
Lawson, John Parker (d. 1852), I, 903; III, 33
Lawson, W. R. (*fl.* 1885), III, 807
Lawson, William (*fl.* 1618), I, 391, 706
Lawton, C. H. J. (*fl.* 1871), III, 778
Lawton, F. W. (*fl.* 1870), III, 77
Lawyer's and Magistrates' Magazine, The (1790), II, 681, 688
Lawyer's Magazine, The (1761), II, 678
Lawyer's Magazine, The (1773), II, 679
Lay Monastery (1727), II, 661
Lay Monk, The (1713), II, 661
Lay-Folks' Catechism (M.E.), I, **186**
Lay-Folks' Mass-Book (M.E.), I, **184**
Lay-Folks' Prayer-Book (M.E.), I, **186**
Lay of Havelock (M.E.), I, 29, 39, 42, **148** f.
Layamon (*fl.* 1200), I, 32, 39, **163** f.
Layard, Sir Austen Henry (1817–1894), III, 153, **1016**
Laycock, F. N. (*fl.* 1895), III, 978
Laycock, Thomas (1812–1876), III, 965
'Layman, A' (1838), III, 121
Layng, H. (*fl.* 1744–8), II, 810, 814
Lazarillo de Tormes, I, 344, 815
Lea, Arthur Sheridan (*fl.* 1892), III, 964
Leach, Edmund (*fl.* 1653), I, 718
Leach, Frederick (*fl.* 1642–95), I, 753, 760; II, 706
Leach, George Pemberton (*fl.* 1891), III, 987
Leacroft, S. (*fl.* 1785), II, 799
Lead, Jane (1623–1704), II, 859
Leadbeater, Mary (1758–1826), II, 159
Leadbetter, Charles (*fl.* 1728), II, 129
Leader, The (1850), III, 814
Leaf, Walter (1852–1927), III, 155
Leaflet Newspaper, The (1888), III, 818
League, The (1843), III, 817
Leake, John (*fl.* 1696), II, 706

Leake, Stephen Martin (1666–1740), II, 150
Leake, Stephen Martin (fl. 1860–78), III, 985, 987
Leake, William Martin (1777–1860), III, 995
Leakey, Caroline Woolmer (1827–1881), III, 1094
Leakey, E. P. (fl. 1882), III, 1094
Leanerd, John (fl. 1677), II, 424
Leapor, Mary (1722–46), II, 370
Lear, Edward (1812–1888), III, 567, 991
Learmont, John (fl. 1791), II, 972
Leask, William (1812–1884), III, 819
Leathermore, — (fl. 1669), II, 826
Leathley, Mrs (fl. 1860), III, 573
Le Bas, Charles Webb (1779–1861), III, 207
Leblanc, Jean Bernard, II, 34, 141
Le Blanc, Vincent, I, 785
Le Blond, Abraham (1819–1894), III, 91
Le Blond, Robert (1816–1863), III, 91
Le Bone Florence de Rome (M.E.), I, 158
Le Bossu, René, II, 40, 786
Le Bovier de Fontenelle, Bernard, II, 786
le Breton, Philip Henry (fl. 1864), III, 882
Le Cabinet des Fées (18 cent.), II, 566
Le Cène, Charles, II, 786
Le Challeux, Nicholas, I, 786
Lechford, Thomas (fl. 1642), I, 795
Lechler, G. V. (fl. 1841), II, 939
Leckie, Daniel R. (fl. 1800), II, 751
Lecky, William Edward Hartpole (1838–1903), III, 911 f.
Le Clerc, Georges Louis, Comte de Buffon, II, 35, 786
Le Clerc, Jean, II, 33, 787
L'Écluse, Jean de, I, 760; II, 719
Le Comte, Louis, II, 787
Lecount, P. (fl. 1839), III, 679
Le Courayer, Pierre François, II, 787
Ledesma, Antonio Colmenero de, I, 795
Ledger, F. (fl. 1840?), III, 821
Lediard, Thomas (1685–1743), I, 44; II, 542, 745, 878
Ledyard, John (1751–1788), II, 742
Lee, Charles (1731–1782), II, 631
Lee, F. B. (fl. 1771), II, 802
Lee, Francis (1661–1719), II, 848, 859
Lee, George Henry, Earl of Lichfield (1718–1772), II, 337
Lee, Harriett (1757–1851), II, 549, 551; III, 405
Lee, Henry (fl. 1702), D.D., II, 942
Lee, Henry (fl. 1744), translator of Sallust, II, 767
Lee, Henry (1765–1836), author of 'Caleb Quotem', III, 583
'Lee, Holme', i.e. Harriet Parr (1828–1900), III, 491 f.
Lee, J. N. (fl. 1900?), III, 810
Lee, John (1779–1859), I, 354
Lee, Nathaniel (1649?–1692), II, 43, 271, 412 f.
Lee Priory Press, III, 86

Lee, Samuel (1783–1852), III, 122, 1013
Lee, Sir Sidney (1859–1926), III, 1040
Lee, Sophia (1750–1824), II, 548, 552, 770; III, 405 f.
'Lee, Vernon', i.e. Violet Paget (1856–1935), III, 749 f.
Lee, W. (fl. 1861), III, 149
Lee, William (d. 1645), I, 476
Lee-Hamilton, Eugene Jacob (1845–1907), III, 346
Lee-Warner, Sir William (1846–1914), III, 1078
Leech, David (fl. 1628–53), I, 911
Leech, John (fl. 1622), I, 861
Leech, John (1817–1864), III, 91
Leech, Richard (fl. 1849), III, 1074
Leeds
    Grammar School, I, 372
    Magazines, II, 684 (1738–98)
    Newspapers, II, 724 f.
Leeds, Francis Osborne, Duke of (1751–1799), II, 165, 456
Leeds and Yorkshire Mercury (1901), II, 725
Leeds Daily News, The (1872), III, 804
Leeds Intelligencer, The (1754), II, 725
Leeds Magazine, The (1738), II, 684
Leeds Mercury, The (1718), II, 725
Leeds Mercury, The (1861), III, 803
Lees, John (fl. 1768), II, 755
Lees, William Nassau (1825–1889), III, 1077
Lefanu, Alicia (fl. 1812–26), II, 458
Le Fanu, Joseph Sheridan (1814–1873), III, 492
Lefanu, Philip (fl. 1755–90), II, 782
Le Feavre, Amy (fl. 1898), III, 574
Lefebore, Denys ('Syned') (fl. 1907), III, 1089
Lefevre, Charles Shaw —, Viscount Eversley (1794–1888), III, 971
Le Fevre, R., I, 261–2
Lefèvre, T. (fl. 1723), II, 772
Lefroy, Edward Cracroft (1855–1891), III, 346
Leftley, Charles (fl. 1798), II, 486
Legal Literature
    Old English Period, I, 96 f. (O.E. laws)
    Middle English Period, I, 118. See also under Writings in Latin, I, 280 f.
    Renaissance to Restoration, I, 717 f. (17 cent. satires), 847 f. (principal works)
    Restoration to Romantic Revival, II, 96 (trade catalogues), 926 (dictionaries of legal terms), 962 f. (principal works)
    Nineteenth Century, III, 845 (legal year books), 919 f. (legal history), 985 f. (principal writers)
Le Gallienne, Richard (b. 1866), III, 551 f.
Legenda Aurea (15 cent.), I, 266
Legendre, Adrien — Marie, III, 652
Legendre, Louis, II, 787
Legends
    Gloucestershire, I, 40
    Saints, I, 93 (O.E.), 168 f. and 173 f. (M.E.)

Legge, Edward (*fl.* 1876), III, 814
Legge, James (1815–1897), III, **1020**
Legge, Thomas (1535–1607), I, 657
Legh, Gerard (d. 1563), I, 395
Le Gobien, Charles, II, 787
Legouvé, Ernest, III, 598
Legrand, Antoine (d. 1699), I, 879; II, 787
Legrand, J., I, 262
Le Grand, Joachim, II, 787
Le Grand, Marc Antoine, II, 787
Le Grand d'Aussy, Pierre Jean Baptiste, II, 787
Le Grice, Charles Valentine (1773–1858), III, 123, **237**, 634
Le Grys, Sir Robert (d. 1635), I, 811
Leguat, François, II, 788
Lehmann, Rudolf (1819–1905), III, 153
Lehmann, Rudolf Chambers (*fl.* 1889–97), III, 763, 779, 835
Leibniz, Gottfried, Wilhelm von, II, 53
Leibbrandt, H. C. V. (*fl.* 1887), III, 1091
LEICESTER
   Library, I, 362
   Newspapers, II, 725
Leicester and Nottingham Journal, The (1753), II, 725
Leicester Chronicle, The (1792), II, 725
Leicester Daily Express, The (1892), III, 806
Leicester Daily Mail, The (1869), III, 803
Leicester Daily Post, The (1872), III, 804
Leicester Evening News, The (1872), III, 804
Leicester Herald, The (1792), II, 725
Leicester Journal, The (1795), II, 725
Leicester, Records of the Borough of (M.E.), I, 121
Leicester Weekly Express, The (1870), III, 803
LEICESTERSHIRE
   Bibliography, I, 9
Leigh, Edward (1602–1671), I, 777, 855–6, 858; II, 120
Leigh, Henry Sambrooke (1837–1883), III, **346**
Leigh, John (1689–1726), II, **440**
Leigh, N. (*fl.* 1568), I, 665
Leigh, Percival (1813–1889), III, **719**
Leigh, R. Austen (*fl.* 1892), III, 835
Leigh, Richard (b. 1649), II, **283**
Leigh, Sir Samuel Egerton (*fl.* 1797), II, 551
Leigh Hunt's Journal (1850), III, 828
Leigh Hunt's London Journal (1834), III, 818
Leighton, A. (*fl.* 1786), II, 687
Leighton, Alexander (1800–1874), III, 188
Leighton, Robert (1611–1684), I, **698**
Leighton, Robert (1822–1869), III, **294**
Leighton, Sir William (*fl.* 1603–14), I, 476, 485, 679
Leinster Journal, The (1799), II, 737
Leisewitz, Johann Anton, II, 60
Leishman, M. (*fl.* 1851), I, 906
Leishman, Thomas (1825–1904), I, 904
Leisure Hour, The (1852), III, 828
Leisure Hour Improved, The (19 cent.), II, 256

LEITH
   Newspapers, II, 733
Leith Commercial List (1797), II, 719
Leland, John (1506–1552), I, 359, 381, 519, 767, 815, **823**
Leland, John (1691–1766), II, 863, 947
Leland, Thomas (1722–1785), II, 546, 760, **887**
Le Maire, Jacques Joseph, II, 788
Le Marchant, Sir Denis (1795–1874), II, 838
Lémery, Louis, II, 788
Lémery, Nicolas, II, 738, 793
Le Mesurier, Thomas (*fl.* 1795), II, 812
Lemierre, Antoine Marin, II, 788
Lemnius, I, 888 (2)
Lemoine, Henry (1756–1812), II, 823
Le Moine, M. (*fl.* 1785), II, 770
Lemon, Mr — (*fl.* 1782), II, 821
Lemon, Mark (1809–1870), III, 598, **603**
Lemon, Robert (1800–1867), I, 407
Le Monde Élégant, or the World of Fashion (1880), III, 826
Le Morte Arthur (Stanzaic) (M.E.), I, 138
Lemprière, John (1765?–1824), III, 50
Lempriere, William (d. 1834), II, 749
Le Nain de Tillemont, Louis Sébastien, II, 788
Lenclos, Ninon de, II, 788
Le Neve, John (1679–1741), II, 193
Lenfant, Jacques, II, 788
L'Enfant Sage (M.E.), I, **187**
Leng, Sir John (1828–1906), III, 807
Leng, Robert (*fl.* 1587), I, 768
Leng, Sir William Christopher (1825–1902), III, 802
Lenglet du Fresnoy, Nicolas, II, 788
Lennard, Samson (d. 1633), I, 781; II, 775
Lennox, Charlotte (1720–1804), II, **475** f., 544 (2), 545–6, 621 (2), 622 (3), 760, 763, 769, 771, 773, 784
Lennox, John (1794–1853), III, 786
Lennox, Lady Sarah (1745–1826), II, 138
Lennox, Lord William Pitt (1799–1881), III, 152, 766
Le Noble de Tennelière, Eustache, II, 122, 541–2, 788
Le Noir, Elizabeth Anne, née Smart (1755?–1841), II, 339
Lenormand d'Étioles, Jeanne Antoinette, Marquise de Pompadour, II, 788
Lenton, Francis (*fl.* 1630–40), I, 723
Leonard, A. G. (*fl.* 1896), III, 1092
Leonard, Eliza Lucy (*fl.* 1815), III, 571
Leonard, G. S. (*fl.* 1879), III, 1078
Leonard, H. B. (*fl.* 1852), I, 534
Leoni, Giachimo (or James) (1686–1746), II, 807, 812
Leonowens, Anna Harriette (*fl.* 1870), III, 1077
Leopardi, Giacomo, III, **39**, 299
Le Pays, René, Sieur du Plessis Villeneuve, II, 788

Lepell, Mary, Lady Hervey (1700–1768), II, 136

Le Pesant, Pierre, Sieur de Bois-Guillebert, II, 788

Le Petit, Jean François, I, 779

Le Prestre de Vauban, Sébastien, II, 788

Le Prince d'Amour (17 cent.), II, 173, 175

Le Prince de Beaumont, Jeanne-Marie, II, 47, 566, 677, 788

Leprohon, Rosanna Eleanor, née Mullins, III, 1086–7

Leroy, Miss ('Esmé Stuart') (*fl.* 1877), III, 573

Le Roy (Regius), Loys, I, 800

Le Roy, Marin, Sieur de Gomberville, II, 788

Lesage, Alain René, II, 47, 541 (2), 543, 788

Lesage, G. L., II, 140

Le Sage, Sir J. M. (1837–1926), III, 799

Lescarbot, Marc, I, 794

Leslie, Charles (1650–1722), non-juror and controversialist, II, 498 (2), 575, 659 (2), 942, 1001

Leslie, Charles (*fl.* 1740), historian of Jamaica, II, 754

Leslie, Charles Robert (1794–1859), III, 608–9, 704

Leslie, John (1527–1596), I, 774, 905

Leslie, John (1727–1790), of Aberdeen University, II, 1000

Leslie, Sir John (1766–1832), mathematician, III, 937

Leslie, Mary E. (*fl.* 1858), III, 1068

Leslie, Thomas Edward Cliffe (1827?–1882), III, 971, 983

Leslie, W. M. (*fl.* 1891), III, 802

Leslie, William (d. 1654?), I, 908

Lesse, Nicholas (*fl.* 1550), I, 665, 810, 816

Lessing, Gotthold Ephraim, II, 51, 58, 60, 62, 71, 303, 486, 806; III, **33**, 49

Lessius, Leonardus, I, 452

Lester, J. W. (*fl.* 1847), III, 7

L'Estrange, Sir Hamon (1605–1660), I, 796, 840

L'Estrange, Sir Roger (1616–1704), II, 33, 38, 69, 533–4, **567**f., 657, 702 (3), 703, 716

Le Sueur, G. (*fl.* 1913), III, 1090

Lesuire, Robert Martin, II, 789

Le Tans'ur, William (*fl.* 1776), II, 231

Lethbridge, Sir Roper (*fl.* 1882), III, 1084

Leti, Gregorio, II, 811

Le Tourneur, Pierre, II, 72

Letsome, Samuel (*fl.* 1734–53), II, 95

LETTER-WRITERS, II, 120

LETTERS

Anglo-Saxon period. See under WRITINGS IN LATIN, I, 98 f.

Middle English Period, I, 115 f.

Fifteenth Century, I, 265 f. See also for 11 to 15 cents. under WRITINGS IN LATIN, I, **280** f.

Renaissance to Restoration, I, **381** f.

Restoration to Romantic Revival, II, 46 (French-English), **133** f., 156 (Scottish), 158 f. (Irish), **827** f. (Chesterfield, Walpole, etc.)

Nineteenth Century, II, **14** f. (literary), 136 f. (educational), 145 f. (political), 149 f. (miscellaneous)

Letters and Poems In Honour of Margaret, Dutchess of Newcastle (17 cent.), II, 177, 178

Letters from a Moor at London (18 cent.), II, 540

Letters from the Living to the Living (18 cent.) II, 185–6

Letters from the Westminster Journal (1741), II, 663

Letters In Prose and Verse, To Polly Peachum (18 cent.), II, 199

Letters of an Italian Nun and an English Gentleman (18 cent.), II, 548

Letters of Abelard and Eloisa [etc.] (18 cent.), II, 240–1

Letters of Abelard and Heloise (18 cent.), II, 541

Letters of the Critical Club (1738), II, 663

Letters of Wit, Politicks and Morality (18 cent.), II, 185

Letters, Poems, and Tales (18 cent.), II, 194

Letters Supposed to have been Written by Yorick and Eliza (18 cent.), II, 548

Lettice, John (1737–1832), II, 157

Lettsom, William Nanson (1796–1865), III, 1028

Leuins, P. (*fl.* 1570), I, 375

Leunclavius, J., I, 781

Leuwenhock, Antonius van, II, 365

Le Vassor, Michel, II, 789

Le Vayer, François de la Mothe, II, 785

Le Vayer de Boutigny, Rolland, II, 534, 789

Lever, Charles James (1806–1872), III, **492** f.

Lever, Christopher (*fl.* 1627), I, 476

Lever, Ralph (d. 1585), I, 873

Lever, Thomas (1521–1577), I, 682

Leveridge, Richard (1670?–1758), II, 183–4, 198

Leverson, M. R. (*fl.* 1854), III, 94

Leveson-Gower, Lord Granville (1773–1846), II, 138, 165

Lévesque de Burigny, Jean, II, 789

Lévesque de Pouilly, Louis Jean, II, 789

Levett, Christopher (*fl.* 1623–8), I, 792

Levett, John (*fl.* 1634), I, 893

Levi, Leone (1821–1888), III, 979

Levis, Pierre Marc Gaston, Duc de, II, 142

Levitt, William (*fl.* 1647), I, 720

Levy, Amy (1861–1889), III, **346**

Levy, Joseph Moses (1812–1888), III, 786

LEWES

Newspapers, II, 725

Lewes, George Henry (1817–1878), III, 644, 814, 829–30, **869** f.

Articles and reviews by, III, 70, 161, 383, 464, 636

Lewicke, Edward (*fl.* 1562), I, 437
Lewin, T. H. (*fl.* 1873-85), III, 1072, 1078
Lewin, Thomas (1805–1877), III, 987
Lewis, D. (*fl.* 1841), I, 702
Lewis, David (1683?–1760), II, 198, 200
Lewis, Sir George Cornewall (1806–1863), III, 832, 944, 975, 981, 999f.
Lewis, Harold (*fl.* 1860?), III, 802
Lewis, John (1675–1747), I, 774; II, 880, 910, 929
Lewis, Leopold David (1828–1890), III, 603
Lewis, Lady Maria Theresa (1803–1865), III, 149
Lewis, Matthew Gregory (1775–1818), III, 25, 41, 406f., 587
Lewis, R. (*fl.* 1787), II, 159
Lewis, Stephen (*fl.* 1715), II, 29
Lewis, Thomas (1689–1749?), II, 662
Lewis, Thomas Taylor (1801–1858), I, 386
Lewis, William (1787–1870), II, 826
Lewis, William David (*fl.* 1843), III, 987
Lewis, William Lillington (*fl.* 1767), II, 768
Lewkenor, Sir Lewis (*fl.* 1599), I, 812
Leybourn, William (1626–1700?), I, 881; II, 129
Leyden, John (1775–1811), I, 902; II, 157; III, 237
Leyden Glossary (O.E.), I, 35
Leyden Riddle (O.E.), I, 37
L'Héritier, L. F., III, 677
L'Hôpital, Guillaume François Antoine de, Marquis de Sainte-Mesme, II, 789
Libeaus Desconus (M.E.), I, 134
Libelle of Englyshe Polycye, The (15 cent.), I, 117, 264
Liber Cure Cocorum (15 cent.), I, 43
Liber Exemplorum ad usum praedicantium (M.E.), I, 301
Liber Metricus de Henrico Quinto (15 cent.), I, 265
Liber Vitae (O.E.), I, 35, 36
Liberal, The (1829), III, 812
'Liberal, Lady Letitia' (1810), III, 111
Liberal or, Verse and Prose from the South, The (1822), III, 832
LIBERAL THEOLOGY, III, 846f.
Liberalitie and Prodigalitie, A Pleasant Comedie (16 cent.), I, 516
LIBRARIANSHIP, III, 105f.
LIBRARIES, III, 104f.
    Catalogues, I, 4f., 360f. (15–17 cents.); II, 102f. (17, 18 cents.)
    Circulating libraries, II, 99 (18 cent.); III, 102 (19 cent.)
Library Circular, The (1862), III, 101
Library of Anglo-Catholic Theology, The (19 cent.), III, 856
Library; Or, Moral and Critical Magazine, The (1761), II, 678
Lichfield, George Henry Lee, Earl of (1718–1772), II, 337

Lichfield, Nicholas (*fl.* 1582), I, 782
Lichfield, William (d. 1447), I, 264
Lichfild, Henry (*fl.* 1613), I, 486
Lichtenberg, Georg Christoph, II, 51, 138, 141, 160
Liddell, Christina Catherine Fraser, née Tytler (b. 1848), III, 360f.
Liddell, Henry George (1811–1898), III, 1000
Liddon, Henry Parry (1829–1890), III, 856, 858f.
Lidgett, John Scott (b. 1854), III, 851
Liébault, Jean, I, 706
Lieven, Doroteya Khristoforovna, Princess, III, 144
Life (1879), III, 814
Life, Adventures, and History of Miss Moreton, The (18 cent.), II, 549
Life and Adventures of a Cat, The (18 cent.), II, 545
Life and Adventures of a Fly, The (18 cent.), II, 563
Life and Adventures of Bampfylde-Moore-Carew, The (18 cent.), II, 544
Life and Adventures of Capt. John Avery, The (18 cent.), II, 536
Life and Death of Jacke Straw, The (16 cent.), I, 538
Life and Opinions of Bertram Montfichet, The (18 cent.), II, 545
Life and Opinions of Miss Sukey Shandy of Bow Street, The (18 cent.), II, 545
Life in London (1822), III, 811
Life of St Ursula, Guiscard and Sigismund, The (15 cent.), I, 266
Light (1876), III, 814
Light, A. W. (*fl.* 1830), III, 975
Light Blue, The (1866), III, 834
Light Blue Incorporated with the Light Green, The (1873), III, 835
Light Green, The [Cambridge] (1872), III, 835
Light Greens [Cambridge] (1875), III, 835
LIGHT VERSE, III, 159
Lightfoot, John (1602–1675), I, 681, 856
Lightfoot, Joseph Barber (1828–1889), III, 848, 1013
Lighthall, William Douw (*fl.* 1889), III, 1085
Ligon, Richard (*fl.* 1657), I, 796
Lille, Jacques de, II, 789
Lillie, Arthur (*fl.* 1897), III, 775
Lillie, Charles (*fl.* 1725), II, 198
Lillie, John (*fl.* 1844), III, 819
Lilliputian History, The (18 cent.), II, 563
Lilliputian Magazine, The (18 cent.), II, 564
Lilliputian Story Teller, The (18 cent.), II, 564
Lillo, George (1693–1739), II, 43, 61, 70, 440
Lilly, John (*fl.* 1710), II, 964
Lilly, William (d. 1522), II, 128
Lilly, William (1602–1681), I, 386, 840, 884; II, 808
Lillywhite, Frederick (d. 1866), III, 773–4

Lillywhite, James (*fl.* 1872–1900), III, 773
Lillywhite, John (d. 1874), III, 773
Lily, William (1468?–1522), I, 374
LIMERICK
  Magazines, II, 668 (1751–90)
  Newspapers, II, 738
  Printing, II, 90
Limerick Chronicle, The (1768), II, 738
Limerick Chronicle, The (1795), II, 738
Limerick Herald, The (1787), II, 738
Limerick Herald and Munster Advertiser, The (1788), II, 738
Limerick Journal, The (1739), II, 738
Limerick Journal, The (1779), II, 738
Limerick Magazine, The (1752), II, 688
Limerick Weekly Magazine; Or, Miscellaneous Repository, The (1790), II, 688
Linacre, Thomas (1460?–1524), I, 374, **664**, 882, 887
Linche (or Lynche), Richard (*fl.* 1596–1601), I, **433**
LINCOLN
  Newspapers, II, 725
Lincoln Diocesan Documents (15–16 cents.), I, 46
Lincoln Gazette; Or, Weekly Intelligencer, The (1729), II, 725
Lincoln, Rutland and Stamford Gazette, The (1793), II, 729
Lincoln, Rutland and Stamford Mercury, The (1784), II, 729
LINCOLNSHIRE
  Bibliography, I, 8
Lincolnshire Domesday, The (M.E.), I, 121
Lind, James (1716–1794), II, 746
Lindesay, Patrick (d. 1753), II, 998
Lindley, A. F. (*fl.* 1873), III, 1092
Lindley, John (1799–1865), III, 821, 951, **960**
Lindley, Nathaniel, Baron (1828–1921), III, 987
Lindsay, Alexander (*fl.* 1546), I, 773
Lindsay, Alexander William Crawford, Earl of Crawford and Balcarres (1812–1880), I, 898
Lindsay, Sir David (1490?–1555), I, 514, **897f.**
Lindsay, John (*fl.* 1758), II, 749
Lindsay, Patrick (d. 1753). See Lindesay
Lindsay, Robert (1500?–1565?), of Pitscottie, I, 905
Lindsay, Robert (*fl.* 1725), II, 591
Lindsay, Thomas Martin (1843–1914), III, 851
Lindsay, William Lander (1829–1880), III, 961
Lindsell, W. H. B. (*fl.* 1889), III, 986
Lindsey, Theophilus (1723–1808), II, 862
Ling, Nicholas (*fl.* 16 cent.), I, 352
Lingard, G. (1810), I, 56. A misprint for John Lingard
Lingard, John (1771–1851), III, **879f.**
Lingard (or Lyngard), Richard (1598?–1670), II, 122
Lingen, William (*fl.* 1705), II, 734
Lingham, John (*fl.* 1584), I, 738

Linguet, Simon Nicolas Henri, II, 789
Link, The (1888), III, 818
Linley, George (1798–1865), III, 711
Linnet, The (1749), II, 213
Linnet: A collection of an Hundred and Thirty Choice Songs, The (1792), II, 247
Linnet or Chearful Companion, The (1783), II, 237
Linnets, The (18 cent.), II, 232
Linschoten, Jan Huighen van, I, 782
Linton, Eliza Lynn, née Lynn (1822–1898), III, **493f.**, 640
Linton, William James (1812–1898), III, **294f.**, 817, 828, 977
Linwood, William (1817–1878), III, **1000**
Lion, The (1828), III, 816
Lion University Magazine, The (1858), III, 834
Lipscomb, George (1773–1846), III, **902**
Lipscomb, William (1754–1842), I, 210
Lisander or the Souldier of Fortune (17 cent.), II, 530
Lisboa, Diego Fernandes, I, 344
Lisieux, Zacharie de ('Louis Fontaines'), II, 781
Lisle (or L'Isle), William (1569?–1637), I, 91, 802, 809, 818
Lisle de la Drévetière, Louis François, II, 41, 789
Lister, Harriet (*fl.* 1834), III, 494
Lister, Joseph (1627–1709), I, 387
Lister, Joseph, Baron (1827–1912), III, 963
Lister, Martin (1638?–1712), II, 744
Lister, T., Baron Ribblesdale (1854–1925), III, 761
Lister, Thomas Henry (1800–1842), III, 494
LISTS OF BOOKS. See BIBLIOGRAPHIES and CATALOGUES
Litohfield, R. B. (*fl.* 1859), III, 117
Literary Annals; or, the Reviewers Reviewed (1765), II, 679
Literary Chronicle and Weekly Review, The (1823), III, 818
Literary Courier of Grub-Street, The (1738), II, 714
Literary Examiner, The (1823), III, 818
Literary Fly, The (1779), II, 665
Literary Garland (1838), III, 1088
Literary Gazette, The (1817), III, 818
Literary Gazette, The (1865), III, 101
LITERARY HISTORIANS AND ANTIQUARIES, II, 892f. (1660–1800); III, 1021f. (19 cent.)
LITERARY HISTORIES (general)
  All periods, I, 9f.
  Anglo-Saxon period, I, 53f.
  Middle English period, I, 113f.
  Renaissance to Restoration, I, 319f.
  Restoration to Romantic Revival, II, 4f. See also II, **892f.**
  Nineteenth Century, III, 4f.

LITERARY HISTORIES (special)
Criticism, I, 867f. (16, 17 cents.); II, 9f. (1660–1800)
Drama, I, 274f. (M.E.), 492f. (16, 17 cents.); II, 393f. (17, 18 cents.); III, 581f. (19 cent.)
English Bible, I, 672f.
Journalism, I, 745f. (17 cent.); II, 689f. (1660–1800); III, 779f. (19 cent.)
Language, I, 24f., 30
Latin writings, 98f. (6–11 cents.), 280f. (12–15 cents.)
Law, I, 847f.
Miscellaneous, III, 4f. (19 cent.)
Philosophy, I, 868 (16, 17 cents.); II, 939f. (1660–1800); III, 861f. (19 cent.)
Poetry, I, 60f. (O.E.), 406f. (16, 17 cents.); II, 169 (17, 18 cents.); III, 156f. (19 cent.)
Prose fiction, I, 726f. (16, 17 cents.); II, 488f. (1660–1800); III, 364f. (19 cent.)
Religious writings, I, 664, 679f. (16 cent.), 694 (17 cent.); II, 845f. (1660–1800)
Romances (M.E.), I, 128f.
Scholarship, I, 852f. (17 cent.)
Science, I, 879f. (16, 17 cents.)
Scottish literature, I, 10 (general), 255 (Middle Scots), 895 (1500–1660); II, 966f.
Translations into English, I, 820f. (16, 17 cents.); II, 758f. (1660–1800)
Travel books, I, 796f. (16, 17 cents.); II, 739f. (1660–1800)
Literary Journal, A (1730), II, 675
Literary Journal, The (1744), II, 687
Literary Journal, The (1803), III, 824
Literary Journal, The (1818), III, 818
Literary Leisure; or, The Recreations of Solomon Saunter, Esq. (1799), II, 667
Literary Magazine, The (1735), II, 675
Literary Magazine, The (1756), II, 673
Literary Magazine and British Review, The (1788), II, 681
Literary Magazine; Or, Select British Library, The (1735), II, 677
Literary Magazine; Or, Universal Review, The (1756), II, 678
Literary Mirror, The (1793), II, 687
Literary Miscellany, The (1756), II, 678
Literary Miscellany, The (1799), II, 254
Literary Miscellany, The (1800), II, 685
LITERARY MOVEMENTS AND IDEAS, I, 321f. (16, 17 cents.); II, 5f. (17, 18 cents.), 171f. (poetry, 17, 18 cents.), 395f. (drama, 1660–1800); III, 6f. (19 cent.), 46f., 157f. (poetry, 19 cent.)
Literary Museum, The (18 cent.), II, 247
Literary Museum; A Weekly Magazine, The (1793), II, 688
Literary Panorama, The (1806), III, 824
Literary Panorama and National Register, The (1814), III, 824f.

Literary Register, The (1769), II, 685
LITERARY RELATIONS WITH CONTINENT, I, 216f. (Chaucer), 325f. (1500–1660); II, 31f. (1660–1800); III, 17f. (19 cent.)
Literary Review and Political Journal, The (1794), II, 682
LITERARY REVIEWS, II, 674f. (1679–1800); III, 818 (19 cent. weeklies)
LITERARY THEORY. See CRITICISM (LITERARY)
Literature (1897), III, 818
Lithgow, William (1582–1645?), I, 783, 900
Lithographer, The (1870), III, 88
Little, Clemens (d. 1580), I, 363
Little, Richard (fl. 1645), I, 757
Little Child's Picture Magazine, The (1859), III, 577
Little Female Orators, The (18 cent.), II, 562
Little Folks (1871), III, 578
Little Master's Miscellany (18 cent.), II, 561
Little Review; Or, An Inquisition of Scandal, The (1705), II, 659
Little Songs for me to Sing (19 cent.), III, 575
Little Times, The (1867), III, 801
Little Warbler of the Cottage, The (19 cent.), III, 575
Littlebury, Isaac (fl. 1699–1709), II, 535, 760
Littledale, Sir Joseph (1767–1842), I, 408, 431
Littledale, Richard Frederick (1833–1890), I, 473; III, 301
Littleton, Adam (1627–1694), II, 128, 936
'Littleton, Master Tommy' (1771), II, 562
LITURGICAL BOOKS
Latin (Irish), I, 101 (5–7 cents.)
LITURGICAL DRAMA (M.E.), I, 274f.
Lively Character of the Malignant Partie, The (17 cent.), I, 724
Lively Jester, The (19 cent.), II, 256
LIVERPOOL
Magazines, II, 684f. (1797–1800)
Newspapers, II, 725
Printing and bookselling, II, 87
Liverpool, Robert Banks Jenkinson, Earl of (1770–1828), III, 973
Liverpool Advertiser, The (1756), II, 725
Liverpool and Bootle Evening Times, The (1884), III, 805
Liverpool and Lancaster Herald, The (1788), II, 725
Liverpool and Southport Daily News, The (1877), III, 803
Liverpool Chronicle and Marine Gazetteer, The (1757), II, 725
Liverpool Courant, The (1712), II, 725
Liverpool Courier, The (1808), III, 793
Liverpool Daily Albion, The (1871), III, 804
Liverpool Daily Mail, The (1857), III, 802
Liverpool Daily Post, The (1879), III, 793, 802
Liverpool Echo, The (1879), III, 805
Liverpool Evening Mercury, The (1861), III, 803

Liverpool Journal of Commerce, The (1861), III, 803
Liverpool Mercury, The (1858), III, 802
Liverpool Phoenix, The (1790), II, 725
Liverpool Post, The, III, 793
Liverpool Songster, The (18 cent.), II, 236–7
Liverpool Times, The (1829), II, 725
Liverpool Trade List, The (1794), II, 719
Liverpool Weekly Herald, The (1792), II, 725
Lives of the most Famous English Poets, The (17 cent.), II, 180
Lives of Women Saints, The (17 cent.), I, 684
Living World, The (1750), II, 677
Livingston, Peter (fl. 1855), III, 714
Livingston, William (fl. 1753), II, 754
Livingstone, Charles (1821–1873), III, 991
Livingstone, David (1813–1873), III, 1091
Livingstone, John (1603–1672), II, 924, 993
Livingstone, Michael (fl. 1680), II, 968 f.
Livingstone, Thomas (fl. 1440), I, 302
Livy, I, 803; II, 766
Ll., O. (fl. 1653), I, 845
Lloyd, Charles (1735–1773), secretary to George Grenville, II, 632
Lloyd, Charles (1775–1839), poet, III, 237 f.
Lloyd, David (1635–1692), II, 763, 871
Lloyd, Edward (fl. 1696–1726), II, 706, 718, 775
Lloyd, Edward (1818–1890), III, 438, 441 (2), 442, 812
Lloyd, Evan (1734–1776), II, 370
Lloyd, G. (fl. 1815), III, 764
Lloyd, Hannibal Evans (1771–1847), II, 59, 805; III, 818
Lloyd, Henry (fl. 1771), II, 959
Lloyd, Humphrey (1800–1881), III, 938
Lloyd, J. (fl. 1862), I, 420
Lloyd, John (fl. 1780), II, 159
Lloyd, L. (fl. 1879), III, 830
Lloyd, R. (fl. 1832), I, 825
Lloyd, Richard (fl. 1653), I, 376
Lloyd, Robert (1733–1764), II, 59, 340, 370, 552, 678
Lloyd, T. A. (fl. 1794), II, 950
Lloyd, Sir W. (fl. 1840), III, 1080
Lloyd, W. (fl. 1890), III, 1084
Lloyd, William Watkiss (1813–1893), I, 549
Lloyd, William (1627–1717), II, 936
Lloyd, William Forster (1794–1852), III, 975, 981
Lloyd's Evening Post and British Chronicle (1757), III, 809
Lloyd's Illustrated London Newspaper (1842), III, 812, 815
Lloyd's List (1726), II, 718
Lloyd's London Magazine (1882), III, 830
Lloyd's Magazine (1895), III, 830
Lloyd's Magazine, with which is incorporated The Poet's Magazine (1879), III, 830
Lloyd's Monthly Volume of Amusing and Instructive Literature (1845), III, 828

Lloyd's News (1696), II, 692, 706
Lloyd's Penny Sunday Times (1843), III, 812
Lloyd's Quarterly Magazine (1886), III, 830
Lloyd's Register (1764), II, 698
Lloyd's Register of British and Foreign Shipping (1834), II, 718
Lloyd's Register of Shipping (1730), II, 718
Lloyd's Weekly News (1842), III, 793
Lloyd's Weekly Newspaper (1843), III, 812
Lloyd's Weekly Volume of Amusing Literature (1847), III, 828
Lluelyn, Martin (1616–1681), I, 477, 829
Llwyd, Humphrey (1527–1568), I, 774, 802, 815, 825, 888
Llwyd, Morgan (1619–1659), II, 859
Loan-Words, I, 33 f.
Lobeira, Vasco, III, 181
Local History, I, 823 f. (1500–1660); II, 864 f. (1660–1800, minor writers, 879–81, 890–2); III, 877 f. (19 cent., minor writers, 882–6, 902–6, 927–30)
Locher, Jacob, I, 411
Lock, David (d. 1780), II, 157
Lock, Thomas (fl. 1653), I, 762 (2)
Lock, W. (fl. 1889), III, 851
Locke, Sir C. S. (fl. 1890), III, 976
Locke, James (fl. 1860), III, 770
Locke, John (1632–1704), II, 38, 53, 55, 65, 109, 759, 940 f.
Locker, Algernon (fl. 1895), III, 798, 800
Locker, Arthur (1828–1893), III, 809, 815
Locker, John (1693–1760), II, 911
Locker-Lampson, Frederick (1821–1895), III, 295 f.
Lockhart, George (1673–1731), II, 876
Lockhart, John Gibson (1794–1854), II, 985; III, 369, 373, 676
    Reviews and articles by, II, 528; III, 207, 223, 257, 302, 308, 393, 400, 419, 423, 497, 677
Lockman, John (1698–1771), II, 29, 399, 542, 764, 774, 782, 784 (2), 789, 794, 803
Lockroy, Joseph-Philippe Simon, III, 593
Lockyer, Charles (fl. 1711), II, 750
Lockyer, Sir Joseph Norman (1836–1920), III, 821, 944, 948
Locrine, The Lamentable Tragedie of (16 cent.), I, 579
Loddell, Robert (fl. 1867), III, 771
Loder, R. (fl. 1786), I, 387
Lodge, Edmund (1756–1839), I, 397; II, 871
Lodge, John (d. 1774), I, 837
Lodge, Thomas (1557–8?–1625), I, 527 f., 729, 803, 815, 818, 845, 864, 889
Lodwick, Charles (fl. 1692), II, 752
Lofft, Capel, the elder (1751–1824), I, 466; II, 85, 257, 635, 917; III, 227
Lofft, Capel, the younger (1806–1873), III, 296
Loftus, Smyth (fl. 1778), II, 883
Logan, George (1678–1755), II, 1000 f.

Logan, John (1748–1788), II, **370**
Logan, W. H. (*fl.* 1835), II, 404
Logan, William (*fl.* 1745), II, 754
Loggan, David (1635–1700?), II, 153–4
Logic, Ontology and the Art of Poetry (18 cent.), II, 232
Loiterer, The (1789), II, 666
Lok, Henry (1553–1608), I, 430, 678
Lom d'Arce, Louis Armand de, Baron de Lahontan, II, 789
Lomazzo, Giovanni Paolo, I, 815
LONDON
  Dialect (M.E.), I, 38
  Libraries, II, 103 f.
  Life in, I, 389 (16, 17 cents.); 145 f. (17, 18 cents.)
  Magazines, II, 676 f. (1731–1800)
  Newspapers, II, 700 f. (1660–1800); III, 798 f., 809 f. (19 cent.)
  Printers and Booksellers of, I, 351 f. (16, 17 cents.); II, 99 f. (17, 18 cents.)
  Stage and theatres, II, 403 f. (17, 18 cents.)
  Texts (M.E.), I, 41
  University, III, 125 f., 836 (magazines)
London, William (*fl.* 1658), I, 358 f., 855
London Acting Drama, The (19 cent.), III, 585
London Advertiser and Literary Gazette, The (1751), II, 709
London and Country Journal; With the History of the Old and New Testament, The (1739), II, 714
London and Dublin Magazine, The (1734), II, 687
London and Edinburgh Philosophical Magazine, The (1832), II, 683
London and Edinburgh Philosophical Magazine and Journal of Science, The (1832), III, 824
London and Edinburgh Polite Songster, The (18 cent.), II, 222
London and Liverpool Advertiser, The (1847), III, 799
London and Provincial Sunday Gazette, The (1808), III, 811
London and Westminster Review, The (1836), III, 832
London Chaunticleres, The (17 cent.), I, 652
London Chronicle, The (1757), II, 698
London Chronicle, The (Dublin, 1758), II, 735
London Chronicle (1760), II, 664
London Chronicle; Or, Universal Evening Post, The (1757), II, 710
London, Chronicles of (M.E. and 15 cent.), I, 115
London Commercial Record, The (1844), III, 820
London Complete Songster, The, II, 244
London Courant, The (1688), II, 704
London Courant, The (1745), II, 708 (2)
London Courant (1779), II, 665
London Courant and Daily Advertiser, The (1782), II, 708 (2)

London Courant and Westminster Chronicle, The (1779), II, 708
London Courant, Noon Gazette and Daily Advertiser, The (1782), II, 708
London Courant; Or, New Advertiser, The (1747), II, 708
London Courant, Westminster Chronicle and Daily Advertiser, The (1781), II, 708
London Courant, Westminster Chronicle and Daily Advertiser, The (1782), II, 708
London Customs Bill of Entry, The (1839), II, 718
London Daily Advertiser, The (1751), II, 709
London Daily Advertiser and Literary Gazette, The (1751), II, 709
London Daily Chronicle and Clerkenwell News, The (1871), III, 799
London Daily Post and General Advertiser, The (1734), II, 708
London Daily Recorder, The (1871), III, 799
London Daily Reporter, The (1869), III, 799
London Dispatch, The (1836), III, 816
London Dispatch, The (1856), III, 813
London Drollery (17 cent.), II, 176
London, Edinburgh and Dublin Philosophical Magazine, The (1832), III, 824
London, Edinburgh and Dublin Philosophical Magazine, The (1851), II, 683
London Entertaining Magazine, The (1845), III, 828
London Entr'acte, The (1869), III, 821
London Evening Post, The (1727), II, 710
London Figaro, The (1870), III, 801
London Financial Guide, The (1888), III, 800
London Gazette, The (1666), II, 698, 702, 720
London Gazette, The (1689), II, 731
London Gazetteer, The (1748), II, 698, 708
London General Advertiser, The (1865), III, 799
London Halfpenny Newspaper, The (1861), III, 813
London Herald and Evening Post, The (1796), II, 711
London Imported (1683), II, 718
London Intelligence, The (1689), II, 705
London Iron Trade Exchange (1874), III, 822
London Journal, The (1719), II, 698, 713
London Journal (1726), II, 663
London Journal, The (1836), III, 813
London Journal and British Journal (1720), II, 662
London Journal and British Journal (1725), II, 662
London Journal and Country Craftsman, The (1743), II, 715
London Lampoon'd Formerly in the Jacobite's Songs (18 cent.), II, 186
London Magazine, The (1732), II, 673
London Magazine (1773), II, 665
London Magazine (1777), II, 665

London Magazine, The (1820), III, 825f.
London Magazine and Monthly Chronicler, The (1741), II, 687
London Magazine; And Monthly Chronologer, The (1736), II, 677
London Magazine; Improved and Enlarged, The (1783), II, 677
London Magazine; Or, Gentleman's Monthly Intelligencer, The (1732), II, 677
London Medical and Physical Journal, The (1815), II, 683
London Medical Journal, The (1781), II, 680
London Medical Review and Magazine, The (1799), II, 683
London Medley, The (18 cent.), II, 201
London Medley: Or, The Humours of the Present Age, The (18 cent.), II, 202
London, Memorials of (M.E.), I, 121
London Mercantile Journal, The (1830), III, 820
London Mercury, The (1669), II, 702
London Mercury, The (1682), II, 704
London Mercury, The (1692), II, 658
London Mercury, The (1780), II, 684
London Mercury, The (1781), II, 235
London Mercury, The (1836), III, 812
London Mercury; Or, Great Britain's Weekly Journal, The (1719), II, 713
London Mercury; Or, Great Britain's Weekly Journal, The (1721), II, 713
London Mercury; Or, Mercure de Londres, The (1696), II, 711, 719
London Mercury; Or, Moderate Intelligencer, The (1688), II, 704
London Mercury; Or, The Orange Intelligence, The (1689), II, 705
London Mercury, Published for Promoting Trade, The (1695), II, 717
London Miscellany, The (18 cent.), II, 200
London Monthly Review, The (1787), II, 681
London Morning (1898), III, 800
London Morning Advertiser, The (1741), II, 707
London Morning Advertiser, The (1742), II, 707-8
London Morning Penny Advertiser, The (1742), II, 708
London Morning Penny Post, The (1751), II, 708
London Museum, The (1770), II, 673
London Museum of Politics, The (1770), II, 679
London Musical Museum, The (18 cent.), II, 254
London New Price Courant, The (1814), II, 718
London Newsletter, with Foreign and Domestick Occurrences, The (1695), II, 706
London Packet, The (1769), II, 711
London Packet, The (1770), II, 698
London Packet (1775), II, 665
London Packet and General Hue and Cry, The (1772), II, 711
London Packet; or, New Evening Post, The (1771), II, 711

London Packet, or New Lloyd's Evening Post (1769), II, 809
London Packet; or, New Lloyd's Evening Post, The (1772), II, 711 (2)
London Packet; or, New Lloyd's Evening Post, The (1776), II, 711
London Phalanx, The (1841), III, 817
London Pioneer, The (1846), III, 813
London Polite Songster, The (18 cent.), II, 222
London Post, The (1644), I, 756
London Post, The (1646), I, 757
London Post, The (1705), II, 706
London Post, The (1715), II, 712
London Post; Or, The Tradesman's Intelligence, The (1717), II, 707
London Post, With Intelligence Foreign and Domestick, The (1699), II, 706
London Post; with the Best Account of the whole week's News, The, (1715), II, 712
London Post, with the Newest Intelligence both Foreign and Domestick, The (1697), II, 706
London Press Journal, The (1858), III, 88
London Price Current, The (1776), II, 718
London Printers' Circular, The (1890), III, 781
London Prodigall, The (17 cent.), I, 579
London, Provincial, and Colonial Press News (1866), III, 782
London Quarterly Review, The (1853), III, 833
London Recorder, The (1783), III, 810
London Recorder and Sunday Reformer, The (1796), III, 810
London Recorder, Or Sunday Gazette, The (1783), II, 716
London Register; Or, Historical Notes of the Present Times, The (1762), II, 678
London Review, The (1809), III, 825
London Review, The (1834), III, 833
London Review and Weekly Journal, The (1860), III, 814
London Review of English and Foreign Literature, The (1775), II, 679
London Slip of News, Both Foreign and Domestick, The (1699), II, 706
London Songster, The (18 cent.), II, 224-5, 229-30, 237 (2), 241
London Songster; Or, Vocal Companion, The (1799), II, 254
London Spy, The (1698), II, 658
London Spy and Read's Weekly Journal, The (1761), II, 712
London Spy Reviv'd, The (1736), II, 707
London Stage, The (19 cent.), III, 585
London Student, The (1868), III, 836
London Students' Gazette, The (1872), III, 836
London Telegraph, The (1848), III, 799
London Terrae Filius, The (1707), II, 660
London Theatre, The (19 cent.), II, 392
London University Chronicle, The (1830), III, 836
London University College Magazine, The (1849), III, 836

London University Inquirer, The (1833), III, 836
London University Magazine, The (1829), III, 836
London University Magazine, The (1842), III, 836
London University Magazine, The (1856), III, 836
London Weekly Gazette, The (1822), III, 813
London Weekly Times, The (1836), III, 812
London-Apprentices Grand Politick Informer, The (1660), II, 701
LONDONDERRY
  Newspapers, II, 738
Londonderry, Charles William Stewart, Marquis of (1778–1854), III, 150
Londonderry Journal and Donegal and Tyrone Advertiser, The (1793), II, 738
Londonderry Journal and General Advertiser, The (1772), II, 738
Londonienses, Annales (M.E.), I, 115
Londons Diurnal (1660), II, 701
Londons Intelligencer (1660), II, 702
Long, Dr — (*fl.* 1757), II, 877
Long, Edward (1734–1813), II, 545, 756
Long, George (1800–1879), III, **1000**
Long, James (1814–1887), III, 1072
Long, John (*fl.* 1791), II, 757
Long, Kingsmill (*fl.* 1625), I, 810
Long, Roger (1680–1770), II, 887
Long Meg of Westminster (16 cent.), I, 714
Long Meg of Westminster, The Life and Pranks of (16 cent.), I, 729
Longe, F. D. (*fl.* 1866), III, 983
Longfield, Mountifort (1802–1884), III, 975, 981
Longinus, I, 804; II, 27
Longland, John (1473–1547), I, 683
Longleat Papers (17 cent.), I, 382
Longman, Charles J. (*fl.* 1894), III, 775
Longman, William (1813–1877), I, 117
Longman's Magazine (1882), III, 831
LONGMANS, GREEN & CO., III, 99
Longstaffe, W. H. D. (*fl.* 1867), I, 387
Longueville, Peter (*fl.* 1727), II, 539
Longus, I, 804; II, 761
Lonicerus, Philippus, I, 778
Lonnergan, A. (*fl.* 1771), II, 823
Lonsdale, Henry (1816–1876), II, 354; III, 170
Look about you (16 cent.), I, 538
Looker-On, The (1792), II, 666
Looking-Glasse for Lawyers, A (17 cent.), I, 717
Lord, E. (*fl.* 1841), III, 111
Lord, Henry (*fl.* 1630), I, 785
Lord, W. B. (*fl.* 1859), III, 770
Lord Chesterfield's Witticisms (18 cent.), II, 229
Lord's Munster Herald; Or General Advertiser (1788), II, 737
Loredano, Giovanni Francesco, I, 733; II, 811
Lorimer, James (1818–1890), III, 121 f.
Lorimer, Peter (1812–1879), I, 901
Lorimer, William (*fl.* 1682), II, 778
Lorleach, — (*fl.* 1740), II, 303
Lorrain, Paul (d. 1719), II, 155, 781

Loseley Manuscripts, The (16 and 17 cents.), I, 382
Losh, James (*fl.* 1798), II, 685
Lossius, Caspar Friedrich, III, 576
Lottery Magazine; Or, Compleat Fund of Literary, Political and Commercial Knowledge, The (1776), II, 680
Loudon, Jane (1807–1858), III, 828
Loudon, John Claudius (1783–1843), III, 826 (2), 827, **959**, 970
Lough, T. (*fl.* 1897), III, 979
LOUGHREA
  Newspapers, II, 738
Loughton, William (*fl.* 1734), II, 931
Lounger, The (1785), II, 666
Lounger's Miscellany, The (1788), II, 666
Louvet de Couvray, Jean Baptiste, II, 789
Love, C. (*fl.* 1792), II, 783
Love, Christopher (1618–1651), I, **698**
Love, David (1750–1827), II, 140
Love, James, earlier Dance (1722–1774), II, 447, 825
Love, John (1695–1750), II, 128
Love and Beauty (18 cent.), II, 226
Love at First Sight (17 cent.), II, 209
Love at First Sight (18 cent.), II, 214, 215
Love Feigned and Unfeigned (16 cent.), I, 516
Love Tales and Elegies (18 cent.), II, 230
Loves Changelinges Change (17 cent.), I, 652
Loves Garland (17 cent.), II, 177
Love's Last Shift [etc.] (18 cent.), II, 195
Love's Repository (19 cent.), II, 256
Loves School (17 cent.), II, 177
Love's Victorie (17 cent.), I, 652
Loveday, John (1711–1789), II, 139
Loveday, Robert (*fl.* 1659), I, 388, 815
Lovelace, D. P. (*fl.* 1659), I, 460
Lovelace, Richard (1618–1657?), I, 460
Lovelich, Henry (*fl.* 15 cent.), I, 138
Lovell (or Lovel), A. (*fl.* 1677–85), II, 534, 781, 790, 801
Lovell, Daniel (d. 1818), III, 800
Lovell, George William (1804–1878), III, **604**
Lovell, John (*fl.* 1880), III, 802
Lovell, Robert (1770?–1796), III, 180
Lover, Samuel (1797–1868), III, **407** f., 826
Lover, The (1714), II, 661
Lover's Best Instructor, The (18 cent.), II, 227, 232
Lovers Cabinet, The (18 cent.), II, 217 (2)
Lover's Instructor, The (18 cent.), II, 232, 249
Lover's Magazine, The (18 cent.), II, 208
Lover's Manual, The (18 cent.), II, 216
Lover's Mass, The (15 cent.), I, 265
Lover's Pacquet, The (18 cent.), II, 203
Loves Garland (17 cent.), I, 104
Lovett, William (1800–1877), III, 152
Lovibond, Edward (1724–1775), II, **370**
Low, David (1786–1859), III, 971
Low, Sampson (1797–1886), III, 100, 101 (2)

Low, Sidney (*fl.* 1888), III, 801
Low, T. (*fl.* 1678), II, 178
Lowde, James (*fl.* 1694), II, 943
Lowe, — (*fl.* 1881), III, 1072
Lowe, George S. (*fl.* 1891), III, 800
Lowe, John (1750–1798), II, **370**
Lowe, Joseph (*fl.* 1822), III, 970
Lowe, Peter (1550?–1612?), I, 802, 891
Lowe, Robert, Viscount Sherbrooke (1811–1892), III, 111, 149, 153
Lowe, Robert William (*fl.* 1877–91), III, **1034**
Lowe, Solomon (*fl.* 1723–37), II, 126, 128–9
Lowell, Percival (b. 1855), III, 945
Lower, Sir William (1600?–1662), I, 647, 812
Lowman, Moses (1680–1752), II, 662, 863
Lowndes, J. J. (*fl.* 1840), III, 94
Lowndes, Richard (*fl.* 1873), III, 987
Lowndes, William (1652–1724), II, 943
Lowndes, William (*fl.* 1790), II, 96
Lowndes, William Thomas (d. 1843), I, 4
LOWNDS AND SON, M., III, 87
Lowne, Benjamin Thompson (*fl.* 1873), III, 954
Lowth, Robert (1710–1787), I, 125; II, 20, 822, 887, 905, 932
Lowth, William (1660–1732), II, 787
Loyal Garland, The (17 cent.), II, 178
Loyal Impartial Mercury, The (1682), II, 704
Loyal Intelligence; Or, News both from City and Country, The (1680), II, 703
Loyal Intelligencer, The (1654), I, 762
Loyal Intelligencer; Or, Lincoln, Rutland, Leicester, Cambridge and Stamford Advertiser, The (1793), II, 729
Loyal London Mercury, The (1682), II, 704
Loyal London Mercury; Or, The Currant Intelligence, The (1682), II, 704
Loyal Messenger, The (1653), I, 762
Loyal Messenger or Newes from Whitehall, The (1654), I, 762
Loyal Mourner, The (18 cent.), II, 193 (2)
Loyal Observator, The (1704), II, 659
Loyal Observator Reviv'd; Or, Gaylard's Journal, The (1722), II, 713
Loyal Poems and Satyrs Upon the Times (17 cent.), II, 179
Loyal Post; With Foreign and Inland Intelligence, The (1705), II, 707
Loyal Protestant and True Domestick Intelligence, The (1681), II, 698, 703
Loyall Scout, The (1659), I, 763 (2)
Loyall Scout, The (1660), II, 702
Luard, Henry Richards (1825–1891), I, 115–6, 299; II, 935 (2)
Lubbock, Sir John, Baron Avebury (1834–1913), III, **915**, 958
Lubin, Eilhard, I, 376
Lucan, I, 804; II, 766
Lucar, Cyprian (*fl.* 1588), I, 819
Lucas, C. P. (*fl.* 1866), III, 145

Lucas, David (1802–1881), III, 91
Lucas, Edward Verrall (1868–1938), III, 570, 836
Lucas, Frederic (1812–1855), III, 786, 819 (2), 836
Lucas, Robert (1748?–1812), II, 125, 761
Lucas, Samuel (1818–1868), III, 224, 799, 814, 818, 830
Lucas, Theophilus (*fl.* 1714), II, 155
Lucas, William (*fl.* 1750), II, 745
Lucas, William (*fl.* 1804–61), III, 151
Lucchini, A. M., II, 471
Luccock, J. (*fl.* 1805), III, 969
Luchetti, Eusebio, I, 660
Lucian, I, 804; II, 288, 761
Lucian's Dialogues, done into English Burlesque (1683), II, 288, 657
Lucian's Dialogues (not) from the Greek, done into English Burlesque (1683), II, 704
Lucifer (1887), III, 831
Lucifers Lacky (17 cent.), I, 724
Luck, Robert (*fl.* 1736), II, 762
Luckman and Sketchley's Coventry Gazette and Birmingham Chronicle (1757), II, 723
Luckombe, Philip (d. 1803), II, 82, 159
Lucretius, I, 804; II, 766; III, 554, 1000
Luctus Britannici for the Death of John Dryden (18 cent.), II, 185
Lucy, Sir Henry William (1845–1924), III, 786, 799, 814
Lucy, William (1594–1677), I, 878
Luders, Alexander (d. 1819), I, 115
Ludgate, The (1895), III, 831
Ludgate Monthly, The (1891), III, 831
Ludger, C. (*fl.* 1792–9), II, 59, 487
LUDLOW
    Newspapers, II, 725
    Printing, II, 87
Ludlow, Edmund (1617?–1692), II, **871**
Ludlow, J. M. (*fl.* 1848–58), III, 486, 817–8, 977, 1076
Ludlow Post-Man; Or, The Weekly Journal, The (1719), II, 725
Ludus Coventriae (15 cent.), I, 39, **277**
Ludwig, Christian (*fl.* 1706), II, 51
Luffman, John (*fl.* 1789), II, 757
Luis de Granada, I, 815
Lukin, Robert (*fl.* 1822), III, 775
Lumby, Joseph Rawson (1831–1895), I, 116, 147
Lumley, Edmund (*fl.* 1875), III, 987
Lumley, Jane, Lady (*fl.* 1555), I, 523, 801
Lumley, William Golden (*fl.* 1875), III, 987
Luna, J. de, I, 815
Lunadoro, Girolamo, I, 781
Lupset, Thomas (1495–1530), I, 516, **670**
Lupton, Donald (d. 1676), I, 723, 781
Lupton, Joseph Hirst (1836–1905), I, 666 (3)
Luscious Poet, The (18 cent.), II, 202
Lushington, Mrs Charles (*fl.* 1829), III, 1079

Lushington, Edmund Law (1811–1893), III, 867, **1000**
Lushington, F. (*fl.* 1851), III, 893
Lushington, Henrietta, Lady, née Prescott (d. 1875), III, 573
Lushington, W. (*fl.* 1808), III, 980
Lusignen, or Parthenay (M.E.), I, **160**
Lussan, H. (*fl.* 1694), II, 769
Lussan, Marguerite de, II, 789
Lusts Dominion (17 cent.), I, 539
Lusus Westmonasterienses (18 cent.), II, 200, 204, 208, 214
Lutel Soth Sermun, A (M.E.), I, **172**
Lutfullah (*fl.* 1857), III, 1083
Luther, Martin, I, 336, 815; II, 53; III, 33
Luttrell, Henry (1765?–1851), III, **238**
Luttrell, Narcissus (1657–1732), II, 162
Lutyens, F. M. (*fl.* 1896), III, 761
Luxborough, Henrietta Knight, Lady (d. 1756), II, 136
Luytel Sarmoun of Good Edificacioun, A (M.E.), I, 172
Lyall, Sir Alfred Comyns (1835–1911), III, **346**, 932 f.
Lyall, Sir Charles James (1845–1920), III, **1020**, 1074
'Lyall, Edna', i.e. Ada Ellen Bayly (1857–1903), III, **552**
Lyall, J. G. (*fl.* 1899), III, 764
Lyall, William Rowe (1788–1857), III, 823
Lyceum, The English (1787), II, 681
Lycidus (17 cent.), II, 180
Lydekker, Richard (1849–1915), III, 953, 958 (2)
Lydgate, John (1370?–1450?), I, 29, 39, 145–6, **250** f.
Lydiat, Thomas (1572–1646), I, 883–4
Lye, Edward (1694–1767), II, **919** f.
Lye, Thomas (1621–1684), II, 130
Lyell, Sir Charles (1797–1875), III, **951**, 967
Lyfe of Alisaunder, or Kyng Alisaunder (M.E.), I, **143**
Lyly, John (1554?–1606), I, 379, 524 f., 692 f., 728
Lyly, William (*fl.* 1522), I, 740
Lynam, Robert (1796–1845), II, 614; III, 886
Lynch, John (1599?–1673), III, 1047
Lynch, Thomas Toke (1818–1871), III, **296**
Lynche (or Linche), Richard (*fl.* 1596), I, **433**
Lyndwood, William (*fl.* 1430), I, **313**
Lyne, Charles E. (*fl.* 1897), III, 1094
Lynes, J. (*fl.* 1825), II, 937
Lyngard (or Lingard), Richard (1598?–1670), II, 122
Lynn, Eliza Lynn, later Linton (1822–1898), III, **493** f., 640
LYNN REGIS
    Magazine, II, 685 (1740)
Lyon, C. J. (*fl.* 1843), I, 125
Lyon, Patrick, Earl of Strathmore (1642–1695), II, 156

Lyra Apostolica (19 cent.), III, 855
Lyre, The (18 cent.), II, 212
Lyric Miscellany; or, the Essence of Harmony and Humour, The (18 cent.), II, 241, 242
LYRIC POETRY (discussions of), II, 21 f. (17, 18 cents.), 169 f. (recent criticism), III, 159 (19 cent.)
Lyric Repository, The (18 cent.), II, 240–1
LYRICS
    Old English. See for details OLD ENGLISH POETRY
    Middle English (to 1500), I, **267** f.
    For later periods see under POETRY
Lyschinska, M. J. (*fl.* 1880), III, 111
Lysias, II, 762
Lysons, Daniel (1762–1834), III, **882** f.
Lysons, Samuel (1763–1819), III, 882, **883**
Lyster, John (*fl.* 1588), I, 366
'Lyster, Lynn', i.e. T. L. Millar (*fl.* 1910), III, 1089
Lyte, Henry (1529?–1607), I, 892
Lyte, Henry (*fl.* 1619), I, 378, 881
Lyte, Henry Francis (1793–1847), III, **238**
Lytille Childrenes Lytil Boke (15 cent.), I, 264
Lyttelton, Arthur Temple (1852–1903), III, 851
Lyttelton, George, Baron (1709–1773), II, 139, 221, 305, **321**, 374, 540, 663, 714
Lyttelton, R. (b. 1854), III, 774
Lyttelton, Sir Thomas (*fl.* 18 cent.), II, 135
Lyttelton, Thomas, Baron (1744–1779), II, 547
Lytton, Edward George Earle Lytton Bulwer-Lytton, Baron (1802–1873), III, **475** f., 597, 599, 636, 647, 827
    Translations from, III, 25, 30, 36, 40, 43, 45
Lytton, Edward Robert Bulwer, Earl of (1831–1891), III, **347**

M., Captain — (*fl.* 1835), III, 765
M., A. (*fl.* 1581), I, 738
M., A. (*fl.* 1621), I, 739
M., A. (*fl.* 1790), II, 563
M., E. J. (*fl.* 1846), III, 131
M., G. (*fl.* 1719), II, 565
M., H. (*fl.* 1597), I, 785
M., H. (*fl.* 1671), II, 32
M., J. (*fl.* 1591), I, 729
M., J. (*fl.* 1692), II, 786
M., M. (*fl.* 1795), II, 771
M., R. (*fl.* 1617), I, 790
M., R. (*fl.* 1629), I, 723
M., R. (*fl.* 1642), I, 390
M., R. (*fl.* 1716), II, 753
M., S. E. (*fl.* 1654), I, 811
M., T. (*fl.* 1599), I, 480
M., T. (*fl.* 1648), I, 910
M., T. (*fl.* 1657), I, 732
M., T. (*fl.* 1659), I, 886
M., T. (*fl.* 1721), II, 196
M., W. (*fl.* 1585), I, 738
M., W. (*fl.* 1609), I, 724

M., W. H. (*fl.* 1849), I, 696
Mabbe, James (1572–1642?), I, 647, 809, 812 (2)
Mabbott, Gilbert (*fl.* 1648–9), I, 756–8, 760
Mabillon, Jean, II, 789
M'Allister, R. (*fl.* 1790), II, 736
M'Anaw, D. (*fl.* 1771), II, 738
Macaroni and Theatrical Magazine, The (1772), II, 665, 679
Macaroni Jester, The (18 cent.), II, 223
Macaroni, Savoir Vivre and Theatrical Magazine, The (1773), II, 679
McArthur, J. (*fl.* 1780), writer on fencing, II, 823
Macarthur, James (1798–1867), III, 1097
Macartney, George, Earl (1737–1806), II, 160, 745
M'Aulay, Alexander (*fl.* 1737), II, 588
Macaulay, Aulay (1758–1819), II, 19, 129
Macaulay, later Macaulay Graham, Catherine (1731–1791), II, 92, 131, 634, 888
Macaulay, George Campbell (1852–1915), III, 1040
Macaulay, Thomas Babington, Baron (1800–1859), III, 125, 683f.
    Translations from, III, 25, 37, 40–1, 43, 45 (2)
Macaulay, Zachary (1768–1838), III, 824
Macbain, Alexander (1855–1907), III, 830
McBane, Donald (*fl.* 1728), II, 823
Macbean, Alexander (d. 1784), II, 623
McCall, Robert (*fl.* 1884), III, 777
MacCarthy, Denis Florence (1817–1882), I, 457; III, 1053
McCarthy, Justin (1830–1912), III, 799, 917
MacCarthy, Justin Huntly (*fl.* 1892), III, 810
M'Clelland, J. (*fl.* 1847), III, 961
Macclesfield Courier and Herald, The, III, 793
McClintock, Sir Francis Leopold (1819–1907), III, 991
McColl, Evan (*fl.* 1888), III, 1086
MacColl, Norman (1843–1904), III, 818
McCombie, Thomas (*fl.* 1845–66), III, 1097
McCombie, William (1809–1870), III, 112, 280, 806
M'Conechy, J. (*fl.* 1847), III, 240
McCorkell, W. (*fl.* 1800?), II, 738
Maccormick, A. D. (*fl.* 1895), III, 1080
McCormick, Charles (1755–1807), II, 635
M'Cosh, James (1811–1894), III, 870, 965
McCoy, Sir Frederick (1823–1899), III, 952
McCrae, George Gordon (1833–1927), III, 1096
McCrae, Hugh R. (*fl.* 1096), III, 1096
MacCray, W. D. (*fl.* 1845), I, 317
McCreery, John (1768–1832), III, 75
McCrie, J. (*fl.* 1871), III, 112
M'Crie, Thomas, the elder (1772–1835), II, 998; III, 886
MacCrie, Thomas, the younger (1797–1875), III, 379, 721, 886 (2)

M'Crie, T. (*fl.* 1846), I, 908
M'Crie, T. (*fl.* 1848), I, 841
M'Crie, T. (*fl.* 1812), I, 904
McCrill, H. (*fl.* 1855), III, 684
McCrindle, J. W. (*fl.* 1877), III, 1077
Maccuen, — (*fl.* 1772), II, 797
MacCullagh, James (1809–1846), III, 942
MacCullagh, W. T., later MacCullagh Torrens (*fl.* 1855), III, 595
MacCulloch, J. M. (*fl.* 1845), I, 673
Macculloch, John (1773–1835), III, 950
McCulloch, John Ramsay (1789–1864), III, 72, 786, 807, 972, 974, 978, 980f.
McCulloh, A. (*fl.* 1743), II, 710
MacDermot, M. (*fl.* 1822), III, 201
MacDiarmid, John (1779–1808), III, 809
McDiarmid, John (1790–1852), II, 631
McDonald, Alexander (*fl.* 1775–9), II, 151
Macdonald, Andrew (1755?–1790), II, 711
Macdonald, Duncan George Forbes (1823?–1884), III, 971
MacDonald, George (1824–1905), III, 494f., 578
Macdonald, J. M. (*fl.* 1896), III, 1070
Macdonald, John (*fl.* 1778), II, 743
Macdonald, K. S. (*fl.* 1879), III, 1078
Macdonald, William Russell (1787–1854), III, 810–1 (2)
Macdonell, James (1842–1879), III, 786, 983
Macdonell, John (*fl.* 1773), II, 757
McDonnell, W. D. (*fl.* 1888), III, 984
McDonnel's Dublin Weekly Journal (1785), II, 736
MacDonough, T. M. (*fl.* 1837), I, 696
McDougall, Mrs (*fl.* 1854), III, 135
Macdowall, Andrew, Lord Bankton (1685–1760), II, 157
MacFall, Frances Elizabeth, née Clarke ('Sarah Grand') (b. 186a), III, 546f.
Macfarlan, James (1832–1862), III, 347
MacFarlane, Charles (d. 1858), III, 665
Macfarlane, John (*fl.* 1887), III, 807
MacFirbis, Duald (1585–1670), III, 1047
McGee, Thomas D'Arcy (1825–1868), III, 1086
McGhie, R. J. (*fl.* 1831), III, 108
MacGilchrist, J. (*fl.* 1868), III, 426
M'Gillivray, Duncan (*fl.* 1794), II, 757
Macgillivray, William (1796–1852), III, 956
McGinty, M. (*fl.* 1832), III, 1047
McGlashan, James (*fl.* 1856), III, 827
McGowan, John (*fl.* 1776), II, 56
Macgregor, A. G. (*fl.* 1879), III, 1078
Macgregor, John (1797–1857), statistician, II, 889
Macgregor, John (1825–1892), traveller, III, 991
McGregor, W. L. (*fl.* 1846), III, 1076
Machiavelli, Niccolò, I, 337–8, 734, 816, 844; II, 811

Machin, Lewis (*fl.* 1608), I, 706
Machlinia, William de (*fl.* 1482–90), I, 351
Machrie, William (*fl.* 1705–11), II, 823, 827
Machyn (or Machin), Henry (1498?–1563?), I, 383
Macintosh, Charles A. (*fl.* 1859), III, 790
Macintosh, William (*fl.* 1782), II, 742
Mackaile, Matthew (*fl.* 1657–96), II, 999
Mackarness, Matilda Anne, née Planché (1826–1881), III, 568
Mackay, Alexander (*fl.* 1796), III, 808
Mackay, Charles (1814–1889), II, 258; III, **296**f., 407, 814–5, 883
Mackay, James Townsend (1775–1862), III, 959
Mackay, Jessie (1864–1938), III, 1095
Mackay, Robert William (1803–1882), III, 848f.
Mackay, T. (*fl.* 1889), III, 976–7
Mackay, William (*fl.* 1913), III, 786
Mackelvie, William (1800–1863), II, 990
MacKendrick, John Gray (b. 1841), III, **964**
Mackenzie, — (*fl.* 1800), II, 557
Mackenzie, Sir Alexander (1755?–1820), III, 991, 1087
Mackenzie, Alexander (*fl.* 1875–88), III, 830
Mackenzie, Anne Maria (*fl.* 1792), II, 550
Mackenzie, Frederick (*fl.* 1775), II, 151
Mackenzie, George, Viscount Tarbat, Earl of Cromarty (1630–1714), II, **869**
Mackenzie, Sir George (1636–1691), II, **869**f., **996**
Mackenzie, George (1669–1725), II, 998
Mackenzie, Georgina Mary Muir (*fl.* 1862), III, 991
Mackenzie, Helen (*fl.* 1853), III, 1083
Mackenzie, Henry (1745–1831), II, 61, 111, 131, 143, 337, 470, 547 (2), 548, 665, 986, 990
Mackenzie, J. (*fl.* 1871), of South Africa, III, 1091f.
Mackenzie, J. C. (*fl.* before 1890), journalist, III, 800
Mackenzie, Roderick (*fl.* 1793), II, 751
Mackenzie, W. D. (*fl.* 1902), III, 1090
McKenzie's Loyal Magazine (1800), II, 688
Mackerell, Benjamin (d. 1738), II, 105
Mackie, S. J. (*fl.* 1858), III, 829
Mackie, William (*fl.* 1877), III, 807
Mackinnon, W. C. (*fl.* 1878), III, 1071
Mackintosh, Alexander (*fl.* 1806), III, 768
Mackintosh, Sir James (1765–1832), III, **880**f.
Mackintosh, R. J. (*fl.* 1835–53), III, 880–1
Mackintosh, Robert (b. 1867), III, 851
Mackintosh, T. S. (*fl.* 1840), III, 977
Mackintosh, William (1662–1743), II, 1001
Macklin, Charles (1697?–1797), II, **476**, 485
Macklin's British Poets (18 cent.), II, 241
Mackmurdo, A. H. (*fl.* 1893), III, 834
Macknight, Thomas (1829–1899), II, 635; III, 426, 808

Mackworth, Sir Humphrey (1657–1727), II, 498
Macky, John (d. 1726), II, 139, 744
Macky, Spring (*fl.* 1728), II, 301, 542, 784, 792
McLachlan, Alexander (*fl.* 1900), III, 1086
Maclachlan, David (*fl.* 1860), III, 987
Maclaine, Archibald (1722–1804), II, 802
Maclaren, Alexander (1826–1910), III, 111
Maclaren, Archibald (1755–1826), II, 971
Maclaren, Charles (1782–1866), III, 807, 950
McLaren, Duncan (1800–1886), III, 979
MacLaren, Samuel Bruce (*fl.* 1900), III, 943
M'Lauchlan, Thomas (1816–1886), III, 906
Maclaurin, Colin (1698–1746), II, 961 (2)
Maclaurin, Colin (*fl.* 1816), II, 651
Maclaurin, John (1693–1754), II, 995
MacLaurin, John, Lord Dreghorn (1734–1796), II, 20, 92
McLean, D. H. (*fl.* 1898), III, 779
Maclean, J. (*fl.* 1883), writer on railways, III, 984
Maclean, J. N. A. (*fl.* 1887), Anglo-Indian novelist, III, 1070
Maclean, Sir John (1811–1895), archaeologist, I, 384–5
Maclean, Letitia Elizabeth, née Landon (1802–1838), III, **294**, 478
Macleane, Arthur, John (1812–1858), III, 1000 (2)
Macleay, John (*fl.* 1900?), III, 802
Macleay, William Sharp (1792–1865), III, 956
M'Lennan, John Ferguson (1827–1881), III, **870**
McLennan, William (*fl.* 1886), III, 1086–7
M'Leod, Allan (d. 1805), II, 711
Macleod, Donald (*fl.* 1852–72), III, 375, 829
'MacLeod, Fiona', i.e. William Sharp (1855–1905), II, **552**f.
Macleod, Henry Dunning (1821–1902), III, 972, 974, 982f.
Macleod, Norman (1812–1872), III, 111, 567, 578, 829, 853
Maclise, Daniel (1806–1870), III, 91
Macliver, P. S. (*fl.* 1858), III, 802
Macmillan, Hugh (1833–1903), III, 853
McMillan, S. (*fl.* 1848), II, 994
MACMILLAN & Co., III, 99
Macmillan's Magazine (1859), III, 829
Macnab, Henry Gray (1761–1823), II, 109; III, 111–2
Macnair, J. (*fl.* 1883), III, 778
MacNally, Leonard (1752–1820), II, **476**f.
Macnamara, Walter Henry (*fl.* 1888), III, 987
MacNeill, Hector (1746–1818), II, 251, **991**
Macneill, Sir John Benjamin (1793?–1880), III, 981
MacNevin, T. (*fl.* 1845), III, 595
M'Nicol, Donald (1735–1802), II, 626
McNicoll, T. (*fl.* 1861), III, 8
Macpherson, Charles (*fl.* 1800), II, 743
Macpherson, David (1746–1816), III, 979

Macpherson, G. (*fl.* 1900), III, 1078
Macpherson, Hector C. (*fl.* 1873), III, 807
Macpherson, Hugh Alexander (*fl.* 1897), III, 763
Macpherson, James (*fl.* 1745), Jacobite historian, II, 1002
Macpherson, James (1736–1796), 'translator' of Ossian, II, 45, 57, 67–8, 71, 343f., 889
Macpherson, John (1710–1765), II, 998
Macpherson, R. (*fl.* 1783), II, 827
Macqueen, D. (*fl.* 1756), II, 952
Macquoid, Gilbert S. (*fl.* 1887), II, 258
Macray, W. D. (*fl.* 1862–9), I, 5, 399; III, 105
Macready, William Charles (1793–1873), III, 152
MacRitchie, William (*fl.* 1795), II, 140
Macro Plays, The (15 cent.), I, 514
M'Robert, Patrick (*fl.* 1776), II, 756
Macropedius, Georgius, I, 328
Macstead, J. P. (*fl.* 1854), III, 936
Macswinney, Robert Forster (*fl.* 1884), III, 987
McWard, Robert (1633?–1687), II, **993**
MADAGASCAR
　　Voyages to, II, 748f.
Madan, Judith, née Cowper (*fl.* 1731), II, 27, 296, 302
Madan, Martin (1726–1790), II, 155, 238, 766
Madden, Sir Frederic (1801–1873), I, 264; III, **1034**f.
Madden, Mary Anne, later Sadlier (*fl.* 1861), III, 1087
Madden, Richard Robert (1798–1886), II, 160; III, 388, 791, 1052 (misprinted D. D. Madden)
Madden, Samuel (1686–1765), II, 160, 539, 621
Maddison, Sir Ralph (1571?–1655?), I, 720
Madox, Thomas (1666–1727), II, **872**
Maffei, Francesco Scipione, II, 66, 811
Maffett, Hugh (*fl.* 1772), II, 767
Magalotti, Lorenzo, II, 140
Magasin de Londres (1749), II, 677
Magasin du Monde Politique, Le (1776), II, 680
Magazine a la Mode; Or, Fashionable Miscellany, The (1777), II, 680
Magazine of Ants; Or, Pismire Journal, The (1777), II, 685
Magazine of Art, The (1878), III, 831
Magazine of Female Fashions of London, The (1798), II, 683
Magazine of Magazines, The (1750), II, 677
Magazine of Magazines, The (1751), II, 688
Magazine of Magazines, The (1758), II, 678
Magazine of Natural History and Journal of Zoology, etc., The (1829), III, 826
Magazine of the Beau Monde, The (1831), III, 826
MAGAZINES
　　Restoration to Romantic Revival, II, 564f. (children's), **668**f. (full list)
　　Nineteenth Century, III, **822**f. (monthlies), **832**f. (quarterlies), 1088 (Canadian)
MAGDALEN COLLEGE (Oxford), I, 368
MAGDALEN COLLEGE SCHOOL, I, 372

MAGDALEN HALL (Oxford), II, 104
Magee, James (d. 1866), III, 809
Magee, John (d. 1809), II, 735
Magee's Weekly Packet (1777), II, 736
Magee's Weekly Packet; Or, Hope's Lottery Journal of News [etc.] (1777), II, 687
Maggi, Carlo Maria, II, 811
'Maggot, Sir Butterfly' (1730), II, 200
MAGIC (writings on), I, 893f. (16, 17 cents.)
Magic and Conjuring Magazine And Wonderful Chronicle, The (1793), II, 682
Maginn, William (1793–1842), III, **677**, 826
　　Reviews and articles by, III, 197, 201, 395, 408, 410
Magnet, The (1837), III, 819
Magnus, Olaus, I, 781
Magnus, Sir P. (*fl.* 1888), III, 111
Magrath, W. (*fl.* 1804), II, 82
Maguire, J. R. (*fl.* 1896), III, 985
Mahaffy, Sir John Pentland (1839–1919), III, 1007
Mahieu, Étienne (*fl.* 1699), II, 717
Mahon, Viscount (1805–1875). See P. H., Earl Stanhope, III, **889**f.
Mahon, A. (*fl.* 1734), II, 823
Mahony, Francis Sylvester (1804–1866), III, **719**f.
MAIDENHEAD
　　Magazine, II, 685 (1797)
Maidment, James (1795?–1879), I, 903 (2); III, 1024, **1026**
MAIDSTONE
　　Newspapers, II, 725
Maidstone and Kentish Journal, The (1853), II, 725
Maidstone Journal, The (1737), II, 725
Maidstone Journal and Kentish Advertiser, The (1786), II, 725
Maidstone Mercury, The (1725), II, 725
Maidwell, Lewis (*fl.* 1705), II, 111, 429
Maier, Jakob, II, 60
Mail, The (1868), III, 809
Mail, The [Portsmouth] (1895), III, 805
Mail and Waterford Daily Express, The (1855), III, 809
Maillard, A. S. (*fl.* 1798), II, 775
Maillet, Benoît de, II, 789
Maimbourg, Louis, II, 789
Main (or Man), James (1700?–1761), I, 910
Main, Robert (1808–1878), III, 944
Maine, Sir Henry James Sumner (1822–1888), III, **893**f.
Maintenon, Madame de, née Françoise d'Aubigné, II, 769
Mainwaring, John (*fl.* 1780–98), II, 25, 373
Mair, Charles (*fl.* 1868), III, 1086
Mair, John (*fl.* 1741–79), II, 128, 757, 767
Maitland, Dollie, later Radford (b. 1858), III, **347**
Maitland, Frederick William (1850–1906), III, **913**

Maitland, G. (*fl.* 1834), I, 836
Maitland, H. (*fl.* 1817), I, 532
Maitland, James, Earl of Lauderdale (1759–1839), III, 973, 978–9
Maitland, Sir John, Baron Thirlstane (1545?–1595), I, 905
Maitland, John (*fl.* 1850?), III, 802
Maitland, Julia Charlotte (*fl.* 1843–54), III, 573, 1083
Maitland, Sir Richard (1496–1586), I, 898
Maitland, Richard, Earl of Lauderdale (1653–1695), II, 768
Maitland, Samuel Roffey (1792–1866), I, 7; III, 854, **900** f.
Maitland, Thomas, Lord Dundrennan (1792–1851), I, 445, 449, 453, 901
Maitland, Thomas (*fl.* 16 cent.), I, 905
Maitland, William (1693?–1757), II, **881**
Maittaire, Michael (1668–1747), II, **938**
Major, John (1469–1550), I, 773, 905
Major, Richard Henry (1818–1891), III, 1076
Makin, Bathsua (*fl.* 1649–73), II, 131
Makluire, John (*fl.* 1630), I, 911
Makower, S. (*fl.* 1892), III, 835
Malabari, Bahramji (*fl.* 1876), III, 1069, 1084
Malachy (*fl.* 1310), I, **301**
Malbie, Sir Nicholas (1530?–1584), I, 393
Malchus (O.E.), I, **93**
Malcolm, Daniel (*fl.* 1739), II, 109
Malcolm, Georgiana (*fl.* 1858), III, 29
Malcolm, James Peller (1767–1815), III, **883**
Malcolm, Sir John (1769–1833), III, **886** f., 1068
Malden, Henry (1800–1876), I, 20
Maldon, The Battle of (O.E.), I, 27, 83 f.
Malebranche, Nicolas, II, 36, 39, 790
Malet, Sir Alexander (1800–1886), III, 134
Malet, H. E. (*fl.* 1876), III, 765
'Malet, Lucas', i.e. Mary St Ledger Kingsley, later Harrison (d. 1931), III, **553** f.
Malham, John (1747–1821), I, 397
Malherbe, J. Fontaine, II, 72
Malim, William (1533–1594), I, 777
Malkin, A. T. (*fl.* 1832), III, 649
Malkin, Benjamin Heath (1769–1842), II, 349
Mall: or the Modish Lovers, The (17 cent.), II, 266
Malleson, George Bruce (1825–1898), III, **932**
Mallet, David (1705?–1765), II, 32, **321** f., 913
Mallet, Paul Henri (1730–1807), II, 70, 74
Mallet, Elizabeth (*fl.* 1701), II, 706
Mallet, Sir Louis (1823–1890), III, 984
Mallet, Robert (1810–1881), III, 952
Mallet du Pan, Jacques François (*fl.* 1797), II, 672, 683 (2)
Mallock, William Hurrell (1849–1923), III, **554**
Mallory, John (*fl.* 1734), II, 964
Malmesbury, James Harris, Earl of (1746–1820), II, 138
Malmesbury, James Edward Harris, Earl of, III, 763

Malmesbury, James Howard Harris, Earl of (1807–1889), III, 146, 149
Malmesbury, William of (d. 1143?), I, 116, 120
Malmesbury Register (M.E.), I, 121
Malone, Edmond (1741–1812), II, **901** f.
Malory, Sir Thomas (*fl.* 1470), I, 30, 33, **263**
Malsachanus (*fl.* 8 or 9 cent.), I, **108**
Maltby, Edward (1770–1859), III, 995
Maltby, William (1763–1854), II, 935
Malthus, David (or Daniel) (*fl.* 1789), II, 553, 771
Malthus, Francis (*fl.* 1629), I, 886
Malthus, Thomas Robert (1766–1834), III, **870**, 975, 979
Malton, Thomas, the younger (1746–1804), II, 146
MALVERN SCHOOL, III, 839
Malynes, Gerard de (*fl.* 1586–1641), I, 846, 850
MAMMONISM, III, 64 f.
MAN, ISLE OF
    Bibliography, II, 87
    Historians, III, 930
Man (or Main), James (1700?–1761), I, 910
Man, Judith (*fl.* 1640), I, 811
Man: a Paper for Ennobling the Species (1755), II, 664
Man in the Moon, The (1660), II, 701
Man in the Moone Discovering a World of Knavery under the Sunne, The (1649), I, 759
Man of Pleasure, The (1771), II, 665
Man of Pleasure's Song Book, The (18 cent.), II, 241
Man of the Town, The (1782), II, 666
Man's Treachery to Woman (18 cent.), II, 186
MANCHESTER
    Booksellers and printers of, I, 353 (17 cent.); II, 87 (18 cent.)
    Chetham's Library, II, 105
    Grammar School, I, 372 f.
    Magazines, II, 685 (1750)
    Newspapers, II, 725 f.
    Victoria University, III, 128
Manchester, W. D. Montagu, Duke of (*fl.* 1864), I, 382
Manchester Chronicle, The (1781), II, 726
Manchester Chronicle, The (1835), II, 726
Manchester Chronicle; Or, Anderton's Universal Advertiser, The (1762), II, 726
Manchester Courier, The (1861), III, 803
Manchester Daily Telegraph (1855), III, 802
Manchester Daily Times, The (1854), III, 802
Manchester, Early Documents of (M.E.), I, 121
Manchester Evening Chronicle, The (1885), III, 806
Manchester Evening Chronicle, The (1897), III, 806
Manchester Evening Mail, The (1874), III, 804
Manchester Evening News, The (1868), III, 803
Manchester Examiner, The (1855), III, 802

Manchester Examiner and Times, The (1855), III, 802

Manchester Examiner Extraordinary, The (1854), III, 802

Manchester Express, The (1854), III, 802

Manchester Gazette, The (1795), II, 726

Manchester Gazette (1824), II, 726

Manchester Guardian, The (1855), III, 793, 802

Manchester Herald, The (1792), II, 726

Manchester Journal, The (1754), II, 726

Manchester Magazine, The (1737), II, 725

Manchester Mercury and Harrop's General Advertiser, The (1766), II, 726

Manchester Songster, The (18 cent.), II, 247

Manchester Weekly Journal, The (1719), II, 725

Mancinus, Dominicus, I, 411

Mandeville, Bernard (1670–1733), II, 45, **599**f., 783

'Mandeville, Sir John' (M.E.), I, **191**, 781

Manet, Jane (*fl.* 1833), III, 981

Mangan, James Clarence (1803–1849), III, **1051**

Mangin, Edward (1772–1852), II, 21, 514, 647, 843

Mangles, James (1786–1867), III, 991

Manilius, II, 766

Maning, Frederick Edward (1812–1883), III, 1097

Mankind (15 cent.), I, 514

Manley, John Jackson (*fl.* 1880), III, 763, 771

Manley, Mary de la Riviere (1663–1724), II, **424**, 531–2, 535 (2), 536–7, 584, 589, 590 (2), 661 (2)

Manley, Thomas (1628–1690), II, 926, 959

Mann, Horace (*fl.* 1846–54), III, 111, 116

Mann, Robert James (1817–1886), III, 257

Mann, T. (*b.* 1856), III, 978

Manners, Catherine, née Pollok, later Lady Stepney (d. 1845), III, **418**

Manners, Lady Catharine Rebecca (*fl.* 1799), II, 27

Manners, James R. (*fl.* 1860), III, 807

Manners, John Henry, Duke of Rutland (*fl.* 1795), II, 140

Manning, Mrs — (*fl.* 1869), III, 1077

Manning, Anne (1807–1879), III, **495**f.

Manning, Francis (*fl.* 1695), II, **440**f., 760, 780, 790

Manning, Henry Edward (1808–1892), III, 855, **859**

Manning, Owen (1721–1801), II, 920–1; III, 882

Manning, Samuel (1822–1881), I, 466

Manning, William Oke (1809–1878), III, 122

Manningham, John (d. 1622), I, 385

Mannyng, Robert, of Brunne (*fl.* 1288–1338), I, 40, **165**f., **183**f.

Mansel, Henry Longueville (1820–1871), III, 127, 868, **870**

Mansel (or Mansell), Sir Robert (1573–1656), I, 739

Mansfield, Charles Blackford (1819–1855), III, 489, 947

Manship, Henry (*fl.* 1562), I, 775

Manson, J. B. (*fl.* 1861), III, 807

Mant, Alicia Catherine (*fl.* 1812–25), III, **571**

Mant, Richard (1776–1848), III, **238**f.

Mant, Walter Bishop (1807–1869), III, 238

Mante, Thomas (*fl.* 1772), II, 755

Mantell, Gideon Algernon (1790–1852), III, 885

Mantuanus, Johannes Baptista Spagnuolus, I, 328, 819; II, 813

Mantz, E. S. (*fl.* 1849), III, 88

MANUALS FOR PREACHERS

    Middle English period, I, 301f. (Latin)

    Renaissance to Restoration, I, 679f. (16 cent.), 694f. (17 cent.)

Manuche (or Manucci) Cosmo (*fl.* 1652), I, 647

Manuel, Niklas, I, 336

Manuel, T. P. (*fl.* 1861), III, 1067

MANUSCRIPTS

    Catalogues, I, 4f. (general), 113 (M.E.)

    Old English Poetry, I, 62f.

Manwaring, Edward (*fl.* 1737–44), II, 22, 25

Manwaring, George (*fl. c.* 1607), I, 783

Manwayring, Sir Henry (*fl.* 1644), I, 390

Manwood, John (d. 1610), I, 394, 850

Manzolli, P. A. (Marcellus Palingenius), I, 329, 817

Manzoni, Alessandro, III, 39

Map, Walter (*fl.* 1190), I, **289**, 610

Maphaeus Vegius, II, 373

Maples, John (*fl.* 1778), II, 817

Maplet, John (d. 1592), I, 884, 892

MAPS. See NAVIGATION, I, 390f. (16, 17 cents.)

    Printing of, II, 106

Maquet, Auguste, III, 456

Mar, John Erskine, Earl of (1675–1732), II, 121

Marana, Giovanni Paolo, II, 534, 811

Marauder, The (1830), III, 836

Marcelline, G. (*fl.* 1625), I, 704

Marcellinus, Ammianus, I, 779

Marcet, Jane (1769–1858), III, 946, 980

March, Charles (*fl.* 1794), II, 666

March, J. (*fl.* 1831), III, 769

March, John (1612–1657), I, 718

March, Thomas (*fl.* 1873), III, 775

Marchand, A. B. (*fl.* 1913), III, 1090

Marchant, Bessie, later Comfort (b. 1862), III, 574

Marchant, John (*fl.* 1746–51), II, 556, 1002

Marche, Olivier de la, I, 334

Marckant, John (*fl.* 1562), I, 678

Marcus Aurelius, I, 800; II, 759f.; III, 1000

Marcus Tullius Cicero (17 cent.), I, 651

'Marforio' (1740), II, 689

Margam, Annals of (15 cent.), I, 115

Margaret, St (O.E.), I, 93

Marguerite D'Angoulême, Queen of Navarre, I, 334, 734; II, 790

Marguetel de Saint-Denis, Charles, Seigneur de Saint-Évremond, II, 790
Marherete, Seinte (M.E.), I, 169f.
Mariana, Juan de, II, 68
Marini, Giovanni Ambrogio, II, 542, 811
Marino, Giambattista, I, 339–40; II, 66, 811
Marishall (or Marshall), Jean (*fl.* 1765), II, 546
Marivaux, Pierre Carlet de Chamblain de, II, 461, **774**
Mark Lane Express, The (1832), III, 793, 819
'Markham, Mrs', i.e. Elizabeth Cartwright, later Penrose (1780–1837), III, 135
Markham, D. F. (*fl.* 1854), I, 707
Markham, Gervase (1568?–1637), I, 380, **705**f., 769, 803, 813
Markham, Violet R. (*fl.* 1900–), III, 1090
Markham, W. O. (*fl.* 1860), III, 821
Markham, William (1719–1807), II, 126
Markland, George (*fl.* 1727), II, 820
Markland, James Heywood (1788–1864), I, 277
Markland, Jeremiah (1693–1776), I, 209; II, **936**
Marlowe, Christopher (1564–1593), I, 33, 46, 404, **531**f., 804–5
Marks, H. H. (*fl.* 1884), III, 800
'Marksman' (1860), III, 762
'Markwell, Marmaduke' (1809), III, 762
Markwell, W. R. S. (*fl.* 1853), III, 604
MARLBOROUGH
   Newspapers, II, 726
MARLBOROUGH COLLEGE, III, 132, 839
Marlborough Journal, The (1771), II, 726
Marlianus, Joannes Bartholomaeus, I, 778
Marmet, Pierre de, II, 427
Marmion, Shakerley (1603–1639), I, 647f.
Marmontel, Jean François, II, 48, 552, 565, 790; III, 22
Maroccus Extaticus (16 cent.), I, 713
Marolles, Louis de, II, 790
Marolles, Michel de, II, 790
Marot, Clément, I, 332–3
MARPRELATE CONTROVERSY, I, 688f.
Marra, John (*fl.* 1772–5), II, 150
MARRIAGE, SATIRES ON, I, 716f. (16, 17 cents.)
Marriage Broker, The (17 cent.), I, 652
Marriage of Wit and Wisdom, The (16 cent.), I, 516
Marriott, Charles (1811–1858), III, 856, **859**
Marriott, Sir James (1730?–1803), II, **371**
Marriott, W. (*fl.* 1838), I, 276
Marrow of Complements, The (17 cent.), II, 179
Marryat, Florence, later Church, later Lean (1838–1899), III, 1069
Marryat, Frank S. (*fl.* 1848), III, 386
Marryat, Frederick (1792–1848), III, **385**f.
Marsden, John Buxton (1803–1870), III, 824, 857
Marsden, John Howard (1803–1891), I, 386; III, 995
Marsden, Reginald G. (*fl.* 1880), III, 987

Marsden, William (1754–1836), I, 782; II, 750, 926
Marse, F. (*fl.* 1872), III, 977
Marsh, Adam (d. 1257), I, **292**
Marsh, Anne, later Marsh-Caldwell, née Caldwell (1791–1874), III, **496**
Marsh, G. P. (*fl.* 1862), I, 213
Marsh, H. (*fl.* 1659), I, 763
Marsh, Herbert (1757–1839), II, 166, 174; III, 107
Marsh, J. B. (*fl.* 1864), I, 549
Marsh, John Fitchett (1818–1880), I, 469
Marsh-Caldwell, Anne (1791–1874), III, **496**
Marshall, — (*fl.* 1788), II, 95, 923
Marshall, Mrs — (*fl.* 1818), III, 571
Marshall, Alfred (1842–1924), economist, III, 983–4
Marshall, Arthur Milnes (1852–1893), III, 955, 958
Marshall, Emma, née Martin (1830–1899), III, 568
Marshall, Francis (*fl.* 1892), III, 775
Marshall, James (*fl.* 1790), II, 468
Marshall, John (*fl.* 1668), II, 749
Marshall, Joseph (*fl.* 1772), II, 746
Marshall, Julian (1836–1903), III, 775
Marshall, M. P. (*fl.* 1879), III, 983
Marshall, Stephen (1594?–1655), I, **698**
Marshall, Thomas (1621–1685), II, 918
Marshall, T. H. (*fl.* 1849), I, 899
Marshall, William (1745–1818), II, 148; III, 969
Marsham, Sir John (1602–1685), II, 938
Marshe, Witham (*fl.* 1744), II, 754
Marshman, John Clark (1794–1877), III, **906**f., 1074
Marshman, Joshua (1768–1837), III, 1017
Marston, Edward (1825–1914), III, 99
Marston, John (1575?–1634), I, **627**f.
Marston, John Westland (1819–1890), III, **604**
Marston, Philip Bourke (1850–1887), III, **347**f.
Marston, R. B. (1853–1927), III, 771
Marston, Roger (d. after 1298), I, **295**
Marteilhe, Jean, II, 790
Martelli, C. (*fl.* 1819), III, 778
Martial, I, 804; II, 766
Martialis Epigrammata Selecta (18 cent.), II, 217
Martianus Capella, I, 125
Martin of Alnwick (d. 1336), I, **304**
Martin, Ann, later Taylor (1759–1829), III, 565
Martin, Arthur Patchett (*fl.* 1876–98), III, 1093, **1095**
Martin, Benjamin (1704–1782), II, 677, 930, 932
Martin, Emma, later Marshall (1830–1899), III, 568
Martin, Frederick (1830–1883), II, 344; III, 219, 1077
Martin, G. (*fl.* 1823), III, 92
Martin, George (*fl.* 1887), III, 1086
Martin, Gregory (d. 1582), I, 676

Martin, Harriet Letitia (1801–1891), III, 387
Martin, James (*fl.* 1577), I, 874
Martin, John (1741–1820), II, 790
Martin, John (1789–1854), painter, III, 91
Martin, John (1791–1855), bibliographer, III, 85
Martin, John William (*fl.* 1882), sporting writer, III, 771
Martin, Martin (d. 1719), II, 157, 744
Martin, Minnie (*fl.* 1903), III, 1093
Martin, Peter John (1786–1860), III, 950
Martin, R. T. (*fl.* 1867), I, 908
Martin, Robert Montgomery (1803?–1868), III, 982, 1075
Martin, Stephen (*fl.* 1666), II, 742
Martin, T. (*fl.* 1838), editor of Urquhart's Rabelais, I, 836
Martin, Sir Theodore (1816–1909), III, **298**
Martin, Thomas (1697–1771), antiquary, II, 102
Martin, Thomas (*fl.* 1763), of Salisbury, II, 289
Martin, Thomas (*fl.* 1837), III, 986
Martin, Sir Thomas Byam (1773–1854), II, 151
Martin, W. B. (*fl.* 1898), Hindu scholar, III, 1074
Martin, William (1801–1867), writer of children's books, III, 567
Martin Burke's Connaught Journal (1769), II, 737
Martin Nonsence His Collections (1648), I, 759
Martin's Bath Chronicle (1763), II, 720
Martindale, Adam (1623–1686), I, 367, 387
Martineau, Harriet (1802–1876), III, **496** f.
Martineau, James (1805–1900), III, 111, 690, 846, 849–50, **870** f., 965
Martinelli, Fioravante, I, 781
Martinengo, Nestore, I, 777
'Martingale', i.e. James (?) White (*fl.* 1840–51), III, 763
Martini, Martinus, I, 786
Martire D'Anghiera, Pietro, I, 763
Martyn, Benjamin (1699–1763), II, **441**
Martyn, Edward (1859–1923), III, **1063**
Martyn, Henry (1781–1812), III, 151
Martyn, John (1699–1768), II, 22, 714, 768, 793
Martyn, Joseph (*fl.* 1621), I, 481
Martyn, Thomas (*fl.* 1785–93), II, 747, 798, 800, 927
Martyrology (O.E.), I, **88**
Marvel, The (1898), III, 578
Marvell, Andrew (1621–1678), I, **460** f.
Marwick, William (*fl.* 1887), III, 705
Mary II, Queen of England (1662–1694), II, 149
Mary of Egypt, St (O.E.), I, **93**
Marzials, Theophilus Julius Henry (b. 1850), III, **348**
Mascall, Leonard (d. 1589), I, 391, 393–4
Mascardi, Agostino, II, 811
Maseres, Francis (1731–1824), I, 400, 467; II, 800, 870

Maskell, William (1814?–1890), I, 693
Mason, C. (*fl.* 1852), writer on lithography, III, 83
Mason, C. M. S. (*fl.* 1886–1919), educationalist, III, 111
Mason, F. (*fl.* 1850), III, 1083
Mason, Francis (1566?–1621), I, 858
Mason, G. Finch (*fl.* 1879–89), sporting writer, III, 761
Mason, G. H. (*fl.* 1855), author of 'Life with the Zulus', III, 1092
Mason, George (*fl.* 1618), musical composer, I, 486
Mason, George (*fl.* 1622), author of 'Grammaire Angloise', I, 44
Mason, George (1735–1806), editor of Hoccleve, II, 915
Mason, George Henry (*fl.* 1800), writer on China, II, 751
Mason, James (*fl.* 1612), I, 893
Mason, John (b. 1582), author of 'The Turke', I, 648
Mason, John (1586–1635), founder of New Hampshire, I, 794
Mason, John (1645?–1694), writer of hymns, II, **283**
Mason, John (*fl.* 1648), schoolmaster, I, 648
Mason, John (1706–1763), writer on elocution, I, 23
Mason, John Monck (1726–1809), Shakespearean commentator, II, **899**
Mason, Peter Hamnett (*fl.* 1853–80), III, **1013**
Mason, R. O. (*fl.* 1798), II, 824
Mason, W. (*fl.* 1810), printer, III, 77
Mason, William (1725–1797), poet, II, 221, **371** f.
Mason, William (*fl.* 1778), of Rotherhithe, II, 915
Mason, William Monck (1775–1859), historian, II, 594
Mason, William Shaw (1774–1853), statist, II, 647
Masonic Miscellanies (18 cent.), II, 252
Masque, The (18 cent.), II, 224–7, 232, 244
Masquerade: Calculated to Amuse all the Good Boys and Girls in the Kingdom, The (18 cent.), II, 562
MASQUES, I, 500 (16, 17 cents.)
Massey, Gerald (1828–1907), III, **298** f., 636
Massey, Stephen (*fl.* 1769), II, 226
Massey, William (1691–1764?), II, 129, 765, 767, 911
Massey, William Nathaniel (1809–1881), III, **898**
Massie, Joseph (d. 1784), II, 959
Massillon, Jean Baptiste, II, 790
Massinger, Philip (1583–1640), I, **630** f.; III, 595
Massingham, H. W. (1860–1924), III, 799

Masson, David (1822–1907), III, **720**, 818, 829
  Articles by, I, 471; III, 225, 651
Master, Streynsham (*fl.* 1675–80), II, 742
Master, William (1627–1684), I, 726
Masterman, C. F. G. (1874–1927), III, 835
Masters, Mary (1694?–1771), II, **322**
Masters, Maxwell Tylden (1833–1907), III, 821, 961
Masters, Robert (1713–1798), I, 370; II, 893
Mathematical Magazine, The (1761), II, 678
MATHEMATICS
  Text-books, I, 377f. (16, 17 cents.); II, **129** (17, 18 cents.)
  Treatises, I, 880f. (16, 17 cents.); III, 940f. (19 cent.). For 1660–1800 see Literature of Science, II, 959f.
Mather, Philip E. (*fl.* 1894), III, 987
Mather, Richard (1596–1669), I, 792
Mathers, Helen Buckingham, later Reeves (1853–1920), III, **554f.**
Mathers, J. (*fl.* 1839), III, 977
Matheson, Annie (1853–1924), III, **348**
Mathew, George Felton (*fl.* 1817), III, 223
Mathews, Mrs — (*fl.* 1838), III, 583
Mathews, A. (*fl.* 1838), III, 605
Mathews, Charles (1776–1835), III, 634
Mathews, Charles Edward (1834–1905), III, 777
Mathews, Charles James (1803–1878), III, **604f.**
Mathewson, T. (*fl.* 1805), III, 778
Mathias, Thomas James (1754?–1835), II, 76, **372f.**
Mathison, T. (*fl.* 1743), II, 827
Matrimonial Magazine, The (1775), II, 680
Mattaire, M. (*fl.* 1743), II, 895
Matteis, Nicola (*fl.* 1696), II, 183–4
Matthew, J. M. (*fl.* 1793), II, 751
Matthew, Patrick (*fl.* 1831), III, 953
'Matthew, Thomas' (1537), I, 675
Matthew, Sir Tobie (1577–1655), I, 385–6, 810, 870 (2)
Matthews, Mrs C. (*fl.* 1806), III, 135
Matthews, E. (*fl.* 1835), III, 135
Matthews, G. K. (*fl.* 1853), III, 375
Matthews, Henry (1789–1828), III, 151
Matthews, J. W. (*fl.* 1887), III, 1092
Matthews, John (*fl.* 1788), II, 749
Matthews, Thomas (*fl.* 1805), II, 450
Matthews, W. H. (*fl.* 1906), III, 1092
Maturin, Charles Robert (1782–1824), III, 25, **408**
Maty, Matthieu (1718–1776), II, 34, 688, 784, 813, 835
Maty, Paul Henry (1745–1787), II, 680
Maude, Gideon Michael Angelo (*fl.* 1831), III, 762
Maude, Thomas (1718–1798), II, 666
Maudslay, Athol (*fl.* 1888), III, 765
Maudsley, Henry (b. 1859), III, 966

Mauger, Claudius (*fl.* before 1667), II, 126
Maugham, Robert (d. 1862), III, 93
Maughan, J. (*fl.* 1854), I, 59
Maundrell, Henry (1665–1701), II, 750
Maunsell, Andrew (d. 1595), I, 358
Maunsell, H. (*fl.* after 1832), III, 809
Maupassant, Guy de, III, **22**
Maupertuis, Pierre Louis Moreau de, II, 795
Maurice of Kirkham (*fl.* 1170), I, **287**
Maurice, Frédéric Guillaume (*fl.* 1796), II, 688
Maurice, John Frederick Denison (1805–1872), III, **720**f., 817 (2)
  Pamphlets, prefaces, etc., II, 858; III, 112, 117, 127, 142, 670, 691, 694, 848–9, 977
Maurice, Thomas (1754–1824), II, **373**, 763
Mauritius de Portu (or O'Fihely) (*fl.* 1488), I, **305**
Maury, Jean Siffrein, II, 29
Maury, Matthew Fontaine (1806–1873), III, 956
Mauve, — de (*fl.* 1756), II, 688
Mauvillon, Éléazar de, II, 790
Maverick, Samuel (*fl.* 1660), I, 796; II, 751
Mavor, J. (*fl.* 1889), III, 984
Mavor, William Fordyce (1758–1837), II, 126, 257, 559, 616, 682–3, 741, 922; III, 135
Mawbey, Sir Joseph (1730–1798), II, 314
Mawer, John (*fl.* 1736), II, 816
Mawson, Robert (*fl.* 1714), II, 712 (2)
Maxims (O.E.), I, **82**
MAXIMS, COLLECTIONS OF, I, 715f. (16, 17 cents.); II, 120 (17, 18 cents.)
Maximus Tyrius, I, 461
Maxse, Frederick Augustus (1833–1900), III, 112
Maxse, L. J. (*fl.* 1900), III, 831
Maxwell, D. (*fl.* 1891), III, 977
Maxwell, E. M. (*fl.* 1883), III, 835
Maxwell, Sir Herbert Eustace (b. 1845), III, 772
Maxwell, James (*fl.* 1629), I, 802
Maxwell, James Clerk (1831–1879), III, 79, **939f.**
Maxwell, John (1590?–1647), I, 909
Maxwell, John (*fl.* 1708), II, 748
Maxwell, P. (*fl.* 1842), II, 354
Maxwell, Sir Peter Benson (1817–1893), III, 987
Maxwell, Shaw (*fl.* 1891), III, 818
Maxwell, William Hamilton (1792–1850), III, **408f.**, 765
May, Charles (*fl.* 1732), II, 753
May, E. (*fl.* 1790), II, 783
May, Frederick (*fl.* 1870), III, 797
May, Henry W. (*fl.* 1871), III, 987
May, John (*fl.* 1613), I, 847
May, Phil (1864–1903), III, 91, 831
May, R. (*fl.* 1660), I, 396
May, Thomas (1595–1650), I, 648, 723, 804, 809, 811 (2), 839

May, Sir Thomas Erskine, Baron Farnborough (1815–1886), III, **901**
May Bee, The [Cambridge] (1884), III, 835
May-Day, or, Anecdotes of Miss Lydia Lively (18 cent.), II, 564
Mayd Emelyn, The Boke of (16 cent.), I, 716
Maydes Metamorphosis, The (16 cent.), I, 539
Mayde(n)stone, Clement (*fl.* 1410), I, 189
Mayer, J. E. (*fl.* 1895), III, 1085
Mayer, John (1583–1664), I, 856
Mayer, John (*fl.* 1815), III, 762
Mayerne Turquet, Théodore de, II, 791
Mayeres, Randulph (*fl.* 1638), I, 772
Mayfair (1877), III, 814
Mayhew, Augustus Septimus (1826–1875), III, **497f.**
Mayhew, E. (*fl.* 1854), II, 817
Mayhew, Henry (1812–1887), III, 799
Mayhew, Horace (1816–1872), III, **721**
Maynard, Edward (1654–1740), II, 864
Maynard, George Henry (*fl.* 1785), II, 761
Maynard, John (*fl.* 1611), I, 485
Maynarde, Thomas (*fl.* 1595), I, 788, 792
Mayne, Jasper (1604–1672), I, **648, 698f.**
Mayne, John (1759–1836), II, 732, 991; III, 800
Mayne, John D. (*fl.* 1856), III, 987, 1084
Mayne, Rutherford (*fl.* 1907–12), III, **1065**
Maynwaring (or Mainwaring), Arthur (1668–1712), II, 661–2
Mayo, Charles (1792–1846), III, 112, 140
Mayo, Elizabeth (1793–1865), III, 112
Mayo, Isabella, née Fyvie (*fl.* 1877) ('Edward Garrett'), III, 573, 786
Mayor, John Eyton Bickersteth (1825–1910), I, 457; III, **1007f.**
Mayor, Joseph Bickersteth (b. 1828), I, 18, 21
Mayow, John (1640–1679), II, 961
Mazarin, Ortensia de la Porte, Duchesse de, II, 785
Mazumdar, P. C. (*fl.* 1882–94), III, 1081
Mazzella, Scipione, I, 781
Mazzini, Giuseppe, III, 211, 657
Mazzoni, Giacomo, I, 339
Mead, R. S. (*fl.* 1900?), III, 831
'Meade, L. T.', i.e. Elizabeth Thomasina, later Toulmin Smith (d. 1914), III, **569f.**
Mead, Richard (1673–1754), II, 961
Mead, Robert (1616–1653), I, 658
Meadowcourt, Richard (1695–1760), II, 911
Meager, Leonard (1624?–1704?), II, 148
Meares, John (1756?–1809), II, 757
Mearne, Samuel (*fl.* 1670), II, 107
Mears, William (*fl.* 1707–32), II, 96, 394
Mease, Peter (*fl.* 1618–27), I, 658
Mechanic's Magazine, The (1823), III, 822
Medalle, née Sterne, Mrs — (*fl.* 1775), II, 522
Medbourne, Matthew (d. 1679), II, 794
Medd, Peter Goldsmith (1829–1908), I, 676
Meddler, The (1744), II, 663
Mede (or Mead), Joseph (1586–1638), I, 856

Medhurst, Walter Henry (1796–1857), III, **1020**
Medical and Chirurgical Review, The (1794), II, 682
Medical and Philosophical Commentaries (1773), II, 686
Medical and Physical Journal, The (1799), II, 683
Medical Commentaries (1780), II, 686
Medical Facts and Observations (1791), II, 680
Medical Magazine, The (1774), II, 679
Medical Museum, The (1763), II, 678
Medical Times, The (1839), III, 821
Medicina Curiosa (1684), II, 674
MEDICINE
   Old English Recipes, I, **97f.**
   Renaissance to Restoration, I, 887f.
   Restoration to Romantic Revival, II, 925 (biographical collections), 927 (dictionaries). See also under Science; II, 959f.
   Nineteenth Century, III, 845 (medical year books), 962f. (physiology)
MEDIEVAL INFLUENCES
   Restoration to Romantic Revival, II, 73f. (modern studies), 74f. (contemporary criticism), 75f. (imitations, etc.), 77f. (translations, editions and collection), 81 (dramatic treatments)
   Nineteenth Century, III, 52f.
Medina, Pedro de, I, 816
MEDITERRANEAN COUNTRIES
   Descriptions of, I, 777 (16, 17 cents.)
   Voyages to, I, 767f. (16, 17 cents.)
Medley, The (1710), II, 661
Medley, The (1712), II, 707 (2)
Medley, The (1738), II, 663
Medley, The (Cork, 1738), II, 737
Medley, or Daily Tatler, The (1715), II, 662
Medleys for the Year, 1711, II, 661
Medlicott, Henry Benedict (1829–1905), III, 1080
Medulla Poetarum Romanorum (18 cent.), II, 206
Medusa or Penny Politician, The (1819), III, 816
Medwall, Henry (*fl.* 1486), I, 514, 517
Medwin, Thomas (1788–1869), III, 206, 215, 769
Meek, D. (*fl.* 1846), I, 908
Meeke, Mary (d. 1816?), III, **409**, 576
Meere, H. (*fl.* 1712–9), II, 708, 712
Meerman, G. (*fl.* before 1774), II, 886
Meery Riddles, the Booke of (17 cent.), I, 716
Meeting of Gallants, The (17 cent.), I, 713
Megrath, Mrs E. R. (*fl.* 1885), III, 1069
Méhégan, Guillaume Alexandre de, II, 791
Mehta, M. N. (*fl.* 1896), III, 1078
Meibom, Heinrich, II, 51
Meier, G. F., II, 806
Meiklejohn, John Miller Dow (1836–1902), III, 32

Meilan, Mark Anthony (*fl.* 1774–1812), II, 552, 566, 799
Meilhac, H., III, 610, 612
Mein, Robert (*fl.* 1661), II, 730
Meister, Jacques Henri, II, 142
Melanchthon, Philipp, I, 327, 816
Melbancke, Brian (*fl.* 1583), I, 729
Melbourne, William Lamb, Viscount (1779–1848), III, 144–5
Melcombe, George Bubb Doddington, Baron (1691–1762), II, 135
Meldola, David (*fl.* 1841), III, 819
Meleager, III, 1006
Mélesville, M., III, 598 (2)
Meliora (1858), III, 833
Mellish, Joseph Charles (*fl.* 1801), III, 34
Mello, Francisco Manuel de, II, 68
Mellon, Francis Hamilton (*fl.* 1890), III, 988
'Melmoth, Courtney,' i.e. S. J. Pratt (1749–1814), II, 26, 148, 257 (2), **377**, 547, 548 (3), 560
Melmoth, William (1710–1799), I, 23; II, 16, 765, 767–8
Melmoth, William Henry (*fl.* 1770–90), II, 232, 768, 799
Melodious Songster, The (18 cent.), II, 240
Melodist, The (18 cent.), II, 253
Melon, Jean François, II, 791
Melpomene (17 cent.), II, 178
Melpomene (18 cent.), II, 216
Melton, Sir John (d. 1640), I, 884
Melusine (M.E.), I, **160**
Melvill, Elizabeth, Lady Culross, the younger (*fl.* 1603), I, 898
Melvill, Henry (1798–1871), III, 853
Melville, Andrew (1545–1622), I, 900
Melville, C. (*fl.* 1841), III, 442
Melville, Sir James (1535–1617), of Hallhill, I, 384, 905
Melville, James (1556–1614), Scottish reformer, I, 905
'Members of the University' (1855), III, 127
Memmie le Blanc, M. A. (*fl.* 1768), II, 784
Memnon, I, 785
Mémoires Littéraires de la Grande Bretagne (1720), II, 688
Mémoires Littéraires de la Grande Bretagne (1768), II, 684
MEMOIRS. See BIOGRAPHIES
Memoirs for the Curious (1701), II, 675
Memoirs for the Ingenious, Containing Several Curious Observations in Philosophy [etc.] (1693), II, 675
Memoirs of Dick the Little Poney (18 cent.), II, 564
Memoirs of Literature (1710), II, 675
Memoirs of Love and Gallantry (18 cent.), II, 539
Memoirs of the Life of Cromwell [etc.] (18 cent.), II, 208
Memoirs of the Life of Mr Theophilus Keene (18 cent.), II, 194

Memoirs of the Life of Pope (18 cent.), II, 211
Memoirs of the Nutrebian Court (18 cent.), II, 544
Memoirs of the Present State (1692), II, 705
Memoirs of the Present State of Europe (1692), II, 676
Memoranda de Parliamento (M.E.), I, 115
Memorial des Marchands à Londres, Le (1681), II, 717
Memorial des Marchands Estant le prix des Marchandises à Londres (1683), II, 717
Menander, II, 762
Mendelssohn, Moses, II, 53
Mendelssohn, Sidney (*fl.* 1910), III, 1088
Mendez, Moses (d. 1758), II, 224, **373**f.
Mendies, J. (*fl.* 1851), III, 1074
Mendoza, Bernardino de, I, 816
Mendoza, Diego Hurtado de, I, 344
Mendoza, Iñigo Lopez de, I, 345
Mendoza, Juan González de, I, 782
Menestrier, C. F., I, 479
Menger, Anton, III, 985
Mennis (or Mennes), Sir John (1599–1671), I, 405
Mennons, James (*fl.* 1783), II, 733
Mennons, John (*fl.* 1782), III, 808
Menologium (O.E.), I, **79**f.
Mensforth, G. (*fl.* 1785), II, 809
Mental Amusement (18 cent.), II, 253 (3)
Menzies, Archibald (1754–1844), II, 757
Merbury, Francis (*fl.* 1579), I, 516
Mercantile Chronicle, The (1821), III, 809
Mercantile Gazette and General Intelligencer, The (1806), II, 721
Mercantile Gazette, and Liverpool and Manchester Daily Advertiser, The (1811), III, 801
Mercator, Gerard, I, 766
Mercator; Or, Commerce Retrieved (1713), II, 660
Mercenary Marriage, The (18 cent.), II, 547
Mercer, Thomas (*fl.* 1774), II, 23
Merchant and His Son (M.E.), I, **163**
MERCHANT TAYLORS' SCHOOL, I, 373; II, 104 (library)
Merchant's News Letter, The (1703), II, 711
Merchant's Remembrancer, The (1679), II, 717
MERCHANTMEN, II, 151 (18 cent.)
MERCIAN TEXTS, I, 36
Mercier, Louis Sébastien, II, 791; III, 590
Mercier-Dupaty, Charles Marguerite Jean Baptiste, II, 791
Mercure Anglois, Le (1644), I, 756
Mercure de France (1800), II, 683
Mercure Historique [etc.] (1750), II, 677
Mercurie Britannique, Le (1711), II, 719
Mercurio Britannico, Il (1799), II, 683
Mercurio Italico (1789), II, 681
Mercurio Volpone or the Fox (1648), I, 759
Mercurius Academicus (1645), I, 757

Mercurius Academicus (1648), I, 758
Mercurius Anglicus (1648), I, 759
Mercurius Anglicus (1650), I, 761
Mercurius Anglicus (1681), II, 704
Mercurius Anglicus, or a Post from the North (1644), I, 756
Mercurius Anglicus; Or, The Weekly Occurrences faithfully transmitted (1679), II, 702
Mercurius Anti-Britannicus (1645), I, 757
Mercurius Anti-Melancholicus (1647), I, 757
Mercurius Anti-Mercurius (1648), I, 759
Mercurius Anti-Pragmaticus (1647), I, 758
Mercurius Aquaticus (1648), I, 759
Mercurius Aulico-Mastix; or, The Whipping Mercury (1644), I, 756
Mercurius Aulicus (1643–5), I, 749 f.
Mercurius Aulicus (1654), I, 762
Mercurius Aulicus againe communcating intelligence from all parts (1648), I, 758
Mercurius Aulicus, communicating the intelligence and affairs of the Court to the rest of the Kingdome (1643) [two examples], I, 754
Mercurius Aulicus communicating intelligence from all parts of the Kingdome (1648), I, 759
Mercurius Aulicus (For King Charls II) (1649), I, 760
Mercurius Aulicus; or, The Court Mercury (1660), II, 701
Mercurius Aulicus; or, the Royal Intelligencer (1660), II, 701
Mercurius Bellicus (1648), I, 758
Mercurius Bellonius (1652), I, 761
Mercurius Bifrons; Or, the English Janus (1681), II, 657
Mercurius Britanicus (1643–6), I, 750
Mercurius Britanicus (1647), I, 757
Mercurius Britanicus alive again (1648), I, 758
Mercurius Britanicus communicating the affairs of Great Britaine (1646), I, 755
Mercurius Britanicus giving a perfect accompt (1648), I, 758
Mercurius Britanicus stating the affairs (1648), I, 758
Mercurius Britannicus (1652), I, 761
Mercurius Britannicus (1653), I, 762
Mercurius Britannicus (1718), II, 676
Mercurius Britannicus, or a Collection of such real and faithful intelligence [etc.] (1659), II, 730
Mercurius Britannicus; Or, The London Intelligencer turned Solicitor (1690), II, 658
Mercurius Britannicus; Or, The Weekly Observer (1692), II, 658
Mercurius Brittanicus communicating his most remarkable intelligence unto the Kingdome (1648), I, 758
Mercurius Brittanicus communicating intelligence from all parts, and handling the humours and conceits of Mercurius Pragmaticus (1649), I, 760

Mercurius Caledonius Comprising the affairs now in agitation in Scotland (1661), II, 702, 730
Mercurius Cambro-Britannus, The British Mercury or the Welch Diurnall (1643), I, 755
Mercurius Candidus (1646), I, 757
Mercurius Candidus (1647), I, 757
Mercurius Carolinus (1649), I, 760
Mercurius Catholicus (1648), I, 759
Mercurius Censorius (1648), I, 758
Mercurius Cinicus (1652), I, 761
Mercurius Civicus (1643–6), I, 750, 754
Mercurius Civicus; Or, A True Account of affairs both foreign and domestick (1680), II, 703
Mercurius Civicus or the Cities Intelligencer (1660), II, 701
Mercurius Civicus; or, The Cities Intelligencer (1660), II, 701
Mercurius Clericus or Newes from Syon communicated to all who love (and seek) the Peace of Jerusalem (1647), I, 758
Mercurius Clericus or Newes from the Assembly of their last III years in the Holy Convocation at Westminster (1647), I, 758
Mercurius Critticus (1648), I, 758
Mercurius Democritus (1652–3; 1659), I, 750, 761
Mercurius Democritus (1654), I, 762
Mercurius Democritus Communicating faithfully the affairs both in City and Countrey (1659), I, 763
Mercurius Democritus, his last Will and Testament (17 cent.), I, 719
Mercurius Democritus in Querpo (1660), II, 702
Mercurius Democritus or a perfect Nocturnall (1659), I, 763
Mercurius Democritus or a true and perfect Nocturnall communicating wonderfull news of the World in the Moon (1652), I, 761
Mercurius Democritus or the Smoaking Nocturnal (1661), II, 702
Mercurius Diutinus (1646), I, 757
Mercurius Diutinus (not Britanicus) (1646), I, 757
Mercurius Dogmaticus (1648), I, 758
Mercurius Domesticus (1648), I, 758
Mercurius Elencticus (1651), I, 761
Mercurius Elencticus, Britanicus, Melancholicus and Aulicus, The Hue and Cry after (17 cent.), I, 720
Mercurius Elencticus communicating intelligence from all parts (1649), I, 759
Mercurius Elencticus communicating the unparallell'd proceedings at Westminster (1647), I, 758
Mercurius Elencticus communicating the unparallell'd proceedings at Westminster (1649) [two examples], I, 759

Mercurius Elencticus communicating the un-parallell'd proceedings of the rebells at Westminster (1649) [two examples], I, 759, 760

Mercurius Elencticus (For King Charls II.) communicating intelligence from all parts (1649), I, 760

Mercurius Elencticus (For King Charles the II.) (1650), I, 760

Mercurius Eruditorum (1691), II, 675

Mercurius &c. (1644), I, 756

Mercurius Fidelicus (1648), I, 759

Mercurius Fumigosus (1654), I, 762

Mercurius Fumigosus (1660), II, 701

Mercurius Gallicus (1648), I, 758

Mercurius Heraclitus (1652), I, 761

Mercurius Hibernicus, or Ireland's Intelligencer (1663), II, 733

Mercurius Honestus or Newes from Westminster (1648), I, 758

Mercurius Honestus or Tom Tell-Truth (1660), II, 701

Mercurius Hybernicus (1649), I, 760

Mercurius Impartialis or an Answer to that Treasonable Pamphlet Mercurius Militaris, together with the Moderate (1648), I, 759

Mercurius Infernus (1680), II, 657

Mercurius Infernus; Or, News from the other World (1680), II, 703

Mercurius Insanus Insanissimus (1648), I, 758

Mercurius Jocosus or the merrie Mercurye (1654), I, 762

Mercurius Latinus (1746), II, 719

Mercurius Librarius (1668), II, 717

Mercurius Librarius; Or, A Faithfull Account of all Books (1680), II, 717

Mercurius Mastix (1652), I, 761

Mercurius Medicus or a Soveraigne Salve for these sick times (1647), I, 758

Mercurius Mediterraneus (1694), II, 706

Mercurius Melancholicus (1647–9), I, 750, 757 (2)

Mercurius Melancholicus communicating the general affaires of the Kingdome (1649), I, 759

Mercurius Melancholicus for King Charls the Second (1649), I, 760

Mercurius Melancholicus; or Newes from Westminster and the head quarters (1648), I, 759

Mercurius Militaris communicating intelligence from the Saints dissembled at Westminster (1648), I, 758

Mercurius Militaris or The Armies Scout (1648), I, 759

Mercurius Militaris or The People's Scout (1649), I, 760

Mercurius Militaris or Times only Truth-Teller (1649), I, 760

Mercurius Morbicus (1647), I, 750

Mercurius Morbicus or Newes from Westminster and other parts (1647), I, 757

Mercurius Musicus (1699), II, 676

Mercurius Nullus, or the Invisible Nuncio (1654), I, 762

Mercurius Pacificus (1648), I, 759

Mercurius Pacificus (1649), I, 760

Mercurius Phanaticus or Mercury Temporising (1660), II, 701

Mercurius Philo-Monarchicus (1649), I, 759

Mercurius Phreneticus (1652) [two examples], I, 761

Mercurius Poeticus (1654), I, 762

Mercurius Poeticus (1660), II, 702

Mercurius Politicus (1650–60), I, 750

Mercurius Politicus (1716), II, 676

Mercurius Politicus, Communicating Advertisements from the three Kingdoms (1660), II, 701

Mercurius Politicus; Comprising the Sum of Foreign Intelligence [etc.] (1653), II, 730

Mercurius Politicus comprising the summ of all intelligence (1650), I, 760

Mercurius Politicus; Or, an Antidote to popular misrepresentation (1705), II, 660

Mercurius Populi (1647), I, 758

Mercurius Pragmaticus (1647–50), I, 750

Mercurius Pragmaticus (1652) [two examples], I, 761

Mercurius Pragmaticus (1653), I, 762

Mercurius Pragmaticus (1658?), I, 763

Mercurius Pragmaticus (1659), I, 763

Mercurius Pragmaticus communicating his Weekly Intelligence (1659), I, 763

Mercurius Pragmaticus communicating Intelligence from all parts (1647) [three examples], I, 757

Mercurius Pragmaticus (For King Charles II) (1649), I, 759–60

Mercurius Pragmaticus Impartially communicating the true state of affairs (1659), I, 763

Mercurius Pragmaticus Revived and from the shades of his Retirement return'd again (1651), I, 761

Mercurius Psitacus or the Parroting Mercury (1648), I, 758

Mercurius Publicus, Being a Summary of the whole week's Intelligence (1680), II, 703

Mercurius Publicus Communicating emergent occurrences (1648), I, 758

Mercurius Publicus, Comprising the Sum of forraign Intelligence, II, 701

Mercurius Reformatus (1690), II, 731

Mercurius Reformatus; Or, The New Observator (1689), II, 658

Mercurius Reformatus; Or, The True Observator (1691), II, 658

Mercurius Republicus (1649), I, 760

Mercurius Rhadamanthus (1653), I, 762

Mercurius Rusticans (17 cent.), I, 662

Mercurius Rusticus (1647), I, 758

Mercurius Rusticus, or a Countrey Messenger (1643), I, 755

Mercurius Rusticus, or the Countries Complaint (1643), I, 755

Mercurius Scommaticus (1651), I, 761

Mercurius Scoticus (1648), I, 759

Mercurius Scoticus (1651), II, 730

Mercurius Scoticus or the Royal Messenger (1651), I, 761

Mercurius Theologicus (1700), II, 661, 676

Mercurius Theologicus; or, The Monthly Instructor (1700), II, 675

Mercurius Urbanicus; or, Newes from London and Westminster (1648), I, 758

Mercurius Urbanus (1643), I, 755

Mercurius Vapulans (1647), I, 758

Mercurius Verax or Truth appearing after seaven yeares Banishment (1649), I, 760

Mercurius Veridicus (1644), I, 756

Mercurius Veridicus (1660), II, 702

Mercurius Veridicus Communicating intelligence from all parts of England (1681), II, 703

Mercurius Veridicus communicating Intelligence from all parts of Great Britaine (1648), I, 758

Mercurius Veridicus, or True Informations (1645), I, 756

Mercurius Zeteticus (1652), I, 761

Mercury of England, Giving An Account of All Publick Events with Historical Observations, The (1704), II, 711

Mercury; or Advertisements concerning Trade, The (1678), II, 716

Mercury, or the Northern Reformer, The (1717), II, 662

Mercury publishing Advertisements, The (1667), II, 716

Méré, Antoine Gombaud, Chevalier de, II, 781

Meredith, C. (*fl.* 1909), III, 1090

Meredith, George (1828–1909), III, **467**f.

Meredith, Hal (*fl.* 1894), III, 574

Meredith, Louisa Anne, née Twamley (*fl.* 1846–91), III, **1097**

'Meredith, Owen', i.e. Edward Robert Bulwer Lytton, Earl of Lytton (1831–1891), III, **347**

Meredith, Royston (*fl.* 1714), II, 610

Meres, Francis (1565–1647), I, 715, 815, 865

Meres, John (1698–1761), II, 676, 698, 710

Meriton, George (1634–1711), I, 850; II, 964

Meriton, Thomas (b. 1638), I, 648

Meritt, Paul (d. 1895), III, **626**

Merivale, Charles (1808–1893), III, **895**

Merivale, Herman (1806–1874), III, **907**

Merivale, Herman Charles (1839–1906), III, 608, **626**f.

Merivale, John Herman (1779–1844), III, **239**

Merle, Gibbons (*fl.* 1817–29), III, 789, 800 (2), 816

MERLIN LEGEND, I, 131

Merlin; The Weekly Monitor (1692), II, 658

Merlinus Phanaticus (1660), II, 701

Mermaid; Or, Nautical Songster, The (18 cent.), II, 251

Merrett (or Merret), Christopher (1614–1695), II, 104, 812

Merrick, James (1720–1769), II, **374**

Merrick, Leonard, originally Miller (1864–1938), III, **555**

Merrick, Rice (d. 1587), I, 774

Merrick, William (*fl.* 1788), II, 817

Merrie Dialogue, Betweene Band, Cuffe, and Ruffe, A (17 cent.), I, 661

'Merriman, Henry Seton', i.e. Hugh Stowell Scott (1862–1903), III, **555**

Merriman, Nathaniel James (1810–1882), III, 1092

'Merriman, Tim' (1729), II, 200

Merry, J. (*fl.* 1791), II, 625

Merry, Robert (1755–1798), II, **374**

Merry, William Walter (1835–1918), III, **1008**

Merry and Wise (1865), III, 830

Merry Companion, The (18 cent.), II, 229

Merry Companion; Or, Feast for the Sons of Comus, The (18 cent.), II, 239

Merry Companion, Or Humourous Miscellany, The (18 cent.), II, 215

Merry Companion, or Universal Songster, The (18 cent.), II, 207, 209, 211, 214

Merry Devill of Edmonton, The (17 cent.), I, 652

Merry Droll, The (18 cent.), II, 226

Merry Drollery (17 cent.), II, 173–5, 182

Merry England (1883), III, 831

Merry Fellow, The (18 cent.), II, 216, 218 (2)

Merry Jeste of a Shrewde and Curste Wyfe lapped in Morrelles Skin, A (16 cent.), I, 716

Merry Lad, The (18 cent.), II, 216

Merry Man's Companion, The (18 cent.), II, 214

Merry Medley, The (18 cent.), II, 210, 211 (2), 213 (2), 214

Merry Mercury; Or, A farce of Fools, The (1700), II, 659

Merry Miscellany, Being the Second Part of Daniel Gunston's Jests, The (18 cent.), II, 234

Merry Mountebank, The (18 cent.), II, 202

Merry Musician, The (18 cent.), II, 193, 199, 200 (3), 201, 203

Merry Quack Doctor, The (18 cent.), II, 233

Merry-Thought, The (18 cent.), II, 201 (5), 202 (3)

'Merryman, Dr' (*fl.* 1703), II, 186

'Merrypin, Margery' (1745), II, 211

'Merton, Ambrose', i.e. William John Thoms (1803–1885), III, 576

MERTON COLLEGE (Oxford), I, 368f.

Library, I, 361

Mery geste of Robyn Hoode, A (16 cent.), I, 520

Meryon, Charles Lewis (1783–1877), III, 150
Meslier, —, I, 735
Mesmes, Jean Antoine de, Count d'Avaux, II, 791
Meston, William (1688?–1745), II, 579, **973**
Metamorphoses of the Town, The [etc.] (18 cent.), II, 210
METAPHYSICAL POETRY. See under Jacobean and Caroline Poets, I, 440f.
METAPHYSICS. See PHILOSOPHY
Metastasio, Pietro Antonio Domenico Bonaventura, II, 812
Metastasio, Pietro Trapassi, II, 66
Metcalf, John (1717–1810), II, 136
Metcalfe, Charles Theophilus, Baron (1785–1846), III, 151
Meteors, The (19 cent.), II, 256
Meteren, E. van, I, 769
Meteyard, Eliza (1816–1876), III, **899**
Metham, John (*fl.* 15 cent.), I, 265
Methinks the Poor Town has been troubled too long (17 cent.), II, 177 (2)
Methodist, The (1874), III, 819
Methodist Magazine, The (1798), III, 823
Methodist Magazine; Or, Evangelical Repository, The (1798), II, 684
Methodist Monitor, The (1796), II, 682, 684
Methodist Monthly, The (1892), III, 827
Methodist Recorder, The (1861), III, 819
Methodist Times, The (1867), III, 819
Methold, William (d. 1653), III, 1079
Methuen, Sir Algernon (1856–1924), III, 99
Methuen, H. H. (*fl.* 1846), III, 1091
METRES. See Prosody, I, 13f.
Metrical Homilies (M.E.), I, 39
Metropolitan, The (1831), III, 826
Metropolitan Conservative Journal, The (1836), III, 813
Metropolitan Magazine, The (1831), III, 826
Metropolitan Nuncio, The (1649), I, 760
Mewe, William (*fl.* 1620–50), I, 658
Mexia, Pedro, I, 344, 734, 816
Meyler, William (*fl.* 1779), II, 449
Meynell, Alice, née Thompson (1847–1922), III, **348**f.
Meynell, Wilfrid (*b.* 1852), III, 819 (2), 831
Meyrick, Frederick (1827–1906), I, 696; III, 691, 853
Meyrick, Sir Samuel Rush (1783–1848), I, 390
Meyrick, T. (*fl.* 1844), III, 856
Meysey-Wigley, Caroline, later Clive (1801–1873), III, **479**
Miall, A. (*fl.* 1841), III, 819
Miall, Edward (1809–1881), III, 786
Micanzio, Fulgentio, II, 812
Michael of Cornwall (*fl.* 1250), I, **300**
Michael, Dan (*fl.* 1340). See *Ayenbite of Inwyt*, I, 184f.
Michael, James Lionel (1824–1868), III, 1094
Michael, W. H. (*fl.* 1872), III, 987

Michel of Northgate (M.E.), I, 184f.
Michel, Francisque, II, 918; III, 891 (2)
Michele, C. E. (*fl.* 1833–49), III, 798
Michell, Sir Lewis (1842–1928), III, 1090
Mickle, William Julius (1735–1788), II, 23, **374**
Mickleburgh, G. T. (*fl.* 1859), III, 73
Microcosm, The (1757), II, 664
Microcosm, The (1786), II, 356, 666
Microcosmus (17 cent.), I, 662
Microscope; Or, Minute Observer, The (1799), II, 688
MIDDLE AGES. See MEDIEVAL INFLUENCES
MIDDLE ENGLISH
    Language, I, 26, **28**f., 32, 37f.
MIDDLE ENGLISH LITERATURE
    Bible Renderings, I, 187f.
    Bibliographies, Surveys, Anthologies, I, 113f.
    Chaucer, I, 208f.
    Chronicles and Prophecies, I, 163f.
    Gower, I, 205f.
    Moral and Religious Instruction, I, 177f.
    Pearl Group, I, 201f.
    Richard Rolle and Associated Pieces, I, 191f.
    Romances, I, 128f.
    Sermons and Saints' Legends, I, 168f.
    Tales, I, 161f.
    The Thre Ages, Wynnere and the Piers Plowman Series, I, 161f.
    Travels, I, 190f.
    Wycliffe and Associated Writings, I, 203f.
    See also FIFTEENTH CENTURY, I, 250f., SONGS AND BALLADS, I, 267f. and MEDIEVAL DRAMA, I, 274f.
MIDDLE ENGLISH POETRY
    General. See under Bibliographies, Surveys, Anthologies, I, 113f.
    Bible Renderings, I, 187
    Chaucer, I, 208f.
    Chronicles and Prophecies, I, 163f.
    Gower, I, 205f.
    Moral and Religious Instruction, I, 177f.
    Pearl Group, I, 201f.
    Rolle and Associated Pieces, I, 191f.
    Romances, I, 128f.
    Sermons and Saints' Legends, I, 168f.
    Tales, I, 161f.
    The Thre Ages, Wynnere and Piers Plowman Series, I, 195f.
    See also under FIFTEENTH CENTURY, I, 250f. and SONGS AND BALLADS, I, 267f. For Latin verse 11 to 15 cents. see under WRITINGS IN LATIN, I, 280f.
MIDDLE SCOTS WRITERS, I, 254f.
MIDDLE TEMPLE LIBRARY, II, 104
MIDDLESEX
    Dialect, I, 41
Middlesex Chronicle, The (19 cent.), III, 793
Middlesex Journal and Evening Advertiser, The (1773), II, 710

Middlesex Journal, and London Evening Post, The (1785), II, 710
Middlesex Journal; Or, Chronicle of Liberty, The (1769), II, 710
Middlesex Journal; Or, Universal Evening Post, The (1772), II, 710
Middleton, C. S. (*fl.* 1858), III, 215
Middleton, Christopher (1560?–1628), I, 395, 730
Middleton, Christopher (d. 1770), II, 743
Middleton, Conyers (1683–1750), II, 101, 714, 765, **878**
Middleton, Erasmus (1739–1805), I, 698; II, 924
Middleton, John (*fl.* 1789), II, 822
Middleton, John Henry (1846–1896), III, **1008**
Middleton, Richard (*fl.* 1283), I, **294**
Middleton, Thomas (1570?–1627), I, **611**f., 733
Middleton, Thomas (*fl.* 1677), Scottish divine, II, 998
Middleton, Thomas Fanshaw (1769–1822), II, 666; III, 823
MIDDLEWICH
    Newspapers, II, 726
Midgley, Robert (1653–1723), II, 534, 796, 810
Midland Counties Evening Express, The (1874), III, 804
Midland Daily Telegraph, The [Coventry] (1891), III, 806
Midland Echo, The [Birmingham] (1883), III, 805
Midland Echo, The [Wolverhampton] (1879), III, 805
Midland Evening News, The [Wolverhampton] (1884), III, 805
Midland Mercury, The (1794), II, 726
MIDLANDS
    Dialects (M.E.), I, 38
    Texts (M.E.), I, 42
'Midnight, Mary' (1751), II, 303
Midsummer Holydays; or, A Story for Young Folk (18 cent.), II, 563
Midwife; Or, Old Woman's Magazine, The (1750), II, 677
Miege, Guy (1644–1718?), I, 461; II, 182–3, 565, 719, 743, 931
Miers, John (1789–1879), III, 991
Mifflin, Benjamin (*fl.* 1764), II, 755
Mignault, Claude, I, 479
Milbourne, Luke (1649–1720), II, 25, 272
Miles, Alfred Henry (*fl.* 1889), III, 574
Miles, Henry Downes (*fl.* 1846–80), II, 815; III, 22, 766 (2)
Miles, William Augustus (1753?–1817), II, 166, 448, 635
Military Actions of Europe, The (1646), I, 757
Military Magazine, The (1793), II, 682
Military Register, The (1814), III, 821
Military Scribe, The (1644), I, 756

MILITARY TEXTBOOKS, I, 389f. (16, 17 cents).
Milkmaid, The (19 cent.), III, 575
Mill, Humphrey (*fl.* 1646), I, 477
Mill, James (1773–1836), II, 954; III, 112, **871**, 965, 980
Mill, John (1645–1707), II, 933, 948
Mill, John (1740–1803), II, 156
Mill, John Stuart (1806–1873), III, 21, 25, 152, 833 (2), **871**
    Reviews, essays, etc. by, III, 112, 122, 157f., 257 (2), 686
Millais, Sir John Everett (1829–1896), III, 91
Millais, John Guille (*fl.* 1892), III, 763
Millar, John (1735–1801), II, 998
Millar, T. L. ('Lynn Lyster') (*fl.* 1910), III, 1089
Millard, J. (*fl.* 1836), III, 104
Millard, John (*fl.* 1770), II, 746
Miller, — (*fl.* 1761), II, 28
Miller, Anne, Lady (1741–1781), II, 231 (4), 232, 235, **374**f.
Miller, Edmond (*fl.* 1717), II, 116
Miller, G. (*fl.* 1833), bookseller, III, 103
Miller, George (1764–1848), divine, II, 20, 666
Miller, Hugh (1802–1856), III, **721**f., 819
Miller, J. (*fl.* 1738), II, 823
Miller, J. (*fl.* 1839), I, 910
Miller, James (1706–1744), II, **441**, 485, 794 (2), 797, 803
Miller, Johann Martin, II, 63, 806
Miller, John (*fl.* 1695), writer on New York, II, 752
Miller, John (*fl.* 1754), naval surgeon, II, **375**
Miller, John Cale (1814–1880), III, 118
Miller, Josiah (1832–1880), III, 312
Miller, Lydia Falconer, née Fraser (1811?–1876) ('Harriet Myrtle'), III, 572, 721
Miller, M. (*fl.* 1761), II, 770
Miller, M. (*fl.* 1872), III, **827**
Miller, R. K. (*fl.* 1871), III, 834
Miller, Thomas (1807–1874), poet, III, **299**, 407
Miller, Thomas (*fl.* 1858), of Dublin, III, 971
Miller, William (1810–1872), III, 299
Miller, William Allen (1817–1870), III, 947
Miller, William Hallows (1801–1880), III, 941
Milles, Jeremiah (1714–1784), II, 344
Milles, Thomas (d. 1627?), I, 396, 816, 847
Milligen, George (*fl.* 1770), II, 755
Milligen, Julius (*fl.* 1831), III, 207
Milliken, E. J. (*fl.* 1896), III, 774
Millikin, Richard Alfred (1767–1815), II, 688; III, **1051**
Millot, Claude François Xavier, II, 791
Mills, Charles (1788–1826), I, 127
Mills, John (d. 1784?), II, 817
Mills, John (*fl.* 1841), III, **498**
Mills, Joseph (*fl.* 1775), II, 762
Mills, L. H. (*fl.* 1894), III, 1082
Mills, R. H. (*fl.* 1857), III, 974
Mills, William (*fl.* 1780), II, 768

Milman, Henry Hart (1791–1868), III, 234, 887f.
Milne, J. (fl. 1899), III, 1090
Milne, William (1785–1822), III, 1020
Milner, Mrs — (fl. 1850), III, 577
Milner, Henry M. (fl. 1820–30), III, 199, 591
Milner, John (1628–1702), II, 883, 943
Milnes, Richard Monckton, Baron Houghton (1809–1885), III, 299
  Editions by, I, 386; II, 651; III, 220–1 (2)
  Reviews and prefaces by, III, 257, 332, 341, 429
Milns, William (fl. 1797), II, 253
Milton, Frances, later Trollope (1780–1863), III, 419
Milton, John (1608–1674), I, 463f.
  Bibliographies, I, 463
  Biography and Criticism, I, 468f. (books), 471f. (articles), 748
  Collected Works, I, 463f.
  Influence, II, 45, 57, 67, 71, 171; III, 25, 45
  Separate Publications, I, 465f., 654, 760, 828
Milton, William Charles de Meuron Went-worth Fitzwilliam, Viscount (1839–1877), III, 990
Milton State Papers (17 cent.), I, 400
Milward, Richard (1609–1680), I, 874
Minadoi, Giovanni Tommaso, I, 785, 816
Minchin, George Minchin (1845–1914), III, 943
Mind (1876), III, 833
Mind of Men (O.E.), I, 82
Mind, Will and Understanding (15 cent.), I, 514
Miner and Workman's Advocate, The (1863), III, 817
Miners' Advocate, The [Middlesbrough] (1873), III, 817
Miner's Weekly News, The [Coventry] (1873), III, 817
Minerva Magazine, The (1793), II, 688
MINING (writings on), III, 969f.
Mining Journal The, (1835), III, 822
Minor British Drama (1834), III, 585
Minor Poets, The (18 cent.), II, 215
Minor Theatre, The (1794), II, 392
Minor's Pocket-Book, The (18 cent.), II, 564
Minot, Lawrence (1300?–1352?), I, 39, 270f.
Minsheu, John (fl. 1617), I, 377, 855
Minstrell, The (18 cent.), II, 234, 248
Minto, Sir Gilbert Elliot, Earl of (1751–1814), II, 137, 166
Minto, W. H. Elliot-Murray-Kynynmound, Earl of (fl. 1863), III, 770
Minto, William (1845–1893), III, 750f., 810
Minton, F. D. (fl. 1883), III, 984
Minton, S. (fl. 1851), III, 691
Mirabeau, Honoré Gabriel Riquetti, Comte de, II, 797
MIRACLE PLAYS, I, 275f.
Miriam (1800), II, 551
Mirk, John (fl. 1043), I, 175, 265, 302

Mirror, The (1779), II, 665
Mirror for Magistrates, A (16 cent.), I, 413f.
Mirror, late Bonner and Middleton's Journal, The (1804), II, 721
Mirror of Literature, Amusement and Instruction, The (1822), III, 815
Mirror of the Times, The (1796), III, 813
Mirrour, The (1719), II, 662
Mirth and Glee (18 cent.), II, 236
Mirth Diverts all Care (18 cent.), II, 188 (2)
Mirth in Abundance (17 cent.), I, 715
Mirth's Magazine (18 cent.), II, 225
Miscellanea (17 cent.), II, 182
Miscellanea (1727), I, 199 (2)
Miscellanea Aurea (18 cent.), II, 195
Miscellanea Curiosa (18 cent.), II, 204–5
Miscellanea Magna (17 cent.), I, 718
Miscellanea Nova et Curiosa (18 cent.), II, 213
Miscellanea Sacra (17 cent.), II, 183–4
Miscellanea Sacra (18 cent.), II, 187 (2), 188, 203
Miscellaneous and Fugitive Pieces (18 cent.), II, 229, 230 (2)
Miscellaneous Collection of Poems, A (18 cent.), II, 196
Miscellaneous Collection of Songs, Ballads & Elegies, A (18 cent.), II, 251, 253
Miscellaneous Collection of the best English & Irish Songs, A (18 cent.), II, 244
Miscellaneous Extracts, Chiefly Poetical (18 cent.), II, 247
Miscellaneous Letters (1694), II, 675
Miscellaneous Letters and Essays (17 cent.), II, 182
Miscellaneous Pieces (18 cent.), II, 215 (2)
Miscellaneous Pieces in Prose and Verse: By Leonard Howard [etc.] (18 cent.), II, 223 (2)
Miscellaneous Pieces of Poetry (18 cent.), II, 223
Miscellaneous Pieces: Original and Collected (18 cent.), II, 240
Miscellaneous Poems and Translations (18 cent.), II, 190–1, 195–6, 198–9, 203
Miscellaneous Poems and Translations Publish'd by Richard Savage (18 cent.), II, 198
Miscellaneous Poems [etc.]. By Vincent Bourne (18 cent.), II, 229
Miscellaneous Poems (Manchester, 1790), II, 244
Miscellaneous Poems on Several Occasions By Mr. Dawson [etc.] (18 cent.), II, 205
Miscellaneous Poems on State-Affairs (18 cent.), II, 193
Miscellaneous Poems, Original and Translated, Published by Mr. Concanen (18 cent.), II, 197
Miscellaneous Poems Published by D. Lewis, II, 198
Miscellaneous Poems Publish'd By Mr Ralph (1729), II, 200, 210

Miscellaneous Poetical Novels or Tales (18 cent.), II, 187

Miscellaneous Tracts (18 cent.), II, 216

Miscellaneous Works Of Prior [etc.] (18 cent.), II, 208 (3)

Miscellaneous Works of...the Late Earls of Rochester And Roscommon, The (18 cent.), II, 187 (2), 189, 192, 194 (2), 196, 202 (2), 205, 208 (2), 215 (2)

Miscellaneous Works of...The Late Earls of Rochester And Roscommon, The (18 cent.), II, 217, 218 (3), 225, 228, 230, 233, 256

Miscellaneous Works, Written by Duke of Buckingham (18 cent.), II, 186 (2)

Miscellaniae Curiosae (1734), II, 685

MISCELLANIES (poetical), I, 403 f. (16, 17 cents.); II, 173 f. (1660–1800)

Miscellanies (18 cent.), II, 199 (2), 201, 203 (7), 205 (5), 207 (2), 209 (3), 211 (2), 212–3, 215

Miscellanies by Dr. Swift, Dr. Arbuthnot, Mr. Pope and Mr. Gay (18 cent.), II, 247

Miscellanies in Prose and Verse (1721), II, 196

Miscellanies in Prose and Verse (1785), II, 239

Miscellanies in Prose and Verse (Edinburgh, 1791), II, 246

Miscellanies in Prose and Verse By Swift and Pope (18 cent.), II, 200, 203

Miscellanies Moral and Instructive (18 cent.), II, 240

Miscellanies over Claret (1697), II, 183–4, 676

Miscellany, A (1753), II, 216

Miscellany, The (1711), II, 661

Miscellany, The (1732), II, 663

Miscellany, The (1768), II, 665

Miscellany, Being A Collection of Poems By Several Hands (17 cent.), II, 179

Miscellany: Giving an Account of the Religion [etc.], *The* (1732), II, 714

Miscellany of Ingenious Thoughts, A (18 cent.), II, 196

Miscellany of Lyric Poems, A (18 cent.), II, 208

Miscellany Of New Poems, A (18 cent.), II, 206

Miscellany of Original Poems Collected by Mr. Theobald, A (18 cent.), II, 203

Miscellany of Poems Publish'd by J. Husbands, A (18 cent.), II, 201

Miscellany Poems (17 cent.), II, 183

Miscellany Poems... by the most Eminent Hands (17 cent.), II, 179 (2), 182 (3), 185–9, 193, 199

Miscellany Poems and Translations By Oxford Hands (17 cent.), II, 179

Miscellany Poems upon Several Occasions (17 cent.), II, 182

Misogonus (16 cent.), I, 521

Miss Catley and Miss Weiwitzer's New London and Dublin Song-Book (18 cent.), II, 227

Misselden, Edward (*fl.* 1608–54), I, 847

Missionary Magazine, The (1796), II, 686

Misson, François Maximilien, II, 791

Misson, Henri, II, 140, 791

Missy, Caesar de, II, 672, 680

Mist, Nathaniel (d. 1737), II, 712

Mist's Weekly Journal (1725), II, 712

Mistaken Beauty, or the Lyar, The (17 cent.), II, 485

Mistaken Husband, The (17 cent.), II, 266

Mister, Mary (*fl.* 1816), III, 571

Mr Henr Purcell's Favourite Songs (18 cent.), II, 197

Mr Redhead Yorke's Weekly Political Review (1805), III, 816

Mrs. Crouch's Favourite Pocket Companion (18 cent.), II, 243, 244 (2)

Mrs. Pilkington's Jests (18 cent.), II, 219, 222

Mitchel, J. (*fl.* 1711), II, 769

Mitchel, John (1815–1875), III, 1051

Mitchell, — (*fl.* 1816), III, 807

Mitchell, Alexander Ferrier (1822–1899), I, 677

Mitchell, Sir Andrew (1708–1771), II, 167

Mitchell, C. (*fl.* 1846), III, 797

Mitchell, Hugh (*fl.* 1799), II, 927

Mitchell, later Mrs Ives Hurry (*fl.* 1803), III, 570

Mitchell, John (1724–1793), II, 961

Mitchell, Joseph (1684–1738), II, 322

Mitchell, Thomas (1783–1845), III, 995

Mitchell, W. H. (*fl.* 1863), III, 78

Mitchell, Sir William (1811–1878), III, 801

Mitchell, William Andrew (*fl.* 1824), III, 768, 826

Mitford, Bertram (*fl.* 1882), III, 1089, 1093

Mitford, John (1781–1859), poet and editor, I, 464 (2); II, 334, 837; III, 239, 636

Mitford, John (1782–1831), humorous and scandalous writer, III, 210, 820

Mitford, John Freeman, Baron Redesdale (1748–1830), II, 890

Mitford, Mary Russell (1787–1855), III, 409 f.

Mitford, William (1744–1827), II, 890

Mitra, Piyarichand (*fl.* 1879), III, 1081

Mitra, Rajendralala (*fl.* 1878), III, 1072, 1074, 1077

Mitra, Vihári-Lála (*fl.* 1891), III, 1073

Mitre and Crown (1748), II, 677

Mitter, G. C. (*fl.* 1870), III, 1081

Mivart, Saint George (1827–1900), III, 954, 966

Moberly, George (1803–1885), III, 122, 858

Moberly, Robert Campbell (1845–1903), III, 851

Mock Press, The (1681), II, 657

Mock Songs and Joking Poems (17 cent.), II, 177

MOCK TESTAMENTS, I, 719 f. (17 cent.)

MOCK-HEROIC, II, 170 (recent criticism). See also BURLESQUE

Mocket (Moket or Moquet), Richard (1577–1618), I, 852

Mocquet, Jean, II, 791
Modena, Leon, I, 780; II, 812
Moderate communicating martial affaires to the Kingdome of England, The (1648), I, 758
Moderate Informer, The (1659), I, 763
Moderate Intelligence impartially communicating martial affairs to the Kingdom of England, A (1649), I, 760
Moderate Intelligencer, The (1649), I, 760
Moderate Intelligencer, The (1652), I, 761
Moderate Intelligencer, The (1653) [two examples], I, 762
Moderate Intelligencer, The, (1654), I, 762
Moderate Intelligencer, The (1682), II, 704
Moderate Intelligencer Impartially communicating Martiall Affaires to the Kingdome of England, The (1645), I, 756
Moderate Mercury, The (1649), I, 760
Moderate Messenger, The (1646), I, 757
Moderate Messenger, The (1647), I, 757
Moderate Messenger, The (1649), I, 760
Moderate Messenger, The (1653), I, 761
Moderate Occurrences (1653), I, 762
Moderate Publisher of every Dayes Intelligence, The (1653), I, 761–2
Moderate Publisher of Every Dayes Intelligence, The (1654), I, 762
Moderator, The (1692), II, 658
Moderator, The (1705), II, 660
Moderator, The (1710), II, 661
Moderator, The (1719), II, 662
Modern Advertising (1900), III, 780
Modern Authors (1895), III, 830
Modern Beauties In Prose and Verse (18 cent.), II, 248
Modern British Drama, The (1811), II, 392
Modern Catch-Club, The (18 cent.), II, 227
MODERN ENGLISH
    Language, I, 26, 29f., 32f., 43f.
Modern English Comic Theatre, The (1843), III, 585
Modern Freemason's Pocket Book, The, II, 230
Modern History; Or, A Monethly Account of Occurrences (1687), II, 675
Modern History; or The Monthly Account of all considerable occurrences (1687), II, 704
Modern Intelligencer, The (1651), I, 761
Modern Miscellany, The (18 cent.), II, 210
Modern Monitor, The (1770), II, 665
Modern Musick-Master, The (18 cent.), II, 200–1, 207
Modern Poems (1776), II, 231
Modern Poets (1892), III, 830
Modern Review, The (1880), III, 834
Modern Songster, The (18 cent.), II, 244
Modern Syren, The (18 cent.), II, 235, 244
Modern Theatre, The (1809), II, 392
Moderne Intelligencer, The (1647), I, 757
Modernism, III, 161f.

Modest Narrative of Intelligence Fitted for the Republique of England and Ireland, A (1649), I, 759
Modus tenendi Parliamentum (M.E.), I, 117
Moe, Jörgen, III, 576
Moens, Simon Bernelot (*fl.* 1817), III, 576
Moestissimae ac Laetissimae Academiae Cantabrigiensis Affectus [on Charles II's death] (17 cent.), II, 179
Moffat, A. S. (*fl.* 1865), III, 770
Moffat, J. S. (*fl.* 1885), III, 1090
Moffat, Robert (1795–1883), III, 1091
Moffat, Thomas (*fl.* 1599), I, 480
Moffett (or Moffet), Thomas (1553–1604), I, 892f.; II, 895
Mogridge, George (1787–1854), III, 567
Mohan Lal (*fl.* 1834), III, 1080
Moir, David Macbeth (1798–1851), III, 235, 410, 677
Moir, J. M. (1868), III, 815
Moivre, Abraham de (*fl.* 1716), II, 826
Mole, John (1743–1827), II, 129
Moleswood, J. T. (*fl.* 1851), III, 1074
Molesworth, Sir G. L. (*fl.* 1894), III, 975
Molesworth, Mary Louisa, née Stewart (d. 1921), III, **569**
Molesworth, Robert, Viscount (1656–1725), II, 159, 322, 662, 744, 783
Molesworth, Sir William (1810–1855), I, 871
Molesworth, William Nassau (1816–1890), III, **916**
Molière, Jean Baptiste Poquelin de, II, 41f., 319, 794; III, 605
Mollineux, Mary, later Southworth (1651–1695), II, **283**
Molloy, Charles (d. 1767), II, **441**, 663, 712, 794
Molteno, P. A. (*fl.* 1900), III, 1090, 1092
Molyneux, Sir C. (*fl.* 1820), II, 943
Molyneux, T. (*fl.* 1709), II, 159
Molyneux, William (1656–1698), II, 777, 943
Momerie, Alfred Williams (1848–1900), III, 851
Mommsen, Theodor, III, 33
Momus (1866) [Cambridge], III, 834
Momus Ridens; Or, Comical Remarks on the Publick Reports (1690), II, 658
Momus's Cabinet of Amusement (19 cent.), II, 256
MONAGHAN
    Magazine, II, 688 (1798)
    Newspaper, II, 738
Monardes, Nicolás, I, 794
Monboddo, James Burnett, Lord (1714–1799), II, 955
Monckton, Sir Philip (1620?–1679), I, 387, 842
Moncrieff, William Thomas (1794–1857), III, 440, **592**
Moncrif, François Auguste Paradis de, II, 541
MONETARY QUESTIONS (writings on), III, 973f.

Monetary Times and Banker's Circular, The (1858), III, 820
Monethly Intelligencer, The (1660), II, 701
Money Market Review, The (1860), III, 820
Monfart, Henri de Feynes de, I, 783
Monget, M. (*fl.* 1806), III, 571
Mongredien, Augustus (1807–1888), III, 983
Monier-Williams, Sir Monier, earlier Williams (1819–1899), III, **1018**, 1071, 1081
Monings, Edward (*fl.* 1596), I, 739
Monipennie, John (*fl.* 1594), I, 775
Monitor, The (1714), II, 661
Monitor, The (1724), II, 662
Monitor; or, British Freeholder, The (1755), II, 664
Monitor; or, Green Room laid open, The (1767), II, 665
Monk, James Henry (1784–1856), II, 900; III, 123, **995**f.
Monk, Mary (d. 1715), II, **322**
Monk, William Henry (1823–1889), III, 313
Monk of Evesham (15 cent.), I, 46
Monkhouse, T. (*fl.* 1767), I, 399
Monkhouse, William Cosmo (1840–1901), III, **349**
'Monkshood' (Francis Jacox?) (1855), III, 651
Monmouth, Geoffrey of (d. *c.* 1152), I, 133, 285
Monmouth, Henry Carey, Earl of (1596–1661), II, 808, 810
Monro, Alexander (d. 1715?), II, **993**
Monro, C. J. (*fl.* 1872), I, 21
Monro, David Binning (1836–1905), III, **1008**
Munro, Donald (*fl.* 1549), I, **774**
Monro, Edward (1815–1866), III, 853
Monro, J. (*fl.* 1893), III, 1082
Monro (or Munro), Robert (d. 1633), I, 772
Monro, Thomas (1764–1815), II, 666, 759
Monroe, Robert (d. 1680), I, 841
Monsey, R. (*fl.* 1665), II, 288
Monson, Sir William (1569–1643), I, 390, 771, 837
Monstrous Droll Songs (18 cent.), II, 251, 253–4
Monstrous Good Songs (18 cent.), II, 248–9, 250–1, 253–4
Monstrous Magazine, The (1770), II, 687
Montagu (or Montague), Anthony Maria Browne, Viscount (d. 1629), I, 384
Montagu, Lady Barbara (d. 1765), II, 545, 556
Montagu, Charles, Earl of Halifax (1661–1715), II, **282**
Montagu (or Mountagu), Edward, Earl of Sandwich (1625–1672), II, 743
Montagu, Elizabeth (1720–1800), II, **842**
Montagu, George (1751–1815), II, 822
Montagu, John, Earl of Sandwich (1718–1792), II, 748
Montagu, Lady Mary Wortley, née Pierrepont (1689–1762), II, **834**f.
Montagu, Matthew (*fl.* 1809), II, 842

Montagu, Richard (1577–1641), I, 847, 857 (2), 858
Montagu, W. D., Duke of Manchester (*fl.* 1864), I, 382
Montagu, Walter (1603?–1677), I, 648, 726
Montagu Papers (16–18 cents.), I, 382
Montague, C. E. (1867–1928), III, 786
Montague, F. C. (*fl.* 1885–1930), III, 976–7
Montague, William (*fl.* 1672–96), II, 744, 772
Montaigne, Michel de, I, 332, 816; II, 36, 791
Montalba, Anthony (*fl.* 1849), III, 576
Montalban, Juan Perez de, I, 344, 734
Montalvo, García Ordoñez de, I, 344; III, 41
Montanus, Arnoldus, I, 908
Montchrétien, Antoine de, I, 334
Montefiore, Claude Joseph Goldsmid (b. 1858), III, 834, 851
Montefiori, Joshua (*fl.* 1802), II, 93
Monteith, Robert (*fl.* 1621–60), I, 910
Monteith, Robert (*fl.* 1704), II, 186, 191
Montemayor, Jorge de, I, 344f., 816
Montesquieu, Charles de Secondat, Baron de la Brède et de, II, 29, 36, 542, 800
Montfaucon, Bernard de, II, 791
Montfaucon de Villars, Nicolas de, II, 791
Montgomerie (or Montgomery), Alexander (1556?–1610?), I, 678, **898**
Montgomery, Florence (1843–1923), III, 569
Montgomery, H. R. (*fl.* 1860), III, 186
Montgomery, James (1771–1854), I, 464; II, 987; III, **239**f.
Montgomery, Jemina, later Baroness Tautphoeus (1807–1893), III, **509**
Montgomery, Robert (1807–1855), I, 700; II, 633; III, **299**f.
Month, The (1864), III, 830
Monthly Account, The (1645), I, 756
Monthly Account of the Present State of Affairs, The (1700), II, 676
Monthly Amusement, The (1709), II, 541, 676
Monthly and Critical Review, The (1756), II, 677
Monthly Banquet of Apollo, The (18 cent.), II, 251
Monthly Beauties; or, The Cabinet of Literary Genius (1793), II, 682
Monthly Catalogue, The (1714), II, 717
Monthly Catalogue; Or A General Register of Books [etc.], *The* (1723), II, 717
Monthly Chronicle, The (1728), II, 676
Monthly Chronicle, The (1838), III, 827
Monthly Collection of Songs, The (18 cent.), II, 198
Monthly Collector of Elegant Anecdotes, The (1798), II, 683
Monthly Communications (1793), II, 682
Monthly Epitome, The (1797), II, 717
Monthly Epitome; Our Readers their own Reviewers, The (1802), II, 717

Monthly Extracts; Or, Beauties of Modern Authors (1791), II, 681
Monthly Intelligence Relating the Affairs of Quakers, A (1662), II, 702
Monthly Journal of the Affairs of Europe, The (1704), II, 676
Monthly Ledger; Or, Literary Repository, The (1773), II, 679
Monthly Literary Advertiser, The (1805), II, 717; III, 101
Monthly Magazine (1796), II, 666
Monthly Magazine, The (1839), III, 824
Monthly Magazine, The (Chelmsford, 1800), II, 684
Monthly Magazine And British Register, The (1796), II, 682; III, 824
Monthly Magazine of Fiction, The (1885), III, 831
Monthly Magazine; or British Register of Literature, Sciences and Belles Lettres, The (1826), III, 824
MONTHLY MAGAZINES, III, 822f. (19 cent.)
Monthly Mask of Vocal Music, The (18 cent.), II, 186
Monthly Masks of Vocal Musick (1703), II, 676
Monthly Masque, The (18 cent.), II, 218
Monthly Melody, The (1760), II, 678
Monthly Mirror (1795), II, 666
Monthly Mirror, Reflecting Men and Manners, The (1795), II, 682
Monthly Miscellany, The (1707), II, 675
Monthly Miscellany; Or, Gentleman and Lady's Compleat Magazine, The (1774), II, 679
Monthly Miscellany; Or, Irish Review and Register, The (1796), II, 688
Monthly Packet of Advice from Parnassus, The (1722) II, 676
Monthly Packet of Evening Readings, The (1851), III, 828
Monthly Preceptor, The (1800-2), II, 564
Monthly Preceptor, or, Juvenile Library, The (1800), II, 683
Monthly Record of Literature, The (1767), II, 679
Monthly Recorder of All True Occurrences, The (1682), II, 704
Monthly Register, The (1703), II, 676
Monthly Remembrancer, The (1730), II, 676
Monthly Repository of Theology and General Literature, The (1806), III, 824
Monthly Review, The (1749), II, 673
Monthly Review, The (1826), III, 822f.
Monthly Review, The (1900), III, 832
Monthly Review Or Literary Journal, The (1749), II, 677
Monthly Review, or Literary Journal Enlarged, The (1790), III, 822
Monthly Visitor And Entertaining Pocket Companion, The (1797), II, 683
Monthly Weather Paper, The (1711), II, 675

Montholieu, Mme — de, III, 577
Monti, T., III, 595
Monti, Vincenzo, III, 229
Montolieu, Mrs — (*fl.* 1798), II, 789
Montolieu, Jeanne Isabelle Polier de Bottens, Baronne de, II, 552
Montresor, James Gabriel (1702–1776), II, 755
Montresor, John (1736–1788?), II, 756
Montreux, Nicolas de, I, 434, 734
Montrion, W. A. (*fl.* 1856), III, 1071
MONTROSE Magazine, II, 687 (1793)
Monumenta Anglicana (18 cent.), II, 193, 194 (2), 195 (2)
Monumenta Westmonasteriensia (17 cent.), II, 178–9
Moodie, Donald (d. 1861), III, 1092
Moodie, D. C. F. (*fl.* 1888), III, 1090
Moodie, Susanna, née Strickland (1803–1885), III, 1088
Moody, Catherine Grace Frances, later Gore (1799–1861), III, **396**f.
Moody, Christopher Lake (*fl.* 1798), II, 748
Moon, G. W. (*fl.* 1863), III, 276
Moon (or Moone), R. (*fl.* 1654), I, 762 (3)
Moonshine (1879), III, 793, 820
Moor, Edward (1771–1848), II, 751; III, 1080, 1082
Moor, James (1712–1779), II, 759, **1001**
Moor, L. (*fl.* 1857), III, 229
Moorcroft, William (1765?–1825), II, 818; III, 1080
Moore, Alexander Leys (*fl.* 1890), III, 798
Moore, Andrew (*fl.* 1660), I, 781
Moore, Arthur William (1853–1909), III, **930**
Moore, Aubrey Lackington (1848–1890), III, 851
Moore, Benjamin (*fl.* 1899), III, 964
Moore, Charles (*fl.* 1790), writer on suicide, II, 823
Moore, C. (*fl.* 1797), translator of Lavater, II, 52
Moore, D. (*fl.* 1795), II, 779
Moore, E. (*fl.* 1867), III, 127
Moore, Edward (1712–1757), II, 43, 61, 70, **323**
Moore, F. F. (b. 1855), III, 786
Moore, Frances, later Brooke (1724–1789), III, 1086
Moore, Francis (*fl.* 1744–73), II, 149, 749, **754**
Moore, George (1857–1933), III, **526**f.
Moore, Giles (*fl.* 1635–79), II, 134
Moore, Sir Harrison (*fl.* 1910), III, 1098
Moore, J. Sheridan (*fl.* 1864), III, 1094
Moore, John (1595?–1657), I, 699, 845
Moore, John (1729–1802), II, 24, 523, 549–51, 746, 986
Moore, John H. (*fl.* 1785), editor of books of travel, II, 741

Moore, Sir John Henry (1756–1780), poet, II, 232, **375**

Moore, Sir Jonas (1617–1679), II, 819

Moore, Morris (*fl.* 1853), III, 694

Moore, Stuart Archibald (1842–1907), III, 987

Moore, Thomas (*fl.* 1829), Devonshire clergyman, III, 885

Moore, Thomas (1779–1852), poet, III, **184 f.**, 207, 245

  Translations from, III, 25, 37, 40, 45

Moore, Thomas (1821–1881), botanist, III, 960–1

Moore, William, II, 665 (3)

Moraes, Francisco de, III, 181

Moral and Entertaining Magazine, The (1777), II, 680

Moral and Political Magazine, The (1796), II, 683

Moral Ballade, A (M.E.), I, **254**

MORAL INSTRUCTION (writings embodying), I, 78 f. (O.E. poems), 94 (O.E. prose), 177 f. (M.E.). See also under EDUCATION and RELIGION.

Moral Instructions of a Father to his Son (18 cent.), II, 230 (2)

Moral Instructor; Consisting of Miscellaneous Essays, The (18 cent.), II, 250

Moral Miscellany, The (18 cent.), II, 218, **225**, 240

Moral World, The (1845), III, 817

MORALITIES, THE, I, 513 f.

Moralizer, The (1799), II, 666

Moran, E. R. (*fl.* before 1865), III, 800

Morande, Charles Théveneau de (1748–1803); II, 696, 719

Morando, Bernardo, II, 542

Morant, Philip (1700–1770), II, 788, **891**

Moranville, — (*fl.* 1666), II, 719

Moratín, Leandro Fernandez de, II, 73

Mordaunt, Sir C. (*fl.* 1896), III, 761

More, Cresacre (1572–1649), I, 840

More, Edward (1537?–1620), I, 716

More, Gertrude (1606–1633), I, 699

More, Hannah (1745–1833), II, 38, 109, 131, 556, **844 f.**; III, 143

More, Henry (1614–1687), I, **875 f.**; II, 32

More, Jacob (1740–1793), II, 26

More, John (*fl.* 1533), I, 781

More, Sir John (*fl.* 1703), II, 819

More, Richard (d. 1643), I, 856

More, Sir Thomas de la (*fl.* 1327–51), I, 11

More, Sir Thomas (1478–1535), I, 46, 329, **666 f.**

More, Sir William (1520–after 1576), I, 363

More, Sir Thomas (16 cent.), I, **576 f.**

Moreau, Charles François Jean Baptiste, III, 456

Moreau, Simeon (*fl.* 1783), II, 154

Moreau de Maupertuis, Pierre Louis, II, 791

Morell, John Daniel (1816–1891), III, **871**

Morell, Thomas (1703–1784), II, 77 f., 102, 206, 758, 760, 768, 814

Moréri, Louis, II, 36

Mores, Edward Rowe (1731–1778), II, 82

Moreto y Cabaña, Agustin, II, 68

Moreton, A. H. (*fl.* 1836), III, 981

Moreton, J. B. (*fl.* 1790), II, 757

Morfill, William Richard (1834–1909), III, **934**

Morfitt, John (*fl.* 1788), II, 823

Morgan, Conwy Lloyd (b. 1852), III, 955, 959, 966

Morgan, E. (*fl.* 1787), II, 776 (2)

Morgan, George (*fl.* 1770), II, 815

Morgan, Sir Henry (1635?–1688), II, 752

Morgan, Henry James (*fl.* 1867–98), III, 1085 (2)

Morgan, J. (*fl.* 1728–39), translator and historical compiler, I, 736; II, 785, 801

Morgan, J. (*fl.* 1829), physician, III, 963

Morgan, James (*fl.* 1678), II, 773

Morgan, John (*fl.* 1888), III, 695

Morgan, John Minter (1782–1854), III, 125, 976

Morgan, M. S. (*fl.* 1870), III, 820

Morgan, Matthew (1652–1703), II, 763

Morgan, Nicholas (*fl.* 1609), I, 393

Morgan, R. C. (1827–1908), III, 99

Morgan, Sydney, Lady, née Owenson (1776–1859), III, **412 f.**

Morgan, Thomas (d. 1743), II, **948**

Morgan, Thomas (*fl.* 1800), II, 922

Morgan, Sir Thomas Charles (1783–1843), III, 412 (2)

Morgan, William (*fl.* 1677), cartographer, I, 389

Morhof, Daniel Georg, II, 31, 51

Morice, E., III, 677

Morier, James Justinian (1780–1849), III, **410 f.**

Morier, Sir Robert Burnett David (1826–1893) III, 154

Morindos, a King of Spain, The Famous & Renowned History of (17 cent.), I, 731

Morison, James Augustus Cotter (1832–1888), III, **900**

Morison, Sir Richard (d. 1556), I, 802

Morison, Robert (1722–1791), II, 245, 672, 687, 914

Moritz, Karl Philipp (1757–1796), II, 114, 141

Morland, Sir Samuel (1625–1695), I, 781; II, 125, 129, 961

Morland, Thomas Hornby (*fl.* 1792), II, 817

Morley, Frank (*fl.* 1893), III, 943

Morley, George (1597–1684), I, **699**

Morley, Henry (1822–1894), I, 525; III, **722 f.**, 810, 836

Morley, John, Viscount Morley of Blackburn (1838–1923), III, 112, 166, **751**

  Periodicals edited by, III, 799, 801, 814, 818, 829

Morley, Thomas (1557–1606?), I, 392, **482f.**, 484
'Morna' (T. M. O'Keefe) (*fl.* 1849), III, 451
Mornay, Philippe de, Seigneur du Plessis-Marly, I, 333, 816; II, 791
Morning (1892), III, 800
Morning Advertiser, The (1794), III, 793, 798
Morning Bulletin [Glasgow], III, 807
Morning Chronicle, The (1769), III, 798
Morning Chronicle and London Advertiser, The (1769), II, 709
Morning Chronicle And Public Advertiser, The (Dublin, 1799), II, 736
Morning Gazette, The (1837), III, 799
Morning Herald, The (1780), III, 798
Morning Herald, The (1899), III, 800
Morning Herald and Daily Advertiser, The (1780), II, 709
Morning Journal, The (1828), III, 799
Morning Journal, The (1858) [Glasgow], III, 807
Morning Leader, The (1892), III, 800
Morning Mail, The (1864), III, 799
Morning Mail, The (1885), III, 800
Morning Mail, The [Dublin] (1870), III, 809
Morning News, The (1856), III, 799
Morning News [Belfast] (1882), III, 808
Morning News, The [Dublin] (1859), III, 809
Morning News, The [Sheffield] (1855), III, 802
Morning Post, The (1772), II, 698; III, 793f., 798
Morning Post, And Daily Advertiser, The (1776), II, 709
Morning Post and Daily Advertising Pamphlet, The (1772), II, 709
Morning Post; Or, Cheap Daily Advertiser, The (1772), II, 709
Morning Post; Or, Dublin Courant, The (1793), II, 736
Morning Star, The (1789), II, 709, 711
Morning Star, The (1805), III, 798
Morning Star, The (1856), III, 799
Morning Walk, The (18 cent.), II, 215
Morning's Discourse of a Bottomless Tubb, A (18 cent.), II, 536
Morosini, Francesco, II, 812
Morphew, J. (*fl.* 1706), II, 712
Morrell, — (*fl.* 1596), I, 662
Morrell, T. B. (*fl.* 1854), III, 290
Morrell, William (*fl.* 1625), I, 795, 893
Morrice, Bezaleel (*fl.* 1732), II, 16
Morrice, D. (*fl.* 1802), III, 129
Morris, Corbyn (d. 1779), II, 16, 447
Morris, E. E. (*fl.* 1898), III, 1098
Morris, Francis Orpen (1810–1893), III, 91
Morris, H. (*fl.* 1890), III, 1078
Morris, Isaac (*fl.* 1750), II, 754
Morris (or Morys), Lewis (1700–1765), II, 685
Morris, Sir Lewis (1833–1907), III, **349**
Morris, Maurice O'Connor (*fl.* 1877), III, 760

Morris, Richard (1833–1894), I, 185; III, **1040f.**
Morris, Thomas (*fl.* 1753–1806), infantry captain and song-writer, II, 409, 757
Morris, Thomas (*fl.* 1787), publisher, II, 718
Morris, William (1834–1896), III, **314f.**, 706, 818, 977
Morris, William O'Connor (1824–1904), III, 786
Morrison, Eliza (*fl.* 1839), III, 1020
Morrison, J. M. (*fl.* 1835), I, 884
Morrison, James (*fl.* 1789), II, 757
Morrison, Sir Richard (*fl.* 1540), I, 819
Morrison, Robert (1782–1834), III, **1020**
Morrison, Sir T. (*fl.* 1879), III, 1078
Morselli, Adriano, II, 66
Morte Arthure (Alliterative) (M.E.), I, 39, **136f.**
Morte, Le, Arthur (Stanzaic) (M.E.), I, 39, **138**
Morthland, John (*fl.* 1796), II, 732
Mortimer, C. E. (*fl.* 1805), I, 469
Mortimer, Favell Lee, née Bevan (1802–1878), III, 567
Mortimer, George (*fl.* 1791), II, 757
Mortimer, James (*fl.* 1870), III, 814
Mortimer, John (1656?–1736), II, 819
Mortimer, John Hamilton (1741–1779), I, 593
Mortimer, Thomas (1730–1810), II, 792, **921**
Mortoft, Francis (*fl.* 1658), I, 773
Morton, Charles (1716–1799), I, 773, 834
Morton, J. (*fl.* 1819), editor of John Leyden's poems, III, 237
Morton, J. (*fl.* 1841–53), middle English scholar, I, 169, 179
Morton, John Chalmers (1821–1888), III, 820
Morton, John Maddison (1811–1891), III, **605**
Morton, S. G. (*fl.* before 1854), III, 1015
Morton, Thomas (*fl.* 1642), I, 720
Morton, Thomas (d. 1646), I, 795
Morton, Thomas (1764?–1838), II, **477**
Morton, W. (*fl.* 1832), III, 1070
Morvan de Bellegarde, Jean Baptiste, II, 792
Morwyng (or Morwen), Peter (1530?–1573?), I, 813
Moryson, Fynes (1566–1630), I, 770, 838
Mosan, J. (*fl.* 1598), I, 889
Moschus, I, 804; II, 762
Moseley, Henry (1801–1875), III, 120
Moseley, Henry Nottidge (1844–1891), III, 958
Moseley, Humphrey (d. 1661), I, 352
Moseley, W. M. (*fl.* 1792), II, 824
Moses, H. (*fl.* 1750), III, 1079
Moslem in Cambridge, The (1870), III, 835
Moss, Joseph William (1803–1862), III, 996
Moss, Robert (1666–1729), II, 893
Moss, T. (*fl.* 1761), II, 678
Mosse, Miles (*fl.* 1580–1614), I, 719, 845
Most Agreeable Companion, The (18 cent.), II, 236
Most pleasant Comedie intituled, A knacke to knowe a knave, A (16 cent.), I, 538

Most pleasant Comedie of Mucedoras, A (16 cent.), I, 579

Mote, Humphrey (*fl.* 1585), I, 738, 768

Motets, Madrigals, and Other Pieces (18 cent.), II, 212

Mother Chit-Chat's Curious Tales and Puzzles (18 cent.), II, 563

Mother Goose's Melody (18 cent.), II, 251 (2), 554

Motherless Mary (19 cent.), III, 575

Motherwell, William (1797–1835), III, 163, **240**

Motier, Marie Madeleine, Comtesse de la Fayette, II, 792

Mott, Albert Julius ('A. J. Barrowcliffe'), III, **473**

Motte, Andrew (d. 1730), II, 961

Motteux, Peter Anthony (1663–1718), II, 28, **424**f., 531, 535, 676

Motteville, Françoise Langlois de, II, 785

Mottley, John (1692–1750), I, 825; II, **441**f., 540

Mottley's Telegraph (1802), II, 727

Mottoes of the Spectators, Tatlers and Guardians, The (18 cent.), II, 205 (2), 206

Moufet, Thomas (1553–1604). See Moffett

Mouhy, Charles de Fieux, Chevalier de, II, 551, 780

Moule, Handley Carr Glyn (1841–1920), III, 853

Moule, Thomas (1784–1851), I, 395

Moulton, Thomas (*fl.* 1539?), I, 888

Moulton, William Fiddian (1835–1898), III, **1014**

Moultrie, John (1799–1874), II, 334; III, **240**

'Mountain, Didymus'. See Thomas Hill (*fl.* 1590)

Mountain Piper; or, The History of Edgar and Matilda, The (18 cent.), II, 563

MOUNTAINEERING (books on), III, 777

Mountcashell, Viscount (*fl.* 1725), II, 592

Mountcastle, Clara H. ('Caris Sima') (*fl.* 1882), III, 1086

Mountfort, Walter (*fl.* 1632), I, 648

Mountfort, William (1664–1692), II, **425**

Mourt, G. (*fl.* 1622), I, 791

Movement, Anti-Persecution Gazette and Register of Progress, The (1843), III, 817

Moxon, Edward (1801–1858), III, **300**, 634

Moxon, John (*fl.* 1782), II, 236

Moxon, Joseph (1627–1700), II, 82, 129

Moyle, Walter (1672–1721), II, 762 (2), 763

Moysie, David (*fl.* 1582–1603), I, 905

Mozeen, Thomas (d. 1768), II, 544

Mozley, James Bowling (1813–1878), III, 854, **859**

Mozley, Thomas (1806–1893), III, 833, 854, 859

Mucedorus, A Most Pleasant Comedie of (16 cent.), I, 579

Muddiman, Henry (1629–1692), I, 748, 763; II, 696, 701 (4)

Mudford, W. H. (*fl.* 1874), III, 799, 801

Mudford, William (1782–1848), II, 523; III, **411**, 800

Mudie, Alexander (*fl.* 1682), II, 157

Mudie, Robert (1777–1842), III, 93, 789

Mueller, Karl Wilhelm (*fl.* 1757), II, 688

Muenchhausen, K. F. H., II, 807

Muffet, Thomas (1553–1604). See Moffett

Mughouse-Diversion (18 cent.), II, 193 (3), 195

Muir, John (1810–1882), III, 1072

Muir, Moncrieff Pattison (b. 1848), III, 949

Muir, Sir William (1819–1905), III, **933**f., 1081

Muirhead, Claud (*fl.* 1820), II, 731

Muirhead, James (*fl.* 1710), II, 731

Mukerji, Charuchandra (*fl.* 1890), III, 1072

Mukherji, T. N. (*fl.* 1883), III, 1084

Mulcaster, Richard (1530?–1611), I, 44, 261, 366, 376, 395

Mulgrave, Constantine John Phipps, Baron (1744–1792), II, 743

Mulgrave, John Sheffield, Earl of (1648–1721), II, 21, 44, 196, **283**, 456

Mullens, Joseph (1820–1879), III, 1081

Müller, Friedrich Max (1823–1900), III, **1018**f.

Müller, Karl Otfried, III, 997, 1000

Müller, L. C. (*fl.* 1835), I, 93

MULLINGAR
Newspaper, II, 738

Mullinger, J. Bass (*fl.* 1867), I, 853

Mullins, J. D. (*fl.* 1869), III, 105

Mullins, Rosanna Eleanor, later Leprohon (*fl.* 1881), III, 1086–7

Mullis, Grace Jennings, earlier Carmichael (*fl.* 1895), III, 1095

Mulock, Dinah Maria, later Craik (1826–1887), III, **498**f.

Multum in Parvo (17 cent.), I, 718

Mum, Sothsegger (M.E.), I, **200**

Mumford, Erasmus (*fl.* 1750), II, 826

Mumford, John (*fl.* 1689), II, 705

Mummery, Albert Frederick (1855–1895), III, 777, 984

Mun, Thomas (1571–1641), I, 847; II, 959

Munby, Arthur Joseph (1828–1910), III, **300**

Munday, Anthony (1553–1663), I, **535**f., 729, 738, 768, 810, 815, 818, 825

Munday, Henry (1623–1682), II, 32

Mundus & Infans, A propre newe Interlude of (16 cent.), I, 515

Mundy, Francis Noel Clarke (*fl.* 1768), II, **375**

Mundy, John (1560?–1630), I, 483

Mundy, Peter (*fl.* 1617–58), I, 771f., 784; II, 742

Mundy, R. (*fl.* 1832), III, 1080

Munro, Hugh Andrew Johnstone (1819–1885), III, **1000**f.

Munro, Innes (d. 1827), II, 751

Munsell, Joel (*fl.* 1850), III, 790
Munshi, Ziauddin Gulam Moheiddin (*fl.* 1889), III, 1071
Münster, Sebastian, I, 335, 765, 777
Munster Journal, The (1749), II, 738
Munster Packet, The (1788), II, 738
Muralt, Béat Louis de, II, 29, 140, 792
Murat, Henriette Julie, Comtesse de, II, 535, 778
Muratori, Lodovico Antonio, II, 812
Murchbank, Richard (*fl.* 1758), II, 735
Murchison, Sir Roderick Impey (1792–1871), III, **951**
Murdin, W. (*fl.* 1740), I, 399
Murdoch, J. (*fl.* 1888), III, 1084
Murdoch, John (1747–1824), II, 29, 786, 810
Murdoch, Patrick (d. 1774), II, 305
Murdock, John (1747–1824). See Murdoch
Mure, Elizabeth (1700–1790), II, 156
Mure, James (*fl.* 1875?), III, 807
Mure, Sir William (1594–1657), of Rowallan, I, **900**, 906
Mure, William (1799–1860), III, **1001**
Murimuth, Adam (1275?–1347), I, 116
Murison, J. W. (*fl.* 1893), III, 835
Murphy, Anna Brownell, later Jameson (1794–1860), III, 1088
Murphy, Arthur (1727–1805), II, 26, **478** f., 485, 664, 794
Murphy, James Cavanah (1760–1814), II, 748
Murphy, Joseph John (1827–1894), III, 300 f.
Murray, — (*fl.* 1793), II, 687
Murray, A. D. (*fl.* after 1860?), III, 803
Murray, Alexander Stuart (1841–1904), III, **1008**
Murray, Amelia Matilda (1795–1884), III, 129
Murray, Charles (b. 1864), III, 1089
Murray, Sir Charles Augustus (1806–1895), III, **499**
Murray, Sir David, of Gorthy (1567–1629), I, 900
Murray, Eustace Clare Grenville (*fl.* 1857), III, 790
Murray, Lord George (1700?–1760), II, 1003
Murray, George (*fl.* 1891), III, 1086
Murray, Henry (*fl.* 1909), III, 786
Murray, Hugh (1779–1846), I, 782
Murray, Sir John Archibald, Lord (1779–1859), I, 776
Murray, James (1732–1782), II, 233, 672, 685 (3), 686
Murray, Sir James Augustus Henry (1837–1915), III, **1041**
Murray, John (1745–1793), publisher, III, 99
Murray, John (1778–1843), publisher, III, 99, 206, 786
Murray, John (1786?–1851), scientific writer, III, 72
Murray, John (1808–1892), publisher, III, 99
Murray, Lindley (1745–1826), II, 932; III, 140

Murray, P. J. (*fl.* 1857), III, 387
Murray, R. (*fl.* 1779), II, 811
Murray, R. W. (*fl.* 1894), III, 1090
Murray, Robert Fuller (1863–1894), III, 350
'Murray, Hon. Mrs. Sarah', i.e. Sarah Aust (1744–1811), II, 157
Murray, T. B. (*fl.* 1845), II, 834
Murray, Thomas (1792–1872), II, 909, 951, 966
Murray, Thomas Archibald (*fl.* 1796–1801), II, 146
Murray, Thomas C. (b. 1873), III, **1066**
Murray, W. H. (*fl.* 1855), III, 807
Murray's Magazine (1887), III, 831
Murrell, John (*fl.* 1615–30), I, 396
Musae Berkhamstedienses (18 cent.), II, 249
Musae Cantabrigiensis, Serenissimis Principibus Wilhelmo et Mariae (17 cent.), II, 181
Musae Seatonianae (18 cent.), II, 229 (2), 240
Musæus, I, 804
Musaeus, J. C. A., II, 807; III, 603
Musapaedia (18 cent.), II, 195 (2)
Musarum Cantabrigiensium Threnodia [on Monke's Death], II, 175
Musarum Lachrymae (18 cent.), II, 195
Musäus, Johann Karl August, II, 63
Muscovite, The (1714), II, 661
Muse in a Moral Humour, The (18 cent.), II, 218 (2)
Muse in Good Humour, The (1744), II, 210, 211 (2), 212, 215, 218, 224, 227, 239
Muse in Good Humour; or Momus's Banquet, The (1785), II, 239
Muse in Masquerade, The (18 cent.), II, 211
Muse's Banquet, The (1752), II, 215
Muses Banquet, or Compleat Songster, The (1760), II, 219
Muses Banquet; or, Vocal Repository, The (1790), II, 244, 246–7
Muses Delight, The (1754), II, 216
Muse's Delight: Or, The Songster's Jovial Companion (1760), II, 219
Muses Farewel to Popery and Slavery, The (17 cent.), II, 181 (3)
Muses Holiday, The (18 cent.), II, 200, 218
Muses Library, The (1737), II, 206 (2), 209
Muses Library, and Young Gentlemen and Ladies Polite Instructor, The (1760), II, 219
Muses Mercury, The (1707), II, 673, 676
Muse's Mirrour, The (18 cent.), II, 233, 237
Muse's Pocket Companion, The (18 cent.), II, 236, 239–40, 256
Muse's Vagaries, The (18 cent.), II, 211
Muses and Graces on a Visit to Grosvenor Square, The (18 cent.), II, 230
Muses' Choice, The (18 cent.), II, 216, 219, 227
Muses' Delight; or, The London Polite Songster, The (1766), II, 224
Muses' Gazette, The (1720), II, 662

Museum, The (1746), II, 674
Museum, The (1796), II, 688
Museum for Young Gentlemen and Ladies, A (18 cent.), II, 222, 561
Museum of Wit (19 cent.), II, 256
Museum; Or, The Literary and Historical Register, The (1746), II, 677
Museum Rusticum et Commerciale (1763), II, 678
Musgrave, Agnes (*fl.* 1796–1808), III, **411**
Musgrave, Sir Anthony (1828–1888), III, 983
Musgrave, Samuel (1732–1780), II, 900 (3)
MUSIC
    Books on, I, 392, 506; II, 30
    Printing of, II, 106
    See also SONGS
Music and Dancing (18 cent.), II, 246
Musica Oxoniensis (17 cent.), II, 184
Musica Transalpina (16 cent.), I, 482–3
Musicae Vocalis Deliciae (18 cent.), II, 244
Musical and Poetical Relicks of the Welsh Bards (18 cent.), II, 237, 249, 256 (2)
Musical Banquet, The (1800), II, 256
Musical Banquet of Choice Songs, The (1797), II, 253
Musical Bouquét; or Popular Songs, and Ballads, The (18 cent.), II, 254
Musical Charmer, or Warbler in the Woods, The (18 cent.), II, 247
Musical Companion, The (1745), II, 211
Musical Companion, The (1759), II, 219
Musical Companion, The (1765), II, **223**
Musical Companion, The (1777), II, 232
Musical Companion, containing Catches and Rounds (1667), II, 175
Musical Companion: or Lady's Magazine, The (1741), II, 209
Musical Companion; or, Songster's ever new Miscellany, The (1791), II, 246
Musical Companion; Or, Songster's Magazine, The (1777), II, 680
Musical Entertainer, The (18 cent.), II, 207 (2), 208
Musical Magazine, The (1760), II, 225 (2), 226–9, 678
Musical Magazine: By Mr. Oswald, The (1761), II, 220
Musical Mason, The (18 cent.), II, 230
Musical Miscellanies (1784), II, 237
Musical Miscellany, The (1729), II, 200 (2), 201
Musical Miscellany, The (1760), II, 219
Musical Miscellany, The (1786), II, 239
Musical Miscellany, The (1789), II, 243 (2)
Musical Miscellany, The (1790), II, 244
Musical Olio, The (18 cent.), II, 256
Musical Repository, The (18 cent.), II, 254
Musicall Banquet, A (1610), I, 485
Musick's Delight on the Cithren (17 cent.), II, 174
Musket, R. (*fl.* 1810), III, 973

Musset, Alfred de, III, 353
Mustafā, Hāji (*fl.* 1799), III, 1070
Musters, George Chaworth (1841–1879), III, 992
My Real Friend (19 cent.), III, 575
Myers, Ernest James (1844–1921), III, **350**
Myers, Frederic (1811–1851), III, 849
Myers, Frederic William Henry (1843–1901), III, 258, **350**, 848
Myers, Thomas (1774–1834), III, 112, 975
Mylne, James (d. 1788), II, 76, 81
Mynshul, Geffray (1594?–1668), I, 717, 722, 725
Myrc, John (*fl.* 1403), I, 302
'Myrtle, Harriet', i.e. Lydia Falconer Miller, née Fraser (1811?–1876), III, 572, 721
Myrtle, The (18 cent.), II, 217
Myrtle and Vine, The (19 cent.), II, 256
Mysteries of Love & Eloquence, The (17 cent.), II, 180
MYSTERY PLAYS (M.E.), I, **275** f.
MYSTICS (18 cent.), II, 857 f.
MYSTICAL WRITERS
    Middle English. See RICHARD ROLLE AND ASSOCIATED PIECES, I, 191 f.
MYTHOLOGY (Germanic). See under GERMANIC BACKGROUND, I, 54 f.

N., Rev. Mr — (*fl.* 1776), II, 805
N., A. (*fl.* 1608), I, 769
N., F. (*fl.* 1651), I, 761
N., G. (*fl.* 1642), I, 776
N., J. (*fl.* 1691), II, 283
N., J. (*fl.* 1765), II, 223, 230, 233, 237, 239, 253, 254 (3)
N., N. (*fl.* 1672), II, 796
N., N. (*fl.* 1704), II, 808
N., N. (*fl.* 1724), II, 813
N., N. (*fl.* 1766), II, 101
N., S. (*fl.* 1678), II, 178
N., W. (*fl.* 1661), II, 173
Nabbes, Thomas (1605–1641?), I, 648 f.
Naden, Constance Caroline Woodhill (1858–1889), III, **350**
Nagle, David A. (*fl.* 1856), III, 808
Nairne, Caroline Oliphant, Baroness (1766–1845), II, **991**
Naismith, J. (*fl.* 807), III, 969
Nalson, John (1638?–1686), I, 400; II, 790
NAMES
    Personal names, I, 48
    Place names, I, 47 f.
    See also under VOCABULARY, I, 30 f.
Nancrede, P. J. G. de (*fl.* 1791), II, 773
Nani, Giovanni Battista Felice Gasparo, II, 812
Nannini, Remigio, I, 817
Naogeorgos, Thomas, I, 437
Napier, Alexander (1814–1887), II, 846
Napier, Sir Charles James (1782–1853), III, 1076

Napier, E. E. (*fl.* 1849), III, 1091
Napier, Sir Joseph (1804–1882), II, 946
Napier (or Neper), John (1550–1617), I, 378, 881
Napier, Macvey (1776–1847), III, 832
Napier, Mark (1798–1879), III, **905**
Napier, Sir William Francis Patrick (1785–1860), III, **900**, 1076
Napleton, John (1738?–1817), II, 118
Narbrough, Sir John (1640–1688), II, 752
Narcissus A Twelve Night Merriment (17 cent.), I, 662
Nares, Robert (1753–1829), I, 44; II, 666; III, **1026**
Narratio de Virtate Missarum (M.E.), I, **163**
Narrative of the Life and Astonishing Adventures of John Daniel, A (18 cent.), II, 544
Narrative of the Proceedings at the Contested Election Norwich (18 cent.), II, 234
Nash, Joseph (1809–1878), I, 392
Nash, Rowland (*fl.* 1831), III, 800
Nash, Treadway Russell (1725–1811), II, 914
Nashe (or Nash), Thomas (1567–1601), I, **533**f., 692, 730, 864, 884, 893
Nasmyth, James (*fl.* 1777), librarian, II, 104
Nasmyth, James (1808–1890), engineer, III, 944
Nasse, E. (*fl.* 1871), III, 971
Nassyngton, William (*fl.* 1375), I, 195
Nathan, Isaac (1791?–1864), III, 404
Nation, The (1824), III, 801
National, The (1839), III, 817
National, The (1846), III, 814
National Adviser, The (1811), III, 810
National Agricultural Labourers' Chronicle, The (1875), III, 818
National Graphic (1932), III, 815
National Journal; Or, The Country Gazette, The (1746), II, 708
National Magazine, The (1830), III, 826
National Magazine, The (1856), III, 829
National Magazine and Dublin Literary Gazette, The (1832), III, 826
National Observer, The (1890), III, 814
National Reformer, The (1844), III, 817
National Register, The (1808), III, 811
National Review, The (1855), III, 833
National Review, The (1883), III, 831
National Scout, The (1659), I, 763
NATURAL DESCRIPTION, II, 171 (18 cent.); III, 160 (19 cent.). See also under OLD ENGLISH POETRY, I, 61 f.
NATURAL HISTORY (writings on), I, 892f. (1500–1660); III, 955f. (19 cent.). For 1660–1800 see under LITERATURE OF SCIENCE, II, 959f.
Natural History Review, The (1861), III, 833
NATURALISM, III, 67
Naturalist's Miscellany, The (1789), II, 681
Nature (1870), III, 821

Naubert, Christiane Benedikte, II, 63, 553, 807
Naudé, Gabriel, II, 100, 792
Naunton, Sir Robert (1563–1635), I, 838
Naval and Military Gazette, The (1833), III, 821
Naval Chronicle, The (1799), II, 683
Naval Glory (18 cent.), II, 244
Naval Magazine; Or, Maritime Miscellany, The (1799), II, 683
Naval Songster, The (19 cent.), II, 256
Navarre, Marguerite d'Angoulême, Queen of, I, 334, 734; II, 790
NAVIGATION (Textbooks of), I, 390f., 884f. (16, 17 cents.)
NAVY, II, 150f. (17, 18 cents.), 924f. (biographical collections), III, 924f. (19 cent. naval historians)
Nayland Miscellany (18 cent.), II, 205
Nayler, James (*fl.* 1716), II, 857
Naylor, B. S. (*fl.* 1833), III, 374
Neade, William (*fl.* 1625), I, 394
Neal, Daniel (1678–1743), II, **877**
Neal, John (*fl.* 1869), III, 833
Neale, Edward Vansittart (1810–1892), III, 977
Neale, John Mason (1818–1866), I, 684; III, 301, 689
Neale, R. (*fl.* 1724), II, 197–8
Neale, Thomas (1614–1646?), I, 658; II, 120
Neale, William Johnson (1812–1893), III, **499**
Neave, B. (*fl.* 1785), II, 761
Neaves, Charles, Lord (1800–1876), III, **301**
Necker, Jacques, II, 792; III, 181
Necker de Saussure, Louis Albert, II, 158
Neckham, Alexander (d. 1217), I, **297**
Ned Ward's Jests (18 cent.), II, 218
Needham, H. C. (*fl.* 1900), III, 775
Needham (or Nedham), Marchamont (1620–1678), I, 748f.
    Pamphlets by, I, 750; II, 119
    Periodicals ed. by, I, 755, 757, 760, 761 (2), 762 (3), 763 (2); II, 701 (2), 716
Needham's Post-Man; Containing Foreign and Domestick News (1724), II, 734
Negri de Bassano, Francesco, I, 817
Negro Slaves, The (18 cent.), II, 486
Negus, Samuel (*fl.* 1724), II, 699
Neighbourhood, The (1800), II, 551
Neil, G. (*fl.* 1831–55), I, 906–7
Neil, Robert Alexander (1852–1901), III, **1019**
NEILL & CO., III, 87
Neilson, Samuel (1761–1803), II, 736
Nelson, Abraham (*fl.* 1654), I, 719
Nelson, Francis (*fl.* 1651), I, 761
Nelson, James (1710–1794), II, 109
Nelson, Robert (1665–1715), II, 799, 845–6, 848
Nelson, William (*fl.* 1710–20), II, 820, **964**
Nelson, William (1816–1887), III, 99
Nemesius, I, 447
Nemnich, Philipp Andreas, II, 142

'Nemo' (1845), III, 125
'Nemo' (1847), III, 128
Nenna, Giovanni Baptista, I, 417.
Nennius (fl. 796), I, 100, 132
Neot, St (O.E.), I, 93
Neri, Antonio, II, 812
Néricault Destouches, Philippe, II, 792
Nero, The Tragedy of (17 cent.), I, 652f.
Nesbit, Edith, later Bland (1858–1924), III, 350f., 570
Nethercote, Henry (fl. 1888), III, 761
NETHERLANDS, THE
   Literary Relations with, I, 345 (1500–1660); II, 69f. (1660–1800); III, 45 (19 cent.)
Netter, Thomas, or Walden (d. 1430), I, 120, 313
Nettle, The (18 cent.), II, 243
'Nettlebottom, Nehemiah' (1820), III, 185
Nettleship, Henry (1839–1893), III, 1008
Nettleship, John (fl. 1831), III, 762
Nettleship, John Trivett (1841–1902), III, 261
Neuman, Henry (fl. 1799), II, 487
Neve, Philip (fl. 1770–89), I, 469; II, 917
Nevile, Henry (1620–1694), I, 716, 731; II, 530, 811
Nevile, Thomas (d. 1781), II, 375
Nevill, William (1497–c. 1540), I, 438
Neville, Alexander (1544–1614), I, 807
Neville, Henry (1620–1694). See Nevile
Neville, Richard Griffin, Baron Braybrooke (1783–1858), II, 831
Nevinson, Evelyn, née Sharp (fl. 1897), III, 570
Nevyle, Alexander (1544–1614), I, 522
New Academy, A (17 cent.), II, 184
New Academy of Complements, The (17 cent.), II, 175 (2), 190
New Academy of Compliments (17 cent.), II, 175, 183, 195
New Anatomie, A (17 cent.), I, 724
New & Complete Collection of Scots Songs, A (18 cent.), II, 241, 244
New and Choice Collection of Loyal Songs, A (18 cent.), II, 213
New and mery Enterlude, called the Triall of Treasure, A (16 cent.), I, 517
New Annual Register, The (1780), II, 684
New Anti-Roman Pacquet, The (1680), II, 657
New Ayres and Dialogues Composed for Voices and Viols (17 cent.), II, 178
New Boghouse Miscellany (18 cent.), II, 220
New Bon Ton Magazine, or Telescope of the Times, The (1818), III, 825
New Book of Songs, A (17 cent.), II, 183–4, 198
New British Songster, The (18 cent.), II, 239, 253
New Buck's Delight, The (18 cent.), II, 224
New Canting Dictionary [etc.], A (18 cent.), II, 198
New Carolls (17 cent.), II, 174–5, 178, 198

New Case put to an Old Lawyer, A (17 cent.), I, 718
New Century Review, The (1897), III, 831
New Children's Friend, The (18 cent.), II, 566
New Christian Uses upon the Weekly True Passages (1643), I, 755
New Christian's Magazine, The (1782), II, 680
New Christmas Carrols (18 cent.), II, 198
New Collection of Miscellany Poems, A (18 cent.), II, 192
New Collection of New Songs and Poems, A (17 cent.), II, 177
New Collection of Original Poems, A (18 cent.), II, 192
New Collection of Original Scotch Songs, A (18 cent.), II, 200
New Collection of Poems and Songs, A (17 cent.), II, 177 (3), 178
New Collection of Poems on Several Occasions, A (18 cent.), II, 185 (2), 192
New Collection of Poems on Several Occasions, A. By Mr Prior [etc.] (18 cent.), II, 198
New Collection of the Choicest Songs, A (17 cent.), II, 177
New Collection Of the Choicest Songs As they are Sung at Court, A (17 cent.), II, 178
New Cork Evening Post, The (1791), II, 737
New Court-Songs, and Poems (17 cent.), II, 176
New Crown Garland of Princely Pastime and Mirth, The (17 cent.), II, 181
New Custome, A new Enterlude entituled (16 cent.), I, 516
New Daily Advertiser, The (1756), II, 709
New Dialogue between Somebody and Nobody, A (1681), II, 657
New Edinburgh Gazette, The (1710), II, 731
New Edinburgh Musical Miscellany, The (18 cent.), II, 249
New Edinburgh Review, The (1821), III, 825
New Election Budget, The (18 cent.), II, 239
New English Drama, The, III, 585
New English Theatre, The (1776), II, 392
New Enterlude called Thersytes, A (16 cent.), I, 520
New Enterlude entituled new Custome, A (16 cent.), I, 516
New enterlude for chyldren to playe, named Jacke Jugeler, A (16 cent.), I, 521
New enterlude of Impacient Poverte, A (16 cent.), I, 515
New enterlude of queene Hester, A (16 cent.), I, 515
New Entertaining Frisky Songster, The (18 cent.), II, 230
New Entertaining Humorist, The, II, 227, 233
New European Magazine, The (1822), III, 826
New Evening Post, The (Dublin, 1782), II, 736
New Farmer's Journal, The (1833), III, 819
New Foundling Hospital for Wit, The (18 cent.), II, 225 (3), 226 (2), 228 (2), 229 (2), 237, 240

New Frisky Songster (18 cent.), II, 249

New, General, and Complete Weekly Magazine, The (1796), II, 683

New General Songster, The (19 cent.), II, 256

New Globe, The (1823), III, 800

New Help to Discourse, The (17 cent.), II, 175–6, 178–9, 183, 185, 193, 196, 203

New Heraclitus Ridens (1689), II, 658

New Heraclitus Ridens; Or, An Old Dialogue between Jest and Earnest revived (1689), II, 705

New Introduction to Enfield's Speaker, A (19 cent.), II, 256

New Jerusalem Journal, The (1772), II, 682

New Jerusalem Magazine, The (1790), II, 681

New Lady's Magazine, The (1786), II, 674

New Lady's Magazine; Or, Polite Companion for the Fair Sex, The (1785), II, 681

New Liverpool Songster, The (18 cent.), II, 243

New London & Country Jester, The (19 cent.), II, 256

New London and Country Songster, The (18 cent.), II, 235

New London Drollery, The (17 cent.), II, 180

New London Jester, The (18 cent.), II, 250

New London Magazine, Being an Universal Repository of Knowledge, The (1785), II, 681

New London Medical Journal, The (1792), II, 681

New London Price Courant, The (1786), II, 718

New London Review, The (1799), II, 683

New Magazine, The (1799), II, 688

New Magazine of Knowledge, The (1791), II, 681

New Magazine; Or, Moral and Entertaining Miscellany, The (1799), II, 688

New Memoirs of Literature (1725), II, 675

New Merry Companion, The (1720), II, 195

New Merry Companion, or Complete Modern Songster, The (18 cent.), II, 229, 233

New Ministry, The (18 cent.), II, 209 (2), 210

New Miscellaneous Poems (18 cent.), 193 (2), 194 (2), 198

New Miscellany, A (1726), II, 198

New Miscellany, A (1730), II, 200

New Miscellany, The (18 cent.), II, 195

New Miscellany for the Year, A (1734), II, 204, 207 (2), 208, 684

New Miscellany In Prose and Verse, A (18 cent.), II, 209

New Miscellany Of Original Poems, A (18 cent.), II, 195, 208

New Miscellany Published For the Benefit of John Maxwell, A (18 cent.), II, 213

New Monthly, The (1882), III, 825

New Monthly Magazine, The (1872), III, 825

New Monthly Magazine and Humourist, The (1837), III, 825

New Monthly Magazine and Literary Journal, The (1821), III, 825

New Monthly Magazine and Universal Register, The (1814), III, 825

New Monthly Review, The (1854), III, 829

New Moral World, The (1834), III, 816

New Morning Post, The (1776), II, 709

New Musical and Universal Magazine, The (1774), II, 230–2, 679

New News, Strange News, True News (1648), I, 758

New News-Book, A (1681), II, 703

New Novelist's Magazine, The (18 cent.), II, 549

New Novelist's Magazine; Or, Entertaining Library of Histories [etc.], The (1786), II, 681

New Observator (1704), II, 659

New Observator on the Present Times, A (1701), II, 659

New Observer, The (1821), III, 811

New Olio, The (18 cent.), II, 250

New Paradise of Dainty Devices, The (18 cent.), II, 232

New Pleasing Instructor: or, Entertaining Moralist, The (18 cent.), II, 562

New Polite Instructor, The (18 cent.), II, 228

New Political State of Great Britain, The (1730), II, 676

New Print Magazine, The (1795), II, 682

New Quarterly Magazine, The (1873), III, 833

New Quarterly Review, The (1844), III, 833

New Quarterly Review and Digest of Current Literature, The (1852), III, 833

New Register Book of Shipping (1799), II, 718

New Review, The (1889), III, 831

New Review, with Literary Curiosities, A (1782), II, 680

New Rolliad, The (18 cent.), II, 239

New Royal and Universal Magazine, The (1759), II, 677

New School of Love, The (18 cent.), II, 240 (2), 248, 256

New Scots Spy, or Critical Observer, The (1777), II, 665

New Select Collection of Epitaphs, A (18 cent.), II, 230

New Spectator, with Opinions of John Bull, The (1784), II, 666

New Spiritual Magazine, The (1783), II, 680

New Sporting Magazine, The (1831), III, 759

New Sporting Magazine, The (1846), III, 823

New Spouters Companion, The (18 cent.), II, 253

New Spouter's Companion, The (19 cent.), II, 256

New State of Europe, Both as to Publick Transactions and Learning, The (1701), II, 711

New State of Europe, Or a True Account of Publick Transactions and Learning, The (1701), II, 706

New Story-Teller, The (18 cent.), II, 236
New Syren, The (18 cent.), II, 254
New Tea-Table Miscellany, A (18 cent.), II, 214 (2)
New Testament Prose Selections (M.E.), I, **190**
New Theatre of Fun, The (18 cent.), II, 233
New Theatrical Songster, The (19 cent.), II, 256
New Theological Repository, The, II, 685
New Thespian Oracle, The (18 cent.), II, 246
New Times, The (1817), III, 799
New Tom Spring's Life in London and Sporting Times (1843), III, 812
New Town and Country Magazine, The (1787), II, 681
New Treasury of Musick, The (17 cent.), II, 183
New Universal Magazine, The (1751), II, 677
New Universal Magazine, The (1775), II, 680
New Universal Magazine, The (1814), III, 822
New Universal Magazine of Knowledge, The (1788), II, 681
New Universal Story-Teller, The (18 cent.), II, **232**
New Vocal Companion, The (1794), II, 249
New Vocal Enchantress, The (18 cent.), II, 241, 243, 246
New Vocal Miscellany, The (18 cent.), II, 201
New Vocal Miscellany, by W. Collins (18 cent.), II, 240
New Weekly Chronicle; Or, Universal Journal, The (1758), II, 715
New Weekly Dispatch, The (1833), III, 812
New Weekly Miscellany, The (1741), II, 715
New Whim of the Day, The (18 cent.), II, 244 (2)
New Wonderful Magazine, The (1793), II, 682
NEW ZEALAND (literature of), III, 1093 f.
NEWARK
  Magazines, II, 685 (1782–94)
  Newspapers, II, 726
  Printers and booksellers, II, 87
Newark Herald, The (1791), II, 726
Newbery, Elizabeth (*fl.* 1800), II, 554
Newbery, Francis (1743–1818), II, 709
Newbery, John (1713–1767), II, 25, 27 (2), 30, 100, 560 f., 672, 696, 741, 931
Newbery, Nathaniel (*fl.* 1622), I, 745
Newbery House Magazine, The (1889), III, 831
Newbolt, Sir Henry John (1862–1937), III, **351**, 832
Newburgh, Brockill (*fl.* 1769), II, 18
Newcastle, Margaret Cavendish, Duchess of (1624?–1674), II, 529 (2)
Newcastle Advertiser; Or, General Weekly Post, The (1788), II, 726
Newcastle Chronicle, The (1764), II, 726; III, 794, 802
Newcastle Courant, With News Foreign and Domestick, The (1711), II, 726
Newcastle Daily Chronicle, The (1862), III, 802
Newcastle Daily Courant, The (1874), III, 804

Newcastle Daily Journal, The (1861), III, 803
Newcastle Daily Leader, The (1895), III, 806
Newcastle Daily Telegraph, The (1869), III, 803
Newcastle Evening Courant, The (1870), III, 804
Newcastle Evening News, The (1893), III, 806
Newcastle Evening Telegraph, The (1871), III, 803
Newcastle Gazette; Or, Northern Courant, The (1710), II, 726
Newcastle Gazette; Or, Tyne Water Journal, The (1744), II, 726
Newcastle General Magazine, The (1747), II, 685
Newcastle Intelligencer, The (1755), II, 726
Newcastle Journal, The (1739), II, 726
Newcastle Journal, The (1832), III, 803
Newcastle Magazine, The (1785), II, 685
Newcastle Magazine, The (1820), III, 826
Newcastle Mercury, The (1722), II, 726
Newcastle Morning Mail, The (1898), III, 806
Newcastle Morning Telegraph, The (1870), III, 803
Newcastle Noah's Ark (M.E.), I, 279
Newcastle Weekly Chronicle, The (1764), II, 726
Newcastle Weekly Chronicle, The (1864), II, 726
Newcastle Weekly Courant, The (1884), II, 726
Newcastle Weekly Journal and Courant, The (1902), II, 726
Newcastle Weekly Magazine, The (1776), II, 685
NEWCASTLE-ON-TYNE
  Magazines, II, 685 (1747–99)
  Newspapers, II, 726
  Printing in, I, 353 (17, 18 cents.)
Newcomb, Thomas (1682?–1762), II, 602, 605
Newcome, Henry (1627–1695), II, 134
Newcome, Thomas (*fl.* 1763), II, 56
Newcome, Thomas (*fl.* 1825), II, 849
Newcome, William (1729–1800), I, 672
Newdigate, Sir Richard (1602–1678), II, 134
Newe mery Comedie of Jacob and Esau, A (16 cent.), I, 521
Newell, Robert Hasell (1778–1852), II, 648
Newenham, Thomas (1762–1831), II, 159
Newes, The (1663), II, 702
Newes come from Hell (16 cent.), I, 719
Newes from Graves End (17 cent.), I, 714
Newes from Rome (17 cent.), I, 714
Newes or the Ful Particulars of the Last Fight, The (1653), I, 762
Newes, True Newes, Laudable Newes (17 cent.), I, 720
Newest Collection of the Choicest Songs, The (17 cent.), II, 179
Newgate Monthly Magazine, or Calendar of Men, Things and Opinions, The (1824), III, 826
Newhall, Isaac (*fl.* 1831), II, 632

Newland, Henry Garrett (1804–1860), III, 770, 854

Newlands, H. (*fl.* 1851), III, 118

Newlands, John Alexander (1837–1898), III, 948

Newman, Francis William (1805–1897), III, 302, 849, 982

Newman, John (*fl.* 1685), II, 763

Newman, John Henry (1801–1890), I, 677, 684, 685 (3); III, **686f.**, 828, 833, 854–5, 856 (2)

Newman, Thomas (*fl.* 1627), I, 649, 808

Newman, William (*fl.* 1788), II, 964

Newmarch, Rosa (b. 1857), III, **351**

Newmarch, William (1820–1882), III, 974

Newminster, Cartulary of (M.E.), I, 121

Newnes, Sir George (1851–1910), III, 787, 814, 831

Newnham, William (1790–1865), III, 112

NEWRY
    Newspaper, II, 738

Newry Journal, The (1775), II, 738

News, The (1805), III, 810

News Expositour, The (1694), II, 658

News from Parnassus (1681), II, 657

News from the Dead (1715), II, 676

News from the Land of Chivalry (1681), II, 657

News Journal, English and French, The (1723), II, 713, 719

News Letter (1685), II, 733

News Letter, The (1716), II, 712

NEWS-LETTER, II, 692

News of the World, The (1843), III, 794, 812

NEWS-SHEETS AND NEWS-BOOKS, I, 736f. (1500–1660)

Newsagent and Advertiser's Record, The (1889), III, 780

Newsagent and Bookseller's Review, The (1890), III, 780

Newsagents' Chronicle, The (1895), III, 780

Newsman, The (1864), III, 813

Newsmen's Weekly Chronicle, The (1837), III, 780

Newspaper and Poster Advertising (1900), III, 780

Newspaper Owner and Manager, The (1898), III, 780

Newspaper Press, The (1866), III, 782

NEWSPAPERS, I, 736f. (1500–1660); II, 688f. (1660–1800); III, 779f. (19 cent.); 1088 (Canadian)

Newstead, Christopher (1597–1662), I, 716

Newsvendor, The (1873), III, 780

Newte, Thomas (*fl.* 1791), II, 140

Newton, Alfred (1829–1907), III, 829

Newton, Sir Charles Thomas (1816–1894), III, 1001

Newton, Sir Isaac (1642–1727), II, 32, 125, 934, 961 (2)

Newton, John (1622–1678), II, 109, 126

Newton, John (1725–1807), II, 341, 749, **853**, 915

Newton, Richard (1676–1753), II, 118

Newton, Samuel (1628–1718), II, 153

Newton, Thomas (1542?–1607), translator, I, 509, 713, 801, 807, 888

Newton, Thomas (1704–1782), bishop of Bristol, II, 850, 912f.

Newton, William (*fl.* 1730), II, 853

New Year's Gift, The (18 cent.), II, 198

New-Years Gift for Batchelors, A (18 cent.), II, 187

New Year's Miscellany, The (1715), II, 192

New-Year's Miscellany, The (1747), II, 212

Niccols, Richard (1584–1616), I, 413, 477

Nice wanton, A Preaty Interlude called (16 cent.), I, 515

Nichol, John (1833–1894), III, 351

Nichol, John Pringle (1804–1850), III, 936, 944

Nicholas of Fakenham (d. *c.* 1407), I, **305**

Nicholas, Sir Edward (1593–1669), I, 385–6, 400

Nicholas, Sir H. (*fl.* 1834), I, 115

Nicholas, H. N. (*fl.* 1827), I, 206

Nicholas, Sir N. H. Misprint for Sir Nicholas Harris Nicolas (1799–1848)

Nicholas, Thomas (*fl.* 1560–96), I, 785, 787 (2)

Nicholas Hussey's Weekly Post (1728), II, 734

Nicholl, John (*fl.* 1605), I, 789

Nicholls, A. B. (*fl.* 1857), III, 461

Nicholls, Charlotte, née Brontë (1816–1855), III, **461**f.

Nicholls, Sir George (1781–1865), III, 971, 976

Nicholls, John (*fl.* 1820), II, 165

Nicholls, Norton (1742?–1809), II, 334

Nicholls, T. (*fl.* 1776), II, 308

Nicholls, William (1664–1712), II, 781

Nichols, James (1785–1861), I, 835 (3)

Nichols, John (1745–1826), II, 19, 83, 139, 232, 234 (2), 235 (2), 236, 238, 295, 700, **885**f., **904** (2)f.

Nichols, John Bowyer (1779–1863), II, 464, 886, 890; III, 87, 822, 879

Nichols, John Gough (1806–1873), I, 265, 383 (3), 384 (2), 399, 500, 824 (4); III, 87 (3), 822

Nichols, Philip (*fl.* 1575), I, 791

Nichols, Thomas (*fl.* 1554), I, 785

Nicholson, — (*fl.* 1805), II, 922

Nicholson, George (1760–1825), II, 251 (2), 252 (3), 253 (3), 254 (2), 256, 336

Nicholson, Henry Alleyne (1844–1899), III, 953

Nicholson, H. W. B. (*fl.* 1836), I, 140

Nicholson, J. S. (1850–1927), III, 974, 978

Nicholson, John (1790–1843), III, **240**

Nicholson, N. A. (*fl.* 1868), III, 974

Nicholson, Renton (1809–1861), III, 812–3, 815

Nicholson, Thomas (*fl.* 1746), II, 754

Nicholson, William (1753–1815), man of science and inventor, II, 469, 683, 927; III, 946
Nicholson, William (1655–1727). See Nicolson
Nicholson, William (1782?–1849), Galloway poet, III, 240
Nicholson, William (*fl.* 1843), editor of archbishop Grindal's writings, I, 682
Nicholson's Weekly Register (1842), III, 820
Nickolls, John (1710?–1745), I, 468
Nicodemus, Gospel of (O.E.), I, 93
Nicol, Alexander (*fl.* 1739), II, 973
Nicol, G. (*fl.* 1813), I, 842
Nicol, James (1810–1879), III, 950, 952
Nicolai, C. F., II, 807
Nicolai, Friedrich, II, 63
Nicolas, Sir Nicholas Harris (1799–1848), I, 387; II, 976; III, 104, 246, 826, **1026f.**
Nicolay, Nicolas de (*fl.* 1585), I, 768, 773
Nicole, Pierre, II, 36, 769, 792
Nicoll, Alexander (1793–1828), III, 994
Nicoll, John (*fl.* 1650), II, 996
Nicoll, Robert (1814–1837), III, **302**
Nicoll, Sir W. R. (1851–1923), III, 814, 831
Nicolls, Thomas (*fl.* 1550), I, 808
Nicolson, William (1655–1727), I, 59; II, 134, **848**, 886
Niebuhr, Barthold Georg, III, 33, 670
Nierembergius, Johannes Eusebius, I, 461
Nietzsche, Friedrich, III, **33**
Nieuwentydt, Bernard, II, 69
Nigel de Longchamps (*fl.* 1190), I, **289**
Night Post, The (1711), II, 710
Night Walker, The (1697), II, 658
Nightingale, The (1738), II, 207, 209–10, 219, 227 (2), 231, 239, 254
Nightingale; or, Vocal Songster, The (18 cent.), II, 239
Nilsson, Sven (*fl.* 1868 or earlier), III, 915
Nimble Heave, The (18 cent.), II, 208
'Nimrod' (1788), II, **822**
'Nimrod', i.e. Charles James Apperley (1779–1843), III, 759f.
Nimrod (1827), III, 811
Nimrod's Songs of the Chace (18 cent.), II, 241
Nine Muses upon the Death of Drydon, The (18 cent.), II, 185
Nineteenth Century, The (1877), III, 830
NINETEENTH-CENTURY CRITICAL AND MISCELLANEOUS PROSE
 Early Nineteenth-Century Essayists (Cobbett–Carlyle), III, 629f.
 Late Nineteenth-Century Critics and Miscellaneous Writers (Stephen–Pater), III, 727f.
 Literature of Sport, III, 757f.
 Mid-Nineteenth Century Essayists (Macaulay–Ruskin), III, 683f.
 Minor Critics and Essayists, 1800–1835, III, 663f.
 Minor Critics and Essayists, 1835–1870, III, 707

 Minor Critics and Essayists, 1870–1900, III, 732f.
 Newspapers and Magazines, III, 779f.
 Writings on Religion, III, 846f.
NINETEENTH-CENTURY DRAMA
 Dramatists of the Irish Revival, III, 1063f.
 Early Nineteenth-Century Drama, 1800–1835, III, 586f.
 General Introduction, III, 580f.
 Late Nineteenth-Century Drama, 1870–1900, III, 610f.
 Mid-Nineteenth Century Drama, 1835–1870, III, 597f.
NINETEENTH-CENTURY FICTION
 Anglo-Indian Fiction, III, 1069f.
 Australian-New Zealand Fiction, III, 1096f.
 Bibliographies, Histories and Critical Studies, III, 364f.
 Canadian Fiction, III, 1086f.
 Children's Books, III, 564f.
 Early Nineteenth-Century Novelists (Maria Edgeworth–Marryat), III, 366f.
 Later Nineteenth-Century Novelists ('Lewis Carroll'–Kipling), III, 513f.
 Mid-Nineteenth Century Novelists (Borrow–Meredith), III, 421f.
 Minor Fiction, 1800–1835, III, 387f.
 Minor Fiction, 1835–1870, III, 471f.
 Minor Fiction, 1870–1900, III, 534f.
 South African Fiction, III, 1089f.
NINETEENTH CENTURY, INTRODUCTION TO
 Bibliographies, Literary Histories and Special Studies, Prose-Selections, and Literary Memoirs and Reminiscences, III, 3f.
 Book Production and Distribution, III, 70f.
 Education, III, 106f.
 Intellectual Background, III, 46f.
 Literary Relations with the Continent, III, 17f.
 Political and Social Background, III, 143f.
NINETEENTH-CENTURY LITERATURES OF THE DOMINIONS
 Anglo-Indian Literature, III, 1067f.
 Anglo-Irish Literature, III, 1045f.
 English-Canadian Literature, III, 1085f.
 English-South African Literature, III, 1088f.
 Literature of Australia and New Zealand, III, 1093f.
NINETEENTH-CENTURY PHILOSOPHY, HISTORY, SCIENCE, AND OTHER FORMS OF LEARNING
 Books of Travel, III, 988f.
 Classical, Biblical and Oriental Scholarship, III, 993f.
 Economics and Political Theory, III, 969f.
 English Scholarship, III, 1021f.
 History, Biography and Archaeology, III, 877f.
 Literature of Science, III, 936f.
 Philosophy, III, 861f.
 Writers on Law, III, 985f.

NINETEENTH-CENTURY POETRY
Anglo-Indian Poetry and Drama, III, 1068f.
Australian and New Zealand Poetry, III, 1093f.
Early Nineteenth-Century Poets (Rogers–Hood), III, 164f.
English-Canadian Poetry, III, 1085f.
English-South African Poetry, III, 1089
Later Nineteenth-Century Poets (Morris–Francis Thompson), III, 314f.
Mid-Nineteenth Century Poets (Praed–the Rossettis), III, 247f.
Minor Verse, 1800–1835, III, 225f.
Minor Verse, 1835–1870, III, 275f.
Minor Verse, 1870–1900, III, 327f.
Poets of the Irish Revival, III, 1051f.
Surveys, Critical Studies and Anthologies, III, 156f.
'Ninnyhammer, Nickydemus' (1715), II, 301
'Nipclose, Sir Nicholas' (1772), II, 409
Nisbet, Hay (fl. 1833), II, 732
Nisbet, James (1785–1854), III, 99
Nisbet, Murdoch (fl. c. 1520), I, 260
Nitsch, F. A. (fl. 1796), II, 52
Nivernois, Louis Jules Henri Barbon Mazarini Mancini, Duke of, II, 770
Nixon, Anthony (fl. 1602), I, 740, 783
Nixon, J. (fl. 1885), III, 1090
Nixon, Robert (fl. 1620), II, 783
Noad, Henry Minchin (1815–1877), III, 938
Noah's Ark (Newcastle) (M.E.), I, 279
Noailles, Louis Antoine de, II, 792
Nobbes, Robert (1652–1706?), II, 819
NOBILITY (biographical collections of), II, 924
Noble, J. (fl. 1877), III, 1092
Noble, James Ashcroft (1844–1896), III, 352
Noble, John (1827–1892), III, 979
Noble, Mark (1754–1827), I, 396; II, 888
'Nobleman, A' (1810), III, 127
'Nobody, A.', i.e. Frederick Gordon Browne (d. 1932), III, 574
No-Body and Some-Body (17 cent.), I, 653
Nodder, Richard P. (fl. 1789), II, 681
Noehden, Georg Heinrich, II, 51, 61, 486
Noel, Lady Augusta (1838–1902), III, 556
Noel, Baptist Wriothesley (1798–1873), III, 853
Noel, Edward Henry (d. 1884), III, 34, 352
Noel, Henry (d. 1597), I, 523
Noel, Nathaniel (fl. 1676), II, 177
Noel, Roden Berkeley Wriothesley (1834–1894), III, 352, 706
Noel-Fearn, Henry, earlier Christmas (1811–1868), III, 818, 848
Nolle, Heinrich, I, 461
NON-CYCLIC ROMANCES (M.E.), I, 147f.
Nonconformist, The (1841), III, 819
NONCONFORMISTS, WRITINGS BY
Bibliographies, I, 9
Restoration to Romantic Revival, II, 861f.
None-Such Charles, The (17 cent.), I, 720

Nonpareil, The (18 cent.), II, 218, 677
Nonsense of Common Sense, The (1737), II, 663, 714
Noon Gazette and Daily Spy, The (1781), II, 709
Noorthouck, John (1746?–1816), II, 145, 922
Norden, John (1548–1625?), topographer, I, 775, 826, 883, 885
Norden, John (fl. 1600), devotional author, I, 684
NORFOLK
Bibliography, I, 8
Printers and booksellers, II, 87
Norfolk, John Howard, Duke of (1430?–1485), I, 120
Norfolk, Thomas Howard, Duke of (1443–1524), I, 120
Norfolk Chronicle; or, The Norwich Gazette, The (1769), II, 727
Norfolk Daily Standard, The (1886), III, 806
Norfolk Evening Standard, The (1903), III, 806
Norfolk Guilds (M.E.), I, 42
Norfolk News, The, III, 794
Norfolk Poetical Miscellany, The (18 cent.), II, 210
Norgate, Thomas Starling (1772–1859), II, 666
Norman, George Warde (1793–1882), II, 972, 974, 978
Norman, H. W. (fl. 1849), I, 90
Norman, J. H. (fl. 1839), III, 974
Norman, Robert (fl. 1581), I, 885
Normanby, Constantine Henry Phipps, Marquis of (1797–1863), III, 413
Norris, — (fl. 1743), II, 105
Norris, Edwin (1795–1872), I, 279; III, 967, 1016
Norris, Isaac (fl. 1745), II, 754
Norris, John (1657–1711), poet and philosopher, II, 283, 763, 943
Norris, John (fl. 1704), editor of 'The Athenian Gazette', II, 658
Norris, John (fl. 1712), writer on America, II, 753
Norris, John Pilkington (1823–1891), III, 112
Norris, Robert (d. 1791), II, 749
NORSE, OLD. See under SCANDINAVIAN, I, 33
'North, Christopher', i.e. John Wilson (1785–1854), III, 668, 682f.
North, Dudley, Baron (1581–1666), I, 724, 726
North, Sir Dudley (1641–1691), II, 943
North, Francis, Baron Guilford (1637–1685), II, 30
North, Frederick, Earl of Guilford (1732–1792), II, 165
North, George (1561–81), I, 777, 813, 817
North, H. (fl. 1797), II, 786
North, Roger (1653–1734), II, 820, 872

North, Sir Thomas (1535?–1601?), 1, 806, 811, 814
North and South Shields Gazette, The (1855), III, 802
North British Advertiser, The (19 cent.), III, 794
North British Daily Mail [Glasgow] (1847), III, 807
North British Intelligencer; Or, Constitutional Miscellany, The (1776), II, 686
North British Magazine; Or, Caledonian Miscellany, The (1782), II, 686
North British Miscellany; Or, Dundee Amusement, The (1778), II, 687
North British Review, The (1844), III, 828
North Briton, The (1762), II, 664
North Country Journal; Or, The Impartial Intelligencer, The (1734), II, 726
North Eastern Daily Gazette, The (1881), III, 804
North London Press, The (1889), III, 818
North of England Magazine, The (1842), III, 828
North of England Magazine and Bradshaw's Journal, The (1843), III, 828
North Tatler, The (1710), II, 661
North Western Daily Mail, The [Barrow] (1898), III, 806
Northall, John (1723?–1759), II, 745
NORTHAMPTON
   Magazine, II, 685 (1721)
   Newspapers, II, 726
Northampton Daily Chronicle, The (1881), III, 805
Northampton Daily Reporter, The (1885), III, 805
Northampton Journal, The (1723), II, 726
Northampton Mercury, The (1720), II, 726
Northampton Mercury Daily Reporter, The (1880), III, 805
Northampton Miscellany, The (1721), II, 674, 685
NORTHAMPTONSHIRE
   Bibliography, I, 8
   Printers and booksellers, II, 87
Northamptonshire Geld Roll (M.E.), I, 121
Northamptonshire Journal, The (1741), II, 726
Northbrooke, John (*fl.* 1568–79), I, 509f.
Northcliffe, Alfred C. W. Harmsworth, Viscount (1865–1922), III, 787
Northcote, James (1746–1831), II, 630; III, 149
Northcote, Sir Stafford, Earl of Iddesleigh (1818–1887), III, 153
Northern Alliterative Prophecies (M.E.), I, 168
Northern Counties Daily Mail, The [Newcastle] (1872), III, 804
Northern Daily Express, The [Newcastle] (1855), III, 802
Northern Daily Mail, The [West Hartlepool] (1883), III, 805
Northern Daily Telegraph, The [Blackburn] (1886), III, 806
Northern Daily Times [Liverpool] (1853), III, 801f.
Northern Echo, The [Darlington] (1870), III, 804
NORTHERN ENGLISH
   Dialect (M.E.), I, 38
   Texts (M.E.), I, 43
Northern Evening Express, The (1866), III, 803
Northern Evening Mail, The [West Hartlepool] (1877), III, 805
Northern Express, The [Darlington] (1854), III, 802
Northern Express and Lancashire Daily Post, The (1821), III, 801
Northern Gazette, Literary Chronicle and Review, The (1787), II, 732
Northern Homily Cycle (M.E.), I, 173f.
Northern Liberator, The [Newcastle-on-Tyne] (1837), III, 816
Northern Liberator and Champion, The (1840), III, 816
NORTHERN OCEAN, VOYAGES TO, II, 743
Northern Star, The (Belfast, 1792), II, 736
Northern Star and Leeds General Advertiser, The [Leeds] (1837), III, 816
Northern Telegraph [Edinburgh] (1854), III, 807
Northern Telegraphic News [Aberdeen] (1855), III, 806
Northern Times [Liverpool] (1857), III, 801
Northern Times, The [Oldham] (1877), III, 805
Northern Whig, The [Belfast] (1858), III, 808
Northleigh, John (1657–1705), II, 264, 744
Northmore, Thomas (1766–1851), II, 763
NORTHUMBERLAND
   Bibliographies, I, 8
Northumberland, Elizabeth Percy, Duchess of, II, 746
Northumberland Garland, The, II, 248
Northumbrian Genealogies (O.E.), I, 35, 37
NORTHUMBRIAN TEXTS (O.E.), I, 36f.
Norton, Andrews (*fl.* 1826), III, 210
Norton, Caroline Elizabeth Sarah, née Sheridan, later Lady Stirling-Maxwell (1808–1877), III, 302, 824
Norton, John Bruce (1815–1888), III, 1076
Norton, J. N. (*fl.* 1861), II, 945
Norton, Robert (d. 1635), I, 390, 827, 880–1
Norton, Thomas (*fl.* 1477), I, 253, 314, 886
Norton, Thomas (1532–1584), I, 523, 678, 808, 811
NORTON LIBRARY, II, 105
NORWAY
   Literary Relations with, II, 70f. (1660–1800); III, 42f. (19 cent.)
   Loan-words, I, 33
NORWICH
   Library, I, 362; II, 105
   Newspapers, II, 726f.

Norwich Courant; Or, Weekly Packet, The (1714), II, 727
Norwich Gazette, The (1761), II, 727
Norwich Gazette or the Loyal Packet, The (1725), II, 727
Norwich Grocers' Play (Adam and Eve) (M.E.), I, 279
Norwich Journal, The (1723), II, 727
Norwich Leet (M.E.), I, 121
Norwich Mercury, The (1725), II, 727
Norwich Post, The (1701), II, 727
Norwich Postman, The (1706), II, 727
Norwood, Colonel — (*fl.* 1649), I, 793
Norwood, Richard (1590?–1675), I, 390, 791, 881 f.
Notes and Queries (1849), III, 818
Nott, George Frederick (1767–1841), I, 212, 403, 412
Nott, John (1751–1865), I, 449
Nott, J. (*fl.* 1812), I, 621
Nott, J. (*fl.* 1816), I, 677
Nott, John (1751–1865), II, 764, 767, 812
Nott, J. C. (*fl.* 1854–7), III, 1015 (2)
NOTTINGHAM
    Newspapers, II, 727
Nottingham Charters (M.E.), I, 121
Nottingham Chronicle, The (1772), II, 727
Nottingham Courant, The (1732), II, 727
Nottingham Daily Express, The (1860), III, 802
Nottingham Daily Guardian, The (1861), III, 803
Nottingham Evening News, The (1885), III, 806
Nottingham Evening Post, The (1878), III, 805
Nottingham Journal, The (1787), II, 727
Nottingham Mercury, The (1715), II, 727
Nottingham Post, The (1710), II, 727
Nottingham Weekly Courant, The (1710), II, 727
NOTTINGHAMSHIRE
    Bibliography, I, 8
    Printers, II, 87
Nottinghamshire Gazette, The (1780), II, 727
Nottola (17 cent.), I, 662
Nougaret, Pierre Jean Baptiste, II, 142
Nourse, Timothy (d. 1699), II, 148
Nouveau Magasin Français, Le (1750), II, 677
Nouvelle Bibliothèque Angloise (1756), II, 688
Nouvelles Ordinaires de Londres (1650), I, 760
Nova Scotian (1828), III, 1088
'Novalis' (Friedrich Leopold von Hardenberg), III, 33
NOVEL, THE, I, 11 (general histories)
    Middle English Period, I, 161 f.
    Renaissance to Restoration, I, 726 f.
    Restoration to Romantic Revival, II, 488 f.
        (recent criticism), 490 f. (principal novelists), 529 f. (minor fiction and translations), 553 f. (children's books)

Nineteenth Century, III, 364 f. (bibliographies, recent studies), 366 f. (Edgeworth–Marryat), 387 f. (minor fiction, 1800–35), 421 f. (Borrow–Meredith), 471 f. (minor fiction, 1835–70), 513 f. (Carroll–Kipling), 534 f. (minor fiction, 1870–1900), 564 f. (children's books)
Novel Reader, The (1800), II, 683
Novel Review, The (1892), III, 830
Novelist's Magazine, The (1780), II, 680
Novello, Mary Victoria Cowden, later Clarke (1809–1897), III, 711
NOVELLO, EWER & CO., III, 99
Now or Never (17 cent.), I, 717
Nowell, Alexander (1507?–1602), I, 376
Nowell, Robert (*fl.* 1568–80), I, 384
Nuce, Thomas (d. 1617), I, 522, 807
Nucius, Nicander, of Corcyra, I, 383
Nugae Antiquae (18 cent.), II, 226, 231, 234, 247
Nugent, Lady Maria, III, 150
Nugent or Craggs, Robert, Earl of Nugent (1702–1788), II, 323
Nugent, Thomas (1700?–1772), II, 28 (2), 34, 51, 127, 552, 745, 774, 778, 782 (2), 785, 798, 800, 803, 809
Nuggets (1892), III, 821
No. I of Macklin's British Poets (18 cent.), II, 241
'Nurse Truelove' (1750), II, 561
Nursery Morals (19 cent.), III, 575
Nus, Eugene, III, 456, 608
Nut-Cracker, The (18 cent.), II, 215, 219, 226
Nuttall, P. A. (*fl.* 1840), I, 835
Nyren, John (1764–1837), III, 773

O., H. (*fl.* 1632), I, 725
O., J. (*fl.* 1689), I, 458
O., J. (*fl.* 1700), II, 185
O., N. (*fl.* 1682), II, 771
O., R. (*fl.* 1642), I, 753
O., W. (*fl.* 1818), III, 194
Oakeley, Frederick (1802–1880), III, 854, 859
Oakes, A. F. (*fl.* 1850), III, 765
OAKHAM SCHOOL, I, 373
Oaten Pipe, The (18 cent.), II, 239
O'Brien, James Bronterre (1805–1864), III, 812, 816 (3), 817 (2), 977
O'Brien, John (d. 1767), III, 1047
O'Brien, M. D. (*fl.* 1892), III, 977
O'Brien, William (d. 1815), actor and dramatist, II, 479, 800
O'Brien, William (*fl.* 1843), Dublin prosodist, I, 17
Observations Historical, Political and Philosophical upon Aristotle's First Book of Political Government (1654), I, 762
Observations on the Morning and Evening Papers published by the Coffee-men (1729), II, 693

Observations on the Most Remarkable Occurrences (1693), II, 705
Observations on the Weekly Bill (1686), II, 657, 674
Observations upon Occurrences in our Weekly News (1693), II, 658
Observeator, The (1702), II, 659
Observator, The (1704), II, 659
Observator, The (1718), II, 662
Observator, being a Sequel to the Englishman, The (1715), II, 661
Observator in Question and Answer, The (1681), II, 657
Observator Observ'd, The (1681), II, 657
Observator Observ'd; Or, Protestant Observations upon Anti-Protestant Pamphlets, The (1681), II, 704
Observator, or a Dialogue between a Countryman and a Schoolmaster (1705), II, 659
Observator Reformed, The (1704), II, 659
Observator Reviv'd, The (1707), II, 660
Observator, with a Summary of Intelligence, The (1654), I, 762
Observer, The (1773), II, 665
Observer, The (1786), II, 666
Observer, The (1791), II, 698, 716; III, 810
Observer of the Times, The (1821), III, 811
Observer of the Times and Constitution, The (1823), III, 811
Observer; Or, A Delineation of the Times, The (1793), II, 686
Occasional Courant, The (1717), II, 660
Occasional Paper, The (1697), II, 661, 675
Occasional Paper, The (1716), II, 662
Occasional Poems On the Late Dutch War (18 cent.), II, 190
Occasional Writer, The (1727), II, 663
Occasional Writer, The (1738), II, 663
Occasionalist, The (1768), II, 665
Occleve (or Hoccleve), Thomas (1368?–1450?), I, 29, 39, 252 f.
Occurrences from Foreign Parts (1659), I, 763
Occurrences of Certain Special and Remarkable Passages (1644), I, 755
Ochino, Bernadino, I, 342, 817
Ockland (or Ocland), Christopher (d. 1590), I, 375
Ockley, Simon (1678–1720), II, 748, 812, 877
O'Clery, Lughaidh (fl. 1609), III, 1047
O'Clery, Michael (1575–1643), III, 1047
O'Connell, Daniel (1775–1847), III, 144, 148
O'Connell, John (1810–1858), III, 144
O'Connor, Arthur (1763–1852), II, 736
O'Connor, Dermod (fl. 1712–29), III, 1047
O'Connor, Feargus (1794–1855), III, 971
O'Connor, Roger (1762–1834), II, 737
O'Connor, T. P. (1848–1929), III, 787, 801 (2), 813
O'Conor, Charles (1710–1791), III, 1047
Octavian (M.E.), I, 156

O'Curry, Eugene (1796–1862), III, 1048
Odd Fellow's Song Book, The (18 cent.), II, 252
Odell, J. (fl. 1806), I, 17
Odell, Thomas (1691–1749), II, 442
Odes (19 cent.), II, 256
Odes and Satyrs of Horace, The (18 cent.), II, 192 (2), 193, 196, 201
Odes, Cantatas, Songs etc. (18 cent.), II, 231
Odgers, William Blake (fl. 1881), III, 987
Odingsells, Gabriel (1690–1734), II, 442
Odling, William (1829–1921), III, 948
Odo of Cheriton (d. 1247), I, 298
O'Donovan, Edmund (1844–1883), III, 992
O'Donovan, John (1809–1861), III, 1049
O'Dowd, Bernard (fl. 1903–12), III, 1096
Oeconomist; Or, Edlin's Weekly Journal, The (1733), II, 714
Oeconomist; Or, Englishman's Magazine, The (1798), II, 685
Oedipus; Or, The Postman Remounted (1730), II, 706
Oehlenschläger, Adam Gottlob, III, 298, 422
Offelen, Heinrich, II, 50
OFFICIAL DOCUMENTS
    Middle English Period, I, 115
    Renaissance to Restoration, I, 380 f., 396 f., 497 f. (theatrical)
    Restoration to Romantic Revival, II, 161 f.
    Nineteenth Century, III, 120 f. (education), 843 f. (year books)
Offor, George (1787–1864), I, 675; II, 490, 491 (2), 492–3
Offray de la Mettrie, Julien, II, 792
Offspring of Fancy; Or, Suffolk, Norfolk and Essex, The (18 cent.), II, 249
Offspring of Russell, The (18 cent.), II, 550
Offspring of Wit and Harmony, The (18 cent.), II, 235
O'Fihely (Mauritius de Portu) (fl. 1488), I, 305
O'Flaherty, Roderic (1629–1718), III, 1047
O'Flanagan, Theophilus (fl. 1795), III, 1047
Ogden, James (1718–1802), II, 23, 139
Ogilby, John (1600–1676), I, 389 (misprinted Ogilvy), 799, 803, 809, 861; II, 174, 761
Ogilvie, James (fl. 1729–35), I, 910; II, 810
Ogilvie, John (1733–1813), II, 18, 23, 76, 375
Ogilvie (or Ogilvy), William (1736–1819), II, 104, 959
Ogilvie, William Henry (b. 1869), III, 1095
Ogilvy, John, I, 389. Misprint for John Ogilby (1600–1676)
Ogle, George (1704–1746), II, 76, 209, 238, 323, 812
Ogle, Nathaniel (fl. 1826), II, 605
Oglethorpe, James Edward (1696–1785), II, 753
O'Gorman, — (fl. 1845), III, 769
O'Grady, Standish (1846–1928), III, 1050

O'Grady, Standish Hayes (1832–1915), III, **1050**
Ogston, William (d. 1667), I, 911
O'Halloran, Sylvester (1728–1807), II, 888, 952; III, **1048**
O'Hara, Kane (1714?–1782), II, **479**
O'Hara, R. P. (*fl.* 1858), III, 834
'Oinophilus, Boniface' (1723), II, 197, 210
Oke, George Colwell (1821–1874), III, 987
O'Keefe, T. M. ('Morna', *fl.* 1849), III, 451
O'Keeffe, Adelaide (1776–1855), II, 481; III, **571**
O'Keeffe, John (1747–1833), II, **479**f.
Okely, Francis (1719?–1794), II, 859, 861
Olcott, H. S. (*fl.* 1882), III, 1081
Old and New Interest, The (18 cent.), II, 216 (2)
Old and Young (1891), III, 821
Old British Spy, The (1779), II, 715
'Old Calabar' (1873), III, 766
Old Common Sense (1737), II, 663
Old Common Sense; Or, The Englishman's Journal (1737), II, 714
Old England (1824), III, 811
Old England (1832), III, 813
Old England; Or, The Broad Bottom Journal (1747), II, 715
Old England; Or, The Constitutional Journal (1743), II, 715
Old England; Or, The National Gazette (1751), II, 715
Old England's Journal (1753), II, 715
OLD ENGLISH
  Language, I, 25f., 26f., 30f., 34f.
Old English Drama, The (1825), I, 488
Old English Drama, The (1830), I, 488
OLD ENGLISH LITERATURE
  General, I, 53ff.
  Poetry, I, 60ff.
  Prose, I, 85ff.
OLD ENGLISH POETRY
  General, I, 60f.
  Caedmon School, I, 73f.
  Cynewulf School, I, 75f.
  Elegiac Poems, I, 70f.
  Heroic Poems, I, 63f.
  Historical Poems, I, 83f.
  Miscellaneous Poems, I, 84f.
  Religious and Didactic Poems, I, 78f.
  Riddles, I, 72f.
OLD ENGLISH PROSE
  General, I, 85
  Alfredian Prose, I, 85f.
  Chronicles, I, 88f.
  Gospels and Psalters, I, 95f.
  Later Prose, I, 89f.
  Laws and Charters, I, 96f.
  Science and Medicine, I, 97f.
OLD ENGLISH SCHOLARSHIP, II, 918f. (1660–1800). For 19 cent. see under ENGLISH SCHOLARSHIP, III, 1021f.

Old Englishman, And Anti-Jacobin Examiner, The (1798), II, 716
Old Exeter Journal and Weekly Advertiser, The (1755), II, 723
'Old Herbert' (*fl.* 1793), II, 635
Old Maid, The (1755), II, 664
Old Merry's Monthly (1872), III, 830
Old Post-Master, The (1696), II, 706
Old Testament Passages in Long Verses (M.E.), I, **190**
Old Testament Strophic Passages (M.E.), I, **190**
Old Whig, The (1719), II, 604
Old Whig; or, The Consistent Protestant, The (1735), II, 663, 714
Old Woman, The (1798), II, 666
Olde (or Old), John (*fl.* 1545–55), I, 665
Oldenberg, Hermann, III, 1081
Oldenburg, Henry (1615?–1677), II, 771
Oldes, Alexander (*fl.* 1700–21), II, 535, 798
Oldfield, Henry George (d. 1791?), II, 824
Oldham, John (1653–1683), II, 44, **283**f., 759
Oldham Daily Standard, The (1882), III, 805
Oldham Evening Chronicle, The (1882), III, 805
Oldham Evening Express, The (1869), III, 803
Oldham Evening Standard, The (1882), III, 805
Oldisworth, William (1680–1734), II, **323**f., 444, 503, 599, 660, 761
Oldmixon, John (1673–1742), II, 28, 191 (2), 661–2, **876**f.
Oldys, Alexander (*fl.* 1700), II, 272
Oldys, William (1696–1761), I, 423; II, 403, **894**f.
O'Leary, Ellen (1831–1889), III, 352
Oley, Barnabas (1602–1686), I, 452 (2), 698
Olio, The (1792), II, 247–8, 252
Olio; Or, Anything Arian Magazine, The (1800), II, 688
Olio; or Museum of Entertainment, The (1828), III, 826
Oliphant, Charles (*fl.* 1695), II, 999
Oliphant, George Henry Hewitt (*fl.* 1847), III, 987
Oliphant, Laurence (1829–1888), III, **499**f.
Oliphant, Margaret Oliphant, née Wilson (1828–1897), III, **500**f.
  Articles and reviews by, III, 410, 478 (2), 497, 706
Oliphant, Robert (*fl.* 1789), II, 666
Oliva, Palmerin de, I, 344
Olivari, T. (*fl.* 1797), II, 812
Oliver, Abbé —. See Olivier
Oliver, Daniel (b. 1830), III, 961
Oliver, Peter (*fl.* 1784), II, 928
Oliver, T. (*fl.* 1831), III, 971
Olivier, Abbé —, II, 48, 541 (misprinted Oliver), 792
Olivier, J. (*fl.* 1771), II, 823
Olla Podrida (1787), II, 666
Olley, J. B. (*fl.* 1827), III, 135

Ollier, Edmund (1827–1886), III, 634, 644, 647, 811

Ollier's Literary Miscellany in Prose and Verse (1820), III, 832

Olliffe, G. (*fl.* 1731), II, 155

O'Malley, William (b. 1853), III, 787

Oman, J. C. (*fl.* 1889–1903), III, 1082

O'Meara (or Meara), Dermod (*fl.* 1610), III, 590

'Omnium, Jacob', i.e. M. J. Higgins (1810–1868), III, 131

Once a Month (1861), III, 829

Once a Month (1870), III, 830

Once a Week (1859), III, 818

O'Neil, F. (*fl.* 1715), II, 1003

'O'Neill, Moira', i.e. Nesta Higginson, later Skrine (*fl.* 1900–24), III, **1057**

Onosander, I, 804

Opera Miscellany, The (18 cent.), II, **201**

Operative, The (1838), III, 812

Operative, The (1851), III, 817

Opie, Amelia, née Alderson (1769–1853), II, 666; III, **411** f.

Opie, John (1761–1807), II, 31

Oppian, II, 315

Opus Chronicorum (M.E.), I, 115

Oracle, The (1715), II, 708

Oracle, The (1789), III, 798

Oracle, The (1792), II, 709

Oracle and Daily Advertiser, The (1798), III, 798

Oracle and the Daily Advertiser, The (1798), II, 709

Oracle, Bell's New World, The (1789), II, 709

Oracle of Reason, The (1841), III, 817

Oracle of Rural Life, The (1839), III, 759

Oracle; or, Bristol Weekly Miscellany, The (1742), II, 721

Oracle; Or, Sunday Gazette, The (Dublin, 1797), II, 736

Oracle, Public Advertiser, The (1794), II, 709

Orange Gazette, The (1688), II, 705

Orange Gazette (1689), II, 731

Oratory Magazine, The (1748), II, 677

Ord, John Walker (1811–1853), III, **302** f.

Ordericus Vitalis (1075–1143?), I, 116

Ordinances of Exeter Tailors' Guild (15 cent.), I, 46

Ordinances of Worcester (15 cent.), I, 46

Ordoyne, Charles Sambrooke, II, 723

O'Reilly, Edward (d. 1829), III, 1048

O'Reilly, John Boyle (1844–1890), III, **1055**

Orfeo, Sir (M.E.), I, **151** f.

Orford, Horace Walpole, Earl of (1717–1797), II, **836** f.

ORIEL COLLEGE (Oxford), I, 369

Oriental Herald and Colonial Review, The (1824), III, 826

Oriental Masonic Muse, The (18 cent.), II, 246

ORIENTAL SCHOLARSHIP

Restoration to Romantic Revival, II, 938 f.

Nineteenth Century, III, 1014 f. See also ANCIENT HISTORY, III, 894 f., 913 f.

Origen, II, 766

Original and Genuine Letters sent to the Tatler and Spectator (18 cent.), II, 198

Original Ipswich Journal, The (1774), II, 724

Original London Post; Or, Heathcote's Intelligence, The (1719), II, 537, 707

Original London Post or Heathcote's Intelligence, The (1738), II, 707

Original Mercury, York Journal, or Weekly Courant, The (1728), II, 730

Original Poems and Translations (18 cent.), II, 191

Original Prologues [etc.] (1756), II, 217

Original Prologues, Epilogues, And other Theatrical Pieces (1766), II, 224

Original Star, And Grand Weekly Advertiser, The (1788), II, 715

Original Weekly Journal, The (1715), II, 712

Original York Journal; Or, Weekly Courant, The (1724), II, 730

Orion Adams's Manchester Journal; or, the Lancashire and Cheshire Advertiser (1752), II, 726

Orion Adams's Weekly Journal; or, The Manchester Advertiser (1752), II, 726

O'Riordan, Conal Holmes O'Connell (b. 1874), III, **1065**

Orleans, Charles, Duke of, I, 264

Orlebar Chronicles (16–18 cents.), I, 383

Orm (*fl.* 1200?), I, 29, 40

Orme, E. (*fl.* 1807), III, 89

Orme, Robert (1728–1830), II, 888; III, 1074 f.

Orme, William (1787–1830), I, 672, 699

Ormerod, George (1785–1873), III, **902** f.

Ormonde Papers (17 cent.), I, 400

Ormulum (M.E.), I, **171**

Ornsby, George (1809–1886), I, 696

Ornsby, Robert (1820–1889), III, **921**

Orosius, Paulus, I, 87 f. (O.E. version), 125

Orpen, C. E. H. (*fl.* 1815), III, 112

Orpen, F. H. S. (*fl.* 1875), III, 1092

Orpen, J. M. (*fl.* 1857–1908), III, 1090, 1092

Orphan Reviv'd; Or, Powell's Weekly Journal, The (1718), II, 713

Orphan, with Reflections Political and Moral, The (1716), II, 712

Orpheus (18 cent.), II, 213

Orpheus Britannicus (1698), II, 184–5, 187, 190 (2), 196, 211

Orpheus Britannicus (1745), II, 211

Orpheus Britannicus (1760), II, 219

Orpheus Caledonius (18 cent.), II, 198, 203, 204

Orr, A. P. (*fl.* 1858), III, 1076

Orrery, Charles Boyle, Earl of (1676–1731), II, 15

Orrery, John Boyle, Earl of (1707–1762), I, 384; II, 593, 767, 773
Orrery, Roger Boyle, Earl of (1621–1679), II, 425 f., 530
Ortelius, Abraham (1527–1598), I, 766
'Orthodoxus, Philanax' (1665), II, 779
ORTHOEPISTS. See GRAMMARIANS (16, 17 cents.), I, 43 f.
Ortigue, Pierre d', Sieur de Vaumorière, II, 37, 49, 122, 532, 802
Orton, Job (1717–1783), II, 152, 811
Orton, John (fl. 1844), III, 763
Ortúñez de Calahorra, Diego, I, 817
Orville, Adrien de la Vieuville d', II, 792
Osbaldeston, George (1787–1866), II, 822 (autobiography incorrectly entered under W. A. Osbaldiston)
Osbaldiston, W. A. (fl. 1792), II, 822
Osbern of Gloucester (fl. 1150), I, 286
Osbert of Clare (d. c. 1136), I, 285
Osbertus Anglicus (fl. 1344), I, 312
Osborn's Penny Post; Or The London Mercury (1733), II, 707
Osborne, Dorothy (1627–1695), I, 388
Osborne (or Osborn), Francis (1593–1659), I, 724, 726, 781, 840; II, 122
Osborne, Francis, Duke of Leeds (1751–1799), II, 165, 456
Osborne, Lord Sidney Godolphin (1808–1889), III, 971
Osborne, Thomas (d. 1767), II, 741
Oseney Abbey, Register of (15 cent.), I, 46
Oseney, Annals of (15 cent.), I, 115
O'Shaughnessy, Arthur William Edgar (1844–1881), III, 1055
O'Shea, John Augustus (1839–1905), III, 787
Osiander, L., I, 680
Osmer, William (fl. 1756), II, 816
Osorio da Fonseca, Jeronimo, I, 327, 817
Ossian, II, 343 f.
Ossington, John Evelyn Denison, Viscount (1800–1873), III, 152
O'Sullivan, Samuel (1790–1851), III, 246
Oswald de Corda (d. 1437), I, 313
Oswald, J. (fl. 1761), editor of Edinburgh song-collections, II, 220–1
Oswald, James (1715–1769), politician, II, 951, 955
Oswald, James Francis (fl. 1892), III, 987
Otter, William (1768–1840), III, 137, 203, 870
Otterbourne, Thomas (fl. 1400), I, 265
Ottley, R. L. (fl. 1889), III, 851
Ottoboni, III, 425
Otuel (M.E.), I, 140
Otway, Thomas (1652–1685), II, 44, 62, 70–1, 413 f., 485
Oudney, Walter (1790–1824), III, 990
Oughtred, William (1575–1660), I, 378, 881 f.
'Ouida', i.e. Marie Louise de la Ramée (1839–1908), III, 556

Oulton, Walley Chamberlain (1770?–1820?), II, 60, 380, 392, 394, 403, 666
Our Boys' Magazine (1887), III, 578
Our Darlings (1881), III, 578
Our Little Dots (1887), III, 578
Our Little Ones (1881), III, 578
Our Tiny Folks' Weekly Budget (1871), III, 578, 821
'Ouranius' (1800), II, 858
Oure Ladyes Myroure (15 cent.), I, 266
Ouseley, Sir Gore (1770–1844), III, 1021
Ouseley, Sir William (1767–1842), III, 1021
OUTDOOR BALL-GAMES, III, 772 f.
Outlook, The (1885), III, 814
Outram, George (1805–1856), III, 303, 808
Outram, Sir James (1803–1863), III, 900
Ouvry, Frederic (1814–1881), I, 706
Overbury, Sir Thomas (1581–1613), I, 722, 779, 805
Overs, John (fl. 1844), III, 449
Overton, John Henry (1835–1903), III, 923
Overton, Robert (1859–1924), III, 574
Ovid, I, 805
Ovid de Arte Amandi (17 cent.), II, 174, 176, 178 (2), 179, 181, 187
Ovid. Epistles translated by Several Hands (17 cent.), II, 182
Ovid's Art of Love (1692), II, 182
Ovid's Art of Love Together with his Remedy of Love (1709), II, 189–90, 195, 205, 212–3, 218, 223, 231–2, 236, 246, 248, 254
Ovid's Epistles, Translated by Several Hands (17 cent.), II, 178 (2), 180, 182, 185, 187, 190, 193, 196
Ovid's Epistles : With his Amours (18 cent.), II, 198–200, 206, 213, 220, 225, 231, 251
Ovid's Metamorphoses. A New Translation (1717), II, 193, 197, 204
Ovid's Metamorphoses, Translated by the most Eminent Hands (1717), II, 193, 196, 199, 203, 206, 215, 229, 249
Ovid's Metamorphosis (1697), II, 183
Ovidius Exulans (17 cent.), II, 288
Ovington, John (fl. 1696), II, 749
Owen, Edward (1728–1807), II, 766
Owen, Sir Hugh (1804–1881), III, 112
Owen, Humphrey (1712–1768), II, 886
Owen, James (1654–1706), of Shrewsbury, II, 119, 498
Owen, John (1560–1622), epigrammatist, I, 328 f., 859; II, 32
Owen, John (1616–1683), theologian, I, 699
Owen, John (fl. 1796), traveller, II, 748
Owen, John (fl. 1844), of Calcutta, III, 1083
Owen, John (1836–1896), critic, III, 751
'Owen Junior' (1800), i.e. George Hardinge (1743–1816), II, 255
Owen, Nicholas (fl. 1746), II, 742
Owen, Sir Richard (1804–1892), I, 471; III, 952, 956, 963, 967

Owen, Robert (1771–1858), III, 112, 140, 787, 816 (2), 817 (2), **872, 976,** 980
Owen, Robert Dale (1801–1877), III, 112, **872,** 975
Owen, William (*fl.* 1767), II, 715
Owen's Weekly Chronicle (1763), II, 665
Owen's Weekly Chronicle; Or, Universal Journal (1758), II, 715
Owenson, Sydney, later Lady Morgan (1776–1859), III, **412** f.
Owl and the Nightingale, The (M.E.), I, 29, 40, **181** f.
Oxberry, William (1784–1824), III, 583, 585
Oxberry's New English Drama (1818), II, 393
Oxenford, John (1812–1877), I, 20; III, 548, 600, **605** f.
Oxenham, Henry Nutcombe (1829–1883), III, 303
OXFORD, I, 8 (bibliographies)
    Middle English Period, I, 124–5 (University)
    Renaissance to Restoration, I, 353 (printing at), 361–2 f. (libraries), 368 f. (University)
    Restoration to Romantic Revival, II, 88 (printing at), 104 (libraries), 117 f. (university), 152 f. (university), 685 (magazines), 727 (newspapers)
    Nineteenth Century, III, 126 f. (university), 836 f. (university and college magazines)
Oxford, Edward de Vere, Earl of (1550–1604), I, 439, 546
Oxford and Cambridge Miscellany Poems (18 cent.), II, 188
Oxford and District Morning Echo, The (1898), III, 806
Oxford Charters (M.E.), I, 121
Oxford Diurnall communicating the intelligence and affaires of the Court to the rest of the Kingdome, The (1643), I, 754
Oxford Drollery (17 cent.), II, 175, 178
Oxford Flying Weekly Journal, and Cirencester Gazette, The (1746), II, 727
Oxford Gazette, The (1665), II, 702
Oxford Gazette, and Reading Mercury, The (1745), II, 728
Oxford Journal and County News, The (1898), II, 727
Oxford Magazine, The (1768), II, 674
Oxford Magazine; or, University Museum, The (1768), II, 679
Oxford Mercury and Midland County Chronicle, The (1795), II, 727
Oxford Morning Echo, The (1899), III, 806
OXFORD MOVEMENT, III, 854 f.
Oxford Sausage, The (18 cent.), II, 223–4, 229, 232
Oxfordshire Contest, The (18 cent.), II, 216
Oxinden Letters, The (17 cent.), I, 385
'Oxonian' (1820), III, 210
'Oxonian, An' (1825), III, 126
'Oxonian, An Old' (1863), III, 681

Ozanam, Jacques (*fl.* 1708), II, 826
Ozell, John (d. 1743)
    Original writings, II, **24,** 676
    Translations from French, II, 769 (2), 771, 776, 778, 784, 787, 791, 793 (3), 794, 795 (3), 796, 799 (2), 800, 803 (2)
    Translations from other languages, II, 69, 761

P., A. (*fl.* 1760), II, 448
P., B. (*fl.* 1694), II, 928
P., E. (*fl.* 1558), I, 669
P., E. (*fl.* 1685), II, 797
P., G. (*fl.* 1584), I, 742
P., H. (*fl.* 1646), I, 799
P., H. (*fl.* 1672), II, 556
P., J. (*fl.* 1683), II, 861
P., J. (*fl.* 1696), II, 788
P., J. (*fl.* 1811), II, 382
P., N. (*fl.* 1671), II, 928
P., P. (*fl.* 1660), I, 814
P., R. (*fl.* 1585), I, 817
P., R. (*fl.* 1642), I, 752
P., R. (*fl.* 1659), I, 767
P., T. (*fl.* 1673), II, 491
P., T. (*fl.* 1713), II, 766
P., T. C. (*fl.* 1797), II, 827
P., T. F. (*fl.* 1706), II, 787
P., W. (*fl.* 1585), I, 884
P., W. (*fl.* 1598), I, 379
P., W. (*fl.* 1618), I, 815
P., W. (*fl.* 1677), II, 178
P., Hon. W. (*fl.* 1728), II, 826
P., W. P. (*fl.* 1856), III, 463
P., Theophilus (*fl.* 1648), I, 718
Pace, Richard (1482?–1536), I, 681
Pace-Sanfelice, G. (*fl.* 1868), I, 557
PACIFIC
    Voyages in, II, 751 f.
Pack, Richardson (1682–1728), II, 27, **324,** 792
Packet of Letters, The (1646), I, 757
Packet of Letters from Sir Thomas Fairfax his Quarters, A (1645), I, 757
Packets of Letters (1648), I, 758
Pacquet from Parnassus, A (1702), II, 185 (2), 659
Pacquet from Will's, A (18 cent.), II, 185
Pacquet of Advice from France, The (1691), II, 658
Pacquet of Advice from Rome, A (1678), II, 657
Pacquet of Advice from Rome Restored, The (1689), II, 658
Pacquet-Boat from Holland, The (1695), II, 706
Paddy Whack's Bottle Companion (18 cent.), II, 246
Paddy's Resource (18 cent.), II, 254
Pagan, Blaise François de, II, 792
Pagan, James (1811–1870), III, 808
Pagan Prince, The (17 cent.), II, 531
Page, John (*fl.* 15 cent.), I, 265

Page, Samuel (1574–1630), I, 434, 477

Page, Thomas (*fl.* 1746–67), II, 821, 823

Page (or de Pagula), William (*fl. c.* 1325), I, **301**

Pageant, The (1896), III, 831

PAGEANTS, I, 500 (16, 17 cents.)

Paget, Francis (1851–1911), III, 851

Paget, Francis Edward (1806–1882), III, 572, **859**

Paget, John (1811–1898), III, 685

Paget, Thomas Catesby, Lord Paget (1689–1742), II, **324**

Paget, Violet ('Vernon Lee') (1856–1935), III, 749 f.

Pagitt, Ephraim (1575?–1647), I, 767

Paglia, Antonio Dalla, I, 817

Pain, Barry (1864–1928), III, 814

Paine, T. (*fl.* 1642), I, 753

Paine, Thomas (1737–1809), II, **955** f.

Painter, W. (*fl.* 1787), II, 827

Painter, William (1540?–1594), author of 'The Palace of Pleasure', I, 728, 814, 883; II, 537

Painter, William (*fl.* 1623), compiler of 'Chaucer new painted', I, 715

PAINTING (books on), I, 392 (16, 17 cents.); II, 30 f. (17, 18 cents.)

PAISLEY
  Newspaper, III, 808

Paisley Daily Express, The (1874), III, 808

Palace Miscellany, The (18 cent.), II, 204

PALAEOGRAPHY
  Latin Script, I, 58
  Runic Script, I, 59

Palatrat, Jean, II, 812

Pale, W. (*fl.* 1864), III, 918

Paleario, A., III, 996

Paley, William (1743–1805), author of 'Evidences of Christianity', II, 114, **956**

Paley, William (*fl.* 1814), lawyer, III, 987

Palgrave, Sir Francis (1788–1861), I, 62; III, **896**

Palgrave, Francis Turner (1824–1897), III, **303**, 636
  Editions by, III, 220, 253, 264, 369

Palgrave, Sir R. H. I. (*fl.* 1873), III, **973**

Palgrave, William Gifford (1826–1888), III, 992

Palingenius, Marcellus (P. A. Manzolli), I, 329, 817

Pall Mall Budget, The (1868), III, 814

Pall Mall Gazette, The (1865), III, 794, 801

Pall Mall Magazine, The (1893), III, 831

Pall-Mall Miscellany, The (18 cent.), II, 203 (4), 205

Palladio, Andrea, II, 812

Palladium, The (1825), III, 818

Palladius on Husbondrie (15 cent.), I, 40, 265

Pallavicino, Ferrante, I, 833; II, 812

Pallavicino, Sforza, II, 812

Palmer, — (*fl.* 1776), II, 746

Palmer, Arthur (1841–1897), III, **1008**

Palmer, Charles John (1805–1882), I, 775

Palmer, Charlotte (*fl.* 1780–97), II, 548

Palmer, E. (*fl.* 1843), III, 75

Palmer, Edward Henry (1840–1882), III, 834, **1020** f.

Palmer, Sir Francis Beaufort (*fl.* 1877), III, 987

Palmer, G. J. (*fl.* 1863), III, 819

Palmer, George (*fl.* 1648), I, 720

Palmer, H. J. (*fl.* 1870), III, 803

Palmer, Herbert (1601–1647), I, 699, 726

Palmer, James (*fl.* 1783), II, 733

Palmer, James F. (*fl.* 1835), III, 955

Palmer, John (1650?–1700?), traveller, II, 752

Palmer, John (1742?–1798?), actor, II, 256, 463

Palmer, Mary (1716–1794), II, 148

Palmer, Roger, Earl of Castlemaine (1634–1705), II, 743

Palmer, Roundell, Earl of Selborne (1812–1895), III, 140, 149

Palmer, Samuel (d. 1724), pamphleteer, II, 119

Palmer, Samuel (1741–1813), nonconformist biographer, II, 627

Palmer, Samuel (1805–1881), landscape painter, II, 349; III, 91

Palmer, T. (*fl.* 1599), I, 616

Palmer, T. A. (*fl.* 1861), III, **627**

Palmer, Thomas (*fl.* 1410), I, **306**

Palmer, Sir William (1803–1885), theologian and antiquary, III, 859

Palmer, William (1811–1879), archaeologist, III, **859**

Palmerston, Henry John Temple, Viscount (1784–1865), III, **677** f.

Palmerston, Henry Temple, Viscount (1739–1802), II, 747

Palsgrave, John (d. 1554), I, 43, 521

Paltock, Robert (1697–1767), II, 544

Paman, Clement (*fl.* 1660), I, 477

PAMPHLETEERS, I, 704 f. (1500–1660); II, 567 f. (1660–1800)

PAMPHLETS, I, 736 f. (1500–1660); II, 567 f. (1660–1800); III, 117 f. (educational)

Pancharis Queen of Love (18 cent.), II, 196 (2), 197

Panciroli, Guido, II, 812

'Panglos, Peter' (1806), II, 405

Panizzi, Sir Anthony (1797–1879), III, 104

Panthalia (17 cent.), I, 732

Pantin, Thomas Pindar (1792–1866), II, 85

Panton, Edward (*fl.* 1671), II, 122

Papendick, George (*fl.* 1798), II, 60, 486

Papendiek, Charlotte Louisa Henrietta (*fl.* 1761–92), II, 150

PAPER, I, 345 f. (1500–1660); II, 82 (1660–1800); III, 71 f. (19 cent.)

Paper and Printing Bits (1898), III, 73

Paper and Printing Trades Journal, The (1872), III, 73

Paper and Pulp (1898), III, 73

Paper Box and Bag Maker (1896), III, 73

Paper Consumers' Circular, The (1879), III, 73

Paper Exchange News, The (1895), III, 73

Paper Maker, The (1891), III, 73

Paper Makers' Circular, The (1874), III, 73

Paper Record, The (1886), III, 73

Paper Trade News, The (1860), III, 73

Paper Trade Review, The (1862), III, 73

Paper Trade Review, The (1883), III, 73

Papermakers' Circular, The (1861), III, 73

Papermakers' Monthly Journal, The (1863), III, 73

Papermaking (1881), III, 73

Papers sent from the Scotts Quarters (1646), I, 757

Paphian Doves, The (18 cent.), II, 239

Papillon, Thomas (1623–1702), II, 134

Papin, Denis (1647–1712?), II, 961

Papworth, John Woody (1820–1870), III, 105

Papworth, Wyatt (1822–1894), III, 97, 105

Paracelsus, Aureolus Philippus, I, 327, 887 (3), 888

Paradin, Claudius, I, 479

Paradis de Moncrif, François Auguste, II, 541

Paradyse of Daynty Devises, The (16 cent.), I, 403

Pardon, George Frederick (1824–1884), III, 821

Paré, Ambroise, I, 891

Pare, William (1805–1873), III, 976

Parfite Life of Petronylla, The (15 cent.), I, 265

Pargiter, Edmund (*fl.* 1745), II, 759

Pargiter, F. E. (*fl.* 1888), III, 1072

Parini, Giuseppe, II, 812

Paris, John Ayrton (1785–1856), III, 946

Paris, Matthew (d. 1259), I, 116

Paris Gazette, The (1706), II, 731

Paris Gazette English'd, The (1704), II, 712

Paris Pendant L'année (1795), II, 682

Parish, John (*fl.* 1789), II, 747

Park, Sir James Alan (1763–1838), II, 964

Park, Mungo (1771–1806), II, 749; III, 992

Park, Thomas (1759–1834), III, 1027

Parke, Ernest, III, 801, 818

Parke, Gilbert (*fl.* 1798), II, 162

Parke, Robert (*fl.* 1588), I, 782

Parker, Charles Stuart (1829–1910), III, 109

Parker, D. (*fl.* 1810?), III, 824

Parker, George (1732–1800), II, 405

Parker, Henry (d. 1470), I, 266

Parker, Henry, Baron Morley (1476–1556), courtier and author, I, 438

Parker, Henry (1604–1652), political writer, I, 747, 817, 847

Parker, Henry Meredith (*fl.* 1827–51), III, 1068

Parker, John Henry (1806–1884), writer on architecture, III, 822, **1002**

Parker, John William (1792–1870), publisher and printer, III, 102, 826

Parker, Martin (d. 1656?), I, 721, 757

Parker, Mary Ann (*fl.* 1795), II, 742

Parker, Matthew (1504–1575), I, 363, 371, **671**, 678, 825

Parker, Richard (1572–1629), I, 371

Parker, Samuel (1640–1688), II, 14, 660, 675 (2), 761, 764, **848** f.

Parker, William (*fl.* 1816–23), III, 975

Parker's General Advertiser and Morning Intelligencer (1782), II, 709

Parker's London News; Or, The Impartial Intelligencer (1719), II, 707

Parker's Penny Post (1725), II, 707

Parkes, B. R. (*fl.* 1854), III, 143

Parkes, Sir Henry (1815–1896), III, **1094**

Parkes, Joseph (*fl.* 1827–67), III, 907

Parkes, Kineton (b. 1865), III, 705

Parkhurst, Ferdinand (*fl.* 1653), I, 887

Parkin, Charles (1689–1765), II, 881

Parkinson, James (*fl.* 1808), writer of children's books, III, 571

Parkinson, James (d. 1824), geologist, III, 949

Parkinson, John (1567–1650), I, 391, 892

Parkinson, Richard (1748–1815), agricultural writer, III, 969–70

Parkinson, Richard (1797–1858), canon of Manchester, I, 387 (2); II, 859

Parkinson, Sydney (1745?–1771), II, 742

Parks, William (d. 1750), II, 696

Parks's Juvenile Library (18 cent.), II, 564

Parkyns, Sir Thomas (1664–1741), II, 827

Parlement of the Thre Ages (M.E.), I, **196**

'Parley, Peter' (1835), III, 566

PARLIAMENT, I, 401 f. (16, 17 cents.); II, 167 f. (17, 18 cents.)

Parliament of Women, The (1640), I, 716

Parliament of Women, The (1656), I, 717

Parliament Porter or the Door Keeper of the House of Commons, The (1648), I, 759

Parliament Scout communicating his Intelligence to the Kingdome, The (1643), I, 755

Parliament-Kite or the Tell Tale Bird, The (1648), I, 758

Parliamentary Intelligencer, The (1659), I, 763

Parliamentary Register, The (1774), II, 679

Parliamentary Review and Family Magazine, The (1833), III, 827

Parliamentary Spy, The (1769), II, 665

Parliaments Post, The (1645), I, 756

Parliaments Scouts Discovery, The (1643), I, 755

Parliaments Scriche Owle, The (1648), I, 758

Parliaments Vulture, The (1648), I, 758

Parminter, Jane (*fl.* 1784), II, 747

Parmoor, C. A. Cripps, Baron (*fl.* 1881), III, 986

Parnassian Garland, The (18 cent.), II, 253

Parnassium, The (18 cent.), II, 221

Parnassus Biceps (17 cent.), I, 405

Parnassus Trilogy, The (17 cent.), I, 662

Parnell, Sir Henry, Baron Congleton (1776–1842), III, 972–3, 978

Parnell, James (1637?–1656), II, 857

Parnell, Thomas (1679–1718), II, 22, 25, **324**
Parr, Harriet ('Holme Lee') (1828–1900), III, 491f.
Parr, Richard (1617–1691), I, 385
Parr, Samuel (1747–1825), II, 109, **936**f., 947
Parr, Wolstenholme (1762–1845), II, 810, 917
Parrain de Durette, François, II, 792
Parrain, Jacques, Baron des Coutures, II, 792
Parrot, Henry (*fl.* 1606–26), I, 480
Parrot, The (1746), II, 663
Parrott, The (1728), II, 663
Parry, Catherine (*fl.* 1784), II, 548
Parry, Sir Charles Hubert Hastings (1848–1918), III, **751**f.
Parry, Sir Edward Abbott (b. 1863), III, 574
Parry, John (*fl.* 1772), II, 711
Parry, R. (*fl.* 1787), II, 801
Parry, Robert (*fl.* 1595), I, 730
Parry, Thomas (*fl.* 1823), III, 190
Parry, William (*fl.* 1601), I, 782
Parry, William (*fl.* 1823–5), friend of Lord Byron, III, 206
Parry, Sir William Edward (1790–1855), arctic explorer, III, **992**
Parsley's Fashionable Lyric Companion (18 cent.), II, 240 (2)
Parsley's Lyric Repository (18 cent.), II, 242, 243 (2), 244 (2)
Parsloe, J. (*fl.* 1878), III, 983
Parson's Daughter [etc.], *The* (18 cent.), II, 193
Parsons, Benjamin (1797–1855), III, 112
Parsons, D. (*fl.* 1836), I, 842
Parsons, Eliza (d. 1811), II, 550, 794; III, **413**
Parsons, John Weddell (*fl.* 1790), II, 20
Parsons, Philip (1594–1653), I, 658
Parsons, Philip (1729–1812), II, 817
Parsons, Robert (1546–1610), jesuit, I, 684, 844
Parsons, Robert (1647–1714), archdeacon of Gloucester, II, 276
Parsons, William (*fl.* 1785–1807), poet, II, **375**, 780
Parsons, William, Earl of Rosse (1800–1867), astronomer, III, 938, 943
Part of Lucian's Dialogues done into Rhyme (17 cent.), II, 288
Parthenay, or Lusignen (M.E.), I, **160**
Parthenia (17 cent.), I, 662
Parthenon, The (1862), III, 818
Parthenope of Blois (M.E.), I, **159**
Partiall Law, The (17 cent.), I, 653
Particular Advice from the Office of Intelligence, A (1659), I, 763
Particular Relation of the most remarkable occurrences from the united forces in the North, A (1644), I, 756
Particular Relation of the Successes of the Earl of Manchesters Army, A (1644), I, 756
Partington, Charles Frederick (d. 1857?), III, 76, 81
Partridge, I. (*fl.* 1570), I, 738

Partridge, John (1644–1715), II, 661
Partridge, Seth (1603–1686), II, 125
Pascal, Blaise, I, 817; II, 36, 792
Paschoud, M. (*fl.* 1726), II, 769
Pascoe, C. E. (*fl.* 1870), III, 583
Pasha of Aleppo (17 cent.), I, 653
Paske, C. T. (*fl.* 1892), III, 772
Paskell, Thomas (*fl.* 1683), II, 752
Pasley, Sir Thomas (1734–1808), II, 742
Pasqualigo, Luigi, I, 340
Pasquils Jests (17 cent.), I, 714
Pasquin (1722), II, 662
Pasquin (1726), II, 663
Passages concerning the King, the army, city and Kingdom (1648), I, 759
Passages in Parliament, The (1642), I, 752
Passfield, Sidney Webb, Baron (b. 1859), III, 977
Passion of Our Lord (M.E.), I, **188**
Passionate Pilgrime, The (16 cent.), I, 404
Paston Letters, The (15 cent.), I, 46, 116, 266
Pastor Fidus (17 cent.), I, 662
Pastoral Lessons and Parental conversations (18 cent.), II, 564
Pate, William (1666–1746), II, 658
Pater, Walter Horatio (1839–1894), III, **731**f.
Paternoster (O.E.), I, 81
Paterson, A. B. (b. 1864), III, **1095**
Paterson, James (*fl.* 1744), II, 913
Paterson, James (1805–1876), I, 258; II, 984; III, 787, 987
Paterson, Ninian (*fl.* 1678), II, 969
'Paterson, P.', i.e. J. G. Bertram (*fl.* 1858), III, 583
Paterson, Samuel (1728–1802), II, 546, 665
Paterson, Thomas (*fl.* 1843), III, 817
Paterson, William (1658–1719), II, 753
Paterson, William (1755–1810), III, 1091
Pathomachia (17 cent.), I, 663
Patience (M.E.), I, **202**
Patmore, Coventry Kersey Dighton (1823–1896), I, 21; III, **270**f., 706, 813
Patmore, Peter George (1786–1855), III, 636, **678**
Paton, Sir Joseph Noel (1821–1901), III, 303
Paton, William Roger (1856–1921), III, **1008**
Patot, Simon Tyssot de, II, 802
Patrician, The (1719), II, 662
'Patricius' (1806), II, 458
Patrick, St (d. 463), I, **101**
Patrick, Mrs F. C. (*fl.* 1798), II, 551
Patrick (or Pattrick), Nathaniel (1560?–1595), I, 483
Patrick, Samuel (1684–1748), II, 765, 768
Patrick, Simon (d. 1613), translator, I, 813
Patrick, Simon (1626–1707), bishop of Ely, II, 195, 204, **849**
Patrick's Purgatory, St (M.E.), I, 177
Patriot, The (1714), II, 661
Patriot, The (1740), II, 663, 686, 731

Patriot, The (1762), II, 665
Patriot, The (1792), II, 666
Patriot, The (1832), III, 819
Patriot and General Advertiser, The (1789), II, 709
Patriot; Or, Political Repository, The (1792), II, 682
Patriot's Calendar, The (18 cent.), II, 248–9
Patriot's Weekly Chronicle, The (1794), II, 732
Patriotic Miscellany, The (18 cent.), II, **226**
Patriotic Songster, The (18 cent.), II, 254
Patrizi, Francesco, I, 327
Patsall, J. (*fl.* 1774), 767
Patten, Robert (*fl.* 1715–7), II, 1002
Patten, William (*fl.* 1548–80), I, 738, 824
Patterson, H. S. (*fl.* 1854), III, 1015
Patterson, J. P. (*fl.* 1893), III, 984
Patterson, Robert (1802–1872), I, 545
Patterson, Robert Hogarth (1821–1886), III, 704, 800, 808, 810
Patteson, Sir John (1790–1861), III, 128
Pattie, James (*fl.* 1839), III, 585
Pattie's Play (1838), III, 585
Pattie's Universal Stage (1839), III, 585
Pattison, Mark (1813–1884), III, 121, **723**
Pattison, William (1706–1727), II, 199, **324**
Paul, C. Kegan (1828–1902), III, 99, 833
Paul, H. H. (*fl.* 1851), III, 828
Paul, Hamilton (1773–1854), II, 975
Paul, James Balfour (*fl.* 1875), III, 776
Paul, John (1707–1787), II, 821
Pauley, T. (*fl.* 1783), II, 742
Pauli, Christianus, II, 55
Pauli, Reinhold, III, 1028
Pauline Epistles (M.E.), I, 190
Paulini, Annales (M.E.), I, 115
Paull, Mrs H. B. (*fl.* 1867), III, 576
Paulton, Abraham Walter (1812–1876), III, 802, 817
PAUPERISM (writings on), III, 975f.
Pausanias, II, 762
Pauw, Cornelius de, II, 793
Payn, James (1830–1898), III, **501**f.
Payne, — (*fl.* 1672), II, 750
Payne, Edward John (1844–1904), III, **933**
Payne, Henry Nevil (d. *c.* 1710), II, **426**
Payne, J. W. H. (*fl. c.* 1821), III, 194
Payne, John (d. 1787), II, 100, 621, 715
Payne, John (1842–1916), III, **352**f.
Payne, Joseph (1808–1876), III, 112
Payne, Robert (*fl.* 1589), I, 775
Payne, Roger (1739–1797), II, 107
Payne, Thomas (*fl.* 1722), II, 713
Payne, William (*fl.* 1756), II, 621–2, 826
Payne and Sorowe of Evyll Maryage, The (16 cent.), I, 716
Payne's Universal Chronicle (1758), II, 664, 715
Payne-Gallwey, Sir Ralph W. F. (1848–1916), III, 763

Paynell, Thomas (*fl.* 1528–68), I, 411, 665, 801, 809–10, 812, 815, 819, 887
Peacham, H. (*fl.* 1577), author of 'The Garden of Eloquence', I, 376
Peacham, Henry (1576?–1643?), miscellaneous writer, I, 379, 389, 392, 479 ('The Mirrour of Majestie' here attrib. to Peacham is really by H. G., perhaps Sir Henry Goodere), 481, 714, 725; II, 122
Peachey, Caroline (*fl.* 1846), III, 576
Peacock, E. (*fl.* 1868), I, 265
Peacock, George (1791–1858), III, 123, 937, 941
Peacock, Lucy (*fl.* 1785–1816), II, 548, 550, 558, 564
Peacock, Thomas Love (1785–1866), III, **384**f., 593
Peake, Richard Brinsley (1792–1847), III, **592**, 762
Peake, Thomas (*fl.* 1655), I, 796
Peaps, William (*fl.* 1649), I, 649
Pearce, Thomas (*fl.* 1722–56), II, 965
Pearce, Thomas (*fl.* 1872), III, 766
Pearce, Zachary (1690–1774), I, 468; II, 623, 850, 911, 937 (2)
Peard, William (*fl.* 1865), III, 771
Pearl (M.E.), I, 38, **201**f.
Pearne, Thomas (*fl.* 1786–93), II, 903–4
Pears, Steuart Adolphus (1815–1875), I, 384
Pearson, Mrs (*fl.* 1823), III, 575
Pearson, Sir C. Arthur (1866–1921), III, 787
Pearson, Charles Henry (1830–1894), III, **917**f.
Pearson, Edwin (*fl.* 1870), III, 771
Pearson, G. (*fl.* 1834–46), I, 669 (2); III, 122
Pearson, John (1613–1686), I, **699**, 856
Pearson, Karl (1857–1936), III, 955, 966, 977
Pearson, R. (*fl.* 1660), I, 856
Pearson, William (1767–1847), III, 943
Pearson's Magazine (1896), III, 831
Pearson's Weekly (1890), III, 814
Pease, Sir Alfred Edward (1857–1939), III, 767
Pease, Edward (1767–1858), III, 149
Pebody, Charles (1839–1890), III, 803 (2)
Pecham, John (*fl.* 1279–92), I, **294**f.
Peck, Francis (1692–1743), I, 593, 776; II, 95, 202, 911
Pecke, Samuel (*fl.* 1645), I, 747, 749, 752–3, 754 (2), 755 (2), 756, 757 (4), 760
Pecke, Thomas (*fl.* 1655–64), I, 804, 859
Peckham, Sir George (d. 1608), I, 787
Peckham, Harry (*fl.* 1772), II, 746
Pecock, Reginald (1395?–1460?), I, 29, 40, **260**f., 313
Pecquet, Antoine, II, 793
Pecuniae obediunt Omnia (17 cent.), II, 184
Pedie, J. (*fl.* 1841), III, 974
Pedlers Prophecie, The (16 cent.), I, 517
Pedley, later Deverell, Robert (1760–1841), II, 685
Peebles, William (*fl.* 1811), II, 984

Peeke (or Pike or Peake or Peecke), Richard (*fl.* 1626), I, 741
Peel, Sir Robert (1788–1850), III, 140, 148, 684, 972
Peele, F. (*fl.* 1803), III, 975
Peele, George (1557?–1596), I, 526f., 715
Peend, Thomas (*fl.* 1565), I, 438, 805
Peeper, The (1788), II, 666
PEERAGE (lists of), III, 843
Peerson, Martin (1580?–1650), I, 486
Pegasus, with News, an Observator, and a Jacobite Courant (1696), II, 658
Pegge, Samuel (1704–1796), II, 828, 886, 887(2), 920, 927
Peggs, J. (*fl.* 1828), III, 1083
Peile, John (1838–1910), III, **1008**f.
Peile, Thomas Williamson (1806–1882), III, 1002
Peirce, James (1674?–1726), II, 863
Pelham, Henry Francis (1846–1907), III, **916**
Pelham-Holles, Sir Thomas, Duke of Newcastle (1693–1763), II, 164
Pelican, The (1889), III, 814
Pell, Albert (1820–1907), III, 154
Pellew, George (1793–1866), III, 149
Pellham, Edward (*fl.* 1631), I, 743, 771
Pellico, Silvio, III, 679
Pellisson, Georges, II, 793
Pellisson-Fontanier, Paul, II, 793
Pelopidarum Secunda (17 cent.), I, 653
Peltier, Jean Gabriel (*fl.* 1793), II, 682, 719
Pem, The (1893), III, 835
Pemberton, E. (*fl.* 1711), II, 825
Pemberton, Henry (*fl.* 1738), II, 22
Pemberton, Sir Max (b. 1863), III, 829
Pemble, William (1592?–1623), I, 766, 885
'Pembrochian' (1803), III, 123
Pembroke, George Robert Charles Herbert, Earl of (1850–1895), III, 977, 991
Pembroke, Mary Herbert, Countess of (1555?–1621), I, 417, 678
Pembroke, Philip Herbert, Earl of (1619–1669), II, 173
PEMBROKE COLLEGE (Oxford), I, 369
Pen and Pencil (1855), III, 815
Pendleton, J. (*fl.* 1894), III, 984
Pendragon (17 cent.), II, 288
Pendred, John (*fl.* 1785), II, 90, 699
Pendred, W. (*fl.* 1646), I, 757
Pengelly, William (1812–1894), III, 967
Pengry, Moses (*fl.* 1676), I, 861
Penhallow, Samuel (*fl.* 1726), II, 753
Penington, Isaac (1616–1679), II, **856**
Penington, Mary (*fl.* 1681), II, 857
PENITENTIALS (O.E.), I, **94**
Peniworþ of Witte (M.E.), I, **162**
Penkethman, John (*fl.* 1623–38), I, 800, 809
PENMANSHIP. See HANDWRITING
Penn, Granville (1761–1844), II, 833; III, 192
Penn, John (1760–1834), II, 24, 400, 756

Penn, Richard (1784–1863), III, 769
Penn, Sir William (1621–1670), admiral, I, 773, 793
Penn, William (1644–1718), quaker, I, 833; II, 122, 560, 744, 752, 854–5, **856**
Pennant, Thomas (1726–1798), II, 140, 145, 157, 746, 827; III, 1082
Pennecuick, Alexander (1652–1722), II, 969
Pennecuik, Alexander (d. 1730), II, 214, 217, 226, 240, 827, 972, **973**
Pennell, Harry Cholmondeley (1837–1915), III, 771
Pennington, Montagu (1762–1849), II, 842–3
Pennington, Penelope (*fl.* 1788–1821), II, 131
Pennington, Lady Sarah (*fl.* 1761), II, 131, 143
Penny, Anne (*fl.* 1761), II, 56, **375**
Penny Illustrated Paper, The (1861), III, 815
Penny London Morning Advertiser, The (1744), II, 708
Penny London Post; Or, The Morning Advertiser, The (1744), II, 708
Penny Medley, The (1746), II, 677
Penny Medley; Or, Weekly Entertainer, The (1746), II, 715
Penny Newsman and Sunday Morning Mail and Telegraph, The (1860), III, 812f.
Penny Pictorial News, The (1877), III, 815
Penny Pictorial Weekly, The (1891), III, 815
Penny Post, The (1715), II, 712
Penny Post; Or, Tradesman's Select Pacquet, The (1717), II, 707
Penny Satirist, The (1837), III, 813
Penny Sunday Times and People's Police Gazette, The (1840), III, 812
Penny Weekly Journal; Or, Saturday's Entertainment, The (1720), II, 713
Pennyman, Lady Margaret (d. before 1740), II, 302
Penrose, Bernard (*fl.* 1775), II, 756
Penrose, Francis Cranmer (1817–1903), III, 1002
Penry, John (1559–1593), I, 691
Penton, Stephen (1639–1706), II, 122
People, The (1881), III, 813
People's Conservative and Trades Union Gazette, The (1834), III, 816
People's Paper, The (1852), III, 817
People's Pocket Story Books, The (1867), III, 578
People's Press, The (1890), III, 818
People's Press; Radical, The (1890), III, 818
Pepin, Philip (*fl.* 1779), II, 234
Pepper, W. (*fl.* 1798), II, 824
Pepys, Samuel (1633–1703), II, **831**f.
Pepys, Sir William Weller (1758–1825), II, 138
PEPYSIAN LIBRARY, II, 832
Perceval, Arthur Philip (1799–1853), III, **859**
Perceval, John, Earl of Egmont (1683–1748), II, 136
Perceval, John (*fl.* 1838–68), III, 118, 975

Perceval (or Percyvall), Richard (1550–1620), I, 377
PERCEVAL LEGEND, I, 131 f.
Percival, E. F. (*fl.* 1847), I, 369
Percival, Sir John (*fl.* 1709–53), II, 135
Percival, P. (*fl.* 1854–64), III, 1074, 1080
Percival, Thomas (1740–1804), II, 19
Percy, Elizabeth, Duchess of Northumberland, II, 136, 746
Percy, Henry Algernon (Earl of Northumberland) (1478–1527), I, 383
Percy, Henry, Earl of Northumberland (1564–1632), I, 379
Percy, Thomas (1729–1811), bishop, I, 403; II, 23, 56, **78** f., 223–5, 231, 244, 246, 249, 552, 620, 646–7, 905 (2)
Percy, Thomas, the younger (1768–1808), II, 624
Percy, William (1574–1627), I, 433
Percy Folio Ballads (M.E.), I, 140
Percyvall (or Perceval), Richard (1550–1620), I, 377
Percyvelle of Galles (M.E.), I, **137** f.
Perdou de Subligny, Adrien Thomas, II, 48, 534, 801
Peregrination of Jeremiah Grant, The (18 cent.), II, 546
Perfect Account of the Daily Intelligence, A (1651), I, 761
Perfect and Impartial Intelligence together with A Politick Commentary on the Life of Caius Julius Caesar (1654), I, 762
Perfect and more particular relation, A (1649), I, 760
Perfect Collection of the Several Songs Now in Mode, A (17 cent.), II, 177 (2)
Perfect Declaration, A (1645), I, 756
Perfect Diary of Passages of the Kings Army, A (1648), I, 758
Perfect Diurnal of Every Day's Proceedings in Parliament, The (1660), II, 701
Perfect Diurnal of Some Passages of Parliament, A (1650), I, 761
Perfect Diurnal of the Daily Proceedings in the Conventicle of the Phanatiques, A (1660), II, 701
Perfect Diurnal; Or, The Daily Proceedings in Parliament, The (1660), II, 701
Perfect Diurnall Occurrences of Certain Military Affairs (1654), I, 762
Perfect Diurnall of Passages in Parliament, A (1649), I, 760
Perfect Diurnall of Some Passages and Proceedings of and in relation to the Armies, A (1649), I, 760
Perfect Diurnall of Some Passages in Parliament and from other parts of this Kingdom, A (1643), I, 755
Perfect Diurnall of the Passages in Parliament, A [1642; nine examples], I, 752–4

Perfect Diurnall; or, Occurrences of Certain Military Affairs, A (1654), I, 762
Perfect Narrative of the Whole Proceedings of the High Court of Justice in the Tryal of the King, A (1649), I, 759
Perfect Occurrences (1654), I, 762
Perfect Occurrences of both Houses of Parliament (1646), I, 755
Perfect Occurrences of Every Dayes Journall in Parliament (1647), I, 756
Perfect Occurrences of Parliament (1644), I, 755
Perfect Occurrences of the most remarkable passages in Parliament (1660), II, 701
Perfect Particulars of Every Daies Intelligence (1651), I, 761
Perfect Passages of Each Dayes Proceedings in Parliament (1644), I, 756
Perfect Passages of every Daies Intelligence (1650), I, 761
Perfect Proceedings of State Affaires (1655), I, 760
Perfect Relation, Or Summarie, A (1642), I, 754
Perfect Summarie of Chiefe Passages in Parliament, A (1648), I, 758
Perfect Summary, A (1648), I, 759
Perfect Summary of an Exact Diarye, A (1649), I, 759
Perfect Summary of Chiefe Passages in Parliament, A (1647), I, 757
Perfect Summary of Exact Passages, A (1649), I, 759
Perfect Weekly Account, The (1647), I, 755
Perfect Weekly Account, The (1648), I, 758
Perfect Weekly Account, The (1650), I, 761
Perfidious Brethren, The (18 cent.), II, 537
Perfidus Hetruscus (17 cent.), I, 663
Perfuming of Tobacco (17 cent.), I, 718
Periodical Essays (1780), II, 666
PERIODICAL PUBLICATIONS, I, 736 f. (1500–1660); II, 656 f. (1660–1800); III, 779 f. (19 cent.), 1088 (Canadian)
PERIODICALS (Special)
    Advertising, II, 716 f. (18 cent.); III, 780
    Agricultural Papers, III, 819 f.
    Book Trade, III, 101 f.
    Financial and Commercial Papers, III, 820
    Humorous Papers, III, 820
    Illustrated Papers, III, 814 f.
    Journals of English Studies, I, 3
    Juvenile, III, 577 f., 820 f.
    Librarianship, III, 106
    Literary Reviews, II, 674 (17, 18 cents.); III, 818 (19 cent. weeklies)
    Paper trade, III, 73
    Printing trade, III, 88 f.
    Radical Journals, III, 815 f.
    Religious Papers, III, 818 f.
    Secondhand books, III, 103

Periodicals (*cont.*)
Sporting, III, 758f., 820
Theatrical, III, 585
See also under DIALOGUE PAPERS, ESSAYS, MAGAZINES, and NEWSPAPERS
Perkin, Sir William Henry (1838–1907), III, **948**
Perkins, John (d. 1545), I, 850
Perkins, William (1558–1602), I, 680, 683, 874, 893; II, 55
Perlin, Estienne, I, 331, 381
Pernety, Antoine Joseph, II, 793
Perowne, T. T. (*fl.* 1853), I, 671
Perplexed Prince, The (17 cent.), II, 530
Perrault, Charles, II, 33, 40, 48, 111, 542, 565, 793
Perrault, Claude, II, 793
Perrin, Pierre, II, 42
Perronet, Edward (1721–1792), II, **376**
Perronet, Vincent (1693–1785), II, 948
Perrot, Charles (*fl.* 1666), II, 702
Perry, Charles (1698–1780), II, 750
Perry, G. W. (*fl.* 1846–8), III, 971
Perry, George Gresley (1820–1897), church historian, I, 192, 264
Perry, James (1756–1821), II, 670, 672, 680, 696, 709 (2); III, 194
Perry, John (1670–1732), traveller, II, 744
Perry, John (*fl.* 1779), translator, II, 469, 804
Perry, Sampson (1747–1823), II, 709; III, 800
Perry, William (*fl.* 1775), II, 931–2
PERSE SCHOOL, I, 373
PERSIAN SCHOLARS, III, 1021
Persius, II, 767; III, 284
Person, David (*fl.* 1635), I, 725
PERSONAL NAMES, I, 48
PERTH
Magazines, II, 687 (1772–83)
Printing, II, 89
Perth Magazine of Knowledge and Pleasure, The (1772), II, 687
Pervigilium Veneris, I, 806
Peshall (or Pechell), Sir John (1718–1788), II, 867
Pestalozzi, Jean Henri, III, 112, 116
Pestel, Thomas (1584?–1659?), I, 477
Petchford, W. (*fl.* 1659), I, 907
Peter of Blois (*fl.* 1170), I, **287**f.
Peter of Candia (*fl.* 1409), I, **305**
Peter Hoey's Publick Journal (1771), II, 735
Peter Parley's Annual (*c.* 1840), III, 577
Peter Parley's Magazine (1840), III, 827
PETERBOROUGH
Library, I, 361
Peterborough Chronicle (M.E.), I, 121
PETERHOUSE (Cambridge), I, 370
Library, I, 362
Peterhouse Magazine, The (1893), III, 836
Peterkin, Alexander (1780–1846), II, 975–6, 987

Peters, H. T. (*fl.* 1896), III, 775
Peters, Hugh (1598–1660), I, 699
Peters, J. G. (*fl.* 1835), III, 765
Peterson, Robert (*fl.* 1576–1606), I, 766, 812
Peterson, Sir William (1856–1921), III, **1009**
Petheram, John (d. 1858), I, 693; II, 918; III, 97
Petis de la Croix, François, II, 541
Petit, Jean Louis, II, 793
Peto, Sir Samuel Morton (1809–1889), III, 979
Petöfi, S., III, 228
Petowe, Henry (*fl.* 1598–1612), I, 438, 740
Petrarca, Francesco, I, 339, 512, 817; II, 812; III, 39, 229 (2), 247
Petre, E. (*fl.* 1849), I, 365
Petrie, Adam (*fl.* 1720), II, 122
Petrie, George (1789–1866), III, **1048**
Petrie, Henry (1768–1842), I, 88; III, 898
Petronius, II, 534, 767
Petronylla, The Parfite Life of (15 cent.), I, 265
Petrus de Hibernia (*fl.* 1240), I, **298**f.
Pett, Phineas (1570–1647), I, 385, 841
Petter, G. W. (*fl.* 1860), III, 73
Pettie, George (1548–1589), I, 728, 814
Pettingal (or Pettingall), John (1708–1781), II, 783
Pettman, C. (*fl.* 1913), III, 1088
Petty, W. T. (*fl.* 1830), I, 673
Petty, Sir William (1623–1687), I, 366, 846; II, 145, **943**, 959
Petty, William, Earl of Shelburne (1737–1805), II, 631–2
Petvin, John (*fl.* 1753), II, 111
Petyt, William (1641?–1707), II, **871**
Peyton, Thomas (1595–1626), I, 479
Peyton, V. J. (*fl.* 1759), II, 930
Pfeiffer, Emily, née Davis (1827–1890), III, **303**f.
Phaer (or Phayer), Thomas (1510?–1560), I, 808, 888
Phanatick Intelligencer, The (1660), II, 701
Pharaoh (O.E.), I, **82**
Pharos (1786), II, 666
Phelan, Charlotte Elizabeth, née Browne, later Tonna (1790–1846), III, 827
Phelips, W. (*fl.* 1750), II, 790
Phelps, Mrs — (*fl.* 1811), III, 136
Philadelphian Magazine, The (1788), II, 681
'Philalethes' (1779), II, 952
'Philalethes, Mercurius' (*fl.* 1660), I, 717
'Philander' (*fl.* 1660), I, 477
Philanthropic Gazette, The (1817), III, 813
Philanthropist, The (1795), II, 666
'Philanthropus, Timotheus' (1768), II, 769
Philibert de Vienne, I, 379, 817
Philidor (or Danican), François André (1726–1795), II, 826
Philip, George (*fl.* 1900), III, 99
Philip, James (*fl.* 1689), II, 1003
Philip, John (1775–1851), III, 1092
Philip, Robert (1791–1858), II, 491–3; III, 1090

Philipot, John (*fl.* 1674), II, 177
Philipott (or Philipot), Thomas (d. 1682), I, 477, 777; II, 759
Philipps, Fabian (1601–1690), I, 720
Philipps, Jenkin Thomas (d. 1755), II, 129
Philippson, Joannes (Sleidanus), I, 817
Philips, Ambrose (1675?–1749), II, 22 (2), 191, 197, **324** f., 485, 762, 789
Philips, Charles (*fl.* 1816), II, 458
Philips, Erasmus (*fl.* 1726), II, 662
Philips, Joan (*fl.* 1679), II, 280
Philips, John (1676–1709), poet, II, **325**
'Philips, John' (1715), II, 1001
Philips, John (*fl.* 1744), traveller, II, 741
Philips, Katherine (1632–1664), II, **284**
Philips (or Phillips), Samuel (*fl.* 1705), II, 187 (3), 188, 203, 676
Philips, Sir Thomas (*fl.* 1635), I, 845
Philips, William (d. 1734), II, **442**
Phillimore, Sir Robert Joseph (1810–1885), II, 321, 963; III, 987
Phillip, Arthur (1738–1814), II, 751
Phillip, John (*fl.* 1566), I, 520
Phillip, William (*fl.* 1596–1619), I, 769, 782 (2), 791
Phillipps, C. S. March (*fl.* 1869), III, 760
Phillipps, Sir Thomas (1792–1872), I, 5, 91 (misprinted Philipps), 774
Phillips, Ambrose. See Philips
Phillips, C. P. (*fl.* 1863), III, 94
Phillips, Edward (1630–1696?), Milton's nephew, I, 399; II, 21, 180, 922
Phillips, Edward (*fl.* 1730–9), dramatist, II, **442**
Phillips, George Searle, i.e. 'J. Searle' (1815–1889), III, 233
Phillips, Giles Firman (1780–1867), III, 83
Phillips, H. A. D. (*fl.* 1885), III, 1072
Phillips, J. F. (*fl.* 1897), writer on Hinduism, III, 1082
Phillips, J. H. (*fl.* 1867), advocate of free libraries, III, 105
Phillips, J. S. R. (*fl.* 1889–91), editor of 'The Manchester Examiner', III, 802
Phillips, John (1631–1706), II, 21, 67–8, **284** f., 288, 532, 533 (2), 675–6, 760, 762, 777, 800 (2), 801
Phillips, John (*fl.* 1785–1803), writer on inland navigation, III, 979
Phillips, John (1800–1874), geologist, III, **951** (2)
Phillips, Sir L. (*fl.* 1905), III, 1092
Phillips, Peregrine (*fl.* 1787), I, 457
Phillips, Sir Richard (1767–1840), II, 564, 605, 697; III, 99, 824 (2), 825, 988
Phillips, S. C. (*fl.* 1884), III, 73
Phillips (or Philips), Samuel (*fl.* 1705), II, 187 (3), 188, 203, 676
Phillips, Samuel (1814–1854), III, **502**
Phillips, Stephen (1864–1915), III, **627**

Phillips, Theresia Constantia (1709–1765), II, 332
Phillips, Thomas (*fl.* 1732), II, 742
Phillips, Watts (1825–1874), III, **606**
Phillips, William (1773–1828), III, 950
Phillips, William A. (*fl.* 1860–86), III, 977
Phillpotts, Eden (b. 1862), III, 570
Phillpotts, Henry (1778–1869), III, 879
'Philo Junius' (1771), II, 630
'Philo-Scoticus' (1797), II, 972
Philological Miscellany, The (1761), II, 678
PHILOLOGY. See under LANGUAGE. See also under ARABIC SCHOLARS, ASSYRIOLOGISTS, BIBLICAL SCHOLARS, CHINESE SCHOLARS, EGYPTOLOGISTS, GAELIC SOURCES, GREEK, INDIA, IRELAND, LATIN, SANSKRIT, etc.
'Philolyrister' (1782), II, 337
Philomel (18 cent.), II, 210
Philon, Francis (*fl.* 1685), II, 795
Philosopher, The (1777), II, 665
Philosophical Collections (1679), II, 674
Philosophical Magazine, The (1798), III, 824
Philosophical Magazine; or Annals of Chemistry [etc.], *The* (1827), III, 824
Philosophical Observator, The (1695), II, 658
Philosophical Quixote, or Memoirs of Mr. David Wilkins, The (18 cent.), II, 548
PHILOSOPHICAL RADICALS, III, 59 f.
PHILOSOPHY
  Anglo-Saxon Period. See under WRITINGS IN LATIN, I, 98 f.
  Middle English Period, I, 119 (political). See also under WRITINGS IN LATIN, I, 280 f.
  Renaissance to Restoration, I, 868 f. See also under WORKS ON SPECIAL SUBJECTS, I, 321 f. and EDUCATION, I, 364 f.
  Restoration to Romantic Revival, II, 35 f. (English-French influences), 52 f. (English-German influences), 65 f. (English-Italian influences), 939 f. (principal writers). See also under LITERARY MOVEMENTS AND IDEAS, II, 5 f.
  Nineteenth Century, III, 46 f. (intellectual background), 159 f. (poets' philosophy), 861 f. (principal writers). See also PSYCHOLOGY, III, 964 f.
Philotus (17 cent.), I, 517, 900
Philp, Robert Kemp (1819–1882), III, 828
Philpot, Charles (*fl.* 1799), II, 917
Philpott, Henry (1807–1892), I, 370
Phipps, Constantine Henry, Marquis of Normanby (1797–1863), III, **413**
Phipps, Constantine John, Baron Mulgrave (1744–1792), II, 743
Phipps, Edmund (1808–1857), III, 149
Phiston (or Fiston), William (*fl.* 1571–1609), I, 714, 815, 817
Phoenix (O.E.), I, **77**
Phoenix, The (1808), III, 816

Phoenix Nest, The (16 cent.), I, 404
Phoenix of Europe or the Forraine Intelligencer, The (1646), I, 757
Phoenix; Or, Weekly Miscellany Improv'd, The (1792), II, 687
PHONOLOGY
    Old English, I, 34 f.
    Middle English, I, 37 f.
    Modern English, I, 43 f.
PHRASE-BOOKS, II, 120 (17, 18 cents.)
Phreas (or Free), John (d. 1465), I, 313
PHYSICIANS, ROYAL COLLEGE OF Library, I, 362
PHYSICS (writings on), III, 936 f.
Physiologus (O.E.), I, **78**
PHYSIOLOGY (writings on), III, 962 f. (19 cent.).
    For earlier writings see under MEDICINE
Pianoforte Magazine, The (1796), II, 682
Pic, Jean, II, 793
Pic-Nic, The (1803), II, 358
Piccolomini, Alessandro, I, 340
Piccolomini, Enea Silvio [i.e. Pope Pius II, known as Æneas Silvius], I, 734, 818 (2); II, 813
Pichot, Amédée, III, 20
Pick, Samuel (*fl.* 1639), I, 405
Pick, William (*fl.* 1785), II, 815
Picken, Andrew (1788–1833), III, **413**
Picken, Ebenezer (1769–1816), II, 972
Pickering, Amelia (*fl.* 1789), II, 63
Pickering, Danby (*fl.* 1737–69), II, 167
Pickering, John (*fl.* 1567), I, 523
Pickering, Roger (*fl.* 1755), II, 409
Pickering, William (*fl.* 1556–71), I, 352
Pickering, William (1796–1854), I, 205; III, 99, 102
Pickering, Honor of (M.E.), I, 121
Pickersgill, Mrs — (*fl.* 1827), III, 1068
Pickersgill, Richard (*fl.* 1782), II, 741
Pickersgill, Robert (*fl.* 1768), II, 225
Pico Della Mirandola, Giovanni, I, 327, 338
Pictet, Auguste, II, 688
Pictet, Marc Auguste, II, 142
Picton, James Allanson (1832–1910), III, **872**
Pictorial Juvenile, The (1853), III, 577
Pictorial Magazine for Little Children, The (1855), III, 577
Pictorial News, The (1888), III, 815
Pictorial Times, The (1844), III, 815
Pictorial World, The (1874), III, 815
Picture Exhibition, The (18 cent.), II, 562
Picture Magazine, The (1863), III, 577
Picture Times, The (1855), III, 815
Piddington, Henry (1797–1858), III, 1083
Pidou de Saint Olon, II, 425
Pieces of Ancient Popular Poetry (18 cent.), II, 246
Pieces on the Subjects of Love and Marriage (18 cent.), II, 253
Pieces Selected from the Italian Poets (18 cent.), II, 233, 238

Piecope, J. G. (*fl.* 1857), I, 380
Pierce, Eliza (*fl.* 1751–75), II, 137
Pierce, Thomas (1662–1691), I, 878
Pierce Egan's Life in London and Sporting Guide (1824), III, 811
Pierce Egan's Weekly Courier (1829), III, 812
Pierce the Ploughman's Crede (M.E.), I, **200**
Piers Plowman (M.E.), I, 29, 32, 40, **197** f.
Pietas Academiae Cantabrigiensis in Funere Principis Wilhelminae Carolinae (18 cent.), II, 207
Pietas Academiae Oxoniensis in Obitum Reginae Carolinae (18 cent.), II, 207
Pietas et Gratulatio Collegii Cantabrigiensis Apud Novanglos (18 cent.), II, 220
Pietas Universitatis Oxoniensis In Obitum Georgii I (18 cent.), II, 199
Pietas Universitatis Oxoniensis in Obitum Georgii II et Gratulatio In Georgii III Inaugurationem (18 cent.), II, 220
Pigafetta, Filippo, I, 782
Pigafetta, Marc-Antonio, I, 768
Piggott (or Pigott), Charles (d. 1794), II, 635
Piggott, S. (*fl.* 1818), III, 246
Pigot (or Pigott), Robert (1736–1794), I, 479; II, 85
Pigott, Harriet ('Mrs Thomson') (1766–1846), II, 549
Pig's Meat (1793), II, 682
Pike, J. R. (*fl.* 1860), III, 971
Pike (or Peeke), Richard (*fl.* 1626), I, 741
Piles, Roger de, II, 793
Pilgrim, The (1711), II, 661
Pilgrimage to Parnassus, The (17 cent.), I, 662
Pilkington, Francis (1562?–1636), I, 485
Pilkington, Gilbert (*fl.* 1350), I, 265, 278
Pilkington, James (1520?–1576), I, 741
Pilkington, Laetitia (1712–1750), II, 136, 219
Pilkington, Mary Hopkins (1766–1839), II, 551, 559, 790
Pilkington, Matthew (*fl.* 1730), II, **325**, 591, 928
Pill to Purge Melancholy, A (17 cent.), I, 718
Pill to Purge State-Melancholy, A (18 cent.), II, 192–4
Pillans, James (1778–1864), III, 113, **122**
PILLANS AND WILSON, III, 87
Pillet, René Martin, II, 142
Pills to Expel Spleen (18 cent.), II, 215
Pills to Purge Melancholy (18 cent.), II, 235
Pilon, Frederick (1750–1788), II, **481**
Pilot, The (1807), III, 800
Pimlyco (17 cent.), I, 713
Pinchard, Mrs — (*fl.* 1791), of Taunton, II, 558 f.
Pindar, II, 762; III, 229, 1001, 1008
Pinder of Wakefield, The (17 cent.), I, 731
Pine, J. B. (*fl.* 1824), III, 818
Pinero, Sir Arthur Wing (1855–1934), III, **615** f.

Pinkerton, John (1758–1826), II, 75, **907**f.

Pinkethman's Jests (18 cent.), II, 196 (2), 205

Pinkney, Miles, i.e. Thomas Car (or Carre) (1599–1674), I, 456

Pinnell, Richard (*fl.* before 1781), II, 750

Pinto, Fernão Mendes, I, 784

Pinto, Isaac de (*fl.* 1767), II, 826

Piot (or Pyott), Lazarus (*fl.* 1595), I, 804, 810

Piozzi, Hester Lynch, earlier Thrale (1741–1821), II, **843**f.

Pipe, H. E. (*fl.* 1831–96), III, 143

PIRATES, II, 151 (18 cent.)

'Piscator' (1826), III, 768

'Piscator' (1872), III, 776

Pistill of Susan (M.E.), I, 189f.

Pistorius, H. A., II, 955

Pitcairn, E. R. (*fl.* 1836), I, 901

Pitcairn, Robert (1793–1855), I, 905; III, 1026

Pitcairne, Archibald (1652–1713), II, **999**

Pitiscus, I, 881

Pitman, Henry (*fl.* 1689), II, 752

Pitman, Sir Isaac (1813–1897), III, 99

Pitman, John Rogers (1782–1861), I, 699; II, 851

Pits, John (1560–1616), I, 9, 359

Pitt, Anne (*fl.* 1734–68), II, 136

Pitt, Christopher (1699–1748), II, 28, 33, **325**f.

Pitt, George Dibdin (*fl.* 1834–44), III, **606**

Pitt, James (*fl.* 1738), II, 713

Pitt, Moses (*fl.* 1654–96), II, 100, 143

Pitt, William, Earl of Chatham (1708–1778), II, 116, 164, 632 (2)

Pitt-Rivers, Augustus Henry Lane, earlier Fox (1827–1900), III, **915**

Pittis, William (1674–1724), II, 272, 499, 659–60, 676, 697, 713

Pittman, Philip (*fl.* 1770), II, 755

Pitton de Tournefort, Joseph, II, 793 (2)

Pitts, Joseph (1663–1731?), II, 748

Pius II (Enea Silvio Piccolomini), II, 813

Pix, Mary (1666–1720?), II, **442**

Pixérécourt, R. C. Guilbert de, III, 586, 593

Place, Francis (1771–1854), III, 113, 143, 816, 872, 971

PLACE-NAMES, I, 47f.

Plain Dealer, The (1712), II, 661

Plain Dealer, The (1724), II, 201, 204, 662

Plain Dealer, The (1729), II, 663

Plain Dealer, The (1763), II, 665

Plain Dealer, The (1775), II, 665

Plain Dealer's Intelligencer, The (1728), II, 663

Plain Sermons (19 cent.), III, 856

Plaisted, Bartholomew (*fl.* 1757), II, 750

Planché, James Robinson (1796–1880), II, 891 (2), 111, 576, **592**f.

Planché, Matilda Anne, later Mackarness (1826–1881), III, 568

Planet, The (1837), III, 812

Plant, George (*fl.* 1880), III, 814

Plantagenet, Beauchamp (*fl.* 1648), I, 796

Plantin, Arabella (*fl.* 1727), II, 539

Plarr, Victor Gustave (1863–1929), III, **353**

Platina, Bartholomaeus, De, II, 813

Plato, I, 806; II, 762; III, 997, 999, 1001, 1002 (2)

Platt, Sir Hugh (1552–1611?), I, 391, 396

Platte, T. (*fl.* 1616), I, 742

Platters, Thomas (*fl.* 1599), I, 385

Plattes, Gabriel (*fl.* 1638), I, 886

Plautus, I, 661, 806; II, 767; III, 1009

Players Tragedy, The; or Fatal Love (17 cent.), II, 531

Playfair, J. G. (*fl.* 1822), III, 949

Playfair, John (1748–1819), III, 949 (2)

Playfair, Lyon (1819–1898), III, 113, 937, 947

Playfair, William (1759–1823), III, 979

Playfere, Thomas (1561?–1609), I, 683

Playford, Henry (1657–1706?), II, 179, 180 (3), 183, 184 (2), 185–6, 676 (3)

Playford, John (1623–1686?), I, 392, 395, 451, 486 (2); II, 30, 173, 176 (2), 180

Play-house Journal, The (1750), II, 663

PLAYS. See DRAMA

Pleasant Comedie Called The Two Merry Milke-maids, A (17 cent.), I, 653

Pleasant Comedie, Called Wily Beguilde, A (17 cent.), I, 663

Pleasant Comedie Shewing the contention betweene Liberalitie and Prodigalitie, A (16 cent.), I, 516

Pleasant Comedie, called Look about you, A (16 cent.), I, 538

Pleasant commodie of faire Em, A (17 cent.), I, 579

Pleasant Comoedie, The wit of a Woman, A (17 cent.), I, 654

Pleasant Conceited Comedie, called, A knacke to know an honest Man, A (16 cent.), I, 538

Pleasant conceited Comedie, how a man may chuse a good Wife, A (17 cent.), I, 623

Pleasant Conceited Historie, called The Taming of a Shrew, A (16 cent.), I, 555

Pleasant Conceyted Comedie of George a Greene, A (16 cent.), I, 538

Pleasant Musical Companion, The (18 cent.), II, 192

Pleasing Companion, The (1799), II, 254

Pleasing Companion, or Guide to Fame, The (1798), II, 254

Pleasing Instructor or Entertaining Moralist, The (18 cent.), II, 562

Pleasing Jester, The (18 cent.), II, 247

Pleasing Melancholy (18 cent.), II, 248

Pleasing Reflections on Life and Manners (18 cent.), II, 240, 242

Pleasing Songster, The (18 cent.), II, 240

Pleasing Variety (18 cent.), II, 249

Pleasure for a Minute (18 cent.), II, 197 (2)

Pleasure Improved, Or, an Account of Mrs. Wishwell's Scholars (18 cent.), II, 562

Pleasures of Coition, The (18 cent.), II, 196 (2)
Plebeian, The (1719), II, 662
Plesner, Augusta (*fl.* 1867), III, 576
Plessis Villeneuve, René le Pays, Sieur du, II, 788
Plessis-Marly, Philippe de, Seigneur du, II, 791
Pliny, the elder, I, 765, 806
Pliny, the younger, I, 806; II, 767
Plotinus, II, 762
'Plough, Patrick' (1842), III, 982
Plowden, Edmund (1518–1585), I, 850
Plowman, J. (*fl.* 1824), III, 89
Plowman's Tale (M.E.), I, 200
Pluche, Noël Antoine, II, 793
Plumer, Francis (*fl.* 1754–72), II, 18, 516
Plumpton Correspondence, The (15 cent.), I, 120
Plumpton Correspondence (16 cent.), I, 382
Plumptre, Anne or Anna (1760–1818), II, 51, 60 (5), 63, 486, 807
Plumptre, Bell (*fl.* 1799), II, 59, 805
Plumptre, Edward Hayes (1821–1891), III, 304, 363
Plumptre, James (1770–1832), II, 257, 918, 983
Plunket, William Conyngham, Baron (1764–1854), III, 148–9
Plunkett, Edward John Moreton Drax, Baron Dunsany (b. 1878), III, 1067
Plutarch, I, 461, 734, 806; II, 763; III, 265, 999, 1000
Plymouth
    Magazines, II, 685 (1758–72)
    Newspapers, II, 727
Plymouth Magazine, The (1772), II, 685
Plymouth Magazine; or, the Universal Intelligencer, The (1758), II, 685
Plymouth Weekly Journal, The (1718), II, 727
Pocket Book for the German Flute or Violin, A (18 cent.), II, 233, 238, 244
Pocket Book for the Guitar (18 cent.), II, 233
Pocket Companion and History of Free-Masons, The (18 cent.), II, 216, 219, 223
Pocket Companion for Free-Masons, A (18 cent.), II, 205 (2), 215 (3), 220, 222–3, 228, 247, 253
Pocket Companion For Gentlemen and Ladies, A (18 cent.), II, 197–8
Pocket Companion for the Guittar, The (18 cent.), II, 217
Pocket Magazine, The (1794), II, 682
Pocket Magazine, The (1827), III, 825
Pocket Magazine of Classic and Polite Literature, The (1818), III, 825
Pocock, Isaac (1782–1835), III, 593
Pocock, Lewis (1808–1882), II, 491
Pocock, Nicholas (1814–1897), I, 697; II, 867
Pocock, Robert (1760–1830), III, 87
Pocock's Everlasting Songster (19 cent.), II, 256

Pococke, Edward, the elder (1604–1691), I, 786; II, 939
Pococke, Edward, the younger (1648–1727), II, 533, 939
Pococke, Richard (1704–1765), II, 139, 157, 159, 749
Pöllnitz, Karl Ludwig von, II, 141, 154, 543, 807
Poema Morale (M.E.), I, 180
Poemata partim reddita, partim Scripta (18 cent.), II, 238
Poematia, Latine reddita A V. Bourne (18 cent.), II, 204–5, 210, 214, 223
Poems, A Chosen Collection (18 cent.), II, 206
Poems and Epistles on several Occasions (18 cent.), II, 189
Poems and Translations (18 cent.), II, 191 (2), 195
Poems by a Literary Society (18 cent.), II, 238
Poems by Eminent Ladies (18 cent.), II, 217–8, 229, 235
Poems, By S. T. Coleridge [etc.] (18 cent.), II, 253
Poems by Several Gentlemen of Oxford (18 cent.), II, 218
Poems by Several Hands, And on Several Occasions (17 cent.), II, 180
Poems By the Earl of Roscomon, The Earl of Mulgrave, Richard Duke (18 cent.), II, 194
Poems, Chiefly by Gentlemen of Devonshire and Cornwall (18 cent.), II, 247
Poems, Divine and Moral (18 cent.), II, 216
Poems Divine, Moral and Philosophical (18 cent.), II, 212
Poems for Ladies (18 cent.), II, 232
Poems for Young Ladies (18 cent.), II, 225, 227, 239
Poems in English and Latin on the Archers (18 cent.), II, 198
Poems in the Scottish Dialect (18 cent.), II, 213
Poems, Moral and Divine. Collected from the Best Authors (18 cent.), II, 219
Poems, Moral, Elegant and Pathetic (18 cent.), II, 252
Poems of Ben Johnson Junior, The (17 cent.), II, 176
Poems of Horace, The (17 cent.), II, 175 (2), 178
Poems of Mr. Cowley and Others (17 cent.), II, 175
Poems on Affairs of State (17 cent.), II, 183, 184 (4), 185, 186 (4), 187 (2), 189, 193
Poems on Affairs of State, Collected from the Papers (18 cent.), II, 204
Poems on Miscellaneous Subjects, Composed and Selected By Charlotte Beverley (18 cent.), II, 247
Poems on moral and divine subjects (18 cent.), II, 215
Poems on Several Occasions (Dublin, 1748), II, 213

Poems on Several Occasions. A Pastoral Courtship (18 cent.), II, 194

Poems on Several Occasions By a Lady (18 cent.), II, 200

Poems on Several Occasions By Mary Barber and others (18 cent.), II, 204–6

Poems on Several Occasions By Matthew Prior [etc.] (18 cent.), II, 199, 210

Poems on Several Occasions. By Michael Bruce [etc.] (18 cent.), II, 227

Poems on Several Occasions By Mr. Addison (18 cent.), II, 195, 197

Poems on Several Occasions by the Duke of Buckingham [etc.] (18 cent.), II, 194

Poems on Several Occasions Collected from the Spectators [etc.] (18 cent.), II, 209

Poems on Several Occasions, from Genuine Manuscripts of Dean Swift, Mr. H—m, Mr. C—r etc. (18 cent.), II, 213

Poems on Several Occasions. Originals, and Translations (17 cent.), II, 183

Poems on Several Subjects. By a Land-Waiter (18 cent.), II, 209

Poems on the Death of Queen Mary (18 cent.), II, 189

Poems on Various Subjects (1756), II, 217

Poems on Various Subjects (1776), II, 231

Poems on Various Subjects (1782), II, 236, 248, 256

Poems on Various Subjects (1786), II, 240, 243

Poems Selected and Printed By a small Party of English (18 cent.), II, 247

Poems to the Memory Of Edmond Waller (17 cent.), II, 180

Poems upon Divine and Moral Subjects (18 cent.), II, 195, 204

Poems, Written by… Pembroke…answered by …Ruddier (17 cent.), II, 173

Poems Written occasionally by John Winstanley [etc.] (18 cent.), II, 210, 215

Poet's Magazine, The (1876), III, 830

Poetical Amusements at a Villa near Bath (18 cent.), II, 231 (4), 232, 235

Poetical Beauties of Modern Writers (18 cent.), II, 254

Poetical Blossoms (18 cent.), II, 248

Poetical Blossoms; or, The Sports of Genius (18 cent.), II, 562

Poetical Calendar, The (18 cent.), II, 222

Poetical Courant, The (1706), II, 187, 676

Poetical Dictionary, A (18 cent.), II, 220

Poetical Entertainer, The (18 cent.), II, 190 (2)

Poetical Epitome, The (18 cent.), II, 247

Poetical Farrago, The (18 cent.), II, 249

Poetical Magazine, The (1779), II, 680

Poetical Magazine, The (18 cent.), II, 223

Poetical Magazine, The (1809), III, 825

Poetical Magazine; Or, The Muses' Monthly Companion, The (1764), II, 679

Poetical Miscellanies (18 cent.), II, 191, 198–9

Poetical Miscellanies Published by Mr. J. Gay (18 cent.), II, 200

Poetical Miscellany, The (1754), II, 216

Poetical Miscellany, The (1762), II, 221, 226, 233

Poetical Monitor, The (18 cent.), II, 252, 254

Poetical Museum, The (18 cent.), II, 238

Poetical Observator, The (1702), II, 659

Poetical Observator Reviv'd, The (1703), II, 659

Poetical Pieces (18 cent.), II, 215

Poetical Preceptor, The (18 cent.), II, 232, 239

Poetical Rapsody, A (1602), I, 404

Poetical Recreations (17 cent.), II, 180

Poetical Tell-Tale, The (18 cent.), II, 222

Poetical Works of that Witty Lord John Earl of Rochester, The (18 cent.), II, 220

Poetical Works Of the Honourable Sir Charles Sedley Baronet, The (18 cent.), II, 187, 189

POETRY, I, 10 f. (general histories), 12 f. (general anthologies)
   Old English, I, 60 f. For details see OLD ENGLISH POETRY. For Latin verse 6 to 10 cents. see under WRITINGS IN LATIN, I, 98 f.
   Middle English, I, 113 f., 128 f. For details see MIDDLE ENGLISH POETRY. For Latin verse 11 to 15 cents. see under WRITINGS IN LATIN, I, 280 f.
   Fifteenth Century, I, 250 f., 264 f. See also SONGS AND BALLADS, I, 267 f.
   Renaissance to Restoration, I, 403 f. For details see RENAISSANCE TO RESTORATION (POETRY OF)
   Restoration to Romantic Revival, II, 169 f. For details see RESTORATION TO ROMANTIC REVIVAL (POETRY OF)
   Nineteenth Century, III, 156 f. For details see NINETEENTH-CENTURY POETRY. See also under IRELAND, INDIA, CANADA, SOUTH AFRICA, AUSTRALIA AND NEW ZEALAND

Poetry Made familiar and easy (18 cent.), II, 213, 221, 226–7

Poetry of the Anti-Jacobin (18 cent.), II, 254, 256

Poetry of the World, The (18 cent.), II, 242, 246 (2)

Poetry of Various Glees, The (18 cent.), II, 254

Poetry: Original and Selected (19 cent.), II, 256

Poets of Great Britain, The (1776), II, 259

Poggio, I, 409

Pogson, F. (*fl.* 1872), III, 1084

Pointer, John (1668–1754), II, 118

Poiret, Jean Louis Marie, II, 793

Poiret, Pierre, II, 793

Poisson de Gomez, Madeleine Angélique, II, 793

Poivre, Pierre, II, 793

POLAND
Literary Relations with, II, 71 (1660–1800); III, 43f. (19 cent.)
Polanus, Amandus, I, 680
Pole, Thomas (1753–1829), III, 113, 117
Police Gazette; or Hue and Cry, The (1828), II, 717
Polidori, John William (1795–1821), III, 205, 413
Polier, Charles de (fl. 1791), II, 20
Polite Companion, The (1749), II, 213
Polite Companion, or Wit a-la-Mode, The (1760), II, 219
Polite Correspondence, The (18 cent.), II, 201
Polite Instructor; or, Youth's Museum, The (18 cent.), II, 561
Polite Jester, or Theatre for Wit, The (18 cent.), II, 252
Polite Miscellany, The (18 cent.), II, 223
Polite Preceptor, The (18 cent.), II, 230
Polite Singer, The (18 cent.), II, 235
Polite Songster, The (18 cent.), II, 218, 219
Polite Songster, The (19 cent.), II, 256
Polite Songster; Or, Vocal Melody, The, II, 248–9
Politeuphuia; wits commonwealth (16 cent.), I, 404
POLITICAL BACKGROUND
Anglo-Saxon Period. See under ARCHAEO-LOGY AND HISTORY, I, 56f.
Middle English Period, I, 115f.
Renaissance to Restoration, I, 396f.
Restoration to Romantic Revival, II, 161f.
Nineteenth Century, III, 143f. (general), 1074f. (Anglo-Indian), 1090f. (South Africa)
Political Cabinet, The (1744), II, 677
Political Controversy, The (1762), II, 665, 678
Political Entertainer, The (1712), II, 676
Political Herald and Review, The (1785), II, 681
Political History of Europe, The (1697), II, 676
Political Letter and Pamphlets (1830), III, 816
Political Magazine, The (1794), II, 682
Political Magazine And Parliamentary, Naval, Military and Literary Journal, The (1780), II, 680
Political Merriment (18 cent.), II, 191–2
Political Miscellanies. By the Authors of the Rolliad (18 cent.), II, 240, 244
POLITICAL POEMS
Middle English, I, 270f.
Political Register and Impartial Review of New Books, The (1767), II, 679
Political Review of Edinburgh Periodical Publications (1792), III, 685–6
POLITICAL SATIRES, I, 719f. (16, 17 cents.)
Political State of Europe, The (1792), II, 681
Political State of Great Britain, The (1711), II, 676

POLITICAL SUMMARIES (periodical), II, 675f. (1687–1730)
Political Tatler, The (1716), II, 662
POLITICAL THEORY (writings on), I, 843f. (16, 17 cents.); III, 969f. For 1660–1800 see under Philosophy, II, 939f.
Politick Spy; Or, the Weekly Reflexions on the State, The (1701), II, 659
Politicks in Miniature (18 cent.), II, 210
Politicks of Europe, The (1690), II, 676
Politics for the People (1793), II, 682
Politics for the People (1848), III, 817
Politique Informer, The (1654), I, 762
Politique Post, The (1654), I, 762
Pollen, John Hungerford (1820–1902), III, 859
Pollexfen, John (fl. 1675–97), II, 959
Pollock, Edith Caroline ('Ismay Thorn') (fl. 1878), III, 569
Pollock, Sir Frederick (1845–1937), III, 353, 834
Pollock, J. M. (fl. 1860), II, 342
Pollock, Juliet, Lady (fl. 1874), III, 573
Pollock, Walter Herries (1850–1926), III, 353f., 573, 778, 814, 834
Pollock, Sir William Frederick (1815–1888), III, 383
Pollok, Catherine, later Manners, later Lady Stepney (d. 1845), III, 418
Pollok, D. (fl. 1843), III, 241
Pollok, Robert (1798–1827), III, 241
POLO (books on), III, 775
Polo, Marco, I, 782, 818
Polwhele, Richard (1760–1838), II, 23, 247, 376, 765
Polyaenus, II, 380
Polybius, I, 777, 806; II, 703; III, 1010
Polyhymnia (1769), II, 226
Polyhymnia, The (1799), II, 254
Pomet, Pierre, II, 793
Pomfret, John (1667–1702), II, 196, 204, 326
Pompadour, Jeanne Antoinette Lenormand d'Étioles, Marquise de, II, 788
Pomponius Mela, I, 766, 804
Pond, John (fl. 1752–7), II, 718, 815
Ponet (or Poynet), John (1514?–1556), I, 671, 817
Ponsonby, Lady Caroline, later Lamb (1785–1828), III, 404
Pont, Timothy (fl. c. 1644), I, 776
Pontey, W. (fl. 1810–22), III, 824, 970
Pontis, Louis de, II, 46, 794
Ponz, Antonio, II, 141
Pool, John J. (fl. 1892), writer on India, III, 1082
Poole, J. (fl. 1813), educationalist, III, 129
Poole, John (1786–1872), dramatist and miscellaneous writer, II, 523; III, 594
Poole, Joshua (fl. 1632–46), I, 377, 867; II, 177
Poole, Matthew (1624–1679), I, 368, 856
Poole, Reginald Lane (b. 1857), III, 834

Poole, Reginald Stuart (1832–1895), III, **1015**
Poole, Robert (1708–1752), II, 745, 754
Poor Gillian (1677), II, 657
Poor Gillian; Or, Mother Redcap's Weekly Advice (1677), II, 702
Poor Man's Advocate, The [Manchester] (1832), III, 816
Poor Man's Guardian, The (1831), III, 816
Poor Robins Collection of Antient Prophecyes (17 cent.), II, 176
Poor Robin's Intelligence (1676), II, 656
Poor Robin's Intelligence newly Revived (1679), II, 657
Poor Robin's Memoirs (1677), II, 656
Poor Robin's Publick and Private Occurrences and Remarks (1688), II, 658
Pope, Alexander (1688–1744), II, **294**f.
   Biography, II, 301
   Collected Works, II, 294f.
   Later criticism, 303f.
   Letters, II, 295f.
   Popiana, II, 301f.
   Separate Works, II, 296f. (pbd in Pope's life), 300 (pbd after Pope's death)
   Translations from, II, 39, 46, 58–9, 67, 71
   Works edited by, II, 300f.
Pope, Sir Joseph (*fl.* 1894), III, 1087
Pope, Walter (d. 1714), II, **285**, 812
Pope's Bath Chronicle (1766), II, 665, 720
Pope's Miscellany (18 cent.), II, 194 (3)
Popish Mass Display'd, The (1681), II, 657
Popping, Sarah (*fl.* 1711–22), II, 707, 710, 713
Popple, William (d. 1708), merchant, II, 940
Popple, William (1701–1764), dramatist, II, **442**f.
POPULAR AND MISCELLANEOUS PROSE, I, 704f. (1500–1660); II, 567f. (1660–1800); III, 629f. (19 cent.)
Popular Ballads Preserved in Memory (18 cent.), II, 251
POPULATION (writings on), III, 975f.
Poquelin de Molière, Jean Baptiste, II, 41f., 319, 794
Porcupine, The (1800), III, 798
Pordage, John (1607–1681), I, 878; II, 54, 861
Pordage, Samuel (1633–1691?), II, **285**
Porder, Richard (*fl.* 1570), I, 845
Porée, Charles, II, 794
Porson, Richard (1759–1808), II, **934**f.
Portal, Abraham (*fl.* 1763), II, **376**f., 758
Portal, Hyate Stanley (*fl.* 1909), III, **1090**
Portal, W. B. (*fl.* 1789), II, 666
Porter, Anna Maria (1780–1832), III, **413**f.
Porter, Endymion (1587–1649), I, 385
Porter, George Richardson (1792–1852), III, 113, 116, 981
Porter, Henry (*fl.* 1596–99), I, 537
Porter, Sir James (1710–1786), II, 745
Porter, James Biggs (*fl.* 1884), III, 987
Porter, Jane (1776–1850), II, 666; III, **414**, 570

Porter, John (*fl.* 1720), literary critic, II, 22
Porter, John (*fl.* 18 cent.?), writer on Arabia, II, 750
Porter, John (1838–1922), sportsman, III, 764
Porter, P. (*fl.* 1673–8), II, 785, 792, 802
Porter, Sir Robert Ker (1777–1842), II, 666; III, 992
Porter, Stephen (*fl.* 1798), II, 60
Porter, Thomas (*fl.* 1655), cartographer, I, 767, 776
Porter, Thomas (1636–1680), dramatist, II, **426**
Porter, Walter (1590?–1659), I, 486
Porteus, Beilby (1731–1808), II, 125, 853 (2)
Portfolio, The (1870), III, 830
Portland, William Henry Cavendish Bentinck, Duke of (1738–1809), II, 632
Portlock, Nathaniel (1748?–1817), II, 742
PORTSMOUTH
   Newspapers, II, 727
Portsmouth and Gosport Gazette, The (1747), II, 727
Portsmouth and Gosport Gazette, and Salisbury Journal, The (1752), II, 728
Portsmouth Gazette and Weekly Advertiser, The (1793), II, 727
Portsmouth Telegraph, The (1799), II, 727
PORTUGAL
   Literary Relations with, I, 342f. (1500–1660); II, 67f. (1660–1800); III, 41f.
Portwine, Edward J. (*fl.* 1836), III, 101–2
Pory, John (1570?–1635), I, 785, 791
Porzio, Luca Antonio, II, 813
Post, Christian F., II, 755
POST OFFICE, II, 692f.
Post-Angel, The (1701), II, 659
Post Boy, The (1710), II, 707
Post-Boy, The (Dublin, 1718), II, 734
Post-Boy, And Historical Account, &c., The (1695), II, 708
Post Boy, Foreign and Domestick, The (1695), II, 706
Post-Man, Le (1704), II, 719
Poste, Edward (1823–1902), III, **1002**
Posthumous Works by Mr Samuel Butler (18 cent.), II, 192 (5), 193 (2), 194 (2), 195, 201, 203, 216
Postlethwayt, Malachy (d. 1767), II, 111, 926, 959
Postman and the Historical Account, The (1695), II, 706
Postman: And the Historical Account, The (Dublin, 1707), II, 734
Postmaster; Or, The Loyal Mercury, The (1718), II, 723
Postmaster; Or, The Loyal Mercury, The (1720), II, 707
Post-Office Intelligence (18 cent.), II, 206
Pote, Joseph (1703?–1787), II, 91
Potent Ally, The (18 cent.), II, 209

Potter, Beatrice, later Webb (b. 1858), III, 984
Potter, Christopher (1591–1646), I, 818
Potter, Frederick Scarlett (*fl.* 1876), III, **573**
Potter, George (1832–1893), III, 817
Potter, Humphrey T. (*fl.* 1790), II, 930
Potter, J. P. (*fl.* 1828), III, 113
Potter, John (1674?–1747), archbishop of Canterbury, II, 937
Potter, John (*fl.* 1754–1804), II, 665, 679
Potter, L. J. A. de, III, 679
Potter, R. (*fl.* 1644), I, 390
Potter, Robert (1721–1804), II, 19, 758, 760, 763
Pottinger, Sir Henry (1789–1856), III, 1079
Pottinger, Israel (*fl.* 1759–76), II, 457 (2)
Potts, Henry (*fl.* before 1791), II, 735
Potts, J. T. (*fl.* 1846–71), Irish journalist, III, 809
Potts, James (*fl.* 1791–6), Irish journalist, II, 735
Potts, John (*fl.* 1796–1846), Irish journalist, II, 735; III, 809
Potts, Robert (1805–1885), III, 123
Pouilly, Louis Jean Levesque de, II, 29
Poulain de la Barre, François, II, 794
Poullain de Saint-Foix, Germain François, II, 795
Poulter, John (*fl.* 1754), II, 155
Poulton, Edward Bagnall (b. 1856), III, 955
Povey, Charles (1652?–1743), II, 516, 661, 697, 707
Povoleri, J. (*fl.* 1789), II, 791
Powel (or Powell), Vavasor (1617–1670), II, 928
Powell, A. J. C. (*fl.* 1866), III, 88
Powell, Baden (1796–1860), III, 113, 848–9
Powell, David (1552?–1598), I, 826
Powell, Ellis T. (*fl.* 1884), III, 800
Powell, Elizabeth (*fl.* 1716), II, 712
Powell, Frederick York (1850–1904), III, **935**
Powell, George (1658?–1714), II, **426**
Powell, James (*fl.* 1787–1805), II, 63
Powell, Thomas (1572?–1635?), I, 438, 713
Powell, Thomas (*fl.* 1840–50), I, 210; III, 7, 644, 646 f.
Powell, Walter (*fl.* 1606–54), I, 385
Power, Henry (1623–1668), II, 961
Power, James (*fl.* 1814–40), III, 184
Power, Joseph (1798–1868), III, 104
Power, Marguerite, later Countess of Blessington (1789–1849), III, **388**
Powis Castle, or Anecdotes of an Antient Family (18 cent.), II, 549
Pownall, Thomas (1722–1805), II, 19, 756, 959
Powys, Mrs Lybbe (*fl.* 1756–1808), II, 138
Poynder, John (1779–1849), III, 789
Poynet (or Ponet), John (1514?–1556), I, 671, 817
Poynting, John Henry (1852–1914), III, 940
Poyntz, Sir Francis (d. 1528), I, 800
Poyntz, Sydnam (*fl.* 1624–50), I, 772, 841
Praed, Mrs Campbell (*fl.* 1881–1902), III, **1096**
Praed, Winthrop Mackworth (1802–1839), III, 247 f.
Pranceriana (18 cent.), II, 231 (2), 234
Pratensis, Felix, I, 677
Prater, The (1756), II, 664
Pratt, — (*fl.* 1596), I, 662
Pratt, John Tidd (1797–1870), III, 987
Pratt, Josiah (1768–1844), I, 697; III, 824, 852
Pratt, Samuel Jackson ('Courtney Melmoth') (1749–1814), II, 26, 148, 257 (2), **377**, 547–8 (3), 560
Pratt, William (*fl.* 1554), I, 765
Prattler, The (1740), II, 663
PRAYER BOOK, THE, I, 676 f.
PRAYERS
  Latin. See under Writings in Latin, I, 98 f. (5–10 cents.)
  Old English, I, 80 f.
  Prayer Book, I, 676 f.
PREACHING, MANUALS ON, I, 301 f. (M.E.), 679 f. (16 cent.), 694 f. (17 cent.); II, 24 f. (17, 18 cents.)
Preaty Interlude called, Nice Wanton, A (16 cent.), I, 515
Preceptive, Moral, and Sentimental Pieces (18 cent.), II, 253
Préchac, Sieur de, II, 534, 795
Precipitate Choice, The (18 cent.), II, 547
PRE-HISTORY (writings on), III, 913 f.
Prelleur, P. (*fl.* 1745), II, 200, 211, 215, 227, 239
Prendergast, G. L. (*fl.* 1857), I, 463
Prendergast, John Patrick (1808–1893), III, 928 f.
Prendeville, J. (*fl.* 1840), I, 466
Prentice, Archibald (1792–1857), II, 993
PRERAPHAELITISM, III, 160
PRESBYTERIAN WRITERS, II, 862 f.
Prescot, Kenrick (*fl.* 1773), I, 593; II, 18
Prescott, Henrietta, later Lady Lushington (d. 1875), III, 573
Prescott, W. H. (*fl.* 1850), III, 376
Prescott's Manchester Journal (1771), II, 726
Present for Children, A (18 cent.), II, 561
Present State of Europe, The (1690), II, 674, 676, 705 (2)
Present State of Europe; Or, The Monthly Account of All Occurrences, The (1692), II, 676, 705
Present State of the Republic of Letters, The (1728), II, 675
President's Guide, The (18 cent.), II, 255
PRESS, THE. See under NEWSPAPERS
Press, The (Dublin, 1797), II, 736
Press, The (1853), III, 794, 814
PRESS AGENCIES, III, 782
Press and St James's Chronicle, The (1866), II, 710
Pressly, David L. (*fl.* 1879), III, 806 (2)

PRESSWORK, III, 78f.

Prest, Thomas Peckett (*fl.* 1837), III, 438, 441 (2), 442

PRESTON

Newspapers, II, 727f.

Preston, John (1587–1628), I, 699

Preston, Richard (1768–1850), II, 965

Preston, Richard Graham, Viscount (1648–1695), II, 121, 764

Preston, Samuel Tolver (b. 1844), III, 940

Preston, Thomas (1537–1598), I, 520, 523

Preston, William (1753–1807), II, 19, 23, 229, 477

Preston Journal, The (1744), II, 727

Preston Review and County Advertiser, The (1793), II, 728

Preston Songster, The (18 cent.), II, 243

Prestwich, Edmund (*fl.* 1651), I, 477, 649, 807

Prestwich, Sir Joseph (1812–1896), III, 952

Pretended Saint and the Prophane Libertine, The (17 cent.), I, 719

Pretie new Enterlude of Kyng Daryus, A (16 cent.), I, 516

Pretty Little Poems for Pretty Little Children (18 cent.), II, 563

Pretty Plaything for children of all Denominations, A (18 cent.), II, 562

Pretyman, J. R. (*fl.* 1878), III, 976

Prevost, Sir George (1804–1893), III, 855–6

Prévost d'Exiles, Antoine François, II, 33, 48, 72, 140, 542–3, 795

Price, Bonamy (1807–1888), III, 127, 974

Price, David (1762–1835), III, 1070, 1075

Price, Ellen, later Mrs Henry Wood (1814–1887), III, 571f.

Price, Frederick George Hilton (1842–1909), III, 973

Price, H. (*fl.* 1736), II, 761

Price, James (*fl.* 1673), II, 808

Price, John (1600–1676?), classical scholar, I, 863

Price, John (*fl.* 1728), translator, II, 786

Price, Joseph (*fl.* 1783), II, 143

Price, L. L. F. R. (b. 1862), III, 975, 984

Price, Laurence (*fl.* 1625–80?), I, 732

Price, Martin (*fl.* 1821), III, 768

Price, Sir R. D. G. (*fl.* 1885), III, 761

Price, Richard (1723–1791), II, 109, 797, **956**

Price, Richard John Lloyd (*fl.* 1884), III, 767

Price, T. (*fl.* 1837–50), III, 824

Price, Sir Uvedale (1747–1829), II, 20, 30, 148, 762

Price, William (d. 1666), I, 695

Price, William Charles (*fl.* 1777), II, 761

PRICES OF MERCHANDISE (newspapers advertising), II, 717f.

Prices of Merchandise in London, The (1667), II, 717

Prichard, H. M. (*fl.* 1880), III, 1092

Prichard, Iltudus Thomas (*fl.* 1864–80), III, 1069, 1077

Prichard, James Cowles (1786–1848), III, 892, 963, **967**

Pricke of Conscience (M.E.), I, **185**

Pride of Life, The (16 cent.), I, 514

Prideaux, Frederick (1817–1891), III, 987

Prideaux, Humphrey (1648–1724), II, **875**

Prideaux, John (1578–1650), I, 695

Prideaux, John Selby (1788–1867), III, 956

Priestley, Joseph (1733–1804)

Educational works, II, 18, 109, 119

Miscellaneous works, II, 18, 113, 126, 635, 681, 883

Philosophical writings, II, 952, **956**

Scientific writings, II, 961; III, 945

Primaleon, I, 818

Primer (M.E.), I, **186**

Primer, or, Office of the B. Virgin, The (1706), II, 187

Primerose, James (d. 1659), I, 890

Primi-Ammonio, Giovanni Battista, II, 813

Prince, John (1643–1723), I, 688

Prince, John Critchley (1808–1866), III, **304**

Prince, William (*fl.* 1789), II, 718

Prince d'Amour, Le (17 cent.), II, 173, 175

Prince of Priggs Revels, The (17 cent.), I, 653

Prince's London Price Current (1796), II, 718

Prince's United with The London Price Current (1823), II, 718

Princely Pellican, The (17 cent.), I, 720

Principles of Free-Masonry Delineated, The (18 cent.), II, 232

Pringle, Thomas (1789–1834), III, **241**, 825

Pringle-Pattison, Andrew, earlier Seth (1856–1931), III, **873**

Prinsep, Henry Thoby (1792–1878), III, 1075

Prinsep, James (1799–1840), III, 1076

Printer, The (1843), III, 88

PRINTERS, I, 350f. (1500–1660); II, 83 (1660–1800), 90f. (1660–1800); III, 86f. (19 cent.)

Printers' Journal, The (1865), III, 88

Printers' Register, The (1863), III, 88

PRINTING, I, 348f. (1500–1660), 585f. (Shakespeare); II, 82f. (1660–1800); III, 75f. (19 cent.)

Printing style, III, 85

Private printing, III, 85f.

Prior, Sir James (1790?–1869), II, 635, 637, 647, 903

Prior, Matthew (1664–1721), II, 21, 56, 58, 198, 289f., 589, 776

Prior, Melton (1845–1910), III, 787

Prior, Richard Charles Alexander (*fl.* 1872), III, 775

Prior, Robert (*fl.* 1730), II, 200

Prior, Thomas (1682?–1751), II, 160

PRISON TRACTS, I, 717f. (16, 17 cents.); II, 155f. (17, 18 cents.)

Pritchard, Andrew (1804–1882), III, 956
Pritchard, Charles (1808–1893), III, 938
Pritt, T. E. (*fl.* 1888), III, 772
PRIVATE DOCUMENTS, I, 381f. (16, 17 cents.),
    498 (theatrical). See also LETTERS,
    DIARIES, AUTOBIOGRAPHIES, etc.
Privateer, The (1892), III, 836
PRIVATEERS, II, 151 (18 cent.)
Prix Courant des Marchandises à Londres
    (1668), II, 717
Prize for Girls and Boys, The (1876), III, 578
Proast, Jonas (*fl.* 1690), II, 943
Probationary Odes (18 cent.), II, 239 (4), 240,
    246
Probyn, May (*fl.* 1881), III, **354**
Proclamation of Henry III (M.E.), I, 41
Proclus, I, 765
Procopius, I, 781
Procter, Adelaide Anne (1825–1864), III, **304**,
    433
Procter, Bryan Waller, i.e. 'Barry Cornwall'
    (1787–1874), III, **241**, 248, 636, 643
Proctor, Henry (*fl.* 1773), II, 827
Proctor, John (1521?–1584), I, 738, 824
Proctor, Percival (*fl.* 1774), II, 541, 799
Proctor, Richard Anthony (1837–1888), III,
    944
Proctor, Thomas (*fl.* 1578–84), I, 390, 403
Proctor's Price-Courant (1706), II, 717
Prodigal Son, The (16 cent.), I, 522
PRODIGAL SON PLAYS, I, 521f. (16 cent.)
PRODUCTION (theatrical), II, 405f. (17, 18
    cents.)
Professional Collection of Glees, The (18 cent.),
    II, 244
Profitable Advertising (1899), III, 780
Progress (1883), III, 831
Progresses of Queen Elizabeth, The (18 cent.),
    II, 242
Projector, The (1721), II, 662
Prologue, and an Epilogue, A [etc.] (18 cent.),
    II, 204
PROLOGUES AND EPILOGUES, COLLECTIONS OF,
    II, 393
*Prologues and Epilogues, Celebrated for their
    Poetical Merit* (18 cent.), 235
*Prologues And Epilogues, Written for the
    L.D.T.* (18 cent.), II, 255
Prolusiones Poeticae (18 cent.), II, 242
Prolusions (18 cent.), II, 220
Prompter, The (1734), II, 663
Prompter, The (1789), II, 666
Prompter, The (1830), III,.816
Promptorium Parvulorum (M.E.), I, 26
PRONUNCIATION. See PHONOLOGY, I, 34f.
Propertius, II, 767; III, 1001
PROPHECIES (M.E.), I, **167**f.
Prophecy of the Six Kings (M.E.), I, 167f.
*Propre newe Interlude of the Worlde and the
    chylde, A* (16 cent.), I, 515

PROSE, I, 11 (general histories), 12f. (general
    anthologies)
  Old English, I, 85f. For details see OLD
    ENGLISH PROSE. For Latin from 6 to 10
    cents. see under WRITINGS IN LATIN, I,
    98f.
  Middle English. For details see MIDDLE
    ENGLISH LITERATURE
  Fifteenth Century, I, 260 (Scottish), 260f.
    (English), 265f. For Latin prose 11 to 15
    cents. see under WRITINGS IN LATIN, I,
    280f.
  Renaissance to Restoration, I, 664f. (religious
    prose), 704f. (popular and miscellaneous
    prose), 823f. (history, philosophy, science
    and other forms of learning), 900f.
    (Scottish prose)
  Restoration to Romantic Revival, II, 488f.
    (fiction), 567f. (miscellaneous), 864f.
    (history, philosophy, science and other
    forms of learning), 992f. (Scottish prose)
  Nineteenth Century, III, 13f. (selections),
    364f. (fiction), **629**f. (critical and miscel-
    laneous), **861**f. (philosophy, history,
    science and other forms of learning)
Prose Alexander (M.E.), I, 144
PROSE FICTION, I, 11 (general histories)
  Middle English period, I, 161f.
  Renaissance to Restoration, I, 726f.
  Restoration to Romantic Revival, II, 488f.
    (recent criticism), 490f. (principal
    novelists), 529f. (minor fiction and
    translations), 553f. (children's books)
  Nineteenth Century, III, 364f. (biblio-
    graphies, histories, studies), 366f. (Edge-
    worth–Marryat), 387f. (minor fiction,
    1800–35), 421f. (Borrow–Meredith), 471f.
    (minor fiction, 1835–70), 513f. (Carroll–
    Kipling), 534f. (minor fiction, 1870–
    1900), 564f. (children's books), 1069f.
    (Anglo-Indian), 1086f. (Canadian), 1089f.
    (South African), 1096f. (Australia–New
    Zealand)
Prose Life of Jesus (M.E.), I, **190**
Prose Merlin (M.E.), I, **138**f.
Prose Psalter (M.E.), I, **189**
PROSE RHYTHM, I, 23f.
PROSODY
  Before Chaucer, I, 13f.
  Modern English, I, 15f. See also Chaucer's
    Versification, I, 218
Protestant Courant Imparting News, The (1682),
    II, 704
Protestant Dissenter's Magazine, The (1794), II,
    682
Protestant (Domestick) Intelligence (1680), II, 702
Protestant (Domestick) Intelligence, The (1680),
    II, 702
Protestant Garland Of Joy and Delight, The
    (17 cent.), II, 181

Protestant Intelligence, The (1724), II, 713
Protestant Intelligence, With News Foreign and Domestick, The (1724), II, 713
Protestant Medley; Or, Weekly Courant, The (1717), II, 712
Protestant Mercury. Occurrences Foreign and Domestick, The (1697), II, 706
Protestant Mercury; Or, The Exeter Post-Boy, The (1715), II, 723
Protestant Observator; Or, Democritus Flens, The (1681), II, 657
Protestant Orange Garland, The (17 cent.), II, 181
Protestant Oxford Intelligence, The (1681), II, 703
Protestant Packet, The (1716), II, 712
Protestant Packet, The (1780), II, 685
Protestant Postboy, The (1711), II, 707
Protestant Post-Boy, The (Dublin, 1712), II, 734
Protestant York Courant, The (1750), II, 730
Protestant's Magazine, The (1761), II, 678
Protester, on Behalf of the People, The (1753), II, 664
Prothero, Sir G. W. (1848–1922), III, 832
Prothero, M. (*fl.* 1895), III, 985
Prothero, R. E., Baron Ernle (*fl.* 1888), III, 832, 972
Proude Wyves Pater Noster, The (16 cent.), I, 716
Prout, William (1786–1850), III, 946
Provand, G. (*fl.* 1809), I, 902
Proverbs of Alfred (M.E.), I, 40, **180**
Proverbs of Hendyng (M.E.), I, **183**
PROVINCES, LITERATURE OF
  Bibliographies, I, 8 f.
  Magazines, II, 684 f. (1660–1800)
  Newspapers, II, 720 f. (1701–1800); III, 801 f. (19 cent.)
  Printers and Booksellers in, I, 352 f. (1500–1660); II, 86 f. (1660–1800)
  Provincial dialects, I, 45; II, 927 f.
  Stage and theatres, II, 404 f. (1660–1800)
Provincial Typographical Circular, The (1852), III, 88
Prowett, C. G. (*fl.* 1876?), III, 811
Prowse, William Jeffery Nicholas (1836–1870), III, **354**
Prude, The (18 cent.), II, 538
Pruen, Thomas (*fl.* 1804), III, 777
'Pry, Peter' (1809), III, 378
Pryce, George (1801–1868), II, 345
Pryce, Sir John (*fl.* 1573), I, 774
Pryce, William (1725?–1790), II, 927
Pryme, Abraham de la (1672–1704), II, 134
Pryme, George (1781–1868), III, 151, 980
Prynne, William (1600–1669), I, 369, 510, 714, 720, 750, **831** f.
Pryor, William (*fl.* 1659), I, 718
'Psalmanazar, George' (1679?–1763), II, 135

PSALMS (VERSIONS OF), I, **80**
  Old English, I, 80
  Middle English, I, 189
  Renaissance to Restoration, I, 677 f.
PSALTERS
  Old English, I, 80 (metrical), **95** f. (prose), 26, 32, 35, 36
  Middle English, I, 40 (prose and verse)
PSEUDO-CHAUCERIAN PIECES, I, 254
Psyche et Filii ejus (17 cent.), I, 663
PSYCHOLOGY (writings on), III, 964 f. See also under PHILOSOPHY
Public Advertiser, The (1734), II, 698
Public Advertiser, The (1752), II, 708
Public Advertiser (1768), II, 665
Public Advertiser (1779), II, 665
Public Advertiser (1792), II, 666
Public Advertiser; Or, The Theatrical Chronicle, The (Dublin, 1773), II, 736
PUBLIC DOCUMENTS
  Middle English period, I, 115
  Renaissance to Restoration, I, 380 f., 396 f., 497 f. (theatrical)
  Restoration to Romantic Revival, II, 161 f.
  Nineteenth Century, III, 120 f. (education), 843 f. (year books)
Public Gazeteer, The (1758), II, 735
Public Ledger, The (1760), II, 664–5; III, 798
Public Ledger and Evening Report, The (1870), III, 801
Public Ledger; Or, Daily Register of Commerce, The (1760), II, 709
Public Magazine, The (1760), II, 678
Public Monitor; Or, New Freeman's Journal, The (Dublin, 1772), II, 736
Public Occurrences Truely Stated (1688), II, 731
Public Opinion (1861), III, 814
Public Prompter, And Irish Journal, The (1765), II, 735
Public Register; Or, Freeman's Journal, The (Dublin, 1763), II, 735; III, 809
PUBLIC SCHOOLS, I, 125. See also SCHOOLS
Publick Advertisements (1666), II, 716
Publick Adviser, The (1657), I, 750, 763
Publick Adviser Weekly, The (1657), II, 716
Publick Intelligence (1665), II, 702
Publick Intelligence, The (1650), II, 701
Publick Intelligencer, The (1655), I, 762
Publick Intelligencer, The (1660), II, 701
Publick Intelligencer. Communicating occurrences within England, Scotland and Ireland, The (1655), II, 701
Publick Journal, The (Dublin, 1771), II, 735
Publick Occurrences Truely Stated (1688), II, 704
Publick Register; Or, Weekly Magazine, The (1741), II, 677, 715
Publisher, The (18 cent.), II, 211
Publisher, Containing Miscellanies in Prose and Verse, The (1745), II, 677

PUBLISHERS
Author's relations with, I, 349 (16, 17 cents.),
585 f. (Shakespeare); III, 96 f. (19 cent.)
Memoirs of, II, 694 f. (1660–1800); III, 97 f.
(19 cent.)
Publishers' Circular, The (1837), III, 101
Puccini, Vincenzo, II, 812
Puckle, James (1667?–1724), II, 122
Pudsey, Hugh (*fl.* 1183), I, 121
Pue, James (*fl.* 1762), II, 733
Pue, Richard (*fl.* 1762), II, 733
Pue, Sarah (*fl.* 1763), II, 733
Pue's Occurrences (1731), II, 733
Pufendorf, Samuel, II, 32
Puget de la Serre, Jean, II, 795
Pugh, John (*fl.* 1787), II, 136
Pughe, William Owen (William Owen) (1759–
1835), II, 75, 81
Pugin, Augustus Charles (1762–1832), III, 884
Pugin, Augustus Welby Northmore (1812–
1852), III, **723** f.
Pulci, Luigi, III, 39
Pullain, John (1517–1565), I, 678
Pullan, Richard Popplewell (1825–1888), III,
1001
Pullein, Samuel (*fl.* 1734–60), II, 33
Pullen, N. (*fl.* 1696), II, 791
Pullen, P. H. (*fl.* 1820), III, 112
Pullen (or Pullus), Robert (d. *c.* 1147), I, **285**
Pullin, A. W. (*fl.* 1900), III, 774
Pulman, George Philip Rigney (1819–1880),
III, 769
Pulteney, John (*fl.* 1680), II, 27
Pulteney, Richard (1730–1801), II, 925
Pulteney, William, Earl of Bath (1684–1764), II,
662
Pulton, Ferdinando (1536–1618), I, 850
Punch in Cambridge (1832), III, 834
Punch, or the London Charivari (1841), III, 794,
820
Punshon, William Morley (1824–1881), II, 493
Purbeck, the Misses (*fl.* 1791), II, 549
Purchas, Samuel (1575?–1626), I, 764, 766
Purdon, Edward (1729–1767), II, 448
Puritaine, The (17 cent.), I, 579
*Puritaine Or The Widdow of Watling Streete,
The* (17 cent.), I, 653
Puritane set forth in his Lively Colours, A
(17 cent.), I, 724
Purity (Cleanness) (M.E.), I, **202** f.
Purnell, Thomas (1834–1889), III, 70, 150
Purney, Thomas (1695–1728?), II, 22, **326**
Purser, J. (*fl.* 1746), II, 708
Purshouse, A. (*fl.* 1782), II, 19
'Purves, George' (Simon Gray), III, 975, 980
Purvey, John (1353?–1428?), I, 29, 40
Pusey, Edward Bouverie (1800–1882), III, 127,
687, 691, 856 (2), **860**
Pusey, Philip (1799–1855), III, 856, 976
Puttenham, George (d. 1590), I, 865

'Puzzlebrains, Peregrine' (1799), II, 564
'Puzzlewell, Peter' (1792), II, 564
Pycroft, James (1813–1895), III, 113, 127, 773 f.
Pye, B. (*fl.* 1766), II, 808
Pye, Henry James (1745–1813), II, 18, 26,
377 f., 550, 807, 815
Pye, John (1782–1874), III, 81
Pyle, Edmund (*fl.* 1729–63), II, 150
Pyne, William Henry (1769–1843), II, 146
Pynson, Richard (*fl.* 1510), I, 351
Pyrrye, C. (*fl.* 1569?), I, 716
'Pythias' (1812), III, 111

'Q', i.e. Sir Arthur Thomas Quiller-Couch
(b. 1863), III, **556** f.
Quadratum Musicum (17 cent.), II, 180
Quadrio, Francesco Saverio, II, 73
Quain, Richard (1800–1887), III, 113
QUAKERS, EARLY, II, 854 f.
Quakers Art of Courtship, The (17 cent.), II, 181,
189, 207
Quaritch, Bernard (1819–1899), III, 103
Quarles, Francis (1592–1644), I, **450** f., 478,
726; II, 56
Quarles, John (1624–1665), I, 477, 719
Quarles, William (*fl.* 17 cent.), I, 663
Quarterly Musical Magazine and Review, The
(1818), III, 832
Quarterly Review, The (1809), III, 832
Queen, The (1861), III, 815
Queen, Or The Excellency Of Her Sex, The
(17 cent.), I, 653
QUEEN'S COLLEGE (Oxford), I, 369
Queen's Quarterly (1894), III, 1088
Queene Hester, A new enterlude of (16 cent.), I,
515
QUEENS' COLLEGE (Cambridge), I, 370
Quelch, H. (*fl.* 1886), III, 818
Quesnay, François, II, 36
Quesnel, Pasquier, II, 795
Quesvedo Villegas, Francisco de, I, 343, 734;
II, 69, 534
Quick, Robert Herbert (1831–1891), II, 113,
140
'Quid', i.e. R. A. Fitzgerald (*fl.* 1866), III,
774 (2)
Quiller-Couch, Sir Arthur Thomas ('Q.')
(b. 1863), III, **556** f.
Quillet, Claude (*fl.* 1712), II, 312, 795
Quillinan, Dorothy (1804–1847), III, 242
Quillinan, Edward (1791–1851), III, **242**
Quilter, Harry (1851–1907), III, 829, 831
Quin, Edward (d. 1823), III, 800
Quin, James (1693–1766), II, 224
Quin, Michael Joseph (1796–1843), III, 823,
1069
Quin, Windham Thomas Wyndham, Earl of
Dunraven (1841–1926), III, 992
Quin's Jests (18 cent.), II, 224
Quinault, Philippe, II, 795

Quincey, Thomas (*fl.* 1775), II, 139
Quincy, John (d. 1722), II, 927
Quintana, Don Francisco de, II, 69, 541
Quintessence of English Poetry, The (18 cent.), II, 208
Quintilian, II, 767
Quintus Curtius, II, 765
Quinze Joyes de Mariage, Les, I, 818
Quirós, Pedro Fernández de, I, 790
Quita, Domingo, III, 597
Quittenton, Richard M. H. ('Roland Quiz') (*fl.* 1865), III, 573, 578
Quiver, The (1861), III, 829
'Quiz' (1816), III, 1068
'Quiz, Roland', i.e. Richard M. H. Quittenton (*fl.* 1865), III, 573, 578
'Quiz, Ronald' (1868), III, 575
Quiz, The (1796), II, 666
'Quizem, Caleb' (1809), III, 765
Quizzical Gazette and Merry Companion, The (1831), III, 820
QUOTATIONS, COLLECTIONS OF, I, 715f. (16, 17 cents.)
Quotidian Occurrences in and about London (1642), I, 754

R., A. (*fl.* 1614), I, 742
R., C. (*fl.* 1569), I, 741
R., C. (*fl.* 1689), II, 705
R., C. (*fl.* 1728), II, 786
R., E. (*fl.* 1678), II, 816
R., G. (*fl.* 1675), II, 787
R., H. (*fl.* 1594), I, 769
R., H. (*fl.* 1616), I, 770
R., H. (*fl.* 1757), II, 218
R., J. (*fl.* 1688), II, 271
R., J. B. (*fl.* 1795), II, 654
R., R. (*fl.* 1766), II, 626
R., T. (*fl.* 1654), I, 652
R., T. (*fl.* 1675), II, 811
R., T. (*fl.* 1698), II, 15
R., T. (*fl.* 1774), II, 449
R., W. (*fl.* 1591), I, 741
Rabaut Saint-Étienne, Jean Paul, II, 795
Rabelais, François, I, 331, 818; II, 48, 795
Rabener, Gottlieb Wilhelm, II, 58
Rabutin, Roger de, Comte de Bussy, II, 47, 542, 795
Race at Sheriff-Muir [etc.], *A* (18 cent.), II, 193
Racine, Jean, II, 42f., 485, 795
Racine, Louis, II, 796
RACING
    Books on, III, 763f.
    Calendars, II, 815f.
    Newspapers, II, 718
Racing Calendar, The (1773), II, 718
Racing Times, The (1851), III, 820
Racing World, The (1887), III, 820
RACKETS (books on), III, 775
Radcliffe, Alexander (*fl.* 1669-96), II, **285**

Radcliffe, Ann, née Ward (1764-1823), II, 14, 24; III, **414f.**, 587 (2)
Radcliffe, E. Delmé (*fl.* 1872), III, 778
Radcliffe, F. P. Delmé (*fl.* 1839), III, 760
Radcliffe, Sir George (1593-1657), I, 385
Radcliffe, John (*fl.* 1791), II, 105
Radcliffe, Richard (*fl.* 1755-83), II, 113
Radcliffe, William (*fl.* 1826), III, 414, 809
Radford, Dollie, née Maitland (b. 1858), III, **347**
Radford, Ernest (*fl.* 1882-1920), III, **354**
Radical, The (1880), III, 818
RADICAL JOURNALS, III, 815f.
RADLEY COLLEGE, III, 133
Rae, G. (*fl.* 1885), III, 973
Rae, John (*fl.* 1834), political economist, III, 981
Rae, John (*fl.* 1884-95), writer on socialism, III, 977, 985
Rae, Peter (1671-1748), II, 1002
Rae, William Fraser (1835-1905), III, 984
Raffles, Thomas (1788-1863), III, 246
Raffles, Sir Thomas Stamford (1781-1826), III, 1075
Rag, The [Cambridge] (1896), III, 835
Raigersfeld, J., Baron de, II, 151
Raikes, Harriet (*fl.* 1861), III, 150
Raikes, Robert (d. 1756), II, 697
Raikes, Thomas (1777-1848), III, 150
Railway Director, The (1845), III, 801
Railway Gazette, The (1846), III, 822
Railway Magazine, The (1897), III, 831
Railway News, The (1864), III, 822
Railway Review, The (1880), III, 818
Railway Times, The (1837), III, 821
Raimbach, Abraham (1776-1843), III, 91
Raimbach, M. T. S. (*fl.* 1843), III, 91
Raine, James (1791-1858), I, 121, 277, 286, 383 (2)
Raines, Francis Robert (1805-1878), I, 382, 385
Rainier, J. S. (*fl.* 1822), III, 970
Rainolde (or Reynolds), Richard (d. 1606), I, 376
Rainolds (or Reynolds), John (1549-1607), I, 510, 683, 857, 863
Rainolds, William (1544?-1594), I, 858
Raithby, John (1766-1826), II, 550
Raj Laksmi Debi (*fl.* 1876), III, 1069
Rajagopaul, P. (*fl.* 1820), III, 1080
Ralegh, Sir Walter (1552?-1618), I, 384, 404 (2), 768, 788, 790f., 806, **827**f.; II, 122
Raleigh, Sir Walter Alexander (1861-1922), III, **752**
Ralph de Hengham (d. 1311), I, **311**
Ralph of Acton (*fl.* 1390), I, **302**
Ralph, James (1705?-1762), II, 200, 415, 443, 663 (3), 697, 710, 713, 794
Ralph, T. S. (*fl.* 1847), I, 892

Ralston, William Ralston Shedden (1828–1889), III, 671

Ram, W. (*fl.* 1606), I, 892

Ramazzini, Bernadino, II, 812

Ramberti, Benedetto, I, 777

Ramble Round the World, A (1689), II, 658, 705

Rambler, The (1712), II, 661

Rambler, The (1750), II, 664

Rambler, The (1848), III, 828

Rambler's Magazine, The (1783), II, 680

Ramesey (or Ramsay), William (*fl.* 1645–76), I, 884; II, 122

Ramsay, Alexander (1822–1909), III, 972

Ramsay, Allan, the elder (1686–1758), II, 969 f.
    Anthologies by, II, 197 (2), 199, 201, 204, 208, 214, 216, 218, 220–3, 225 (2), 227, 231, 236–7, 242, 249 (2), 250

Ramsay, Allan, the younger (1713–1784), II, 18, 665

Ramsay, Andrew (1574–1659), I, 900

Ramsay, Sir Andrew Crombie (1814–1891), II, 949, **952**

Ramsay, Andrew Michael (1686–1743), II, 796

Ramsay, Edward Bannerman (1793–1873), III, 152

Ramsay, Sir George (1800–1871), philosopher, III, 981

Ramsay, George Gilbert (*fl.* 1869), editor of William Ramsay, III, 1002

Ramsay, John (*fl.* 1811), writer on curling, III, 777, 806

Ramsay, John (*fl.* 1848), editor of 'The Aberdeen Journal', III, 806

Ramsay, Thomas (*fl.* 1849), III, 401

Ramsay (or Ramesey), William (*fl.* 1645–76), I, 884; II, 122

Ramsay, William (1806–1865), classical scholar, III, **1002**

Ramsay, Sir William (1852–1916), chemist, III, **949**

Ramsay, Sir William Mitchell (1851–1939), theologian, III, 851

Ramsay's Waterford Chronicle (1782), II, 738

Ramsey Cartulary (M.E.), I, 122

Ramus (Pierre de la Ramée), I, 327 f., 680

Ramusio, Giovanni Battista, I, 764

Ranade, M. G. (*fl.* 1898), III, 1078

Rand, Theodore Harding (*fl.* 1900), III, 1085–6

Randall, John (*fl.* 1732), II, 433

Randall, John (*fl.* 1873), III, 760, 776

Rander, William (*fl.* 1800), II, 552

Randolph, Bernard (1643–1690?), II, 744

Randolph, John (1749–1813), II, 104

Randolph, Robert (*fl.* 1638), I, 658

Randolph, Thomas (1605–1635), I, 379, **658**

Randolph, Thomas (1701–1783), II, 115, 883 (2)

Random de Bérenger, Charles, Baron de Beaufain, III, **762**

Rands, William Brighty (1823–1882), III, 228, **304**

Ranelaugh Concert, The (18 cent.), II, 231

Ranger, The (1794), II, 666

Ranjitsinghi, K. S., Maharajah Jam Sahib of Nawanagar (d. 1933), III, 774

Rankine, William John Macquoon (1820–1872), III, **939**

Rankins, William (*fl.* 1587–1601), I, 480, 510, 713

Rann, Joseph (1733–1811), II, 915

Ransome, Arthur (*fl.* 1907), III, 787

Ranulf de Glanville (d. 1190), I, 117, **289**

Rape of the Smock (18 cent.), II, 194, 199, 206

Raper, Elizabeth (*fl.* 1756–70), II, 137

Rapin, René, II, 40, 796

Rapin-Thoyras, Paul de (1661–1725), II, 796, 876

Rare Triumphs of Love and Fortune, The (16 cent.), I, 520

Rashdall, Hastings (1858–1924), III, 851

Rask, Rasmus Christian, III, 1028

Raspe, Rudolph Erich (1737–1794), II, 59, 64, 486, 548 f., 806

Rastell, John (1470?–1536), I, 351, 514, 517, 667, 812, 851, 884

Rastell, William (1508?–1565), I, 351, 667, 851

Rarities of Richmond, The (18 cent.), II, 206 (2)

Rathmore, Lord D. R. P. (*fl.* 1867), III, 149

Rational Amusement, The (18 cent.), II, 216

Ratis Raving (M.E.), I, 40, 43

Ratseis Ghost (17 cent.), I, 717

Ratsey, *The Life and Death of Gamaliel* (17 cent.), I, 717

Rattle for Grown Children, A (18 cent.), II, 224

Ratts Rhimed to Death (17 cent.), II, 173

Rauf Coilyar (M.E.), I, 40, 43

Raunce, John (*fl.* 1650), I, 884

Ravenscroft, Edward (*c.* 1650–*c.* 1700), I, 659; II, 62, **426** f., 776, 794

Ravenscroft, Thomas (1583?–1633?), I, **485**

Raven-Hill, L. (*fl.* 1893), III, 831

Ravenstone, P. (*fl.* 1821), III, 980

Raverty, H. G. (1825–1906), III, 1071, 1074

Rawdon, Marmaduke (1610–1669), I, 386

Rawdon-Hastings, Francis, Marquis of Hastings (1754–1826), III, 149

Rawlet, John (1642–1686), II, **285**

Rawley, William (1588?–1667), I, 868, 869 (3), 870

Rawlidge, Richard (*fl.* 1627), I, 511

Rawlin, Thomas (*fl.* after 1610), I, 886

Rawlins, Edward (*fl.* 1682), II, 657, 703

Rawlins, John (*fl.* 1622), I, 771

Rawlins, Thomas, the elder (1620?–1670), medallist and playwright, I, 649

Rawlins, Thomas, the younger (*fl.* 1677), dramatist, II, **427**

Rawlins, Thomas (*fl.* 1706), pamphleteer, II, 499

Rawlinson, Christopher (1677–1733), II, 920
Rawlinson, George (1812–1902), III, **913f.**
Rawlinson, Sir Henry (Reswicke) (1810–1895), III, **1016**
Rawlinson, Richard (1690–1755), I, 843; II, 102, 788, 811, **874**
Rawlinson, Thomas (1681–1725), II, 102
Rawlinson New Testament Strophic Passages (M.E.), I, **189**
Rawlinson Prose Siege of Thebes (M.E.), I, **146**
Rawlinson Prose Troy Piece (M.E.), I, **145**
Rawnsley, Hardwicke Drummond (1850–1920), III, **354f.**
Rawstorne, Lawrence (*fl.* 1837), III, 762
Ray, James (*fl.* 1745–6), II, 151, 1002
Ray (or Wray), John (1627–1705), naturalist, I, 854; II, 740, 743, 818, 927, **961f.**
Ray, John (*fl.* 1686–90), Dublin printer, II, 733
Raya Raja Ramomohana (*fl.* 1820), III, 1073, 1081, 1082, 1083
Rayleigh, John William Strutt, Baron (1842–1918), III, 940
Raymond, G. (*fl.* 1845), III, 584
Raymond, H. (*fl.* 1897), III, 1090
Raymond, J. G. (*fl.* 1807), III, 232 (2)
Raymond, John (*fl.* 1646), I, 772
Raymond, Oliver (*fl.* 1866), III, 771
Raymond, Richard John (*fl.* 1818), III, **594**
Raymond, Samuel (*fl.* 1854), II, 625
Raymond, Thomas (*c.* 1610–*c.* 1681), I, 386
Raynal, Guillaume Thomas François, II, 796
Raynalde, Thomas (*fl.* 1540–1551), I, 890
Rayner, G. (*fl.* 1887), III, 578
Rayner, William (*fl.* 1797), II, 763
Rayner's London Morning Advertiser (1742), II, 707
Rayner's Morning Advertiser (1735), II, 707
Reach, Angus Bethune (1821–1856), III, **724**
Read, Alexander (1586?–1641), I, 891
Read, Carveth (1848–1931), III, **872**
Read, Sir Charles Hercules (1857–1929), III, 969
Read, J. M. (*fl.* 1860), III, 78
Read, James (*fl.* 1715), II, 712
Read, John (*fl.* 1587), I, 891
Read, S. (*fl.* 1821–9), III, 975, 981
Read, T. (*fl.* 1724), II, 713
Read, Walter William (1855–1907), III, 774
Read's Weekly Journal; Or, British Gazetteer (1730), II, 712
Reade, Charles (1814–1884), III, **455f.**
Reade, John (*fl.* 1870), III, 1086
Reade, John Edmund (1800–1870), III, 200
Reade, William Winwood (1838–1875), III, 872, 992
Reader, The (1714), II, 661
Reader, The (1863), III, 818
READERS
 Old English, I, 36. See also ANTHOLOGIES, I, 54, 62, 85

 Middle English. See COLLECTIONS OF SELECTED PIECES, I, 114
 Modern English. See BOOKS OF EXTRACTS, I, 46
READING
 Magazine, II, 685 (1794)
 Newspapers, II, 728
 University, III, 128
Reading, John (1588–1667), I, 720
Reading, William (1674–1744), II, 104 (2)
Reading Journal and Weekly Review, The (1741), II, 728
Reading Mercury, and Oxford Gazette, The (1745), II, 728
Reading Mercury and Oxford Gazette, The (1767), II, 728
Reading Mercury; Or, Weekly Entertainer, The (1723), II, 728
Reading Mercury; or, Weekly Post, The (1737), II, 728
Real John Bull, The (1821), III, 811
REALISM, III, 67
Reaper, The (1796), II, 666
Reardon, J. P. (*fl.* 1848), I, 511 (2), 580
Reasoner, The (1784), II, 666
Reasoner, The (1846), III, 817
Rebellion of Naples, The (17 cent.), I, 653
Recommendation to Mercurius Morbicus, A (17 cent.), I, 724
Reconciler, The (1713), II, 661
Record, The (1818), III, 818
Record, The (1828), III, 810
Recorde, Robert (1510?–1588), I, 378, 880, 882, 888
Records of Love (1710), II, 676
Recreations in Agriculture [etc.] (1799), II, 683
Recuyell of the Histories of Troye (M.E.), I, 145
Red Republican, The (1850), III, 817
Redding, Cyrus (1785–1870), II, 528; III, 184, 212, 219, 787, 800, 825
Rede, Leman Thomas (d. 1832), II, 771, 922
Rede, William Leman (1802–1847), III, **606f.**
Redesdale, John Freeman Mitford, Baron (1748–1830), II, 890
Redford, John (d. 1547), I, 515
Redgrave, Alexander (*fl.* 1878), III, 987
Redgrave, Jasper A. (*fl.* 1878), III, 987
Redhouse, Sir James William (1811–1892), III, **1021**
Redi, Francesco, III, 39
Redpath, Robert (*fl.* 1860?), III, 803
Reece, Robert (1838–1891), III, **627f.**
Reed, Sir Charles (1819–1881), III, 105
Reed, Daniel (*fl.* 1872), III, 808
Reed, Sir Edward James (1830–1906), III, 822
Reed, Edward (*fl.* 1709–20), II, 153
Reed, Isaac (1742–1807), II, **904**
Reed, Joseph (1723–1787), II, **481f.**, 906
Reed, T. A. (*fl.* 1869), III, 781
Reed, Talbot Baines (1852–1893), III, 569

Reed, W. (*fl.* 1809), i, 849
Rees, Abraham (*fl.* 1778–1819), ii, 119
Rees, Josiah (1744–1804), ii, 685
Rees, Thomas (1777–1864), iii, 93
Rees, William Jenkins (1772–1855), i, 98
Reeve, Clara (1729–1807), ii, 24, 31, 548 (2), 549, 551
Reeve, Henry (1813–1895), i, 773, 834; iii, 787, 790, 832
Reeve, Lovell Augustus (1814–1865), iii, 818, 952
Reeves, Helen Buckingham, née Mathers (1853–1920), iii, 554f.
Reeves, John (*fl.* 1757), ii, 816
Reeves, John (1752?–1829), legal historian, i, 848
Reeves, W. (*fl.* 1857), i, 102
Reeves, William (1815–1892), iii, 1047, 1049 (2)
Reeves, William Pember (*fl.* 1898), iii, 977, 1095
Referee, The (1877), iii, 813
REFERENCE, WORKS OF
General Literary Reference-Books, i, 3f., 11f. See also DICTIONARIES, LITERARY HISTORIES, etc.
Reflections, Moral, Comical, Satyrical &c. (18 cent.), ii, 187 (3), 188 (5)
Reflector, The (1811), iii, 832
Reflector, The [Cambridge] (1888), iii, 835
Reformer, The (1748), ii, 663
Reformer, The (1776), ii, 665
Reformist's Register and Weekly Commentary, The (1817), iii, 816
Regimen Animarum (M.E.), i, 301
Reginald of Canterbury (d. *c.* 1109), i, 283
Register Book of Shipping, The (1760), ii, 718
Register of the Times, The (1794), ii, 682
Register of the Trade of the Port of London, A (1776), ii, 719
Regius (Loys Le Roy), i, 800
Regnard, Jean François, ii, 43, 796
Regnauld de Segrais, Jean, ii, 533f., 792, 797
Rehearsal, The (1704), ii, 659
Rehearsal Rehears'd In a Dialogue between Bayes and Johnson, The (1706), ii, 660
Reid, A. (*fl.* 1897), iii, 779
Reid, Alexander (1640–1706), ii, 993
Reid, Andrew (d. 1767?), ii, 675
Reid, H. L. (*fl.* 1888), iii, 979
Reid, Sir Hugh Gilzean (*fl.* 1859–68), ii, 991; iii, 791, 804
Reid, John (1808–1841?), i, 353; iii, 797
Reid, Peter (*fl.* 1780), ii, 665
Reid, Thomas (1710–1796), ii, 956
Reid, Thomas Mayne (1818–1883), iii, 503f., 801, 821
Reid, Sir Thomas Wemyss (1842–1905), iii, 803, 814, 919
Reid, Walter (*fl.* after 1858), iii, 802

Reid, William Hamilton (*fl.* 1793–1816), ii, 858
Reilly's Weekly Oracle (1736), ii, 735
Reitz, F. W. (*fl.* 1913), iii, 1090
Relhan, Anthony (*fl.* 1761), ii, 154
RELIGION (writings on)
Old English, i, 78f. (religious and didactic poems), 95f. (gospels and psalters). See also under CAEDMON SCHOOL, i, 73f., CYNEWULF SCHOOL, i, 75f., ALFREDIAN PROSE, i, 85f., LATER PROSE, i, 89f. For Latin works (5–10 cents.) see under WRITINGS IN LATIN, i, 98f.
Middle English, i, 168f. (sermons and saints' legends), 177f. (moral and religious instruction), 191f. (Rolle and associated pieces), 201f. (Pearl group), 203f. (Wycliffe and associated writings). For Latin works (11–15 cents.) see under WRITINGS IN LATIN, i, 280f.
Renaissance to Restoration, i, 376 (catechisms), 664f. (humanists and reformers), 672f. (English Bible), 676f. (Prayer Book), 677f. (versions of Psalms), 679f. (sermons and devotional writings, 1500–1620), 688f. (Marprelate controversy), 694f. (Caroline divines), 855f. (biblical scholars), 856f. (edns of early fathers and schoolmen), 857f. (disputational learning), 858f. (ecclesiastical and theological learning), 900f. (Scottish writers)
Restoration to Romantic Revival, ii, 845f. (Restoration divines), 850f. (18 cent. divines), 854f. (early Quakers), 857f. (mystics), 861f. (dissenters)
Nineteenth Century, iii, 60f. and 68f. (religion and science), 159f. (religion and poetry), 818f. (religious weeklies), 844 (religious year books), 846f. (liberal theologians and evangelicals), 854f. (Oxford movement and high churchmen), 920f. (ecclesiastical historians)
Religious Magazine, The (1760), ii, 686
Reliques of Ancient English Poetry (18 cent.), ii, 223 (2), 224–5, 231, 244, 246, 249
Reliquiae Wottonianae (17 cent.), ii, 176, 180
Relph, Josiah (1712–1743), ii, 326
Remains Concerning Britain (17 cent.), ii, 177
Remarkable Occurrences from the High Court of Parliament (1642), i, 753
Remarkable Passages (1643), i, 755
Remarkable Passages, or a Perfect Diurnall of the weekly proceedings in both Houses of Parliament (1642), i, 754
Remarkeable Passages in Parliament (1642), i, 753
Remedies against Discontentment (16 cent.), i, 725
Remedium Melancholiae (17 cent.), ii, 182
Remembrancer, The (1747), ii, 663
Remembrancer, The (1766), ii, 665

Remembrancer; Or, Impartial Repository of Public Events, The (1775), II, 680

Remonstrance of Londons Occurrences, A (17 cent.), I, 720

RENAISSANCE, CULT OF, III, 53f.

RENAISSANCE TO RESTORATION, DRAMA OF
Bibliographies, Collections of Plays, General Criticism, I, 487f.
Early Comedies, I, 517f.
Early Tragedies, I, 522f.
Jacobean and Caroline Dramatists (Chapman–Shirley), I, 609f.
Later Elizabethan Dramatists (Lyly–Nashe), I, 524f.
Minor Elizabethan Drama (1580–1603), I, 534f.
Minor Jacobean and Caroline Drama (1603–60), I, 640f.
Moralities, I, 513f
Shakespeare, I, 539f.
University Plays (1500–1642), I, 654f.

RENAISSANCE TO RESTORATION, HISTORY, PHILOSOPHY, SCIENCE, ETC. OF
Economists and Political Theorists, I, 843f.
Historians, Biographers and Antiquaries, I, 823f.
Legal Writers, I, 847f.
Literary Criticism, I, 863f.
Philosophical Writers, I, 868f.
Scholars and Scholarships, I, 852f.
Science and Pseudo-Science, I, 879f.

RENAISSANCE TO RESTORATION, INTRODUCTION TO
Bibliographies and Collections of Reprints, I, 317f.
Book Production and Distribution, I, 345f.
Education, I, 364f.
Literary Histories, etc., I, 319f.
Literary Relations with the Continent, I, 325f.
Political Background, I, 396f.
Social Background, I, 380f.

RENAISSANCE TO RESTORATION, POETRY OF
Elizabethan Sonneteers, I, 427f.
Emblem Books, I, 478f.
Epigrammatists and Formal Satirists, I, 479f.
Jacobean and Caroline Poets (Donne–Traherne), I, 440f.
Milton, I, 463f.
Minor Jacobean and Caroline Verse (1603–60), I, 473f.
Minor Tudor Verse (1500–1603), I, 434f.
Miscellanies, Anthologies, Critical Surveys, I, 403f.
Song Books, I, 481f.
Tudor Poets (Skelton–Barnfield), I, 408f.
See also under MINOR POPULAR LITERATURE, I, 712f. and TRANSLATIONS INTO ENGLISH, I, 799

RENAISSANCE TO RESTORATION, POPULAR AND MISCELLANEOUS PROSE OF
Books of Travel, I, 763f.
Character-Books and Essays, I, 721f.
Minor Popular Literature, I, 712f.
News-Sheets and News-Books, I, 736f.
Pamphleteers and Miscellaneous Writers (Rich–Brathwaite), I, 704f.
Prose Fiction, I, 726f.
Translations into English, I, 799f.

RENAISSANCE TO RESTORATION, RELIGIOUS PROSE OF
Caroline Divines (1620–60), I, 694f.
English Bible, I, 672f.
Hooker, I, 685f.
Humanists and Reformers (Linacre-Fulke), I, 664f.
Marprelate Controversy, I, 688f.
Prayer Book, I, 676f.
Sermons and Devotional Writings (Fisher–Donne), I, 679f.
Versions of Psalms, I, 677f.

RENAISSANCE TO RESTORATION, SCOTTISH LITERATURE OF
General Introduction, I, 895f.
Poetry and Drama, I, 896f.
Prose, I, 900f.

Render, William (*fl.* 1790–1801), II, 51, 61, 63, 486 (2)

Rennell, James (1742–1830), III, 1075

Rennell, James Rennell Rodd, Baron (b. 1858), III, **356**

Renneville, René Augustin Constantin de, II, 797

Rennie, James (1787–1867), II, 841

Rennie, S. (*fl.* 1866), III, 1077

Renouf, Sir Peter le Page (1822–1897), III, 1015

Renowned History of Primrose Prettyface, The (18 cent.), II, 562

Renton, A. Wood (*fl.* 1897), III, 986

Renwick, William (1740?–1814), II, 549

Repertory of Arts and Manufactures, The (1794), III, 823

Repertory of Patent Inventions, and Other Discoveries in Arts, Manufactures and Agriculture, The (1825), III, 823

Reply of Friar Daw Thopias (M.E.), I, **200**

Repository, The (1752), II, 215

Repository; or, General Review, The (1756), II, 217, 678

Repository, The (1777), II, 232, 237 (2), **244**

Repository, The (1788), II, 681

Repository; Containing Various Political Articles, The (1782), II, 680

Repository; Or, Library of Fugitive Pieces, The (1763), II, 687

Repository; or, Treasury of Politics and Literature, The (1769), II, 679

Repository; Or, Treasury of Politics and Literature, The (1770), II, 679

Repository; Or, Weekly General Entertainer, The (1770), II, 684
Representative, The (1821), III, 811
Representative, The (1826), III, 799
Reprisal, The (1717), II, 662
REPTON SCHOOL, I, 373; III, 839
Repton, Humphrey (1752–1818), II, 30, 148; III, 701
Republican, The (1817), III, 816
Republican Herald, The (1873), III, 817
Reresby, Sir John (1634–1689), I, 388, 773
Reresby, Tamworth (*fl.* 1721), II, 16, 196
'Resident Member of the University' (1835), III, 123
Restif de la Bretonne, Nicolas Anne Edme (*fl.* 1790), II, 797
Respublica (16 cent.), I, 515
RESTORATION TO ROMANTIC REVIVAL, DRAMA OF
Adaptations and Translations, II, 40f. (French-English), 43f. (English-French), 59f. (German-English, English-German), 484f.
Catalogues (Trade), II, 96 (1660–1800)
Early Eighteenth-Century Dramatists, II, 430f.
General Introduction, II, 392f. (collections of plays), 393 (collections of prologues and epilogues), 393f. (dictionaries of plays and dramatists, general histories), 395f. (special studies), 397f. (dramatic theory and criticism), 400f. (Collier controversy)
LaterEighteenth-CenturyDramatists,II,445f.
Minor Drama, 1660–1700, II, 417f.
Minor Drama, 1700–1750, II, 434f.
Minor Drama, 1750–1800, II, 459f.
Restoration Dramatists, II, 410f.
Theatres and Actors, II, 402f. (theatres and theatrical history), 405f. (production, costume, etc.), 407f. (actors and acting)
RESTORATION TO ROMANTIC REVIVAL, HISTORY, PHILOSOPHY, SCIENCE, ETC. OF
Classical and Oriental Scholars, II, 933f.
Historians, Biographers and Antiquaries, II, 864f.
Legal Literature, II, 962f.
Literary Historians and Antiquaries, II, 892f.
Literature of Science, II, 959f.
Philosophers, II, 939f., 957f. (economic theory)
RESTORATION TO ROMANTIC REVIVAL, INTRODUCTION TO
Bibliographies, II, 3f.
Book Production and Distribution, II, 81f.
Education, II, 107f.
Literary Histories, II, 4f.
Literary Relations with the Continent, II, 31f.
Literary Theory, II, 9f.
Medieval Influences, II, 73f.
Political Background, II, 161f.
Social Background, II, 132f.

RESTORATION TO ROMANTIC REVIVAL, MISCELLANEOUS PROSE OF
Books of Travel, II, 739f.
Diarists and Letter-Writers, II, 827f.
Essayists and Pamphleteers, II, 567f.
Literature of Sport, II, 814f.
Periodical Publication, II, 656f. (dialogue papers), 660f. (periodical essay), 668f. (magazines and reviews), 688f. (newspapers)
Religious Prose, II, 845f.
Translations into English, II, 757f.
RESTORATION TO ROMANTIC REVIVAL, POETRY OF
Anthologies (modern), II, 257f.
Collections, II, 259f.
Early Eighteenth-Century Poets, II, 289f.
Later Eighteenth-Century Poets, II, 333f.
Minor Verse, 1660–1700, II, 277f.
Minor Verse, 1700–1750, II, 308f.
Minor Verse, 1750–1800, II, 350f.; Influences, II, 45f. (French-English, English-French), 55f. (German-English, English-German), 66f. (Italian-English, English-Italian)
Miscellanies, II, 173f.
Recent Criticism, II, 169f.
Restoration Poets, II, 260f.
RESTORATION TO ROMANTIC REVIVAL, PROSE FICTION OF
Children's Books, II, 553f.
French-English, II, 46f.
English-French, II, 49f.
German-English, II, 62f.
English-German, II, 64f.
English-Italian, II, 67
Spanish-English, II, 68f.
English-Dutch, II, 70
Minor Fiction and Translations, II, 529f.
Principal Novelists, II, 490f.
Recent Criticism, II, 488f.
RESTORATION TO ROMANTIC REVIVAL, SCOTTISH LITERATURE OF
General Introduction, II, 966f.
Poetry and Drama, II, 967f.
Prose, II, 992f.
Restorer, The (1711), II, 661
Resurrection of Our Lord, The (16 cent.), I, 515
Retail Booksellers' and Bookbuyers' Advocate, The (1836), III, 101
Retingdon, Philip (d. 1424), I, 313
Retired Pleasures (18 cent.), II, 241, 246
Retrospector, The (1754), II, 664
Retrospective Review, The (1820), III, 826
Returne from Parnassus, The (17 cent.), I, 662
Retz, Cardinal de (Paul de Gondi), II, 781
Retzer, Joseph (*fl.* 1783), II, 236, 238–9
Reuss, Jeremias David (*fl.* 1780–1804), II, 924
Revelations of Saint Birgitta, The (15 cent.), I, 266

Reveller, The (18 cent.), II, **220** (2)
Revenge for Honour (17 cent.), I, 653
Reveur, The (1737), II, 663
Review and Sunday Advertiser, The (1789), II, 716; III, 810
Review of Historical Publications relating to Canada (1897), III, 1088
Review of Reviews, The (1890), III, 831
Review of the Affairs of France, The (1704), II, 659
Review of the State of the British Nation, A (1709), II, 659
Review of the State of the English Nation, A (1705), II, 659
REVIEWS (literary), II, 668f.; III, 818 (weeklies)
Revival, The (1859), III, 819
Revived. The Delicate Jester (19 cent.), II, 256
Rewle of Sustris Menouressess (15 cent.), I, 46
Reynard the fox (17 cent.), II, 807
Reynardson, Charles Thomas Samuel Birch (*fl.* 1875), III, 765
Reynardson, Francis (1694?–1725), II, 409
Reynold (or Rainolde), Richard (d. 1606), I, 376
Reynolds, Beatrice (*fl.* 1855), III, 507
Reynolds, Edward (1599–1676), I, 366, **699**
Reynolds, Edward (*fl.* 1880), III, 812
Reynolds, Emerson (1843–1920), III, 949
Reynolds, Frederick (1764–1841), II, **482**f., 486
Reynolds, George William McArthur (1814–1879), III, 440, **504**f., 787, 812, 814, 817
Reynolds, Henry (*fl.* 1627–32), I, 649, 805, 819, 866
Reynolds, James (1805–1866), III, **1021**
Reynolds (or Rainolds), John (1549–1607), I, 683, 857, 863
Reynolds, John (*fl.* 1621–50), I, 461, 731; II, 121
Reynolds, John (*fl.* 1685), novelist, II, 531
Reynolds, John Hamilton (1796–1825), III, 223, 233–4, **242**
Reynolds, Sir Joshua (1723–1792), II, 14, 616, 625, **629**f., 748
Reynolds, Osborne (1842–1912), III, 940
Reynolds, Samuel William (1773–1835), III, 91
Reynolds, Thomas (1771–1836), II, 159
Reynold's Miscellany (1847), III, 814
Reynolds's Newspaper, III, 794
Reynolds's Political Instructor (1849), III, 817
Reynolds' Weekly Newspaper (1850), III, 812
Rhapsodist, The (1757), II, 664
Rhapsody, The (1712), II, 661
Rhapsody, The (1750), II, 214
RHETORIC, TEXTBOOKS OF, I, 376 (16, 17 cents.)
Rhind, William (*fl.* 1833), III, 405
Rhoades, James (1841–1923), III, **355**
Rhodes, Hugh (*fl.* 1550), I, 264, 378, 396
Rhodes, William Barnes (1772–1826), III, **594**
RHYME. See under PROSODY, I, 13ff.
Rhyming Poem (O.E.), I, **84**f.

Rhynd, M. (*fl.* 1804), III, 77
RHYTHM
  Prose, I, 23f.
  Verse. See under PROSODY, I, 13f.
Riach, T. (*fl.* 1890?), III, 803
Ribaut, Jean, I, 786
Ribblesdale, T. Lister, Baron (1854–1925), III, 761
Ricardo, David (1772–1823), III, 972–3, 978, **980**
Ricaut (or Rycaut), Sir Paul (1628–1700), II, 68, 743, 813, **869**
Riccoboni, Luigi, II, 31, 797
Riccoboni, Marie Jeanne, II, 48, 552, 797
Rice, James (1843–1882), III, 764
Rice, John (*fl.* 1765–79), I, 16; II, 131
Rich, Barnabe (1540?–1617), I, **704**, 718, 725, 728, 775, 802
Rich, Claudius James (1787–1820), II, 992
Rich, Edmund (d. 1240), I, **301**
Rich, Jeremiah (d. 1660?), II, 129
Rich, Mary, Countess of Warwick (1625–1678), II, 133
Rich, Richard (*fl.* 1610), I, 790
Rich Cabinet, The (17 cent.), I, 725
Richard de Coniton (or Conyngton) (*fl.* 1310), I, **303**
Richard of Bury (1281–1345), I, **311**
Richard of Devizes (*fl.* 1189–92), I, 116
Richard of Hexham (*fl.* 1138–54), I, 116
Richard of St Victor (d. *c.* 1173), I, **287**
Richard of Salerno (d. 1252), I, **299**
Richard of Wendover (d. 1252), I, **299**
Richard Rufus of Cornwall (*fl.* 1250), I, **292**
Richard the Englishman (or of Wendover and of Salerno) (d. 1252), I, **299**
Richard, John (*fl.* 1780), II, 746
Richard Coer de Lyon (M.E.), I, **150**
Richard Reilly. The Dublin News-Letter (1736), II, 735
Richard the Redeless (M.E.), I, **200**
Richard the Third, The True Tragedie of (16 cent.), I, 538
Richards, Alfred Bate (1820–1876), III, 798–9, 811
Richards, George (1767–1837), II, 23, 77
Richards, Godfrey (*fl.* 1668), II, 812
Richards, Grant (b. 1872), III, 99
Richards, J. (*fl.* 1822), III, 978
Richards, John (*fl.* 1697–1702), II, 135
Richards, Nathaniel (1612?–1654?), I, 477
Richardson, Mrs — (*fl.* 1808), III, 571
Richardson, David Lester (1801–1865), III, 7, 1068, 1083
Richardson, Gabriel (d. 1642), I, 779
'Richardson, Henry Handel', i.e. Henrietta Richardson, later Robertson (*fl.* 1908), III, 1097
Richardson, J. (*fl.* 1755), of Newent, II, 17
Richardson, J. Hall (b. 1857), III, 787

Richardson, John (*fl.* 1773), of York, II, 58, 63, 552
Richardson, John (1741–1811 ?), orientalist, III, 1073, 1075
Richardson, Sir John (1787–1865), arctic explorer, III, 956
Richardson, John (1797–1863), Canadian journalist, III, 1086–7
Richardson, Jonathan, the elder (1665–1745), II, 17, 30, 909
Richardson, Jonathan, the younger (1694–1771), II, 294, 301, 909
Richardson, Joseph (1755–1803), II, **378**
Richardson, Richard (*fl.* 1747), I, 468
Richardson, Robert (1663–1741), botanist and antiquary, II, 965
Richardson, Robert (1850–1901), III, 1095
Richardson, Samuel (1689–1761), II, 50, 64, 67, 69, 70, 92, **514**f., 615, 789
Richardson, Thomas (*fl.* 1828), III, 585
Richardson, W. H. (*fl.* 1864), III, 71
Richardson, William (1698–1775), antiquary, I, 838
Richardson, William (1743–1814), Glasgow critic, II, 25, 746, 755
Richardson's New Minor Drama, III, 585
Richardus Anglicus (*fl.* 1196), I, **289**
Richey, Alexander George (1830–1883). See Richie
Richie (or Richey), Alexander George (1830–1883), III, **906**
Richmond, L. (*fl.* 1864), III, 976
Richmond, Legh (1772–1827), III, 572
Richmond, Mary Elizabeth (*fl.* 1898), III, 1095
Richmond and Derby, Margaret Beaufort, Countess of (1443–1509), I, 266
Richmond (Yorks.) Register (M.E.), I, 122
Richson, Charles (1806–1874), III, 118
Richter, Johann Paul Friedrich ('Jean Paul'), III, 33 f.
Rickards, Sir George Kettilby (1812–1889), III, 976
Rickards, R. (*fl.* 1829), III, 1075
Rickets, J. (*fl.* 1625–33), I, 658
Rickman, John (*fl.* 1781), II, 742
Rickman, Thomas ('Clio') (1761–1834), II, 252
Rid, Samuel (*fl.* 1612), I, 717
Riddell, Mrs J. H., née Charlotte Elizabeth Lawson Cowan (1832–1906), III, **557**f.
Riddell, James (1823–1866), III, 999, **1002**
Riddell, Maria (*fl.* 1792), II, 757
RIDDLES
  Latin (Irish), I, 103, 104
  Old English, I, 28, 32, 35, **72** f.
  Renaissance to Restoration, I, 716
Rider, Henry (*fl.* 1638), I, 803
Rider, John (1562–1632), I, 375
Rider, William (*fl.* 1655), I, 649
Rider, William (1723–1785), II, 552, 923
Ridge, L. L. (*fl.* 1868), III, 102

Ridgeway, Sir William (1853–1926), III, 968
Ridgway, J. (*fl.* 1810), III, 668
RIDING (books on), I, 393 (1500–1660), II, 815 f. (1660–1800); III, 765 f. (19 cent.). See also RACING and HUNTING
Ridley, James (1736–1765), II, 546, 664
Ridley, Mark (1560–1624), I, 885
Ridley, Nicholas (1500?–1555), I, **670**
Ridout, Matilda, later Lady Edgar, III, 1087
Ridpath, George (d. 1726), whig journalist, I, 910; II, 156, 401, 675, 697, 706
Ridpath, George (1717?–1772), Scottish historian, II, 994, 998
Ridpath, Philip (1721–1788), II, 764
Riedesel, Friderike Charlotte Luise von, Baroness, II, 151
Riem, Andreas, II, 141
Riesch, Isaak Wolfgang de, Baron, II, 141
Rievaulx Cartulary (M.E.), I, 122
Rigby, Edward (1747–1821), II, 747; III, 970
Rigby, Elizabeth, later Lady Eastlake (1809–1893), III, 435, **712**f.
Rigg, J. C. (*fl.* 1848), III, 819
Rigg, James Harrison (1821–1909), III, 721
Rights of Irishmen; Or, National Evening Star, The (1790), II, 736
Riley, Henry Thomas (1816–1878), I, 115 (2), 121–2
Riley, John (*fl.* 1870?), III, 819
Riley, W. Harrison (*fl.* 1873), III, 817
Rimbault, Edward Francis (1816–1876), I, 267, 405, 534, 621, 707, 713, 722; II, 872
Ringer, Sidney (1835–1910), III, 964
Ringrose, Basil (d. 1686), II, 752
Rintoul, Robert Stephen (1787–1858), III, 787, 811, 813
Ripa, Cesare, II, 813
Ripley, George (d. 1490?), I, 253, 886
Ripley, George (*fl.* 1793), II, 716
Rippingille, Edward Villiers (1798?–1859), III, 694
Riquetti, Honoré Gabriel, Comte de Mirabeau, II, 797
Rishanger, William (1250?–1312?), I, 115
Ritchie, A. D. (*fl.* 1891), III, 777
Ritchie, Anne Isabella, Lady, née Thackeray (1837–1923), III, **561**
Ritchie, David George (1853–1903), III, **872**
Ritchie, J. E. (*fl.* 1860), III, 487, 815
Ritchie, Leitch (1800?–1865), III, 376, **505**, 604, 821
Ritchie, T. E. (*fl.* 1887), II, 951
Ritson, Isaac (1761–1789), II, 928
Ritson, Joseph (1752–1803), II, **905**f., 908
Rittenhouse, David (*fl.* 1765–75), II, 60
Rival Beauties, The (18 cent.), II, 229
Riverius, Lazarus, II, 797
Rivers, Anthony (*fl.* 1601–6), I, 382
Rivers, Anthony Wydeville, Earl (1442?–1483), I, 262 (3)

Rivers, David (*fl.* 1797), II, 800, 924
Rivers, George (*fl.* 1639), I, 731
Rivers, H. J. (*fl.* 1862), III, 443
Rivers, Marcellus (*fl.* 1659), I, 793
Rivière, Pierre, I, 411
Rivington, John (1720–1792), II, 697
RIVINGTON & Co., III, 99
Rizzetti, G., II, 826
Roach, Richard (1662–1730), II, **859**
Roach's Beauties of the Poets of Great Britain
    (18 cent.), II, 249
Road to Hymen, The (18 cent.), II, 244
Robarts (or Roberts), Henry (*fl.* 1585–1616), I,
    729
Robb, — (*fl.* 1863), III, 775
Robberds, J. W. (*fl.* 1843), III, 182
Robe, James (1688–1753), II, 686
Robe, Jane (*fl.* 1723), II, 485
Roberd of Cisyle (M.E.), I, **157**
Roberson, G. (*fl.* 1859), III, 911
Robert of Chester (*fl.* 1140), I, **285**
Robert of Cricklade (*fl.* 1170), I, **288**
Robert of Gloucester (*fl.* 1260–1300), I, 40, **165**
Robert of Melun (d. 1167), I, **287**
Robert of Torigni (*fl.* 12 cent.), I, 116
Robert of Ware (*fl.* 1268), I, **293**
Robert of York (*fl.* 1348), I, **306**
Robert and Adela, or, The Rights of Women
    (18 cent.), II, 550
Robert the Devil (Sir Gowther) (M.E.), I, **153**
Robert Owen's Journal (1851), III, 817
Roberts, Alexander (*fl.* 1616), I, 893
Roberts, Daniel (*fl.* 1746), II, 857
Roberts, Eliza (*fl.* 1788), II, 798
Roberts, Emma (1794?–1840), III, 294, 1068
Roberts, Francis (1609–1675), I, 679
Roberts, Frederick Sleigh, Earl (d. 1914), III,
    1078
Roberts, George (*fl.* 1721–6), II, 742
Roberts, George (d. 1860), I, 385, 388
Roberts, Henry (*fl.* 1585–1616), I, 739 (2), 740,
    742, 788
Roberts, Henry (*fl.* 1760), II, 816
Roberts, James (*fl.* 1760), II, 816
Roberts, John (*fl.* 1729), II, 911
Roberts, John (*fl.* 1869), III, 777
Roberts, Lewis (1596–1640), I, 767, 847
Roberts, Margaret (*fl.* 1814), III, 412
Roberts, Morley (b. 1857), III, 992
Roberts, O. O. (*fl.* 1838), III, 971
Roberts, Miss R. (*fl.* 1763–74), II, 783, 790
Roberts, Sir Randal H. (*fl.* 1860–87), III, 767,
    770
Roberts, Samuel (1763–1848), III, 149, 975
Roberts, Thomas (*fl.* 1801), II, 822
Roberts, Walworth Howland (*fl.* 1881), III, 987
Roberts, William (1767–1849), II, 666, 845
Roberts, William Hayward (d. 1791), II, 26,
    378
Robertson, C. (*fl.* 1850?), III, 113

Robertson, E. P. (*fl.* 1854), III, 1074
Robertson, Eric Sutherland (*fl.* 1883), III, **355**
Robertson, Frederick William (1816–1853),
    III, 849
Robertson, G. (*fl.* 1830), political economist,
    III, 981
Robertson, George (*fl.* 1651), I, 377
Robertson, George Croom (1842–1892), III,
    833, **872**
Robertson, Henrietta, earlier Richardson
    (*fl.* 1908–17) ['Henry Handel Richard-
    son'], III, 1097
Robertson, James (*fl.* 1770), II, **378**
Robertson, James Craigie (1813–1882), I, 839
Robertson, James Logie (1846–1922), III, 355
Robertson, John (*fl.* 1772–90), II, 731
Robertson, John Mackinnon (1856–1933), III,
    752 f., 831
Robertson, Joseph (1726–1802), divine, I, 17
Robertson, Joseph (1810–1866), Scottish
    historian, III, 807, 819, **906**
Robertson, Joseph Clinton (1788–1852), III,
    822
Robertson, R. (*fl.* 1770), translator of Jacques
    Saurin, II, 800
Robertson, Robert (1742–1829), physician, II,
    742
Robertson, T. W. (*fl.* 1835), journalist, III, 822
Robertson, Thomas (d. 1799), divine, I, 593;
    II, 19, 732, 934
Robertson, Thomas William (1829–1871), III,
    597 f., 801
Robertson, William (d. 1686?), lexicographer,
    I, 376
Robertson, William (1721–1793), historian, II,
    38, 53 f., 68, 71, **881** f.
Robertson, William (*fl.* 1865), III, 763
Robie, James (*fl.* 1855), III, 807
Robin, The (1749), II, 213
Robin, The (1774), II, 230, 231
Robin Conscience, The Booke in Meeter of
    (16 cent.), I, 719
Robin Good-Fellow (17 cent.), I, 715
Robin Hood (1795), II, 251
Robin Hood and the Sheriff of Nottingham
    (15 cent.), I, 520
Robin Hoods Garland (1663), II, 174–5, 181,
    186, 207, 212, 226, 233–4, 239, 243, 247,
    249, 251 (2), 252, 255
Robin Hood's Garland (1787), II, 241
Robin's Last Shift; Or, Weekly Remarks (1716),
    II, 712
Robin's London and Dublin Magazine (1827),
    III, 826
Robin's Panegyrick (18 cent.), II, 200–1, 203
Robins, Benjamin (1707–1751), II, 962
Robins, Robert (*fl.* 1647), I, 718
Robinson, Agnes Mary Frances, later Dar-
    mesteter, later Duclaux (b. 1857), III,
    355 f.

Robinson, B. Fletcher (*fl.* 1897), III, 775
Robinson, Charles Best (*fl.* 1857), I, 387
Robinson, Clement (*fl.* 1566–84), I, 404
Robinson, Edward Jewitt (*fl.* 1855–85), III, 1084
Robinson, Emma (*fl.* 1844–68), III, **505**
Robinson, Francis (*fl.* 1712), II, 717
Robinson, G. (*fl.* 1826), I, 531
Robinson, Hastings (1792–1866), I, 382
Robinson, Henry Crabb (1775–1867), III, **678**, 798
Robinson, Hugh (1584?–1655), II, 128
Robinson, J. (*fl.* 1860?), Dublin journalist, III, 809
Robinson, John (1576?–1625), pastor of the Pilgrim Fathers, I, 725
Robinson, John (1650–1723), bishop of London, II, 744
Robinson, John (1727–1802), politician, II, 168
Robinson, John (*fl.* 1794), novelist, II, 550
Robinson, John (*fl.* 1860), Bengalee translator, III, 1074
Robinson, Sir John (1839–1903), Prime Minister of Natal, III, 1090
Robinson, Sir John Richard (1828–1903), journalist, III, 787, 799, 801
Robinson, Lennox (b. 1886), III, **1065** f.
Robinson, Mary ('Perdita') (1758–1800), II, **379**, 456, 550–1
Robinson, Mary Elizabeth (*fl.* 1804), editor of 'The Wild Wreath', III, 406
Robinson, Matthew (1628–1694), I, 387
Robinson, Philip (*fl.* 1887), III, 811
Robinson, Philip Stewart (1847–1902), III, 1084
Robinson, Ralph (*fl.* 1542–51), I, 666
Robinson, Richard (*fl.* 1576–1600), I, 349, 384, 396, 735, 769, 815–6
Robinson, Robert (1735–1790), II, 119, 776, 800, 863
Robinson, Samuel (1794–1884), III, 34
Robinson, Thomas (*fl.* 1620), I, 477
Robinson, Thomas (d. 1747), lawyer, II, 965
Robinson, Thomas (*fl.* 1737), editor of Hesiod, II, 937
Robinson, Thomas (1790–1873), divine, III, 234
Robinson Crusoe's London Daily Evening Post (1742), II, 710
Robinson's Merchant's Weekly Remembrancer (1712), II, 717
Robinson, Sir John (1778–1843), III, 937
Robothan, T. (*fl.* 1643), I, 375
Robson, Charles (1598–1638), I, 771
Robson, Horatio (*fl.* 1784), II, 666, 776
Robson, J. (*fl.* 1842–55), I, 129, 201
Robson, Joseph (*fl.* 1752), II, 754
Robson, Mary, later Hughs (*fl.* 1813), III, 566
Roby, Henry John (1830–1915), III, 122, **1009**
Roby, John (1793–1850), III, 205, 378

Roch, Jeremy (*fl.* 1665), II, 742
Rochdale Observer, The, III, 794
Roche, Eugenius (1786–1829), III, **204**, 787, 798 (2), 799, 800, 811
Roche, John (*fl.* 1813), II, 632
Roche, Regina Maria, née Dalton (1764?–1845), III, **415**
Rocheford, Jorevin de, II, 140, 159
Rochester, John Wilmot, Earl of (1648–1680), II, 56, **276** f.
Rochester Register (M.E.), I, 122
Rochon, Alexis Marie, II, 797
Rodd, James Rennell, Baron Rennell (b. 1858), III, **356**
Rodd, Thomas (d. 1849), III, 103
Roderick, Richard (d. 1756), II, 912
Roderyck Mors, The True Coppy of the Complaint of (17 cent.), I, 720
Rodger, Alexander (1784–1846), III, **242**
Rodgers, William (*fl.* 1642), I, 753
Rodney, George Brydges, Baron (1719–1792), II, 755
Rodrigo, Francisco Vasquez de Ciudad, I, 345
Rodriguez, E. A. (*fl.* 1841), III, 1081
Rodwell, George Herbert Buonaparte (1800–1852), III, **607**
Roe, — (*fl.* 1642–6), I, 841
Roe, John (*fl.* 1763), II, 733
Roe, Richard Baillie (d. 1853), I, 17
Roe, Sir Thomas (1581?–1644), I, 784, 818, 847
Roe, Sir Thomas (*fl.* 1732), III, 1079
Roebuck, John Arthur (1801–1879), III, 140, 790
Roeer, H. H. E. (*fl.* 1845), III, 1071
Rösslin, Eucharius, I, 890
Roger of Hereford (*fl.* 1176), I, **288**
Roger, C. (*fl.* 1847), I, 673
Roger, Robert (*fl.* 1704), II, 719
Rogers, A. (*fl.* 1895), III, 1069
Rogers, Benjamin Bickley (1828–1919), III, **1009**
Rogers, Charles (1711–1784), II, 809
Rogers, Charles (1825–1890), III, **929**
Rogers, Francis (*fl.* 1665), II, 742
Rogers, Francis Newman (1791–1851), III, 987
Rogers, Henry (1806–1877), I, 836; III, 832, 853
Rogers, James Edwin Thorold (1823–1890), III, **925** f.
Rogers, John (1500?–1555), martyr, I, 675, 816
Rogers, John (*fl.* 1560–80), perhaps author of 'The Glasse of Godly Love', I, 713
Rogers, John (1627–1665?), controversialist, I, 718
Rogers, Richard (1550?–1618), I, 384
Rogers, Robert (1727–1800), II, 755
Rogers, Samuel (*fl.* 1764), minor poet, II, 379
Rogers, Samuel (1763–1855), poet, banker and talker, III, 40, **164**

Rogers, T. (*fl.* 1578), translator, I, 845 (2)
Rogers, T. (*fl.* 1879), III, 1072
Rogers, Thomas (1574?–1609?), poet, I, 438
Rogers, Thomas (d. 1616), protestant divine, I, 678, 685, 810
Rogers, William (1819–1896), III, 140
Rogers, Woodes (d. 1732), II, 741
Roget, Peter Mark (1779–1869), III, 937
ROGUE PAMPHLETS, I, 717 f. (16, 17 cents.); II, 155 f. (17, 18 cents.)
Rojas Zorrilla, Francisco de, II, 68
Roland, George (*fl.* 1823), III, 778
Roland, Joseph (*fl.* 1809), III, 778
Roland, Manon Jeanne, II, 141
Roland and Vernagu (M.E.), I, **140**
Roland, Song of (M.E.), I, **141** f.
Rolando, Guezman (*fl.* 1822), III, 778
Rolf (or Rolfe), John (1585–1622), I, 790
Rolland, John (*fl.* 1555–60), of Dalkeith, I, 899
Rolland, William (*fl.* 1720), II, 731
Rolle, Henry (1589?–1656), II, 965
Rolle, Richard, de Hampole (1290?–1349)
    English works, I, 29, 32, **191** f.
    Latin works, I, **306** f.
Rolleston, Charles (*fl.* 1890), III, 830
Rolleston, George (1829–1881), III, 958
Rolleston, Thomas William Hazen (1857–1920), III, **1056**
Rolliad, The (18 cent.), II, 251–2, 391
Rollin, Charles, II, 29, 797
Rollington, Ralph (*fl.* 1879), III, 821
Rollinson, F. (*fl.* 1596), I, 663
Rollock, Robert (1555?–1599), I, 683
Rollos, G. (*fl.* 1762), II, 221
Rolt, Richard (1725?–1770), II, 339, 677, 812, 924, 926
Romaine, William (1714–1795), II, **853**
ROMAN CULTURE, III, 49 f.
Roman Post-Boy, The (1689), II, 658, 705
ROMANCES (M.E.), I, 128 f.
    Alexander Romances, I, 142 f.
    Arthurian Romances, I, 130 f.
    Breton Lais, I, 151
    Charlemagne Romances, I, 140 f.
    English Heroes (Romances of), I, 147 f.
    Godfrey of Bouillon Romances, I, 146
    Miscellaneous Romances, I, 153 f.
    Troy Romances, I, 144 f.
Romanes, George John (1848–1894), III, 356, **872**, 955, 966
Romans, Bernard (1720?–1784?), II, 756
ROMANTICISM
    Restoration to Romantic Revival. See II, 5 f. (LITERARY MOVEMENTS AND IDEAS), 9 f. (LITERARY THEORY), 73 f. (MEDIEVAL INFLUENCES), 171 f. (poetry)
    Nineteenth Century, III, 156 f. See also LITERARY MOVEMENTS AND IDEAS, III, 6 f.
Rome Rhym'd to Death (17 cent.), II, 179
Rome, The Seven Sages of (M.E.), I, 155

Romei, Annibale, I, 338, 818
Romeus et Julietta (17 cent.), I, 663
Romilly, Sir Samuel (1757–1818), II, 797; III, 149, **872**
Ronalds, Alfred (*fl.* 1836), III, 769
Rondeau, —, later Mrs Vigor (*fl.* 1775), II, 746
Ronge, B. (*fl.* 1855), III, 109
Ronge, J. (*fl.* 1855), III, 109
Ronksley, William (*fl.* 1712), II, 556
Ronsard, Pierre de, I, 333
Rood-Tree, The History of (M.E.), I, 40
Rooke, Sir George (1650–1709), II, 744
Rooke, Henry (*fl.* 1783), II, 751
Rooke, John (*fl.* 1729), translator, II, 759, 787
Rooke, John (1780–1856), political economist, III, 981
Rookes, Thomas (*fl.* 1667), II, 93
Roome, Edward (d. 1729), II, 313
Rooney, William (1873–1901), III, 1059
Rooper, George (*fl.* 1867), III, 771
Rooper, Thomas Godolphin (1847–1903), III, 113, 140
Rope for Pol, A (17 cent.), I, 719
Roper, Abel (1665–1726?), II, 697, 706
Roper, Margaret (1505–1544), I, 665
Roper, W. J. D. (*fl.* 1847), III, 130
Roper, William (1496–1578), I, 824
Ros, Sir Richard (*fl.* 15 cent.), I, 254
Roscoe, C. (*fl.* 1830), III, 213
Roscoe, Edward Stanley (*fl.* 1878), III, 988
Roscoe, Henry (1800–1836), III, 887, 988
Roscoe, Sir Henry Enfield (1833–1915), III, **948**
Roscoe, Thomas (1791–1871), II, 517, 523, 582; III, 38, **678** f.
Roscoe, William (1753–1831), III, **887**
Roscoe, William Caldwell (1823–1859), III, 305
Roscoe, William Stanley (1782–1843), III, 243
Roscommon, Wentworth Dillon, Earl of (1663?–1685), II, 204, **285** f.
Rose, George (1744–1818), statesman, III, 149, 975
Rose, Sir George Henry (1771–1855), diplomatist, II, 165
Rose, George Maclean (*fl.* 1886), III, 1085
Rose, H. (*fl.* 1891), III, 984
Rose, Hugh (*fl.* 1698), II, 752
Rose, Hugh James (1795–1838), III, 29, 122, 854, 860, 891
Rose, J. Holland (b. 1855), III, 985
Rose, P. (*fl.* 1814), III, 77
Rose, William (1719–1786), II, 340, 677, 765, 767
Rose, William Stewart (1775–1843), III, **243**
Rose-Belford's (1878), III, 1088
'Rosicrucian' (*fl.* 1656), I, 887
Rosier, James (1575–1635), I, 789
Ross, Miss — (*fl.* 1817), III, 818
Ross, Alexander (1591–1654), I, 477, 767, 834, 866, 877, 883, 890, 909
Ross, Alexander (1699–1784), II, 251, 973

Ross, Alexander (1783–1856), III, 1088
Ross, C. H. (*fl.* 1884), III, 820
Ross, David (*fl.* 1883), III, 1080
Ross, F. (*fl.* 1783), II, 736
Ross, Hugh (*fl.* 1702), II, 786
Ross, J. C. (*fl.* 1866), III, 834
Ross, Sir James Clark (1800–1862), III, 992
Ross (or Rous), John (1411?–1491), I, 265
Ross, Sir John (1777–1856), III, 992
Ross, R. B. (*fl.* 1888), III, 835
Ross, Thomas (d. 1675), II, 768
Ross, W. (*fl.* 1836), III, 33
ROSSALL SCHOOL, III, 839
Rosse, William Parsons, Earl (1800–1867), III, 938, 943
Rosseter, Philip (1572?–1623), I, 484
Rossetti, Christina Georgina (1830–1894), III, 273 f.
Rossetti, Dante Gabriel (1828–1882), III, 271 f., 277, 289
Rossetti, Gabriele (*fl.* 1824–50), III, 724
Rossetti, William Michael (1829–1919), III, 724
    Articles by, III, 269, 706
    Editions by, III, 271, 274
Rossi, Giacomo, II, 813
Rosslyn, Francis Robert St Clair Erskine, Earl of (1833–1890), III, 340
Rossy, Thomas (d. 1409), I, 302
Rost, Reinhold (1822–1896), III, 1019
Roswall and Lillian (M.E.), I, 160
Rota, J. M., I, 811
Rotch, B. (*fl.* 1841), III, 79
Rotterdam's Courant, The (1680), II, 703
Rotuli Hundredorum (M.E.), I, 120
Rotuli Parliamentorum (M.E. and 15 cent.), I, 115
Rouillé, Pierre Jean, II, 775
Round, James Thomas (*fl.* 1838–45), II, 848
Roundelay or the New Syren (18 cent.), II, 235, 236 (2), 237, 244, 251
Rouquet, J. B., II, 141
Rous, Francis (1579–1659), I, 725
Rous, Francis, the younger (*fl.* 1637), I, 780
Rous, G. (*fl.* 1791), II, 635
Rous, Henry John (1795–1877), III, 763
Rous (or Ross), John (1411?–1491), I, 265
Rous, John (1584–1644), I, 386
Rouse, W. H. D. (b. 1863), III, 1073
Rousseau, Jean Baptiste, II, 797
Rousseau, Jean Jacques
    Influence of, II, 37, 46, 48; III, 22
    Quarrel with Hume, II, 951
    Translations from, II, 110, 552, 797
Rousseau de la Valette, Michel, II, 798
Rousselet, L., III, 1080
Roussillon, G. (*fl.* 1721), II, 769
Routh, Bernard (1695–1768), II, 25
Routh, Edward John (1831–1907), III, 942
Routh, Martin Joseph (1755–1854), II, 869; III, 860

ROUTLEDGE & CO., III, 99
Rovenzon, John (*fl.* 1613), I, 886
Rover, The (18 cent.), II, 536
Row, C. A. (*fl.* 1850), III, 127 (2)
Row, John (1586–1646), I, 910
Row, John (1598?–1672?), I, 911
Row, W. (*fl.* 1680), I, 841
Row, W. (*fl.* 1796–1839), III, 824
Row, Walter (*fl.* 1796–1822), II, 682
Rowbothum, James (*fl.* 1562), I, 395
Rowcroft, Charles (*fl.* 1843), III, 1096
Rowe, Elizabeth (1674–1737), II, 58, 326, 539 (2)
Rowe, John (*fl.* 1709), II, 767
Rowe, Nicholas (1674–1718), II, 44, 193, 431 f., 909
Rowe, Richard P. L. (*fl.* 1858), III, 1094
Rowe, Theophilus (*fl.* 1737), II, 326, 777
Rowe, Thomas (1687–1715), II, 326
Rowe-Mores, Edward (1731–1778), II, 921
Rowell, J. (*fl.* 1749), II, 785
ROWING (books on), III, 778 f.
Rowland, David (*fl.* 1569–86), I, 815
Rowland, John (1606–1660), I, 893
Rowland, William (*fl.* 1652), I, 884; II, 797
Rowlande, Duke, and Sir Ottuell (M.E.), I, 141
Rowlands, Richard, later Verstegen (*fl.* 1565–1620), I, 778
Rowlands, Samuel (1570?–1630?), I, 707 f., 717
Rowlands, William (1802–1865), I, 7
Rowlandson, Thomas (1756–1827), II, 154, 818, 823–4; III, 92
Rowley, Samuel (d. 1624), I, 537
Rowley, William (1585?–1642?), I, 636, 713; III, 593
Roworth, C. (*fl.* 1798), II, 824
Rowson, Susanna, née Haswell (1762–1824), II, 549 (2)
ROXBURGHE CLUB, III, 86
Roxby, Robert (1809?–1866), III, 770
Roy, Pratapchandra (*fl.* 1883), III, 1072
Roy, William (*fl.* 1525–31), I, 665, 668, 675
ROYAL COLLEGE OF PHYSICIANS LIBRARY, II, 104
Royal Female Magazine, The (1760), II, 678
Royal Garland Of Love and Delight, The (17 cent.), II, 177
Royal Gazette, The (1762), II, 708
Royal Gazette And Universal Chronicle, The (1761), II, 708
Royal Glosses (O.E.), I, 36
Royal Informer, The (1660), II, 701
Royal Jester, The (18 cent.), II, 247
Royal Magazine, The (1750), II, 677
Royal Magazine, The (1788), II, 681
Royal Magazine, The (1898), III, 831
Royal Magazine; Or, Gentleman's Monthly Companion, The (1759), II, 678
ROYAL SOCIETY
    Foundation, II, 959 f.
    Library, II, 104

Royal Toastmaster, The (18 cent.), II, 246 (2), 248
Royal Westminster Journal And London Political Miscellany, The (1763), II, 715
Royall Diurnall, The (1648), I, 759
Royall Diurnall (for King Charls II), The (1650), I, 760
Royalty Songster, The (18 cent.), II, 242
Roye, E. de (*fl.* 1489), I, 262
Royle, J. F. (*fl.* 1839), III, 1083
Rozas, Fernando de, I, 343
Rud, Edward (*fl.* 1709–20), II, 116
Rud, T. (*fl.* 1825), I, 6
Ruddier (or Rudyerd), Sir Benjamin (1572–1658), II, 173
Ruddiman, Thomas (1674–1757), I, 445; II, 102, 104, 697, 731, 870, 909f., 1001
Ruddiman, Walter (*fl.* 1759–73), II, 229, 672, 686 (2), 731–2
Ruddiman's Weekly Mercury (1777), II, 732
Ruding, Rogers (1751–1820), III, 973
Rudler, Frederick William (*fl.* 1889), III, 953
Ruffhead, Owen (1723–1769), II, 301, 664
Ruffini, John, i.e. Giovanni Domenico Ruffini (1807–1881), III, 505
RUGBY SCHOOL, I, 373; III, 133, 839
Rugeley, Rowland (*fl.* 1763), II, 379
Rugeley-Powers, S. (*fl.* 1867), III, 576
Ruggle, George (1575–1622), I, 659
Ruin, The (O.E.), I, 71
Rule, Gilbert (1629?–1706), II, 993
Rule, William Harris (1802–1890), III, 823
Rule of St Benedict (M.E.), I, 39, 178f.
Rulhière, Claude Carloman de, II, 798
Rumbold, Sir Horace (1829–1913), III, 154
'Rumfish, John' (1750), II, 214
Rumford, Sir Benjamin Thomson, Count (1753–1814), II, 962; III, 936f.
Rump, The (17 cent.), II, 173, 174 (2), 201
Runcie, J. (*fl.* 1905), III, 1089
Runciman, James (1852–1891), III, 787
Rundall, Thomas (*fl.* 1850), I, 784, 790
Rundle, Elizabeth, later Charles (1828–1896), III, 283f.
Rune-Song (O.E.), I, 85
RUNES, I, 59f.
Runne Red-cap (17 cent.), I, 713
Rural Songster, The (19 cent.), II, 256
Ruscelli, Girolamo, I, 809
Rusden, George William (1819–1903), III, 1097
Ruse, G. (*fl.* 1860), III, 77 (2)
Rushton, W. L. (*fl.* 1858–97), lawyer, I, 318, 544; III, 776
Rushton, William (*fl.* 1850–69), of University College, London, III, 6
Rushworth, John (1612?–1690), I, 399, 749, 755, 756 (2), 757, 760
Ruskin, John (1819–1900), III, 25f., 691f.
Russel, Alexander (1814–1876), III, 787, 807
Russel, George (1728–1767), II, 786

Russel, Richard (*fl.* 1730), II, 714
Russell, Thomas (*fl.* 1602), I, 886
Russell, Alexander (1715?–1768), II, 750
Russell, Arthur Tozer (1806–1874), I, 836
Russell, Charles (*fl.* 1742), II, 151
Russell, Charles (*fl.* 1867), III, 799, 808
Russell, Sir Edward (1834–1920), III, 787, 802
Russell, F. W. (*fl.* 1859), I, 399
'Russell, Fox' (1887), III, 761
Russell, Francis, Earl of Bedford (1527?–1585), I, 363
Russell, Francis (*fl.* 1786), II, 747
Russell, Francis (*fl.* 1849), III, 988
Russell, George William (1867–1935) ['A.E.' or 'Æ'], III, 1058f.
Russell, H. A., Duke of Bedford (*fl.* 1897), III, 972
Russell, John (*fl.* 1450), I, 264, 378–9
Russell, John, Duke of Bedford (1710–1771), II, 164
Russell, John (*fl.* 1750), traveller, II, 745
Russell, John (*fl.* 1794), writer of children's books, II, 559
Russell, Lord John, Earl (1792–1878), III, 113, 122, 594, 897
Russell, John, Viscount Amberley (1842–1876), III, 146
Russell, John (*fl.* 1888), assistant master, University College School, III, 112
Russell, John Abraham (*fl.* 1825), archdeacon of Clogher, III, 246
Russell, Michael (1781–1848), I, 838
Russell, Rachel, Lady (1636–1723), II, 135
Russell, Thomas (1762–1788), poet, II, 379
Russell, earlier Cloutt, Thomas (1781?–1846), divine and scholar, I, 699
Russell, William (*fl.* 1425), I, 305
Russell, William (1741–1793), II, 801, 889
Russell, William Clark (1844–1911), III, 558f.
Russell, Sir William Howard (1820–1907), III, 787, 1080
Russell, Sir William Oldnall (1785–1833), III, 988
Russell, Memoirs of the House of (17 cent.), I, 382
RUSSIA
  Literary Relations with, II, 71 (1660–1800); III, 43f. (19·cent.)
Rust, George (d. 1676), II, 943
Rustaing de Saint Jory, Louis, II, 798
'Rutherford, Mark', i.e. William Hale White (1831–1913), III, 559f.
Rutherford, Samuel (1600–1661), I, 857, 909
Rutherford, T. (*fl.* 1751), II, 951
Rutherford, William (*fl.* 1788), II, 26
Rutherford, William Gunion (1853–1907), III, 1009
Rutherforth, Thomas (1712–1771), II, 600
Ruthven, J. (*fl.* 1820), III, 83

Ruthwell Cross (O.E.), I, 36, 59f.
Rutland, John Henry Manners, Duke of (*fl.* 1795)
Rutland Papers, The (16 cent.), I, 382
Rutledge, Jean Jacques, II, 798
Rutt, G. T. (*fl.* 1828), I, 388
Rutt, John Towill (1760–1841), I, 401; II, 938, 956
Rutter, Joseph (*fl.* 1637), I, 649, 812
Ryall, M. Q. (*fl.* 1843), III, 817
Ryan, Michael (1800–1841), I, 889
Ryan, Richard (1796–1849), III, 584
Rycaut (or Ricaut), Sir Paul (1628–1700), II, 68, 743, 813, **869**
Ryder, Dudley, Earl Harrowby (1762–1847), III, 148
Rye, Peter (*fl.* 1793), II, 749
Rye, William Brenchley (1818–1901), I, 320, 790
Ryland, John (1717?–1798), II, 619
Ryland, John Collett (1723–1792), II, 863
Ryland, Jonathan Edwards (1798–1866), III, 669, 824
Ryland, R. (*fl.* 1813), III, 832
Rylands, John (*fl.* 1792), II, 20
Ryle, Herbert Edward (1856–1925), III, 853
Ryley, Samuel William (1759–1837), III, 584
Ryley, T. (1758), II, 773
Ryman, James (*fl.* 15 cent.), I, 265
Rymer, Thomas (1641–1713), I, 872; II, 15 (2), 29, 276, **875**
Rypon, Robert, of Durham (*fl.* 14 cent.), I, **312**
Ryves, Bruno (1596–1677), I, 755
Ryves, Elizabeth (1750–1797), II, 549, 784

S., A. (*fl.* 1697), II, 819
S., A. (*fl.* 1782), II, 817
S., D. (*fl.* 1573), I, 741
S., E. (*fl.* 1680), II, 773
S., E. G. (*fl.* 1627), I, 801
S., G. (*fl.* 1626), I, 444
S., G. (*fl.* 1741), II, 820
S., H. (*fl.* 1791), II, 564
S., H. W. (*fl.* 1860), III, 651
S., I. (*fl.* 1655), I, 793
S., I. M. (*fl.* 1632), I, 592
S., J. (*fl.* 1597), I, 437
S., J. (*fl.* 1639), I, 731
S., J. (*fl.* 1651), I, 653
S., J. (*fl.* 1660), I, 651
S., J. (1690), II, 531
S., J. (*fl.* 1693), II, 182
S., J. (*fl.* 1697), II, 429, 819
S., J., Gent. (*fl.* 1697), II, 819
S., J. (*fl.* 1704), II, 780
S., J. (*fl.* 1704), II, 781
S., M. (*fl.* 1581), I, 738
S., M. (*fl.* 1622), I, 845
S., N. (*fl.* 1671), II, 816

S., N. (*fl.* 1684), II, 801
S., O. (*fl.* 1700), II, 185 (2)
S., P. (1591), I, 479
S., R. (*fl.* 1593), I, 404
S., R. (*fl.* 1653), I, 718
S., R. (*fl.* 1661), II, 173
S., R. (*fl.* 1670), II, 175
S., R. (1684), II, 530
S., R. (*fl.* 1774), II, 624
S., S. (*fl.* 1616), I, 652
S., S. (*fl.* 1653), I, 726
S., T. (*fl.* 1614), I, 394
S., T. (*fl.* 1660), II, 808
S., T. (*fl.* 1681), II, 530 (2)
S., W. (*fl.* 1672), II, 176
Saavedra, Miguel de Cervantes, I, 344
Sabie, Francis (*fl.* 1587–96), I, 438
Sabine, Sir Edward (1788–1883), III, 937
Sabine, Henry (*fl.* 1732?), II, 722
Sablé, Marquise de (*fl.* 1694), II, 785
Sacchi, Bartholomaeus (De Platina), II, 813
Sacheverell, Henry (1674?–1724), II, 119
Sacheverell, William (*fl.* 1702), II, 744
Sacheverells, Letters of the Sitwells and (17, 18 cents.), I, 383
Sachs, Hans, I, 336
Sack-Full of Newes, The (16 cent.), I, 714
Sackville, Charles, Earl of Dorset (1638–1706), II, **280**
Sackville, George Sackville German, Viscount (1716–1785), II, 632 (2)
Sackville, Thomas, Earl of Dorset (1536–1608), I, 413f., 523
Sackville-West, R. W. (*fl.* 1859), I, 523
Sacrae Scripturae Locorum Quorundam Versio Metrica (18 cent.), II, 206
Sacred Miscellanies (18 cent.), II, 190
Sacred Oratorios, The (18 cent.), II, 255
Sacred Poems (18 cent.), II, 215
Sacy, Louis de, II, 798
Sade, Jacques François Aldonce de, II, 798
'Sadeur, Jacques', i.e. Gabriel de Foigny, II, 798
Sa'di, III, 1071
Sadler, — (*fl.* 1791), of Chippenham, II, 549
Sadler, John (d. 1595?), divine, I, 808
Sadler, John (1615–1674), master of Magdalene College, Cambridge, I, 659; II, 529
Sadler, Michael Thomas (1780–1835), III, 975
Sadler, Sir Ralph (1507–1587), I, 397
Sadler, Thomas (1822–1891), III, 226
Sadlier, Mary Anne, née Madden (*fl.* 1861), III, 1087
Sagas (influence of), III, 42, 52
Sage, John (1652–1711), II, 909–10, **993**
Sailing (books on), III, 778f.
St Albans
    Printing in, I, 353 (15 cent.)
St Albans, Chronicles of (M.E.), I, 115

St Andrews
  Library, I, 363
  Printing in, I, 354
  University, III, 128, 838 (magazines)
St Augustine's Soliloquies (O.E.), I, **88**
St Bartholomew's Church, History of (M.E.), I, 41
Saint Birgitta, The Revelations of (15 cent.), I, 266
St Catharine's College (Cambridge), I, 370; II, 104 (library)
St Cecilia (18 cent.), II, 234, 236 (2)
St Chad (O.E.), I, **93**
St Christopher (O.E.), I, **93**
St Clair, R. (*fl.* 1697), II, 813
'St Clair, Rosalia' (1819–35), III, **415**
St Editha and St Ethelreda (M.E.), I, 41
Saint-Étienne, Jean Paul Rabaut, II, 795
Saint-Évremond, Charles Marguetel de Saint-Denis, Seigneur de, II, 29, 40, 149, 790
Saint-Foix, Germain François Poullain de, II, 795
Saint-Gelais, Louis François Dubois de, II, 140
St German, Christopher (1460?–1540), I, 851
St Guthlac (O.E.)
  In verse, I, 28, 31, 35, **78**
  In prose, I, **93**
Saint Hyacinthe, Hyacinthe Cordonnier de, II, 543
St Ives
  Newspapers, II, 728
St Ives Mercury, The (1719), II, 728
St Ives Post, The (1716), II, 728
St Ives Post-Boy; Or, The Loyal Packet, The (1718), II, 728
St James Chronicle (1761), II, 664
St James's Chronicle, The (1761), III, 809
St James's Chronicle; Or, British Evening Post, The (1761), II, 710
St James's Evening Post (1715), II, 710
St James's Evening Post, The (Dublin, 1719), II, 734
St James's Evening Post, Or Nightly Pacquet (1715), II, 710
St James's Gazette, The (1880), III, 801
St James's Journal, With Memoirs of Literature, The (1722), II, 713
St James's Magazine, The (1762), II, 678
St James's Magazine, The (1776), II, 679
St James's Magazine, The (1861), III, 829
St James's Miscellany, The (18 cent.), II, 200
St James's Post, The (1715), II, 707
St James's Register, The (18 cent.), II, 206
St James's Tatler, The (18 cent.), II, 204
St James's Weekly Journal (1717), II, 712
St James's Weekly Journal; Or, Hanover Postman (1719), II, 713
St James's Weekly Packet, The (1732), II, 714
St John, Mrs — (*fl.* 1863), III, 766
St John, Charles William George (1809–1856), III, 766

St John, Henry, Viscount Bolingbroke (1678–1751), II, 17, 39, 111, **612**f.
St John, Holles (*fl.* 1742), II, 209
St John, James Augustus (1801–1875), I, 466 (2), 829, 834; II, 835, 940; III, 816
St John, Percy Bolingbroke (1821–1889), III, 568, 815
St John, Vane (1839–1911), III, 821
St John's College (Cambridge), I, 370
Saint-Lambert, Jean François de, II, 798
St Leger, Francis Barry Boyle (1799–1829), III, **415**
St Leonards, Edward Burtenshaw Sugden, Baron (1781–1875), III, 900, 988
St Margaret (O.E.), I, **93'**
St Mary of Egypt (O.E.), I, **93**
St Neot (O.E.), I, **93**
St Neot's
  Printers, II, 88
St Patrick's Purgatory (M.E.), I, **177**
St Paul's (1867), III, 839
St Paul's School, I, 373; II, 104 (library); III, 133
St Serfe or Sydserf, Sir Thomas (*fl.* 1658), II, **427**
St Stephen's Review (1883), III, 814
St Swithun (O.E.), I, **93**
St Ursula, The Life of (15 cent.), I, 266
St Veronica (O.E.), I, **93**
Saint-Réal, César Vichard de, II, 48, 533, 802
Sainte-Marthe, Scévole de, the elder, II, 798
Sainte-Marthe, Scévole de, the younger, II, 798
Sainte-Maure de Beaulieu, Charles de, II, 798
Sainte-Mesme, Guillaume François Antoine de L'Hôpital, Marquis de, II, 789
Sainte-Palaye, Jean Baptiste La Curne de (1697–1781), II, 29, 75
Saints' Legends and Lives
  Old English, I, 89, 93. For Latin, see under Writings in Latin, I, 98f. (5 to 10 cents.)
  Middle English, I, 168f., 173f.
Saintsbury, George Edward Bateman (1845–1933), III, **753**f.
Saker, Austen (*fl.* 1580), I, 729
Sala, Angelo, I, 719
Sala, George Augustus Henry (1828–1896), III, **505**f., 601
Sala's Journal (1894), III, 818
Saladin, Charles (*fl.* 1801), II, 142
Salas Barbadillo, Alonzo Geronimo de, II, 68, 533
Saldkeld, T. (*fl.* 1730), II, 121
Sale, George (1697?–1736), II, 939
Salesbury (or Salisbury), William (1520?–1600?), I, 44, 806
Salignac de la Mothe Fénelon, François de, II, 798
Salisbury
  Magazines, II, 685 (1786)
  Newspapers, II, **728**

Salisbury, Robert Arthur Talbot Gascoyne Cecil, Marquis of (1830–1903), III, 149
Salisbury, Robert Cecil, Earl of (1563?–1612), I, 384–5, 399
Salisbury, W. (fl. 1776), II, 774
Salisbury and Winchester Journal, The (1773), II, 728
Salisbury and Winchester Journal and Hampshire Chronicle, The (1784), II, 729
Salisbury Journal, The (1729), II, 728
Salisbury Journal, The (1772), II, 728
Salisbury Journal; Or, Weekly Advertiser, The (1739), II, 728
Salisbury Post-Man, The (1715), II, 728
Salisbury Register (M.E.), I, 122
Sallust, II, 767
Salmon, — (fl. 1855), III, 82
Salmon, George (1819–1904), III, 851, 942
Salmon, Nathaniel (1675–1742), II, **880**
Salmon, Thomas (1679–1767), II, 742
Salmon, William (1644–1713), II, 657
Salmon's Mercury (1777), II, 720
Salomon and Marcolphus, The Dyalogus Betwixt (15 cent.), I, 266
Salomon and Saturnus (O.E.), I, 82 (in verse), 94 (in prose)
Salopian Journal and Courier of Wales, The (1794), II, 728
Salt, Henry (1780–1827), III, 992
Salter, Robert (fl. 1811), III, 768
Salter, Samuel (d. 1778), I, 879
Salter, Thomas (fl. 1581), I, 713
Salter, Thomas Frederick (fl. 1814–26), III, 768
Salterne, George (b. 1568), I, 659
Saltmarsh, John (d. 1647), I, 699, 749–50
Saltonstall, Charles (fl. 1636), I, 390, 885
Saltonstall, Wye (fl. 1630–40), I, 723, 766, 805, 858, 885
Salusbury, Sir John (fl. 1600), poet, I, 581
Salusbury, John (fl. 1695), printer, II, 706
Salusbury, T. (fl. 1660–5), II, 182, 777, 808, 810
Saluste, Guillaume de, I, 333, 766, 818
Salviati, L., I, 661
Salvin, Francis Henry (1817–1904), III, 778 (2)
Salvin, Osbert (1835–1898), III, 829, 958
Salzmann, Christian Gotthilf, II, 566
Sam. Farley's Bristol Newspaper (1730), II, 721
Sam. Farley's Bristol Post-Man (1713), II, 721
Sam. Farley's Exeter Post-Man (1701), II, 723
Samber, Robert (fl. 1729), II, 121, 541–2, 565, 744, 783, 793, 809
Sammes, Aylett (1636?–1679?), II, 920
Sampson, Henry (1841–1891), III, 813–5, 820
Sampson, T. (fl. 1842), III, 75
Sampson, William (1590?–1636?), I, 649f., 803
Samuel, E. (fl. 1807), III, 800
Samuelson, Sir Bernhard (1820–1905), III, 120
Samuelson, James (fl. 1868–90), III, 791, 1078

Samwell, David (d. 1799), II, 756
San Pedro, Diego Hernandez de, I, 343
Sanatt, J. H. (fl. 1808), III, 777
Sancroft, William (1617–1693), I, 368, 699f.
Sanday, William (1843–1920), III, 851
Sandby, Paul (1725–1809), II, 161
Sandeman, F. (fl. 1892), III, 772
Sanden, Thomas (fl. 1781–1817), II, 101
Sanderman, Robert (fl. 1763), II, 24
Sanders, Nicholas (1530?–1581), I, 826, 845
Sanderson, John (d. 1602), I, 769, 874
Sanderson, Robert (1587–1663), bishop of Lincoln, I, 700, 874
Sanderson, Robert (1660–1741), historian, II, 875
Sanderson, Thomas (1759–1829), II, 326
Sanderson, Sir William (1586?–1676), I, 840
Sandford, Sir Daniel Keyte (1798–1838), III, 126
Sandford, Francis (1630–1694), II, 798
Sandford (or Sanford), James (fl. 1567–9), I, 801, 806
Sandford, John (1801–1873), III, 129
Sandford, Robert (fl. 1666), II, 752
Sandham, Elizabeth (fl. 1788–1815), II, 549, 560; III, 136
Sandwich, Edward Montagu, Earl of (1625–1662), II, 743
Sandwich, John Montagu, Earl of (1718–1792), II, 748
Sandys, Edwin (1516?–1588), archbishop of York, I, 683
Sandys, Sir Edwin (1561–1629), statesman, I, 679, 687, 779
Sandys, Frederick (1829–1904), III, 91
Sandys, George (1578–1644), I, 444, 679, 770, 805, 809
Sandys, William (1792–1874), I, 267
Sanford (or Sandford), James (fl. 1567–9), I, 714, 809, 880
Sanford, John (fl. 1573), I, 814
Sangs of the Lowlands of Scotland (18 cent.), II, 255
Sangster, Charles (fl. 1856), III, 1086
Sannazaro, Giacomo, I, 342
SANSKRIT SCHOLARS, III, 1017f.
Sansom, J. (fl. 1843), I, 696
Sanson, Nicolas, II, 800
Sansovino, Francesco, I, 338, 818
Sapientia Salomonis (16 cent.), I, 663
Sappho, II, 763
Sappho (18 cent.), II, 216
Sarah Farley's Bristol Journal (1777), II, 721
Saravia, Hadrianus (1531–1613), I, 687
Sardi, Pietro, II, 813
Sardou, Victorien, III, 22, 456, 598, 608
Sargant, William Lucas (1809–1889), III, 977, 979, 982
Sargent, Harry R. (fl. 1895), III, 761
Sargent, John Young (1829–1915), III, **1002**

Saris, Edward (*fl.* 1617), I, 784
Saris, John (d. 1646), I, 783
Sarkar, K. L. (*fl.* 1898), III, 1082
Sarmun, A (M.E.), I, **172**
Sarpi, Pietro (Paolo Servita), I, 818; II, 813
Sarrasin, Jean François, II, 800
Sastres, Francesco (*fl.* 1789), II, 681
Sastri, Mahamamahopadhyaya (*fl.* 1897), III, 1082
Satelite; Or, Repository of Literature, The (1798), II, 684
SATIRE
    Middle English Period. See under TALES, I, **161**f. and PIERS PLOWMAN SERIES, I, **195**f.
    Renaissance to Restoration, I, 479f. (formal satirists), 713f. (popular satire)
    Restoration to Romantic Revival, II, 24 (criticism), 44f. (French-English), 58f. (German-English, English-German), 170 (recent criticism)
Satirist, The (1807), II, 391
Satirist, or Censor of the Times, The (1831), III, 812
Satirist, or Monthly Meteor, The (1808), III, 825
Satthianadhan, Samuel (*fl.* 1886), III, 1084
Saturday Analyst and Leader, The (1860), III, 814
Saturday Review, The (1856), III, 794, 814
Saturday's Post, The (1716), II, 712
Satyre Ménippée, La, I, 331
Satyrical, Humourous, & Familiar Pieces (18 cent.), II, 251
Satyrical Works of Titus Petronius Arbiter, The (18 cent.), II, 188–9, 191 (2)
Saul, Arthur (*fl.* 1614), I, 395
Saulnier, Gilbert, Sieur Du Verdier, I, 734
Sault, Richard (d. 1702), II, 658, 790
Saumières, Jacques de Langlade, Baron de, II, 785
Saunder's Irish Daily News (1878), III, 808f.
Saunders, Charles (*fl.* 1681), II, 268
Saunders, George (1762–1839), II, 403
Saunders, Henry (*fl.* 1755), II, 735
Saunders, James (*fl.* 1724), II, 820
Saunders, John (1810–1895), I, 210; III, 829
Saunders, T. H. (*fl.* 1855), III, 71
Saunders, Thomas (*fl.* 1584), I, 768
Saunders, William (1823–1895), III, 799, 802, 803 (2), 807
Saunders' Irish Daily News (1878), II, 735
Saunders' News-Letter (1755), II, 735 (2)
Saunders's News-Letter [Dublin] (1777), III, 808
Saunders' News-Letter and Daily Advertiser (1784), II, 735
Saurin, Jacques, II, 800
Saussure, César de, II, 140
Saussure, Horace Bénédict de, II, 800
Savage, James (1767–1845), III, 789

Savage, John (1673–1747), II, 744, 790, 800, 869
Savage, Marmion W. (1803–1872), III, **506**f., 810
Savage, Richard (1697?–1742), II, 198, 202 (2), **326**f., 662
Savage, William (1770–1843), III, 73, 75, 79
Savary, Jacques, II, 926
Savery, Thomas (1650–1715), II, 962
Savigny, Friedrich Karl von, III, 34, 718
Savile, Bourchier Wrey (1817–1888), III, 29, 59, 162
Savile, George, Marquis of Halifax (1633–1695), II, **570**f.
Savile, Sir Henry (1549–1622), scholar, I, 312, 807, 857–8, 861
Savile, Henry (*fl.* 1596), voyager, I, 788
Savile, Henry (1568–1617), of Banke, I, 363
Savile, Henry (1642–1687), diplomatist, II, 134
Saviolo, Vincentio (*fl.* 1595), I, 379, 394
Savoy et de Fontenai, Jean Baptiste de la Fontaine, Seigneur de, II, 784
Savoy, The (1896), III, 834
Sawles Warde (M.E.), I, 40, **168**f.
Sawyer, Edmund (d. 1759), I, 397
Sawyer, J. R. (*fl.* 1867), III, 82
SAXON PATOIS TEXTS, I, 36
Say, Charles (*fl.* 1748–95), II, 709, 715–6
Say, Jean Baptiste, II, 142
Say, Samuel (1676–1743), II, 22
Sayer, B. (*fl.* 1833), III, 978
Sayer, Joseph (*fl.* 1768), II, 965
Sayers, Frank (1763–1817), II, 20, 26, 81, **379**
Scamozzi, Vincenzio, II, 813
SCANDINAVIA
    Literary Relations with, II, 70f. (1660–1800); III, 42f. (19 cent.)
    Loan-Words from, I, 33
Scarborough Daily Post, The (1876), III, 804
Scarborough Evening News, The (1882), III, 805
Scarborough Mercury, The, III, 794
Scarborough Miscellany, The (18 cent.), II, 203, 204 (3)
Scarborough Post, The (1887), III, 804
Scargill, M. A. (*fl.* 1837), III, 416
Scargill, William Pitt (1787–1836), III, **415**f., 634
Scarlatti, Alessandro, II, 66
Scarron, Paul, II, 44f., 48, 533, **800**
'Scarronnomimus, Naso' (1673), II, 288
Scattergood, Antony (1611–1687), I, 856
SCENERY (theatrical), I, 506 (16, 17 cents.); II, 405f. (18 cent.)
Schaefer, Sir Edward Albert Sharpey (b. 1850), III, 964
Schaw, Janet (*fl.* 1776), II, 742, 756
Scheffel, Joseph Viktor von, III, 34
Schelling, Friedrich Wilhelm Joseph von, III, 47

Schemer or Universal Satirist, The (1760), II, 664

Schenck, F. (*fl.* 1857), III, 83

Schiller, Johann Christoph Friedrich von, II, 60f., 63; III, 34, 46, 50
  Translations from (18 cent.), II, 60f, 63, 553, 807
  Translations from (19 cent.), III, 34, 406, 594, 597, 670

Schink, A. (*fl.* 1798), II, 60

Schlegel, August Wilhelm von, II, 71; III, 34

Schlegel, Friedrich, III, 34, 50

Schleiermacher, F. D. E., III, 34, 47, 894

Schlesinger, Max (*fl.* 1853), III, 790

Schloss, D. F. (*fl.* 1892), III, 984

Schmitz, Leonhard (1807–1890), III, 670

Schnitzler, Arthur, III, 35

Schoenaich, C. O., II, 807

Schoenberg, L. (*fl.* 1841), III, 75

Schofield's Middlewich Journal; Or, General Advertiser (1756), II, 726

Scholae Edinensis in Caroli II Redditum (17 cent.), II, 174

Schole Howse of Women, The (16 cent.), I, 716

Scholefield, James (1789–1853), II, 934; III, 853, 994 (2)

Schomberg, Alexander Crowcher (1756–1792), II, 23, 27

Schomberg, Raphael (1714–1792), II, 373

Schomburgk, Sir Robert Hermann (1804–1865), I, 790

School for Honour, The (18 cent.), II, 486

School of Venus, The (18 cent.), II, 208

SCHOOL PLAYS, I, 521f. (16 cent.)

SCHOOL-BOOKS, I, 125 (O.E. and M.E.), 374f. (16, 17 cents.); II, 125f. (1660–1800); III, 135f. (19 cent.)

SCHOOLS, I, 371f. (16, 17 cents.); II, 122f. (17, 18 cents.); III, 128f. (19 cent.)
  Public Schools, I, 125 (M.E.)
  Textbooks, I, 125 (M.E.), 374f. (1500–1660); II, 125f. (1660–1800); III, 135 (19 cent.)

Schopenhauer, Arthur, III, 35, 47

Schort Memoriale, The (M.E.), I, 260

Schottus, Franciscus, I, 781

Schreiner, Olive (1865–1920), III, 560

Schulz, Johann Christoph Friedrich, II, 63

Schuman, F. (*fl.* 1770), II, 227

Schorman, Anna Maria, II, 130

Schurtleff, N. B. (*fl.* 1856), III, 105

SCIENCE (literature of)
  Old English, I, 97f. See also under WRITINGS IN LATIN, I, 98f.
  Middle English, I, 215 (in Chaucer). See also under WRITINGS IN LATIN, I, 280f.
  Renaissance to Restoration, I, 545 (in Shakespeare), 879f. (principal writers)
  Restoration to Romantic Revival, II, 674f. (magazines), 959f. (principal writers)
  Nineteenth Century, III, 60f. and 68f. (science and religion), 160 (science and poetry), 936f. (principal writers)

Science of Love, The (18 cent.), II, 247

Scientific Magazine and Freemasons' Repository, The (1797), II, 682

Scientific Receptacle, The (1795), II, 682

'Scipio, C.' (1807), II, 832

Sclater, P. L. (*fl.* 1859), III, 829

Scobell, Henry (d. 1660), I, 760, 851

Scoble, A. R. (*fl.* 1856), I, 400

Scoble, J. (*fl.* 1900), III, 1092

Scogan, Henry (*fl.* 15 cent.), I, 254

Scoggin, His Jestes (16 cent.), I, 714

Scoloker, Anthony (*fl.* 1548), I, 819

Scoresby, William (1789–1857), III, 992

Scory, John (d. 1585), I, 810

Scot, Elizabeth (*fl.* 1801), II, 983

Scot, Sir John (1585–1670), of Scotstarvet, I, 910

Scot, Michael (d. before 1236), I, 298

Scot (or Scott), Reginald (1538?–1599), I, 391, 893

Scot, Thomas (*fl.* 1610–25), I, 481

Scotch Intelligencer, Relating the Weekly News from Scotland, the Court and other places, The (1643), I, 755

Scotch Mercury; Giving a true Account of Occurrences in Scotland, The (1692), II, 705

Scotchman, The (1772), II, 665

Scotish Ballads and Songs (18 cent.), II, 252, 254

Scotish Dove sent out and returning, The (1643), I, 755

Scotish Poems, Reprinted from Scarce Editions (18 cent.), II, 247

Scotish Songs (18 cent.), II, 249, 250

SCOTLAND
  Bibliographies and Library Catalogues, I, 7; II, 966
  Cultural and Social Background, I, 895f. (16, 17 cents.); II, 156f. and 966f. (17, 18 cents.)
  Descriptions, I, 773f. (16, 17 cents.); II, 156f. (1660–1800)
  Historians and Antiquarians, I, 909f. (17 cent.); II, 995f. (1660–1800); III, 886, 904f., 928f. (19 cent.)
  Jacobite Literature, II, 1001f.
  Literary Histories, I, 10; II, 966
  Magazines, II, 685f. (1739–1800)
  Middle Scots Writers, I, 254f.
  Newspapers, II, 730f. (1642–1800); III, 806f. (19 cent.)
  Poetry and Drama, I, 896f. (16, 17 cents.); II, 967f. (17, 18 cents.); III, 163 (19 cent., anthologies)
  Printers and Booksellers, I, 353f. (16, 17 cents.); II, 89f. (18 cent.)

Scotland (*cont.*)
Prose, i, 900f. (16 cent.); ii, 992f. (1660–1800)
Saints' Legends, i, 175
Social Background, ii, 156f. (1660–1800)
Theology and Religious Controversy, i, 906f. (17 cent.); ii, 992f. (1660–1800)
Universities, i, 124–5 (M.E.)
Scots Angler, The (1896), iii, 768
Scots Chronicle, The (1796), ii, 732
Scots Courant, The (1710), ii, 731
Scots Farmer, The (1772), ii, 686
Scots Magazine, The (1739), ii, 674, 686; iii, 822
Scots Magazine and Edinburgh Literary Miscellany, The (1804), iii, 822
Scots Memoirs (1683), ii, 657
Scots Memoirs, by way of dialogue between John and Elymas (1683), ii, 704
Scots Musical Museum, The (18 cent.), ii, 241–2, 245, 247, 253
Scots Nightingale, The (18 cent.), ii, 233–4
Scots Observator Being Remarks upon the affairs of the North of Britain (1708), ii, 660
Scots Observer, The [Edinburgh] (1888), iii, 814
Scots Postman, or New Edinburgh Gazette, The (1708), ii, 731
Scots Scourge (18 cent.), ii, 222
Scots Scourge, The (18 cent.), ii, 223
Scots Spy, or Critical Observer, The (1776), ii, 665
Scots Town and Country Magazine, The (1778), ii, 686
Scots Vocal Miscellany, The (18 cent.), ii, 235
Scots Weekly Magazine; Or, Grand Repository, The (1776), ii, 686
Scotsman, The [Edinburgh] (1860), iii, 794, 807
Scott, A. (*fl.* 1793), journalist, ii, 732
Scott, A. (*fl.* 1840), dramatist, iii, 379
Scott, A. de C. (*fl.* 1862), of the Ordnance Survey, iii, 83
Scott, Alexander (1525?–1584), i, 899
Scott, C. P. (1846–1932), iii, 787, 802
Scott, Caroline Lucy, Lady (1784–1857), iii, 389
Scott, Clement (1841–1904), iii, 600 (2), 787, 830
Scott, Constance Margaret (*fl.* 1919), iii, 787
Scott, Dukinfield Henry (b. 1854), iii, 962
Scott, Edmund (*fl.* 1606), i, 783
Scott, Ernest (b. 1868), iii, 1098
Scott, Firth (*fl.* 1897), iii, 1097
Scott, G. (*fl.* 1772), editor of Camden, i, 827
Scott, G. (*fl.* 1781), publisher, ii, 709
Scott, George (*fl.* 1683), editor of Sir James Melville's 'Memoirs', i, 384
Scott, Helenus (1760–1821), ii, 548

Scott, Hew (1791–1872), iii, 904
Scott, Hugh Stowell (1862–1903) ('Henry Seton Merriman'), iii, **555**
Scott, J. A. (*fl.* 1877), journalist, iii, 809
Scott, James (1733–1814), ii, 665
Scott, John (1730–1783), of Amwell, poet, ii, 221, **379**
Scott, John (1747–1819), later Scott-Waring, agent of Warren Hastings, ii, 456, 634, 709
Scott, John, Earl Eldon (1751–1817), ii, 112
Scott, John (*fl.* 1792–1828), of Emmanuel College, Cambridge, iii, 123
Scott, John (1777–1834), divine, ii, 853
Scott, John (*fl.* 1815), of Gala, friend of Sir Walter Scott, iii, 375
Scott, John (1783–1821), journalist, iii, 223, 798 (2), 800, 810–1, 825
Scott, John Robert (*fl.* 1804), ii, 20
Scott, Joseph Nicol (1703?–1769), ii, 761
Scott, Michael (1789–1835), iii, **416**
Scott (or Scot), Reginald (1538?–1599), i, 391, 893
Scott, Robert (1811–1887), iii, 1000
Scott, Robert Pickett (*fl.* 1877–92), iii, 113
Scott, S. (*fl.* 1687), ii, 180
Scott, Sarah (d. 1795), ii, 545f., 546, 556, 645, 770
Scott, T. C. (*fl.* 1813), educationalist, iii, 113
Scott, Thomas (1580?–1626), political writer, i, 737
Scott, Thomas (*fl.* 1696), dramatist, ii, **427**
Scott, Thomas (1705–1775), of Ipswich, iii, 405
Scott, Thomas (1747–1821), rector of Aston Sandford, ii, **853**, 916
Scott, Walter (1614?–1694?), ii, 996
Scott, Sir Walter (1771–1832), iii, **369**f., 414
Dramatic adaptations from, iii, 586–7, 591, 593 (3), 595, 604
Reviews by, ii, 343, 381, 834, 987; iii, 86, 165, 192 (2), 196, 210, 368, 383, 411, 1028
Translations from, iii, 26, 37, 40, 42–3, 45 (2)
Scott, William (*fl.* 1820), educationalist, iii, 130
Scott, William (1813–1872), divine, i, 698; iii, 854
Scott, William Bell (1811–1890), iii, **305**
Scott-Moncrieff, W. G. (*fl.* 1661–78), ii, 158
Scott-Waring, John (1747–1819). See Scott
Scottish Alexander Buik (M.E.), i, **144**
Scottish Congregational Magazine, The (1835), ii, 686
Scottish Farmer and Horticulturalist, The (1861), iii, 819
Scottish Feilde (M.E.), i, **201**
SCOTTISH LANGUAGE
Dialects, i, 38
Dictionaries, ii, 927
Texts, i, 43

Scottish Leader, The [Edinburgh] (1887), III, 807
Scottish Legend Collection (M.E.), I, **175**
SCOTTISH LITERATURE. See SCOTLAND
Scottish Mercury, The (1643), I, 755
Scottish News, The [Glasgow] (1886), III, 808
Scottish Register; Or, General View of History [etc.], *The* (1794), II, 686
Scottish Review, The (1853), III, 833
SCOTTISH TEXTS (M.E.), I, 43
Scottish Tragic Ballads (18 cent.), II, 235, 237
Scottish Troy Fragments (M.E.), I, **145**
Scottish Typographical Circular, The (1857), III, 88
Scougal, Henry (1650–1678), II, 993
Scoundrel's Dictionary, The [etc.] (18 cent.), II, 216
Scourge, The (1717), II, 662
Scourge, The (1752), II, 664
Scourge, The (1780), II, 665
Scourge: or Monthly Expositor of Imposture and Folly, The (1811), III, 825
Scrafton, Luke (*fl.* 1763), II, 750
Scrapeana (18 cent.), II, 247 (2)
Scribe, Augustin Eugène, Adaptations from, III, 587–8, 591 (3), 595 (2), 598 (2), 600, 604, 626, 711
Scriven, John (*fl.* 1823), III, 988
Scrivener, Frederick Henry Ambrose (1813–1891), III, **1014**
Scrivener, Matthew (*fl.* 1660–88), II, 142
Scrivener, S. C. (*fl.* 1891), III, 972
Scroggs, Sir William (1623?–1683), II, 965
Scrope, George Poulett (1797–1876), III, 951, 971, 978, 981
Scrope, J. (*fl.* 1765), II, 779
Scrope, R. (*fl.* 1767), I, 399
Scrope, William (1772–1852), III, 766, 769
Scrutator, The (1764), II, 665
Scrutton, Sir T. E. (*fl.* 1886), III, 988
Scudamore, James (*fl.* 1664), II, 288
Scudéry, Georges de, II, 43
Scudéry, Madeleine de, I, 819; II, 48f. 533, **800**
Scully, W. C. (*fl.* 1886–1913), III, 1089 (2), 1090, 1092
SCULPTURE (books on), I, 392 (16, 17 cent.)
Scupoli, Lorenzo, II, 813
Seafarer, The (O.E.), I, **70**f.
Seager, Francis (*fl.* 1549–63), I, 678
Seal, Sir Brajendranath (*fl.* 1899), III, 1082
Seale, E. W. (*fl.* 1858), III, 811
Seall, Francis (*fl.* 1592), I, 768f.
Seally, John (1747?–1795), II, 20, 678–9
Sealy, H. N. (*fl.* 1858), III, 974
Seaman, William (1606–1680), I, 781
SEAMANSHIP (Handbooks of), I, 390f. (16, 17 cents.)
'Searle, January', i.e. George Searle Phillips (1815–1889), III, 170, 233
Searle, W. G. (*fl.* 1850), I, 370

Seasonable Writer, The (1727), II, 663
Sebright, Sir John Saunders (1767–1846), III, 778
Secker, Thomas (1693–1768), 132, 152, II, **853**
Second Book of the Pleasant Musical Companion, The (17 cent.), II, 180 (2)
Second Booke of Ayres, The (17 cent.), I, 486
Second Collection of Miscellanies, A (18 cent.), II, 196
Second Maiden's Tragedy, The (17 cent.), I, 653
Secondat, Charles de, Baron de Montesquieu, II, 800
Secret History of Mama Oello, The (18 cent.), II, 539
Secret Mercury, The (1702), II, 661
Secret Mercury; Or, The Adventures of Seven Days, The (1702), II, 659
Secreta Secretorum (15 cent.), I, 266
Secrets of the Free-Masons Revealed, The (18 cent.), II, 219
Secular Review, The (1877), III, 819
Secular World, The (1862), III, 817
Secundus, Johannes, I, 329, 819; II, 201
Sedaine, Michel-Jean, II, 43, 800
SEDBERGH SCHOOL, I, 373
Sedgwick, Adam (1785–1873), geologist, III, 122–3, 140, **950**
Sedgwick, Adam (1854–1913), zoologist, III, 959
Sedgwick, Joseph (*fl.* 1653), I, 368
Sedgewick (or Sedgwick), O. (*fl.* 1737–42), II, 540
Sedley, Sir Charles (1639?–1701), II, **275**, 794
Sedulius Scottus (*fl.* 850), I, **108**f.
Seebohm, Frederic (1833–1912), III, **926**f.
Seege of Troy (M.E.), I, **145**
Seeley, Harry Govier (1839–1909), III, 953
Seeley, Sir John Robert (1834–1895), III, 836, **932**
Seeley, Robert Benton (1798–1886), III, 853
Seely, John Benjamin (*fl.* 1824), III, 1079
Segar (or Seager), Francis (*fl.* 1549–63), I, 264
Segar, Sir William (d. 1633), I, 379, 394, 396, 724
Sege of Jerusalem, or Distructio Jerusalem (M.E.), (Alliterative Version), I, **158**
Sege of Melayne (M.E.), I, **141**
Segneri, Paolo, II, 813
Segrais, Jean Regnauld de, II, 533f., 792, 797
Seinte Marherete (M.E.), I, **169**f.
Selborne, Roundell Palmer, Earl of (1812–1895), III, 140, 149
Selby, Charles (1802?–1863), III, 442, **607**
Selden, John (1584–1654), I, 379, **851**, 863, **874**
Select and Remarkable Epitaphs (18 cent.), II, 218
Select Ayres and Dialogues (1659), I, 486
Select Ayres and Dialogues (1669), II, 175 (2)
Select Beauties of Ancient English Poetry (18 cent.), II, 241

Select British Theatre, A (1816), II, 392
Select Collection of English Plays, A (1755), II, 392
Select Collection of English Songs, A (18 cent.), II, 237
Select Collection of Epigrams, A (18 cent.), II, 252
Select Collection of Epitaphs from Tombstones, A (18 cent.), II, 219
Select Collection of Farces, A (1762), II, 392
Select Collection of Favourite Scotish Ballads, A (18 cent.), II, 245
Select Collection of Favourite Scots Songs (18 cent.), II, 245
Select Collection of Modern Poems, A (1713), II, 191, 201
Select Collection of Modern Poems, A (1744), II, 210, 214, 218, 222
Select Collection of New, Favourite and Popular Songs, A (18 cent.), II, 252
Select Collection of New Songs, A (1780), II, 235
Select Collection of Novels and Histories, A, II, 542
Select Collection of Original Scottish Airs, A (18 cent.), II, 248
Select Collection of Poems, A (18 cent.), II, 235 (2), 236, 238
Select Collection of Poems, From Admired Authors, A (18 cent.), II, 245
Select Collection of Poems, From the most approved Authors, A (1768), II, 225, 229
Select Collection of Scots Poems, A (18 cent.), II, 232, 239
Select Collection of the Most Admired Songs, Duetts, A (18 cent.), II, 234, 251
Select Collection Of the Original Love Letters of several Eminent Persons, A (18 cent.), II, 217
Select Collection of Vocal Music, A (18 cent.), II, 228
Select Epigrams (18 cent.), II, 253
Select Epigrams of Martial (18 cent.), II, 217
Select Epitaphs (18 cent.), II, 217
Select Essays from the Batchelor (18 cent.), II, 229 (2)
Select Fables (18 cent.), II, 238
Select Lessons in Prose and Verse (18 cent.), II, 223, 230, 233, 237, 239, 253, 254 (3)
Select Letters between the late Duchess of Somerset, William Shenstone, Esq. and others (18 cent.), II, 233
Select Musicall Ayres (17 cent.), I, 486
Select Musicall Ayres and Dialogues (17 cent.), I, 486
Select Pieces of Poetry, Intended to promote Piety and Virtue in Young People (18 cent.), II, 251
Select Poems (1783), II, 237
Select Poems and Ballads (18 cent.), II, **232**

Select Poems from a Larger Collection (18 cent.), II, 231
Select Poems from Ireland, II, 201
Select Poems of Dr Akenside [etc.], *The* (18 cent.), II, 221
Selection of Fables From the best English Writers, A (18 cent.), II, 254
Selection of favourite Catches, A (18 cent.), II, 253, 255
Selection of Masonic Songs, A (18 cent.), II, 223, 254
Selection of Scots Songs, A (18 cent.), II, 250
Selection of the most Favourite Scots Songs, A (18 cent.), II, 245, 247
SELECTIONS. See ANTHOLOGIES, MISCELLANIES and READERS
Selector, The (1776), II, 680
Selector, The (1797), II, 253
Selector; Or Say's Sunday Reporter, The (1795), II, 716; III, 810
Sell, Edward (*fl.* 1896), III, 1082
Sellar, William Young (1825–1890), III, **1009**
Seller, John (*fl.* 1700), II, 129
Sellman, Edward (*fl.* 1578), I, 787
Sellon, Mary A. (*fl.* 1810), III, 374
Selous, F. C. (*fl.* 1881), III, 1092
Selwyn, George (1719–1791), II, 136f.
Selwyn, T. K. (*fl.* 1829), III, 130, 779
Selwyn, William (1806–1875), III, 124
SEMANTICS. See under VOCABULARY, I, 30f.
SEMI-OFFICIAL PAPERS, II, 718f.
Semmedo, Alvaro, I, 786
Sempill, Sir James (1566–1625), I, 709, 909
Sempill, Robert (1595?–1665?), I, 905f.
Sempills, The (1530?–1665?), I, 900
Semple, Robert (1766–1816), III, 1091
Sen, Guruprasada (*fl.* 1891), III, 1082
Sen, Kesabchandra (*fl.* 1886), III, 1082
Senator, The (1728), II, 663
Senator; Or, Clarendon's Parliamentary Chronicle, The (1790), II, 681
Seneca, I, 807; II, 767
SENECAN TRAGEDIES, I, 522f. (16 cent.)
Senefelder, Alois, III, 92
Senhouse, John (*fl.* 1730), II, 767
Senilis Amor (17 cent.), I, 663
Senior, Nassau William (1790–1864), III, **151**, 872f., 974, 976
Senior, William (d. 1920), III, 771, 815
Sentences and Maxims Divine (18 cent.), II, 190
Sentimental and Masonic Magazine, The (1792), II, 688
SENTIMENTAL COMEDY, II, 395f. (18 cent.)
Sentimental Magazine, The (1773), II, 679
Sentimental Spouter, The (18 cent.), II, 230
Sentinel, The (1843), III, 814
Sepulchrorum Inscriptiones (18 cent.), II, 199
Séran de la Tour, Abbé, II, 801
SERBIA
    Literary Relations with, III, 43f.

Sergeant, John (1622–1707), II, 943
Serious Thoughts (1710), II, 661
Serle, Ambrose (1742–1812), II, 19
Serle, John (*fl.* 1745), II, 303
Serle, Thomas James (*fl.* 1819–47), III, **594f.**, 810
Serlio, Sebastiano, I, 392
Serlo of Wilton (*fl.* 1170), I, **288**
Sermo in Festo Corporis Christi (M.E.), I, **172**
Sermon against Miracle Plays (M.E.), I, **172**
SERMONS
    Anglo-Saxon Period. See HOMILIES, I, 89f., 92f. and under WRITINGS IN LATIN, I, 98f.
    Middle English Period, I, 168f. and under WRITINGS IN LATIN, I, 280f.
    Renaissance to Restoration, I, 679f. (1500–1620), 694f. (1620–60)
    For later periods see under RELIGION (writings on)
    See also PREACHING (manuals on)
Serre, Jean de la, I, 334
Serres, Jean de, I, 331, 819
Serres, Olivier de, I, 893
Servita, Paolo (Pietro Sarpi), I, 818; II, 813
Session of the Critics [etc.], *The* (18 cent.), II, 201
Seth, Andrew, later Pringle-Pattison (1856–1931), III, **873**
Seton, Sir Henry Wilmot (*fl.* 1830), III, 988
Seton, John (1498?–1567), I, 880
Settle, Dionyse (*fl.* 1577), I, 787
Settle, Elkanah (1648–1724), II, 270–1, 401, **427**, 704, 810
Seven Sages of Rome, The (M.E.), I, **155**
SEVENTEENTH CENTURY. For years 1600–60 see RENAISSANCE TO RESTORATION, I, 317f.; for 1660–1700 see RESTORATION TO ROMANTIC REVIVAL, II, 3f.
Several Copies of Verses on the Death of Mr. Abraham Cowley (17 cent.), II, 175
Several Letters from Scotland (1651), I, 761
Severall Proceedings in Parliament (1649), I, 760
Severall Proceedings of Parliament (1653), I, 762
Severall Proceedings of Parliament (1654), I, 760
Severall Proceedings of State Affaires (1653), I, 760
Severall Proceedings of State Affaires (1655), I, 760
Severn, C. (*fl.* 1839), I, 387
Severn, Joseph (1793–1879), III, 223
Sévigné, Marie de Rabutin-Chantal, Marquise de, II, 46, 801
Seville, Isidore of, I, 125
Seward, Anna (1747–1809), II, 23, 77, **380**
Seward, William (*fl.* 1740), traveller, II, 754
Seward, William (1747–1799), miscellaneous writer, II, 337, 904
Seward, William Wenman (*fl.* 1783–1804), Irish topographer, II, 159
Sewel, William (1654–1720), II, 855

Sewell, Anna (1820–1878), III, 568
Sewell, Elizabeth Missing (1815–1906), III, **507**
Sewell, George (1690?–1726), II, 191, 193, **327**, 602, 759, 766, 910, 929, 1001
Sewell, Gregory (*fl.* 1728), II, 327 (2)
Sewell, William (1804–1874), III, 113, 122 (2), 126–7, 507 (2), 860
Sex, The [Cambridge] (1897), III, 836
Seyd, E. (*fl.* 1872), III, 973–4
Seymour, E. H. (*fl.* 1805), I, 588
Seymour, Michael Hobart (1800–1874), I, 824
Seymour, Richard (*fl.* 1720), II, 826
Seymour, Robert (*fl.* 1794), II, 718
Seymour, Mrs Robert (*fl.* 1860?), III, 440
Seymour family, letters of (16, 17 cents.), I, 382
Seyssel, C. de, I, 808
Shacklock, Richard (*fl.* 1565), I, 817
Shadgett's Weekly Review of Cobbett, Wooler [etc.] (1819), III, 816
Shadwell, Charles (*fl.* 1710), II, **443**, 774, 794
Shadwell, J. L. (*fl.* 1877), III, 983
Shadwell, Thomas (1642?–1692), II, **411f.**, 794
Shaftesbury, Anthony Ashley Cooper, 3rd Earl of (1671–1713), II, 39, 54, 117, **948**
Shaftesbury, Anthony Ashley Cooper, 7th Earl of (1801–1885), III, 119
Shairp, John Campbell (1819–1885), III, **725**
Shakespear, John (1774–1858), III, 1074
Shakespear's Garland (18 cent.), II, 226 (5)
Shakespeare, William (1564–1616), I, **539f.**
    All's Well that Ends Well, I, 569
    Antony and Cleopatra, I, 572f.
    Apocryphal plays, I, 576f.
    As You Like It, I, 564; II, 358
    Attributed plays, I, 576f.
    Authenticity, I, 587
    Baconian theory, I, 546
    Bibliography, I, 540f.
    Biographies, I, 541f.
    Characters, I, 595f.
    Collected Works, I, 546f.
    Comedy of Errors, The, I, 554
    Continent, Shakespeare on, I, 599f.; II, 71f. (1660–1800)
    Coriolanus, I, 573
    Criticism, I, 590f.
    Cymbeline, I, 573f.
    Dramatic technique, I, 597
    Dramatic types, I, 597f.
    Education of, I, 543
    Edward the Third, I, 577f.
    Extracts and vulgarisations, I, 551f.
    Folios, I, 546f.
    France, Shakespeare in, I, 599f.; II, 72 (1660–1800)
    Geographical knowledge of, I, 545
    Germany, Shakespeare in, I, 604f.; II, 71f. (1660–1800)
    Hamlet, I, 565f.; II, 358

Shakespeare (*cont.*)
Henry the Eighth, I, 575f.
Henry the Fifth, I, 562f.
Henry the Fourth, I, II, I, 561f.
Henry the Sixth, I, II, III, I, 552f.
Influence abroad, I, 599f.
Influence of theatrical conditions, I, 596f.
Influence on successors, I, 599
Influences on, I, 584f.
Interests of, I, 543f.
Julius Caesar, I, 563f.
King John, I, 559f.
King Lear, I, 571f.
Language, I, 30, 33, 46, 588f.
Law in, I, 544f.
Life of, I, 541f.
Love's Labour's Lost, I, 556f.
Lover's Complaint, A, I, 583
Lucrece, I, 580f.
Macbeth, I, 572
More, Sir Thomas, I, 576f.
Measure for Measure, I, 569f.
Merchant of Venice, The, I, 560f.
Merry Wives of Windsor, The, I, 568
Midsummer Night's Dream, A, I, 559f.
Much Ado About Nothing, I, 562
Natural history in, I, 545
Netherlands, Shakespeare in, II, 72 (1660–1800)
Order of plays, I, 586f.
Othello, I, 570f.
Passionate Pilgrim, The, I, 581
Pericles, I, 578
Personality of, I, 543f.
Philosophy of, I, 544
Phoenix and the Turtle, The, I, 581
Poems, I, 580f.
Politics of, I, 544
Printing and publishing of, I, 585f.
Prosody, I, 590
Punctuation, I, 588
Quartos, I, 551
Religion of, I, 544
Richard the Second, I, 558
Richard the Third, I, 553f.
Romeo and Juliet, I, 557f.
Science in, I, 545
Sir Thomas More, I, 576f.
Societies and periodicals, I, 541
Sonnets, I, 581f.
Sources, I, 583f.
Stage-history of plays, I, 598
Style, I, 590
Supernatural in, I, 544
Taming of the Shrew, The, I, 555f.
Tempest, The, I, 574f.
Textual criticism, I, 587f.
Timon of Athens, I, 573
Titus Andronicus, I, 554f.
Translations of, I, 509f.

Travels (alleged) of, I, 545
Troilus and Cressida, I, 568f.
Twelfth Night, I, 564f.
Two Gentlemen of Verona, The, I, 556
Two Noble Kinsmen, The, I, 578f.
Venus and Adonis, I, 580
Vocabulary, I, 33, 589f.
Winter's Tale, The, I, 574
Shamrock, The (1772), II, 229 (2), 230
Shamrock, The (1800), II, 256
Shand, Alexander Innes (1832–1907), III, 767 787
Shand, C. F. (*fl.* 1845), I, 908; II, 993
Shannon, Charles (1863–1937), III, 92
Shannon, Charles Hazelwood (*fl.* 1896), III, 831
Shannon, E. N. (*fl.* 1821), III, 205
Sharkey, Pat. (*fl.* 1790), II, 815
Sharp, Bartholomew (*fl.* 1684), II, 752
Sharp, Sir Cuthbert (1781–1849), II, 258
Sharp, Evelyn, later Nevinson (b. 1869), III, 570
Sharp, Granville (1735–1813), III, 980
Sharp, J. (*fl.* 1883), III, 819
Sharp, John (1645–1714), II, **849**
Sharp, M. R. (*fl.* 1859), III, 819
Sharp, Richard (1759–1835), II, 20
Sharp, Samuel (1700?–1778), II, 745
Sharp, Thomas (1693–1758), divine, II, 849
Sharp, Thomas (*fl.* 1722), publisher, II, 713
Sharp, Thomas (1770–1841), antiquary, I, 275, 277, 279
Sharp, William (1855–1905) ('Fiona Macleod'), III, **552**f.
Sharpe, Charles Kirkpatrick (1781?–1851), I, 272; II, 996 (2); III, 119
Sharpe, Gregory (1713–1771), II, 773, 938
Sharpe, John (*fl.* 1704), II, 753
Sharpe, L. (*fl.* 1794), II, 344
Sharpe, Lewis (*fl.* 1640), I, 650
Sharpe, R. S. (*fl.* 1823), III, 575
Sharpe, Roger (*fl.* 1610), I, 481
Sharpe, Samuel (1799–1881), III, 164
Sharpe, Timothy (*fl.* 1751 or perhaps a pseudonym), II, 214
Sharpe (or Sharp), William (1770–1841), antiquary, II, 17
Sharpe, William (*fl.* 1859), of Highbury, III, 164
Sharpe's British Theatre (1804), II, 392
Sharpe's London Journal (1849), III, 828
Sharpe's London Magazine (1845), III, 828
Sharpe's London Magazine of Entertainment (1852), III, 828
Sharpham, Edward (1576–1608), I, 650, 717
Shatterall, Robert (*fl.* 1676), II, 421
Shaw, Cuthbert (1738–1771), II, **380**
Shaw, Ferdinando (*fl.* 1730), II, 928
Shaw, George (1751–1813), II, 681
Shaw, George Bernard (b. 1856), III, **617**f., 977
Shaw, J. Dods (*fl.* 1860), III, 802

Shaw, James (*fl.* 1786), II, 747
Shaw, John (1559–1625), II, 130
Shaw, John (*fl.* 1778), II, 932
Shaw, Lachlan (1692–1777), II, 998
Shaw, Lawrence Stebbing (1762–1802), II, **892**;
    III, 662
Shaw, Peter (1694–1763), II, 110, 664, 802, 911
Shaw, Samuel (1635–1696), II, 52
Shaw, Stebbing (1762–1802). See Lawrence
    Stebbing Shaw
Shaw, Thomas (1694–1751), African traveller,
    II, 749
Shaw, Thomas (*fl.* 1808), III, 1079
Shaw, William (1749–1831), biographer, II, 624
Shaw, William (*fl.* 1801), Rector of Chelry, III,
    113
Shaw, William (1797–1853), agriculturalist,
    III, 819
Shaw, William A. (b. 1865), economist, III,
    975
Shaw-Lefevre, Charles, Viscount Eversley
    (1794–1888), III, 971
Shaw-Lefevre, Sir John George (1797–1879),
    III, 972
Shawe, John (*fl.* 1608–64), I, 382
Shaylor, Joseph (1844–1924), III, 99
Sheares, Henry (*fl.* 1768), II, 665, 737
Sheares, W. (*fl.* 1633), I, 627
Shearman, Montague (1857–1930), III, 775
Shears (or Sheeres), Sir Henry (d. 1710), II,
    762–3, 937
Shebbeare, John (1709–1788), II, 141, 545 (2)
Shee, M. A. (*fl.* 1860), III, 595
Shee, Sir Martin Archer (1769–1850), III, **595**
Sheehan, — (*fl.* 1832), III, 809
Sheeres (or Shears), Sir Henry (d. 1710), II,
    762–3, 937
Sheffard, William (*fl.* 1622), I, 744
SHEFFIELD
    Newspapers, II, 728
    Printers and booksellers, II, 88
    University, III, 128
Sheffield, John, Earl of Mulgrave (1648–1721),
    II, 21, 44, 196, **283**
Sheffield, John Baker Holroyd, Earl of (1735–
    1821), II, 884; III, 975
Sheffield Advertiser, The (1792), II, 728
Sheffield Daily Advertiser, The (1863), III, 803
Sheffield Daily Argus, The (1859), III, 802
Sheffield Daily News, The (1856), III, 802
Sheffield Daily Post, The (1882), III, 804
Sheffield Daily Telegraph, The (1855), III, 794,
    802
Sheffield Evening Star and Daily Times, The
    (1865), III, 803
Sheffield Evening Telegraph, The (1887), III, 806
Sheffield Independent, The, III, 794
Sheffield Iris, The (1828), II, 728
Sheffield Post, The (1873), III, 804
Sheffield Register, The (1787), II, 728

Sheil, Richard Lalor (1791–1851), III, **595**
Shelburne, William Petty, Earl of (1737–
    1805), II, 631–2
Sheldon, Gilbert (1598–1677), I, 700
Shelley, Elizabeth (*fl.* 1810), III, 213
Shelley, George (1666?–1736?), II, 125, 190
Shelley, J., Lady (*fl.* 1859), III, 215
Shelley, Mary Wollstonecraft, née Godwin
    (1797–1851), III, 212–4, **416**, 591
Shelley, Percy Bysshe (1792–1822), III, **212**f.
    Translations from, III, 26, 37, 40, 45 (2)
Shelton, Maurice (*fl.* 1735), II, 918
Shelton, Thomas (*fl.* 1612–20), I, 812; II, 68
Shelvocke, George (*fl.* 1690–1728), II, 741
Shenstone, William (1714–1763), II, 18 (2),
    221, **307**f.
Shepheard, H. (*fl.* 1857), III, 463
Shepherd, Richard (1732–1809), II, **380**
Shepherd, Richard Herne (1842–1895), III, 258
Shepherd, William (1768–1847), III, 113
Shepherd, The (1759), II, 664
Shepherd, The (1834), III, 816
Shepherd's Pastime, The (18 cent.), II, 234,
    243
Sheppard, Elizabeth Sara (1830–1862), III, **507**
Sheppard, John (1785–1879), divine, II, 381;
    III, 669 (2)
Sheppard, John George (*fl.* 1845–70), writer
    on education, III, 114
Sheppard, Miss S. (*fl.* 1841), III, 294
Sheppard, Samuel (*fl.* 1646), I, 477, 731, 747,
    749, 757, 758 (3), 759 (2), 761 (5), 867
Sheppard, William (d. 1675?), I, 851; II, 965
SHERBORNE
    Magazine, II, 685 (1773)
    Newspapers, II, 728
*Sherborne, Dorchester and Taunton Journal,
    The* (1886), II, 728
Sherborne Journal, The (1773), II, 728
*Sherborne Mercury; Or, Weekly Advertiser,
    The* (1737), II, 728
Sherbrooke, Robert Love, Viscount (1811–
    1892), III, 111, 149, 153
Sherburne, Sir Edward (1618–1702), I, 807–8;
    II, 28, 56, **286**
Sherburne, John (*fl.* 1639), I, 805
Sherer, J. W. (*fl.* 1883–97), III, 1070, 1084
Sheridan, Caroline Elizabeth Sarah, later
    Norton, and afterwards Lady Stirling-
    Maxwell (1808–1877), III, **302**
Sheridan, Frances (1724–1766), II, 461, **483**,
    545–6
Sheridan, Helen Selina, later Blackwood
    (Baroness Dufferin) (1807–1867), III, **1052**
Sheridan, Richard Brinsley (1751–1816), II,
    44, 62, 66, **454**f., 487; III, 26
Sheridan, Thomas (*fl.* 1661–1703), Irish
    historian, I, 427; II, 782
Sheridan, Thomas (1687–1738), friend of
    Swift, II, 232, 234 (2), **327**f., 663

Sheridan, Thomas (1719–1788), actor and lecturer, I, 16, 46; II, 17, 110, 126, 581, 589, 593, 794
Sheridan's and Henderson's Practical Method of Reading English Poetry (18 cent.), II, 252
Sherley (or Shirley), Sir Anthony (1565–1635?), I, 783
Sherley (or Shirley), Thomas (1638–1678), II, 791
Sherlock, Martin (d. 1797), II, 19, 746
Sherlock, Thomas (1678–1761), II, **853**
Sherlock, William (1641?–1707), II, 847, **849**
Sherman, Francis (*fl.* 1896), III, 1086
Sherring, Matthew Atmore (1826–1880), III, 1084
Sherry (or Shirrye), Richard (*fl.* 1550), I, 376, 800
Sherwin, W. T. (*fl.* 1817), III, 816
Sherwin's Weekly Political Register (1817), III, 816
Sherwood, Henry (d. 1849), III, 417
Sherwood, Mary Martha, née Butt (1775–1851), II, 556; III, 136, **416**f., 1069
Shields, Alexander (1660?–1700), II, **993**
Shields, Michael (*fl.* 1699), II, 995
Shields Daily Gazette, The (1884), III, 794, 802
Shields Daily News, The (1864), III, 803
Shiels, Robert (d. 1753), II, 923
Shift Shifted, Or Weekly Remarks, The (1716), II, 712
Shift's Last Shift; or Weekly Journal, The (1717), II, 712
Shilleto, Richard (1809–1876), III, **1002**
Shilling Magazine, The (1865), III, 830
Shipley, Sir Arthur Everett (1861–1927), III, 959
Shipley, Orby (*fl.* 1866), III, 274, 925
Shipley, William (*fl.* 1838), III, 769
Shipman, Thomas (1632–1680), II, **286**
Shipp, W. (*fl.* 1861), II, 890
Shippen, William (1673–1743), II, 265
SHIPPING (newspapers), II, 718
Shipping and Mercantile Gazette, The (1836), III, 801
Shipping Gazette and Lloyd's List, The (1884), II, 718
Shipping World, The (1883), III, 820
Shipton, J. (*fl.* 1699), II, 790
Shirley (or Sherley), Sir Anthony (1565?–1635?), I, 783
Shirley, Henry (d. 1627), I, 650
Shirley, James (1596–1666), I, 374, 376, **638**f., 799, 863; III, 595
Shirley, John (1366?–1456), I, 257
Shirley, John (1648–1679), biographer of Ralegh, I, 829
Shirley (or Shurly), John (*fl.* 1680–1702), anthologist, II, 179, 180–1
Shirley, Thomas (*fl.* 1784), II, 822
Shirley, Walter Waddington (1828–1866), I, 120, 203–4, 310, 313

Shirley, William (*fl.* 1739), II, **443**f.
Shirreff, Emily Anne Eliza (1814–1897), III, 142–3
Shirreff, Maria Georgina, later Grey (1816–1906), III, 110, 142
Shirrefs, Andrew (1762–1807?), II, 687 (2)
Shirrefs, J. (*fl.* 1799), I, 908
Shirrye (or Sherry), Richard (*fl.* 1550), I, 376, 800
Shirwood, John (d. 1494), **314**
Shoard, J. (*fl.* 1863), III, 94
SHOOTING (books on), III, 762f.
Shore, Arabella (*fl.* 1855), III, 305 (3)
Shore, John Baron Teignmouth (1751–1834), II, 368; III, 1075
Shore, Louisa Catherine (1824–1895), III, **305**
Shore, Margaret Emily (1819–1839), III, 154
Shoreham, William of (*fl.* 14 cent.), I, 271f.
Short, Frederick Hugh (*fl.* 1890), III, 988
Short, John (*fl.* 1887), III, 988
Short, Peter (*fl.* 16 cent.), I, 352
Short, Thomas (1690?–1772), II, 146
Short Metrical Chronicle (M.E.), I, **165**
Shorter, Clement K. (1857–1929), III, 787, 815 (3), 831
Shorter, Dora Mary, née Sigerson (1866–1918), III, **1057**f.
SHORTHAND, I, 377, 586 (Shakespeare), II, 129 (17, 18 cents.)
Shorthouse, Joseph Henry (1834–1903), III, **560**, 820
Shotterel, Robert (*fl.* 1676), II, 823
Shower, Sir Bartholomew (1658–1701), II, 104
SHREWSBURY
  Newspapers, II, 728
  Printers and Booksellers, I, 353 (17, 18 cents.)
  School, I, 373; III, 133, 839
Shrewsbury Chronicle; Or, Wood's British Commercial Pamphlet, The (1772), II, 728
Shrewsbury Officium Pastorum (M.E.), I, 277
Shrigley, Nathaniel (*fl.* 1669), II, 752
SHROPSHIRE
  Booksellers and printers, II, 88
Shropshire Journal, The (1737), II, 714
Shrubsole, E. S. (*fl.* 1893), III, 772
Shrubsole, W. G. (*fl.* 1870), III, 82
Shuckburgh, Evelyn Shirley (1843–1906), III, 834, **1009**f.
Shurley, T. (1681). Misprint for John Shurley or Shirley (*fl.* 1680–1702), II, 807
Shurly, John (*fl.* 1680–1702). See Shirley
Shute, John (*fl.* 1550–70), architect, I, 392
Shute, John (*fl.* 1562–73), translator, I, 777
Shute, W. (*fl.* 1612), I, 779
Shutte, R. N. (*fl.* 1861), III, 854
Shuttleworth Accounts, The (16–17 cents.), I, 46, 384
Sibbald, James (1590?–1650?), I, 911

Sibbald, James (1745–1803), I, 10, 898; II, 672, 686, 732

Sibbald, Sir Robert (1641–1712), II, **996f.**

Sibbes, Richard (1577–1635), I, **700**

Sibthorp, John (1758–1796), III, 959

Sidebotham, J. S. (*fl.* 1865), III, 130

Sidgwick, Arthur (*fl.* 1883), III, 109

Sidgwick, Henry (1838–1900), III, **873f.**

Reviews, etc., III, 109, 265, 269, 849

Sidmouth, Henry Addington, Viscount (1757–1844), III, 149

Sidnam, Jonathan (*fl.* 1630), I, 650, 814

Sidney, Algernon (1622–1683), II, 134

Sidney, Henry, Earl of Romney (1641–1704), II, 134, 163

Sidney, Mary, later Herbert, Countess of Pembroke (1561–1621), I, 537, 817

Sidney, Sir Philip (1554–1586), I, 335, 337, **419f.**, 678, 726; II, 70

Sidney, Samuel (1812–1883), III, 766

Sienkiewicz, Henryk, III, 44

Sigerson, Dora Mary, later Shorter (1866–1918), III, **1057f.**

Sigerson, George (1839–1925), III, 1050, **1054**

Sigmond, G. G. S. (*fl.* 1848), II, 454

Sikes, George (*fl.* 1662–6), II, **871**

'Silence, Samuel' (1743), II, 210 (3), 212 (3), 213 (2), 222 (2)

'Silence, Timothy' (1743), II, 210

Silent Monitor, The (1711), II, 661

Silent Monitor, The (1712), II, 661

Silesio, Mariano, I, 734

Silius, Italicus, II, 768

Silke, Robert (or Spicer) (*fl.* 1320), I, **301**

Sill, Richard (*fl.* 1797), II, 903

Silvanus (16 cent.), I, 663

Silver, George (*fl.* 1599), I, 395

Silver Court Gazette, The (1728), II, 734

Silver Crescent, The [Cambridge] (1890), III, 835

Silvester, Tipping (1700–1768), II, 820

Silvestre, J. B., III, 1034

Silvius, Aeneas, I, 734

Sim, John (*fl.* 1806), II, 374

Simcoe, John Graves (1752–1806), II, 756

Simcoe, Mrs John Graves (*fl.* 1792), II, 757

Simcox, Edith (*fl.* 1877–94), III, 874

Simcox, George Augustus (b. 1841), III, **356f.**, **1010**

Simcox, William Henry (1843–1889), III, 1010

Sime, D., II, 247–8

Sime, S. H. (*fl.* 1895), III, 831

Sime, T. (*fl.* 1772), II, 152

Simeon, Charles (1759–1836), III, 852

Simeon, Cornwall (*fl.* 1860), angler, III, 770

Simeon (or Simons), Joseph (1594–1671), I, 659

Simm, Alexander (*fl.* 1753), II, 216

Simmond's Colonial Magazine (1844), III, 828

Simmonds, P. L. (*fl.* 1841), III, 790

Simmons, G. (*fl.* 1849), III, 119

Simmons, M. (*fl.* 1642–9), I, 753, 760

Simmons, Samuel Foart (1750–1813), II, 680

Simon de Henton (*fl.* 1360), I, 306

Simon of Faversham (1240?–1306), I, **311**

Simon, Sir John (1816–1894), III, 176

Simon, Richard, II, 801

Simond, Louis (*fl.* 1815), II, 142

Simonde de Sismondi, J. C. L., III, 629

Simons, T. (*fl.* 1802), III, 114

SIMPKIN, MARSHALL & CO., III, 99

Simpson, James (1781–1853), III, 114

Simpson, John Palgrave (1807–1887), III, **608**

Simpson, Joseph (*fl.* 1750), II, 615

Simpson, Richard (1820–1876), III, 828, **899**

Simpson, Thomas (1710–1761), mathematician, II, 826

Simpson, Thomas (*fl.* 1814), of Newham, III, 970

Simpson, Sir Walter Grindlay (1843–1898), III, 775

Simpson, William (1823–1899), III, 787

Sims, John (1749–1831), III, 823

Simson (or Symson), Andrew (1638–1712), I, 731

Simson (or Symson), Archibald (1564?–1628), I, 858, **909**

Simson, Matthew (*fl.* 1745), II, 733

Simson, Patrick (1556–1618), I, 910

Sinclair, Captain — (*fl.* 1800), II, 824

Sinclair, A. G. (*fl.* 1792), II, 817

Sinclair, Alexander (*fl.* 1845), III, 787

Sinclair, Archibald (*fl.* 1894), III, 776

Sinclair, Catherine (1800–1864), III, **507f.**

Sinclair, George (d. 1696), II, 999

Sinclair, Hannah (*fl.* 1852), III, 508

Sinclair, John (1683–1750), Master of Sinclair, II, 504, 1003

Sinclair, Sir John (1754–1835), II, 157–8; III, **969**, 980

Singer, G. A. (*fl.* 1897), III, 831

Singer, John (*fl.* 1594–1602), I, 714

Singer, Samuel Weller (1783–1858), III, **1027**

Reprints ed. by, I, 449, 460, 475 (2), 528, 531, 667, 824 (2)

'Single, John' (1742), II, 209, 211 (2), 212 (2)

Singleton, Hugh (*fl.* 16 cent.), I, 351

Singleton, Mary Montgomerie, née Lamb, later Lady Currie, pseudonym 'Violet Fane' (1843–1905), III, **345**

SION COLLEGE (London), Library, I, 361, 362; II, 104

Sir Amadace (M.E.), I, **154f.**

Sir Cleges (M.E.), I, **158**

Sir Degare (M.E.), I, **153**

Sir Degrevant (M.E.), I, **158**

Sir Eger, Sir Grime and Sir Graysteele (M.E.), I, **160**

Sir Eglamour of Artois (M.E.), I, **157**

Sir Firumbras (M.E.), I, **141**

Sir Gawayne and the Grene Knight (M.E.), I, 32, **135** f., 203
Sir Gowther (Robert the Devil) (M.E.), I, **153**
Sir Gyles Goosecappe (17 cent.), I, 653
Sir Isumbras (M.E.), I, **156** f.
Sir John Fielding's Jests (18 cent.), II, 228
Sir John Old-castle, The first part Of the true and honorable historie, of the life of (17 cent.), I, 580
Sir Lambewell (M.E.), I, **153**
Sir Lamwell (M.E.), I, **153**
Sir Landeval (M.E.), I, **152**
Sir Launfal (M.E.), I, **152**
Sir Orfeo (M.E.), I, **151** f.
Sir Percyvelle of Galles (M.E.), I, **137** f.
Sir Thomas More (16 cent.), I, **576** f.
Sir Thomas Overbury His Wife (17 cent.), II, 174, 189
Sir Torrent of Portyngale (M.E.), I, **159**
Sir Triamour (M.E.), I, **159**
Sir Tristrem (M.E.), I, **133** f.
Siraudin, Paul (*fl.* 1854), III, 456
Siris, P. (*fl.* 1706), II, 825
Sisley, Charles P. (*fl.* 1877–92?), III, 815
Sitwell, George (d. 1667), I, 383
Sitwells and Sacheverells, Letters of the (17, 18 cents.), I, 383
Six-Pennyworth of Wit (18 cent.), II, 562
Sixpenny Magazine, The (1861), III, 829
Sixpenny Miscellany, The (18 cent.), II, 198
SIXTEENTH CENTURY. See RENAISSANCE TO RESTORATION
SKATING (books on), III, 779
Skeat, Walter William (1835–1912), III, **1041** f.
Skeats, H. S. (*fl.* 1857), III, 114, 118
Skeen, Robert (*fl.* 1876), III, 87
Skelton, John (1460?–1529), I, 46, **408** f., 515, 714
Skelton, Sir John (1831–1897), III, **754** f.
Skelton, Joseph (*fl.* 1820–50), III, 127
Skelton, Philip (1707–1787), II, 600; III, 886
Skene, James (1775–1864), III, 379
Skene, William Forbes (1809–1892), I, 888; III, **906**
Skeptic; or, Unbeliever, The (1773), II, 665
Sketch, The (1893), III, 815
Sketchley, J. (*fl.* 1769), II, 721
Sketchley, William (*fl.* 1793), II, 827
Sketchy Bits (1893), III, 820
Skeyne, Gilbert (1522?–1599), I, 888
Skilbeck, W. Wray (*fl.* 1900?), III, 830
Skinner, John (1721–1807), song-writer, II, 983–4, **991**
Skinner, John (1744–1816), bishop of Aberdeen, II, 991
Skinner, John (1772–1839), antiquary, II, 153
Skinner, S. (*fl.* 1844), III, 114
Skinner, Stephen (1623–1667), II, 930
Skinner, Thomas (1800?–1843), III, 1080
Skinner, Vincent (*fl.* 1568), I, 813

Skippon, Sir Philip (*fl.* 1700?), II, 744
Skipsey, Joseph (1832–1903), III, **357**
Skrefsrund, L. O. (*fl.* 1873), III, 1074
Skrine, F. H. B. (*fl.* 1892), III, 1078
Skrine, Henry (1755–1803), II, 157
Skrine, Nesta, née Higginson (*fl.* 1900–24) ['Moira O'Neill'], III, **1057**
Skylark, The (1730), II, 201
Sky-Lark, The (1772), II, 229
Sky Lark, The (1775), II, 231
Sky Lark, or the Lady's and Gentleman's Harmonious Companion, The (1788), II, 242
Skylark, The (1795), II, 251
Skylark; being an Elegant Collection of the Best and Newest Songs in the English Language, The (1791), II, 246, 256
Slack, Henry James (1818–1896), III, 811
Slade, John (*fl.* 1753), II, 664, 762
Sladen, Douglas Brooke Wheelton (b. 1856), III, **357**, 1093
Slaney, B. A. (*fl.* 1817), III, 978
SLANG, II, 930 (dictionaries)
Slater, F. C. (*fl.* 1905), III, 1089
Slater, Samuel (d. 1704), II, **286**
Slatter, Henry (*fl.* 1852), III, 88
Slatyer, William (1587–1647), I, 679
Sleater, William (*fl.* 1758), II, 735
Sleeman, Sir William Henry (1788–1856), III, 978, 992, 1083
Sleidanus, i.e. Joannes Philippson, I, 813, 817
Slezer, John (d. 1714), II, 158
'Slick, Sam', i.e. Thomas Chandler Haliburton (*fl.* 1836), III, 1086
SLIGO
  Newspapers, II, 738
Sligo Journal, The (1771), II, 738
Sligo Morning Herald, The (1793), II, 738
Slingsby, Sir Henry (1602–1658), I, 387, 842
Slingsby, Sir William (*fl.* 1596), I, 769
Sloane, Sir Hans (1660–1753), II, 753
Smale, F. G. (*fl.* 1897), III, 811
Small, Anne H. (*fl.* 1894), III, 1085
Small, John (1828–1886), I, 173, 897
Smaller Vernon Legend Collection (M.E.), I, 175
Smalridge, George (1663–1719), II, **853**
Smaragdus of St Mihiel (*fl.* 1800), I, **108**
Smart, Christopher (1722–1771), II, **338** f., 545, 677 (2)
Smart, Henry Hawley (1833–1893), III, **561**
Smart, W. (*fl.* 1891), III, 984
Smedley, Edward (1788–1836), III, 833
Smedley, Francis Edward (1818–1864), III, **508**
Smedley, Jonathan (1671–1729?), II, 199, **328**, 713
Smedley, Menella Bute (1820–1877), III, **305** f.
Smee, Alfred (1818–1877), III, 75, 938
Smeeton, George (*fl.* 1800–28), II, 506

Smellie, William (1740?–1795), II, 672, 686, 697, 786, 951
Smetham, James (1821–1889), III, **306**
Smeton, Thomas (1536–1583), I, 904
Smiles, Samuel (1812–1904), III, **925**
Smith, A. M. (*fl.* 1886), political economist, III, 984
Smith, Adam (1723–1790), I, 16; II, 17, 110, **953**
   Translations from, II, 54; III, 26, 37, 40, 42
Smith, Albert Richard (1816–1860), III, 445 (2), **508**f., 724, 790, 827
Smith, Alexander (*fl.* 1714–26), II, 155, 536f., 539, 930
Smith, Alexander (*fl.* 1786), II, 239
Smith, Alexander (1829–1867), II, 492; III, **306**
Smith, Arthur (*fl.* 1860), III, 770
Smith, Bernard (*fl.* 1868), III, 723
Smith, C. (*fl.* 1800), translator of Kotzebue, II, 60
Smith, C. M. (*fl.* 1857), III, 87
Smith, Charles Manby (*fl.* 1854), III, 788
Smith, Charles Manley (*fl.* 1852), III, 988
Smith, Charles Roach (1807–1890), III, **903**
Smith, Charlotte (1749–1806), II, **380**f., 549, 550 (5), 559
Smith, D. B. (*fl.* 1868), III, 1080
Smith, E. (*fl.* 1688), II, 760
Smith, E. T. (*fl.* 1856), III, 811
Smith, Edmund (1672–1710), II, **444**, 485
Smith, Egerton (*fl.* 1811), III, 802
Smith, Elizabeth Thomasina Toulmin, née Meade (d. 1914) ('L. T. Meade'), III, **569**f.
Smith, Ernest (*fl.* 1900), III, 788
Smith, Francis (*fl.* 1659–1688), II, 84, 100, 697, 703
Smith, G. H. (*fl.* 1859), of Liverpool, III, 978
Smith, G. H. (*fl.* 1890), journalist, III, 811
Smith, George (*fl.* 1643–6), journalist, I, 749, 755 (4)
Smith, George (*fl.* 1702), translator of Pliny, II, 767
Smith, George (1693–1756), nonjuring divine, I, 59; II, 821, 874, 920
Smith, George (*fl.* 1783), captain, II, 237
Smith, George (1824–1901), publisher, III, 100, 788, 807
Smith, George (1840–1876), Assyriologist, III, **1017**
Smith, George Barnett (*fl.* 1879–92), III, 715, 984
Smith, Goldwin (1823–1910), III, **930**f.
Smith, Gyles (*fl.* 1754), II, 114f.
Smith, Sir H. L. (*fl.* 1888), III, 984
Smith, Sir Harry George Wakelyn (1787–1860), III, 1090
Smith, Henry (1550?–1591), I, 683, 836, 845
Smith, Henry John Stephen (1826–1883), III, 942

Smith, Horatio (1779–1849), III, 243, **417**f.
Smith, Hubert Llewellyn (*fl.* 1892), III, 106
Smith, I. Gregory (*fl.* 1862), I, 452
Smith, J. (*fl.* 1641), publisher, I, 753
Smith, J. (*fl.* 1786), contributor to 'The Microcosm', II, 356
Smith, J. Murray (*fl.* 1870), III, 808
Smith, James (1605–1667), poet and divine, I, 405, 478
Smith, James (*fl.* 1768), author of 'The Art of Living in London', II, 146
Smith, James (1775–1839), humorist, III, 243, 418
Smith, Sir James Edward (1759–1828), botanist, II, 747; III, **959** (2)
Smith, James Elimalet (Elishama) (1801–1857), divine, III, 816 (2), 853
Smith (or Smythe), Sir John (1534?–1607), diplomatist and military writer, I, 390, 394
Smith, John (1567–1640), author of 'Lives of the Berkeleys', I, 382
Smith, John (1580–1631), captain and colonist, I, 789, 845 (2)
Smith, John (1618–1652), Cambridge Platonist, I, 878
Smith, John (*fl.* 1626), sea-captain, I, 390
Smith, John (*fl.* 1633–70), writer on trade, II, 815
Smith, John (*fl.* 1649), translator of Horace, I, 803
Smith, John (*fl.* 1657), writer on rhetoric, I, 867
Smith, John (*fl.* 1680), publisher, II, 703–4
Smith, John (*fl.* 1696), angler, II, 819 (2)
Smith, John (1662–1717), editor of Bede, II, 920
Smith, John (*fl.* 1713), poet, II, **328**
Smith, John (*fl.* 1747), author of 'Memoirs of Wool', II, 148
Smith, John (1747–1807), Gaelic scholar, II, 75
Smith, John (1749–1831), painter and traveller, II, 747
Smith, John (*fl.* 1820), Pepys transcriber, II, 831–2
Smith, John Frederick (*fl.* 1856), III, 673
Smith, John Pye (1774–1851), III, 847
Smith, John Russell (1810–1894), I, 8
Smith, John Thomas (1766–1833), III, **883**
Smith, John William (1809–1845), III, 988
Smith, Joseph (*fl.* 1867), I, 9
Smith, Lucy Toulmin (1838–1911), III, **1042**
Smith, M. (*fl.* 1702–13), poet, II, 190, 192
Smith, M. (*fl.* 1715), publisher, II, 708
Smith, Miles (d. 1624), I, 856
Smith, P. A. (*fl.* 1860), I, 853
Smith, R. (*fl.* 1786), contributor to 'The Microcosm', II, 356
Smith, R. A. (*fl.* 1821), III, 163
Smith, R. J. (1857–1916), III, 829

Smith, Reginald Bosworth (1839–1908), III, **915**

Smith, Richard (1590–1675), book-collector, II, 101

Smith, Richard (*fl.* 1769), traveller in America, II, 755

Smith, Robert (1689–1768), mathematician, II, 962

Smith, Robert (*fl.* 1768), rat-catcher, II, 821

Smith, Robert Angus (1817–1884), III, 946

Smith, Robert Payne (1819–1895), III, **1014**

Smith, Samuel (*fl.* 1746), II, 103

Smith, Samuel (*fl.* 1887), III, 974

Smith, Sarah (1832–1911) ('Hesba Stretton'), III, **569**

Smith, Southwood, III, 56

Smith, Sydney (1771–1845), III, **679**f., 832
Reviews by, III, 129, 186

Smith, T. (*fl.* 1755), author of 'Printer's Grammar', II, 82

Smith, Sir Thomas (1513–1577), statesman and scholar, I, 44, 367, 383, 400, 774, 826, 844, 851

Smith, Thomas (*fl.* 1600–27), soldier, I, 390

Smith, Thomas (1638–1710), nonjuror and scholar, I, 827; II, 743, 813, **939**

Smith, Thomas (*fl.* 1770), angler, II, 321

Smith, Thomas (*fl.* 1807–21), London accountant, III, 973, 980

Smith, Thomas (*fl.* 1838), sporting writer, III, 760

Smith, V. (*fl.* 1848), II, 837

Smith, W. J. (*fl.* 1852–3), II, 632

Smith, Walter (*fl.* 1525), I, 714

Smith, Walter Chalmers (1824–1908), III, **306**

Smith, Wareham (b. 1874), III, 788

Smith, Wentworth (*fl.* 1601–23), I, 650

Smith, William (1550?–1618), herald, I, 381, 774

Smith, William (*fl.* 1596), poet, I, 433

Smith, William (*fl.* 1684), seaman, II, 749

Smith, William (*fl.* 1726–44), II, 749

Smith, William (*fl.* 1729), numismatist, II, 580

Smith, William (*fl.* 1735), freemason, II, 205

Smith, William (*fl.* 1745), author of 'The Natural History of Nevis', II, 754

Smith, William (1711–1787), translator, II, 28, 763–4

Smith, William (*fl.* 1765), writer on Ohio Indians, II, 755

Smith, William (*fl.* 1770), author of 'The Student's Vademecum', II, 130

Smith, William (1769–1839), geologist, III, 950f.

Smith, William (1769–1847), historian of Canada, III, 1087

Smith, William (*fl.* 1848), Edinburgh translator, III, 29

Smith, Sir William (1813–1893), lexicographer, III, 33, 832, **1002**f.

Smith, William (*fl.* 1863), acting manager New Adelphi Theatre, III, 779

Smith, William Henry (1808–1872), philosopher, III, 849

Smith, William Henry (1825–1891), statesman, III, 100

Smith, William Robertson (1846–1894), III, 851

Smith and His Dame (M.E.), I, **162**

Smith's Currant Intelligence (1680), II, 703

Smith's Protestant Intelligence (1681), II, 703

Smithson, Peter (*fl.* 1750?), II, 718

Smollett, Tobias George (1721–1771), II, 50, 65, 69, 340, **523**f., 535, 541, 664 (2)

Smuts, J. C. (b. 1870), III, 1092

Smyth, A. (*fl.* 1828), III, 981

Smyth, G. C. (*fl.* 1847), III, 1076

Smyth, James (*fl.* 1692), II, 288

Smyth, John F. D. (*fl.* 1784), II, 756

Smyth, Nicholas (*fl.* 1550), I, 802

Smyth, Richard (1590–1675), I, 364

Smyth, Thomas Scott (*fl.* 1831), III, 234

Smyth, W. C. (*fl.* 1860), III, 1074

Smyth, William (1765–1849), historian, III, **907**

Smyth, William Henry (1788–1865), scientific writer, III, 943

Smythe, Elizabeth Ann (*fl.* 1840), III, 572

Smythe (or Smith), Sir John (1534?–1607), I, 390, 394

Smythe (or Smith), James Moore (1702–1734), II, 331, 713

Smythe, Robert (*fl.* 1808), III, 130

Smythies, H. M. G. (*fl.* 1840), III, 400

Snaith, J. C. (*fl.* 1899), III, 774

Snape, Andrew (*fl.* 1683), II, 816

Snape, Andrew (1675–1742), II, 893

Snape, Edward (*fl.* 1791), II, 817

Snarl, The (1899), III, 835

Snart, Charles (*fl.* 1801), III, 768

Snelgrave, William (*fl.* 1734), II, 749

Snelling, Thomas (b. 1614), I, 659

Snob, The [Cambridge] (1829), III, 834

Snotty-Nose Gazette, The (1679), II, 657

Snow, Herbert, later Kynaston (1835–1910), III, **1007**

Soames (or Soame), Sir William (*fl.* 1683), II, 771

Soane, George (1790–1860), III, 29, **595**f.

'Sobersides, Solomon' (1780), II, 562

SOCIAL BACKGROUND
Middle English Period, I, 119f. See also SOCIAL AND ECONOMIC HISTORY, I, 118f. and EDUCATION, I, 124f.
Renaissance to Restoration, I, 380f.
Restoration to Romantic Revival, II, 132f.
Nineteenth Century, III, 143f. (general), 1082f. (Anglo-Indian). See also ILLUSTRATIVE MATTER under EDUCATION, III, 118f.

Social Harmony (18 cent.), II, 222, 231, 235
Social Harmony (19 cent.), II, 256
SOCIAL HISTORIANS, III, 925 f. See also under
    SOCIAL BACKGROUND
Social Magazine, The (19 cent.), II, 256
*Social Magazine; Or, Monthly Cabinet of Wit,
    The* (1800), II, 683
SOCIALISM (writings on), III, 976 f.
Socialist, The (1888), III, 818
Society (1879), III, 814
SOCIETY FOR PROPAGATION OF GOSPEL, library,
    II, 104
Soldier's Pocket Magazine, The (1798), II, 683
Solicitors' Journal, The (1857), III, 821
Solinus, Julius, I, 766
Solitary Walks (18 cent.), II, 231, 241
Solleysel, Jacques de, II, 816
Solomon, — (*fl.* 1811), III, 801
Solorzano, Castillo, II, 534
Soltan, G. W. (*fl.* 1819), III, 768
Solyman and Perseda, The Tragedye of (16
    cent.), I, 538
Solymannidæ Tragœdia (16 cent.), I, 663
Some, Henry (*fl.* 1657), II, 29, 793
Some (or Solme), Thomas (*fl.* 1540–53), I,
    669
*Some Special Passages from London, West-
    minster, Yorke* (1642), I, 753
*Some Speciall and Considerable Passages from
    London, Westminster* (1642), I, 753
Some Speciall Passages from divers parts (1642),
    I, 753
Somebody, Avarice and Minister (16 cent.), I,
    515
Somer, John (*fl.* 1380), I, **305**
Somers (or Sommers), John, Baron (1651–
    1716), II, 271
Somers, Robert (1822–1891), III, 807 (2), 973
Somers Tracts (18 cent.), II, 881
SOMERSET
    Bibliography, I, 9
Somerset, Charles A. (*fl.* 1827–34), III, **596**
Somerset, Edward, Marquis of Worcester
    (1601–1667), II, 962
Somerset, Frances, Duchess of, II, 136, 233
Somerset House Gazette, The (1824), III, 818
Somervile (or Somerville), William (1675–
    1742), II, **328**
Somerville, Elizabeth (*fl.* 1801), III, 570
Somerville, John Southey, Baron (1765–1819),
    III, 969
Somerville, Mary, née Fairfax (1780–1872),
    III, 937, 943
Somerville, Thomas (1741–1830), II, **889**
Sommers, T. (*fl.* 1803), II, 991
Somner, William (1598–1669), I, 776, **843**, 851,
    855; II, 875, 920, 928
Song Book for 1798 (18 cent.), II, 254
Song of Roland (M.E.), I, 141 f.
Songes and Sonettes (16 cent.), I, 403

SONGS
    Middle English (to 1500), I, 267 f.
    Renaissance to Restoration, I, 481 f.
Songs and Chorusses in the Tempest (18 cent.),
    II, 232
Songs and Poems of Love and Drollery (17 cent.),
    I, 405
Songs, Chorusses, &c. (18 cent.), II, 226, 232
Songs Compleat (18 cent.), II, 195
Songs. Descriptive, Moral, and Pastoral (18
    cent.), II, 252, 255
*Songs, Duets, Choruses, &c. &c. now singing at
    Vauxhall, The* (18 cent.), II, 248
Songs. Elegiac. Sea (18 cent.), II, 252, 255
Songs for Little Folks (19 cent.), III, 1865
*Songs for 1 2 & 3 Voyces Composed by Henry
    Bowman* (17 cent.), II, 178 (3)
Songs for One Two and Three Voices Composed
    By R. King (17 cent.), II, 182, 183
Songs, Hymns, and Psalms, II, 237
Songs of Love in a Village, The [etc.] (18 cent.),
    II, 243
Songs, Political, Satyrical, and Convivial
    (18 cent.), II, 250
Songs set by Signior Pietro Reggio (17 cent.), II,
    178
*Songs sung in the Several Lodges of the Order of
    Bucks* (18 cent.), II, 216
*Songs, Trios, Choruses, &c. as performed at
    Sadler's Wells* (18 cent.), II, 249
Songs, Trios, Glees, &c., The (18 cent.), II, 253
Songster for the year 1800, The (19 cent.), II,
    256
Songster's Companion, The (1787), II, 241–3,
    245, 247, 249, 251–2, 254–6
Songster's Companion, The (1800), II, 256
Songster's Delight, The (18 cent.), II, 222
Songster's Favourite, The (1780), II, 235
Songster's Favourite, The (1785), II, 239
Songster's Favourite Companion, The (1800), II,
    256
Songster's Miscellany, The (18 cent.), II, 245,
    256
Songster's Pocket Book, The (18 cent.), II, 228
Songster's Polite Tutor, The (18 cent.), II, 231,
    245
Songster's Repository, The (18 cent.), II, 249
SONNET, THE, I, 427 (Elizabethan); II, 170
    (18 cent.); III, 159 (19 cent.)
Soowthern, John (*fl.* 1584), I, 431
Sophocles, II, 763; III, 286, 997, 999, 1004,
    1006
Soranzo, Lazzaro, I, 778
Sorbière, S. de, II, 33
Sorby, Henry Clifton (1826–1898), III, 952
Sorel, Charles, I, 734
Sorley, William Ritchie (1855–1935), III, **874**
Sotheby, Miss — (*fl.* 1798), II, 808
Sotheby, Samuel (1771–1842), auctioneer, II,
    97

Sotheby, Samuel Leigh (1805–1861), auc-
tioneer, I, 346–7, 469
Sotheby, William (1757–1833), III, **243**
SOTHERAN & CO., III, 103
Soulsby, L. H. M. (*fl.* 1899), III, 114
SOUND-CHANGES. See PHONOLOGY, I, 34 f.
South, Robert (1634–1716), II, 320, 744, **849**
SOUTH AFRICA (literature of, in English), III,
1088 f.
*South London Observer, Camberwell and Peck-
ham Times, The* (1874), III, 810
South London Press, The (1865), III, 810
SOUTH SEAS
Voyages to, II, 751 f.
South Wales Argus, The [Newport, Mon.]
(1892), III, 806
South Wales Daily News, The (1872), III, 804
South Wales Daily Post, The (1893), III, 806
South Wales Daily Times, The (1889), III, 805
South Wales Echo, The (1884), III, 805
South Wales Evening Telegram, The (1891), III,
804
SOUTH-EASTERN ENGLISH
Dialect (M.E.), I, 38
Texts (M.E.), I, 41
South-Sea Pills (18 cent.), II, 196
SOUTHAMPTON
Newspapers, II, 728 f.
Southern, Henry (1799–1853), III, 825–6
Southern Daily Mail, The [Portsmouth] (1896),
III, 805
Southern Echo, The [Southampton] (1888), III,
806
*Southern Echo and Bournemouth Telegraph,
The* (1891), III, 806
SOUTHERN ENGLISH
Dialect (M.E.), I, 38
Texts (M.E.), I, 41
Southern Legend Collection (M.E.), I, **174** f.
Southern Passion, The (M.E.), I, 40
Southern Reporter, The [Cork] (1855), III, 808
Southerne, Thomas (1659–1746), II, 44, 62,
272, **427** f.
Southesk, James Carnegie, Earl of (1827–
1905), III, 989
Southey, C. C. (*fl.* 1844), III, 136, 181 (3)
Southey, Caroline Anne, earlier Bowles (1786–
1854), III, **228**
Southey, Robert (1774–1843), II, 684, 922; III,
180
Reviews, etc. by, I, 408; II, 345; III, 107,
186, 238, 240, 636, 880
Southport Daily News, The (1875), III, 803
Southport Independent, The (1861), III, 803
Southport News, The (1872), III, 803
Southwell, Charles (*fl.* 1843), III, 817
Southwell, Robert (1561–1595), I, 416, **421** f.,
685
Southworth, Mary (1651–1695), II, 283
Sowdone of Babylone (M.E.), I, **142**

Sowerby, James (1757–1822), III, 949
Sowerby, James de Carle (1787–1871), III, 949
Sowler, John (*fl.* 1826), III, 803
Sowler, Sir Thomas (*fl.* 1874), III, 803–4
Spagnuoli, Baptista (Mantuan), I, 818–9; II,
813
SPAIN
Literary Relations with, I, 342 f. (1500–
1660); II, 67 f. (1660–1800); III, 41 f.
Spalding, Augustine (*fl.* 1614), I, 785
Spalding, John (*fl.* 1650), I, 910
Spalding, William (1809–1859), I, 588; III, 192,
725
Spallanzani, Lazzaro, II, 813
Spanish Libertines, The (18 cent.), II, 540
Sparke, Michael (*fl.* 1641), I, 357 (2)
Sparrow, J. (*fl.* 1743), 793
Sparrow, John (1615–1665?), II, 860–1
Sparrowe, Thomas (*fl.* 1630–3), I, 659
SPAS, II, 154 f. (17, 18 cents.)
Spavan, J. (*fl.* 1720), II, 778
Speaker, The (18 cent.), II, 230, 239, 243, 245
Speaker, The (1890), III, 814
Spearman, Robert (1703–1761), II, 781
Spears, Robert (1825–1899), III, 788
*Speciall Passages and certain information from
severall places* (1642), I, 753
Speciall Passages and Certain Informations
(1642), I, 754
Speciall Passages and Certaine Informations
(1642–3), I, 750
*Specimen of a Book, Intituled, Ane Compendious
Booke, of Godly and Spiritual Sangs, A*
(18 cent.), II, 223
Specimens of the Early English Poets (18 cent.),
II, 245
Spectakle of Luf, The (M.E.), I, 260
Spectator, The (1711), II, 35, 52, 69, 603, 661
Spectator, The (1715), II, 661
Spectator, The (1716), II, 662
Spectator, The (1753), II, 664
Spectator, The (1828), III, 794, 813
Speculatist, The (1725), II, 662
Speculator (1780), II, 665
Speculator, The (1790), II, 666
Speculum Gy de Warewyke (M.E.), I, **172**
Speculum Laicorum (M.E.), I, 301
Spedding, James (1808–1881), III, **725** f.
Reviews and articles by, I, 576; III, 257, 269,
385, 446
SPEECHES
Collections of political speeches, III, 148 f.
Speed, John (1552?–1629), I, 766, 775, 837
Speedy, Thomas (*fl.* 1884), III, 767
Speght, Rachel (*fl.* 1617), I, 716
Speidell, John (*fl.* 1616–28), I, **881**
Speke, John Hanning (1827–1864), III, 992
SPELLING
Textbooks of, I, 376 f.
Spelling Reformer, The (1849), III, 1030

Spelman, Clement (1598–1679), I, 843 (2)
Spelman (or Yallop), Edward (d. 1767), II, 760, 763 (2)
Spelman, Sir Henry (1564?–1641), historian, I, 789, **843**, 851
Spelman, Henry (*fl.* 1609), writer on Virginia, I, 789
Spelman, Sir John (1594–1643), I, 855
Spelman, William (*fl.* 1595?), I, 769
Spence, Catherine Helen (*fl.* 1854–68), III, **1096**
Spence, Elizabeth Isabella (1768–1832), II, 984
Spence, Ferrand (*fl.* 1683), II, 29, 122, 534 (2), 762, 790, 795, 802
Spence, George (1787–1850), III, 978
Spence, Joseph (1699–1768), II, **895**f.
Spence, Thomas (1750–1814), II, 85, 672, 682; III, 976
Spence, William (1783–1860), III, 955, 979
Spencer, Sir Baldwin (1860–1929), III, 1098
Spencer, Edward (*fl.* 1654), I, 811
Spencer, Herbert (1820–1903), III, 62, 114, **874, 954**, 963, 965, 976
    Translations from, III, 26, 37, 40, 42
Spencer, John (*fl.* 1650), II, 104
Spencer, Nicholas (1758, pseud.?), II, 678
Spencer, R. (*fl.* 1726–30), I, 657; II, 772
Spencer, T. (*fl.* 1840), III, 75
Spencer, Walter T. (*fl.* 1880–1920), III, 103
Spencer, William (*fl.* 1658), I, 857
Spencer, William Robert (1769–1834), III, **244**
Spender, Edward (*fl.* 1860), III, 802
Spender, J. A. (b. 1862), III, 788 801, 803
Spendthrift, The (1766), II, 665
Spens, — (*fl.* 1757), II, 710
Spens, H. (*fl.* 1763), II, 762
Spenser, Edmund (1552?–1599), I, 33, 46, **417**f., 776, 806, 808, 817, 844
Spenser, John (1559–1614), I, 686
Sphere, The (1900), III, 815
Sphynx, The (1827), III, 812
Spicer, Robert (or Silke) (*fl.* 1320), I, **301**
Spie, The (1644), I, 756
Spielmann, M. H. (b. 1858), III, 831
Spiers, Alexander (1807–1869), I, 17
Spiess, C. H., II, 807
Spilman, James (*fl.* 1742), II, 750
Spilsbury, F. (*fl.* 1776), II, 646
Spinnet, The (18 cent.), II, 214
Spinoza, Benedictus de, II, 32; III, 46
Spinster, The (1719), II, 662
Spirit of the Age, The (1848), III, 817
Spirit of the Nation, The (19 cent.), III, 1046
Spirit of the Public Journals, The (1798), II, 684
Spirit of the Times, The (1849), III, 87
Spiritual Bee, The (17 cent.), II, 560
Spiritual Magazine, The (1761), II, 678
Splenetick Pills (18 cent.), II, 214
Spon, Jacob, II, 801

SPORT, LITERATURE OF, I, 393 f. (16, 17 cents.); II, 814 f. (1660–1800); III, 757 f. (19 cent.), 820 (sporting papers), 845 f. (sporting annuals)
Sporting Almanack, The (1842), III, 759
Sporting Annual, The (1900), III, 759
Sporting Calendar, The (1751), II, 718
Sporting Calendar: Containing An Account of the Plates [etc.]*, The* (1769), II, 718
Sporting Chronicle, The (1871), III, 804
Sporting Clipper, The (1872), III, 820
Sporting Gazette, The (1862), III, 820
Sporting Life, The (1859), III, 759
Sporting Life (1883), III, 799 f.
Sporting Magazine, The (1792), II, 674, 682
Sporting Magazine or Monthly Calendar of the Transactions of the Turf, etc., The (1793), III, 758
Sporting Magazine; or Monthly Calendar of the Turf [etc.]*, The* (1793), III, 823
Sporting Oracle, The (1841), III, 759
Sporting Repository, The (1822), III, 758
Sporting Review, The (1839), III, 827
Sporting Review, The (1846), III, 823
Sporting Telegraph, The (1860), III, 800
Sporting Times, The (1865), III, 794, 820
Sportive Wit (17 cent.), I, 405
Sports of the Muses, The (18 cent), II, 215
Sportsman, The (1834, 1836), III, 827
Sportsman, The (1846), III, 823
Sportsman, The (1865), III, 759
Sportsman, The (1876), III, 799
Sportsman and Veterinary Recorder, The (1835), III, 827
Sportsman's Evening Brush, The (18 cent.), II, 246, 251
Sportsman's Magazine, The (1845), III, 759
Sportsman's Magazine, or Chronicle of Games and Pastimes, The (1823), III, 758
Sportsman's Weekly Guide to the Turf, The (1880), III, 820
Spottiswoode, John (1565–1639), I, 838
Spottiswoode, William (1825–1883), III, 942
SPOTTISWOODE & CO., III, 87
Spouter's Companion, The (18 cent.), II, 228
Spouter's New Guide, The (18 cent.), II, 252
Spranger, John (*fl.* 1754), II, 154
Sprat, Thomas (1635–1713), II, 14, **286**
Spratt, Thomas Abel Brimage (1811–1888), III, 1003
Spratt, William (1842–1920), III, 1010
Sprengell, Sir Conrad Joachim (*fl.* 1708), II, 761
Sprenger, Jacob, I, 328
Sprigg, William (*fl.* 1657), I, 724, 726
Sprigge, Joshua (1618–1684), I, 400, 839
Sprightly Muse, The (18 cent.), II, 228
Spring-Garden Journal, The (1752), II, 664
Springer, Balthasar (*fl.* 1509), I, 781
Sproat, G. M. (*fl.* 1870), III, 114

Sprott, George Washington (1829–1909), I, 904

Spry, Henry Harpur (1804–1842), III, 1075

Spurgeon, Charles Haddon (1834–1892), III, 854

Spurstow, William (1605–1666), I, 700

Spy, The (1811), III, 165

Squire, Samuel (1713–1766), II, 763

Squyr of Lowe Degre (M.E.), I, **159**f.

Sreeram, Lala (*fl.* 1885), III, 1082

Staal, Marguerite Jeanne de, II, 801

Stables, William Gordon (1840–1910), III, **569**

Stace, M. (*fl.* 1810), I, 400

Stack, Richard (d. 1812), I, 593; II, 19

Stackhouse, Thomas (1677–1752), II, 91, 152, 542, 782

Stacy, John (*fl.* 1820), III, 198

Staël-Holstein, Mme de, III, 22

Staffetta Italiana, La (1728), II, 719

Stafford, Anthony (1587–1645?), I, 725

Stafford, J. (*fl.* 1635), I, 616

Stafford, R. (*fl.* 16 cent.), I, 523

Stafford, Sir Thomas (*fl.* 1633), I, 776, 838

Stafford, William (1554–1612), I, 713

Stafforde, Robert (*fl.* 1607), I, 766

STAFFORDSHIRE
Bibliographies, I, 9

Staffordshire Advertiser, The (1795), II, 729

Staffordshire Daily Sentinel, The (1873), III, 804

Staffordshire Sentinel, The (1883), III, 804

STAGE
Puritan attack on, I, 507 f. (16, 17 cents.); II, 400 f. (Collier controversy)
See ACTORS and THEATRES

Stage, The (1881), III, 821

Stage-coach, The (18 cent.), II, 545

Stage Directory, The (1880), III, 821

STAGING, I, 504 f. (16, 17 cents.)

Stähele, A. (*fl.* 1828), III, 126

Staicie, J. (*fl.* 1737), II, 769

Stair, James Dalrymple, Viscount (1619–1695), II, 963

Stallenge, William (*fl.* 1609), I, 893

STAMFORD
Newspapers, II, 729

Stamford Mercury, The (1784), II, 729

Stamford Mercury; Being Historical and Political Observations on the Transactions of Europe, The (1715), II, 729

Stamma, Philip (*fl.* 1745), II, 826

STAMP DUTIES, II, 691 f. (18 cent.); III, 795 f. (19 cent.)

Stamper, Francis (*fl.* 1754), II, 409

Stampiglia, Silvio, II, 425

Stanbridge, John (1463–1510), I, 374

Stanbury, G. (*fl.* 1851), III, 83

Standard, The (1827), III, 794, 801

Standard, The (1857), III, 799

Standard of Freedom, The (1848), III, 817

Standish, Arthur (*fl.* 1611), I, 391, 847

Stanfield, James Field (d. 1824), II, 749

Stanford, C. S. (*fl.* 1833), III, 827

Stanford, Edward (*fl.* 1880), III, 100

Stanhope, Charles (*fl.* 1786), journalist, II, 681

Stanhope, Charles, Earl (1753–1816), II, 635; III, 87

Stanhope, Eugenia (*fl.* 1774), II, 835

Stanhope, George (1660–1728), II, 760, 764, 775, 796

Stanhope, Lady Hester Lucy (1776–1839), III, 150

Stanhope, Leicester Fitzgerald Charles, Earl of Harrington (1784–1862), III, 206

Stanhope, Mrs Leicester (*fl.* 1846), III, 411

Stanhope, Louisa Sidney (*fl.* 1808–35), III, **418**

Stanhope, Philip, Earl of Chesterfield (1633–1713), II, 134

Stanhope, Philip Dormer, Earl of Chesterfield (1694–1773), II, 121, 196, 229, 437, 632, 663, **835**f.

Stanhope, Philip Henry, Earl (1805–1875), III, 684, **889**f.

Stanley, Arthur Penrhyn (1815–1881), III, **901**f.
Pamphlets, etc., III, 126, 670, 889

Stanley, Lady Augusta, née Bruce (d. 1876), III, 154

Stanley, Edward, Earl of Derby (1508–1572), I, 383

Stanley, Edward (*fl.* 1786), traveller, II, 749

Stanley, Edward (*fl.* 1827), writer on horsemanship, III, 764

Stanley, Edward George Geoffrey Smith, Earl of Derby (1799–1869), III, **306**f.

Stanley, Edward Henry, Earl of Derby (1826–1893), III, 149

Stanley, Edward Lyulph, Baron (1839–1925), III, 114

Stanley, Eliza (*fl.* 1736), II, 776

Stanley, Ferdinando, Earl of Derby (1559?–1594), I, 546

Stanley, Sir Henry Morton (1841–1904), III, 992

Stanley, John Thomas, Baron (*fl.* 1796), II, 55

Stanley, Thomas (1625–1678), I, **478**, 799, 800, 819, 878; II, 758

Stannard, W. J. (*fl.* 1860), III, 81

Stans Puer ad Mensam (15 cent.), I, 264

Stanton, Daniel (*fl.* 1772), II, 755

Stanton, Samuel (*fl.* 1790), II, 823

Stanyan, Abraham (1669?–1732), II, 744

Stanyhurst, Richard (1547–1618), I, 678, 774, 808, 864

Stanzaic Life of Christ (M.E.), I, **190**

Staples, John C. (*fl.* 1898), III, 831

Stapleton, Augustus Granville (1800–1880), III, **898**

Stapleton, Richard (*fl.* 1598), I, 610

Stapleton (or Stapylton), Sir Robert (1605?–1669), I, 803–4, 806, 809; II, 47, **428**
Stapleton, Thomas (1535–1598), I, 811, 827
Stapleton, Thomas (1805–1849), I, 120–1, 382
Stapylton, C. B. (*fl.* 1652), I, 802
Stapylton, H. E. C. (*fl.* 1864), III, 131
Stapylton (or Stapleton), Sir Robert (1605?–1669), I, 803–4, 806, 809; II, 47, **428**
Star, The (1788), II, 711; III, 800
Star, The [Glasgow] (1870), III, 808
Star, The (1888), III, 801
Star, The [Newport] (1892), III, 805
Star and Evening Advertiser, The (1788), II, 711
Star and National Trades Journal, The (1837), III, 816f.
Star of Freedom, The (1852), III, 817
Stark, H. A. (*fl.* 1892), III, 1078
Stark, Malcolm (*fl.* 1915), III, 788
Starke, John (*fl.* 1730), II, 110
Starke, Mariana (1762?–1838), II, 748, 788
Starkey, George (d. 1655), I, 887
Starkey, Thomas (1499?–1538), I, 383
Starkie, Thomas (1782–1849), III, 988
Starling, Ernest Henry (1866–1927), III, 964
State Bell-Man's Collection of Verses, The (18 cent.), II, 189
State Garland of Antient and Modern Loyal Songs (18 cent.), II, 208
State Poems (18 cent.), II, 193
State-Amusements (18 cent.), II, 190
State-Poems (17 cent.), II, 184
Statesman, The (1806), III, 800
Statesman and Weekly True Sun, The (1840), III, 799
Statham, F. R. (*fl.* 1881–1901), III, 1089, 1090 (2), 1092
Stationer, The (1859), III, 101
STATIONERS' COMPANY, I, 356 (15–17 cents.); II, 99f. (17, 18 cents.)
Stationers', Printers', and Bookbinders' Monthly Journal, The (1861), III, 73
Stationery World (1892), III, 73
Stations of Jerusalem (M.E.), I, **191**
Stations of Rome (M.E.), I, **190**
Statist, The (1878), III, 820
Statius, I, 807; II, 768
Statutes of the Realm (M.E. 18 cent.), I, 115
Staundford (Stanford or Stamford), Sir William (1509–1558), I, 851
Staunton, Sir George Leonard (1737–1801), diplomatist, II, 751
Staunton, Sir George Thomas (1781–1859), writer on China, I, 782
Staunton, Howard (1810–1874), I, 371; III, 777
Stayner, Sir Richard (d. 1662), I, 785
Stead, William Thomas (1849–1912), III, 788, 801, 804, 818, 831
Stearne, J. (*fl.* 1648), I, 894
Stearns, Charles (*fl.* 1798), II, 253

Stebbing, Beatrice, later Batty (*fl.* 1873), III, 573
Stebbing, Henry (1799–1883), I, 446, 464, 466; II, 490; III, 818
Stedman, John (*fl.* 1782), II, 19, 766
Stedman, John Gabriel (1744–1797), II, 757
Steed, Henry Wickham (b. 1871), III, 788
Steel, Flora Annie (1847–1929), III, 1070
Steele, Anne (1717–1778), II, **381**
Steele, Elizabeth (*fl.* 1787), II, 798
Steele, Joshua (1700–1791), I, 16
Steele, Richard (1629–1692), II, **849**
Steele, Sir Richard (1672–1729), II, 39, 44, 62, 66, 77, 110, 120, **608**f., 661–2, 702, 809
Steele, W. J. (*fl.* 1856), III, 940
Steere, Edward (1828–1882), II, 946
Steevens, George (1736–1800), I, 820; II, 295, 624, **901**
Steevens, George Warrington (1869–1900), III, 788
Stein, Sir M. Aurel, III, 1073
Steinbach, Henry (*fl.* 1845), III, 1080
Stenhouse, William (1773?–1827), I, 272; II, 984
Stennett, Joseph (1663–1713), II, 863
Stephen of Easton (d. 1252), I, **299**
Stephen, Sir George (1794–1879), III, 760, 982
Stephen, Henry John (1787–1864), III, 988
Stephen, James (1758–1832), III, 979
Stephen, Sir James (1789–1859), III, 803, **907**
Stephen, Sir James Fitzjames (1829–1894), III, **919**f.
Stephen, James Kenneth (1859–1892), III, **357**, 835 (2)
Stephen, Sir Leslie (1832–1904), III, **727**f., 830
Stephens, A. (*fl.* 1685), II, 179
Stephens, Edward (d. 1706), pamphleteer, II, 801
Stephens, Edward (*fl.* 1751), poet, II, **381**
Stephens, Frederic George (1828–1907), III, **726**
Stephens, George (1813–1895), I, 59, 69, 78, 154
Stephens, Henry (1795–1874), III, 971
Stephens, James Brunton (1833–1902), III, **1094**f.
Stephens, Jeremiah (*fl.* 1629–46), I, 843 (2)
Stephens, John (*fl.* 1615), I, 650, 722
Stephens (or Stevens), John (d. 1726), II, 68 (5), 69 (4), 151, 534, 540, 740, 864
Stephens, Robert (1665–1732), II, 909
Stephens, Thomas (*fl.* 1648), I, 807, 861
Stephens, William (1647?–1718), whig divine, II, 499
Stephens, William (1671–1753), president of Georgia, II, 754
Stephens, William Richard Wood (1839–1902), III, **923**, 1081
Stepney, Catherine, Lady, née Pollok, later Manners (d. 1845), III, **418**
Stepney, George (1663–1707), II, **287**, 605

STEREOTYPE, III, 75
Sterling, Edward (1773–1847), III, 788
Sterling, James (*fl.* 1718–55), II, 762
Sterling, John (1806–1844), III, **680**
  Reviews by, III, 257, 657
Sterling, Joseph (*fl.* 1781–9), II, 70, 75–6
Sterndale, Robert Armitage (*fl.* 1879–87), III, 1070
Sterne, Laurence (1713–1768), II, 50, 55, 65, 67, 136, **521**f.
Sternhold, Thomas (d. 1549), I, 677f.
Sterry, Joseph Ashby (b. 1838), III, **357**
Sterry, Peter (1613–1672), I, **700**
Sterry (or Stirry), Thomas (*fl.* 1641), I, 479
Stettin-Pomerania, Philip Julius, Duke of, I, 385
Steuart (or Stewart), Sir James, later Denham (1712–1780), II, 956; III, 972, 979
Steuart, John (*fl.* 1715–52), of Inverness, II, 156
Steven, W. (*fl.* 1849), III, 130
Stevens, B. (*fl.* 1906), Australian anthologist, III, 1093
Stevens, B. F. (*fl.* 1890), bookseller, III, 103
Stevens, Catherine, later Crowe (1800?–1876), III, **482**f.
Stevens, Charles (*fl.* 1866), III, 820
Stevens, George Alexander (1710–1784), II, 24, 228, **328**f., 545
Stevens, J. (*fl.* 1752), II, 215
Stevens (or Stephens), John (d. 1726), II, 68 (5), 69 (4), 151, 534, 540, 740, 864
Stevens, Phineas (*fl.* 1749), II, 754
Stevens, R. (*fl.* 1775), III, 1075
Stevens, Sacheverell (*fl.* 1756), II, 745
Stevens, William Bagshaw (1756–1800), II, 76
Stevenson, Elizabeth Cleghorn, later Gaskell (1810–1865), III, **427**f.
Stevenson, George (1799–1856), III, 800
Stevenson, Joseph (1806–1895), I, 95, 99 (misprinted Stephenson), 100, 120, 139, 181, 184, 257, 277, 384 (2)
Stevenson, John Hall (1718–1785), II, **381**, 626
Stevenson, Matthew (*fl.* 1654–85), I, **478**; II, 818
Stevenson, Robert Alan Mowbray (1847–1900), III, **755**
Stevenson, Robert Louis (1850–1894), I, 21; III, **520**f.
Stevenson, Thomas George (*fl.* 1868), II, 258
Stevenson, William (*fl.* 1553–60), I, 520, 659
Stevenson, William (*fl.* 1722–60), II, 799
Stevenson's Daily Express [Nottingham] (1855), III, 802
Stevin, Simon, I, 881, 885
Steward, Charles (*fl.* 1821), III, 764
Steward, Richard (1593?–1651), I, 700
Stewart, Balfour (1828–1887), III, **939**
Stewart, C. B. (*fl.* 1796), II, 458

Stewart, Charles William, Marquis of Londonderry (1778–1854), III, 150
Stewart, Dugald (1753–1828), II, 881, **957**
Stewart, Sir James (d. 1713), II, 993
Stewart (or Steuart), Sir James, later Denham (1712–1780), II, 956; III, 972, 979
Stewart, James (*fl.* 1792), II, 757
Stewart, John (*fl.* 1600), of Baldynneis, I, 432
Stewart, John (1749–1822), III, 976
Stewart, Mary Louisa, later Molesworth (d. 1921), III, **569**
Stewart, Randolph, Earl of Galloway (*fl.* 1854), III, 132
Stewart, Robert, Viscount Castlereagh (1769–1822), III, 150
Stewart, Thomas Brown Phillips (*fl.* 1887), III, 1086
Stewart, W. C. (*fl.* 1857–74), angler, III, 770
Stewart, William (1481?–1550?), I, 901
Stewart, William J. (*fl.* 1857–63), novelist, III, 29
Stibbs, Bartholomew (*fl.* 1723), II, 749
Stickney, Sarah, later Ellis (1810?–1872), III, **483**
Stiles, Ezra (*fl.* 1754), II, 754
Still, A. W. (*fl.* 1900), III, 803
Stillingfleet, Edward (1635–1699), II, 271, **849**f.
Stillingfleet, James (*fl.* 1735), II, 850
Stillman, W. J. (1828–1901), III, 788
Stinton, George (*fl.* 1770–9), II, 853
Stirling, Edward (*fl.* 1837–48), III, 441, 442 (2), 445, **608**
Stirling, James Hutchison (1820–1909), III, 176, **874**f.
Stirling, John (*fl.* 1751), II, 127, 765, 766 (2)
Stirling, P. J. (*fl.* 1846), III, 982
Stirling-Maxwell, Caroline Elizabeth Sarah, née Sheridan, later Norton, Lady (1808–1877), III, **302**
Stirling-Maxwell, Sir William (1818–1878), III, **908**
Stirling Observer, The, III, 794
Stirry (or Sterry), Thomas (*fl.* 1641), I, 479
Stock, Joseph (1740–1813), II, 944
Stockdale, Mary R. (*fl.* 1798–1821), II, 566
Stockdale, Percival (1736–1811), II, 18, 26, 85, 110, **381**f., 678, 797
Stockenstrom, Sir Andries (*fl.* 1887), III, 1090
Stocker, Thomas (*fl.* 1569), I, 801
Stockport Echo, The (1883), III, 805
STOCKS AND SHARES (newspapers), II, 718
STOCKTON
  Magazine, II, 685 (1793)
Stockton Bee; or, Monthly Miscellany, The (1793), II, 685
Stockwood, John (d. 1610), I, 375–6, 511, 819
Stocqueler, Joachim Hayward (1800–1885), III, 811, 1083
Stoddart, A. M. (*fl.* 1866), III, 307

Stoddart, Isabella (*fl.* 1819) ('Martha Blackford'), III, 571
Stoddart, Sir John (1773–1856), II, 61, 486; III, 798–9, 808
Stoddart, Thomas Tod (1810–1880), III, **307**
Stoicus Vapulans (17 cent.), I, 663
Stokes, Sir George Gabriel (1819–1903), III, **939**
Stokes, R. (*fl.* 1657), I, 882
Stokes, Whitley (1763–1845), professor of medicine, II, 160
Stokes, Whitley (1830–1909), Celtic scholar, I, 279; III, **1049** f.
Stokes, William (*fl.* 1652), I, 395
Stokoe, J. (*fl.* 1882), III, 903
Stolberg, Friedrich Leopold, Graf zu, II, 56, 470
STOLEN GOODS (newspapers advertising), II, 717
Stone, Edmund (d. 1768), II, 789
Stone, Francis (1738?–1813), II, 635
Stone, Marcus (1840–1921), III, 92
Stone, Samuel (*fl.* 1842), III, 988
Stone, Samuel John (1839–1900), III, **357** f.
'Stonehenge', i.e. John Henry Walsh (1810–1888), III, 766, **776**
Stoney, George Johnstone (1826–1911), III, 939
Stonhill, W. J. (*fl.* 1883), III, 73
Stonor Letters and Papers, The (M.E. and 15 cent.), I, 116
STONYHURST COLLEGE, III, 133
Stonyhurst Pageants (M.E.), I, 279
Storace, Stephen (*fl.* 1761–71), II, 810
Storer, Nathaniel (*fl.* 1716), II, 712
Storer, Thomas (1571–1604), I, 438
Stork, William (*fl.* 1766), II, 755
Storm, Theodor, III, 35
Story, George (*fl.* 1800), III, 823
Story, Robert (1795–1860), Northumbrian poet, III, **244**
Story, Robert Herbert (1835–1907), principal of Glasgow University, III, 155 (misprinted Robert Henry)
Story, Thomas (1670?–1742), II, 754
Story of the St. Alb–n's Ghost, The (18 cent.), II, 536
Stothard, Anna Eliza, née Kempe, later Bray (1790–1883), III, **389**
Stothard, Charles Alfred (1786–1821), III, 389
Stothard, Thomas (1755–1834), III, 92
Stoughton, John (1807–1897), III, **920** f.
STOURPORT
   Magazine, II, 685 (1800)
Stourton, W., Baron (*fl.* 1821), III, 970, 978
Stout, B. (*fl.* 1820), III, 1091
Stout, George Frederick (b. 1859), III, 833, **875**
Stout Stukley, The Famous History of (17 cent.), I, 731
Stovin, Aistroppe (*fl.* 1794), II, 817
Stow, David (1793–1864), III, 114, 116

Stow, G. W. (*fl.* 1905), III, 1093
Stow, John (1525?–1605), I, 775, **825**
Stowe, Harriet Beecher, III, 483
Stowell, William Hendry (1800–1858), III, 824
Stower, Charles (*fl.* 1787–1814), II, 82; III, 76, 77 (2)
STRABANE
   Magazine, II, 688 (1799)
   Newspapers, II, 738
   Printing, II, 90
Strabane Journal, The (1771), II, 738
Strabane Magazine, The (1800), II, 688
Strabane Newsletter, The (1788), II, 738
Strachan, Andrew (*fl.* 1634), I, 909
Strachey, Sir John (1823–1907), III, 1078
Strachey, John St Loe (1860–1927), III, 788, 813, 829
Strachey, William (*fl.* 1609–18), I, 790
Strada, Famiano, II, 814
Stradling, Sir John (1563–1637), I, 478, 861
Strafford, Passage of, over the River of Styx (17 cent.), I, 719
Strahan, Alexander (*fl.* 1739), II, 768
Strahan, Alexander (*fl.* 1867), III, 99
Strahan, Alexander (*fl.* 1881), III, 100
Strahan, George (1744–1824), II, 616
Strahan, W. (*fl.* 1722), translator from French, II, 778
Strahan, William (1715–1785), II, 100
Straight, Sir Douglas (*fl.* 1896), III, 801, 831
Strains of the British Muses, The (18 cent.), II, 234
Straker, C. (*fl.* 1860), III, 77
Strand Magazine, The (1891), III, 831
Strang, John (1795–1863), III, 807
Strang, William (1859–1921), III, 92
Strange, James (*fl.* 1786), II, 756
Strange Histories, Of Kings, Princes, Dukes &c. (17 cent.), I, 404
Strange Metamorphosis of Man, A (17 cent.), I, 723
Stratford, Agnes (*fl.* 1795), II, 777
Stratford, Nicholas (1633–1707), II, 153
STRATFORD-ON-AVON School, I, 373
Strauss, David Friedrich, III, 35
Strauss, Gustave Louis Maurice (1807–1887), III, 788, 822
STRAWBERRY HILL
   Printing, II, 88. See also under Horace Walpole, II, 836 f.
Strean, Annesley (*fl.* 1808), II, 647
Streater (or Streeter), John (*fl.* 1650–70), I, 749, 762 (3)
Street, Peter (*fl.* 1811), III, 800
Strenae Natalitiae Academiae Oxoniensis in Celsissimum Principem (17 cent.), II, 180
Strephon's Revenge [etc.] (18 cent.), II, 196–7
'Stretton, Hesba', i.e. Sarah Smith (1832–1911), III, **569**

Strickland, Agnes (1796–1874), III, 567, 577, **897**
Strickland, Catherine Parr, later Traill (*fl.* 1850), III, 1087–8
Strickland, Elizabeth (1794–1875), III, **897**
Strickland, Hugh Edwin (1811–1853), III, 952, 957
Strickland, Jane Margaret (1800–1888), III, 577
Strickland, Samuel (1809–1867), III, 1088
Strickland, Susanna, later Moodie (1803–1885), III, 1088
Strindberg August, III, 43
Stringer, Arthur (*fl.* 1714), II, 820
Stringer, Francis A. (*fl.* 1889), III, 988
Strode, Ralph (d. *c.* 1400), I, **313**
Strode, William (1602–1645), I, 478, 659, 700
Strong, Charles (1785–1864), III, 244
Strong, James (*fl.* 1645), I, 716; II, 177
Strong, Sandford Arthur (1863–1904), III, **1021**
Struther, William (*fl.* 1633), I, 909
Strutt, B. (*fl.* 1796), II, 336
Strutt, Jacob George (*fl.* 1814–22), I, 465
Strutt, John William, Baron Rayleigh (1842–1918), III, 940
Strutt, Joseph (1749–1802), II, **891**, 921
Strutton, Richard (*fl.* 1690), II, 744
Struve, Burchard Gotthelff, II, 103
Strype, John (1643–1737), II, **872**
Stuart, Lady Arabella (1575–1615), I, 385
Stuart, Charles (*fl.* 1783), II, 480
Stuart, Daniel (1766–1846), II, 697; III, 176, 788, 798, 800
'Stuart, Esmé', i.e. Miss Leroy (*fl.* 1877), III, 573
Stuart, Gilbert (1742–1786), II, 672, 680–1, 684, 686, **890**, 952
Stuart, James (*fl.* 1892), III, 800–1
Stuart, John (1813–1877), Scottish antiquary, I, 59
Stuart, John McDouall (1815–1866), explorer, III, 992
Stuart, Lady Louisa (*fl.* 1778–1834), II, 137–8, 835
Stuart, Peter (*fl.* 1788–1805), newspaper proprietor, II, 709 (2), 711
Stuart, Peter (*fl.* 1856), III, 84
Stuart, Sophia, Marchioness of Bute (*fl.* 1858), III, 149
Stuart's Star and Evening Advertiser (1789), II, 709, 711
Stuart-Wortley, Lady Emmeline Charlotte Elizabeth (1806–1855), III, **307**
Stuart-Wortley, John, Baron Wharncliffe (1801–1855), II, 835
Stub, Edmund (*fl.* 1632), I, 659f.
Stubbe, Stubbs or Stubbes, Henry (1632–1676), I, 863, 878; II, 809, 813, 959
Stubbes, George (*fl.* 1731), author of 'A Dialogue on Beauty', II, 16
Stubbes, Philip (*fl.* 1581–91), I, **511**

Stubbs, George (1724–1806), animal painter, II, 817
Stubbs, William (1825–1901), III, **909**f.
Stubs, Stubbs or Stubbe, John (1543?–1591), I, 377
Stuchey, V. (*fl.* 1834), III, 972
Student, The (1797), II, 684
Student; Or, The Oxford Monthly Miscellany The (1750), II, 214–5, 685
Studio, The (1893), III, 831
Studley, Christopher (*fl.* 1585), I, 742
Studley, John (b. *c.* 1547), I, 522, 807
Study to be Quiet (17 cent.), I, 720
Stukeley, William (1687–1765), II, **880**f.
Sturgeon, William (1783–1850), III, 937
Sturges, Joshua (*fl.* 1800), II, 827
Sturgess, John (*fl.* 1772), II, 115
Sturgion, John (*fl.* 1657–61), II, 862
Sturt, Charles (1795–1869), III, 992
Sturtevant, Simon (*fl.* 1602–12), I, 799, 886
STYLE, I, 61f. (O.E. poetry); II, 172 (poetry, 1660–1800)
    Treatises on, II, 14f. (1660–1800)
Style, William (1603–1679), I, 851
Styles, John (*fl.* 1824), III, 210
Stymmelius, Christophorus, I, 328
Subligny, Adrien Thomas Perdou de, II, 48, 534, 801
SUBLIME, THE (treatises on), II, 14f. (17, 18 cents.)
'Subscriber, A' (1828), III, 126
Suckling, Alfred Inigo (1796–1856), III, **903**
Suckling, George (*fl.* 1780), II, 756
Suckling, Sir John (1609–1642), I, **456**, 866
Sucquet, A., III, 312
Sudbury, William (*fl.* 1400), I, **313**
Sudbury's New Royal Whim of The Night (18 cent.), II, 250
Sudermann, Hermann, III, 35
Sue, Eugène, III, **22**
Suetonius, I, 807; II, 768
SUFFOLK
    Bibliography, I, 9
Suffolk, H. M. P. Howard, Earl of (*fl.* 1886), III, 764
Suffolk Mercury; Or, St. Edmunds Bury Post, The (1716), II, 722
Sugden, Edward Burtenshaw, Baron St Leonards (1781–1875), III, 900, 988
Suinett, A. P. (*fl.* 1895), III, 975
Sulivan (or Sullivan), Sir Richard Joseph (1752–1806), II, 139
Sullivan, Alexander Martin (1830–1884), III, 809 (2)
Sullivan, Arabella (*fl.* 1820?), III, 229
Sullivan, W. K. (*fl.* 1866), III, 125
Sullivan, William Francis (1756–1830), III, 571
Sully, James (1842–1923), III, 966
Sully, Maximilien de Bethune, Duc de, II, 771

Sulzer, Johann Georg, II, 30
Summary, The (1883), III, 800
Summer Miscellany, The (18 cent.), II, 210
Summer Rambles (19 cent.), III, 574
'Summerly, Felix', i.e. Sir Henry Cole (*fl.* 1841), III, 576
Summersett, Henry (*fl.* 1797), II, 551
Summoning of Everyman, The (15 cent.), I, 515
Sumner, Charles Richard (1790–1874), I, 468; III, 1028
Sumner, J. (*fl.* 1669), I, 843
Sumner, John Bird (1780–1862), III, 852
Sun, The (1792), II, 711; III, 794, 800
Sun, The (1893), III, 801
Sunday Advertiser, The (1807), III, 810
Sunday Advertiser and Weekly Register, The (1821), III, 810
Sunday and Everyday (1914), III, 578
Sunday Chronicle, The (1788), II, 716
Sunday Chronicle, The [Manchester] (1885), III, 813
Sunday Evening Globe, The (1836), III, 812
Sunday Gazette, The (1866), III, 813
Sunday Gazette, The (Dublin, 1796), II, 736
Sunday Graphic, The (1893), III, 813
Sunday Herald, The (1790), II, 716
Sunday Herald, The (1824), III, 811
Sunday Herald, The (1828), III, 810
Sunday Magazine, The (1864), III, 830
Sunday Mail, The (1896), III, 813
Sunday Mercury, The (1891), III, 813
Sunday Monitor, The (1814), III, 810
SUNDAY PAPERS, II, 716 (18 cent.); III, 810f. (19 cent.)
Sunday. Reading for the Young (1872), III, 578
Sunday Reformer and Universal Register, The (1793), II, 716
Sunday Review, The (1796), II, 716
Sunday Review, The (1798), III, 810
Sunday School Magazine, The (1842), III, 577
Sunday School Teachers' Magazine, The (1850), III, 577
Sunday Special, The (1897), III, 813
Sunday Sun, The (1891), III, 813
Sunday Times, The (1822), III, 794, 811
Sunday World, The (1891), III, 818
Sunderland Daily Echo, The (1873), III, 804
Sunderland Daily Post, The (1876), III, 805
Sunderland Daily Shipping News, The (1865), III, 803
Sunderland Daily Times, The (1876), III, 804
Sunderland Morning Mail, The (1898), III, 806
Sundon, Charlotte Clayton, Viscountess (d. 1742), II, 135
Superville, Daniel de, II, 801
Supplement, The (1708), II, 707
Supplement, by way of Postscript to The Weekly Journal, The (1716), II, 712
Supplement to Dr Swift's Works, A (18 cent.), II, 232, 234 (2)

Supplement to Swift's and Pope's Works, A (18 cent.), II, 208
Supplement to the Weekly Journal, The (1715), II, 712
Supplementary Journal to the Advice from the Scandal Club, A (1704), II, 659
Surfeit, The (17 cent.), I, 726
Surflet, Richard (*fl.* 1600–16), I, 391, 706
Surgens Manerius summo Diluculo (M.E.), I, 287
SURGERY (writings on), I, 890f. (16, 17 cents.)
Surprise, The (1711), II, 661
Surr, Thomas Skinner (1770–1847), III, 418
Surrey, Henry Howard, Earl of (1517?–1547), I, 412f., 677, 808
Surtees, Robert (1779–1834), III, 885
Surtees, Robert Smith (1803–1864), III, 509
Surtees Psalter (M.E.), I, 189
Susannah (M.E.), I, 189f.
Susenbrotus Comoedia (17 cent.), I, 663
Susenbrotus, Joannes, I, 376
SUSSEX
    Printing, II, 88
Sussex Advertiser, The (1811), II, 725
Sussex Daily News, The (1868), III, 803
Sussex Evening Times, The (1880), III, 805
Sussex Weekly Advertiser, The (1745), II, 725
Sutcliffe, A. (*fl.* 1633), I, 616
Sutcliffe, Matthew (1550?–1629), I, 394, 680, 687, 693, 858
Suter, William (*fl.* 1865), III, 830
Sutherland, Alexander (1852–1902), III, 1093, 1097f.
Sutherland, David (*fl.* 1790), II, 747
Sutherland, J. (*fl.* 1092), III, 1092
Sutherland, James (*fl.* 1761), II, 749
Sutherland, James (*fl.* 1878), III, 814
Suttner, Bertha von, III, 35
Sutton, Christopher (1565?–1629), I, 685
Sutton, Henry Septimus (1825–1901), III, 307f.
Sutton, Peter (*fl.* 1311), I, 303
Sutton, T. (*fl.* 1858), III, 81
Sutton, T. R. (*fl.* 1875–95), III, 820
Svedenstjerna, Eric Thomas, II, 142
Swadlin, Thomas (1600–1670), I, 757–8, 884
Swain, Charles (1801–1874), III, 308
Swainson, Charles Anthony (1820–1887), III, 921
Swall, A. (*fl.* 1691), II, 788
'Swami Vivekananda', i.e. Narendranath Datta (*fl.* 1896), III, 1082
Swan, C. (*fl.* 1828), III, 39
Swan, John (*fl.* 1742), II, 621
Swansea Daily Shipping Register, The (1877), III, 805
Swansea Gazette, The (1888), III, 805
Swanwick, Anna (1813–1899), III, 30
SWEDEN
    Literary Relations with, II, 70f. (1660–1800); III, 42f. (19 cent.)
    Loan-words, I, 33

Swedenborg, Emanuel, II, 33
Sweeney, J. N. (*fl.* 1861), I, 695
Sweet, Henry (1845–1912), III, **1042**
Sweet Robin (18 cent.), II, 250
Swetnam, Joseph (*fl.* 1617), I, 716
Swetnam, The Woman-Hater (17 cent.), I, 653
Swift, Deane (1707–1783), II, 593
Swift, Jonathan (1667–1745), II, 50, 59, 70–1, 110, **581**f., 661 (2)
SWIMMING (books on), III, 776
Swinburne, Algernon Charles (1837–1909), III, **317**f.
    Articles and reviews by, III, 161, 269, 348, 998
Swinburne, Henry (1560?–1623), I, 851
Swinburne, Henry (1743–1803), II, 746
Swinden, John (*fl.* 1833), II, 632
Swinhoe, Gilbert (*fl.* 1658), I, 650
Swinney's Birmingham and Stafford Chronicle (1773), II, 721
Swinney's Birmingham and Stafford Chronicle; and Coventry Gazette (1781), II, 721
Swinney's Birmingham and Stafford Chronicle and Piercy's Coventry Gazette (1778), II, 721
Swinney's Birmingham and Warwickshire Chronicle and Staffordshire Advertiser (1792), II, 721
Swinny (or Swiney), Owen Mac (d. 1754), II, 425 794
Swinton, Andrew (*fl.* 1792), II, 747
Swithun, St (O.E.), I, **93**
Switzer, Stephen (*fl.* 1718), II, 148
SWITZERLAND
    Literary relations with, III, 45
Swynnerton, Charles (*fl.* 1884–1903), III, 1072
Sydenham, Floyer (1710–1787), II, 762
Sydenham, Sir Philip (*fl.* 1727), II, 102
Sydenham, Thomas (1624–1689), II, 621, 962
Sydney, George Frederic (*fl.* 1795), II, **765**, 767
Sydserf, Thomas (1581–1663), bishop of Galloway, II, 702, 730
Sydserf (or St Serfe), Sir Thomas (*fl.* 1658), dramatist, II, **427**
Sykes, Arthur Ashley (1684?–1756), II, 714
Sykes, Sir Mark Masterman (1771–1823), I, 251
Sykes, William Henry (1790–1872), III, 1075
Sylph, The (1795), II, 666
Sylph; a Novel, The (1779), II, 548
Sylvae (17 cent.), II, 180
Sylvester, James Joseph (1814–1897), III, 942
Sylvester, Joshua (1563–1618), I, 478, 652, 718, 818
Sylvester, Matthew (1636?–1708), I, 695
Sylvia's Home Journal (1878), III, 830
Sylvia's Journal (1892), III, 830
Sylvius, Aeneas (Enea Silvio Piccolomini, later Pope Pius II), I, 329
Syme, David (1827–1908), III, 983

Syme, J. B. (*fl.* 1853), III, 646
Symes, Michael (1753?–1809), II, **751**
Symes, R. (*fl.* 1815), III, 764
Symmons, Mr — (*fl.* 1725), II, 538
Symmons, Caroline (*fl.* before 1804), III, 247
Symmons, Charles (1749–1826), I, 466
Symmons, Edward (*fl.* 1648), I, 719
Symonds, — (*fl.* 1798), II, 61
Symonds, A. R. (*fl.* 1845), III, 1080
Symonds, Henry (*fl.* 1899), III, 761
Symonds, John Addington (1840–1893), III, **358**f.
Symonds, William (1556–1616?), I, 845
Symonds, William Samuel (1818–1887), III, 721
Symons, Arthur (b. 1865), III, **359**f., 834
Symson (or Simson), Andrew (1638–1712), II, 731
Symson (or Simson), Archibald (1564?–1628), I, 858, **909**
Symson, William (*fl.* 1715), II, 750
Synge, John Millington (1871–1909), III, **1062**f.
Synopsis Musicae (17 cent.), II, 182
Synopsis of Vocal Musick (17 cent.), II, 178
SYNTAX, ENGLISH, I, 26f.
Syre Gawane and the Carle of Carlyle (M.E.), I, 138
Syren, The (1735), II, 205, 207 (2), 208
Syren, The (1765), II, 223, 228
Syren, The (1797), II, 253
Syren or Musical Bouquet, The (1789), II, 243 (2), 247

T., B. A. (*fl.* 1807), III, 575
T., C. (*fl.* 1569), I, 811
T., C. (*fl.* 1615), I, 718
T., C. (*fl.* 1701), II, 744
'T., E.' (1735), II, 540
T., G. (*fl.* 1642), I, 724
T., H. (*fl.* 1659), I, 726
T., J. (*fl.* 1594), I, 431
T., J. (*fl.* 1609), I, 811
T., J. (*fl.* 1742), II, 813
T., W. (*fl.* 1601), I, 814, 817
T., W. (*fl.* 1656), I, 405
Tabacco, A Defence of (17 cent.), I, 718
Tabacco, A New and Short Defense of (17 cent.), I, 718
'Tabby, A' (1808), III, 566
Tablet, The (1840), III, 819
Tabley, John Byrne Leicester Warren, Baron de (1835–1895), III, **361**f.
Tacheron, G. S. (*fl.* 1740), II, 777
Tachmas, Prince of Persia (17 cent.), II, 533
Tacitus, I, 778, 807; II, 768
'Tagg, Thomas' (1758), II, 561
'Tagg, Timothy' (1777), II, 232
Tagore, Sir Saurindramohan (*fl.* 1875), III, 1069, 1072, 1084

Taill of Rauf Coilȝear (M.E.), I, **142**
Tailor, Robert (*fl.* 1614), I, 650
Taisnier, Joannes, I, 885
Tait, Alexander (*fl.* 1790), II, 983
Tait, Archibald Campbell (1811–1882), III, 127
Tait, James Andrew Arnan (*fl.* 1890), III, 775
Tait, Peter Guthrie (1831–1901), III, **940**
Tait, W. (*fl.* 1750), I, 901
Tait, William (1793–1864), III, 827
Tait's Edinburgh Magazine (1832), III, 827
Taitt, David (*fl.* 1772), II, 755
Talbot, Catherine (1721–1770), II, 131, **843**
Talbot, Charles, Duke of Shrewsbury (1660–1718), II, 162
Talbot, E. S. (*fl.* 1889), III, 851
Talbot, Sir Gilbert (*fl.* 1657), I, 650
Talbot, Henry Fox (1800–1877), III, 82
Talbot (or Talbott), James, II, 110, 767
Talbot, Robert (1505?–1558), I, 774
Talbot Papers (16 cent.), I, 397
Tale of Beryn, The (M.E.), I, **254**
TALES, I, **161**f. (M.E.)
For later periods see under FICTION
Tales and Novels in Verse From La Fontaine (18 cent.), II, 205, 221
Tales, and Quick Answers (16 cent.), I, 714
Tales of the Arbor (1800), II, 564
Tales to kill Time (18 cent.), II, 218
Talfourd, Francis (1828–1862), III, 602
Talfourd, Sir Thomas Noon (1795–1854), III, **596**, 636, 642
Talking Bird, The (19 cent.), III, 574
Tallemant, Paul, II, 801
Tallis, John (*fl.* 1859), III, 815
Taming of a Shrew, The (16 cent.), ballad, I, 716
Taming of a Shrew, The (16 cent.), play, I, 555
Tannahill, Robert (1774–1810), III, **244**
Tanner, Thomas (1674–1735), II, 923
Tansillo, Luigi, I, 339; II, 814
'Tantara' (1893), III, 761
Tap (or Tapp), John (*fl.* 1596–1615), I, 378, 812
Taplin, William (*fl.* 1772–1803), II, 821; III, 758
Tarleton, Sir Banastre (1754–1833), II, 756
Tarlton's Jests (17 cent.), I, 715
Tarltons Newes out of Purgatorie (16 cent.), I, 713
Tartaglia, Niccoló, I, 819
Tasker, William (1740–1800), II, 76, **382**
'Tasma', i.e. Jessie Catherine Couvreur, III, 1096
Tasso, Torquato, I, 338, 340f., 819; II, 67, 814; III, 39, 405
Tassoni, Alessandro, II, 67
TASTE (discussions of), II, 14f. (17, 18 cents.)
Taswell, William (*fl.* 1651–82), I, 388
Tate, J. (*fl.* 1687), II, 124
Tate, Nahum (1652–1715), I, 458; II, 21, 180, 183 (3), 190, 192, 250, **428**f., 760, 766, 810
Tate, Thomas (1807–1888), III, 114

Tatham, Edward (1749–1834), II, 635; III, 127
Tatham, F. (*fl.* 1850), II, 349
Tatham, John (*fl.* 1632–64), I, 650
Tatler, The (1709), II, 34, 52, 69, 110, 609, 661, 698, 707
Tatler, The (1711), II, 661 (3)
Tatler, The (1754), II, 664
Tatler, The (1830), III, 799
Tatler in Cambridge, The (1871), III, 835
Tatler Reviv'd, The (1727), II, 663
Tatler Revived, The (1750), II, 664
Tatling Harlot, The (1709), II, 661
Tattersall, George (1817–1849) ('Wildrake'), III, 763
Tattersall, Richard (1724–1795), II, 697
Tattler, The (1887), III, 814
Tatwine (d. 734), I, **104**
Taubman, Matthew (d. 1690?), II, 179
Tauchnitz, Bernhard, III, 100
Taunton, T. H. (*fl.* 1887), III, 764
Taunton, Sir William Elias (1773–1835), II, 666
Tautphoeus, Jemima, Baroness, née Montgomery (1807–1893), III, **509**
Taverner, John (*fl.* 1600), I, 394
Taverner, Richard (1505?–1575), I, 665, 675, 715, 800
Taverner, William (d. 1731), II, **444**
Tavernier, Jean Baptiste, II, 771, 801
Tawney, C. H. (*fl.* 1871), III, 1072
TAXATION, II, 691 (of press); III, 72f. (of paper), 978 (treatises on)
Tayler, James (*fl.* 1888), angler, III, 772
Tayler, John James (1797–1869), divine, II, 862
Tayler, William (*fl.* 1853–78), of Middle Temple, III, 978
Tayler, William (1808–1892), Indian civilian, III, 1084
Taylor, Dr — (*fl.* 1757), II, 887
Taylor, Rev. — (*fl.* 1832), II, 346
Taylor, A. (*fl.* 1802–21), editor of 'The General Baptist Repository', III, 824
Taylor, Alexander (*fl.* 1830–58), II, 849
Taylor, Alfred Swaine (1806–1880), III, 988
Taylor, Ann, née Martin (1759–1829), III, 565
Taylor, Ann, later Gilbert (1782–1866), II, 558, 564; III, 151, 565 (3)
Taylor, Charles (*fl.* 1880), editor of 'The Court Journal', III, 813
Taylor, Charles (1840–1908), master of St John's College, Cambridge, III, **1014**
Taylor, Daniel (1738–1816), II, 672, 683
Taylor, E. J. (*fl.* 1691), II, 861
Taylor, Edgar (1793–1839), III, 576, 701
Taylor, Edward (*fl.* 1691), expositor of Boehme, II, 54
Taylor, Edward (*fl.* 1772–83), Glasgow scholar, II, 400, 762, 783
Taylor, Emily (1795–1872), III, 275, 572

Taylor, G. (*fl.* 1768–9), traveller to North America, II, 755

Taylor, G. W. (*fl.* 1827), I, 264

Taylor, Henry (1711–1785), theologian, II, 883

Taylor, Sir Henry (1800–1886), dramatist, III, 169, **308**

Taylor, Isaac (1759–1829), engraver and writer for the young, III, 565

Taylor, Isaac (1787–1865), artist, author and inventor, III, 114, 136, 565, 847, **875**

Taylor, Isaac (1829–1901), archaeologist and philologist, III, 565

Taylor, James (1788–1863), bimetallist, III, **974**, 978

Taylor, James (*fl.* 1884) writer on curling, III, 778

Taylor, Jane (1783–1824), II, 558; III, 565 (3)

Taylor, Jefferys (1792–1853), III, 565

Taylor, Jeremy (1613–1667), I, **700**f.

Taylor, Jesse Paul (*fl.* 1898), III, 772

Taylor, John (1578–1653), I, **708**f.
  Periodicals by, I, 757, 759 (2), 760 (2)

Taylor, John (1704–1766), classical scholar, II, 617, 887, 937

Taylor, John (1711–1788), friend of Dr Johnson, II, 623

Taylor, John (*fl.* 1761), author of 'History of Travels', II, 745

Taylor, John (*fl.* 1807), editor of Joseph Richardson's remains, II, 378

Taylor, John (d. 1808), writer on India, II, 751

Taylor, John (1750–1826), of Norwich, hymn-writer, II, 666

Taylor, John (1757–1832), journalist and miscellaneous writer, II, **709** (2); III, 209, 374, 788, 800

Taylor, John (1781–1864), publisher, II, 631 f.; III, 100, 218, 825

Taylor, John (*fl.* 1869–95), of Northampton, I, 8

Taylor, John Edward (1791–1844), founder of 'The Manchester Guardian', III, 788, 802

Taylor, John Edward, the younger (1830–1905), art-collector and newspaper-proprietor, III, 802

Taylor, John Pitt (*fl.* 1848), III, 988

Taylor, Joseph (*fl.* 1705), of the Inner Temple, II, 157

Taylor, Joseph (*fl.* 1804–15), III, 570

Taylor, Philip Meadows (1808–1876), III, **509**f.

Taylor, R. S. (*fl.* 1844–8), editor of 'The Manchester Guardian', III, 802

Taylor, Richard (1781–1858), editor of 'The Philosophical Magazine', II, 957; III, 824

Taylor, T. (*fl.* 1818), historian of the Baptists, II, 862

Taylor, T. (*fl.* 1836), biographer of Bishop Heber, III, 234

Taylor, T. D. (*fl.* 1865), editor of 'The Bristol Times', III, 803

Taylor, Thomas (1576–1633), Puritan divine, I, 702

Taylor, Thomas (*fl.* 1692–1704), translator, II, 534, 770, 777, 790, 796, 944

Taylor, Thomas (*fl.* 1782), compiler of a biblical concordance, II, 928

Taylor, Thomas (1758–1835), Platonist, II, 762 (3), 764; III, **876**f.

Taylor, Thomas (*fl.* 1833–9), biographer of Cowper, II, 342

Taylor, Tom (1817–1880), dramatist, III, 443, 456 (2), **608**f.

Taylor, Robert (1784–1844), III, **875**

Taylor, Samuel (*fl.* 1800), II, 822

Taylor, Sarah, later Austin (1793–1867), III, 107, 576, 680

Taylor, Sidney (*fl.* before 1843), III, 798

Taylor, William (*fl.* 1749), of 'The Monthly Review', II, 677

Taylor, William (*fl.* 1792), compiler of 'A Catalogue of Stirling's Library', II, 105

Taylor, William (1765–1836), of Norwich, German scholar, III, **680**f.

Taylor, William Benjamin Sarsfield (1781–1850), painter, III, 124

Taylor, William Cooke (1800–1849), miscellaneous writer, III, 297

Tea Table, The (1715), II, 662

Tea Table, The (1724), II, 662

Tea-Table Dialogues; between Miss Thoughtful, Miss Sterling [etc.] (18 cent.), II, 562

Tea-Table Miscellany, The (18 cent.), II, 197, 199, 201, 204 (2), 208, 214 (2), 216, 220–1, 222–3, 225 (2), 226, 231, 236–7, 242, 249 (2), 250

'Teachem, Toby' (1780), II, 562

Teacher's Offering, The (1840), III, 577

Teall, Sir Jethro J. (1849–1924), III, 953

Teares or Lamentacions of a Sorrowfull Soule, The (17 cent.), I, 485

Tebbutt, A. (*fl.* 1897), III, 779

Tebbutt, C. G. (*fl.* 1894), III, 778–9

Tegg, Thomas (1776–1845), III, 93, 100

Tegg's Magazine of Knowledge (1843), III, 828

Teignmouth, John Shore, Baron (1751–1834), II, 368

Teixeira, José, I, 734, 743

Telang, K. T. (*fl.* 1879), III, 1072 (2)

Telegraph, The (1794), II, 710

Telescope, The (1824), III, 811

Telford, Thomas (1757–1834), II, 138

Tell Tale (17 cent.), I, 653

Tell-Tale, The (19 cent.), III, 575

Tell-Trothes New Yeare's Gift (16 cent.), I, 713

Tell-Truth Remembrancer, The (1702), II, 659

Téllez, Gabriel, I, 343

'Telltruth, Charles' (1766), II, 224

Temperance and Humility (16 cent.), I, 515

Tempest, P. (*fl.* 1709), II, 813

Templar and Literary Gazette, The (1773), II, 665

Templar; Or, Monthly Register of Legal Knowledge, The (1788), II, 681

Temple, Frederick (1821–1902), III, 114, 848

Temple, Henry, Viscount Palmerston (1739–1802), II, 747

Temple, Henry John, Viscount Palmerston (1784–1865), III, **677f.**

Temple, J. W. (*fl.* 1795), II, 654

Temple, Sir Richard (1634–1697), II, 944

Temple, Sir Richard (1826–1902) III, 1070, 1078

Temple, Richard Temple Grenville, Earl (1711–1779), II, 632 (3)

Temple, Sir William (1555–1623), logician, I, 874

Temple, Sir William (1628–1699), statesman and essayist, II, 15, 39, 74, **569f.**

Temple, William Johnstone (1739–1796), II, 138, 625

Temple Magazine, The (1896), III, 831

Temple of Apollo, The (18 cent.), II, 212

Temple of Comus, The (18 cent.), II, 223

Temple of Death, The (17 cent.), II, 183

Temple of Love, The (18 cent.), II, 206

Temple of Mirth, The (18 cent.), II, 238

Temple-Bar (1860), III, 829

Temple-Oge Intelligencer, The (1728), II, 663

Tench, Watkin (1759?–1833), II, 748, 751

Tençin, Claudine Alexandrine Guérin de, II, 551

Tenison, Thomas (1636–1715), II, 402, **850**

Tennant, Charles (*fl.* 1834–69), III, 978

Tennant, William (1784–1848), II, 969; III, **244,** 1075

Tennelière, Eustache Le Noble de, II, 122, 541–2, 788

Tennent, Sir James Emerson (1804–1869), III, 992

Tenniel, Sir John (1820–1914), III, 92

TENNIS (books on), III, 775

Tennyson, Alfred, Baron (1809–1892), III, **253f.**
  Translations from, III, 26, 37, 40f., 42–3, 45 (2)

Tennyson, Charles, later Turner (1808–1879), III, **308**

Tennyson, Frederick (1807–1898), III, **309**

Tenterden, Charles Abbott, Baron (1762–1832), III, 985

Teonge, Henry (1621–1690), II, 150

Terence, I, 808; II, 768; III, 1010

Terens in Englysh (16 cent.), I, 522

Teres, T. (*fl.* 1769), II, 804

Terilo, William (*fl.* 1604), I, 714

Terrae Filius (1721), II, 662

Terrae-Filius (1763), II, 665

Terrae-Filius (1764), II, 665

Terrasson, Jean, II, 29, 542, 801

Terrell, Thomas (*fl.* 1884), III, 988

Terry, Daniel (1780?–1829), III, 379

Terry, Edward (1590–1660), I, 785

Terry, Ellen (1847–1928), III, 155

Test, The (1756), II, 664

Test-Paper, The (1688), II, 658, 731

Testa de Nevill (M.E.), I, 120

Teuthold, Peter (*fl.* 1794), II, 805

Tewkesbury, Annals of (15 cent.), I, 115

TEXTBOOKS, I, 125 (O.E. and M.E.), 374f. (1500–1660); II, 125f. (1660–1800); III, 135f. (19 cent.)

Textor, Johannes Ravisius, I, 328

Thacher, Anthony (*fl.* 1635), I, 792

Thackeray, Anne Isabella, later Lady Ritchie (1837–1923), III, **561**

Thackeray, Francis (1793–1842), II, 164

Thackeray, T. J. (*fl.* 1832), III, 584

Thackeray, William Makepeace (1811–1863), III, 26, **429f.**, 834
  Articles, prefaces, etc., III, 281, 441, 452, 461, 478, 564, 686

Thackwell, E. J. (*fl.* 1851), III, 1576

Thamara, Francisco, I, 765

Theakston, M. (*fl.* 1853), III, 770

Theal, G. McC. (*fl.* 1888–1910), III, 1090–1, 1093

Theater of Mortality, An (18 cent.), II, 186, 191

Theater of Music, The (17 cent.), II, 180 (4)

Theatre, The (1720), II, 662

Theatre, The (1877), III, 830

Théâtre Anglois, Le (1746), II, 392

Theatre of Compliments, The (17 cent.), II, 181

Theatre of Ingenuity, The (18 cent.), II, 186

Theatre of Mirth, The (18 cent.), II, 235

Theatre of Wit, The (18 cent.), II, 212

Theatre: or, Select Works of the British Dramatic Poets, The (1768), II, 392

THEATRES, I, 497f. (16, 17 cents.)
  Elizabethan companies, I, 501f.
  London and provincial, II, 403f. (17, 18 cents.); III, 580f. (19 cent.)
  Puritan attack on, I, 507f. (16, 17 cents.); II, 400f. (17, 18 cents.)

Theatrical Bouquet, The (18 cent.), II, 235

Theatrical Museum, The (18 cent.), II, 232

Theatrical Review, The (1771), II, 665

Theatrical Review; Or, Annals of the Drama, The (1763), II, 678

Theatrical Review; Or, New Companion to the Playhouse, The (1771), II, 679

THEBES, ROMANCES OF, I, **146**

Theloall, Simon (*fl.* 1579), I, 851

Thelwall, John (1764–1834), I, 17; II, 672, 681; III, 135, **244f.**

Thenterlude of Youth (16 cent.), I, 516

Theobald, H. S. (*fl.* 1881), III, 985

Theobald, Lewis (1688–1744), II, 74, 301, **444,** 893f.

Theocritus, I, 808; II, 763

Theognis, II, 362

Theological and Political Comet, The (1819), III, 816

Theological Comet or Free Thinking Englishman, The (1819), III, 816

Theological Magazine, The (1750), II, 677

Theological Miscellany, The (1784), II, 680

Theological Review, The (1864), III, 830

THEOLOGICAL WRITINGS

    Anglo-Saxon period. See under Writings in Latin, I, 98 f.

    Middle English period. See under WYCLIFFE AND ASSOCIATED WRITINGS, I, 203 f. and WRITINGS IN LATIN, I, 280 f.

    Renaissance to Restoration, I, 856 f. See also under RELIGIOUS PROSE, I, 664 f. and under PHILOSOPHICAL WRITERS, I, 868 f. ·

    Restoration to Romantic Revival, II, 39 (French-English, English-French), 54 f. (German-English, English-German), 845 f. (Restoration divines), 850 f. (18 cent. divines), 854 f. (early Quakers), 857 f. (mystics), 861 f. (dissenters). See also under THE PHILOSOPHERS, II, 939 f.

    Nineteenth Century, III, 58 f. (higher criticism), 60 f. and 68 f. (religion and science), 846 f. (liberal theologians and evangelicals), 854 f. (Oxford Movement). See also under PHILOSOPHY, III, 861 f.

Theophania (17 cent.), I, 732

Theophrastus, I, 808; II, 763; III, 1006

Theosophical Review, The (1897), III, 831

Therry, Sir Roger (1800–1874), II, 356, 635

Thersytes (16 cent.), I, 520

Thesaurus Ænigmaticus (18 cent.), II, 198 (2), 199

Thesaurus Dramaticus (18 cent.), II, 197

Thesaurus Musicus (17 cent.), II, 182, 183 (4)

Thesaurus Musicus (18 cent.), II, 210–2

Thespian Magazine and Literary Repository, The (1792), II, 682

Thetford, Launcelot (*fl.* 1655), I, 706

Théveneau de Morande, Charles (1748–1803), II, 696, 719

Thévenot, Melchisedech (*fl.* 1699), II, 827

Thevet, André, I, 786

Thibault (Governor of Talmont), II, 542

Thibaut, G. (*fl.* 1890), III, 1072

Thiboust, Lambert, III, 548

Thicknesse, Philip (1719–1792), II, 154, 631, 745

Thinbleby, J. (*fl.* 1849), III, 974

Third Part of the Works of Mr Abraham Cowley, The (17 cent.), II, 181, 185

Thirlstane, Sir John Maitland, Baron (1545?–1595), I, 905

Thirlwall, Connop (1797–1875), III, 122, **894** f.

Thirty Scots Songs (18 cent.), II, 218, 228 (2), 235, 245 (2)

Thistleton-Dyer, Sir William Turner (1843–1929), III, 962

Thom, John Hamilton (1808–1894), III, 847, 850

Thom, Walter (1770–1824), III, 776

Thom, William (1798?–1848), III, 245

Thomas Anglicus (*fl.* 13 cent.), I, **296**

Thomas de Hibernia (d. 1270), I, **293**

Thomas de Jorz (d. 1310), I, **306**

Thomas of Bungay (d. *c.* 1275), I, **293**

Thomas of Burton (*fl.* 1396), I, 265

Thomas of Eccleston (*fl.* 1250), I, **292**

Thomas of Sutton (*fl.* 1290), I, **296**

Thomas of York (d. *c.* 1260), I, **292**

Thomas, Antoine Léonard, II, 801

Thomas, David (1813–1894), III, 814

Thomas, E. (*fl.* 1695), II, 706

Thomas, Elizabeth (1677–1731), II, 210

Thomas, G. P. (*fl.* 1847), III, 1068

Thomas, Gabriel (*fl.* 1698), II, 752

Thomas, John (*fl.* 1641), II, 752–3

Thomas, John Wesley (1798–1872), III, 198

Thomas, Joshua (1719–1797), II, 862

Thomas, Nathaniel (*fl.* 1761), II, 710

Thomas, Pascoe (*fl.* 1745), II, 741

Thomas, Thomas (1553–1588), I, 375, 861

Thomas, Timothy (1697–1757), II, 909

Thomas, Vaughan (1775–1858), III, 127 (2)

Thomas, W. C. (*fl.* 1861), III, 694

Thomas, William (d. 1554), I, 777, 781

Thomas, William (1670–1738), I, 211; II, 277, 864

Thomas, Sir William Beach (b. 1868), III, 788

Thomas, William Luson (1830–1900), III, 788

Thomas Lord Cromwell, The True Chronicle Historie of the whole life and death of (17 cent.), I, 580

Thomas of Ersseldowne (M.E.), I, **168**

Thomas of Woodstock (17 cent.), I, 539

Thomas Overbury His Wife, Sir (17 cent.), II, 174, 189

Thomason, George (d. 1666), I, 352

Thompson, Alexander (*fl.* 1796), II, 51, 60

Thompson, Alfred (*fl.* 1868), III, 603

Thompson, Alice, later Meynell (1850–1922), III, **348** f.

Thompson, Benjamin (1776?–1816), dramatist and translator, II, 59, 60 (2), 61, 63; III, **596** f.

Thompson, Charles (*fl.* 1744–63), II, 742, 745, 816

Thompson, D'Arcy Wentworth (1829–1902), III, 114

Thompson, Ebenezer (*fl.* 1777), II, 761

Thompson, Edward (1738?–1786), II, **382** f., 916

Thompson, Edward (*fl.* 1837), III, 833

Thompson, Francis (1859–1907), III, **326** f.

Thompson, George (*fl.* 1642), I, 752

Thompson, George (*fl.* 1827), III, 1091

Thompson, H. M. (*fl.* 1892), III, 984

Thompson, Henry (1797–1878), II, 845

Thompson, J. (*fl.* 1657), I, 890
Thompson, John Vaughan (1779–1847), III, 955
Thompson, Joseph T. (*fl.* 1846), III, 1074
Thompson, Nathaniel (*fl.* 1666–1688), II, 179 (2), 697, 702–3
Thompson, Silvanus Phillips (1851–1916), III, 940
Thompson, Thomas (1708?–1773), II, 742
Thompson, Thomas (*fl.* 1803), of Hull, III, 969
Thompson, Thomas Perronet (1783–1869), III, 981
Thompson, William (1712–1767), poet, II, 23, **329**
Thompson, William (1785?–1833), political economist, III, 976
Thompson, William (*fl.* 1845), Dean of Raphoe, I, 449
Thompson, William Hepworth (1810–1886), classical scholar, III, 865, **1003**
Thompson, William Marcus (1857–1907), journalist, III, 812
Thompson's Pocket Companion for the German-Flute (18 cent.), II, 233
Thoms, William John (1803–1885), I, 575, 825; III, 818, **1035**
'Thomson, Mrs' (Harriet Pigott) (*fl.* 1788), II, 549
Thomson, Alexander (*fl.* 1767–98), traveller, II, 743
Thomson, Alexander (1763–1803), poet, II, 20, 768, 827
Thomson, Anthony Francis (*fl.* 1865), III, 114
Thomson, Sir Benjamin, Count Rumford (1753–1814), II, 962, 936f.
Thomson, Charles (*fl.* 1816), III, 195
Thomson, Sir Charles Wyville (1830–1882), III, 958
Thomson, Ebenezer (*fl.* 1815–58), I, 94, 256
Thomson, George (1757–1851), II, 983
Thomson, Hugh (1860–1920), III, 92
Thomson, Isaac (*fl.* 1731), II, **329**
Thomson, J. (*fl.* 1795), artillery captain and translator, II, 793
Thomson, J. (*fl.* 1829–33), antiquary, I, 387 (misprinted I. Thomson), 903
Thomson, James (1700–1748), poet, II, 22, 44, 46, 58, 62, 67, **305**f.
Thomson, James (*fl.* 1747), translator of Marcus Aurelius, II, 760
Thomson, James (1822–1892), professor of engineering, III, 939
Thomson, James (1834–1882), poet and pessimist, III, **316**f.
Thomson, Sir James Arthur (1861–1937), III, 955, 959
Thomson, John (pseud.?) (1732), II, 539
Thomson, John (*fl.* 1875), traveller, III, 992
Thomson, John (*fl.* 1893), golfer and poet, III, 775

Thomson, John Anstruther (*fl.* 1889), foxhunter, III, 761
Thomson, Joseph (1858–1894), African explorer, III, 992
Thomson, Sir Joseph John (1856–1940), physicist, III, **940**
Thomson, Katherine ('Grace Wharton') (*fl.* 1830–60), III, 14
Thomson, Robert (*fl.* 1715), II, 733
Thomson, Thomas (1768–1852), antiquary, I, 260, 839. 905
Thomson, Thomas (1773–1852), chemist, II, 960; III, 825, 937, 945, **946**
Thomson, Thomas (*fl.* 1842–65), clergyman, III, 164, 709
Thomson, W. (*fl.* 1834), author of 'The Age of Harmony', III, 976
Thomson, William (1746–1817), miscellaneous writer, II, 20, 548, 680, 888
Thomson, William (1819–1890), archbishop of York, III, **876**
Thomson, Sir William, Baron Kelvin (1824–1907), III, 824, **939, 952**
Thomson, William Roger (*fl.* 1867), South African poet, III, 1089
Thoresby, Ralph (1658–1725), II, 135, 157, 850, **879**, 927
Thorius, John (*fl.* 1586–93), I, 819
Thorius, Raphael (d. 1625), I, 718
Thorkelin, Grimus J. (*fl.* 1789), II, 921
'Thorn, Ismay', i.e. Edith Caroline Pollock (*fl.* 1878), III, **569**
Thornbury, George Walter (1828–1876), III, **309**
Thorndike, Herbert (1598–1672), I, **702**
Thorne, James (1815–1881), III, 769
Thorne, William (*fl.* 1397), I, 265
Thornes, Edward (*fl.* 1615), I, 775
Thorney Abbey (17 cent.), I, 653
Thornhill, R. B. (*fl.* 1804), III, 762
Thornley, George (*fl.* 1657), I, 804, 863
Thornton, Alfred (*fl.* 1821), III, 199
Thornton, Alice (*fl.* 1629–69), I, 387
Thornton, Bonnell (1724–1768), II, 116, 217–8, 229, 235, **383**, 615–6, 664 (3)
Thornton, Edward (1799–1875), III, 1075
Thornton, Henry (1760–1815), economist, III, 852, 972–3
Thornton, Henry (1818–1905) ('Henry Thornton Craven'), III, **602**
Thornton, R. (*fl.* 1691), II, 733
Thornton, Robert John (1768?–1837), III, 135
Thornton, Thomas (1757–1823), II, 140, 413
Thornton, W. L. (*fl.* 1890?), III, 823
Thornton, William (*fl.* 1784), II, 145
Thornton, William Thomas (1813–1880), social philosopher, III, **876**, 971, 976
Thorold, John (*fl.* 1726), II, 600
Thoroton, Robert (1623–1678), II, **871**
Thorowgood, G. (*fl.* 1656), I, 717

Thorowgood, Thomas (*fl.* 1650), I, 796
Thorpe, Benjamin (1782–1870), I, 77; III, 1027f.
Thorpe, John (1682–1750), I, 122
Thorpe, Sir Thomas Edward (1845–1925), III, 949
Thou, Jacques Auguste de (Thuanus), II, 33, 801
Thoughts Moral and Divine (18 cent.), II, 218–20, 222
Thracian Wonder, The (17 cent.), I, 653
Thrale, Hester Lynch, later Piozzi (1741–1821), II, 843f.
Three Kings' Sons (15 cent.), I, 266
Three Kynges of Coleyn, The (15 cent.), I, 266
Three New Poems (18 cent.), II, 196
Three Poems (18 cent.), II, 196
Three Poems Upon the Death of the Late Usurper Oliver Cromwel (17 cent.), II, 178
Three Select Poems; Viz. Windsor Forest [etc.] (18 cent.), II, 250
Three Songs in English and Latin (18 cent.), II, 214
Threni Cantabrigienses in Exequiis (17 cent.), II, 175
Thring, Edward (1821–1887), III, 114, 141
Throkmorton, Job (1545–1601), I, 692, 693
Throsby, John (1740–1803), II, 871
Thrush, The (18 cent.), II, 213
Thrush and the Nightingale, The (M.E.), I, 183
Thuanus. See J. A. de Thou
Thucydides, I, 808; II, 763; III, 1003
Thurloe, John (1616–1668), I, 400, 760, 763
Thurlow, Edward, later Hovell-Thurlow, Baron (1781–1829), III, 245
Thurnham, John (1810–1873), III, 967
Thursday's Journal, The (1719), II, 713
Thurston, Joseph (*fl.* 1731), II, 329, 826
Thwaites, Edward (1667–1711), II, 919
Thwaites, R. G. (*fl.* 1896), III, 1088
Thyer, Robert (1709–1781), II, 913
Thynne, Francis (1545?–1608), I, 211, 479
Thynne, William (d. 1546), I, 211
Tibullus, II, 768
Tickell, Richard (1751–1793), II, 383, 456
Tickell, Thomas (1685–1740), II, 22, 199, 329f., 820
Tickler, The (1748), II, 663
Tickler, The (1770), II, 665
Tickler; or Monthly Compendium of Good Things, The (1818), III, 825
Tidd, William (1760–1847), II, 965
Tieck, Ludwig, III, 35, 48f., 670
Tierney, George (1761–1830), II, 457
Tighe, Mary, née Blachford (1772–1810), III, 245
Tighe, Richard (*fl.* 1813), biographer of William Law, II, 858
Tighe, Robert Richard (*fl.* 1858), historian of Windsor, I, 826

Tighe, Robert Stearne (*fl.* 1805), writer on Ireland, II, 160
Tilak, Bal Gangadhar (*fl.* 1893), III, 1082
Till Eulenspiegel, I, 819
Tillbrook, Samuel (*fl.* 1822), I, 17
Tillemont, Louis Sebastien le Nain de, II, 788
Tillesley, Richard (1582–1621), I, 847
Tilloch, Alexander (1759–1825), II, 672, 683, 697, 711
Tillotson, John (1630–1694), I, 703 (2), 879; II, 55, 846, 850
Tillotson, John (*fl.* 1853?), III, 829
Tillotson, W. F. (*fl.* 1867), III, 803
Tilney, Edmund (d. 1610), I, 728
Tilsley, Hugh (*fl.* 1849), III, 790
Tilson, — (*fl.*1764), II, 68
Timaeus, Johann Jacob Carl, II, 61, 306, 486
Timberlake, Henry (d. 1626), I, 769
Timberlake, Henry (*fl.* 1762–5), II, 755
Timbs, John (1801–1875), I, 716; III, 99
Time (1879), III, 831
Time's Triumph (17 cent.), I, 653
Times, The (1785), II, 698
Times, The (1788), II, 709; III, 794, 798
Times; Or The Daily Universal Register, The (1788), II, 709
Timms, Thomas (*fl.* 1574), I, 819
Timon (17 cent.), I, 663
Timperley, Charles H. (1794–1846?), III, 70, 75
Tindal, Matthew (1657–1733), II, 32, 55, 84, 787, 948
Tindal, Nicholas (1688–1774), II, 796, 896
Tindale (or Tyndale), William (d. 1536), I, 665, 668, 675 (2)
Tinsley, William (1831–1902), III, 100
Tinsley's Magazine (1867), III, 830
Tiny Tots (1899), III, 579
Tipper, John (d. 1713), II, 676
Tiptoft, John, Earl of Worcester (1427?–1470), I, 362, 800
Tirwhyt, William (*fl.* 1634), I, 810
Tissot, Samuel Auguste André David, II, 801
Tit-Bits (1881), III, 814
Titan, The (1856), III, 828
'Titmore, Timothy' (1785), II, 563
Titt for Tatt (1710), II, 661
Titus (17 cent.), I, 653
Titus and Vespasian (couplet version) (M.E.), I, 157f.
Tlysau yr hen Oesoedd (1735), II, 685
To-Day (1893), III, 814
To-Morrow (1896), III, 831
Toasts of the Rump-Steak Club, The (18 cent.), II, 204 (2)
TOBACCO PAMPHLETS, I, 718 (16, 17 cents.)
Tobin, John (1770–1804), III, 597
TOBOGGANING (books on), III, 779
Toby in Cambridge (1832), III, 834
Tobyas, Thomas (*fl.* 1701), II, 407
Tod, James (1782–1835), III, 1075, 1080

Todd, Alpheus (1821–1884), III, 1087
Todd, Henry John (1763–1845), I, 5; III, 200, 879 (2), **1028**
Todd, James (fl. 1748), II, 110
Todd, James Henthorn (1805–1869), I, 204 (3), 702; III, 124, **1048**
Todd, Robert Bentley (1809–1860), III, 963
Todhunter, Isaac (1820–1884), III, **942**
Todhunter, John (1839–1916), III, 1054f.
Tofte, Robert (1561–2–1620), I, **433**f., 716, 810–11, 818
Tokefield, George (fl. 1663), II, 93
Toland, John (1670–1722), I, 466, 878; II, 55, 499, 505, 744, 759, 767, **948**f.
Toldervy, William (fl. 1755), II, 217
Tollet, Elizabeth (1694–1754), II, **330**
Tolstoi, Leo, III, **44**
Tom Brown's Complete Jester (18 cent.), II, 218
Tom Gay's Comical Jester (18 cent.), II, 233
Tom Gaylove's Compleat Jester (18 cent.), II, 220
Tom Smart's New Comical Jester (19 cent.), II, 256
Tom Spring's Life in London and Sporting Chronicle (1840), III, 812
Tom Thumb's Folio (18 cent.), II, 562
Tom Tyler and his Wife (16 cent.), I, 521
Tomahawk, The (1867), III, 820
Tomahawk or Censor General, The (1795), II, 708
Tombes, John (1603?–1676), I, 702
Tomkins, E. (apparently misprint for Thomas Tomkins, 1743–1816), II, 256
Tomkins, F. G. (fl. 1840), III, 584
Tomkins, Thomas (1573?–1656), I, 486
Tomkins, Thomas (1743–1816), II, 236, 248, 256
Tomkis, Thomas (fl. 1607), I, 660
Tomline, George (fl. 1850), editor of Sir Henry Wotton, I, 426
Tomline, Sir George Pretyman (1750–1827), biographer of Pitt, III, **880**
Tomlins, Frederick Guest (1804–1867), III, 812
Tomlins, Sir Thomas Edlyne (1762–1841), I, 401
Tomlins, Thomas Edlyne (1804–1872), I, 501, 831
Tomlinson, Kellom (fl. 1720), II, 825
Tomlinson, L. (fl. 1780), II, 634
Tommy Thumb's Pretty Song Book (18 cent.), II, 554
Tommy Trip's Valentine Gift (18 cent.), II, 564
Tompson, Charles (1806–1883), III, 1094
Tompson, John (fl. 1737), II, 206, 603
Toms, E. (fl. 1767), II, 810
Tomson, Graham Rosamund, later Marriott Watson (1860–1911), III, **360**
Tomson, Laurence (1539–1608), I, 676
TONBRIDGE SCHOOL, I, 373; III, 133

Tongue, Cornelius (fl. 1851) ('Cecil'), III, 759, 766
Tonkin, Thomas (1678–1742), I, 826
Tonna, Charlotte Elizabeth, earlier Phelan, née Browne (1790–1846), III, 827
Tonstall (or Tunstall), Cuthbert (1474–1559), I, 378, 683, 880
Tooke (earlier Horne), John Horne (1736–1812), II, 630–1, 932, 937, 957
Tooke, Thomas (1774–1858), III, **974**
Tooke, William (1744–1820), II, 31, 58, 63, 224, 339, 547, 748, 778, 922
Tooker, Charles (fl. 1695), II, 97
Tooker, William (1558?–1621), I, 889
Tooly, Thomas (fl. 1719), II, 764
Tootell (or Tootel), Hugh (1672–1743) ('Charles Dodd'), II, 95
Top, Alexandre (fl. 1629), I, 679
Top Book of All, The (18 cent.), II, 554
Toper's Delight, The (18 cent.), II, 210
Tophail, Abi Jaaphar Ebn, II, 533
Topham, Edward (1751–1820), II, 157, 242, 391, 697, 709
Toplady, Augustus Montague (1740–1778), II, 672, 679, **853**
Topley, William (1841–1894), III, 953
TOPOGRAPHICAL DESCRIPTIONS
    Renaissance to Restoration, I, 381, 773f.
    Restoration to Romantic Revival, II, 139f. (England), 157f. (Scotland), 159 (Ireland)
Topsell, Edward (d. 1638?), I, 813, 893
Torkyngton (or Torkington), Rychard (fl. 1518), I, 767
Torquemada, Antonio de, I, 345, 819
Torr, John (fl. 1838–43), letter-writer, III, 153
Torr, John Berry (fl. 1838–49), editor of 'The Court Gazette', III, 813
Torrens, Henry Whitelock (1806–1852), III, 1083
Torrens, Robert (1780–1864), III, 800, 970, 972–3, 979
Torrent of Portyngale, Sir (M.E.), I, **159**
Tory Pill, A (18 cent.), II, 192 (2)
Tory Tatler, The (1710), II, 661
Totenham, The Turnament of (15 cent.), I, 265
Tottel, Richard (d. 1594), I, 351, 402
Tottel's Miscellany (16 cent.), I, 46, 402
'Touchstone, Timothy' (1820), III, 379
Toulmin, John (fl. 1892), III, 806
Toulmin, Joshua (1740–1815), II, 761, 862, 877
Toulons, Earl of (M.E.), I, 153
Toup, Jonathan (1713–1785), II, **937**
Tour, Abbé Seran de la, II, 801
Tournay, Charles de Brosses, Comte de, II, 773
Tournefort, Joseph Pitton de, II, 793 (2)
Tourneur, Cyril (1575?–1626), I, **628**f.
TOURS. See TRAVEL
Tousey, George Philip (fl. 1768), II, **383**
Tovey, Duncan Crookes (1842–1912), III, **1042**
Towers, John (fl. 1862), III, 817

Towers, Joseph (1737–1799), II, 262, 624, 626, 922, 952
Towers, Matthew (*fl.* 1742), II, 765
Town, The (1832), III, 812
Town, The (1837), III, 813
Town and Country Jester, The (18 cent.), II, 220
Town and Country Magazine, The (1769), II, 665 (6), 666, 679
Town and Country Magazine and Irish Miscellany, The (1784), II, 687
Town and Country Song-Book, The (18 cent.), II, 245
Town and Country Songster, The (18 cent.), II, 241
Town and Country Songster's Companion, The (18 cent.), II, 254
Town and Country Tales (19 cent.), III, 575
Town and Country Weekly Magazine, The (1785), II, 687
Town Mistress [etc.], *The* (18 cent.), II, 198
Town Spy, The (1704), II, 659
Town Talk (1715), II, 662
Town Talk (1858), III, 814
Towneley Plays (M.E.), I, 277f.
Townesend, George (*fl.* 1667), II, 965
Townley, James (1714–1778), II, 445, **483**
TOWNS AND TOWN LIFE, I, 124 (M.E. period), 389 (1500–1660); II, 145f. (1660–1800)
Townsend, A. (*fl.* 1853), I, 684
Townsend, Aurelian (1583?–1643), I, 453, 478
Townsend, C. (*fl.* 1858), III, 243
Townsend, G. F. (*fl.* 1863), historian of Leominster, III, 909
Townsend, George (1788–1857), theological writer, I, 824 (2)
Townsend, George Henry (d. 1869), compiler and journalist, III, 814
Townsend, J. (*fl.* 1851), III, 817
Townsend, Joseph (1739–1816), II, 747, 957; III, 949
Townsend, Meredith White (1831–1911), III, 788, 813
Townsend, William Charles (1803–1850), III, 127
Townshend, Chauncey Hare (1798–1868), III, 449
Townshend, George, Viscount (1724–1807), II, 665
Townshend, Henry (*fl.* 1640–63), I, 387, 842
Townshend, Heywood (*fl.* 1601), I, 401
Townson, Robert (*fl.* 1795–8), II, 748
'Toxophilite' (1867), III, 775
Toy-Shop, or Sentimental Preceptor, The (18 cent.), II, 564
Toynbee, Arnold (1852–1883), III, 984
Tozer, Henry Fanshawe (1829–1916), III, **1010**
TRACTS, COLLECTIONS OF, I, 712f.
Tracts for the Times (19 cent.), III, 855
Tracy, T. (*fl.* 1841), III, 576

TRADE TERMS (dictionaries of), II, 926
Trade Unionist, The (1891), III, 818
Tragedie of Caesar's Revenge, The (17 cent.), I, 661
Tragedie of Claudius Tiberius Nero, The (17 cent.), I, 651
TRAGEDIES, I, 522f. (16 cent.); II, 396 (heroic tragedy). See also under DRAMA
Tragedy of Alphonsus, The (17 cent.), I, 651
Tragedy of Amurath, The (17 cent.), I, 661
Tragedy of Nero, The (17 cent.), I, 652
Tragedye of Solyman and Perseda, The (16 cent.), I, 538
Tragic and Comic Theatre, The (1778), II, 392
Traherne, Thomas (1637?–1674), I, 462f.
Traheron, Bartholomew (1510?–1558), I, 890
Traheron, William (*fl.* 1604), I, 816
Traill, Catherine Parr, née Strickland (*fl.* 1850), III, 1087–8
Traill, Henry Duff (1842–1900), III, **755**, 810
Train, The (1856), III, 829
Traiteur, The (1780), II, 665
TRALEE
    Newspaper, II, 738
Transatlantic, The (1873), III, 830
TRANSLATION, ART OF, II, 758. See also under OLD ENGLISH POETRY, I, 61f.
TRANSLATIONS
    Old English Poetry, I, 62
    Middle English verse. See Collections of Modern Renderings, I, 114, and for the romances Collections of Abstracts or Modern Renderings, I, 130
    Renaissance to Restoration, I, 732f. (prose fiction), 799f. (Greek and Latin), 809f. (medieval and contemporary), 820f. (criticism)
    Restoration to Romantic Revival, II, 27f. (literary criticism), 532f. (novels, 1660–1700), 540f. (novels, 1701–39), 551f. (novels, 1740–1800), 565f. (children's books), 758f. (from Greek), 764f. (from Latin), 769f. (from French), 804f. (from German), 807f. (from Italian)
    Nineteenth Century, III, 576f. (children's books), 1070f. (from Indian languages)
Trapaud, Elisha (*fl.* 1774–88), II, 751, 790
Trapham, Thomas (*fl.* 1679), II, 752
Trapp, Joseph (1679–1747), I, 466; II, 13, 22, **330**
Trapp, Joseph (*fl.* 1796), II, 63, 797
'Trapwit, T.' (1758), II, 561
TRAVEL, BOOKS OF
    Middle English Period, I, 191f.
    Renaissance to Restoration, I, 763f. (general collections and accounts), 765f. (general geographical descriptions), 767f. (Europe and Mediterranean countries), 781f. (Africa and Asia), 786f. (America), 796f. (critical and historical works)

Travel, Books of (*cont.*)
  Restoration to Romantic Revival, II, 120
  (treatises on), 139f. (tours of England),
  157f. (tours of Scotland), 159 (tours of
  Ireland), 739f. (modern studies), 740f.
  (collections of voyages), 741f. (voyages
  round the world), 743 (voyages to northern
  ocean), 743f. (voyages in Europe), 748f.
  (Africa), 749f. (Asia, East Indies, Austra-
  lia), 751f. (Americas and South Seas)
  Nineteenth Century, III, 988f. (principal
  works), 1079f. (India), 1087f. (Canada),
  1090f. (South Africa), 1097f. (Australia,
  New Zealand)
Traveller, The (1801), III, 800
Traveller, The (1871), III, 830
*Travellers Magazine; Or, Gentleman and Lady's
  Agreeable Companion, The* (1749), II,
  677
Travels of Don Francesco de Quevedo, The
  (17 cent.), II, 530
Travels of Sir John Mandeville (M.E.), I, **191**
Travers, H. (*fl.* 1731), II, **330**, 820
Travers, Walter (1548?-1635), I, 687, 691
TRAVESTIES. See BURLESQUES
Travis, George (1741-1797), II, 883
Tream, W. (*fl.* 1892), III, 972
Treasury of Divine Raptures, A (17 cent.), II,
  175
Treasury of Musick, The (17 cent.), II, 175
Treasury of Wit, The (1786), II, 240
Treasury of Wit, The (1788), II, 242
Treatise of a Galaunt, A (16 cent.), I, 713
Treaty Traverst, The (1648), I, 759
Tregelles, Samuel Prideaux (1813-1875), I,
  673; III, **1014**
Trelawny, Edward John (1792-1881), III,
  681
Tremellius, Immanuel, I, 679
Trench, Frederick Herbert (1865-1923), III,
  1057
Trench, Richard Chenevix (1807-1886), III,
  168, **309**f.
Trenchard, John (1662-1723), II, 497 (2),
  662 (2), 713 (2)
Trenchfield, Caleb (*fl.* 1671), II, 122
Trenck, Friedrich von der, II, 55, 807
Trend, W. (*fl.* 1801), III, 973
Trentalle Sancti Gregorii (M.E.), I, **162**
Tresham, Sir Thomas (1543?-1605), I, 382
Tressan, Abbé de la Verne de, II, 786
Tresswell, Robert (*fl.* 1605), I, 769
TREVECCA
  Printing at, II, 88
Trevelyan, Sir C. L. [Misprint for Sir Charles
  Edward Trevelyan] (1807-1886), I, 382
Trevelyan, Sir Charles Edward (1807-1886), I,
  382; III, 1073
Trevelyan, Sir George Otto (1838-1928), III,
  728, 834, **918**f.

Trevelyan, Hannah, Lady, née Macaulay
  (*fl.* 1810-60), III, 683
Trevelyan, Sir Walter Calverley (1797-1879),
  I, 382
Trevelyan Papers (17 cent.), I, 382
Trevisa, John de (1326-1412), I, 40, **167**, 880
Trevytham (or Tryvytlam), Richard (*fl.* 1400),
  I, **305**
Trewman's Exeter Evening Post (1769), II, 724
Trewman's Exeter Flying Post (1770), II, 724
Treyssac de Vergy, Pierre Henri, II, 547 (2)
TRI-WEEKLY NEWS PAPERS, III, 809f.
Triall of Treasure, A new Enterlude called the
  (16 cent.), I, 517
Triamour, Sir (M.E.), I, **159**
*Triana, Or a Threefold Romanza of Mariana
  Paduana Sabina* (17 cent.), I, 732
Tribune, The (1729), II, 663
*Tribune. A Publication consisting chiefly of the
  Lectures of J. Thelwall, The* (1795), II, 682
Tribute to Liberty, A (18 cent.), II, 249, 256
Tricks of State; or more Westminster Projects
  (1648), I, 758
Tricoupi, Spiridion, III, 206
Trident, The [Cambridge] (1889), III, 835
Trifle, or Gilded Toy, The (18 cent.), II, 561
Trifler, The (1786), II, 666
Trifler, The (1788), II, 666
Trifler, The (1795), II, 666
Trimen, Henry (1843-1896), III, 962
Trimmer, Sarah (1741-1810), II, III, 125-6,
  554, 558, 564, 681; III, III, 114, 117, 136
TRINITY COLLEGE (Cambridge), I, 370
TRINITY COLLEGE (Dublin), I, 362 (library)
Trinity College Homilies (M.E.), I, 40, **170**
Triphook, R. (*fl.* 1814), I, 317
Trissino, Giovanni Giorgio, I, 341
Tristram, Henry Baker (1822-1906), III, 992
Tristram, Thomas Hutchinson (*fl.* 1881), III,
  988
Tristram, William Outram (*fl.* 1888), III, 765
TRISTRAM LEGEND, I, 132
Tristrem, Sir (M.E.), I, **133**f.
Triumph of Wit, The (17 cent.), II, 181, 186,
  188, 190, 197, 205, 220
Triumphs of Bacchus, The (18 cent.), II, 200
Triumphs Of Female Wit (17 cent.), II, 179
Triumphes of Oriana, The (17 cent.), I, 484
'Triviator' (1877), III, 760
Trivet, Nicolas (d. 1328), I, **306**
Trogus Pompeius, I, 808
Trojan Tales, related by Ulysses [etc.] (18 cent.),
  II, 536
Trokelowe, John de (*fl.* 1330), I, 115
Trollope, Anthony (1815-1882), III, 94, **457**f.
Trollope, Frances, née Milton (1780-1863),
  III, **419**
Trollope, Thomas Adolphus (1810-1892), III,
  510
Trollope, William (1798-1863), III, 634

Trotter, Alys Fane (*fl.* 1900), III, 1091

Trotter, Catharine, later Cockburn (1679–1749), II, **444f.**

Trotter, John Bernard (1775–1818), III, 638

Trotter, L. J. (*fl.* 1866), III, 1077

Trotti de la Chétardie, Joachim, II, 122

Troublesome Raigne of John King of England, The (16 cent.), I, 537

Troughton, Thomas (*fl.* 1751), II, 749

Troup, George (1811–1879), III, 788, 807

TROY, ROMANCES OF, I, 144f.

Trublet, Nicolas Charles Joseph, II, 29

Trubner, Nicholas (1817–1884), III, 100

True and Impartial Account of Accidents, Casualties and other Transactions, A (1688), II, 704

True and Impartial Collection of Pieces [on] *The Westminster Election, A* (18 cent.), II, 213

True and Perfect Diurnall of all the Chiefe Passages in Lancashire, A (1642), I, 753

True and Perfect Diurnall of the passages in Parliament, A (1642), I, 754

True and Perfect Dutch Diurnall, The (1653), I, 762

True and Perfect Dutch Diurnall, The (1654), I, 762

True and Perfect Informer, The (1654), I, 762

True and Perfect Journall of the Warres in England, A (1644), I, 756

True Anti-Pamela, The (18 cent.), II, 543

True British Courant; Or, Preston Journal, The (1745), II, 728

True Briton, The (1723), II, 662

True Briton, The (1751), II, 664, 677

True Briton, The (1793), III, 798

True Briton, The (1820), III, 800

True Briton, The [Boston] (1819), III, 816

True Character of an Untrue Bishop, The (17 cent.), I, 724

True Character of Mercurius Aulicus, The (17 cent.), I, 724

True Character of Mercurius Urbanicus and Rusticus, The (1667), II, 716

True Chronicle Historie of Thomas Lord Cromwell, The (17 cent.), I, 580

True Chronicle History of King Leir, The (17 cent.), I, 539, 571

True Diurnal Occurrances, or the Heads of the Proceedings of Both Houses of Parliament, The (1642), I, 752

True Diurnal of the Passages in Parliament, A (1642), I, 753

True Diurnall, A Continuation of the (1642), I, 749

True Diurnall Occurrences; or, Proceedings in the Parliament this last weeke, A (1642), I, 752

True Diurnall of The Last Weekes Passages In Parliament, A (1642), I, 752

True Diurnall of the Last Weeks Passage in both Houses of Parliament, A (1642), I, 752

True Diurnall of the Last Weeks Passages in Parliament, A (1642), I, 752

True Diurnall of the Passages in Parliament, A (1642), I, 752

True Diurnall, or the Passages in Parliament, A (1642), I, 752

True Domestick Intelligence, The (1679), II, 702

True History of a Little Old Woman who found a Silver Penny, A (19 cent.), III, 574

True Informer, The (1651), I, 761

True Informer, The (1654), I, 762

True Informer containing a collection of the most speciall and observable passages, The (1643), I, 755

True Informer containing a perfect collection of the Proceedings in Parliament, The (1645), I, 756

True Informer or Monthly Mercury being the certain intelligence of Mercurius Militaris, The (1648), I, 759

True Intelligence from the Head Quarters (1650), I, 761

True Inventory of the Goods and Chattels of Superstition, A (17 cent.), I, 719

True Loyalists, The (18 cent.), II, 234

True News; Or, Mercurius Anglicus (1679), II, 702

True Patriot, and the History of Our Own Times, The (1745), II, 663, 715

True Post Boy, The (1710), II, 707

True Protestant (Domestick) Intelligence, The (1680), II, 702

True Protestant Mercury, The (1680), II, 703

True Protestant Mercury, The (1689), II, 705

True Protestant Mercury; containing three general heads, The (1690), II, 705

True Protestant Mercury; Or, Occurrences, Foreign and Domestick, The (1681), II, 704

True Relation of Certaine Speciall and Remarkable Passages, A (1642), I, 753

True Sun, The (1832), III, 801

True Tablet, The (1842), III, 819

True Tragedie of Richard Duke of York, The (16 cent.), I, 552f.

True Tragedie of Richard the Third, The (16 cent.), I, 538

True Tragi-Comedie formarly acted at Court, The (17 cent.), I, 653

Trumph, E. (*fl.* 1877), III, 1072

Truro, C. C. (*fl.* 1853), I, 901

Trusler, John (1735–1820), II, 122, 137, 143, 160, 556, 672, 682, 699 (2)

Trussell, John (*fl.* 1636–1642), I, 839

Truth (M.E.), I, 227

Truth (1877), III, 794, 814

Tryall of Chevalry, The History of the, I, 653

Tryon, Thomas (1634–1703), II, 816, **859**

Trysorfa Gwybodaeth (1770), II, 685

Trysorfa Ysprydol (1799), II, 685
Tryvytlam (or Trevytham), Richard (*fl.* 1400), I, **305**
Tschinck, Cajetan, II, 63
T--t--m and V--d-t (18 cent.), II, 213 (2)
Tubbe, Henry (1618-1655), I, 478
Tubières de Grimoard de Pestels de Levis, Anne Claude, Comte de Caylus, II, 802
Tubières de Grimoard de Pestels de Levis, Marthe Marguerite Hippolyte de, Marquise de Caylus, II, 802
Tucker, Abraham (1705-1774), I, 16; II, **957**
Tucker, Charlotte Maria (1825-1893) ('A.L.O.E.'), III, **568**
Tucker, Edward (*fl.* 1858), III, 101
Tucker, H. (*fl.* 1909), III, 1089
Tucker, Henry St George (1771-1851), III, 907, 1075
Tucker, Josiah (1712-1799), II, 146, 634, 959
Tucker, Thomas (*fl.* 1656), I, 776
Tuckett, Elizabeth (*fl.* 1870), III, 573
Tuckett, H. (*fl.* 1840), III, 1075
Tuckett, John Debell (*fl.* 1846), III, 971
Tuckey, Humphrey (*fl.* 1642), II, 752
Tuckwell, W. (*fl.* 1865), III, 114
Tudor, Owen Davies (*fl.* 1854), III, 988
TUDOR DRAMA, I, 487f. (histories, etc.), 513f. (moralities), 517f. (early comedies), 522f. (early tragedies), 524f. (later major dramatists), 534f. (minor drama, 1580-1603)
TUDOR POETRY, I, 408f. (major poets), 427f. (sonneteers), 434f. (minor verse)
Tuer, Andrew White (1838-1900), II, 555; III, 73, 87
Tuesdaies Journall, A (1649), I, 760
Tuke, Sir Brian (d. 1545), I, 211
Tuke, Sir Samuel (*c.* 1620-1674), II, **429**
Tuke, Thomas (d. 1657), I, 725
'Tulip, Timothy' (1732), II, 202
Tulloch, John (1823-1886), I, 322; III, 826, **876**
Tunbridge-Miscellany, The (18 cent.), II, 190, 191 (2), 195-6, 201, 204, 208
Tuner, The (1754), II, 664
Tunstall (or Tonstall), Cuthbert (1474-1559), I, 378, 683, 880
Tunstall, William (*fl.* 1716), II, 192
Tuomy, Martin (*fl.* 1790), II, 760
Tupper, J. L. (*fl.* 1869), III, 112
Tupper, Martin Farquhar (1810-1889), III, **310**
Turbervile, George (1540?-1598), I, 403, **438** f.
Turchill Compotista (*fl.* 1115), I, **284**
Turgeniev, Ivan, III, 44
Turgot, Anne Robert Jacques, Baron de L'Aulne, II, 802
Turke and Gowin (M.E.), I, **139**
Turle, Henry Frederic (1835-1883), III, 818
Turlerus, Hieronymus, I, 778
Turnament of Totenham, The (15 cent.), I, 265
Turnbull, George (1562?-1633), I, 906

Turnbull, George (*fl.* 1740-2), II, 110, 771, 778
Turnbull, William Barclay David Donald (1811-1863), I, 149-50, 177, 421, 445, 457, 514, 901
Turner, B. B. (*fl.* 1897), III, 973
Turner, B. N. (*fl.* 1818), II, 901
Turner, Catherine Ann, later Dorset (1750?-1817?), III, 566
Turner, Charles (1774-1857), engraver, III, 92
Turner, Charles, earlier Tennyson (1808-1879), poet, III, **308**
Turner, Daniel (1710-1798), II, 627
Turner, Dawson (1775-1858), I, 347; II, 908
Turner, Edward (1796-1837), III, 947
Turner, Elizabeth (d. 1846), III, 566
Turner, Ethel, later Curlewis (b. 1872), III, 570
Turner, G. W. (*fl.* 1860), III, 811
Turner, Gyles (*fl.* 1904), III, 1098
Turner, H. G. (*fl.* 1898), III, 1093
Turner, Sir James (1615-1686), I, 387
Turner, Joseph Mallord William (1775-1851), III, 378
Turner, Margaret (*fl.* 1790), II, 971
Turner, Philip (*fl.* 1778), II, 757
Turner, Richard (1753-1788), III, 136
Turner, Robert (*fl.* 1640-64), I, 809, 887
Turner, Samuel (1749?-1802), Asiatic traveller, II, 751
Turner, Sharon (1768-1847), III, **881**
Turner, Sydney (1814-1879), III, 881
Turner, T. (*fl.* 1735), of York, II, 685
Turner, Thomas (*fl.* 1659), I, 718
Turner, Thomas (*fl.* 1754-65), of East Hoathly, II, 137
Turner, Sir Tomkyns Hilgrove (1766?-1843), I, 120
Turner, William (d. 1568), I, 396, 437, 892 (2)
Turnough, John (*fl.* 1788), II, 241
Turnour, George (1799-1843), III, 1071
Turquet, Théodore de Mayerne, II, 791
Turton, John (*fl.* 1836), III, 769
Turton, Thomas (1780-1864), III, 122
Tusser, Thomas (1524?-1580), I, 391, **439**, 846
Tutchin, John (1661?-1707), II, **287**, 498, 659, 697
Tuting, William (*fl.* 1769), II, 718, 817
Tuvil, Daniel (*fl.* 1608), I, 725
Twamley, Josiah (*fl.* 1784), II, 148
Twamley, Louisa Anne, later Meredith (*fl.* 1837-91), III, 679, **1097**
'Twas Wrong to Marry him; or, The History of Lady Dursley (18 cent.), II, 547
Tweddell, John (1769-1799), II, **383**
Tweddell, R. (*fl.* 1815), II, 383
Tweedie, Mrs Alec (*fl.* 1912), III, 788
Tweedsmuir, John Buchan, Baron (1875-1940), III, 1092
Twelfth Cake, The (18 cent.), II, 563
Twells, Leonard (d. 1742), II, 850, 939
Twelve Arietts or Ballads (18 cent.), II, 205

Twelve New Songs (17 cent.), II, 184
Twelve New Songs (18 cent.), II, 199
Twenty New Songs Compos'd by Mr. James Graves (18 cent.), II, 196
Twenty New Songs Of Humour Compos'd By Wm. Turner (18 cent.), II, 194
[Twenty] *XX Songes* (16 cent.), I, 482
Twining, Thomas (1735–1804), II, 20, 937
Twiss, Horace (1787–1849), III, 149
Twiss, Richard (1747–1821), II, 159, 746
Twiss, Sir Travers (1809–1897), III, 974, 976, 982
Twisse, William (1578?–1646), I, 857–8
Twistleton, Thomas James (*fl.* 1789–1816), II, 666
'Twitcher, Jemmy' (1770), II, 227, 231, 253
Two Candidates, The (18 cent.), II, 213
Two Essays of Love and Marriage (17 cent.), I, 726
Two Merry Milke-Maids, The (17 cent.), I, 653
Two Noble Kinsmen, The (17 cent.), I, **578**f.
Two Noble Ladies, The (17 cent.), I, 653
Two Wise Men (17 cent.), I, 653
Twopence Worth of Hog's Bristles (18 cent.), II, 250
Twycross, J. (*fl.* 1853), III, 300
Twyne, Brian (or Bryan) (1579?–1644), I, 124, 369
Twyne, Thomas (1543–1613), I, 512, 774, 801, 808, 885
Twysden (or Twisden), Sir Roger (1597–1672), I, 843
Tyers, Thomas (1726–1787), II, 304, 606, 624
Tyler, Margaret (*fl.* 1578), I, 817
Tylor, Sir Edward Burnett (1832–1917), III, **968**
Tymme, Thomas (d. 1620), I, 778, 886
Tynan, Katharine, later Hinkson (1861–1931), III, **1057**
Tyndale (or Tindale), William (d. 1536), I, 46, 665, **668**, 675 (2)
Tyndall, John (1820–1893), III, **939**, 963, 992
Tyneside Echo, The (1880), III, 805
TYPES, TYPOGRAPHICAL ORNAMENTS, ETC., I, 348 (1500–1660); II, 82 (1660–1800); III, 74f. (19 cent.)
Typhon: or, The Gyants War with the Gods (17 cent.), II, 288
Typographic Advertiser (1862), III, 88
Typographical Circular, The (1854), III, 88
Typographical Circular, The (1877), III, 88
Typographical Gazette, The (1846), III, 88
Typographical Protection Circular, The (1849), III, 88
Tyranicall-Government Anatomized (17 cent.), I, 654
'Tyro' (1816), III, 195
Tyro, T. (*fl.* 1598), I, 480
'Tyro, Theresa' (1808), III, 566

Tyrrell, George (1861–1909), III, **851**
Tyrrell, James (1642–1718), I, 879
Tyrrell, James Williams (*fl.* 1893), III, 1088
Tyrrell, Robert Yelverton (1844–1914), III, 124, **1010**
Tyrtaeus, II, 763
Tyrwhitt, Thomas (1730–1786), II, **899**f., 929, 937
Tyssot de Patot, Simon, II, 802
Tytler, Alexander Fraser, Lord Woodhouselee (1747–1813), II, 20, 486, 812, 889, 916f., 955, 969; III, 1075
Tytler, Ann Fraser (*fl.* 1839), III, 572
Tytler, Christina Catherine Fraser, later Liddell (b. 1848), III, **360**f.
Tytler, Henry William (1752–1808), II, 760, 798
Tytler, James (1747?–1805), II, 624, 665–6, 673, 686 (3), 697
Tytler, Margaret Fraser (*fl.* 1838–55), III, 572
Tytler, Patrick Fraser (1791–1849), III, **886**
'Tytler, Sarah', i.e. Henrietta Keddie (*fl.* 1868), III, 573
Tytler, William (1711–1792), II, 39, 887, 913

U., T. (*fl.* 1642), I, 753
Ubaldini, Petruccio, I, 768
Udall, John (1560?–1592), I, 683, 691
Udall, Nicholas (1505–1556), I, **519**, 660, 808, 890
Udden, J. A. (*fl.* 1900), III, 1085
Uffenbach, Zacharias Conrad von, II, 113, 140, 153 (2)
Ulrici, Hermann, I, 594
Ulster Echo, The [Belfast] (1874), III, 808
Ulster Examiner, The (1868), III, 808
Ulster Examiner and Northern Star, The (1873), III, 808
Ulster Miscellany, The (1753), II, 688
Umfreville, Edward (*fl.* 1784), II, 756
Umpire, The [Manchester] (1884), III, 813
Underdowne, Thomas (*fl.* 1566–87), I, 802, 805
Underhill, G. F. (*fl.* 1897), III, 761
Underhill, John (d. 1672), I, 795
Underhill, Thomas (*fl.* 1644), I, 756
Underwood, E. (*fl.* 1885), III, 1074
Underwood, J. (*fl.* 1858), III, 74
Underwood, James (*fl.* 1787), II, 823
Unfortunate Dutchess, The (18 cent.), II, 540
Unfortunate Marriage of the Marchioness de Fresne, The (18 cent.), II, 538
Unfortunate Union, The (18 cent.), II, 548
Unhappy Lovers [etc.], *The* (18 cent.), II, 203
Union, The (18 cent.), II, 216, 219–20, 224, 252
Union Chronicle, The [Manchester, Leamington, and Coventry] (1873), III, 818
Union Jack, The (1880), III, 821
Union Jack Library of High-Class Fiction, The (1894), III, 579

Union Journal; or, Halifax Advertiser, The (1759), II, 724
Union Magazine, The (1900), II, 687
Union Song Book, The (1759), II, 219
Union Song-Book, The (1781), II, 235
Union Star, The (Dublin, 1798), II, 736
UNITARIAN WRITERS, II, 862f.
United Kingdom, The (1830), III, 812
United Methodist Free Churches' Magazine, The (1858), III, 827
United Presbyterian Magazine, The (1847), II, 687
United Secession and Relief Magazine, The (1847), II, 686f.
United Secession Magazine, The (1833), II, 686
United Service Gazette, The (1833), III, 821
United Service Journal and Naval and Military Magazine, The (1829), III, 826
United Service Magazine, The (1891), III, 826
United Service Magazine and Naval and Military Journal, The (1842), III, 826
Universal Advertiser, The (1752), II, 735
Universal Catalogue for the year 1772, The, II, 717
Universal Chronicle And Westminster Journal, The (1760), II, 715
Universal Chronicle; Or, Weekly Gazette, The (1758), II, 715
Universal Corn Reporter, The (1832), III, 819
Universal Harmony (18 cent.), II, 210–2
Universal Historical Bibliotheque, The (1687), II, 674
Universal Intelligence, The (1688), II, 704
Universal Intelligence, The (1689), II, 705
Universal Intelligence; comprizing the most remarkable passages weekly published by others, The (1681), II, 704
Universal Jester, The (18 cent.), II, 216
Universal Journal, The (1723), II, 713
Universal Journal, The (1746), II, 735
Universal Journalist, The (Dublin, 1768), II, 735
Universal Librarian, The (1751), II, 677
Universal London Price-Current, The (1784), II, 718
Universal Magazine, The (1804), III, 822
Universal Magazine and Review; Or, Repository of Literature, The (1789), II, 688
Universal Magazine of Knowledge, The (1747), II, 677
Universal Magazine of Knowledge and Pleasure, The (1747), III, 822
Universal Melody, The (18 cent.), II, 224
Universal Mercury, The (1726), II, 676
Universal Museum and Complete Magazine of Knowledge and Pleasure, The (1764), II, 678
Universal Museum; Or, Gentleman's and Lady's Polite Magazine of History, The (1762), II, 678

Universal Museum; Or, The Entertaining Repository for Gentlemen and Ladies, The (1765), II, 684
Universal Musician, The (18 cent.), II, 207 (3), 214
Universal Politician, The (1796), II, 683
Universal Review, The (1760), II, 678
Universal Review, The (1888), III, 831
Universal Scots Songster, The (18 cent.), II, 235
Universal Shuttlecock, The (18 cent.), II, 563
Universal Songster, The (18 cent.), II, 249
Universal Songster Or Harmony and Innocence, The (18 cent.), II, 236, 241, 247, 251
Universal Spectator, The (1728), II, 663
Universal Spectator And Weekly Journal, The (1728), II, 713
Universal Spy, The (1739), II, 677
Universal Spy; or, Aesop the Fabulist, The (1732), II, 714
Universal Spy; Or, London Weekly Magazine, The (1739), II, 714
Universal Spy; Or, The Royal Oak Journal Reviv'd, The (1732), II, 714
Universal Visiter, The (1758), II, 674
Universal Visiter And Monthly Memorialist, The (1756), II, 677
Universal Weekly Journal, The (1739), II, 714
Universalists' Miscellany, The (1797), II, 683
Universe, The (1846), III, 794, 819
UNIVERSITIES
    Middle English Period, I, 124f.
    Renaissance to Restoration, I, 367f.
    Restoration to Romantic Revival, II, 115f., 152f.
    Nineteenth Century, III, 121f., 834f. (magazines)
University College Gazette, The (1895), III, 836
University College, London, Gazette, The (1886), III, 836
University Magazine, The [Dublin] (1878), III, 827
University Magazine and Free Review, The (1897), III, 831
University Miscellany, The (18 cent.), II, 191 (2)
UNIVERSITY PLAYS, I, 654f. (16, 17 cents.)
Unnatural Mother, The (18 cent.), II, 539f.
UNSTAMPED JOURNALS, III, 815f.
Unton, Sir Henry (1557?–1596), I, 384
Unton Inventories, The (16, 17 cents.), I, 384
UNWIN BROTHERS, III, 87
Unzer, J. C., II, 807
Up-to-date Boys (c. 1900), III, 820
Upham, Edward (1776–1834), III, 1081
Upright Protestant, The (17 cent.), I, 723
Upton, Bertha (fl. 1895), III, 570
Upton, James (1670–1749), II, 127, 909
Upton, John (1707–1760), II, **897**
Upton, W. (fl. 1820), III, 572
Urbanitatis (15 cent.), I, 264

Urfé, Honoré d', I, 334, 819
Uri, John (1726–1796), II, 104
Uring, Nathaniel (*fl.* 1726), II, 742
Urquhart, David (1805–1877), III, 788, 790, 829, 978, 1076
Urquhart, David Henry (*fl.* 1787), II, 759
Urquhart, I. (*fl.* 1890), III, 831
Urquhart, Sir Thomas (1611–1660), I, **836**
Urquhart, W. P. (*fl.* 1850–67), III, 979, 982
Urry, John (1666–1715), II, 909
Urstitius, Christianus, I, 881
Ursula, The Life of St (15 cent.), I, 266
Usages of Winchester (M.E.), I, 41
Use and Abuse of Free-Masonry, The (18 cent.), II, 237
Useful Intelligencer. For Promoting of Trade and Commerce, The (1711), II, 717
Useful Transactions in Philosophy (1709), II, 675
Usher, Charles (*fl.* 1699), II, 118
Usher, James (*fl.* 1732), translator, II, 29
Usher, James (1720–1772), schoolmaster, II, 18
Usher, W. (*fl.* 1854), III, 1015
Usk, Adam of (*fl.* 1400), I, 116
Usk, Thomas (d. 1388), I, 187
Ussher, George Neville (*fl.* 1786), II, 932
Ussher (or Usher), James (1581–1656), I, 363, 385, 686, **702**, 780, 857–8, 863; III, 1047
Usurie Araigned and Condemned (17 cent.), I, 719
USURY (writings on), I, 845 (16, 17 cents.)
Utterson, R. (*fl.* 1817–20), I, 129, 146
Utterson, Edward Vernon (1776?–1856), I, 433, 476, 707 (6), 735

V., N. (*fl.* 1690), II, 786
V., R. (*fl.* 1672), II, 176
V., T. (*fl.* 1672), II, 808
Vairasse d'Allais, Denis, II, 533
Valdés, Francisco de, I, 343, 819
Valdés, Juan de, I, 452
Valdin, Monsieur — (*fl.* 1729), II, 823
VALE PRESS, III, 86
Valens, W. (*fl.* 1615), I, 731
Valentia, George Annesley, Viscount (*fl.* 1809), III, 1079
Valentine, Basil, I, 887
Valette, Michel Rousseau de la, II, 798
Valiant Scot, The (17 cent.), I, 654
Valiant Welshman, The (17 cent.), I, 654
Vallancey, Charles (1721–1812), III, **1047**f.
Vallans, William (*fl.* 1578–90), I, 439
Valle, Pietro della, II, 814
Vallenger, Stephen (d. 1581), I, 363
Valpy, Abraham John (1787–1854), II, 295
Van Broeck, Adrian (*fl.* 1709), II, 536
Vanbrugh, Sir John (1664–1726), II, 44, 62, **414**, 794
Vancouver, George (1758–1798), II, 742
Vandenhoff, John M. (1790–1861), III, 151

Van de Pass, Crispin, I, 819
Vanderlint, Jacob (d. 1740), II, 959
Vanderstop, Cornelius (*fl.* 1777), II, 971
Vanderstraeten, F. (*fl.* 1816), III, 970
Van Dyk, H. S. (*fl.* 1824), III, 228
Vaniere, Jacques, II, 360
Vanity Fair (1868), III, 814
Vanity of Human Wishes, Or, The History of Sir James Scudamore, The (18 cent.), II, 547
Van Mildert, William (1765–1836), II, 854
Vanneschi, Francesco, II, 66
Van Oven, J. (*fl.* 1802), III, 975
van Reenen, J. (*fl.* 1792), III, 1091
Van Shaack, Peter, II, 141
'Varamund, Ernest' (François Hotman), I, 742
Varchi, Benedetto, I, 434
Varenius, Bernardus, II, 802
VARIETY ENTERTAINMENTS (16, 17 cents.), I, 506
Varillas, Antoine, II, 802
Varnhagen von Ense, Karl August, III, 35
Vasari, Giorgio, II, 65, 814
Vattel, Emerich de, II, 802
Vauban, Sébastien Le Prestre de, II, 788
Vaughan, Charles John (1816–1897), III, 132
Vaughan, E. T. (*fl.* 1869), III, 690
Vaughan, Henry (1622–1695), I, **461**f., 679, 814
Vaughan, Henry Halford (1811–1885), III, 128
Vaughan, Robert (*fl.* 1542), I, 716
Vaughan, Robert (1795–1868), congregational divine, III, 833, **897**
Vaughan, Robert Alfred (1823–1857), poet and critic, III, **726**
Vaughan, Rowland (*fl.* 1610), I, 846
Vaughan, Thomas (1622–1666), I, 886
Vaughan, Thomas (*fl.* 1761–1820), II, **483**
Vaughan, Walter (*fl.* 1714), II, 750
Vaughan, William (1577–1641), I, 795, 811, 845, 865
Vaumorière, Pierre d'Ortigue, Sieur de, II, 37, 49, 122, 532, 802
Vautor, Thomas (b. *c* 1590?), I, 486
Vaux, Frances Bowyer (*fl.* 1815), III, 571
Vaux, James Hardy (*fl.* before 1819), II, 155
Vaux, Thomas, Baron (1510–1556), I, 439
Vaux, William Sandys Wright (1818–1885), I, 792
Vauxhall Songs For the Year 1795 (18 cent.), II, 251
Vecchj, C. A., III, 428
Vedder, David (1790–1854), III, 374
Veel, Mary Colborne (*fl.* 1894), III, 1095
Veer, Gerrit de, I, 769
Vega, Lope de, I, 343, 734; II, 68
Vegetius Renatus, Flavius, I, 808
Vegius, Maphaeus, I, 808
Veil, Sir Thomas de (*fl.* 1747), II, 146
Veitch, John (1829–1894), III, 868 (3), **876**

Veitch, William (1794–1885), III, 1003
Veley, Margaret (1843–1887), III, 361
Venables, George Stovin (1810–1888), III, 788
Venables, Robert (1612?–1687), I, 793; II, 818
Venkata Ramasvāmi, Kāvali (*fl.* 1829), III, 1075
Venn, Henry (1725–1797), evangelical divine, II, 853
Venn, Henry (1796–1873), divine, II, 853
Venn, John (1759–1813), II, 853
Venn, Thomas (*fl.* 1672), II, 810
Venner, Tobias (1577–1660), I, 718
Ventum, Harriet (*fl.* 1806), III, 571
Venture, The (18 cent.), II, 202
Venus Looking-Glass (18 cent.), II, 185
Venus' Mass (15 cent.), I, 265
'Verax' (1785), II, 654
'Verax' (1847), III, 694
'Verax, Philadelphus' (17 cent.), I, 719
Verbruggen, John (*fl.* 1688–1707?), II, 426
Vercelli Book, The (O.E.), I, 63
    Gospels, I, 26, 32
    Homilies, I, 92
Vere, Edward de, Earl of Oxford (1550–1604), I, 439, 546
Vere, Sir Francis (1560–1609), I, 827
Verelst, Harry (d. 1785), III, 1075
Vergil, Polydore (1470?–1555?), I, 116, 375, 823
Verhaeren, Émile, III, 359
Verie excellent... Treatise intitulit Philotus, Ane (17 cent.), I, 517, 900
Vérité Cachée, La, I, 515
Verity, Arthur Wilson (1863–1937), III, 1042f.
Vermigli, Pietro Martire (1500–1562), I, 519
Verne, Jules, III, 22, 576
Vernet, Jean Jacob, II, 802
Verney, Francis (1584–1615), I, 660
Verney, W. R. (*fl.* 1896), III, 761
Verney Family, Letters and Papers of (17 cent.), I, 382
Vernon, James (1646–1727), II, 162
Vernon, Joseph (1738?–1782), II, 235
Vernon Miracles of Mary (M.E.), I, 162f.
Vernon's Glory (18 cent.), II, 208 (3)
Véron, Jean (d. 1563), I, 820
Veronica, St (O.E.), I, 93
Verrall, Arthur Woollgar (1851–1912), III, 1011
Verri, Alessandro, II, 814
Versatile Ingenium (17 cent.), II, 178
VERSE
    Alliterative. See under PROSODY, I, 13f.
    Blank. See under PROSODY, I, 15f.
    Rhyming. See under PROSODY, I, 13f.
    See also POETRY
Verses by the University of Oxford. On the Death of Sir Bevill Grenvill (17 cent.), II, 179

Verses for Little Children (19 cent.), III, 575
Verses on the Coronation Of King George II and Queen Caroline. Spoken by the Scholars of Westminster School (18 cent.), II, 220
Verses on the Death of Queen Caroline (18 cent.), II, 207
Verses on the Peace (18 cent.), II, 191
VERSIFICATION. See under PROSODY, I, 13f.
Verstegan, Richard (*fl.* 1565–1620), I, 678
Vertewis of the Mess, The (M.E.), I, 260
Vertue, George (1684–1756), II, 838
Vertue Rewarded, or the Irish Princess (17 cent.), II, 531
Very Full and Particular Relation, A (1649), I, 760
Veryard, Ellis (*fl.* 1701), II, 742
Vesalius, Andreas, I, 890
Veseler, George (*fl.* 1620), I, 743
Veslingius, Joannes, I, 890
Vial de Saint Bel, Charles, II, 817
Vicars, John (1580?–1652), I, 400, 711, 809, 859, 884
Vicary, Thomas (1490?–1561), I, 891
Vices and Virtues (M.E.), I, 181
Vichard de Saint Réal, César, II, 802
Vickers, R. (*fl.* 1849), III, 124
Victor, Benjamin (d. 1778), II, 403, 545
Victoria, Queen (1819–1901), III, 144, 154
Victoria Magazine, The (1863), III, 829
VICTORIA PRESS, III, 87
Vida, Marcus Hieronymus, II, 33, 814
Vidler, William (1758–1816), II, 683
Vidocq, François Eugène, III, 23
'Vieille Moustache' (*fl.* 1874), III, 765
Viel de Boisjolin, Jacques François Marie, II, 255
Vieth, G. A. Anthony, III, 136
View of the Beau Monde, A (18 cent.), II, 202, 539
View of the Town, A (18 cent.), II, 202 (2)
Vigilance Gazette, The (1888), III, 781
Vignan, Le Sieur du, II, 802
Vigne, Godfrey Thomas (1801–1863), III, 1080
Vigny, Alfred de, III, 23
Vigor, Mrs —, née Rondeau (*fl.* 1775), II, 746
Vile, Thomas (*fl.* 1682), II, 704
Viles, E. (*fl.* 1869), I, 717
Villars, Nicolas de Montfaucon de, II, 791
Villaut, Nicolas, Sieur de Bellefond, II, 802
Villegagnon, Nicolas Durand de, I, 767
Villette, John (*fl.* 1774–7), II, 155, 360
Villiers, Frederick (1852–1922), III, 788
Villiers, George, Duke of Buckingham (1628–1687), II, 419
Villiers, J. de, II, 802
Villiers, John Charles, Earl of Clarendon (*fl.* 1789), II, 747
Villiers, Pierre de, II, 790, 803
Villon, François, III, 319, 353
Vincent of Beauvais, I, 262

Vincent, John (fl. 1808), III, 762
Vincent, Philip (fl. 1638), I, 795
Vincent, Sir R. (fl. 1794), II, 666
Vincent, Sam (fl. 1674), II, 122
Vincent, Thomas (d. 1633), I, 660
Vincent, William (1739–1815), II, 110, 116, 124, 759, 937 f.; III, 129
Vinculum Societatis (17 cent.), II, 180–2
'Vinegar, Hercules' (1742), II, 303
Vines, Richard (1600?–1656), I, 702
Vines, Sydney Howard (fl. 1886), III, 962
Vint, Mary (fl. 1758–95), II, 715–6
Vinycomb, J. (fl. 1869), III, 74
Violet, Thomas (fl. 1634–62), I, 847
Viret, Pierre, I, 819
Virgil, I, 262, 808 f.; II, 768; III, 243, 247, 284, 299, 314, 355, 474
Virgil, Polydore, I, 773
Virgin Muse, The (18 cent.), II, 194, 197, 202
Virgins Complaint for the losse of their Sweet-Hearts, The [etc.] (17 cent.), I, 720
Vision concerning Piers Plowman (M.E.), I, 197 f.
Vision of St Paul (M.E.), I, 176 f.
Vision of Tundale (M.E.), I, 177
Visions of Sir Heister Ryley, The (1710), II, 661
Visiter, The (1723), II, 662
Vita Edwardi II (M.E.), I, 115
Vives, Johannes Ludovicus (1492–1540), I, 328, 375, 395, 819
Vizetelly, Henry (1820–1894), III, 506, 788, 815 (2)
VOCABULARY, WORD-FORMATION, ETC., I, 30 f.
Vocal Companion, The (1757), II, 218
Vocal Companion, The (1759), II, 219
Vocal Enchanter, The (18 cent.), II, 246
Vocal Enchantress, The (18 cent.), II, 237
Vocal Magazine, The (1778), II, 680
Vocal Magazine. Containing a selection of English, Scots, and Irish Songs, The (18 cent.), II, 253–4, 255 (2)
Vocal Magazine; Or, British Songster, The (1784), II, 680
Vocal Magazine; or, British Songster's Miscellany, The (18 cent.), II, 233–5, 238
Vocal Magazine; Or, Compleat British Songster, The (1781), II, 680
Vocal Magazine; Or, Compleat Songster, The (18 cent.), II, 236
Vocal Medley, The (1749), II, 213, 217
Vocal Melody (18 cent.), II, 215
Vocal Miscellany, The (18 cent.), II, 204 (3), 207 (3)
Vocal Miscellany, a collection of above 400 songs, The (18 cent.), II, 238
Vocal Miscellany of Great Britain and Ireland, The (18 cent.), II, 253
Vocal Music Or The Songsters Companion (18 cent.), II, 228 (2), 229, 231, 233
Vocal Musical Mask, The (18 cent.), II, 210

Voigt, J. C. (fl. 1899), III, 1091
Voiture, Vincent, I, 819; II, 45–6, 803
Volkmann, Johann Jacob, II, 141, 157
Volney, Constantin François Chassebœuf de, II, 775; III, 23
'Volpi, Odoardo' (1836), III, 205
Voltaire, François Arouet de, I, 601; II, 33, 37, 43, 45, 49, 72, 485, 552 (2), 803 f.; III, 23, 236, 339, 723
Volunteer Evening Post, The (Dublin, 1786), II, 736
Volunteer Journal, or Weekly Advertiser, The (Cork, 1782), II, 737
Volunteer's Journal; Or, Irish Herald, The (1783), II, 736
Volusenus, Florentus, II, 310
Vondel, Joost van den, II, 70
von Hügel, Carl A. A., Baron (fl. 1845), III, 1080
Vota Oxoniensia Pro Serenissimis Guilhelmo et Maria (17 cent.), II, 181
Votes of both Houses, The (1660), II, 702
Votes of the House of Commons (1680), II, 703
Votes of the House of Commons at Oxford (1681), II, 703
Votes of the House of Commons (1690), II, 705, 720
Votes of the House of Commons in Ireland (1692), II, 705
Votes of the House of Commons in the Second Session Held at Westminster (1696), II, 706
Votivum Carolo (17 cent.), II, 173
Voules, Horace (fl. 1880), III, 801 (2)
Vox and the Wolf (M.E.), I, 161
Vox Populi Vox Dei (16 cent.), I, 719
Voyage to the New Island Fonseca, A (18 cent.), II, 535
VOYAGES (descriptions of). See BOOKS OF TRAVEL, I, 191 f. (M.E.), 763 f. (1500–1660); II, 139 f. and 157 f. (tours of British Isles, 1660–1800), 739 f. (rest of world, 1660–1800); III, 988 f. (19 cent.)
Vuillier, Gaston, III, 778
Vulpius, Christian August, II, 63
Vyllagon, Nicholas (fl. 1542), I, 742
Vyner, Robert Thomas (fl. 1841), III, 760

'W.' (1739), II, 132
W., B. (fl. 1647), I, 757
W., D. (fl. 1652), I, 761
W., E. (fl. 1615), I, 391
W., G. (fl. 1644), I, 448 (2)
W., H. (fl. 1658), II, 121
W., I. (fl. 1769), II, 127
W., J., Gent. (fl. 1637), I, 654
W., J. (fl. 1641), I, 752
W., J. (fl. 1642), I, 754
W., J. (fl. 1671), II, 816
W., J. (fl. 1682), II, 752
W., J. (fl. 1707), II, 760

'W., J.' (1727), II, 434
W., J. H. (*fl.* 1772), II, 562
W., M. (*fl.* 1662), I, 652
W., M. (*fl.* 1732), II, 753
W., R. (*fl.* 1642), I, 753
W., R. (*fl.* 1659), I, 810
W., R., Gent. (*fl.* 1688), II, 819
W., S. (*fl.* 1805), III, 574
W., T. (*fl.* 1575), I, 801
W., T. (*fl.* 1606), I, 739
W., T. (*fl.* 1639), I, 890
W., T. (*fl.* 1653), I, 762
W., T. (*fl.* 1654), I, 762
W., T. (*fl.* 1662), I, 653
W., T. (*fl.* 1671), II, 789
W., T. (*fl.* 1682), II, 178
W., T. (*fl.* 1698), II, 769
W., T. (*fl.* 1705), II, 556
W., T. (*fl.* 1745), II, 772
W., W. (*fl.* 1670?), II, 192, 194 (2)
Waagen, G. F., III, 712
Wace (*fl.* 1160–70), I, 133
Wace, Henry (1836–1924), III, 854
Wächter, Leonhard ('Veit Weber'), II, 63
Wadding, Luke (1588–1657), I, 282, 293, 302
Waddington, Samuel (1844–1923), III, 361
Wade, Henry (*fl.* 1861), III, 770
Wade, John (1788–1875), II, 631; III, 816, 974
Wade, Thomas (1805–1875), poet, III, 310f., 810, 828
Wade, Sir Thomas Francis (1818–1895), diplomatist, III, 1020
Wade's London Review (1845), III, 828
Wadham, Dorothy (*fl.* 1609–18), I, 386
Wadham, E. (*fl.* 1869), I, 17
WADHAM COLLEGE (Oxford), I, 369
Wadsworth, Arthur (*fl.* 1912), III, 1093
Wadsworth, Benjamin (*fl.* 1694), II, 752
Wadsworth, James (1604–1656?), I, 771, 780, 795
Waerferth, Bishop (d. 915), I, 28, 88
Wafer, Lionel (1660?–1705?), II, 753
Wagenaer, Lucas, I, 778
Wager, Lewis (*fl.* 1566), I, 512, 516
Wager, W. (*fl.* 1565?–9), I, 516
Wagstaffe, John (1633–1677), II, 761
Wagstaffe, Walter (*fl.* 1711), II, 606
Wagstaffe, William (1685–1725), II, 536, 580, 590 (3)
Wainewright, A. (*fl.* 1804), II, 938
Wainewright, Thomas Griffiths (1794–1852), III, 635
Wainwright, L. (*fl.* 1830), II, 956; III, 124
Waite, Arthur Edward (b. 1860), III, 361
Wake, William (1657–1737), II, 95, 779, 944
Wakefield, Benjamin (*fl.* 1749), II, 213
Wakefield, Daniel (1776–1846), II, 959; III, 979
Wakefield, Edward (1774–1854), II, 159
Wakefield, Edward Gibbon (1796–1862), III, 971, 1097

Wakefield, Gilbert (1756–1801), II, 113, 154, 295–6, 304, 333, 766, 938
Wakefield, Priscilla, née Bell (1751–1832), II, 132, 140, 559
Wakefield Evening Herald, The (1874), III, 804
Wakefield Express, The, III, 794
WAKEFIELD SCHOOL, I, 373
Waker, Nathaniel (*fl.* 1663), I, 379; II, 809
Waker, W. (*fl.* 1693), II, 994
Wakley, J. G. (*fl.* 1862?), III, 821
Wakley, Thomas (1795–1862), III, 788, 821
Wakley, Thomas Henry (1821–1907), III, 821
Walbancke, Matthew (*fl.* 1636), I, 395
Walbank, Marke (*fl.* 1642), I, 754 (2)
Walbeck, W. (*fl.* 1785), II, 776
Walbran, F. M. (*fl.* 1889), III, 772
Walcher of Malvern (d. 1135), I, 284f.
Walcot, D. (*fl.* 1769), II, 18
Walcot, James (*fl.* 1748), II, 754
Walcott, Mackenzie Edward Charles (1821–1880), III, 902
Waldegrave, James, Earl (1715–1763), II, 136, 165
Waldegrave, Powle (*fl.* 1649), I, 786
Waldegrave, Samuel (1817–1869), III, 853
Waldere (O.E.), I, 28, 69
Waldron, Francis Godolphin (1744–1818), II, 483f., 916
WALES
    Bibliographies, I, 7f.
    Printing in, I, 354f. (1500–1660); II, 88 (1660–1800)
    University of, III, 128
Wales, William (1734?–1798), II, 937
Walesby, F. P. (*fl.* 1826), II, 651
Walford, Edward (1823–1897), I, 449; III, 668
Walford, William (*fl.* before 1851), III, 920
Walkden, Peter (1684–1769), II, 136
Walker, Adam (1731?–1821), II, 747
Walker, B. (*fl.* 1770), II, 718
Walker, Charles Edward (*fl.* 1900), III, 763, 772
Walker, Charles Vincent (1812–1882), III, 75
Walker, Donald (*fl.* 1834), III, 776
Walker, Sir Edward (1612–1677), I, 400, 840
Walker, Ellis (*fl.* 1692), II, 760
Walker, Ferdinand (*fl.* 1600), I, 819
Walker, George (1581?–1651), I, 720
Walker, George (d. 1777), privateer, II, 742
Walker, George (1734?–1807), dissenter and mathematician, II, 21, 400
Walker, George (1772–1847), novelist, II, 551 (2); III, 419f.
Walker, George Richard (*fl.* 1865), III, 763
Walker, Gilbert (*fl.* 1580?), I, 713
Walker, Henry (*fl.* 1647–60), I, 379, 749, 755–7, 758 (2), 759, 760 (2), 761 (3); II, 701
Walker, J. (*fl.* 1688), translator of Pascal, II, 792
Walker, J. (*fl.* 1844), high churchman, III, 856

Walker, John (1674–1747), ecclesiastical historian, II, 924

Walker, John (1692?–1741), classical scholar, II, 938

Walker, John (1732–1807), lexicographer, I, 16, 44; II, 232, 931

Walker, John (1759–1830), scientist, III, 969

Walker, John (fl. 1792–1800), editor of 'The Copperplate Magazine', II, 681

Walker, John (1770–1831), antiquary, III, 128, 856

Walker, Johnny (fl. before 1857), pugilist, III, 776

Walker, Joseph Cooper (1762?–1810), II, 400; III, 1048

Walker, Josiah (fl. 1811), II, 975, 985

Walker, Lady Mary, née Hamilton (fl. 1776), II, 547

Walker, Obadiah (1616–1699), I, 855; II, 110, 122, 846, 868, 920

Walker, Patrick (d. 1745), II, 995

Walker, R. (fl. 1739), publisher, II, 714

Walker, R. (fl. 1848), Oxford University reformer, III, 128

Walker, R. Bailey (fl. 1871), journalist, III, 817

Walker, Richard (fl. 1839), editor of Richard Zouche, I, 766

Walker, Thomas (fl. 1715), writer on heraldry, II, 871

Walker, Thomas (1822–1898), III, 799

Walker, William (fl. 1601), translator from Dutch, I, 782

Walker, William (1623–1684), schoolmaster, II, 110, 128

Walker, William (fl. 1796), contributor to 'The Flapper', II, 666

Walker, William (fl. 1862), drawing master, III, 936

Walker, William Sidney (1795–1846), critic, III, 1028

Walker's Hibernian Magazine (1786), III, 823

Walker's Weekly Penny Journal (1735), II, 714

Walking Amusements (1775), II, 231

Walkingame, Francis (fl. 1751–85), II, 125

Walkington, Thomas (d. 1621), I, 725

Walkley, Arthur Bingham (1855–1926), III, 755

Walkley, Thomas (fl. 1620), I, 352, 815 (misprinted T. W. Calkley)

Wall, — (fl. 1748), II, 709

Wall, Arnold (fl. 1900), III, 1096

Wall, Richard (1694–1778), II, 816

Wallace, Alfred Russel (1823–1913), III, 954, 957, 978

Wallace, Eglantine, Lady, née Maxwell (d. 1803), II, 747

Wallace, George (fl. 1881), III, 987

Wallace, J. A. (fl. 1867), III, 99

Wallace, J. Bruce (fl. 1890), radical journalist, III, 818

Wallace, James (d. 1688), writer on Orkneys, II, 999

Wallace, James (fl. 1684–1724), physician, II, 998

Wallace, Robert (1697–1771), II, 663, 959, 1001

Wallace, Robert (1791–1850), unitarian divine, II, 862

Wallace, Robert (fl. 1863), writer on India, III, 1077

Wallace, Robert (1831–1899), divine and M.P., III, 807

Wallace, Robert Grenville (fl. 1824), historian of India, III, 1079

Wallace, Thomas (fl. 1759), writer on farriery, II, 927

Wallace, Thomas (fl. 1797), Irish critic, II, 25

Wallace, William (1768–1843), mathematician, III, 881

Wallace, William (1843–1897), philosopher, III, 876

Waller, Augustus (1816–1890), III, 963

Waller, Edmund (1606–1687), I, 455 f.

Waller, John Francis (1810–1894), III, 274, 827 (2)

Walleys, Thomas (d. 1340), dominican, I, 301

Walleys, Thomas (d. c. 1350), franciscan, I, 305

Wallich, George Charles (1815–1899), III, 957

Wallington, Nehemiah (1598–1658), I, 839

Wallis, J. E., III, 819

Wallis, John (1616–1703), I, 44, 702, 863, 877, 882–3; II, 605, 961–2

Wallis, Samuel (1728–1795), II, 742

Wallis, Thomas (fl. 1764), II, 817

Wallwork, James (fl. 1847), III, 770

Walpole, Horace, Baron (1678–1757), II, 837

Walpole, Horace, Earl of Orford (1717–1797), II, 50, 67, 333, 778, 836 f.

Walpole, Sir Robert (1676–1745), II, 503, 607

Walpole, Robert (1781–1856), III, 989

Walpole, Sir Spencer (1839–1907), III, 919

Walpoole, G. A. (fl. 1784), II, 140

Walrond, H. (fl. 1894), III, 775

Walsh, B. D. (fl. 1837), III, 124

Walsh, Edward (1756–1832), army surgeon, II, 748

Walsh, Edward (1805–1850), Irish poet, III, 1051

Walsh, John Edward (1816–1869), II, 159

Walsh, John Henry (1810–1888) ('Stonehenge'), III, 758, 766, 776, 815

Walsh, W. J. (fl. 1893), III, 974

Walsh, William (1663–1708), II, 21, 191 (2), 195, 287

Walsh's Dublin Post Boy (1727), II, 734

Walsh's Dublin Weekly Impartial News Letter (1728), II, 734

Walsingham, Edward (fl. 1643–54), I, 386, 841

Walsingham, Sir Francis (1530?–1590), I, 384 (2), 726

Walsingham, Robert (fl. 1312), I, 311

Walsingham, Thomas (d. 1422?), I, 115, 265
Walsingham, The Foundation of the Chapel of (15 cent.), I, 264
Walter of Evesham (*fl.* 1320), I, **311**
Walter of Henley (*fl.* 13 cent.), I, 120, 845
Walter of Wimborne, Master (*fl.* 12 cent.), I, **286**
Walter the Englishman (*fl.* 1177), I, **288**
Walter, Backhouse (*fl.* 1902), III, 1098
Walter, Henry (1785–1859), I, 668 (3)
Walter, H. (*fl.* 1848), I, 673
Walter, John, the elder (1739–1812), II, 239, 709
Walter, John, the younger (1776–1847), III, 798
Walter, John (*fl.* 1789), II, 711
Walter, John (1818–1894), III, 766
Walter, Richard (1716?–1785), II, 741
Walter, W. J. (*fl.* 1817), I, 422, 685
Walter, William (*fl.* 1520?), I, 716
Walters, John, the elder (1721–1797), II, 74
Walters, John, the younger (1759–1789), II, **383**, 917
Waltham, Roger (d. 1336), I, **311**
Walthoe, John (*fl.* 1722), II, 96
Walton, Brian (1600?–1661), I, 702, 855
Walton, Christopher (1809–1877), II, 858
Walton, E. H. (b. 1856), III, 1092
Walton, H. B. (*fl.* 1869), I, 676
Walton, Izaak (1593–1683), I, 688, **829** f.
Walton, John (*fl.* 1410), I, 265
Walton, W. (*fl.* 1865), III, 942
Walwyn, B. (*fl.* 1782), II, 400
Wanderer, The (O.E.), I, 28, **70**
Wanderer, The (1717), II, 537, 662
Wanderer, The (1798), II, 666
Wandering Jew (German), I, 336
Wandering Spy; Or, Way of the World, The (1705), II, 660
Wandering Whore, The (1660), II, 702
Wanley, Humfrey (1672–1726), II, 15, 101, **919**
Wanley, Nathaniel (1634–1680), II, **287**
Wanostrocht, Nicholas (1804–1876), III, 774
Wansey, Henry (1752?–1827), II, 757; III, 975
Wapull, George (*fl.* 1576), I, 516
War Cry and Official Gazette of the Salvation Army, The (1880), III, 819
War Express and Daily Advertiser, The [Manchester] (1854), III, 802
War Telegraph [Edinburgh] (1854), III, 807
WAR, TEXTBOOKS OF, I, 389 f. (16, 17 cents.)
Warbler, The (1757), II, 218
Warbler, The (1772), II, 229
Warblers Delight, The (18 cent.), II, 225
Warbling Muses, The (18 cent.), II, 213
Warbling Philomell, The (18 cent.), II, 228
Warburton, Bartholomew Eliot George (1810–1852), III, 53, **727**
Warburton, E. (*fl.* 1851), II, 840

Warburton, George Drought (1816–1857), III, 727
Warburton, John (1682–1759), II, 891
Warburton, Rowland Eyles Egerton (1804–1891), III, **286**
Warburton, William (1698–1779), II, 18, 22, 24, 92, 294, 303 (2), 602, 764–5, 865, 912, 949, 952
Warcupp, Edmund (*fl.* 1660), I, 781
Ward, Sir Adolphus William (1837–1924), III, **1043**
Ward, Ann, later Radcliffe (1764–1823), III, **414** f.
Ward, Charles (*fl.* 1806), II, 456
Ward, Edward (1667–1731), II, 187, 190, 218, 532, **596** f., 753, 819
Ward, Frederick William Orde (1843–1922), III, **361**
Ward, G. R. M. (*fl.* 1843), I, 368
Ward, George (*fl.* 1764), II, 54
Ward, Sir Henry George (1797–1860), III, 812
Ward, Harriot (*fl.* 1848), III, 1091
Ward, Harry Marshall (1854–1906), III, 962
Ward, Mrs Humphry, i.e. Mary Augusta Ward, née Arnold (1851–1920), III, **561** f.
Ward, James (1843–1925), III, **876** f.
Ward, John (d. *c.* 1640), composer, I, 485
Ward, John (1648–1679), vicar of Stratford-on-Avon, I, 387
Ward, John (1679?–1758), biographer, II, 113, 129, 932, 939
Ward, John (*fl.* 1771), compiler of a Latin grammar, II, 128
Ward, Richard (*fl.* 1710), I, 876
Ward, Robert (*fl.* 1623–42), I, 390, 660
Ward, Robert, later Plumer Ward (1765–1846), III, **420**
Ward, Samuel (1572–1643), I, 384
Ward, Seth (1617–1689), I, 368, **702**, 878, 882–3
Ward, Thomas Humphry (1845–1926), III, **755** f.
Ward, Wilfrid Philip (1856–1916), III, **924**
Ward, William (1534–1604?), I, 809, 888
Ward, William (*fl.* 1765–85), master of Beverley Grammar School, II, 932, 971
Ward, William (*fl.* 1776), writer on horses, II, 817
Ward, William (1769–1823), baptist missionary, III, 1075
Ward, William George (1812–1882), Roman Catholic theologian, III, 691, 860, 877
Warden, J. (*fl.* 1761), II, 604
Warder, Ann (*fl.* 1786), II, 756
Wardlaw, Elizabeth, Lady (1677–1727), II, 973
Wardlaw, Ralph (1779–1853), II, 152
Ware, Isaac (d. 1766), II, 812
Ware, Sir James (1594–1666), I, 363, 776 (2); II, 925

Waring, Anna Laetitia (1823–1910), III, **311**
Waring, G. (*fl.* 1854–65), I, 95; III, 1022
Waring, Thomas (*fl.* 1814), III, 776
Waring, William (*fl.* 1770), II, 798
Warkworth, John (d. 1500), I, 265
Warner, Ferdinando (1703–1768), II, 912
Warner, G. T. (*fl.* 1899), III, 985
Warner, John (1736–1800), I, 17
Warner, Pelham F. (b. 1873), III, 774
Warner, Richard (1713?–1775), botanist and
    scholar, II, 767, 913
Warner, Richard (1763–1857), divine and
    topographer, II, 140, 154, 321, 613; III,
    379
Warner, William (1558?–1609), I, **439**, 729,
    769, 806
Warning for Faire Women, A (16 cent.), I, 538
Warr, D. (*fl.* 1823), II, 493
Warr, George Charles Winter (1845–1901), III,
    1011
Warr, John (*fl.* 1686), II, 767
Warre, T. (*fl.* 1624), I, 616
Warren, Mrs — (*fl.* 1857), III, 829
Warren, Arthur (*fl.* 1605), I, 439
Warren, C. (*fl.* 1765), II, 223
Warren, George (*fl.* 1667), II, 752
Warren, Hardick (*fl.* 1651), I, 884
Warren, John Byrne Leicester, Baron de
    Tabley (1835–1895), III, **361** f.
Warren, Samuel (1807–1877), III, **510**
Warren, Thomas (*fl.* 1780), II, 222, 234
Warres of Cyrus King of Persia, The (16 cent.),
    I, 538
WARRINGTON
    Booksellers in, I, 353 (17 cent.); II, 88
    (18 cent.)
    Newspapers, II, 729
Warrington Daily Guardian, The (1896), III, 806
Warrington Evening Post, The (1877), III, 805
Wars of Alexander (M.E.), I, **143**
Warter, John Wood (1806–1878), III, 181 (3)
Warton, John (*fl.* 1794), II, 384
Warton, Joseph (1722–1800), II, 20, 26, 221,
    295, **383** f., 544, 914
Warton, Thomas, the elder (1688?–1745), II, **330**
Warton, Thomas, the younger (1728–1790),
    II, 26, 115, 216, 219, 221, 223–4, 229, 232,
    252, 616, **384** f., **899**
Warwick, Arthur (*fl.* 1634), I, 725
Warwick, Mary, Countess of (1625–1678), I,
    387
Warwick, Sir Philip (1609–1683), I, 400
Warwick and Staffordshire Journal, The (1737),
    II, 714
*Warwick and Staffordshire Journal With the
    History of the Holy Bible, The* (1740), II,
    714
*Warwick and Staffordshire Journal, with the
    History of the Life of Jesus Christ, The*
    (1740), II, 714

WARWICK SCHOOL, I, 373
WARWICKSHIRE
    Bibliography, I, 9
    Printing, II, 88
Warwickshire Journal, The (1769), II, 721
*Warwickshire Journal and Hereford Mercury,
    The* (1770), II, 721
Warwickshire Weekly Journal, The (1769), II,
    721
Wase, Christopher (1625–1690), I, 376, 394,
    650, 807, 853, 855, 863; II, 77, 110, 128,
    764
Washbourne, Thomas (1606–1687), I, 478
Washington, J. (*fl.* 1692), I, 467
Washington, T. (*fl.* 1585), I, 768
Wasp, The [Cambridge] (1891), III, 835
Wasse, Joseph (1672–1738), II, 938
Wastel, Simon (d. 1632), II, 130
Watchman, The (1796), II, 666
Watchman, The (1835), III, 819
Water Poetry (18 cent.), II, 231
Waterfield, William (*fl.* 1868), III, 1068
WATERFORD
    Newspapers, II, 738; III, 809
Waterford Chronicle, The (1765), II, 738
Waterford Chronicle, The (1850), II, 738
Waterford Daily Mail, The (1870), III, 809
Waterford Flying Post, The (1729), II, 738
Waterford Herald, The (1791), II, 738
Waterford Journal, The (1765), II, 738
Waterford Mail, The (1823), III, 809
Waterford Mirror and Munster Packet, The
    (1800), II, 738
Waterford Mirror and Tramore Visitor, The
    (1889), II, 738
Waterford Newsletter, The (1740), II, 738
Waterhouse, Edward (*fl.* 1622), I, 794
Waterhouse, Edward (1619–1670), I, 368; II,
    120, 965
Waterhouse, George Robert (1810–1888), III,
    957
WATERING PLACES, II, 154 f. (17, 18 cents.)
Waterland, Daniel (1683–1740), I, 26; II, 116,
    854
Waterlow, A. C. (*fl.* 1854), III, 83
WATERLOW BROTHERS AND LAYTON, III, 87
Watermeyer, E. B. (*fl.* 1850), III, 1090
Waters, B. (*fl.* 1809), III, 970
Waterston, John James (1811–1884), III, 938
Waterton, Charles (1782–1865), III, 955
Wateson, George (*fl.* 1598), I, 889
Watkins, John (d. 1831), I, 669; II, 458, 922;
    III, 206
Watkins, John (*fl.* 1850), III, 233
Watkins, Rowland (*fl.* 1662), I, 478
Watkins, T. (*fl.* 1877), III, 805
Watkins, Thomas (*fl.* 1792), II, 747
Watkinson, John (*fl.* 1774–8), II, 159
Watreman, William (*fl.* 1555), I, 765
Wats (or Watts), Gilbert (d. 1657), I, 869

Watson, Aaron (1850–1926), III, 788, 801, 802 (2), 806
Watson, Alfred Edward Thomas (*fl.* 1880), III, 759, 767
Watson, Christopher (d. 1581), I, 806
Watson, David (1710–1756), II, 938
Watson, Edward (*fl.* 1791), II, 96
Watson, Elkanah, II, 141
Watson, Graham Rosamund Marriott, née Tomson (1860–1911), III, **360**
Watson, Henry (*fl.* 1509), I, 411
Watson, Hewett Cottrell (1804–1881), III, **960**
Watson, James (d. 1722), II, 187–8, 190 (2), 193, 195, 698
Watson, James (1799–1874), III, 788
Watson, John (*fl.* 1890), writer on sport, III, 763, 772
Watson, John Forbes (1827–1892), writer on India, III, 907
Watson, John Selby (1804–1884), classical scholar, II, 935
Watson, Richard (1737–1816), bishop of Llandaff, II, 116f., 883, 957
Watson, Richard (1781–1833), methodist divine, III, 182
Watson, Robert (1730?–1781), II, **888**
Watson, S. B. (*fl.* 1848), III, 175
Watson, Thomas (1513–1584), bishop of Lincoln, I, 661, 683
Watson, Thomas (1557–1592), poet, I, **431**, 483, 819
Watson, Sir William (1715–1787), II, 962
Watson, Sir William (1858–1935), III, **362**
Watson's Limerick Chronicle (1793), II, 738
Watson-Wentworth, Charles, Marquis of Rockingham (1730–1782), II, 164
Watt, James (1736–1819), III, 936, 945
Watt, P. B. (*fl.* 1870), III, 88
Watt, Robert (1774–1819), bibliographer, I, 4, 366
Watt, Robert (*fl.* 1848), economist, III, 978
Watt, William (1793–1859), III, 245, 762
Watton, John (*fl.* 1486), I, 265
Watts, Alaric Alexander (1797–1864), III, 210, **245**, 801, 803, 821
Watts (or Wats), Gilbert (d. 1657), I, 869
Watts, Isaac (1674–1748), II, 22, 110, 124, 326, **330**, 556 (2)
Watts, John (*fl.* 1672), II, 748
Watts, John (1818–1887), III, 114
Watts, Thomas (*fl.* 1722), II, 111
Watts, William (1590?–1649), I, 745, 819
Watts-Dunton, Theodore, earlier Watts (1832–1914), III, **756**
Watzdorf, Heinrich Maximilian Friedrich von, II, 141
Waugh, Edwin (1817–1890), III, **311**
Waugh, G. (*fl.* 1900), III, 830
Waverley, Annals of (15 cent.), I, 115
WAVERLEY BOOK STORE, III, 103

Way, Albert (1805–1874), I, 125
Way, Benjamin (*fl.* 1778), II, 835
Way, G. L. (*fl.* 1796), II, 361, 787
Way, W. A. (*fl.* 1912), III, 1089
Way (or Wey), William (d. 1476), I, **313**
Wayland, John (*fl.* 16 cent.), I, 351
Wayland, T. (*fl.* 1832), III, 976
Waylett, Henry (*fl.* 1791), II, 245
Wayside Words (1879), III, 830
Wayte, William (1829–1898), III, 1011
Wayth, C. (*fl.* 1845), III, 769
Weakest Goeth to the Wall, The (17 cent.), I, 538
Weale, John (1791–1862), III, 903
Weamys, Anne (*fl.* 1651), I, 732
Weatherby, James (*fl.* 1773), II, 718
Weaver, John (1673–1760), II, 403, 825
Weaver, Thomas (1616–1663), I, 405
Webb, Beatrice, earlier Potter (b. 1858), III, 984
Webb, Daniel (1719?–1798), II, 18, 30, 793
Webb, Francis (*fl.* 1790), II, 23
Webb, Mrs J. B. (*fl.* 1839), III, 572
Webb, R. (*fl.* 1869), I, 839
Webb, Sidney, Baron Passfield (b. 1859), III, 977
Webb, T. (*fl.* 1775), II, 230
Webbe, Edward (*fl.* 1590), I, 768
Webbe, George (*fl.* 1629), I, 808
Webbe, Joseph (*fl.* 1612–33), I, 801
Webbe, William (b. 1552?), I, 803, 864
Webber, Alexander (*fl.* 1841), III, 762
Webber, Byron (*fl.* 1879), III, 761
Weber, Carl Maria von, III, 608
Weber, Henry William (1783–1818), III, **1028**
Weber, V., II, 807
Webster, Augusta, née Davies (1837–1894), III, **362f.**
Webster, Benjamin Nottingham (1797–1882), III, 442, 585 (2), **597**
Webster, Charles (*fl.* 1781), II, 999
Webster, D. (*fl.* 1818), editor of Sir Robert Sibbald, II, 997
Webster, David (*fl.* 1885), angler, III, 772
Webster, G. (*fl.* 1838–42), I, 684; III, 93
Webster, J. (*fl.* 1735), translator of Voiture, II, 803
Webster, James (1658?–1720), II, 993
Webster, John (1580?–1625), dramatist, I, **629f.**, 865
Webster, John (1610–1682), puritan and scientist, I, 368, 962
Webster, Pelatiah (*fl.* 1765), II, 755
Webster, R. G. (*fl.* 1880), III, 983
Webster, Thomas (1772–1844), III, 949
Webster, W. F. (*fl.* 1870), III, 1018
Webster, William (1689–1758), II, 714, 790
'Webster, William' (1732), II, 663 (2)
Wedd, N. (*fl.* 1888), III, 835
Wedderburn, Alexander (*fl.* 1755), II, 686
Wedderburn, David (1580–1646), I, 912

Wedderburn, John (*fl.* 1567), I, 678
Weddynge of Sir Gawen (M.E.), I, **139**
Wedel, Liupold von, I, 384
Wedgwood, Josiah (1730–1795), II, 137, 138
Wedlake, George (*fl.* 1897), III, 813
Wedmore, Sir Frederick (1844–1921), III, 303, 756 f.
Wednesday Packet, The (1798), II, 732
Wednesday's Journal, The (1717), II, 712
Wednesday's Mercury, or Speciall Passages and Certain Informations (1643), I, 755
Week, The (1878), III, 814
Week, The (Toronto, 1883), III, 1088
Weekely Post-Master, The (1645), I, 756
Weekes, Nathaniel (*fl.* 1752–65), II, 17
Weekly Abstract, The (1654), I, 762
Weekly Accompt of certain special and remarkable passages from both Houses of Parliament, A (1643), I, 755
Weekly Accompt, or Perfect Diurnall, A (1643), I, 755
Weekly Account, The (1643), I, 755
Weekly Account Faithfully Representing, The most Remarkable Passages in Parliament, The (1659), I, 763
Weekly Account, on the establishment of a free state, The (1659), I, 763
Weekly Advertisement of Books (1680), II, 717
Weekly Advertisements of Things Lost and Stolen (1669), II, 717
Weekly Amusement, The (1734), II, 663
Weekly Amusement, The (1784), II, 680
Weekly Amusement; Or, An Useful Miscellany of Literary Entertainments, The (1763), II, 678
Weekly Amusement; Or, The Universal Magazine, The (1734), II, 714
Weekly Amusement; Or, Universal Magazine, The (1735), II, 687
Weekly Bill of Mortality, The (1602), II, 719
Weekly Character, The (1679), II, 657
Weekly Character; Being the Character of a Pope, The (1679), II, 703
Weekly Chronicle, The (1836), III, 812
Weekly Chronicle and Register, The (1855), III, 812
Weekly Comedy, The (1699), II, 659
Weekly Comedy, The (1707), II, 660
Weekly Courant, The (1716), II, 727
Weekly Discoverer Strip'd Naked, The (1681), II, 657
Weekly Discovery of the Mystery of the Rebellion in England, The (1681), II, 657
Weekly Discovery of the Mystery of the Rebellion in England. Anno 1641, The (1681), II, 703
Weekly Dispatch, The (1801), III, 794, 810
Weekly Dispatch (1816), III, 811
Weekly Entertainer, The (1783), II, 685
Weekly Entertainment, The (1700), II, 659

Weekly Essay; or Middlesex Journal, The (1738), II, 663
Weekly General Post, The (1716), II, 712
Weekly Globe, The (1824), III, 811
Weekly Herald, The (1836), III, 816
Weekly History; Or, an Account of the most Remarkable Passages of the Gospel, The (1741), II, 715
Weekly Information from the Office of Intelligence, The (1657), I, 750, 763; II, 716
Weekly Intelligence, The (1816), III, 811
Weekly Intelligence, communicating News from City and Country, The (1679), II, 703
Weekly Intelligence from severall Parts of this Kingdome (1642), I, 754
Weekly Intelligencer and British Luminary, The (1820), III, 811
Weekly Intelligencer of the Commonwealth, The (1650), I, 761
Weekly Intelligencer of the Commonwealth, The (1659), I, 763 (2)
Weekly Intelligencer of the Commonwealth, The (1660), II, 701
Weekly Journal, The (1716), II, 712
Weekly Journal, The (1757), II, 731
Weekly Journal from London, The (1688), II, 730
Weekly Journal; Or, British Gazetteer, The (1715), II, 712
Weekly Journal; Or, General Post, The (1720), II, 713
Weekly Journal; Or, Saturday's Post, The (1716), II, 712
Weekly Journal, With Fresh Advices, A (1713), II, 712
Weekly Journal, With Fresh Advices Foreign and Domestick, The (1714), II, 712
Weekly Letters to the Human Race (1850), III, 817
Weekly Magazine, The (1759), II, 674
Weekly Magazine and Historical Register, The (1793), II, 688
Weekly Magazine and Literary Review, The (1758), II, 678
Weekly Magazine and Literary Review, The (1779), II, 687
Weekly Magazine; Or, Edinburgh Amusement, The, II, 686
Weekly Magazine; Or, Gentleman and Lady's Polite Companion, The (1759), II, 678
Weekly Medley, The (1718), II, 662
Weekly Medley, The (1729), II, 713, 719
Weekly Medley and Literary Journal, The (1729), II, 713, 719
Weekly Medley; Or, The Gentleman's Recreation, The (1718), II, 712
Weekly Memorial, The (1692), II, 658
Weekly Memorial; or Political Observations on England's Benefits by the War with France, The (1692), II, 705

Weekly Memorials (1689), II, 675

Weekly Memorials for the Ingenious (1682), II, 674 (2)

Weekly Mercury; Or, The Protestant's Packet, The (1721), II, 727

Weekly Mirror, The (1780), II, 665, 686

Weekly Miscellany, The (1701), II, 659

Weekly Miscellany, The (1732), II, 663, 714

Weekly Miscellany, The (Dublin, 1734), II, 735

Weekly Miscellany of Instruction and Entertainment, The (1789), II, 687

Weekly Miscellany; Or Instructive Entertainer, The (1773), II, 685

Weekly Museum, The (1788), II, 681

Weekly News, and Daily Register, The (1730), II, 714

Weekly News and Register, The (1730), II, 714

Weekly News from Forraigne Parts Beyond the Seas, The (1644), I, 756

Weekly News Letter, The (1695), II, 711

Weekly Observator, The (1692), II, 658

Weekly Observator, The (1716), II, 660, 662

Weekly Oracle; Or, Universal Library, The (1734), II, 663, 714

Weekly Oracle; Or, Universal Library, The (Dublin, 1735), II, 735

Weekly Packet, The (1712), II, 712

Weekly Packet, The (1741), II, 715

Weekly Packet of Advice from Ireland, The (1690), II, 705

Weekly Packet, with the Price Courant, The (1718), II, 712

Weekly Pacquet of Advice from Geneva, The (1681), II, 657

Weekly Pacquet of Advice from Geneva; Or, the History of Presbytery, The (1683), II, 657, 704

Weekly Pacquet of Advice from Germany, The (1679), II, 657

Weekly Pacquet of Advice from Rome Restored, The (1680), II, 657

Weekly Pacquet, or Advice from Rome, The (1678), II, 657

WEEKLY PAPERS, II, 711 f. (1660–1800); III, 810 f. (19 cent.)

Weekly Post, The (1654), I, 762

Weekly Post, The (1659), I, 763; II, 701

Weekly Post; Or, A Just Account of All the Principal News, The (1711), II, 712

Weekly Press, The (1823), III, 813

Weekly Register, The (1730), II, 714

Weekly Register, The (1798), II, 716

Weekly Register, The (1823), III, 810

Weekly Register, The (1855), III, 819

Weekly Register, The (1863), III, 860

Weekly Register; or, Universal Journal, The (1732), II, 714

Weekly Remarks and Political Reflections Upon the Most Material News (1715), II, 712

Weekly Remarks on the Transactions Abroad, The (1691), II, 658

Weekly Remembrancer, The (1702), II, 659

Weekly Remembrancer and Discoverer, The (1702), II, 659

Weekly Repository, The (1779), II, 688

Weekly Review of the Affairs of France, A (1704), II, 659, 661

Weekly Review; Or, Literary Journal, The (1799), II, 683

Weekly Review; Or, The Wednesday's Post, The (1717), II, 712

Weekly Sun, The (1891), III, 794, 813

Weekly Survey of the World, The (1696), II, 658, 711

Weekly Test Paper, The (1688), II, 704, 731

Weekly Times, The (1826), III, 812

Weekly Times, The (1835), III, 812

Weekly Times, The (1847), III, 812

Weekly Times and Echo, The (1885), III, 812

Weekly Tribune, The (1849), III, 817

Weekly True Sun, The (1833), III, 812

Weekly Visions of the Late Popish Plot, The (1681), II, 657

Weekly Worcester Journal, The (1709), II, 729

Weekly Worcester Journal, The (1725), II, 729

Weelkes, Thomas (1575–1623), I, 483

Weever, John (1576–1632), I, 478, 480

Wehnert, A. (*fl.* 1869), III, 576

Weir, A. (*fl.* 1834), author of 'Life of Sir Walter Scott', III, 374

Weir, Arthur (*fl.* 1887), Canadian poet, III, 1086

Weir, William (*fl.* 1838), II, 981

Weir, William (1802–1858), III, 799

Weisse, Christian Felix, II, 566

Weisslau, O. E. (*fl.* 1895), III, 978

Wekett, W. (*fl.* 1729), I, 696

Welby, John (*fl.* 1867), III, 760

Welch, J. (*fl.* 1695), II, 717

Welch, Joseph (d. 1805), I, 373

Welch Mercury, communicating remarkable intelligence and true news, The (1643), I, 755

Welcome Hour, The (1878), III, 831

Weld, Charles Richard (1813–1869), I, 853

Weld, Isaac (1774–1856), II, 719, 757

Welde, W. (*fl.* 1615), I, 375

Weldon, Sir Anthony (d. 1649?), I, 776, 842

Weldon's Ladies' Journal of Dress and Fashion (1879), III, 822

Well-Bred Scholar, The (18 cent.), II, 253

Wellesley, Arthur, Duke of Wellington (1769–1852), III, 144

Wellesley, Arthur Richard, Duke of Wellington (*fl.* 1858–72), III, 144

WELLINGTON COLLEGE, II, 839

Wells, Charles Jeremiah (1800–1879), III, **245**

Wells, Edward (1667–1727), II, 125

Wells, Herbert George (b. 1866), III, 778

Wells, Joseph (*fl.* 1842), III, 769

Wells, L. B. (*fl.* 1894), III, 984

Wells, Mary (*fl.* 1781–1812), II, 698, 709

Wells, S. (*fl.* 1830), III, 970

Wells, William Charles (1757–1817), III, 937, 953

Wellwood (or Welwood), James (1652–1727), I, 833; II, 432, 658 (2), 705 (2), 763, 870

Welsh, Charles (*fl.* 1885), II, 554

Welsh Ambassador, The (17 cent.), I, 654

WELSH LITERATURE
   Bibliographies, I, 7 f.
   Magazines, II, 685 (1735–1800)

Welsted, Leonard (1688–1747), II, 16, 27, **331**, 765

Welth, and Helth, An enterlude of (16 cent.), I, 515

Welton, J. (b. 1854), III, 114

Welwood (or Wellwood), James (1652–1727), I, 833; II, 432, 658 (2), 705 (2), 763, 870

Wendeborn, Gebhardt Friedrich August, II, 51, 141

Wendover, Roger of (d. 1236), I, 116

Wenrington, William (*fl.* 1799), II, 553

Wentworth, Charles William, Earl Fitzwilliam (1786–1857), II, 633

Wentworth, John (*fl.* 1797), II, 965

Wentworth, Thomas (1568?–1628), lawyer, I, 851

Wentworth, Thomas, Earl of Strafford (1593–1641), I, 386, 400

Wentworth, Thomas, Earl of Strafford (1672–1739), II, 135, 163

Wentworth, William Charles (1793–1872), III, 1097

Wentworth Papers, The (18 cent.), I, 47

Werge, John (*fl.* 1753), II, **385**

Werner, Zacharias, III, 35

WERTHEIMER, LEA & CO., III, 87

Wesley, Charles (1707–1788), II, **854**

Wesley, John (1703–1791), I, 451; II, 55, 136, 210, 435, 492, 680, 756, 771, 780, 782, **854**

Wesley, Samuel (1662–1735), II, 21, 119, **287** f., 658

Wesley, Samuel, the younger (1691–1739), II, **331**

Wesleyan Methodist Association Magazine, The (1838), III, 827

Wesleyan Methodist Magazine, The (1822), III, 823

Wesleyan Times, The (1849), III, 819

West, Sir Algernon (1832–1921), III, 155

West, Benjamin (1738–1820), II, 30

West, Sir Edward (1782–1828), III, 970, 980

West, Gilbert (1703–1756), II, **331** f., 760, 762 (2)

West, Jane (1758–1852), III, **420**

West, Matthew (*fl.* 1799), II, 487

West, Richard (*fl.* 1607), I, 481

West, Richard (d. 1726), lawyer and playwright, II, 760

West, Richard (1716–1742), poet, II, 334

West, Thomas, Baron de La Warr (1577–1618), I, 790

West, W. (*fl.* 1869), editor of Robert Leighton's works, I, 698

West, William (*fl.* 1568–94), I, 851

West, William (1770–1854), II, 100; III, 97

West Country Intelligence, The (1715), II, 733

West Cumberland Post, The (1897), II, 729

WEST MIDLAND ENGLISH
   Dialect (M.E.), I, 38
   Texts (M.E.), I, 42

WEST SAXON TEXTS, I, 36

Westall, William (1781–1850), III, 1076

Westbury, Richard Bethell, Baron (1800–1873), III, 152

Westcott, Brooke Foss (1825–1901), I, 672; III, 850

Western Counties Daily Herald, The [Plymouth] (1863), III, 803

Western County Magazine, The (1790), II, 685

Western Daily Mercury, The [Plymouth] (1860), III, 794, 802

Western Daily Press, The [Bristol], III, 794, 802

Western Daily Standard, The [Plymouth] (1869), III, 803

Western Flying Post; Or, Sherborne and Yeovil Mercury, The (1749), II, 728

Western Flying Post; Or, Yeovil Mercury, The (1744), II, 729

Western Mail, The [Cardiff] (1869), III, 803

Western Morning News, The [Plymouth] (1860), III, 794, 802

Western Star, The (1807), II, 721

Western Times, The [Exeter] (1866), III, 803

Westerne Informer, The (1646), I, 757

Westgarth, William (1815–1889), III, **1097**

Westlake, W. C. (*fl.* 1867), III, 833

Westmacott, Charles Malloy (*fl.* 1823–46), III, 789, 811

Westmeath Journal, The (1783), II, 738

Westminster and Foreign Quarterly Review, The (1847), III, 832 f.

Westminster Cartulary (M.E.), I, 41

Westminster Gazette, The (1681), II, 703

Westminster Gazette, The (1893), III, 801

Westminster Gazette; Or, Constitutional Evening Post, The (1776), II, 711

Westminster Journal and Imperial Weekly Gazette, The (1813), III, 813

Westminster Journal And London Political Miscellany, The (1764), II, 715

Westminster Journal and old British Spy, The (1794), III, 813

Westminster Journal; Or, New Weekly Miscellany, The (1741), II, 715

Westminster Magazine, The (1750), II, 677

Westminster Magazine (1780), II, 665

Westminster Magazine, The (1772), II, 679
Westminster Projects; or, The Mystery of Darby House Discovered (1648), I, 758
Westminster Projects; or, the Mystery of Iniquity of Darby-House Discovered (1648), I, 758
Westminster Quibbles in Verse (17 cent.), II, 176
Westminster Review, The (1824), (1841), (1852), III, 832
WESTMINSTER SCHOOL, I, 373; III, 134
Westminster-Drollery (17 cent.), II, 175 (2), 176-7
Westmorland, Priscilla Anne Fane, Countess of (1793-1879), III, 152
Weston, Edward (1703-1770), II, 702
Weston, Elizabeth Jane (1582-1612), I, 861
Weston, J. (*fl.* 1824), editor of Robert Bloomfield's poems, III, 228
Weston, James (*fl.* 1727), II, 129
Weston, Joseph (*fl.* 1789), critic, II, 23
Weston, Sir Richard (1591-1652), I, 391
Weston, Stephen (1747-1830), II, 747, 934-5; III, 376
Weston, T. (*fl.* 1730), II, 810
Westrup, William (*fl.* 1913), III, 1090
Westward for Smelts (17 cent.), I, 715
Westwood, John Obadiah (1805-1893), III, 956
Westwood, Thomas (1814-1888), III, 311f., 636
Wetenhall, James (*fl.* 1800?), II, 718
Wetherell, Sir Charles (1770-1846), III, 125
Wetherell, T. F. (*fl.* 1868), III, 828
Wetton, Harry W. (*fl.* 1864), III, 199
Wever, R. (*fl.* 1565?), I, 515
Wewitzer, Ralph (1748-1825), II, 407
WEXFORD
    Newspapers, II, 738f.
Wexford Chronicle, The (1782), II, 739
Wexford Herald, The (1788), II, 739
Wexford Journal, The (1774), II, 738
Wey (or Way), William (d. 1476), I, 313
Weyland, John (1774-1854), III, 114, 975
Weyman, Stanley John (1855-1928), III, 562
Whaley, John (1710-1745), II, 211, 332
Whaley (or Whalley), Thomas (1766-1800), II, 159
Whalley, George Hammond (1813-1878), III, 988
Whalley, Henry (*fl.* 1648), I, 755-6, 758
Whalley, John (1653-1724), II, 734
Whalley, Peter (1722-1791), II, 25, 887f., 914
Whalley, Thomas Sedgwick (1746-1828), II, 154, 385
Whalley Abbey, The Coucher Book of (M.E.), I, 122
Whalley's Newsletter (1714), II, 734
Wharncliffe, John Stuart-Wortley, Baron (1801-1855), II, 835
Wharton, Anne, née Lee (1632?-1685), II, 180

Wharton, Sir George (1617-1681), I, 749, 758, 759 (3); II, 701
Wharton, Henry (1664-1695), I, 260-1, 857; II, 850
Wharton, J. (*fl.* 1655), I, 377
Wharton, Philip, Duke of (1698-1731), II, 200, 210, 662
Wharton, Richard (*fl.* 1804), I, 210
Wharton, Thomas (1614-1673), I, 891
Whartoniana (18 cent.), II, 199, 201, 208
What Not, The (1859), III, 829
What-D'Ye-Call-It, The (1733), II, 663
Whateley, Elizabeth, later Darwell (*fl.* 1764), II, 385
Whateley, Stephen (*fl.* 1712-41). See Whatley
Whateley (or Whately), Thomas (d. 1772), II, 148
Whately, E. J. (*fl.* 1864), biographer of Richard Whately, III, 669, 681-2
Whately, G. N. (*fl.* 1803), III, 969
Whately, Richard (1787-1863), II, 956; III, 114, 383, 681f., 847, 974
Whatley, George (*fl.* 1769), II, 959
Whatley (or Whateley), Stephen (*fl.* 1712-41), II, 706, 745, 786, 788, 796, 802, 807, 813
Whatton, A. P. (*fl.* 1859), I, 883
Wheare, Degory (1573-1647), I, 827
Wheatley, Henry Benjamin (d. 1917), I, 910; III, 1043
Wheatley, Hewett (*fl.* 1849), III, 770
Wheatley, J. (*fl.* 1803), III, 973
Wheatstone, Sir Charles (1802-1875), III, 938, 963
Wheble, John (*fl.* 1779), II, 711
Whedon, D. (*fl.* 1864), I, 873
Wheeldon, J. P. (*fl.* 1894), III, 772
Wheeldon, John (*fl.* 1773), I, 451
Wheeler, C. A. (*fl.* 1867), III, 766
Wheeler, G. B. (*fl.* 1859), III, 809
Wheeler, James Talboys (1824-1897), III, 1076f.
Wheeler, John (*fl.* 1601-8), I, 846
Wheeler, Rosina, later Lady Bulwer-Lytton (1804-1882), III, 478f.
Wheeler's Manchester Chronicle (1792), II, 726
Wheler, George (1650-1723), II, 743
Whellan, T. (*fl.* 1859), III, 303
Whellan, William (*fl.* 1860), III, 890
Whelock (or Wheelock), Abraham (1593-1653), I, 857-8
When All is Done (1689), II, 658
Whethamstede (or Bostock), John (d. 1465), I, 261
Whetstone, George (1544?-1587), I, 440, 512, 520, 523, 728, 864
Whewell, William (1794-1866), I, 846, 874; III, 114, 122, 124, 141, 877, 881, 938, 981
Whibley, Charles (1860-1930), III, 757
Whichcote, Benjamin (1609-1683), I, 879
Whig, The (1779), II, 665

Whig and Tory (18 cent.), II, 190–1
Whig Examiner, The (1710), II, 603
Whig Magazine; Or, Patriot Miscellany, The (1779), II, 680
Whim of the Day, The (18 cent.), II, 245 (2), 246 (4), 247 (2), 249–56
Whimsical Incidents (19 cent.), III, 575
Whimsical Songster, The (18 cent.), II, 255
Whimsies of Senor Hidalgo (17 cent.), I, 654
'Whimsy, Funny' (1796), II, 252
Whincop, Thomas (d. 1730), II, 442
Whip for all scandalous Lyers, A fresh (17 cent.), I, 720
Whipping Post, The (1705), II, 660
Whishaw, Frederick J. (*fl.* 1895), III, 574
Whisperer, The (1709), II, 661
Whisperer, The (1770), II, 665
Whistler, Daniel (1619–1684), I, 890
Whiston, James (*fl.* 1679), II, 717 (2)
Whiston, William (1667–1752), II, 117, 124, 761, 863, **949**
Whiston's Merchant's Weekly Remembrancer (1689), II, 717
Whiston's Merchant's Weekly Remembrancer of the Prices of Goods in London (1691), II, 717
Whitaker, — (*fl.* 1783), II, 680
Whitaker, Alexander (*fl.* 1613), I, 790
Whitaker, Evelyn (*fl.* 1879), III, 573
Whitaker, John (1735–1808), II, 883, **888** f.
Whitaker, Joseph (1820–1895), III, 100, 101 (2)
Whitaker, Thomas Dunham (1759–1821), I, 197; III, **882**
Whitbourne, Sir Richard (*fl.* 1579–1627), I, 791
WHITBY
   Printing, II, 88
Whitby, Daniel (1638–1726), II, 129
Whitchurch, James Wadham, II, 110
White, Andrew (1579–1656), I, 792
White, Charles (1728–1813), III, 966
White, E. (*fl.* 1823), III, 572
White, F. (*fl.* 1716), II, 712
White, Gilbert (1720–1793), II, 337, **841**
White, Henry (*fl.* 1821), III, 810–1
White, Henry Kirke (1785–1806), III, 26, **246**
White, J. D. (*fl.* 1840?), III, 807
White, J. W. Gleeson (*fl.* 1896), III, 831
White, James (*fl.* 1759), translator of Aristophanes, II, 759
White, James (*fl.* 1788–93), translator from French, II, 795, 797
White, James (d. 1799), historical novelist, II, 549, 765
White, James (1775–1820), Charles Lamb's friend, III, 633
White, James (1803–1862), miscellaneous writer, II, 986; III, 375
White, James (?) (*fl.* 1840–51) ('Martingale'), III, 763
White, John (1757–1648), colonist and divine, I, 795

White, John (*fl.* 1642), publisher, I, 754
White, John (*fl.* 1654), versifier of psalms, I, 679
White, John (*fl.* 1731), of Nayland, Essex, II, 279
White, John (*fl.* 1790), voyager to Australia, II, 751
White, John (*fl.* 1802), brother of Gilbert White, II, 841
White, Joseph (1745–1814), orientalist and theologian, II, 883; III, 1070
White, Joseph Blanco, earlier José Maria Blanco (1775–1841), theological writer, III, **847**
White, Percy (*fl.* 1880–94), III, 814
White, R. (*fl.* 1658), translator of Sir Kenelm Digby, I, 887
White, R. (*fl.* 1858), editor of John Leyden's poems, III, 237
White, Robert (*fl.* 1649), publisher, I, 760
White, S. (*fl.* 1688), II, 760
White, T. H. (*fl.* 1819), II, 627
White, Thomas (1550?–1624), divine, I, 512
White, Thomas (1593–1676), philosopher and controversialist, I, 877
White, Thomas (d. 1672?), writer of children's books, II, 556
White, Thomas (*fl.* 1705), writer of children's books, II, 556
White, Thomas (*fl.* 1830), I, 488
White, Walter (1811–1893), III, 215, 992
White, William (*fl.* 1800), traveller, II, 749
White, William Hale (1831–1913) ('Mark Rutherford'), III, **559** f.
White Dwarf, The (1817), III, 816
White Ethiopian, The (17 cent.), I, 654
White Hat, The (1819), III, 816
Whitefield, George (1714–1770), II, 490, 754, **854**
Whitefoord, Caleb (1734–1810), II, 689, 698
Whitefoot, John (*fl.* 1660?), I, 834
Whitefoot, Thomas (*fl.* 1878), III, 799
Whitehall, John (*fl.* 1679), I, 879
Whitehall Evening-Post, The (1718), II, 710
Whitehall Evening Post, The (1746), II, 698
Whitehall Evening-Post; Or, London Intelligencer, The (1746), II, 710
Whitehall Fayre (17 cent.), I, 719
White-Hall Gazette, Containing Foreign and Domestic News, The (1726), II, 734
Whitehall Journal, The (1722), II, 713
Whitehall Review, The (1876), III, 814
Whitehall-Courant, The (1716), II, 707
WHITEHAVEN
   Magazines, II, 685 (1775–81)
   Newspapers, II, 729
Whitehaven Weekly Courant, The (1736), II, 729
Whitehead, Charles (1804–1862), III, **312**, 386
Whitehead, Paul (1710–1774), II, **332**, 373

Whitehead, William (1715–1785), II, **484-5**
Whitehorn, William (*fl.* 1865), III, 817
Whitehorne (or Whithorne), Peter (*fl.* 1550–63), I, 389, 804, 816
Whitehouse, J. Howard (b. 1873), III, 705
Whiteing, Richard (1840–1928), III, 788
Whitelaw, A. (*fl.* 1831), III, 395
Whitelocke, Bulstrode (1605–1675), I, 386, 773, **833** f.
Whitelocke, Sir James (1570–1632), I, 385
Whitelocke, R. H. (*fl.* 1860), I, 834
Whiter, Walter (1758–1832), II, 917
Whitford, Richard (*fl.* 1495–1555?), I, 685
Whitgift, John (1530?–1604), I, 683, 687
Whithorne (or Whitehorne), Peter (*fl.* 1550–63), I, 389, 804, 816
Whiting, John (*fl.* 1708), II, 95
Whiting, Nathaniel (*fl.* 1629–63), I, **478**
Whiting, Thomas (*fl.* 1787–98), II, 682
Whitlaw, C. (*fl.* 1839), III, 971
Whitlock, John (*fl.* 1695), II, 706, 711
Whitmore, W. W. (*fl.* 1823), writer on agriculture, III, 970
Whitmore, Walter Jones (formerly Walter Whitmore Jones) (*fl.* 1868), writer on croquet, III, 774
Whitney, Geffrey (1548?–1601?), I, 479
Whitney, John (*fl.* 1700), II, 819
Whittaker, Frederick (*fl.* 1870), III, 503
Whittaker, Meredith J. (*fl.* 1886), III, 805
Whittaker, T. P. (*fl.* 1890), III, 800
Whittemore, J. (*fl.* 1857–76), III, 496, 819
Whittingham, William (1524?–1579), I, 383, 676, 678
WHITTINGHAM & CO., C., III, 88
Whittington (or Whytynton), Robert (*fl.* 1512–54), I, 375, 665, 800, 807
Whittington, W. D. (*fl.* 1804), III, 834
Whittock, N. (*fl.* 1828), III, 128
Whitty, Edward Michael (1827–1860), III, 808
Whitty, Michael James (1795–1873), III, 802, 826
Whitworth, Charles, Baron (1675–1725), II, 745
Whitworth, Sir Charles (1714?–1778), II, 719, 871, 958
Whitworth's Manchester Advertiser and Weekly Magazine (1757), II, 725
Whitworth's Manchester Gazette (1730), II, 725
Whitworth's Manchester Magazine (1755), II, 725
Whole of the Chapters Circulated during the Election for Hull, The (18 cent.), II, 252
Whole Proceedings of the [old Bailey] Sessions (1674), II, 720
Whole Prophecies, The (18 cent.), II, 194
Whole Volume of Mercurius Musicus, The (17 cent.), II, 184, 185 (3)
Whymper, Edward (1840–1911), III, 777, 992

Whyte, Edward Athenry (*fl.* 1792–7), II, 386, 654
Whyte, Samuel (1733–1811), II, 229, 247, **386**
Whyte-Melville, George John (1821–1878), III, **511**
Whythorne, Thomas (b. 1528), I, 482
Whytynton (or Whittington), Robert (*fl.* 1512–54), I, 375, 665, 800, 807
Wiat (or Wyatt), Sir Thomas (*fl.* 1549), I, **411** f., 677
Wibourne, Nathaniel (d. 1613), I, 660
Wickham, Edward Charles (1834–1910), III, 1011
Wickham, Hill (*fl.* 1863), II, 385
Wickins, Nathan (*fl.* 1638), I, 717
Wicks, Frederick (*fl.* 1866), III, 808
Wicks, Philip (*fl.* 1794), II, 718
Wicksteed, P. H. (*fl.* 1888), III, 974, 984
Wicquefort, Abraham de, II, 804
Wide World Magazine, The (1898), III, 832
Widsith (O.E.), I, **69** f.
Wieland, Christoph Martin, II, 56 f., 58, 63, 71, 552, **807**
Wife's Complaint, The (O.E.), I, **71**
Wiffen, Benjamin Barron (1794–1867), III, 246
Wiffen, Jeremiah Holmes (1792–1836), III, 210, **246**
Wigan, Alfred Sydney (1814–1878), III, **609**
Wigan, Eleazar (*fl.* 1695), II, 125
Wigan, Horace (1818?–1885), III, 605
Wiggers, G. (*fl.* 1840), III, 894
Wight, Andrew (*fl.* 1778–84), II, 157
Wight, O. W. (*fl.* 1852), III, 21
Wigley, B. (*fl.* 1782), II, 800
Wignell, John (d. 1774), II, 386
Wigstead, Henry (*fl.* 1797), II, 140, 154
Wilberforce, Edward (*fl.* 1857), III, 199
Wilberforce, H. G., III, 856
Wilberforce, Henry William (1807–1873), III, 819, **860**
Wilberforce, Robert Isaac (1802–1897), III, **860**, 898
Wilberforce, Samuel (1805–1873), II, 830; III, 151–2, 898
Wilberforce, William (1759–1833), II, 138, 165; III, 852
Wilbraham, Sir Roger (*fl.* 1593–1616), I, 384
Wilbye, John (1574–1638), I, 483
Wilcocke, Samuel Hull (*fl.* 1797–1807), II, 53
Wilcocks, J. C. (*fl.* 1865), III, 771
Wilcox, C. B. (*fl.* 1840), III, 834
Wilcox, Dora (*fl.* 1905), III, 1096
Wilcox, Thomas (1549?–1608), I, 687, 713
Wild, Robert (1609–1679), II, **288**, 827
Wilde, George (1610–1665), I, 660
Wilde, Jane Francesca, Lady (1826–1896), née Elgee, III, 1049, **1054**
Wilde, Oscar Fingall O'Flahertie Wills (1856–1900), III, 37 f., **620** f.
Wilde, Sir William Robert (1815–1876), II, 594; III, 967, **1049**

Wilderspin, Samuel (1792?–1866), III, 114
'Wildrake', i.e. George Tattersall (1817–1849), III, 763
Wilford, John (*fl.* 1723–42), II, 94, **717**, 924
Wilkes, John (1725–1797), II, 165, 340, 626, 664–5, 678, 698
Wilkes, Thomas (d. 1786), II, 403, 416, 915
Wilkes, Wetenhall (*fl.* 1740–7), II, 143, 820
Wilkes's Jest Book (18 cent.), II, 228
Wilkie, William (1721–1772), II, 23, **386**
Wilkin, M. H. (*fl.* 1855), III, 1028
Wilkin, Simon (1790–1862), III, **1028**
Wilkins, Augustus Samuel (1843–1905), III, **1011**
Wilkins, Sir Charles (1749?–1836), III, **1019**, 1073
Wilkins, David (1685–1745), I, 851; II, 920, 929
Wilkins, George (*fl.* 1605–1608), I, 651, 715, 731, 808
Wilkins, Henry Musgrave (1822–1887), III, **1003**
Wilkins, John (1614–1672), I, **702**f., 883
Wilkins, W. (*fl.* 1725), II, 713
Wilkins, W. J. (*fl.* 1882), writer on Hindu mythology, III, 1082
Wilkins, William Henry (1860–1905), biographer, III, **919**
Wilkins, William Walker (*fl.* 1860), literary antiquary, I, 450; II, 258, 871
Wilkinson, Charles Henry (*fl.* 1804), physicist, III, 937
Wilkinson, H. (*fl.* 1824), author of 'Cain, a Poem', III, 200
Wilkinson, Henry (1616–1690), II, 104
Wilkinson, James John Garth (1812–1899), II, 349
Wilkinson, John (*fl.* 1547–55), translator, I, 799, 810
Wilkinson, John (*fl.* 1618), lawyer, I, 851
Wilkinson, Sir John Gardner (1797–1875), III, 992, **1015**
Wilkinson, Joseph (*fl.* 1810), III, 169
Wilkinson, Joshua Lucock (*fl.* 1798), II, 748
Wilkinson, Robert (*fl.* 1797–1825), II, 146
Wilkinson, Tate (1739–1803), II, 137, 405 (2), 449
Wilks, M. (*fl.* 1822), commentator on 'Peveril of the Peak', III, 379
Wilks, Mark (1760?–1831), writer on India, III, 1075
Wilks, Matthew (*fl.* 1800?), editor of 'The Evangelical Magazine', II, 682
Wilks, Samuel Charles (1789–1872), III, 824
Wilks, Thomas Egerton (*fl.* 1832–50), III, **609**
Will, John Shiress (1840–1910), III, 987–8
Will, Peter (*fl.* 1795–9), II, 52, 63 (2), 533
Willan, Leonard (*fl.* 1650), I, 651, 799
Willet, Andrew (1562–1621), I, 479
Willet, R. (*fl.* 1617), I, 715

Willett, Ralph (1719–1795), II, 102
Willett, W. M. (*fl.* 1809–33), III, 800 (2)
William III, King (1650–1702), II, 166
William de Pagula (or Page) (*fl. c.* 1325), I, **301**
William of Alnwick (*fl.* 1300), I, **303**
William of Conches (*fl.* 1154), I, **286**
William of Drogheda (d. 1245?), I, **298**
William of Hotham (d. 1298), I, **296**
William of Macclesfield (d. 1304), I, **305**
William of Malmesbury (d. 1143?), I, 116, 120
William of Newburgh (1136–1198?), I, 116
William of Nottingham (d. *c.* 1251), I, **292**
William of Nottingham (d. 1336), I, **304**
William of Ockham (d. *c.* 1349), I, 304f.
William of Rymyngton (*fl.* 1372), I, **312**
William of Shoreham (*fl.* 14 cent.), I, 271f.
William of Ware (*fl.* 1240), I, **292**
William the Englishman (*fl.* 1231), I, **298**
William Flynn's Hibernian Chronicle (1772), II, 737
William of Palerne (M.E.), I, 29, 40, **156**
Williams, Anna (1706–1783), II, 332, 622, 812
Williams, B. (*fl.* 1850), I, 116
Williams, Charles (*fl.* 1685), II, 534
Williams, Charles (*fl.* 1848–64), clergyman, III, 567
Williams, Charles (1838–1904), war correspondent, III, 801 (2)
Williams, Sir Charles Hanbury (1708–1759), II, **332**f.
Williams, Charles Hanbury (*fl.* 1900), III, 832
Williams, D. (*fl.* 1725), translator from the French, II, 787
Williams, David (1738–1816), divine and educationalist, II, 110, 448, 804 (3)
Williams, E. E. (*fl.* 1897), III, 972
Williams, E. M. Abdy (*fl.* 1885), III, 831
Williams, Edward (*fl.* 1650), I, 796
Williams, Edward (Iolo Morganwg) (1746–1826), II, 81
Williams, Sir Edward Vaughan (1797–1875), III, 988
Williams, George (1814–1878), topographer and divine, I, 313
Williams, George Phipps (*fl.* 1904), New Zealand poet, III, 1096
Williams, H. L. (*fl.* 1868), translator from the French, III, 22, 608
Williams, Helen Maria (1762–1827), II, **386**f., 252, 553
Williams, Hugh William (1773–1829), III, 203
Williams, Isaac (1802–1865), III, **312**, 856
Williams, J. (*fl.* 1778), Birmingham poet, II, 771
Williams, Sir James (*fl.* 1717), II, 155
Williams, John (1582–1650), I, 363
Williams, John (*fl.* 1735), translator, II, 793
Williams, John ('Anthony Pasquin') (1761–1818), II, **387**

Williams, Sir John Bickerton (1792–1855), I, 466

Williams, Sir Monier, later Monier-Williams (*fl.* 1875–89), III, 779, 1081

Williams, Moses (1686–1742), I, 774; II, 88, 935

Williams, Oliver (*fl.* 1657–60), I, 763 (3); II, 701 (3), 702, 716

Williams, Owen (*fl.* 1828), II, 393

Williams, P. (*fl.* 1808), III, 980

Williams, Robert (*fl.* 1865), editor of 'The Examiner', III, 810

Williams, Robert Folkstone (*fl.* 1840?), biographer of Horace Walpole, II, 840

Williams, Robert G. (*fl.* 1868), lawyer, III, 988

Williams, Sir Roger (1540?–1595), soldier, I, 390

Williams, Roger (1604?–1683), colonist, I, 795

Williams, Sir Roland L. B. Vaughan (1838–1916), III, 988

Williams, Rowland (1817–1870), III, 29, 848

Williams, Sarah (1841–1868), I, 398; III, 363

Williams, T. (*fl.* 1680), lawyer, II, 965

Williams, T. (*fl.* 1810?), editor of 'The Eclectic Review', III, 824

Williams, T. E. (*fl.* 1807), Reading antiquary, II, 839

Williams, Theodore (*fl.* 1833), II, 732

Williams, Thomas (*fl.* 1793), II, 682

Williams, Thomas Walter (1763–1833), I, 851

Williams, W. Phillpotts (*fl.* 1894–9), poet and huntsman, III, 761

Williams, W. S. (*fl.* 1861), editor of a Ruskin selection, III, 692

Williams, Walter Vaughan (*fl.* 1870), lawyer, III, 988

Williams, Zachariah (1673?–1755), II, 621

WILLIAMS'S LIBRARY, DR, II, 104

Williamson, Alexander Williams (1824–1904), III, **948**

Williamson, David (b. 1868), III, 831 (2)

Williamson, J. (*fl.* 1835), III, 114

Williamson, John (*fl.* 1740), II, 820

Williamson, Peter (1730–1799), II, 665 (2), 1001

Williamson, Richard (*fl.* 1845), III, 134

Williamson, Robert (*fl.* 1642), I, 753

Williamson, William Crawford (1816–1895), III, 957, **961**

Williamson's Liverpool Advertiser (1766), II, 725

Willich, Anthony Florian Madinger (*fl.* 1798), II, 30, 52, 683

Willis, Browne (1682–1760), II, **880**

Willis, Francis (*fl.* 1683), II, 759

Willis, H. Norton (*fl.* 1795), II, 926

Willis, John (d. 1628?), I, 377

Willis, R. (*fl.* 1639), I, 385

Willis, Richard (1664–1734), II, 124, 401, 661, 675

Willis, Robert (1799–1878), I, 889

Willis, Thomas (1621–1675), II, 962

Willison, John (1680–1750), II, **995**

Willm, J. (*fl.* 1847), III, 115

Willmer, Charles (*fl.* 1853–61), III, 802 (2)

Willmer's Liverpool Morning News (1859), III, 802

Willmott, Robert Aris (1809–1863), III, **727**

'Willoby, Henry' (*fl.* 1594–1605), I, 440

Willoughby, Cassandra (*fl.* 1702), I, 382

Willoughby, Francis (1635–1672). See Willughby

Willoughby, Robert (*fl.* 1800), II, 256

Willoughby family, Household accounts of (16 cent.), I, 382

WILLS, I, 46 (M.E.)

Wills, Charles James (*fl.* 1883), III, 993

Wills, James (*fl.* 1754), translator of Du Fresnoy, II, 779

Wills, James (1790–1868), Irish poet and journalist, III, 408, 827

Wills, W. R. (*fl.* 1885), III, 1095

Wills, William Gorman (1828–1891), III, **609**

Wills, William Henry (1810–1880), II, 604; III, 447, 449

Willughby, Francis (1635–1672), II, 743, 818, 962

Wilmot, A. (*fl.* 1869–1904), III, 1089, 1090 (3), 1092

Wilmot, John Earl of Rochester (1648–1680), II, 27, **276** f.

Wilmot, Sir John Eardley Eardley- (1810–1892), III, 760

Wilmot, Robert (d. 1597), I, 523

Wilmott, C. (*fl.* 1864), III, 727

Wilson, A. (*fl.* 1806–11), printer, III, 75

Wilson, A. J. (*fl.* 1879), writer on banking, III, 973

Wilson, Alexander (1766–1813), ornithologist, II, **991** f.

Wilson, Alexander (d. 1852), poet, III, 312

Wilson, Andrew (1766–1863), zoologist, III, 955

Wilson, Andrew (1831–1881), traveller, III, 993

Wilson, Anne (*fl.* 1889), III, 1095

Wilson, Anthony (*fl.* 1791–3) ('Henry Bromley'), II, 106, 972

Wilson, Arthur (1595–1652), I, 651, 838

Wilson, B. (*fl.* 1620), II, 801

Wilson, Benjamin (1721–1788), II, 808

Wilson, Caroline, née Fry (1787–1846), III, 852

'Wilson, Charles' (*fl.* 1730), II, 415

Wilson, Charles Henry (*fl.* 1800–8), II, 256, 435, 572, 593, 635

Wilson, Charles Robert (1863–1904), III, 1078

Wilson, Daniel, the elder (1778–1858), bishop of Calcutta, III, 852

Wilson, Daniel, the younger (*fl.* 1863), editor of his father's works, III, 852

Wilson, Sir Daniel (1816–1892), archaeologist, I, 59; II, 345

Wilson, Effingham (1783–1868), III, 100
Wilson, F. W. (*fl.* 1874–92), III, 800, 803
Wilson, George (*fl.* 1607), I, 395
Wilson, Harriette (1789–1846), III, 151
Wilson, Henry (*fl.* 1711), II, 536
Wilson, Henry Bristow (1803–1888), III, 128, 848
Wilson, Henry Schütz (1824–1902), III, 777
Wilson, Horace Hayman (1786–1860), III, **1019**, 1070, 1074–5, 1081
Wilson, J. (*fl.* 1692), editor of Bunyan's 'Works', II, 490
Wilson, J. (*fl.* 1803), author of 'Memorabilia Cantabrigiae', III, 124
Wilson, J. (*fl.* 1835), writer on Presbyterianism, II, 862
Wilson, J. I. (*fl.* 1821), author of 'The History of Christ's Hospital,' III, 634
Wilson, J. P. (*fl.* 1841), editor of Lancelot Andrews, I, 680
Wilson, James (*fl.* 1758–75) ('Claudero'), Scottish poet, II, 992
Wilson, James (*fl.* 1799), missionary in Pacific, II, 757
Wilson, James (1805–1860), political economist, III, 820, 972
Wilson, James Maurice (1836–1931), educationalist, III, 109, 115, 124, 141
Wilson, John (1595–1673), lutenist, I, 486
Wilson, John (1627?–1696), playwright, II, 32, 173, **429**f., 811
Wilson, John (1720–1789), author of 'The Clyde', II, 992
Wilson, John ('Christopher North') (1785–1854), III, **682**f.
    Reviews by, I, 20; II, 987 (2); III, 192, 196 (2), 199, 200, 219, 226, 233, 240, 244, 248, 257, 478, 673
Wilson, John (*fl.* 1827), Shakespearian bibliographer, I, 540
Wilson, John (1804–1875), missionary and orientalist, III, 1081
Wilson, John Mackay (1804–1835), Scottish writer and printer, III, 158
Wilson, Lea (*fl.* 1845), I, 672
Wilson, M. T. (*fl.* 1850?), III, 312
Wilson, Margaret Oliphant, later Oliphant (1828–1897), III, **500**f.
Wilson, R. F. (*fl.* 1833–9), tractarian, III, 855–6
Wilson, Robert (d. 1600), I, 516–7
Wilson, Robert (*fl.* 1826), writer on the corn laws, III, 978
Wilson, Sir Robert Thomas (1777–1849), general, III, 143
Wilson, Samuel (*fl.* 1682), II, 752
Wilson, Thomas (1525?–1581), secretary of state, I, 376, **671**f., 801, 804, 845, 864, 873
Wilson, Sir Thomas (1560?–1629), translator, I, 816

Wilson, Thomas (1663–1755), bishop of Sodor and Man, II, 110, **854**
Wilson, W. (*fl.* 1825), educationalist, III, 115
Wilson, W. (*fl.* 1855), printer, III, 77
Wilson, W. Carus (*fl.* 1826–66), educationalist, III, 577–8
Wilson, Walter (1781–1847), biographer, II, 511
Wilson, William (*fl.* 1784), topographer, II, 159
Wilson, William (1799–1871), botanist, III, 960
Wilson's Musical Miscellany (18 cent.), II, 234, 236 (2)
Wilton, A. G. Egerton, Earl of (*fl.* 1868), III, 766
Wilton, Richard (1827–1903), III, **312**f.
Wily Beguilde, A Pleasant Comedie, Called (17 cent.), I, 663
Wimbledon, Robert (*fl.* 1387), I, 172f.
Winch, Sir Humphrey (1555?–1625), II, 965
Winchcombe Register (M.E.), I, 122
WINCHESTER
    Book trade, I, 353 (16–18 cents.)
    College, I, 373f.; III, 134, 839
    Magazines, II, 685 (1799)
    Newspapers, II, 729
    Printers and booksellers, II, 88
Winchester, Annals of (15 cent.), I, 115
Winchester Journal; Or, Weekly Review, The (1743), II, 728
Winchester Register (M.E.), I, 122
Winchilsea, Anne Finch, Countess of (1666–1720), II, **333**
Winchilsea, Heneage Finch, Earl of (d. 1689), II, 743
Winckelmann, Johann Joachim, II, 53; III, 49
Windham, Sir Charles (1810–1870), III, 153
Windham, William (1717–1761), colonel, II, 745
Windham, William (1750–1810), statesman, II, 138, 165; III, 148–9
Windhus, John (*fl.* 1725), II, 748
Windsor, A. L. (*fl.* 1860), II, 512
Windsor and Eton Journal, The (1746), II, 723
Windsor Drollery (17 cent.), II, 176 (3)
Windsor Forest [etc.] (18 cent.), II, 255
Windsor Magazine, The (1895), III, 831
Windsor Medley, The (18 cent.), II, 202 (3)
Windsor Projects and Westminster Practices (1648), I, 758
Wine, Beere, and Ale (17 cent.), I, 654
Winer, Georg Benedict, III, 1014
Wingate, David (1828–1892), III, **313**
Wingate, Edmund (1596–1656), I, 851f., 881; II, 125
Wingfield, Anthony (1550?–1616?), I, 768
Wingfield, Edward-Maria (*fl.* 1607), I, 789
Wingfield, Lewis Strange (1842–1891), III, 993
Wingfield, Walter (*fl.* 1897), III, 778
Winks, J. F. (*fl.* 1821–54), III, 117, 577
Winkworth, Catherine (1827–1878), III, **313**

Winkworth, Susanna (1820–1884), III, 29, 670
'Winlove, Solomon' (1767), II, 562
Winne, Edward (fl. 1621), I, 791
Winslow, Edward (1595–1655), I, 791 (2)
Winstanley, — (fl. 1779), II, 680
Winstanley, John (1678?–1750), II, 210
Winstanley, William (1628?–1698), II, 21, 175, 180, 532, 656, 921–2, 924
Winston, James (fl. 1808), II, 405
Winston, M. (fl. 1799), II, 255
Winter, Thomas (fl. 1603), I, 818
Winter Evening Tales (18 cent.), II, 539
Winter-Evenings Companion (18 cent.), II, 219–20, 235
Winter Medley, The (18 cent.), II, 230
Wintersted, — (fl. 1771), II, 58
Winterton, Ralph (1600–1636), I, 863
Winthrop, John (1588–1649), I, 793
Wintour, T. (fl. 1781), II, 316
Winwood, Sir Ralph (1563?–1617), I, 397
Winwood Papers (16–18 cents.), I, 382
Winzet, Ninian (1518–1592), I, 906
Wirsung, —, I, 889
Wisden, John, III, 774
Wisdom of Solomon, The (M.E.), I, 260
Wisdom, who is Christ (16 cent.), I, 514
Wisdome of Doctor Dodypoll, The (17 cent.), I, 539
Wise, B. R. (fl. 1913), III, 1098
Wise, Francis (1695–1767), I, 85
Wise, John Richard de Capel (1831–1890), I, 542
Wise, Joseph (fl. 1766), II, 387
Wise, T. A. (fl. 1854), III, 1083
Wiseman, Charles (fl. 1764–78), II, 121, 641
Wiseman, Nicholas Patrick Stephen (1802–1865), III, 860
Wiseman, Sir Robert (fl. 1686), II, 965
Wishart, George (1599–1671), I, 910f.
Wishart, W. (fl. 1742), I, 879
Wit À-la-Mode (1775), II, 231
Wit a-la-mode; Or, Lord Chesterfield's Witticisms [etc.] (1778), II, 233
Wit and Drollery (17 cent.), I, 405; II, 174, 178
Wit and Loyalty Reviv'd (17 cent.), II, 178
Wit and Mirth (1682), II, 179 (2)
Wit and Mirth: Or, Pills to purge Melancholy (1699), II, 184–5, 187 (2), 188 (5), 189–1, 195–6
Wit at a Venture (17 cent.), II, 177
Wit for the Ton! (18 cent.), II, 232, 234
Wit Musically Embellish'd (18 cent.), II, 202
Wit of a Woman, The (17 cent.), I, 654
Wit of the Day, The (18 cent.), II, 238
Wit Restor'd (17 cent.), I, 405
Wit, Women, and Wine (18 cent.), II, 222
Wit's Magazine; Or, Library of Momus, The (1784), II, 680
Wit's Miscellany, Or A Companion for the Choice Spirits, The (1774), II, 230

Wit's Recreations Augmented (17 cent.), I, 405
WITCHCRAFT AND MAGIC, I, 893f. (16, 17 cents.)
Witchell, G. (fl. 1761), II, 678
Witcomb, Charles (fl. 1857–84), I, 18
Withal (Withals or Whithals), John (fl. 1556–62), I, 375
Witham, Henry Thomas (1779–1844), III, 950
Witham, T. W. (fl. 1897), III, 779
Wither, George (1588–1667), I, 446f., 679, 747, 755
Withers, Fabian (fl. 1558–83), I, 883
Withers, J. J. (1863–1939), III, 835
Withers, Philip (fl. 1791), II, 20
Withers, Robert (fl. 1625), I, 779
Witherspoon, John (1723–1794), II, 995
Withington, J. S. (fl. 1880?), III, 827
Withington, Nicholas (fl. 1612–6), I, 783
Witness, The [Edinburgh], III, 819
Wits, The (17 cent.), II, 174, 176–7
Wits Academy: or, The Muses Delight, The (17 cent.), II, 178
Wits Cabinet Or A Companion For Young Men and Ladies (17 cent.), II, 179, 184, 186, 190, 202, 207–8, 211
Wits Interpreter (17 cent.), I, 405; II, 174, 176
Wits Museum (18 cent.), II, 235, 250
Wits Paraphrased, The (17 cent.), II, 288
Wits Secretary (18 cent.), II, 185
Witt, Johan de, II, 540
Witt's Recreations refined (17 cent.), II, 174–5, 179
Witticisms and Strokes of Humour Collected by Robert Baker (18 cent.), II, 225
Wittie (or Witty), Robert (fl. 1640–81), I, 890; II, 154
Witts Recreations (17 cent.), I, 405
Witty Jests, A Choice Banquet of (17 cent.), I, 715
Witty Rogue, The (17 cent.), I, 718
Wodenoth (or Woodnoth), Arthur (1590?–1650?), I, 796
Wodham (or Godham), Adam (d. c. 1358), I, 305
Wodhull, Michael (1740–1816), II, 387
Wodroephe, John (fl. 1623), I, 377
Wodrow, Robert (1679–1734), I, 907; II, 998
WOKINGHAM Newspapers, II, 729
Wolcot, John (1738–1819), II, 387f.
Wolf and Eadwacer (O.E.), I, 72
Wolfe, Charles (1791–1823), III, 246
Wolfe, James (1727–1759), III, 151
Wolfe, John (d. 1601), I, 352
Wolfe, Reynold (or Reyner) (d. 1573), I, 200, 351
Wolferston, Francis (fl. 1661), II, 766
Wolff, C. F., Baron von, III, 46
Wolff, H. W. (fl. 1896), III, 973
Wolff, Sir Henry Drummond Charles (1830–1908), III, 155

Wollaston, William (1660–1724), II, 949
Wollaston, William Hyde (1766–1828), III, **946**
Wolley, Charles (*fl.* 1701), II, 753
Wolley, Edward (d. 1684), I, 819
Wolley (or Woolley), Hannah, later Challinor (*fl.* 1661–75), II, 142, 818
Wolley, Richard (*fl.* 1667–94), II, 675
Wollstonecraft, Mary (later Godwin) (1759–1797), II, 39, 551, 558, 566, **656**, 792
Wolseley, Garnet Joseph, Viscount (1833–1913), III, 155
Wolseley, Robert (1649–1697), II, 15, 276
Wolstenholme, E. C. (1869), III, 143
WOLVERHAMPTON, I, 374 (school); II, 88 (printers), 729 (newspaper)
Wolverhampton Chronicle, The (1789), II, 729
Woman (1890), III, 822
Woman of Samaria (M.E.), I, **188**
Woman's Magazine, The (1928), III, 578
Woman's Wit (18 cent.), II, 235
Womanly Noblesse (M.E.), I, 227
WOMEN, EDUCATION OF, I, 379 f. (16, 17 cents.); II, 130 f. (17, 18 cents.); III, 141 f. (19 cent.)
WOMEN, SATIRES ON, I, 716 f. (16, 17 cents.)
Women will have their Will (17 cent.), I, 717
Women's Suffrage Journal (1870), III, 830
WOMEN-WRITERS, III, 5
Wonder. A Mercury without a Lye in's Mouth, A (1648), I, 759
Wonderful Magazine And Marvellous Chronicle, The (1793), II, 682
Wonderful Magazine; Or, Marvellous Chronicle, The (1764), II, 679
Wonderful Newes from Wood-Street Counter (17 cent.), I, 718
Wonders of Creation (O.E.), I, **80**
Wonders of the East (O.E.), I, **94**
Wood, Abraham (*fl.* 1674), II, 752
Wood, Adam (*fl.* 1659), I, 720
Wood, Anthony à (1632–1695), II, **867**
Wood, C. (*fl.* 1887), editor of 'The Argosy', III, 830
Wood, Sir Charles, Viscount Halifax (1800–1885), III, 684, 1077
Wood, Emma Caroline, Lady (*fl.* 1866–79), III, **563**
Wood, Mrs Henry, née Ellen Price (1814–1887), III, **511** f., 627, 830
Wood, J. (*fl.* 1828), educationalist, III, 115
Wood, J. (*fl.* 1860), printer, III, 75
Wood, John (*fl.* 1694), arctic voyager, II, 743
Wood, John (*fl.* 1705?–1754), architect, II, 154
Wood, John (*fl.* 1757), writer on farriery, II, 816
Wood, John (*fl.* 1765), author of an edition of Milton, II, 914
Wood, John (1811–1871), geographer, III, 993
Wood, Mary Anne Everett, later Green (1818–1895), III, **899**

Wood, R. M. (*fl.* 1860), III, 75
Wood, Robert (*fl.* 1642–52), I, 752, 753 (2), 754 (2), 760, 761 (2?), 762
Wood, Robert (1717?–1771), II, 26, 54, 750
Wood, T. (*fl.* 1615), I, 391
Wood, Thomas (*fl.* 1683), II, 759
Wood, William (*fl.* 1634–9), writer on New England, I, 795
Wood, Sir William (1609–1691), toxophilite, II, 823
Wood, William (*fl.* 1718), Secretary of Customs, II, 959
Wood Pulp (1896), III, 73
WOOD-ENGRAVING, III, 84 f.
Wood-Lark, The (18 cent.), II, 235, 238
Woodall, John (1556?–1643), I, 891
Woodard, Nathaniel (1811–1891), III, 115
Woodes, Nathaniel (*fl.* 1581), I, 516
Woodewarde, Philippe (*fl.* 1608), I, 813
Woodfall, Henry (*fl.* 1734), publisher, II, 708
Woodfall, Henry Sampson (1739–1805), printer and journalist, II, 85
Woodfall, William (1746–1803), parliamentary reporter and dramatic critic, II, 457, 709, 711
Woodfall, William (*fl.* 1802), lawyer, III, 988
Woodfin, Mrs A. (*fl.* 1756–64), II, 545
Woodford, William (d. *c.* 1397), I, **305**
Woodforde (or Woodford), Samuel (1636–1700), I, 15; II, 21
Woodforde, James (*fl.* 1759–73), II, 115, 137
Woodhead, Abraham (1609–1678), I, 810; II, 846
Woodhouse, James (1735–1820), II, **389** f.
Woodhouse, John (*fl.* 1647), I, 776
Woodhouse, Peter (*fl.* 1605), I, 480
Woodhouse, Robert (1773–1827), III, 941
Woodhouselee, Alexander Fraser Tytler, Lord (1747–1813), II, 20, 486, 812, 889, 916 f., 955, 969
Woodner, Robert (*fl.* 1642), I, 753
Woodnoth (or Wodenoth), Arthur (1590?–1650?), I, 796
Woods, James Chapman (*fl.* 1879), III, 363
Woods, Julian Edward Tenison (1832–1889), III, 1097
Woods, Margaret Louisa, née Bradley (b. 1856), III, **563**
Woods, Thomas (*fl.* 1649), I, 780
Woodville (or Wydeville), Anthony, Earl Rivers (1442?–1483), I, 262 (3), 880
Woodward, Ezekias (1590–1675), I, 375
Woodward, George (*fl.* 1717), II, **333**
Woodward, George Moutard (1760?–1809), II, 140
Woodward, Horace Bolingbroke (b. 1848), III, 953
Woodward, Josiah (*fl.* 1699–1706), II, 115, 402, 857
Woodward, R. B. (*fl.* 1863), III, 833

Woodward, Samuel Peckworth (1821–1865), III, 957

Woody, Robert (*fl.* 1642), I, 753

Wooler, Thomas Jonathan (1786?–1853), III, 801, 811, 816

Wooler's British Gazette [Manchester] (1819), III, 811

Wooll, John (1767–1833), II, 384

Woolley (or Wolley), Hannah, later Challinor (*fl.* 1661–75), II, 142, 818

Woolley, Robert (*fl.* 1685), II, 717

Woolman, John (1720–1772), II, 756

Woolmer's Exeter and Plymouth Gazette (1792), II, 724

Woolner, Thomas (1825–1892), III, **313**

Woolnough, C. W. (*fl.* 1853), III, 92

Woolridge, John (*fl.* 1669–98). See Worlidge

Woolrych, Humphry William (1795–1871), I, 427

Woolsey, R. (*fl.* 1790), II, 635

Woolston, Thomas (1670–1733), II, 949

Woolton, John (1535?–1594), I, 685

WORCESTER
    Newspapers, II, 729

Worcester, Florence of (d. 1118), I, 116

Worcester, Edward Somerset, Marquis of (1601–1667), II, 962

Worcester, John Tiptoft, Earl of (1427?–1470), I, 362, 800

Worcester, Annals of (15 cent.), I, 115

Worcester Daily Times and Journal, The (1880), III, 805

Worcester Herald, The (1793), II, 729

Worcester Journal, The (1748), II, 729

Worcester Post; Or, Western Journal, The (1723), II, 729

Worcester Post-Man, The (1713), II, 729

Worcester, Register and Cartulary (M.E.), I, 122

WORCESTERSHIRE
    Bibliography, I, 9
    Libraries, I, 363
    Printing in, I, 353 (16–18 cents.)
    Schools, I, 373

Worcestershire Echo, The (1883), III, 805

Worcestershire Evening Post, The (1881), III, 805

WORD-FORMATION, I, 30f.

Worde, Wynkyn de (d. 1534?), I, 351

WORDS. See VOCABULARY, I, 30f., LOAN-WORDS, I, 33f. and DICTION

Words of Such Pieces As are performed by The Academy of Ancient Music, The (18 cent.), II, 220, 225

Words of the Favourite Pieces, as performed at the Glee Club, The (18 cent.), II, 250

Wordsworth, Charles (1806–1892), I, 585; III, 115, 141, 153

Wordsworth, Christopher (1774–1846), master of Trinity College, Cambridge, II, 933; III, 122

Wordsworth, Christopher (1807–1885), bishop of Lincoln, III, **313**, 879–80, 1003

Wordsworth, Dorothy (1771–1855), III, 683

Wordsworth, John (1843–1911), III, 1011

Wordsworth, William (1770–1850), III, 26, 115, **165**f.

Worgan, John Dawes (*fl.* 1800?), II, 365

Worke for Cutlers (17 cent.), I, 663

Workman, W. R. (*fl.* 1860), III, 818

Workman's Advocate, The (1865), III, 817

Workman's Times, The [Huddersfield] (1890), III, 818

Works of Celebrated Authors, The (18 cent.), II, 214

Works of Geoffrey Chaucer, The (1721), II, 196

Works of Horace in English Verse, The (18 cent.), II, 218–9, 225

Works of Mr John Philips [etc.], *The* (18 cent.), II, 191

Works of Monsr. Boileau Despreaux, The (18 cent.), II, 190 (3), 191, 206

Works of the British Poets, The (1792), II, 260

Works of the English Poets, The (1779), II, 259

Works of the Learned, The (1691), II, 675

Works of the most celebrated Minor Poets, The (18 cent.), II, 213

Works of William Hay, Esq., The [etc.] (18 cent.), II, 250

World, The (1753), II, 664

World, The (1827), III, 819

World, The (1874), III, 814

World as it Goes, The (18 cent.), II, 235

World, Fashionable Advertiser, The (1787), II, 709

World in a Maize, The (17 cent.), I, 719

World of Adventure, The (19 cent.), III, 575

World of Fashion and Continental Feuilletons, The (1824), III, 826

WORLD, VOYAGES ROUND, II, 741 f.

World's Comic, The (1892), III, 821

World's Idol, The (17 cent.), I, 654

World's Paper Trade Review (1891), III, 73

World's Pulp and Paper Industry (1898), III, 73

Worlde and the chylde, A propre newe Interlude of (16 cent.), I, 515

Worlidge, John (*fl.* 1669–98), II, 818

Wormald, R. B. (*fl.* 1880?), III, 811

Wormius, Olaus, II, 70

Wornum, Ralph Nicholson (1812–1877), II, 838

Worrall, John (*fl.* 1736–49), I, 848f.; II, 97

Worsaal, J. J. A., I, 56; III, 1035

Worseley, Ralph (d. 1590), I, 660

Worsfold, W. B. (1858–1939), III, 1090, 1092

Worsley, Charles (*fl.* 1754), II, 104

Worsley, Philip Stanhope (1835–1866), III, **363**

Worth, Richard Nicholls (1837–1896), III, 802

Wortham, B. H. (*fl.* 1886), III, 1072

Worthington, J. W. (*fl.* 1835), III, 833

Worthington, John (1618–1671), I, **703**, 876, 878

Wortley, Francis (1591–1652), I, 724

Wotton, Edward (*fl.* 1552), I, 892

Wotton, Sir Henry (1568–1639), poet and diplomatist, I, 366, 392, **426**, 719, 726

Wotton, Henry (*fl.* 1672), author of 'An Essay on the Education of Children', II, 110

Wotton, William (1666–1727), II, 15, 577, 779, 920, 939

Woty, William (1731–1791), II, 222, **390**

Wrangham, Francis (1769–1842), II, 921; III, **246**f.

Wratislaw, Theodore (1871–1933), III, **363**

Wraxall, Sir Nathaniel William, II, 138, 165, 746

Wray, Mary, Lady (*fl.* 1714), II, 120

Wreaks, Barbara, later Hoole, later Hofland (1770–1844), III, **400**f., 566

Wreath, The (1752), II, 215, 216 (2), 217–8

Wreath, The (1761), II, 220, 229

Wrednott, William (*fl.* 1604), I, 715

Wren, Christopher, the elder (1591–1658), dean of Windsor, I, 660

Wren, Sir Christopher (1632–1723), mathematician and architect, I, 882; II, 30

Wren, Matthew (1585–1665), I, 878

Wren; or, the Fairy of the Green-house, The (18 cent.), II, 563

Wright, A. B. (*fl.* 1890), III, 819

Wright, Abraham (1611–1690), I, 405, 695

Wright, Arnold (*fl.* 1891), III, 1074

Wright, C. N. (*fl.* 1826), III, 379

Wright, David McKee (*fl.* 1897), III, 1095

Wright, E. (*fl.* 1807), I, 547

Wright, Edward (1558?–1615), I, 769, 881, 885

Wright, Edward (*fl.* 1730), II, 744

Wright, George (*fl.* 1775–87), compiler, II, 231 (2), 236, 240, 241 (2), 242, 248 (2), 250, 252 (2), 306, 556

Wright, George Newnham (1790?–1877), editor of philosophical works, II, 944, 956

Wright, Ichabod Charles (1795–1871), III, 39, 268

Wright, J. M. F. (*fl.* 1827), author of 'Alma Mater', III, 124

Wright, James (*fl.* 1663), translator of Martial, II, 766

Wright, James (1643–1713), antiquary and miscellaneous writer, II, 15, 403, **871**

Wright, John (*fl.* 1641), publisher, I, 752 (2), 754

Wright, John (*fl.* 1674), translator of Seneca, II, 767

Wright, John (misprint for James Wright) (1643–1713), II, 864

Wright, John (*fl.* 1727), author of 'Spiritual Songs for Children', II, 130, 556

Wright, John (1770?–1844), bookseller and author, I, 547; II, 651, 837; III, 187

Wright, Leonard (*fl.* 1591), I, 693

Wright, Richard (*fl.* 1805), II, 617

Wright, Samuel (1683–1746), II, 503

Wright, Thomas (*fl.* 1604), scientific writer, I, 616, 884

Wright, Thomas (*fl.* 1693), translator of Molière, II, 794

Wright, Thomas (1711–1786), natural philosopher, II, 710, 962

Wright, Thomas (*fl.* 1798), editor of Goldsmith, II, 638

Wright, Thomas (*fl.* 1800?), journalist, III, 798

Wright, Thomas (1809–1884), geologist, III, 957, 963

Wright, Thomas (1810–1877), antiquary, III, **890**f.

Wright, Thomas (*fl.* 1886–94), journalist, III, 798

Wright, William (*fl.* 1855), writer on angling, III, 770

Wright, William (1830–1889), orientalist, III, **1021**

Wright, William Aldis (1831–1914), English scholar, III, **1043**f.

Wright's Chaste Wife, The (15 cent.), I, 266

Wrightson, Joseph (*fl.* 1838), III, 810

Wrigley, T. (*fl.* 1864), III, 73

Wriothesley, Charles (1508?–1562), I, 823

WRITING MANUALS, I, 346 (16, 17 cents.); II, 129 (17, 18 cents.)

WRITING MASTERS. See HANDWRITING

Writing-Desk, The (18 cent.), II, 487

Wrixon, Sir H. (*fl.* 1896), III, 978

Wroth, Lady Mary (*fl.* 1621), I, 478, 731

Wroth, Sir Thomas (1584–1672), I, 481, 809

Wulf and Eadwacer (O.E.), I, **72**

Wulfstan of Winchester (*fl.* 965), I, **107**

Wulfstan (O.E.), I, 26, 28, 36, **92**

Wyatt, Captain — (*fl.* 1594), I, 788

Wyatt, Benjamin Dean (1775–1850?), II, 403

Wyatt (or Wiat), Sir Thomas (1503?–1542), I, **411**f., 677

Wycherley, William (1640?–1716), II, **410**f., 794

Wyclif (or Wycliffe), John (1320?–1384), I, 29, 40, **203**f., **307**f.

Wydeville (or Woodville), Anthony, Earl Rivers (1442?–1483), I, 262 (3), 880

Wyer, Robert (*fl.* 1529–56), I, 351

Wyeth, Joseph (1663–1731), II, 280

Wykes, Thomas de (*fl.* 1258–93), I, 115

Wylde, Zachary (*fl.* 1711), II, 823

Wylie, James Hamilton (1844–1914), III, **919**

Wylie, William Howie (1833–1891), III, 808

Wyll of the Devil, The (16 cent.), I, 713

WYMAN AND SONS, C. H., III, 88

Wyn (or Wynne), Ellis, (1671–1734), III, 422

Wyndham, Henry Penruddocke (1736–1819), II, 139
Wynfrith or Boniface (d. 755), I, **105**f.
Wyngale, Thomas (*fl.* 1470), I, **302**
Wynn (of Gwydir) Papers, Calendar of (16, 17 cents.), I, 383
Wynne, G. (*fl.* 1890), III, 802
Wynne, John (1667–1743), II, 944
Wynne, John Huddleston (1743–1788), II, 673, 679, 698, 709
Wynne, R. (*fl.* 1752), II, 797
Wynne (or Wynn), Sir Richard (d. 1649), I, 771
Wynne, W. (*fl.* 1697), I, 825
Wynnere and Wastoure (M.E.), I, **196**f.
Wynter, Andrew (1819–1876), III, 821
Wynter, P. (*fl.* 1863), I, 697
Wyntoun, Andrew of (1350?–1420?), I, 41, 43
Wyot, Philip (*fl.* 1586–1608), I, 384
Wyrley, William (1565–1618), I, 396
Wyse, Sir Thomas (1791–1862), III, 115, 117–8
Wyss, Johann David Rudolf, III, 577
Wythers, Stephen (*fl.* 1563), I, 378, 817

Xamolxis and Perindo (17 cent.), I, 654
Xenophon, I, 784, 809; II, 763
Xystus Betuleius, I, 663

Y., D. (*fl.* 1770), II, 771
Y., E. (*fl.* 1739), II, 808
Y Geirgrawn (1796), II, 685
Yalden, Thomas (1670–1736), II, **333**
Yallop (or Spelman), Edward (d. 1767), II, 760, 763 (2)
Yard, Robert (*fl.* 1671), II, 702
Yarington, Robert (*fl.* 1601), I, 537
YARMOUTH
    Printers, II, 88
Yarranton, Andrew (1616–1684?), II, 959
Yarrell, William (1784–1856), III, 956
Yarrow, Joseph (*fl.* 1738), II, 207, 209
Yates, Edmund Hodgson (1831–1894), III, 441, **563**, 814, 829
Yates, James (*fl.* 1582), I, 440
Yates, James (1789–1871), III, 115, 125
Yates, Richard (1769–1834), II, 138
Yates, William (1792–1845), III, 1074
Ye True Blue [Cambridge] (1883), III, 835
YEAR BOOKS, III, 842f.
Year's Sport, The (1886), III, 759
Yeardley, Francis (*fl.* 1654), I, 793
Yearly Chronicle For M,DCC,LXI, The (18 cent.), II, 221
Yearly Subscription or the Harmonious Entertainment, The (18 cent.), II, 196
Yearsley, Ann (1756–1806), II, **390**
Yeats, J. (*fl.* 1870), III, 983
Yeats, William Butler (1865–1939), III, **1059**f.
Yeld, G. (*fl.* 1903?), III, 830
Yeldham, W. (*fl.* 1875), III, 1069

Yellow Book, The (1894), III, 834
Yellow Dwarf, The (1818), III, 816
Yeoman, John (*fl.* 1774), II, 137
YEOVIL
    Newspapers, II, 729
Yeowell, James (1803?–1875), II, 895
Yonde, John (*fl.* 1775), II, 23
Yong, Thomas (*fl.* 1634), I, 792
Yonge, Charlotte Mary (1823–1901), II, 554; III, **512**, 564, 828
Yonge, Walter (1581?–1649), I, 385
Yonge, Sir William (d. 1755), II, 313
Yorick turned Trimmer (18 cent.), II, 228, 253
Yorick's Jests (18 cent.), II, 228, 230, 237
YORK
    Library, I, 361
    Magazine, II, 685 (1734–86)
    Newspapers, II, 729f.
    Printing in, I, 353 (1500–1660); II, 88 (1660–1800)
    Schools, I, 374
York, Edward, Duke of (1373?–1415), I, 266
York Chronicle (1796), II, 666
York Chronicle and General Advertiser, The (1777), II, 730
York Chronicle, and Weekly Advertiser, The (1772), II, 730
York Courant, The (1725), II, 730
York Gazetteer, with News both Foreign and Domestick, The (1741), II, 730
York Herald, The (1790), II, 730
York Herald, The (1874), III, 804
York Journal; Or, The Protestant Courant, The (1745), II, 730
York Mercury, The (1719), II, 730
York Plays (M.E.), I, **278**
Yorke, Charles, Earl of Hardwicke (1722–1770), II, 164
Yorke, Henry Redhead (1772–1813), III, 788
Yorke, Philip, Earl of Hardwicke (1720–1790), II, 164, **887**
YORKSHIRE
    Bibliography, I, 9
Yorkshire Charters (M.E.), I, 122
Yorkshire Evening Post, The (1890), III, 806
Yorkshire Evening Press, The (1905), III, 805
Yorkshire Freeholder, The (1780), II, 665, 730
Yorkshire Garland, The (18 cent.), II, 242
Yorkshire Herald, The (1890), III, 794, 804
Yorkshire Magazine, The (1786), II, 685
Yorkshire Musical Miscellany, The (18 cent.), II, 256
Yorkshire Observer, The (19 cent.), III, 794
Yorkshire Post, The (1866), III, 803
Yorkshire Telegraph and Star, The (1898), III, 806
Yorkshire Tragedy, A (17 cent.), I, 580
Youde, J. (*fl.* 1793), II, 800
Youll, Henry (*fl.* 1608), I, 485

Young, Arthur (1741–1820), II, 148–9, 159, 546–7, 673, 678, 680, **957**; III, **969**
Young, Bartholomew (*fl.* 1577–98), I, 811, 816
Young, Edward (*fl.* 1690?), secretary to Archbishop Tillotson, II, 850
Young, Edward (1683–1765), poet, II, 17, 22, 44, 46, 54, 58, 62, 67–8, 71, **290**f.
Young, Edward (*fl.* 1854), III, 694
Young, George (1777–1848), topographer, II, 381
Young, Sir George (*fl.* 1862–6), literary antiquary, I, 853; III, 247–8
Young, James (*fl.* 1776), II, 804
Young, John (1585–1654), I 385
Young, John (*fl.* 1783), II, 26
Young, L. J. H. (*fl.* 1865), III, 771
Young, M. J. (*fl.* 1806), biographer of Mrs Crouch, II, 408
Young, Matthew (1750–1800), bishop of Clonfert, II, 80
Young, Murdo (*fl.* 1820?), editor of 'The Sun', III, 800
Young, Patrick (1584–1652) (Patricius Junius), I, 857, 859, 863
Young, R. (*fl.* 1725), poet and essayist, II, 606
Young, Robert (*fl.* 1660), Scottish theologian, II, 993
Young, Thomas (1587–1655), I, 703
Young, Thomas (1773–1829), III, **937**
Young, William (*fl.* 1742), translator, II, 759, 761
Young, Sir William (1749–1815), colonial governor, II, 25, 746
Young Briton, The (1869), III, 821
Young Clerks Assistant, The (18 cent.), II, 204
Young England (1880), III, 578
Young Englishman's Journal, The (1867), III, 821
Young Englishwoman, The (1865), III, 830
Young Folks (1871), III, 578
Young Folks (1879), III, 821
Young Folks' Paper (1884), III, 821
Young Folks' Weekly Budget (1876), III, 578
Young Freemason's Assistant, The (18 cent.), II, 238
Young Gentleman's Agreeable Companion, The (18 cent.), II, 249
Young Gentleman's and Lady's Magazine, The (1799), II, 683
Young Gentleman's Complete Jester, The (18 cent.), II, 221
Young Gentleman's Magazine, The (1777), II, 680
Young Men of Great Britain, The (1868), III, 821

Younge, R. (*fl.* 1695), publisher, II, 711
Younge (or Young), Richard (*fl.* 1637–71), Calvinist pamphleteer, I, 720
Younger, John (1785–1860), III, 769
Younghusband, Sir Francis Edward (b. 1863), III, 993
Younghusband, Sir George J. (b. 1859), III, 1078
Youth (1882), III, 821
Youth, Thenterlude of (16 cent.), I, 516
Youth's Entertaining and Instructive Calendar (18 cent.), II, 561
Youth's Instructor, The (1858), III, 578
Youth's Instructor, or Entertaining Story Teller, The (18 cent.), II, 562
Youth's Miscellany of Knowledge and Entertainment, The (1823), III, 577
Youth's Monthly Visitor, The (1822), III, 577
Youth's Play-hour, The (1870), III, 578
Youth's Treasury (17 cent.), II, 181
Ypodigma Neustriae (15 cent.), I, 265
Ypotis (M.E.), I, **187**
Yule, Henry (1820–1889), III, 993, 1074
Yvan, M., III, 605
Yver, Jacques, I, 334
Yvon, Pierre, II, 804
Ywain and Gawain (M.E.), I, **134**

'Z', i.e. John Gibson Lockhart (1794–1854?), III, 223, 647
Z., Z. A. (*fl.* 1841), I, 210
Zachariä, Just Friedrich Wilhelm, II, 59
Zangwill, Israel (1864–1926), III, **563**f.
Zappi, Giovanni Battista Felice, II, 814
Zárate, Agustín de, I, 787
Zeiller, M., I, 381
Zelinda: an Excellent New Romance (17 cent.), II, 530
Zelotypus (17 cent.), I, 663
Zeno, A., II, 810
Zepheria (16 cent.), I, 434
Zimmermann, Johann Georg, II, 53, 312, 807
Zinzendorf, Nikolaus Ludwig, Graf von, II, 55
Zion's Trumpet (1798), II, 684
Zola, Émile, III, **23**, 339, 359
ZOOLOGY (writings on), I, 892f. (16, 17 cents.); III, 955f. (19 cent.): For 1660–1800 see under LITERATURE OF SCIENCE, II, 959f.
Zouch, Henry (1725?–1795), II, 821
Zouch, Thomas (1737–1815), I, 420; II, 915f.
Zouche, Richard (1590–1661), I, 661, 766, **852**; II, 965
Zschokke, Heinrich, III, 35, 406
Zurich Letters, The (16 cent.), I, 382
Zwingli, Ulrich, I, 820

CAMBRIDGE: PRINTED BY
W. LEWIS, M.A.
AT THE UNIVERSITY PRESS